North with Lee and Jackson

Best regards to John, from

James A. Kegel

Dec. 20, 1996

NORTH WITH LEE AND JACKSON

The Lost Story of Gettysburg

James A. Kegel

STACKPOLE
BOOKS

Copyright © 1996 by Stackpole Books

Published by
STACKPOLE BOOKS
5067 Ritter Road
Mechanicsburg, PA 17055

Printed in the United States of America

10   9   8   7   6   5   4   3   2   1

First edition

Permission to reproduce portions of an 1860 map of canals and railroads (page 310) was granted by the Regional Economic History Research Center, Eleutherean Mills Hagley Foundation in Greenville, Delaware.

Library of Congress Cataloging-in-Publication Data

Kegel, James A., 1907–
    North with Lee and Jackson: the lost story of Gettysburg/James A. Kegel.—1st ed.
        p.   cm.
    Includes bibliographical references and index.
    ISBN 0-8117-1128-5
    1. United States—History—Civil War, 1861–1865—Campaigns. 2. Strategy—History—19th Century. 3. Confederate States of America—History, Military. 4. East (U.S.)—History, Military. 5. Lee, Robert E. (Robert Edward), 1807–1870—Military leadership. 6. Jackson, Stonewall 1824–1863—Military leadership. 7. Gettysbrug Campaign, 1863. I. Title.
E470.2.K44   1996
973.7'3—dc20
                                                                                96-141
                                                                                 CIP

*To my wife, Mickey,
in appreciation for her
encouragement and patience during
the long years of research and writing
and for her valued assistance in reading copy*

CONTENTS

LIST OF MAPS

FOREWORD

HINDSIGHT HANDICAPS HISTORIANS. PERSPECTIVE POSES PROBLEMS. Knowing that historical events developed in a certain way sometimes leads the student of history to assume that those events *must have* developed in that way. Then, when those events result in something great and momentous, the student often focuses on that occurrence itself, paying little attention to its prelude and even less to reasonable ways in which the situation might have developed differently.

This approach applies all too often to military history. Awareness that a campaign or campaigns culminated in a great and often decisive battle frequently leads the student to concentrate on that battle and to neglect the preceding campaign. Blenheim thus overshadows the early eighteenth century, Saratoga and Yorktown dominate the Revolutionary War, Austerlitz exalts Napoleon victorious, and Waterloo enshrouds the French emperor in defeat.

The Battle of Gettysburg comparably towers over the American Civil War, especially its Eastern Theater. The fascination with that battle is understandable and the publication of books on it appears endless. In recent years, war games, videos, television documentaries, and movies have joined them. Such offerings appeal to readers and viewers for everyone now knows that military operations in the East during the first twenty-seven months of the war resulted in the epic Battle of Gettysburg.

Such knowledge comes from hindsight. Yet, during those twenty-seven months, that certainty obviously was denied to the Confederate and Federal officers whose strategy eventually brought the Army of

Northern Virginia and the Army of the Potomac to battle at Gettysburg. Those generals could not see the future; they acted in the present in the hope that they could steer the future toward their advantage.

The challenge of the historian is to seek to understand the military situation as the participants might have at the time. That affords keener comprehension of how generals exercised command. Freeing oneself from knowing the outcome of their operations makes one realize that the outcome was not predetermined at all.

James A. Kegel accepts this challenge in his important new book, *North with Lee and Jackson: The Lost Story of Gettysburg.* He analyzes Confederate generalship not as if it would inexorably lead to Little Round Top and Pickett's Charge but as it actually developed. He also does not keep his study within the confines of a campaign. For him, the "Gettysburg Campaign" did not begin in May or June 1863 but rather formed an integral part of a Southern strategic offensive that governed Confederate operations in the Eastern Theater for the entire first half of the war. He recognizes that what we call the Romney Campaign, the Shenandoah Valley Campaign of 1862, the Second Manassas Campaign, the Maryland Campaign, and the Gettysburg Campaign were not separate operations but parts of this strategy.

By approaching events as they unfolded and perceiving their unity over time, he offers fresh understanding of events in the Eastern Theater from 1861 to 1863.

His analysis is supported by forty years of studying the campaigns of Robert E. Lee and Stonewall Jackson. Over those years, Mr. Kegel also served as reporter and assistant city editor of the *Lancaster Intelligencer Journal,* as public information officer of the Pennsylvania Department of Agriculture, and as World War I survey coordinator of the U.S. Army Military History Institute. Since 1976, he has been an active member of the Harrisburg Civil War Round Table.

This interest in the Civil War and experience in writing come through clearly in his book. Equally clear is the breadth of vision and the keenness of insight that characterize his assessments. The result is a significant new interpretation that enhances our understanding of how Lee, Jackson, and other Confederates developed and executed grand strategy during the first half of the Civil War.

Richard J. Sommers
Chief Archivist-Historian
U.S. Army Military History Institute

INTRODUCTION

My interest in the Civil War began in May 1937, when, as a member of the news staff of the *Lancaster Intelligencer Journal* in Pennsylvania, I prepared a special article for Memorial Day. I had to photograph and interview the last Civil War veterans in Lancaster County. There were eleven.

Until that time, Civil War history for me was nothing more than a hazy memory of events studied during school days and of my grandmother recalling her girlhood in southern Lancaster County, when she saw smoke from the burning Columbia-Wrightsville bridge in late June 1863.

In grade school and high school, I had little interest in history. It was dull, with most of its attention focused on dates. But all that changed in May 1937. Talking to those eleven veterans, whose ages ranged from eighty-nine to ninety-seven, sparked my interest in the Civil War and I began to read about it. A few years later, I was given a six-volume set of Carl Sandburg's *Biography of Abraham Lincoln.* I found it very interesting and began to read other Civil War books.

In the last week of 1946, our family moved to Mechanicsburg in Cumberland County. Gradually, my interest began to focus on the Gettysburg battlefield only thirty miles away. As I read more and more about the battle, I began feeling a vague frustration that something was missing or that I was missing something in the books I read and reread.

I had no idea how much was missing until I began asking questions about things I read and then went in search of answers. In doing this, I was following instructions from Earl E. Keyser, city editor of the *Intelligencer Journal* while I was there.

Mr. Keyser was a strict editor. Copy had to meet the requirements of the "who, what, when, and where" rule that prevailed in those days. If something was not clear or seemed not to fully describe what had happened, he immediately asked the writer about which question the reporter was trying to answer. If the writer said, "I don't know," he was told to drop everything and find the answer.

I quickly learned this procedure from Mr. Keyser and, when questioned about what had been written, could point out that I, too, had recognized the question and had started a search for the answer. I was promoted to Mr. Keyser's assistant about 1940 and kept his procedures. As assistant city editor, I ranked third behind the managing editor and city editor.

The lessons I learned from Earl Keyser and his advice on reading and studying copy helped me seek answers to the questions that I had raised about Gettysburg and related Civil War activities.

In the late 1950s, I had concluded to write about the problems that had bothered me and answers that I had perceived. When I mentioned this possibility to a friend, he asked, "Whatever is left to write about Gettysburg?" I explained, "It is not what has been written, but what has been overlooked or forgotten that interests me."

I continued working on the manuscript into the late seventies but was still not satisfied with it. Maybe the problem was that I still was writing as a newsman, not as a historian. Then, in 1976, there was a significant development.

A friend who was the librarian at the U.S. Army Military History Research Collection (renamed the U.S. Army Military History Institute in 1977) at Carlisle Barracks suggested that I might find helpful material there. She was right, and I was amazed at the number of books and other documents available.

More important, however, was that I met Dr. Richard J. Sommers, the chief archivist-historian, who became interested in my study of the Civil War. We had frequent conversations in which he helped me shift my writing to the historical field. His suggestions and guidance were of great help in properly developing the manuscript.

In 1979, it was my good fortune to be employed at the institute to supervise the World War I survey started four years earlier. It was completed in 1983 but my contact with MHI and Dr. Sommers is a continuing friendship.

Without the guidance of Earl Keyser and Dr. Sommers, I would not have been able to do proper research and develop the text that follows.

I am indeed grateful to Dr. Sommers also for his valued services as my mentor in reading the copy I had prepared.

I also appreciate the assistance of my good friend William C. "Jack" Davis, who has had more than thirty Civil War books published. He raised interesting questions about the manuscript that set me in search of answers as Earl Keyser had taught me to do. Jack also added good suggestions at other points.

In pursuing the extensive research for this project, I was helped by many staff members at archives and libraries throughout the nation. I am deeply indebted to them.

I also extend my appreciation to the following for their special assistance: Michael Hammerson of London, England, who made available to me a copy of Lee's letter of April 8, 1863, regarding his health problem and use of quinine; Dr. Joseph Cincotta of Shepherdstown, Pennsylvania, for providing details on the use of quinine; my friend Lowell Reidenbaugh of St. Louis, Missouri (who also was at the *Intelligencer Journal* when I worked there), for background on Stonewall Jackson that he had developed; and Dr. Gerald Brinton and Robert Swift of the Harrisburg Civil War Round Table for maps and notes. Thanks also to Leo L. Ward of Pottsville, Pennsylvania, president of the Historical Society of Schuylkill County, for material on anthracite coal production during the Civil War, and to Robert J. Trout, fellow member of the Stuart-Mosby Historical Society, for providing a photograph of Alexander J. Boteler.

PROLOGUE

Looking Back before the Battle

IT WAS SATURDAY, JUNE 27, IN THE CRITICAL YEAR OF 1863. THE CON-
federate invasion of the North was under way and troops of the Army of
Northern Virginia, already well into Pennsylvania, were moving toward
the Susquehanna River.

In the lead was the 2nd Corps, commanded by Lieutenant General
Richard S. Ewell. Two of its three divisions were at Carlisle on the main
road to Harrisburg. The third division had reached Gettysburg and was
on its way eastward to York and Wrightsville. Behind it, in the Chambersburg area, were the 1st and 3rd corps, commanded by Lieutenant
Generals James Longstreet and A. P. Hill.[1]

Ewell's primary targets were the long bridges across the Susquehanna, one at Wrightsville and two leading from Cumberland County to
Harrisburg on the river's east bank. If they could be seized, the way
would be open for General Robert E. Lee, commander of the Army of
Northern Virginia, to march into the industrial heart of the North. Carrying the war beyond the Susquehanna, it was believed, might well bring
peace and independence to the Confederate States of America.

With 22,000 men, Ewell was preparing to advance to the Susquehanna. Behind him, at Chambersburg, were Longstreet and Hill with
almost 44,000 men. South of the Potomac River, around Washington,
was Major General J. E. B. Stuart with three brigades of cavalry.[2] Most of
the Southerners were battle-hardened and there was not much standing
in their way.

A week earlier, on June 20, there had been only 1,321 troops in the

1

entire Department of the Susquehanna.[3] By June 29, the arrival of volunteers and militia from Pennsylvania, New York, and other states had increased the strength to 16,000. Major General Darius N. Couch, department commander, expressed his opinion that they would be no match for 5,000 seasoned enemy troops.[4]

Everything seemed to be going well, but Lee was uneasy. He had not yet heard from Stuart, who, on June 24, had moved to threaten the rear of the Army of the Potomac and get between it and Washington. On the morning of the 27th, Stuart reached Fairfax Court House, Virginia, and learned that Union troops had crossed the Potomac at Leesburg and were moving toward Frederick, Maryland.[5] He sent a dispatch to Lee describing the Union movement, but the message apparently went astray. It never reached Lee, though a copy, dated June 27, was received in Richmond several days later.[6]

Seated in his tent near Chambersburg on that sultry Saturday afternoon of June 27, Lee studied a map of Pennsylvania. With him was Major General Isaac R. Trimble, who had rejoined the army a few days earlier after recovering from a serious wound suffered in the Second Battle of Bull Run.

Lee told Trimble that he had not yet heard of enemy troops crossing the Potomac but was waiting for word from Stuart. He then asked Trimble, a civil engineer, to describe the topography east of Chambersburg, especially Adams County and its seat, Gettysburg. Trimble, a West Point graduate, had resigned from the army in 1832 and served as a civil engineer and superintendent with several Eastern railroads. Trimble told Lee the area "contained good positions for battle or skillful maneuvering."

Lee said he expected the Union Army to protect Baltimore and Philadelphia and after crossing the Potomac, probably would move northward through Frederick. If so, Lee added, he would hit its advance force, then attack separated units as they came up, "and by successive repulses and surprises before they can concentrate, create a panic and virtually destroy the army." Then, according to Trimble, Lee put his hand on the map over Gettysburg and said:

Hereabout we shall probably meet the enemy and fight a great battle, and if God gives us the victory, the war will be over and we shall achieve the recognition of our independence.

In dismissing Trimble, Lee reportedly said: "General Ewell's forces are by this time in Harrisburg; if not, go and join him and help [him] to take the place."[7]

———————

On the night of June 28, a scout brought bad news to Lee. Union troops had crossed the Potomac and were moving through Maryland into Pennsylvania. Advance units reportedly were marching on several roads leading toward Gettysburg.

The enemy approach in that area discouraged the movement against Harrisburg, so Lee focused his attention on Gettysburg. It was there, almost by chance, that the armies met on July 1 and struggled through three days of battle.[8] More than 163,000 men were involved, 51,000 of whom became casualties. The total number of dead was put at 5,662 to 7,058.[9]

Because of heavy depletion of men and ammunition, Lee abandoned the battle. On the rainy night of July 4, he began to withdraw on the long and painful march back to Virginia, where he would fight out the rest of the war.[10]

Eventually, the Battle of Gettysburg on July 1–3, 1863, was recognized as the high tide of the Confederacy and, along with the Confederate surrender of Vicksburg, Mississippi, on July 4, the turning point in the Civil War. The battlefield itself is well preserved and attracts more than a million visitors a year. Hundreds of cannon stand along the battle lines and more than 1,000 monuments and other markers identify the positions and movements of troops.[11]

———————

The Gettysburg story has been told and retold in countless books, speeches, articles, and other documents.[12] But another side of the story has been overlooked—lost behind the smoke and thunder of battle. It is the story of Confederate strategy that led to Gettysburg, the planning of the campaign to invade Pennsylvania, who originated it, when and how it was conceived, what the Confederates hoped to do, how they hoped to do it, and what went wrong.

To understand that part of Confederate military history, a special viewpoint is needed. Instead of allowing the battle to dominate this study and analysis, time must be turned back to events that preceded it. What was intended must be determined, not what eventually happened.

More than a century and a quarter after the battle, the history of the campaign that led to Gettysburg is still clouded by questions, confusing statements, and misinterpreted facts. The search for answers is like trying to put together a giant jigsaw puzzle when many pieces are missing—or pieces have been brushed aside and lost over time. As missing pieces are found and put into place, the picture takes on new dimension and reveals a new perspective of the campaign.

⋯⋯⋯

Why was this battle fought at Gettysburg? In his preliminary report, dated July 31, 1863, and in the detailed report dated January 20, 1864, Lee stated that he had not intended to fight a general battle at such a distance from his base if it could be avoided. But because of the unexpected approach of the enemy, the battle "had become in a measure unavoidable."[13]

The wording of the reports appears to contradict the idea, supposedly expressed by Lee to Trimble, to attack the enemy unit by unit. Yet Lee himself, just three years after the war, stated to a colleague at Washington College (now Washington and Lee University in Lexington, Virginia) that "he did not want to fight unless he could get a good opportunity to hit them in detail [separated units]."[14] That wording tends to bear out Lee's intention, quoted by Trimble, to hit the enemy unit by unit.

That phase of the Gettysburg story raises another question. Why did Lee take his entire army into Pennsylvania? In a dispatch to Ewell on June 19, twelve days before the battle, Lee made it clear that he preferred to send only one corps into Pennsylvania. The rest of the army, he implied, could prevent the enemy from pursuing the invading column.[15] If Lee had intended to invade Pennsylvania with only one corps, when and how was such a plan changed?

Hindering the search for answers is the absence of postwar accounts by Lee. He had intended to write a history of the Army of Northern Virginia's campaigns and battles, but died on October 12, 1870, before he could begin work. This was tragic because it deprived future historians of many facts known to Lee alone.

Less than four months after the Confederate surrender at Appomattox Court House, Virginia, on April 9, 1865, Lee made known his desire to write this history. In a letter to Colonel Walter H. Taylor, a staff member during the war, Lee said: "I am desirous that the bravery and devotion of the Army of Northern Virginia shall be correctly transmitted to posterity. This is the only tribute that can now be paid to the worth of its noble officers and soldiers."

At that time, however, Lee faced a seemingly insurmountable task. He pointed out to Taylor that all of his official documents "have been lost or destroyed." He asked Taylor if he could provide any information,[16] but he could not offer much help, nor could other former Confederate officers whom Lee contacted.

In the meantime, great public interest in the war and its battles had developed on both sides and in Europe. Publishers were eager to satisfy this demand and sought material from leading participants. Many who knew, or purported to know, important details of the war or of specific battles and campaigns quickly grasped the opportunity.

But when Lee was asked by a number of publishers to prepare a history, he declined. In a letter of October 25, 1865, to the firm of Scranton & Burr in Hartford, Connecticut, Lee stated:

I can not undertake now the work you propose nor can I enter into an engagement to do what I may never be able to perform. It will be some time before the truth can be known and I do not think that period has yet arrived.[17]

On January 19, 1866, Lee wrote to Longstreet and repeated a request for assistance in gathering material for his history. He said:

I shall be in no hurry in publishing, and will not do so until I feel that I have got the true story, as my only object is to disseminate the truth.[18]

Lee's frustrating search was summarized in his letter of June 8, 1866, to Colonel Osmun Latrobe, assistant adjutant general on Longstreet's staff. "I regret to learn that the mass of official papers of Longstreet's Corps were destroyed in the conflagration at Richmond," Lee told Latrobe, then added:

> All my records, reports, returns, orders, &c., were destroyed near Appomattox Courthouse by those in charge of them from needless apprehension. There is no possibility of ever replacing them.[19]

Actually, only some of Lee's and Longstreet's papers had been lost or destroyed, chiefly those of the 1864–65 campaigns. Vast records of Confederate military headquarters, as well as government documents from earlier in the war, had been preserved by Union authorities. From 1880 to 1901, this material and a mass of Union documents were printed in the 128-volume set known as the Official Records.

This was no help to Lee. Early in 1868, however, his efforts to assemble material for his history entered a new—and overlooked—phase.

Lee became president of Washington College on October 2, 1865. On the faculty was Colonel William Allan, who had been an ordnance officer in the Army of Northern Virginia. Allan frequently saw Lee on business, and it was inevitable that conversation occasionally would turn to the war. On February 15, 1868, Allan began to record these talks in a composition book. There were thirty-six handwritten pages covering seven conversations with Lee, starting with February 15. Some corrections in the text are in Lee's writing. Perhaps after each conversation, the book was shown to Lee to ensure its accuracy. The book remained in the Allan family until September 27, 1946, when it was presented to Washington and Lee University, where it was placed in the Cyrus Hall McCormick Library.

The material is a priceless source. It covers a wide range of subjects, including a great deal about the invasion of the North, related incidents, and the Battle of Gettysburg.

Allan apparently wanted to help assemble notes for the history that Lee contemplated. In a conversation dated December 17, 1868, he noted that he had gone to Lee's office to discuss insurance business. While there, Allan wrote, he urged Lee to prepare his history.

Lee expressed reluctance but not for the reason given to Scranton & Burr. Lee was disturbed by some accounts already written. In his notes, Allan stated:

> He [Lee] talked about the difficulties and referred to the many errors which had become rife, and which it would be necessary to correct, as one of the disagreeable things that stood in his way.[20]

In a previous conversation, Lee had referred specifically to Gettysburg and, according to Allan, commented, "Critics talk much of that [which] they knew little about."[21]

In letters to publishers and conversations with Allan, Lee focused on a problem that would affect the early accounts of the war, especially those written by ex-Confederates. Most were memoirs prepared without access to official reports, correspondence, and other documents that would become available later.

In their eagerness to have their views published, many of the early writers drafted accounts based on memory. In his conversations with Allan, Lee also drew on his memory. But, as he pointed out, it was intended only as a foundation for the history he hoped to write, one that would require documentation if he were to "disseminate the truth."

Longstreet, the highest-ranking Confederate at Gettysburg to write about the battle—three magazine or newspaper articles and his book, *From Manassas to Appomattox*—also recognized the problem. Unlike Lee, he did not wait until documentation was available. This created a different problem for Longstreet.

An example is the account of the 1st Corps' movement across the Blue Ridge into the Shenandoah Valley of Virginia in June 1863. Three versions of this movement are presented in the articles and book he wrote. In a letter to Latrobe on February 27, 1866, he asked for help in locating the papers he needed, then added, "One's memory at best should not be relied upon, in writing for the historian of the future."[22]

In the preface of his book, Longstreet expressed his regret that Lee had not been able to write his history. He then noted that in writing his own history thirty years after the war, he found that the "official War Records" had supplied "a great mass of trustworthy statistics."[23]

This remark and the comment in his letter to Latrobe show a problem that still bothers researchers: the questionable reliance on memory alone.

⟶⟶⟶●⟵⟵⟵

In light of Lee's disclosures to Allan and Longstreet's comment, it becomes necessary to re-examine some accepted versions of the Gettysburg story. One is the belief that the campaign originated after the Battle of Chancellorsville. Another is that the invasion movement commenced on June 3, 1863, when Confederate troops left the Fredericksburg, Virginia, area, marched to Culpeper, and, a week later, headed into the Shenandoah Valley on their way northward to Pennsylvania.

True, the first northward steps were taken by Confederate troops in late May and early June. But a chain of evidence links that movement and the one in 1862 into a single effort that should be designated "the invasion campaign."

To understand this, it is necessary to turn away from Gettysburg and the battle there. The search goes back before the war to events that shaped the careers of Lee and Jackson, who had such important roles in the Confederacy's attempt to win its independence.

With the start of the Civil War, it is necessary to follow Lee and Jackson as the invasion plan was developed and then march northward along the road that led first to disappointment at Antietam in 1862 and finally to defeat at Gettysburg in 1863.

PART 1

Invasion Proposed

CHAPTER 1

The Road to War

THE SINGLE-CAMPAIGN CONCEPT IS NOT NEW. COLONEL CHARLES Marshall, aide-de-camp on General Robert E. Lee's staff, wrote after the war:

> The battles and strategic movements which attracted so much attention were not separate and distinct events, entirely independent one of the other, but formed parts of one plan of warfare, adopted by General Lee at the time he took command of the army [of Northern Virginia], and steadily pursued until his means were exhausted. The battles on the Chickahominy and at Manassas, the invasion of Maryland, and the invasion of Pennsylvania, all had a common object.

While the primary purpose was defense of Richmond, Marshall wrote, it was "a plan deemed by General Lee to be the best adapted to meet the necessities of this country, and to secure final success."[1]

Adopting this plan was the first step by Lee to shift from strictly defensive strategy to offensive action. At that time, in the first week of June 1862, Lee endorsed a plan proposed by Major General Thomas J. Jackson to move into Pennsylvania, then remarked that if Jackson could be strongly reinforced, "it would change the character of the war."[2]

The first invasion movement began after the Union commander, Major General George B. McClellan, had been repulsed in the Seven Days Battles in 1862. It was turned back at the Battle of Antietam, however, and Lee and Jackson began a long series of meetings on how to renew the invasion in 1863. This time, the strategy was drastically changed.

The Confederate plan for 1863 first emphasized the intention to avoid a general battle if possible. Instead, Confederate forces were to move freely about the invaded area, threaten cities, and disrupt the Northern economy.

The major objective was to close coal mines, particularly anthracite mines in seven northeastern counties of Pennsylvania, which supplied more than half of the nation's total annual coal production. That would have two important results: It would deprive factories in the northeastern states of fuel and would idle Navy steamships, especially blockaders along the East Coast and in the Gulf of Mexico.

Another objective was to disrupt traffic on railroads and canals, isolating the Union states west of Pennsylvania. These actions would bring economic pressure to bear on the entire North and encourage the people to seek an end to the war.

To understand how and when this strategic plan was developed and set in motion, it is necessary to trace events that brought Lee and Jackson into the military forces of Virginia. One also must recognize that these two differed early in the war on offensive and defensive strategy and know how the differences were resolved. It is also necessary to understand events that brought Lee and Jackson together on the battlefield in June 1862 and the close relationship that developed between them after that.

It also is important to weigh the influence of Northern activities—on the military and home fronts—that affected development of Confederate invasion plans and changes made after they were in motion. Other factors to consider were Virginia's early desire to remain in the Union and the untimely event that resulted in the state's secession.

———✦———

In the spring of 1842 an eighteen-year-old youth in Jacksons Mill, Virginia, made a momentous decision. Thomas Jonathan (then known as Tom) Jackson sought appointment to the United States Military Academy at West Point, New York.

He was one of four youths from western Virginia who sought the appointment. One was too young, and the others took a test that would enable Representative Samuel L. Hays, the district's congressman, to select a candidate.

The result was a bitter disappointment to Tom. He finished second. Gilson J. Butcher was first, and he received a conditional appointment from the secretary of war on April 19, 1842. The next month he left for West Point. After a few days Butcher decided he would not like the strict life of a cadet. Without notifying anyone at the school, Butcher packed his belongings and left West Point on June 2. On his way home he stopped at Jacksons Mill and explained what had happened.[3]

Friends and relatives urged Tom to try again, and he sought the advice of a cousin's husband, Colonel J. M. Bennett, who asked Jackson if he had done anything to prepare himself for the strict standards of the academy. "I am very ignorant, but can make it up by study," Tom replied. "I know I have the energy, and I think I have the intellect."[4]

Impressed by this determination, Bennett wrote a letter of recommendation to Hays, who had returned to Washington. Influential friends, acquaintances, and relatives joined in recommending Jackson for the appointment. Tom left immediately for Washington, arrived at Hays's office on June 17, and presented the recommendations. Among them was a letter from Gilson Butcher. It was his formal resignation from the academy and noted that the letter would be delivered by "Mr. Jackson who is an applicant for the appointment."[5]

The next day Jackson received the appointment.[6] He arrived at West Point on June 19 and learned that he and all the other candidates would be required to take three days of entrance examinations. On June 25, the Academic Board posted the list of those who had been accepted for admission to the academy. The last name was that of Thomas J. Jackson.

On July 1, 1842, twenty-one years to the day before the Battle of Gettysburg began, Jackson entered West Point. At the end of his first year he ranked fifty-first in a class of eighty-three; at the end of his second, he was thirtieth in a class of seventy-eight; in his third, he was twentieth in a class of sixty-two; when he graduated after four years, with the brevet rank of second lieutenant, he was seventeenth in a class of fifty-nine.[7]

In second place was George B. McClellan, whose troops Jackson faced in battle in Virginia and Maryland. Ranking thirteenth, four places ahead of Jackson at graduation, was Darius N. Couch, who as a major general commanded the Department of the Susquehanna during the invasion of Pennsylvania in 1863. In last place was George E. Pickett, who as a Confederate major general made the climactic charge at Gettysburg.[8]

War with Mexico had broken out a few months before his class graduated, and Lieutenant Jackson and a number of his classmates were assigned there. He served bravely and his commanding officers cited him in several battle reports, noting particularly leadership that earned him three rapid promotions. Over eighteen months Jackson was given the brevet ranks of first lieutenant, captain, and major in the 1st U.S. Artillery Regiment.[9]

The war ended and Jackson's command was sent to Fort Hamilton, New York, in June 1848. Two years later, he was transferred to Fort Meade, near Tampa Bay in Florida.[10] On February 4, 1851, Jackson was given an opportunity to return to civilian life.

That day he received a letter from F. H. Smith, superintendent of Virginia Military Institute in Lexington, Virginia, asking if he would serve as professor of natural and experimental philosophy. Jackson agreed and reported on August 13. The new term began on September 1, and Jackson was given additional duties. He was to serve as instructor of artillery for the cadets.[11]

Jackson also developed a deeply religious character at VMI, a trait evident in his career as a Confederate officer. In November 1851, he joined Lexington Presbyterian Church and became a deacon.[12] Jackson accepted religion with intensity and deep feeling, a characteristic that remained throughout the rest of his life.[13]

———⊸◈⊶———

Ten years passed before Jackson returned to military duty. The guns at Fort Sumter, South Carolina, had been silent little more than a week, and the storm clouds of civil war were beginning to roll ominously over the land. Governor John Letcher of Virginia called for volunteers and also requested the services of VMI cadets. On April 21, 1861, Major Jackson led the corps of cadets from Lexington to Richmond, where he was nominated for a commission as colonel of Virginia volunteers.[14]

The appointment was confirmed April 27, and the next day he was ordered to Harpers Ferry to take command of Virginia militia that had seized the U. S. arsenal there. The order came from Robert E. Lee, a new major general who had been placed in command of Virginia's military forces.[15]

———⊸◈⊶———

Lee was Virginia's second choice to take command of the state's forces. Winfield Scott, the Union general in chief, had rejected the assignment.[16]

A descendant of an old and prominent Virginia family, Lee graduated from West Point in 1829 and was commissioned a lieutenant of engineers. He served with distinction in Mexico under Scott and in 1852 was appointed superintendent of West Point. Three years later he was promoted to lieutenant colonel and assigned to the 2nd Cavalry, a new unit organized for duty in Texas at the urging of Secretary of War Jefferson Davis.[17]

While on furlough in Washington in October 1859, Lee was placed in command of a small force sent to Harpers Ferry to put down an incipient revolt by John Brown. With him went a young lieutenant, J. E. B. Stuart, who had volunteered to accompany Lee. Stuart had been a cadet at West Point when Lee was superintendent there.[18]

After the John Brown affair Lee returned to Texas and was on duty there when South Carolina seceded on December 20, 1860. As the wave of secession swept across the South, Lee was shocked and hurt. He expressed his deep concern in letters to his family on January 23, 1861.

He had just finished reading a biography of George Washington and wrote to his wife: "How his spirit would be grieved could he see the wreck of his mighty labors! I will not, however, permit myself to believe, till all ground for hope has gone that the work of his noble deeds will be forgotten by his countrymen. As far as I can judge by the [news]papers we are between a state of anarchy and civil war. May God avert from us both."

To his daughter Agnes he added: "I can however do nothing but trust to the wisdom & patriotism of the nation & to the overruling providence of a merciful God."[19] In a letter to a son he stated: "As an American citizen I take great pride in my country, her prosperity, and her institutions, and would defend any State if her rights were invaded. But I can anticipate no greater calamity for the country than a dissolution of the Union. It would be an accumulation of all the evils we complain of, and I am willing to sacrifice everything but honor for its preservation."[20]

Lee would be called upon, sooner than he expected, to make a painful decision. On February 4 he was ordered to return to Washington and report to the general in chief.[21] When Lee arrived at Scott's office in early March, he naturally was curious about his recall from Texas. Scott said the purpose was to have Lee and several other officers revise Army regulations. Then the talk turned to the growing trouble between North and South. The possibility was mentioned that the Army might have to put down another wave of rebellion, this one much greater than the incident that had taken Lee to Harpers Ferry in 1859. Under these circumstances, Lee told Scott, "he could not go on duty against the South."

In an effort to reassure Lee and allay his fears, Scott produced "a mass" of correspondence from President Lincoln, Secretary of State William H. Seward, and others. Scott said the letters led him to "think there would be no war." Lee described one from Seward as "very pacific in tone." In it, Lee said, Seward was "very emphatic and stated that he would not remain in the cabinet if he thought any thing but peace was contemplated."

Lee feared that the purpose of his recall from Texas was to put him on war duty. If so, he intended to resign before orders could be issued. But he found Scott's remarks reassuring and left Washington for his home across the Potomac River "much relieved." In the next few weeks the only word Lee received from Washington was that he had been promoted to the rank of full colonel. All that time, Lee said, he was convinced that Scott "himself believed that a peaceful solution would be attained."

But on Thursday, April 18, Lee was forced to face reality. That day he met in Washington with Francis P. Blair, a powerful political figure who told Lee that Lincoln and his Cabinet wanted him to command U.S. forces in the field because Scott was too old. Blair's lengthy attempt at persuasion failed. Lee said he prayed war could be averted but that "he could not take arms against the South."

After the meeting Lee went directly to Scott's office and told him of the conversation with Blair. He said he had declined the offer and stated his reasons. Scott "expressed his deep regret" but said he had rather expected it from what Lee had said on his return from Texas.

Still torn between loyalty to the Union and devotion to his native state, Lee went home to struggle with his conscience. He decided to resign rather than risk disobeying orders. The next day, he wrote his resignation, "but kept it by him another night to reflect fully" on his decision.[22]

The next morning, Saturday, April 20, Lee sent the letter to Scott. "Since my interview with you on the 18th instant," he wrote, "I have felt that I ought not longer to retain my commission in the Army. I therefore tender my resignation, which I request you will recommend for acceptance. It would have been presented at once, but for the struggle it has cost me to separate myself from a service to which I have devoted all the best years of my life and all the ability I possessed. Save in defense of my native State, I never desire again to draw my sword." This was followed by a brief message to Secretary of War Simon Cameron announcing that "I have the honor to tender the resignation of my commission as Colonel of the 1st Regt. of Cavalry."[23]

Two other letters were written the same day. One was to Lee's brother, Sydney Smith Lee, who later served in the Confederate Navy. The other was to his sister, Anne Marshall of Baltimore, who was married to Judge William Marshall, a staunch Union man.

To his brother he explained: "I am at any time to be ordered on duty which I could not conscientiously perform. To save me from such a position, and to prevent the necessity of resigning under orders, I had to act at once, and before I could see you again on the subject, as I had wished."

An even more poignant plea for understanding was sent to his sister. He told her:

> I am grieved at my inability to see you. I have been waiting for a more convenient season which has brought to many before me lasting regret. Now we are in a state of war which will yield to nothing. The whole South is in a state of revolution, into which Virginia, after a long struggle, has been drawn; and though I recognize no necessity for this state of things, and would have forborne and pleaded to the end for redress of grievances, real or supposed, yet in my own person I had to meet the question whether I should take part against my native state.
>
> With all my devotion to the Union, and the feeling of loyalty as an American citizen, I have not been able to make up my mind to raise my hand against my relatives, my children, my home. I have therefore, resigned my commission in the Army, and save in defense of my native state (with the sincere hope that my poor services may never be needed) I hope I may never be called upon to draw my sword.
>
> I know you will blame me, but you must think kindly as you can, and believe that I have endeavored to do what I thought right. To show you the feeling and struggle it has cost me I send you a copy of my letter of resignation. I have no time for more. May God guard and protect you and yours and shower upon you everlasting blessings, is the prayer of your devoted brother.[24]

Once the decision was made, Lee was prepared to return to civilian life and spend the rest of his time in retirement.[25] It was not to be. Sunday night, April 21, the day after he had submitted his resignation and written his brother and sister, Lee received an important visitor with an urgent message. It was Judge John Robertson, Virginia's commissioner to other Southern states involved in secession. Robertson informed Lee that the Virginia convention, after voting for secession four days earlier, had sent him to Washington to see Scott and ask him to take command of Virginia's military forces.[26] Scott, born near Petersburg, Virginia, and educated at the College of William and Mary, declined.[27]

"In such a contingency," Lee quoted Robertson as saying, "he had been instructed to see Lee and invite him to Richmond." They talked briefly and Lee agreed to meet Robertson the next morning in nearby Alexandria. After another short talk, they boarded a train to Richmond, where Letcher offered Lee command of Virginia's forces.[28] He accepted and the formal nomination was approved immediately.[29]

The next day, April 23, Lee appeared before the delegates for a brief but solemn ceremony. John Janney, the convention president, told Lee that Virginia "placed her sword in your hand upon the implied condition that in all things you will keep it to the letter and spirit, that you will draw it only in her defense."

Lee responded with a few careful words and a fervent pledge: "Trusting to Almighty God, an approving conscience and the aid of my fellow citizens, I will devote myself to the defense and service of my native State, in whose behalf alone would I have ever drawn my sword."[30]

During the troubled days that followed, Lee kept hoping that war could be averted. On April 25, two days after taking command of Virginia's forces, Lee wrote to a friend:

> No earthly act could give me so much pleasure as to restore peace to my country. But I fear it is now out of the power of man, and in God alone must be our trust. . . . I think our policy should be purely defensive, to resist aggression and allow time to allay the passions and permit Reason to assume sway.[31]

The next day he wrote to his wife, Mary, expressing his fear that war was inevitable and urging her to leave the family home at Arlington. In a letter four days later Lee again urged his wife to leave Arlington and seek safety elsewhere.

"Where to go is the difficulty," he told her. "When war commences no place will be exempt in my opinion, & indeed all the avenues into the State will be the scene of military operations." He explained that he did not expect Virginia "to make war," but doubted that the Federal government would delay taking action against seceding states. To this he added a deeply pessimistic note expressing his belief that "the war may last ten years."[32]

Virginia faced a peculiar predicament regarding secession. It had almost half a million slaves, more than any other state, and free blacks outnumbered slaveholders by more than 5,000. Its sympathies were, naturally, with the slaveholding states, but there also was strong public sentiment for the Union.[33]

Five states had seceded during January: Mississippi on the 9th, Florida on the 10th, Alabama on the 11th, Georgia on the 19th, and Louisiana on the 26th.[34]

As the wave spread across the South, Virginia could not ignore the issue. On January 7, 1861, Letcher called the Virginia General Assembly into special session to consider the situation and determine, if possible, what course the state should follow.

In this troubled atmosphere legislators tried to stay level-headed. On January 14 they ordered a general election for delegates to a convention to consider secession. It was scheduled for February 4.[35]

On January 19 legislators invited representatives of all states to meet in Washington to seek a peaceful solution. Just so there would be no misunderstanding about Virginia's position if the mission failed, the legislators two days later adopted a resolution stipulating that if nothing was accomplished at the conference, then "every consideration of honor and interest demands that Virginia shall unite her destiny with the slaveholding states to the South."[36]

Of the 152 delegates selected February 4, 46 were described as secessionists while the rest were considered moderates who had expressed their desire to save the Union.[37]

The same day, representatives from fourteen Northern states and seven Southern ones met in Washington. Virginia was represented by former President John Tyler, Judge John W. Brockenbrough, William C. Rives, George W. Summers, and James A. Seddon (later a Confederate secretary of war). Nothing concrete was accomplished, though the conferees did draft a reconciliation plan. It was submitted to Congress but rejected.[38]

There was a slight glimmer of hope that could not be overlooked. On February 7 Tyler sent an urgent message to Governor Francis W. Pickens of South Carolina in which the Virginia delegates urged him not to attack Fort Sumter.[39]

Delegates from the six seceded states had met in Montgomery, Alabama, on February 4 and drafted a provisional constitution, naming Montgomery as the provisional Confederate capital. It was adopted

February 8. The next day they elected Jefferson Davis of Mississippi as president and Alexander H. Stephens of Georgia as vice president.[40]

On March 2 Texas was admitted to the Confederacy. Four days later a permanent constitution was adopted, and the provisional president, vice president, and other officers were designated to serve until elections could be held in December.[41]

The Virginia state convention met March 6. After hearing the report on the Washington conference, delegates continued to try to avert a conflict. Another effort was made April 8 when the convention sent three members to Washington to meet with President Lincoln.

The timing could not have been worse. Despite Virginia's plea to South Carolina to spare Fort Sumter, it was bombarded early on April 12. Virginia's peace delegates first met with Lincoln that day. They met again with him on April 13, the day the firing ceased and the fort's garrison prepared to surrender. The only thing the Virginians brought from the conference was a statement by Lincoln declaring his intention to "coerce the seceding states into obedience to Federal authority."[42]

Two days later Lincoln called for 75,000 troops to help suppress rebellion and "maintain the honor, the integrity, and the existence of our National Union." Their first objective, he stated, "will probably be to repossess the forts, places and property which have been seized from the Union."

This was followed by a message from Cameron to governors of loyal states and those in the South that had not seceded. The men were to serve for three months and quotas were assigned to each of twenty-four states. Virginia's was 2,340 officers and men.[43]

Reaction was swift. In an angry letter to Cameron on April 16, Letcher stated:

> I have only to say that the militia of Virginia will not be furnished to the powers at Washington for any such use or purpose as they have in view. Your object is to subjugate the Southern States, and a requisition made upon me for such an object—an object, in my judgment, not within the purview of the Constitution or the act of 1795—will not be complied with.
>
> You have chosen to inaugurate civil war, and having done so, we will meet it in a spirit as determined as the Administration has exhibited toward the South.[44]

Lincoln's call and Letcher's reply brought a dramatic change in public opinion. On Wednesday, April 17, the Virginia convention voted eighty-eight to fifty-five to secede. The ordinance would not be effective unless ratified by Virginia voters in a poll set for Thursday, May 23.[45]

It was not an easy decision for many of the delegates. One of those who voted against the ordinance was Jubal A. Early, who became one of Lee's top field commanders. He was a West Pointer who had fought in the Seminole and Mexican wars, then resigned from the Army to become a lawyer. Early wrote in the preface of his *War Memoirs:*

> I had opposed secession with all the ability I possessed, with the hope that the horrors of civil war might be averted. As a member of the Virginia Convention, I voted against the ordinance of secession on its passage by that body, with the hope that even then, the collision of arms might be avoided and some satisfactory adjustment arrived at.
>
> The passage of that ordinance wrung from me bitter tears of grief. But I at once recognized my duty to abide [by] the decision of my native State, and to defend her soil against invasion.[46]

CHAPTER 2

In Defense of Virginia

AT THE TIME OF SECESSION VIRGINIA WAS THE SECOND-LARGEST CON-
federate state. Only Texas was larger. With 64,000 square miles Virginia
occupied a peculiar geographic position in the Civil War arena. It was the
northernmost of the eleven Confederate states and was the buffer
between South and North. It extended from the Atlantic Ocean to the
Ohio River. It was bounded on the north by Maryland and Pennsylvania,
on the west by Ohio and Kentucky, and on the south by North Carolina
and Tennessee.

In the northwestern corner was a narrow corridor of land between
Pennsylvania and Ohio, the point of which was about ninety miles
from Lake Erie. It was like a dagger almost cutting the North in half,
east from west.

But the northwestern part of Virginia was a land of divided loyalties.
Unrest spread through the area following secession, and steps were taken
to separate that region from the rest of the state. Finally, on June 20,
1863, it was admitted to the Union as West Virginia.

West Virginia occupied about one-third of the total area that had
been Virginia. Of the 148 counties in Virginia in 1860, 50 were transferred to the new state, and 98 remained in what is now Virginia.

Virginia's exposed position made it highly vulnerable to attack.
Union troops could invade from the north along several routes—from
the Washington area into the northeastern corner, from Pennsylvania
through the Cumberland Valley into the Shenandoah Valley, and from
Ohio into western Virginia. In the east the Chesapeake Bay (into which

flowed the Potomac, Rappahannock, York, and James rivers) provided water access to major peninsulas leading inland.

———————

Defense was uppermost in almost everyone's mind after the Virginia convention adopted the secession ordinance on April 17. Adoption of the ordinance, however, was kept secret for two days to allow Virginia authorities to seize the U.S. armory and arsenal in Harpers Ferry, and the Gosport Navy Yard in Norfolk. The installations at Harpers Ferry were seized on April 18 and the navy yard two days later.[1]

That same day, April 20, Governor Letcher called for volunteers as directed in the secession ordinance. He also urged Virginians serving in the U.S. army and navy to resign and enter state service. The next day he instructed volunteer companies to be ready for immediate orders.[2]

On April 25 the Virginia convention took an unusual step. Though the public vote on secession was almost a month away, the convention formed an agreement with Alexander H. Stephens, the Confederate vice president, for a temporary union of Virginia with the Confedercy. Two days later the delegates approved the action by a vote of eighty to sixteen. On May 7 the Confederate Congress ratified a resolution admitting Virginia as the eighth state of the Confederacy.[3]

The agreement with Stephens was followed two days later by an invitation to the Confederacy to make Richmond, "or some other place in this state," the Confederate capital. Congress adopted a resolution May 21 accepting the invitation and directed that the government and its agencies be transferred to Richmond. Jefferson Davis explained that aggressive enemy movements indicated that first efforts were to be directed against Virginia. He added that necessary measures for the state's defense and protection could not be effectively provided unless the capital was in Virginia.[4]

These unusual steps were taken between April 25 and May 21, before Virginians went to the polls on the secession question. The point was moot, however, when the returns came in from May 23; they approved the separation by a vote of 125,950 to 20,373.[5]

———————

Virginia's vulnerability to attack was intensified when the capital was transferred to Richmond in the spring of 1861. Only a little more than

100 miles separated it from the Federal capital, Washington. Richmond, naturally, was a prime target of Union armies.

Defending this area and the rest of Virginia with militia and hastily formed volunteer units presented Lee with difficulties, but his determination to "draw his sword only in defense of Virginia" was evident in his correspondence following his appointment as state commander.

On April 24 he relayed his defensive policies to officers in command at two key points in eastern Virginia. Brigadier General Philip St. George Cocke in Alexandria, just across the Potomac from Washington, was instructed to "let it be known that you intend no attack, but invasion of our soil will be considered an act of war." Brigadier General Daniel Ruggles, stationed in Fredericksburg along the Rappahannock, was told that "you will act on the defensive."[6] Oddly enough, when Lee ordered Jackson to Harpers Ferry three days later, he did not mention any strict defensive policy.

Harpers Ferry is situated on the Virginia (now West Virginia) side of the Potomac where it and the Shenandoah River meet. It is flanked on the Virginia side by two hills, Loudoun Heights to the east and Bolivar Heights to the west. Across the river in Maryland is a third hill, appropriately known as Maryland Heights. Any one of these hills, but especially Maryland Heights, commanded the town.

The Baltimore and Ohio Railroad approached the town from the west along the southern bank of the Potomac. The double-track line crossed the river on a bridge there and continued through Maryland to Washington Junction, where it forked south to the national capital and north to Baltimore. Paralleling the railroad in that area was the Chesapeake and Ohio Canal, which linked Baltimore and Washington to the bituminous coal fields in western Maryland.

The idea of sending Jackson to Harpers Ferry originated with Letcher, not Lee. On April 27, a few days after Jackson's arrival in Richmond with the VMI cadets, Letcher asked Lee to order Jackson to take command at Harpers Ferry. Practically the entire letter dealt with organizational duties, but in a brief passage Letcher told Lee to "give him [Jackson] such general instructions as may be required for the military defenses of the State."[7]

Lee ordered Jackson that day to proceed to Harpers Ferry without delay. He repeated most of the instructions in Letcher's letter but, apparently through an oversight or the pressure of his new duties, did not mention anything about defense.[8]

Jackson left immediately. At Harpers Ferry some found Jackson unimpressive. In an era when soldiering was considered glamorous and officers usually adorned uniforms with as much braid as their rank permitted, Jackson shunned fancy trimmings. His uniform was drab, and some said Jackson lacked "pride, pomp, and circumstance."[9]

It was not long before Lee became concerned, but not about the lack of braid on Jackson's uniform. Jackson had taken a bold step completely at odds with a strict defensive policy: He had sent troops across the river and positioned them on Maryland Heights.

One of the major concerns of the Confederacy was the situation in Maryland. Efforts were being made to woo Maryland away from the Union. Washington would be isolated and the Federal government probably would be forced to withdraw from the capital.

There were indications that Maryland might be leaning toward the South. The state had gone heavily against Lincoln in the election of 1860, and anti-Union feelings were strong in some parts, as they were in Virginia. Baltimore had been torn by rioting, and Southern sympathizers had fired on Union troops passing through the city on their way to Washington. There was open talk of secession, and some Maryland legislators attempted (unsuccessfully, it turned out) to push through a secession ordinance.

In view of this and his own repeated desire to pursue a strict defensive policy, Lee must have been shocked by Jackson's action. "I have occupied the Virginia and Maryland Heights," Jackson informed Lee in a report on May 6. He then stated that he was preparing to construct blockhouses on the Virginia side and that "whenever the emergency calls for it, I shall construct similar works on the Maryland Heights. My object is to put Harpers Ferry in the most defensive state possible."

About the same time Lee wrote to Jackson warning that he "considered it probable that the Government at Washington will make a movement against Harpers Ferry, and occupy the Baltimore and Ohio Railroad, or use the Chesapeake and Ohio Canal for the transportation of troops." If he learned of Union troop movements in that direction, Jackson was to destroy the railroad bridge at Harpers Ferry and to obstruct the passage of the canal "as much as possible."

Lee also suggested that Jackson should arrange with Marylanders to destroy the B&O bridge over the Monocacy River and drain the canal if there was evidence "of the enemy's attempt to make use of either."[10]

Communication between Lee and Jackson was handicapped. The only telegraph service between Richmond and Harpers Ferry was by way of Washington. Rather than risk having messages fall into Federal hands, Lee and Jackson had to rely on couriers or the mail. At least two days were required for mail from one point or the other to reach its destination, so it was difficult for Jackson to keep Lee promptly informed of developments or for Lee to transmit timely instructions.[11]

The situation was further complicated for Lee by new responsibilities. On May 7 Letcher directed Lee to take command of all volunteers in Virginia. Three days later Leroy P. Walker, Confederate secretary of war, notified Lee that he was to assume control of "the forces of the Confederate States in Virginia, and assign them to such duties as you may indicate."[12]

In the midst of organizing Virginia's defenses and in light of his new duties, Lee decided to restrain Jackson's aggressiveness. This becomes increasingly evident in correspondence from May 7 to 12.

Jackson reported that he was determined to fortify Maryland Heights, "be the cost what it may"; that about 4,000 Federal troops were near Chambersburg, Pennsylvania; and that Marylanders with artillery were opposite Shepherdstown, Virginia, and were threatening Confederate troops.

Lee became increasingly stern in his replies. On May 9 he advised Jackson that "it is considered advisable not to intrude upon the soil of Maryland, unless compelled by the necessities of war." On May 10 Lee told Jackson that "you may have been premature in occupying the heights of Maryland. The true policy is to act on the defensive, and not to invite attack." On May 12 Lee expressed concern over the feeling provoked by the Marylanders with artillery and told Jackson to "confine yourself to a strictly defensive course."[13]

————⟶●⟵————

Jackson's letter of May 11, in which he mentioned Marylanders with artillery, is significant for a different reason. Jackson noted that "Col. J. M. Bennett will deliver this [letter] to you, and give important information respecting the northwest [area of Virginia]." Nineteen years earlier, in June 1842, it was Bennett who had encouraged Jackson to seek appointment to West Point and whose letter of recommendation helped Jackson achieve that goal.

In 1861 Bennett was the Virginia state auditor and resided in Richmond. He evidently was visiting at Jackson's headquarters when he was asked to deliver the letter to Lee. In his reply, dated May 12, Lee noted that he had "just received your letter of the 11th instant by Col. Bennett."[14]

Unusual? Perhaps, but not uncommon in Jackson's efforts to convey important information to high authorities. Friends, such as Bennett, would be helpful in presenting his ideas to those authorities and gaining their approval. In addition, Jackson considered it unwise to include important or confidential information in written messages.

<hr />

There were two more letters in this exchange. On May 14 Lee wrote that he was "very much concerned at the condition of things in the country west of you." He asked Jackson to send some help to Virginia troops in Grafton if possible.

A week later, on May 21, Jackson responded with a plan for defense of the northwestern area. "If no better plan is practicable," Jackson wrote, "I suggest that a force destined for the northwest" be assembled in Winchester, Virginia. Upon voter ratification of secession, Jackson added, this force should be rushed to the northwest counties to crush opposition. "You will pardon me for urging promptness in what is to be done for that section of the state," Jackson continued. "Any want of this may be disastrous."[15]

Two days later Jackson was replaced as commander at Harpers Ferry by Brigadier General Joseph E. Johnston, a Confederate officer.[16] Although relieved as overall commander, Jackson still led the 1st Brigade, made up of Virginia volunteers.[17] That day at the polls Virginia voters approved secession.

Federal authorities reacted swiftly. The next day Major General Robert Patterson, commander of the Department of Pennsylvania, was ordered to move toward Frederick, Hagerstown, and Cumberland, in Maryland, to "threaten Harpers Ferry and support Union sentiment in western Virginia."[18] Patterson's force included the troops in Chambersburg whose presence Jackson had reported to Lee on May 9.

At the same time a dispatch was sent from Washington to Major General George B. McClellan, commander of Union troops in the Department of the Ohio. McClellan, Jackson's classmate at West Point, was informed that two companies of Virginia troops reportedly had reached Grafton, a rail junction more than 100 miles west of Harpers

Ferry. They had been sent there, General Scott explained, to counter Union sentiment in western Virginia. McClellan was advised to promptly counteract the move. He immediately sent troops to Grafton and, on May 30, reported that they had occupied the town after its evacuation by the Virginia force.[19]

The more serious threat to Virginia, however, developed in the northeastern corner of the state. Early on May 24, Union troops crossed the Potomac and occupied Arlington Heights and Alexandria.[20] The war that Lee had dreaded had come to Virginia!

———————

At Harpers Ferry it quickly became evident that Jackson and Johnston disagreed on the town's importance. Shortly after taking command Jackson had decided to put Harpers Ferry in "the most defensible state possible." Three days after replacing Jackson Johnston told Lee that "I regard Harpers Ferry as untenable by us at present against a strong enemy."[21]

On June 13, using discretionary power granted him earlier, Johnston prepared to evacuate Harpers Ferry. During the next two days public property was sent to Winchester and bridges over the Potomac at Harpers Ferry and Shepherdstown were destroyed. On June 15 Johnston's troops withdrew toward Winchester. The move was interrupted by a report that Patterson's troops had crossed the Potomac at Williamsport, Maryland. Johnston immediately moved his army northward to counter the threat to Winchester.[22]

———————

The evacuation of Harpers Ferry and Patterson's movements set up Jackson's first encounter with Union troops on July 2 at Falling Waters, south of the Potomac crossing at Williamsport. Compared with battles that followed, it was little more than a skirmish, and Johnston later referred to it merely as "the affair at Falling Waters."

Jackson had been instructed to feel out the enemy and, if he found a superior force, to retire toward Winchester. In addition to his own brigade, Jackson was joined by a Virginia cavalry unit under Lieutenant Colonel J. E. B. Stuart, who had volunteered to accompany Lee to Harpers Ferry during the John Brown uprising in 1859.

Jackson stalled Patterson's advance, then held him in check for several hours. Stuart helped by capturing a company of Union volunteers. Patterson reported on July 3 that the force "we scattered yesterday was thirty-five hundred strong."[23]

In addition to stalling Patterson's advance, the skirmish was important for another reason. It marked the beginning of a strong bond between Jackson and Stuart that became important to Confederate fortunes. It was especially important in the planning and preparation for the Confederate invasion of Pennsylvania in 1863. In his report, Jackson noted that Stuart and his command "merit high praise, and I may here remark that he has exhibited those qualities which are calculated to make him eminent in his arm of the service."[24]

Johnston commented that Jackson had given the enemy "a severe lesson" and recommended that "Colonel Jackson be promoted without delay to the rank of brigadier general." He also recommended Stuart's promotion to the rank of full colonel.[25] A short time later, Jackson was promoted to brigadier general in the Confederate Army; Stuart was promoted on July 16.[26]

The next move marked the beginning of the Jackson legend. It also brought to light a burning desire within him, though few recognized the first tiny flame.

As July slipped away, the Confederacy faced increasing danger in northeastern Virginia. Brigadier General Irvin McDowell, who had been placed in command of Union troops there May 27, was preparing to attack. Confederates under Brigadier General P. G. T. Beauregard had established a defensive line along Bull Run, about twenty-five miles west of Washington, near the junction of the Manassas Gap and the Orange and Alexandria railroads.

Beauregard, with about 22,000 troops, faced a force of more than 35,000. As early as July 9, he asked President Jefferson Davis for more men. When McDowell's intention to attack became evident, Johnston and his force of more than 10,000 was summoned from the Shenandoah Valley to support Beauregard.[27]

On July 18 Johnston and his troops headed eastward. Along with him went Jackson with his brigade of five Virginia regiments. They arrived in Manassas on July 20, and the next morning, advance elements of the opposing armies collided in the Civil War's first major battle.

Union forces secured the upper hand early and, for a time, gained ground against the Southerners. Then the Confederate line stiffened.

It was there at the First Battle of Bull Run (or Manassas, as Southerners called it) that Confederate Brigadier General Barnard Bee, seeking to halt the repulse of his troops, shouted: "Look! There is Jackson standing like a stone wall! Rally behind the Virginians!"[28] Jackson was to be known forever after as Stonewall, and the unit he commanded in that battle was identified as the Stonewall Brigade.

As the Union tide was checked, then reversed, the Yankees began to withdraw. Soon the movement turned into a rout, with much of the defeated army fleeing back to Washington.[29]

———⇒✦⇐———

Far more revealing than his stand at Manassas was Jackson's comment as he watched Federal troops retreat. "Give me ten thousand men," he declared, "and I will be in Washington tonight." Jackson did not get the men and, as the days passed, he waited impatiently for an order to advance. "I have three days' rations cooked," he said. "Why doesn't the order come?"

This was characteristic of Jackson—impatient for action and eager to seize any opportunity he believed would lead to a greater victory. Washington, he claimed, was almost undefended, and the time for attack was "perfectly practicable." While Jackson fretted, the opportunity slipped away. The order to advance was never given and the Southern troops returned to camp.[30]

Unlike Lee, who had adopted a strictly defensive strategy, Jackson intended to go on the offense and end the war quickly. In a letter to his wife on August 22 he said: "Don't put any faith in the assertion that there will be no more fighting till October. It may not be till then; and God grant that, if consistent with His will, it may never be. Surely, I desire no more, if our country's independence can be secured without it."[31]

CHAPTER 3

After Bull Run

THE NORTH WAS STUNNED BY NEWS OF THE DEFEAT AT BULL RUN. Public confidence was shaken, and people soon realized that suppressing the rebellion could become long and difficult.

In Washington, authorities were shocked by the failure of the first "on-to-Richmond" campaign—one the Northern press had eagerly endorsed.[1] Fearful that the Confederates would sweep into the city, they swiftly strengthened defenses of the capital. Their first major move was to summon McClellan from western Virginia to take command.

Officials had been impressed by McClellan's rapid advance from Ohio into western Virginia. On July 14 he received a telegram from Scott: "The General-in-Chief, and what is more the cabinet, including the President, are charmed with your activity, valor, and consequent success. We do not doubt that you will in due time sweep the rebels from West Virginia, but do not mean to precipitate you, as you are fast enough."[2]

A week later, early on Sunday, July 21, as the Battle of Bull Run was taking shape, Scott sent another message to McClellan. Scott was confident as he explained that "Johnston has amused Patterson [north of Martinsburg, Virginia] and re-enforced Beauregard. McDowell is this forenoon forcing the passage of Bull Run. In two hours he will turn the Manassas Junction and storm it today with superior forces."[3]

But how quickly the tide turned. At 1 A.M. July 22 Scott informed McClellan that "after fairly beating the enemy and taking three of his batteries, a panic seized McDowell's army, and it is in full retreat on the Potomac."[4] Later that day, Adjutant General Lorenzo Thomas told

McClellan, "Circumstances make your presence here [in Washington] necessary. . . . Come hither without delay."[5]

McClellan started at daylight the next morning, rode sixty miles to the nearest station, and took a train to Washington. He arrived Friday afternoon, July 26, and the next morning was instructed by Thomas to call on President Lincoln. "I was received cordially," McClellan wrote to his wife, "and informed that he had placed me in command of Washington and all the troops in its vicinity."[6]

The order giving McClellan command had been issued by the War Department on July 25. It also directed that the Department of Washington and the Department of Northeastern Virginia be combined.[7] McClellan's first order was issued July 27, assuming command of the Division of the Potomac and stating that his headquarters would be in Washington."[8]

McClellan was appalled by his tour of the city. "I found no preparations whatever for defence," he wrote. "Not a regiment was properly encamped, not a single avenue of approach guarded." Many men had gone home after their flight from Bull Run, and "all was chaos" in the streets. "If the secessionists attached any value to the possession of Washington, they committed their greatest error in not following up the victory of Bull Run." This opinion was shared by Edwin M. Stanton, who had been attorney general in President James Buchanan's Cabinet and who became Lincoln's secretary of war in January 1862. Five days after Bull Run, in a letter to Buchanan, Stanton wrote: "The capture of Washington seems now to be inevitable. Even now I doubt whether any serious opposition to the entrance of the Confederate forces could be offered."[9]

Both statements seem to echo Jackson's thoughts as he watched Union troops flee from the field. If given 10,000 men, he remarked, he could be "in Washington tonight."

———— ⇒►●◄—— ————

Following Bull Run Lee and Jackson were sent to western Virginia. Lee was first. In a letter to Johnston on August 1 Jefferson Davis said, "General Lee has gone to Western Virginia, and I hope may be able to strike a decisive blow at the enemy in that quarter; or, failing in that, will be able to organize and post our troops so as to check the enemy, after which he will return to this place [Richmond]."[10]

A month later Davis regretted Lee's absence. In a letter to Johnston on September 5 Davis revealed that he had been ill and was so weak that he seldom attempted to write.[11] The day before the Confederate adjutant and inspector general, General Samuel Cooper, had written to Lee, apparently at Davis's request: "He [Davis] has not ceased to feel an anxious desire for your return to this city to resume your former duties, even while satisfied of the importance of your presence in Western Virginia. Whenever in your judgment, circumstances will justify it, you will consider yourself authorized to return."[12]

But Lee was not ready. Union forces were steadily pushing against the divided efforts of two Confederate forces. Complicating the situation was a bitter dispute between the commanders. The two brigadier generals— John B. Floyd, Buchanan's secretary of war, and Henry A. Wise, like Floyd a former governor of Virginia—poured out their differences in nearly eighty letters exchanged in August and September. The torrent of words spilled over into forty or more letters in those months to Davis, Leroy Walker, and Lee.[13]

Lee could not resolve the differences and, following a clash with Union troops at Carnifax Ferry on September 10, the two forces withdrew to separate camps eighteen miles apart.[14] Meanwhile, Lee had undertaken an expedition to Cheat Mountain, hoping to surprise Union forces in that area. A heavy storm delayed his troops on September 11, and a bungled signal the next day disrupted the planned attack. Lee waited three days for some sign of action, then withdrew his troops to their original camp.[15]

In a desperate plea to Wise on September 21 Lee expressed his regret that Wise and Floyd were still separated, then added, "I beg, if [it is] not too late, that the troops be united, and that we conquer or die together."[16] Four days later Wise was ordered to return to Richmond, and he left western Virginia immediately.[17] But trouble had not ended for Lee.

Newspapers had become critical and blamed him for the repulses and retreats in western Virginia. Editorially, they referred to him as "Granny" Lee and "Evacuating" Lee.[18] It was a low point in his career and would not be quickly forgotten by newsmen.

Commenting on this situation to his wife in a letter on October 7, Lee observed: "I am sorry that the movements of the armies cannot keep pace with the expectations of the editors of [news]papers. I know they can regulate matters satisfactorily to themselves on paper. I wish they could do so in the field." To this he added: "General Floyd has the benefit of three editors on his staff. I hope something will be done to please them."[19]

Heavy rain and muddy roads complicated the situation in October and by the end of the month Lee could see no reason to remain in western Virginia. On October 20 he advised Floyd that "on reaching

Meadow Bluff I will inform you of the probable time of my return to Richmond."[20]

Nine days later, writing from Meadow Bluff, he advised Floyd: "I will visit the hospitals at Lewisburg and White Sulphur and proceed thence to Richmond."[21] Lee left for Richmond the next day with Colonel Walter Taylor, and they arrived late in the afternoon of October 31.[22]

The following morning Lee called on Davis. Lee declined to defend himself against the criticism that had been raised but orally reported on the campaign in western Virginia. Later Davis commented, "My confidence in his ability, zeal, and fidelity rested on a foundation not to be shaken by such criticism."[23]

On November 5 Lee was assigned to the command of a new Confederate military department made up of the coasts of South Carolina, Georgia, and eastern Florida.[24] He was especially directed to take up the defense of Savannah, Georgia, and Charleston, South Carolina.[25]

Lee left immediately for his new post and was absent from Richmond for the next four months—a critical period during which the Confederacy almost lost Jackson's services.

The order sending Jackson to the Shenandoah Valley was, in a sense, the result of his own efforts. On August 27, almost six weeks after Bull Run, Jackson wrote to his friend Colonel Bennett: "My hopes for our section of the State [western Virginia] have greatly brightened since General Lee has gone there. Should you ever have occasion to ask for a brigade from this army for the Northwest, I hope that mine will be selected." The comment, he said, was confidential, since duty dictated where he would serve. "But it is natural," he added, "for one's affection to turn to the home of his boyhood and family."[26]

On the morning of October 1 Jackson met Davis while the latter was at Fairfax Court House to discuss war plans proposed by Beauregard, Johnston, and Major General G. W. Smith, commander of the 2nd Corps, Confederate Army of the Potomac. During a brief visit with Davis, Jackson wrote, "the President introduced the subject of the condition of my section of the State, but did not even so much as intimate that he designed sending me there. I told him, when he spoke of my native region, that I felt a very deep interest in it. He spoke hopefully of that region, and highly of General Lee."[27]

On October 5 Andrew Hunter, a member of the Virginia General Assembly, wrote to acting Secretary of War Judah P. Benjamin that people in his district had asked him to inform Confederate authorities about conditions in northwestern Virginia. "The management of military affairs in this quarter is in utterly incompetent hands," Hunter stated, then urged that "some experienced and intelligent officer" be sent there to study the problem and recommend action.

Hunter added that his colleague "Hon. A. R. Boteler will give you full and minute information about the matter."[28] Boteler warned Secretary of State R. M. T. Hunter on October 24 that "the condition of our border is becoming more alarming every day." He also urged the promotion of Lieutenant Colonel Turner Ashby to the rank of full colonel so that he would be free to direct operations of cavalry patrolling the Potomac River.[29]

Three days earlier Benjamin had notified Jackson that the exposed condition of northwestern Virginia and constant appeals from people there had prompted the War Department to form the Valley District of the Department of Northern Virginia. Jackson was to be placed in command.

The selection had been based, Benjamin explained, on Jackson's qualities as a commander and on his "intimate knowledge of the country, its population, and its resources." Benjamin also noted that "the people of that district, with one voice, have made constant and urgent appeals that to you, in whom they have confidence, should their defense be assigned."

The small Confederate force in the area was to be increased as rapidly as possible, Benjamin stated, then he concluded with this invitation: "I will be glad to receive any suggestions you may make to render effectual your measures of defense."[30]

The next day, October 22, the official order was issued creating the Department of Northern Virginia, with Johnston as commander and Jackson in command of the Valley District.[31]

It was during late October that the flame within Jackson grew stronger and brighter. He could keep it hidden no longer. Three months after Bull Run, he suggested a new course of action far more daring than anything he had proposed before. He planned to invade the North!

The idea was not new. One of the earliest proposals was made by Colonel Isaac R. Trimble on June 4, 1861. He suggested to Lee that Confederate troops should cross the Potomac River and attack Federal forces at Hagerstown, Maryland. If successful, the Confederates would "give out" information that the attack was the beginning of a westward thrust toward Cumberland, Maryland. Instead, they would move eastward to attack

Baltimore and Washington. Success there, Trimble said, would force the Federal government to abandon its capital.

Trimble also expressed concern that a strict defensive policy could hurt morale and urged aggressive action to avoid this.[32] There is no evidence that Trimble's proposal was given consideration.

———————

A second plan to cross into Maryland and attack Washington was presented by Beauregard on July 14. He had been called north from Charleston, South Carolina, late in May and met with Davis and Lee on May 31. Later that day Lee placed Beauregard in command of "troops on the Alexandria line." Lee reminded Beauregard of advice given previously to other officers in that area: "The policy of the State [Virginia], at present, is strictly defensive." On June 2 Beauregard replaced Brigadier General M. L. Bonham and established his headquarters in the Manassas area.[33]

———————

In his plan of July 14 Beauregard proposed movements intended to defeat three Union armies that were threatening Virginia from the north and west.

At the time McDowell was preparing to move from Alexandria against Confederate forces at Centreville and Fairfax Court House. The start of his movement was set for July 8, but was delayed more than a week.[34] In the Shenandoah Valley Patterson had advanced a bit south of Martinsburg, but was reluctant to attack Johnston. Instead he maneuvered, hoping to prevent Johnston from moving eastward to unite with Beauregard.[35] In western Virginia McClellan was making rapid progress eastward from Ohio. By July 13 his troops had advanced on a broad front to Grafton, Philippi, Beverley, and Huttonsville near, the western base of the Allegheny Mountains.[36]

On July 13 Beauregard sent an aide, Colonel James Chesnut, to Richmond to present a plan to Davis, Lee, and Cooper. Johnston's troops in the Shenandoah Valley and a Confederate force in Fredericksburg under Brigadier General T. H. Holmes were to unite with Beauregard. This force would attack and defeat McDowell. Then Johnston, reinforced by some of Beauregard's troops, would return to the Valley and crush Patterson's army. After that, Johnston would reinforce Brigadier General Robert

S. Garnett in northwestern Virginia, enabling him to defeat McClellan's army. Garnett then would go east, join Johnston, and their combined force would cross the Potomac and march against Washington from the Maryland side while Beauregard attacked the capital from Virginia.[37]

Chesnut said his listeners gave "respectful and earnest consideration" to the proposal but did not approve it. Davis and Lee observed that enemy forces still were too close to their defenses and reserves to make the plan feasible. They also said that the time was not ripe for such a move but that it might succeed later.[38]

After the meeting Davis explained that there were not sufficient men available to carry out such a plan. He also pointed out that the idea "was based on the improbable and inadmissible supposition that the enemy was to wait everywhere, isolated and motionless, until our forces could effect junctions and attack them in detail."[39]

Early in September Beauregard again considered a plan to cross the Potomac. In a letter to Johnston dated September 6 he suggested that some of Johnston's brigades could be moved toward the Potomac "to keep the enemy constantly alarmed for the safety of Washington." If a large Union force should be sent from Washington to any other point, then Johnston could advance into Maryland.[40] Davis was informed of this suggestion and, on September 8, advised Johnston that "the measure can have little permanence and no material effect on your general plan of operations. We cannot afford to divide our forces unless and until we have two armies able to contend with the enemy's forces at Washington. It is true that a successful advance across the Potomac would relieve other places; but, if not successful, ruin would befall us."[41]

A fourth attempt at an invasion plan was made in late September, this time by Johnston. In a letter on September 26 to Benjamin he explained that he had moved troops forward from Bull Run in preparation for an advance into Maryland. He suggested that Benjamin or Davis come to headquarters near Fairfax Court House to discuss such action. Three days later Benjamin replied that the president would attend the meeting.[42]

Three high-ranking generals—Johnston, Beauregard, and G. W. Smith—met with Davis at Fairfax Court House on October 1 in the meeting Jackson had noted. The generals had no detailed plans or targets to talk about; it was strictly a question of getting sufficient men and munitions to carry the war into enemy country and cut off communications with Washington.

Although sympathetic to a point, Davis explained that the government was unable to support such an undertaking. The generals urged Davis to reconsider; he asked how many men would be needed. Smith estimated 50,000. Johnston and Beauregard agreed the number should be 60,000.

Again Davis stated that such manpower was unavailable and remained firm against attacking at that time. He did, however, suggest "partial operations," including limited attacks against Federal troops in Maryland. This time the generals balked, and the conference ended.[43]

In postwar writings about the conference Davis concluded his remarks with an unusual statement. Referring to the reluctance of the generals to undertake partial operations, Davis noted that a later expedition, in the Shenandoah Valley, "was achieved by another officer not of this council, General T. J. Jackson."[44]

———————

In mid-October Jackson added his voice to those urging invasion of the North. He went to see his corps commander, General Smith, and outlined his own plan. Convinced that the time to strike was while Yankee morale was low, Jackson told Smith, "We ought to invade their country now, and not wait for them to make the necessary preparations to invade ours."

Jackson suggested that Confederate troops cross the Potomac, seize eastern Maryland, occupy Baltimore, and cut off communications with Washington. The move, he stated, would force the Federal government to abandon the capital. That was similar to previous proposals. But then Jackson outlined elements that were startlingly different. He told Smith that Confederate troops should then move northward and do the following:

1. Destroy industrial establishments wherever they found them.
2. Break up the lines of interior commercial intercourse.
3. Close the coal mines.
4. Seize and, if necessary, destroy the manufactories and commerce of Philadelphia, and of other large cities within their reach.
5. Take and hold the narrow neck of country between Pittsburgh and Lake Erie.

6. Subsist mainly on the country they traverse.

7. And, making unrelenting war amidst their homes, "force the people of the North to understand what it will cost them to hold the South in the Union at the bayonet's point."

Jackson then urged Smith to use his influence with Johnston and Beauregard "in favor of immediate aggressive operations." Smith told Jackson that it would be useless for him to do that. When Jackson pressed for an answer, Smith told him of the conference at Fairfax Court House and Davis's decision. Jackson responded, "I am sorry, very sorry." A few days later, Smith noted, Jackson was ordered to the Shenandoah Valley.[45]

———————

It was in the Shenandoah Valley that Jackson developed an invasion plan that conformed with action he could take from his new position. He now proposed a two-pronged drive aimed at eastern and western Pennsylvania.

Jeb Stuart's ordnance officer, John Esten Cooke, noted that the plan was "the deliberate result of Jackson's reflections." He proposed that the Confederates invade the North in two columns, winter in Harrisburg, and in the spring of 1862 advance upon Philadelphia. The result, Jackson believed, would force Federal authorities to "abandon their opposition to secession and agree to an honorable peace." Again Jackson indicated the importance of striking quickly while the Union was discouraged by the defeat at Bull Run. Then, according to Cooke, Jackson outlined these details of his revised plan:

1. He would advance into northwestern Virginia and drive out Union troops occupying the area.

2. He would seek recruits there to raise the strength of his force to 25,000 men.

3. He would then move into western Pennsylvania, cross the Monongahela River, and attack Pittsburgh and the U.S. arsenal there.

4. Then, in conjunction with another column from the Department of Northern Virginia that would have crossed the Potomac River at Leesburg, he would seize Harrisburg and remain there during the winter.

5. When weather permitted, the combined forces would move against Philadelphia.

This plan, Cooke observed, was proposed to Confederate authorities but not adopted. However, Cooke added: "Invasion was his possessing thought, and became the dream of his life. He never ceased to think of it, and the great successes at Port Republic, Cold Harbor, and second Manassas, were chiefly important in his eyes from their bearing on his favorite policy."[46]

<hr />

Jackson tried again after his successful Valley Campaign in the spring of 1862. This time he sent an aide to Richmond to present the plan to Davis. Jackson wanted reinforcements for a move that he said would shift the scene to the banks of the Susquehanna River. Davis reacted favorably but before taking action sought Lee's advice.

Lee felt that if Jackson could be strongly reinforced, it would change the character of the war.[47] It was the first move by Lee from strictly defensive to offensive action that led to the single invasion plan noted above by Colonel Marshall.

In following the development of invasion plans for 1862 and 1863, it is important to recognize the similarity of objectives proposed by Jackson and those adopted by Lee. They are as follows:

1. In late 1861 Jackson had proposed a two-column advance. His own forces would invade western Pennsylvania, seize Pittsburgh, then move east to Harrisburg and join troops from the Army of Northern Virginia that were to cross the Potomac River at Leesburg.

    As Lee was preparing for the 1862 invasion, in several letters he suggested a northward movement by General William W. Loring's Confederate troops in western Virginia. On October 15, however, he advised Loring that the season was too far advanced to consider an expedition into western Pennsylvania "that I once proposed to you."[48]

2. While Jackson suggested wintering in Harrisburg, Lee also indicated that Harrisburg was a primary target of both the 1862 and 1863 summer invasions.[49]

3. Jackson's proposal was for his troops (with another column that would cross the Potomac at Leesburg) to move against Philadelphia after leaving Harrisburg. Lee expressed his intention to move about, maneuver, and alarm the enemy, threaten cities, and hit any blows he could without risking a general battle. Then, toward fall, he planned to return nearer to his base.[50]

4. Jackson and Lee intended to bring pressure on the Northern people to seek an end of the war. As noted above, Jackson wanted to force them to understand what it would cost to hold the South in the Union by force. Lee sought to avoid trouble for the public but to give all the support possible to what he described as the rising peace party of the North.[51]

These similarities not only indicated Lee's transition from defensive to offensive strategy; they also showed his intention to pursue an economic policy to gain the support of people in the North, along the lines suggested by Jackson in his invasion plan.

CHAPTER 4

King Coal versus King Cotton

BEFORE PURSUING MILITARY ACTIONS FURTHER, THE POTENTIAL IMPACT of Jackson's strategic plan for invasion of the North must be considered. Basically, it would have led to an economic conflict intended to pressure Northerners into demanding that the Federal government make peace with the South. That would have meant Confederate independence.

While states' rights, slavery, and secession are generally considered to be the important issues that separated North and South, there was another: the differences between agricultural and industrialized economies. More than two years before war broke out, Jefferson Davis focused attention on these differences. Speaking in Boston on October 12, 1858, he stated:

> Even after railroads had been built—after steam-engines had become a motive power for a large part of manufacturing machinery, the natural causes from which your people [in the North] obtained a manufacturing ascendancy and ours became agriculturists continued to act in a considerable measure to preserve that relation.
>
> Your interest is to remain a manufacturing, and ours to remain an agricultural people. Your prosperity, then, is to receive our staple and to manufacture it, and ours to sell it to you and buy the manufactured goods.

Davis then expressed his hope for a continued friendship between the two sections of the nation: "This is an interweaving of interests which makes us all the richer and happier."[1]

A little more than two years later, the Civil War shattered Davis's hope. On April 19, 1861—five days after the surrender of Fort Sumter—President Lincoln ordered a blockade of the ports of seven states that had seceded: South Carolina, Georgia, Alabama, Florida, Mississippi, Louisiana, and Texas. Eight days later he took similar action against Virginia and North Carolina.[2] The blockade was intended not only to cut off imports of war materials, food, clothing, and other essentials but also to control the export of agricultural products, especially cotton.

━━━►●◄━━━

The South's economy was firmly rooted in the products of farms and plantations—cotton, corn, tobacco, rice, and sugar cane. Cotton was the major cash crop of planters. The area in which it was grown was known as the "cotton kingdom" and the crop as "King Cotton."[3]

The impact of the war and blockade on the cotton trade is clearly described in the annual agricultural reports of the U.S. Patent Office for 1860 and 1861.[4] In the 1860 report S. T. Shugart, acting commissioner of patents, noted that "not many years ago the cotton plant was little better than a mere weed. It now vivifies the commerce of the world."[5]

In the 1861 report D. P. Holloway, then the commissioner of patents, noted that because of "the recent disturbed state of affairs" in the South, cotton could become expensive and scarce. He warned that "our exports of cotton may fall off" and that it probably would be necessary to develop substitutes to keep Northern textile mills operating. He suggested that farmers, particularly those in Northern states, should consider growing flax for linen. Hemp also was mentioned as a possible substitute.[6]

Holloway also urged that a silk industry be developed. He stated that unproductive land could be used, that it would require little expense and labor, and that it would provide "low-priced articles of apparel for all classes of society."[7]

Behind this concern was the realization that U.S. cotton mills, most of which were in the Northeast, represented an investment of about $94 million.[8] Holloway noted, "However this country may be adapted to agricultural products, it is still better fitted for manufacturing industry."

He cited as elements of the successful manufacturing economy an abundance of mineral wealth, especially coal; ample water and steam power; and the vast networks of railroads and canals that were the "instrumentalities of internal commerce in the United States."[9] These were the major objectives targeted by Stonewall Jackson in the invasion plan he outlined only a few months before Holloway's report was issued.

———————

Just as cotton was king in the South, coal drove Northern industrial might. It fueled manufacturing machinery, railroad locomotives, and steamships. Pennsylvania, a major objective of Confederate invasion plans, was the keystone of the nation's coal industry.

In 1860, the year before the Civil War started, coal was mined in twenty-three of the nation's thirty-three states. Total production exceeded twenty million tons.[10] Of that, nearly sixteen million tons (78.3 percent of the nation's output) came from Pennsylvania (table 1).[11] Ranking in following order were Ohio, Illinois, Virginia (including what is now West Virginia), and Maryland (table 2).[12]

Even more important is the fact that more than half of the U.S. coal mined in 1860 was anthracite (hard coal) produced in ten northeastern Pennsylvania counties (table 3).[13] Major anthracite production was concentrated in Carbon, Columbia, Dauphin, Lackawanna, Luzerne, Northumberland, and Schuylkill counties,[14] with additional deposits in Lebanon, Susquehanna, and Wayne counties.[15] These counties are the sole source of U.S. anthracite.

———————

During the first two years of the Civil War anthracite production declined. One factor was the enlistment of many miners and laborers into the Army. Another was a severe rainstorm that swept through Schuylkill County on June 4, 1862. Flooding seriously damaged many mines and filled others. As a result the area's coal trade was shut down for more than a month.[16] Another factor was the activity of a secret miners' organization, the Molly Maguires.

Resolving these problems and the Navy's increasing demand for coal helped increase anthracite production in 1863.

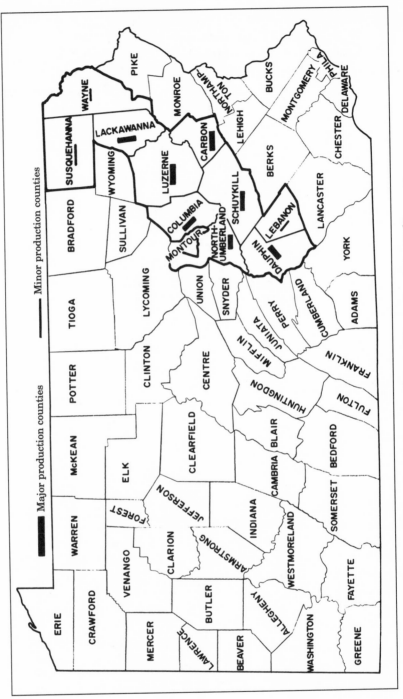

Coal-producing Counties of Central Pennsylvania in 1863. JOHN HEISER

COAL PRODUCTION FROM 1860 TO 1863

PENNSYLVANIA COAL PRODUCTION, ANTHRACITE AND BITUMINOUS,
COMPARED TO ESTIMATED PRODUCTION IN ALL STATES,
NORTH AND SOUTH, FROM 1860 TO 1863.
FROM EAVENSON, COAL, P. 431.

YEAR	Total U.S. Production (tons)	Pennsylvania Production (tons)	Percent of U.S. Production
1860	20,040,859	15,694,372	78.3%
1861	19,000,663	14,807,156	77.9%
1862	19,570,544	15,182,035	77.5%
1863	22,747,407	17,600,046	77.4%

LEADING COAL PRODUCING STATES, TONS MINED,
NORTH AND SOUTH, FROM 1860 TO 1863.
FROM EAVENSON, COAL, PP. 428, 431.

STATES	1860	1861	1862	1863
Pennsylvania	15,694,372	14,807,156	15,182,035	17,600,046
Ohio	1,849,586	1,855,300	1,890,400	1,923,500
Illinois	857,600	948,800	1,038,200	1,198,900
Virginia	477,227	418,556	382,317	388,577
Maryland	438,000	287,073	346,201	877,313

ANTHRACITE COAL PRODUCTION IN PENNSYLVANIA,
COMPARED TO PRODUCTION IN ALL STATES,
NORTH AND SOUTH, FROM 1860 TO 1863.
FROM EAVENSON, COAL, P. 498.

YEAR	Total U.S. Production (tons)	Anthracite Produced in Penna. (tons)	Percent of Total U.S. Production
1860	20,040,859	10,983,972	54.8%
1861	19,000,663	10,245,156	53.9%
1862	19,570,544	10,186,435	52.0%
1863	22,747,407	12,267,446	53.9%

It is hard to underestimate the importance of anthracite at this point and place in history. Early-nineteenth-century tests at the University of Pennsylvania demonstrated that anthracite burned hotter and three to four times longer than bituminous (soft) coal. Anthracite also burned with little flame and smoke. James Woodhouse, one of the researchers, concluded that anthracite "promises to be particularly useful where a long, continued heat is necessary." He also noted that this characteristic would be important "in generating steam to work steam engines."[17]

As the Industrial Revolution gained momentum, these characteristics became increasingly important. Anthracite was recognized as the ideal fuel in manufacturing plants, textile mills, and other industrial establishments where power from steam engines was transferred to machinery through shafts, pulleys, and belts. It also was the ideal fuel for Navy steamships.

Steam power was relatively new in the U.S. Navy in 1860. In 1814 it had acquired its first steamship, a wooden vessel driven by a center wheel. Eight years later a wooden side-wheeler was introduced. In 1843 an iron vessel driven by a propeller was added. Between 1814 and 1854 the Navy acquired twenty steamships.

That was generally considered the experimental period, when numerous propulsion systems were tried. Secretary of the Navy James C. Dobbin stated in his annual report to Congress for 1853, "Steam is unquestionably the great agent to be used on the ocean, as well for purposes of war as [for] commerce." He also recommended the immediate construction of six steam frigates—intermediate-sized warships. Congress quickly authorized construction of "six first-class steam frigates to be provided with screw propellers."

The steam-powered Navy was on its way. Between 1854 and 1860 thirty steam vessels were added to the Navy. Twenty-nine had propellers; the other was a side-wheeler.[18]

On the eve of the Civil War the Navy had sixty-three vessels. Thirty-three were powered by steam. Most of the sailing ships were described as small.[19] The war required rapid expansion of the Navy. In 1861 construction was started on fifty-two steam warships, followed by seventy-seven in 1862. Twenty-eight were completed in 1861 and thirty-four in 1862. In addition, ten monitors (ironclads) and five river ships were completed in the winter of 1862–63.[20] One ironclad, the *Monitor*, had been finished by early 1862—in time for the Battle of Hampton Roads.

These new ships more than tripled the Navy's effective steam-powered strength. But it also created a problem—how to get ample supplies of hard coal from Pennsylvania to ports, fueling stations, and the vessels themselves, especially those blockading squadrons. By late 1862, consumption averaged 950 to 1,000 tons a week just for the South Atlantic squadron, not to mention the three other major squadrons in the war zone.[21]

In 1862 blockade commanders repeatedly asked Union authorities for more coal. In the critical year of 1863, Union Army and Navy officials had difficulties fueling ships on the Mississippi River as part of the Vicksburg campaign.[22]

Railroads (and, in some cases, canals) were vital lines for moving coal to ports. These "lines of commercial intercourse" also were major targets in Jackson's plan.

Just as it dominated coal production, Pennsylvania also was critical to rail transportation between the Midwest and the Northeast. In 1860 there were ninety-seven rail lines with 2,662 miles of track in Pennsylvania. Thirty-two were spur or feeder lines with 454 miles of track that linked coal fields and plants with main railroads.[23]

The Pennsylvania Railroad, with 360 miles of track, was the state's longest line. It extended from Philadelphia through Lancaster and Harrisburg beyond Pittsburgh, where it tied in with midwestern lines. Next was the Philadelphia and Reading Railroad with 152 miles of track from Philadelphia to Reading and Harrisburg. It also had important connections with several lines in the anthracite coal region.[24]

Supplementing these rail lines in 1860 were nineteen canals with a network of 1,295 miles. Major canal systems provided important freight links between Pittsburgh and Philadelphia as well as other eastern terminals. They also connected the anthracite fields to Philadelphia and ports on the Delaware and Chesapeake bays.[25]

Just south of the Pennsylvania Railroad was a major east-west line that was vulnerable to attack in the Civil War. It was the Baltimore and Ohio Railroad, with 418 miles of track through Maryland and northwestern Virginia. From its eastern terminals at Baltimore and Washington, the B&O extended through Harpers Ferry to Cumberland, Maryland, and to its western terminus in Wheeling, Virginia. There it tied into several Ohio lines. Paralleling part of the B&O Railroad was the Chesapeake and Ohio Canal, which linked Baltimore and Washington to the bituminous fields near Cumberland in western Maryland.[26]

The B&O was the first railroad to feel the impact of the war. Before it was first closed in mid-June 1861 by the destruction of track and bridges around Harpers Ferry, trains had run daily through the lines and camps of both armies.[27]

By May 28 Confederates generally controlled more than 100 miles of the Main Stem, "chiefly between Point of Rocks and Cumberland," according to the thirty-fifth annual report of the B&O for the fiscal year that ended September 30, 1861. Occasional movements also were made on sections of the road between Cumberland and Wheeling, and on a spur from Grafton to Parkersburg, Virginia, identified as the Northwestern Virginia Railroad.

As a result 14 locomotives and tenders plus cars, machinery, and parts were moved south for use on Southern railways. In addition 42 locomotives and tenders, 386 cars (mostly for coal), and 17 bridges were destroyed or damaged.

Thirty-six and a half miles of track (between Point of Rocks and Cumberland) were torn up and the rails and other track fixtures removed for use on Southern roads. One hundred and two miles of telegraph lines, two water stations, and other valuable property also were destroyed.[28] A total of 5,801 tons of new iron rails and 151,337 new cross-ties were required to restore 61 3/4 miles of track that had been torn up on the entire B&O line.[29]

As a result the entire B&O, in fiscal year 1861, was open for passenger service for eight months and two days. Freight service, especially from the coal regions near Cumberland to Baltimore, was available only for seven months and twenty-four days. This cut the volume of coal shipped to 213,984 tons—just half the amount shipped in the previous fiscal year.[30]

Jackson was responsible for much of the damage on the double-track line between Point of Rocks, Maryland, and Martinsburg, Virginia. While still in command at Harpers Ferry, he decided to break up traffic on the railroad.

Disturbed by the frequency of trains moving through the Harpers Ferry area, he first complained to the president of the B&O, then persuaded him to schedule all train traffic through the town between

11 A.M. and 1 P.M. When that was accomplished, he sent Captain John Imboden with his troops to Point of Rocks and Colonel Kenton Harper to Martinsburg to set a trap that would halt all traffic.[31]

The first sign of trouble came on May 25, when "a large rock supported by masonry, near the Point of Rocks, was undermined and thrown upon the track."[32] In a few days long lines of trains had been trapped on both tracks. Troops began tearing up rails and shifting locomotives and cars to a branch line leading to Winchester.[33]

The work was interrupted a few days later when Jackson was replaced by Johnston. In mid-June, while near Martinsburg to meet the threatened advance of Patterson across the Potomac, Jackson was instructed by Johnston to send to Winchester as much "rolling stock" as possible. Locomotives, cars, and other equipment that could not be salvaged were to be destroyed, and large supplies of coal were to be sold, if possible, to area residents.[34]

Jackson torched some locomotives and cars, many still loaded with coal, and the flames evidently spread to repair shops and other structures. A short time later, Jackson wrote to his wife from Winchester:

> It was your husband that did so much mischief at Martinsburg. To destroy so many fine locomotives, cars, and railroad property was a sad work, but I had my orders, and my duty was to obey.[35]

Confiscation of B&O stock did not stop when Jackson, with Johnston's main force, moved east to Manassas. Thomas R. Sharpe, described as a special Confederate agent, took over and during the summer of 1861 reportedly moved fourteen more locomotives from Martinsburg to Strasburg, Virginia, on the Manassas Gap Railroad.[36]

When Jackson returned to the Shenandoah Valley in early November, he immediately prepared for aggressive action. This time he had the high government support to drive enemy forces from northwestern Virginia.

But Jackson also injected another course of action, a step undoubtedly prompted by his disruption of the B&O, and by elements of the invasion plan he had recently submitted to General Smith. It was an attempt to disrupt traffic on the C&O Canal and halt coal shipments from western Maryland to Washington.

CHAPTER 5

Jackson's Romney Campaign

ON OCTOBER 7, 1861, GENERAL JOSEPH E. JOHNSTON LEARNED THAT seventeen of his officers had been promoted, four to major general, and thirteen to brigadier general. Two new major generals were James Longstreet and Stonewall Jackson. Five days later, Johnston assigned Longstreet to the 1st Corps in what was then known as the Confederate Army of the Potomac. Jackson was assigned to the 2nd Corps.[1]

On October 22 the name was changed to the Department of Northern Virginia, to be commanded by Johnston. The newly organized army had three districts—the Potomac District under General P. G. T. Beauregard, the Aquia District under Major General T. H. Holmes, and the Valley District under Jackson.

The day before Secretary of War Judah P. Benjamin had notified Jackson of his selection to command the Valley District. In his acknowledgment on October 25 Jackson expressed gratitude and stated that he was ready to move to his new post promptly, "even though it separates me from the brigade which I had hoped to command through the war."[2]

During those weeks developments in the northwestern corner of the Valley affected Jackson's plans in his new post. On October 26 Union troops under Brigadier General Benjamin F. Kelley seized Romney after routing a small Confederate force there.[3]

More than a week passed before Jackson received a formal order to take his new command. After receiving Johnston's order on November 4, Jackson assembled his brigade, bade its members an emotional farewell, and left immediately for Winchester, accompanied by two aides, Lieutenant Colonel J. T. L. Preston and Lieutenant Sandie Pendleton. They arrived that night.[4]

The next day he sent Preston to Richmond with an urgent message for Benjamin. His new command, Jackson stated, consisted of 1,591 militiamen and they were threatened with attack from the north and west. He reported that there were about 1,200 enemy troops in Williamsport, Maryland, and 800 more opposite Shepherdstown, Virginia. At Romney, an important junction forty-two miles west of Winchester, there were 4,000 Federal troops reportedly preparing to advance.

Uppermost in Jackson's mind was "the importance of not only holding Winchester, but also of repelling the invaders from this district before they shall secure a firm lodgment." He urged Benjamin to send him all available troops from the Cheat Mountain region of western Virginia and also requested at least twenty pieces of artillery, plus any other forces that might be available.[5]

Benjamin had anticipated Jackson's need and had moved to strengthen Confederate forces in the district. Benjamin had ordered about 6,000 men from William W. Loring's command in western Virginia to join Jackson, but probably the best news was that his old brigade, plus a battery of artillery, had been ordered to the Valley from Centreville.[6]

Johnston protested, but Richmond was firm. "The brigade of General Jackson was ordered to join him as a matter of urgent necessity," Benjamin informed Johnston on November 7. "The Valley District is entirely defenseless and will fall into the hands of the enemy unless General Jackson has troops sent to him immediately."

Davis also supported Jackson. "General Jackson, for reasons known to you, was selected to command the District of the Valley, but we had only militia and one mounted regiment in the district assigned to him," Davis reminded Johnston on November 10. He pointed out that enemy activity, especially the seizure of Romney, dictated strong reinforcements for Jackson to meet the threat his small force faced.[7]

About ten days later Jackson presented a plan for assuming the offensive from the Shenandoah Valley. On November 20 he urged Benjamin to send all of Loring's troops to Winchester at once. "Deeply impressed with the importance of absolute secrecy respecting military operations, I have made it a point to say but little respecting my proposed movements in the event of sufficient re-enforcements arriving [here]," Jackson stated. Nevertheless, Jackson outlined his intent to capture the Union forces at Romney; to move eastward to support Johnston, if necessary; or to move rapidly westward to the Monongahela River.

"I deem it of very great importance that Northwestern Virginia be occupied by Confederate troops this winter," he stated. If the movement should be postponed until spring, he explained, the enemy probably would be better prepared to meet the attack. "I know that what I have proposed will be an arduous undertaking and cannot be accomplished without the sacrifice of much personal comfort; but I feel that the troops will be prepared to make this sacrifice when animated by the prospects of important results to our cause and distinction to themselves."[8]

Johnston added a note endorsing Jackson's plan and forwarded Jackson's letter to the War Department. Benjamin also endorsed the plan, including the proposed westward movement to the Monongahela. According to Davis, "It was decided to adopt his proposition."[9]

Approval of Jackson's plan was clearly reflected in Benjamin's subsequent correspondence. In a November 24 letter to Loring, Benjamin explained the government's desire to set the plan in motion. Just so there would be no misunderstanding, he enclosed a copy of Jackson's November 20 letter.

"I have for several weeks been impressed with the conviction that a sudden and well-concealed movement of your entire command up the Valley [northward] towards Romney, combined with a movement of General Jackson from Winchester, would result in the entire destruction, and perhaps capture, of the enemy's whole force at Romney," Benjamin stated. He also expressed the opinion that "a continuation of the movement westward would force a general retreat of the whole forces of the enemy" from northwestern Virginia. But "if the farther movement west was found impracticable," Benjamin observed, "a severe blow might be dealt by the seizure of Cumberland" in western Maryland.[10]

Benjamin then noted the risks and that the movement would open mountain passes leading to Staunton in the Shenandoah Valley, and possibly permit enemy troops to get in the rear of Confederate forces.

> We do not desire, under such a state of things to direct the movement above described without leaving you a discretion, and the President wishes you to exercise that discretion. If, upon full consideration, you think the proposed movement objectionable and too hazardous, you will decline to make it, and so inform the Department. If, on the contrary, you approve it, then proceed to execute it as promptly and secretly as possible.
>
> In arriving at a conclusion on the subject you will not, of course, forget the extreme difficulty of keeping open your communications in the coming winter if you adhere to the plan of guarding the passes, and thus wintering some 6,000 or 7,000 men in the severe climate of the mountain region.[11]

The letter seemed to give Loring some choice but also applied firm pressure on him to decide on the move to Winchester. Loring agreed and notified Benjamin of his decision on November 29. But, he added, the move would require two or three weeks.[12]

On December 5 the War Department directed Loring to move his entire command as rapidly as possible to Winchester.[13] The next day, Benjamin notified Jackson: "You will now perceive, by the enclosed copy of a letter received from General Loring, that in accordance with your views, endorsed by this Department, he has commenced a movement for cooperation with you, which will place at your disposal quite an effective force for your proposed campaign, although I regret to observe that his movement cannot be made as promptly as I had hoped."[14]

Jackson was pleased by the endorsement but disappointed by the delay in action. Time was becoming critical, especially if he was to use the Romney movement to initiate a two-column invasion of the North. This movement, Jackson believed, would result in a peace treaty and independence for the South.[15]

Although Jackson's plan reportedly had been proposed to Confederate authorities, it had not been adopted. It also was noted that the suggestion "went no farther than his [Jackson's] friends in the Legislative Assembly [the Confederate Congress]."[16]

A significant step was taken in Congress, however, on December 7, the day after Benjamin notified Jackson that Loring's troops would begin moving toward Winchester. Representative Charles W. Russell, from the Wheeling District of Virginia, introduced the following resolution:

First. Resolved by the Confederate States of America, that the sufferings of the good people of Maryland under the oppression of our enemy excite our profound sympathy and entitle them to speedy and efficient exertions on our part for their relief.

Second. That it is the desire of this Government, by appropriate measures, to facilitate the accession of Maryland, with the free consent of her people, to the Confederate States.

Third. That no peace ought to be concluded with the United States which does not insure to Maryland the opportunity of forming a part of the Confederacy.

The resolution was adopted December 19 by a vote of forty-five to six and was signed by Davis two days later.[17]

The timing of this action raises questions. Was it coincidence or did a friend or friends in Congress know of Jackson's plan? If so, was the action taken in support of Jackson's proposal to follow the Romney movement with an advance north of the Potomac River?

Thirteen Virginia congressmen voted in favor of the resolution, including a special friend of Jackson's, Representative Alexander R. Boteler, from Jefferson County.[18] Boteler was, according to Henry Kyd Douglas, a member of Jackson's staff, "at all times the General's unconditional friend, one whom he admired greatly, and in whom he evinced great confidence. To this gentleman General Jackson wrote more freely than to anyone else."[19]

Boteler lived in Shepherdstown, in what is now West Virginia, and entered politics in 1852 as a delegate to the Whig convention in Richmond. In 1859 he was elected to Congress as a representative from Virginia; he was proposed as a compromise candidate for speaker but declined the position. In 1860 he was chairman of the National Executive Committee of the Constitutional Union Party. During those years, he was a staunch Union man and worked for peaceable settlements of sectional differences.[20]

On the eve of Abraham Lincoln's inauguration, Boteler visited the president-elect and urged him to help defeat legislation, known as the

Force Bill, that had been introduced in Congress a few days earlier. The bill would have given the president complete authority over regular troops and militia throughout the nation for enforcement of laws.

This bill, Boteler told Lincoln, was "bristling all over with war." In Virginia, he said, it would paralyze Unionists and precipitate the state into secession, and "unquestionably involve the whole country in civil war." Lincoln hesitated but then agreed to see what he could do to defeat the bill. His influence was not needed, however, for the House adjourned that night without considering it.[21]

Still, civil war could not be avoided. When Virginia seceded, Boteler cast his lot with his native state. In May 1861 he was elected to the House in the Confederate Congress.[22]

The bond between Jackson and Boteler was evident in a lengthy letter written by Jackson on March 3, 1862. Near the end, he told Boteler: "If you were not so invaluable in Richmond I would like to have you here, but you can serve the country better in Richmond than in the field."[23]

A few months later, Boteler—still a member of Congress but also a volunteer on Jackson's staff—had a major role in presenting Jackson's invasion plan to top officials in Richmond and getting their support for it.

In early December 1861, however, Jackson had a more immediate problem. The twenty-five-mile stretch of the B&O west of Harpers Ferry that Jackson's troops had torn up before the First Battle of Bull Run was still out of service. In late November and early December, workmen were busy removing more track west of Martinsburg.[24] (In the railroad's thirty-sixth annual report, the master of transportation noted that, from October 1, 1861, to March 29, 1862, the road was in operation only at its extremities because 100 miles between Harpers Ferry and Cumberland were still out of use.)

The nearby C&O Canal, however, was open and boats were moving large amounts of freight. Early in December, Jackson attempted to disrupt service there and cut off, if possible, the shipment of supplies (especially coal) to Washington. A small force was sent to break up Dam No. 5—about seven miles upstream from Williamsport, Maryland—where water from the Potomac was diverted into the canal.[25]

On December 9 Jackson notified Benjamin that canal boats had been going westward toward Cumberland "for near a week. They have gone up[stream] in large numbers. To prevent their returning to Washington with coal I attempted to turn the water around the Virginia side of Dam No. 5, but was prevented by the enemy's sharpshooters."[26]

Determined to halt the shipment of bituminous coal from the Cumberland mines to eastern terminals, Jackson decided to try again with a larger force. On December 14 he notified General Johnston of the plan, adding that he had secured some small boats to be used if he had to send troops across to the Maryland side. He then added:

> If this plan succeeds—as through the blessing of Providence it will—Washington will hardly get any further supply of coal during the war from Cumberland.[27]

This time Jackson took his old brigade with him. It left Winchester early on December 16 and the following night began work on the dam. Work was frequently interrupted by rifle and artillery fire and by the hardship of standing waist deep in cold water while attempting to cut dam supports. By December 21 a partial breach had been made and Jackson withdrew his troops to Winchester.[28]

Apparently the breach was not large enough. On December 20 Major General Nathaniel P. Banks, the Union commander in the area, reported that the dam had not been seriously damaged and that repairs would start immediately. Two days later he received a report that boats were operating in both directions.[29]

———◈———

Despite Jackson's intent to maintain "absolute secrecy" about his proposed operations, Union authorities apparently had learned or surmised that their forces at Romney would be a Confederate objective. On December 16, the day Jackson's force left Winchester to attack Dam No. 5, Adjutant General Lorenzo Thomas in Washington notified Brigadier General B. F. Kelley in Romney: "The news from Virginia is that you are to be attacked by some 7,000 or 8,000 men, probably from Winchester." At 10 o'clock that night, Banks notified Colonel Samuel E. Leonard, commanding Union troops at Williamsport: "We have a report that General Kelley may be attacked tonight—perhaps from Winchester. Be ready to assist him with all your disposable force."[30]

Jackson's movement from Winchester apparently had been interpreted as the start of an attack on Romney. At that time, however,

Jackson was still awaiting the arrival of Loring's command for the proposed move against Romney.

———————≫●≪———————

The first of Loring's troops, a brigade consisting of four regiments and commanded by Colonel William B. Taliaferro, had arrived at Winchester on December 8. Two other brigades and Loring himself did not arrive until December 24, when Loring informed Jackson that he had decided not to bring any more of his troops to Winchester.[31]

"I have given the subject much thought," Jackson wrote on December 24 to Major Thomas G. Rhett, assistant adjutant general of the Department of Northern Virginia, "and as the enemy appears to be continually receiving accessions, and as I may receive no more, it appears to me that my best plan is to attack him at the earliest practical moment, and accordingly, as soon as the inspection of General Loring's forces shall be finished and the necessary munitions of war procured, I expect to march on the enemy, unless I receive orders to the contrary."[32] None were received and Jackson prepared to move against Romney.

In another letter to Rhett on December 24 Jackson wrote, "Brig. Gen. W. W. Loring informs me that, in his opinion, the Secretary of War designs his command to be known as the Army of the Northwest and that he should continue to be its immediate commander. This meets with my approbation, and I respectfully request that no action be taken upon my former application for him to command as a division such part of his forces as might be in this district."[33]

———————≫●≪———————

Loring's arrival increased Jackson's effective strength to 10,952, almost double that of a month earlier.[34] Jackson now was ready to begin his first independent campaign of the war and on January 1, 1862, set out for Romney with about 8,500 men.[35] Weather quickly created a problem.

The last few days of 1861 had been mild and pleasant, but the weather turned unseasonably warm on the first day of the year. As the men prepared to march from Winchester, overcoats and blankets were piled on supply wagons that were to follow. In late afternoon, a storm swept in from the northwest, the temperature dropped rapidly, and snow began to fall.

The first day's march halted at Pughtown, eight miles northwest of

Winchester. The wagons had not kept pace and soldiers without their overcoats and blankets had to endure a snowy night without cover. It was the beginning of a long period of bad weather, with temperatures sometimes as low as twenty degrees below zero and the ground covered with snow and ice.[36]

The next morning the column turned to the right on the road leading to Bath, about thirty miles north of Winchester. Jackson wanted to drive about 1,500 Union troops from Bath and, if possible, cross the Potomac into Hancock, Maryland. The enemy was routed and Bath occupied on the night of January 4, but Jackson was not pleased. In his report, he stated that Loring, whose troops were in the lead, had delayed the occupancy of Bath by "prematurely and repeatedly" permitting the head of the column to halt "without sufficient cause."

The move against Hancock was abandoned on January 6 and the next day Jackson sent his force westward toward Romney. The telegraph line had been broken at several points and the B&O bridge across the Big Cacapon River destroyed, disrupting communication and rail service between Romney and the east. On January 10 Union forces evacuated Romney and Jackson's troops occupied the major objective of the campaign.[37]

Again Jackson was beset by trouble. He had contemplated another "important expedition against the enemy"—possibly a move westward toward the Monongahela River—but was forced to abandon it because of the "extent of demoralization" in one of Loring's brigades. Believing it "imprudent to attempt further movements with General Loring's command," Jackson decided to put his army in winter quarters. Loring remained in Romney, small forces were posted in Bath and Martinsburg, and General Richard B. Garnett's brigade returned to Winchester.[38]

After two weeks in Romney eleven of Loring's officers drafted a letter protesting conditions there and requesting that it "may be ordered to some more favorable position." Loring sent the letter to Jackson on January 26 with a request that it be forwarded to Benjamin. Jackson sent the letter to Richmond with a notation, "Respectfully forwarded, but disapproved."[39]

Benjamin's response provoked a bitter reaction from Jackson. On January 30 he informed Jackson that "our news indicates that a movement is being made to cut off General Loring's command. Order him back to Winchester immediately." The next day Jackson acknowledged receipt of the order and informed Benjamin that he had promptly complied with it. Then he added:

With such interference in my command I cannot expect to be of much service in the field, and accordingly respectfully request to be ordered to report for duty to the superintendent of the Virginia Military Institute at Lexington. Should the application not be granted, I respectfully request the President will accept my resignation from the Army.

The letter was sent to Johnston, commander of the Department of Northern Virginia, who held it until February 7, when he sent it to Richmond with this comment: "Respectfully forwarded, with great regret. I don't know how the loss of this officer can be supplied."[40]

———

Jackson's letter touched off a chain reaction. Johnston had written on February 3 and urged Jackson to "reconsider this matter." He explained that he had delayed forwarding Jackson's letter to Richmond in order to "make this appeal to your patriotism, not merely from warm feelings of personal regard, but from the official opinion which makes me regard you as necessary to the service of the country in your present position."[41]

Governor Letcher was drawn into the controversy by a letter from Jackson on January 31. "As a single order like that of the Secretary's may destroy the entire fruits of a campaign, I cannot reasonably expect, if my operations are thus to be interfered with, to be of much service in the field. It now appears to be my duty to return to the [Virginia Military] Institute, and I hope that you will leave no stone unturned to get me there."[42] Letcher's initial reaction was to ask Benjamin on February 3 that Jackson's request to be sent back to the VMI "may be complied with and the requisite order issued."[43]

No action was taken on this request and attention quickly focused on Jackson's decision to resign. Again, prominent people wrote to Richmond, as they had several months earlier when they had urged Jackson's appointment. This time they declared that Jackson's resignation, if accepted, would produce a panic in the Valley.[44]

Boteler wrote on February 3 to Jackson and urged him to reconsider. Two days later Jackson wrote his friend: "I don't see how I can be of any service in the field, so long as that principle which has been applied to me—of undoing at the War Department, what is done in the field— is adhered to."[45]

In the meantime Letcher had reconsidered and joined others in urging Jackson to withdraw his resignation. Apparently he and Boteler had discussed the situation on February 4 and Letcher asked Boteler to deliver an important letter to Jackson in Winchester. Boteler met with Jackson and added his voice to the urgent appeal not to desert Virginia in its great hour of need.[46] It was the one appeal Jackson could not resist.

On February 6 Jackson replied to Letcher, "If my retiring from the Army would produce that effect upon our country that you have named in your letter, I of course would not desire to leave the service, and if, upon receipt of this note, your opinion remains unchanged, you are authorized to withdraw my resignation, unless the Secretary of War desires that it should be accepted." Letcher received the letter February 10 and sent it to the War Department, requesting that "his resignation be sent to me."[47]

The resignation was withdrawn, but Jackson was still bitter. He expressed his feelings in a letter to Boteler on February 12. "An official dispatch received this morning informs me that the enemy are in possession of Moorefield [about 20 miles south of Romney]. Such is the fruit of evacuating Romney. Genl. Loring should be cashiered for his course."[48]

———————

Benjamin provided a strange insight into this entire affair. In a letter to Johnston on February 3, Benjamin stated that the order to return Loring's command to Winchester "was telegraphed [to] General Jackson at the President's insistance."[49]

Six days later Benjamin wrote to Loring, "The President has determined to recognize your services in the past campaign by promoting you to the rank of major-general, and your nomination will be submitted to Congress tomorrow." Benjamin added that it was "the design of the President to assign you to command in Georgia under General Lee."[50] The next day Benjamin ordered two of Loring's regiments to Tennessee; three others went to the Aquia District of Johnston's department. The rest of Loring's force reported to Johnston in Manassas.[51] It left Jackson with 5,267 officers and men present for duty, slightly less than half the force he had when he started for Romney.[52]

On February 25 Benjamin ordered Loring to report to Major General Benjamin Huger, commander of the Department of Norfolk.[53] He remained there until May 8, when he was placed in command of the Department of Southwestern Virginia.[54] Loring's assignment to southwest Virginia eventually led to his involvement with Lee as Lee tried to develop a second column for his first invasion movement of the North.

———————

In the next three weeks Jackson's attitude changed. Despite a buildup of Union forces to the north and the possibility of having to evacuate Winchester, Jackson's mood showed in a letter to Boteler on March 3.

> My plan is to put on as bold a front as possible and to use every means in my power to prevent his [the enemy's] advance.
> What I desire is to hold the country as far as practicable until we are in condition to advance and then with God's blessing, let us make thorough work of it.

Near the end of the letter he stated, "I am delighted to hear you say that Virginia is resolved to consecrate all her resources, if necessary, to the defense of Herself. Now we may look for war in earnest."[55]

PART 2

Jackson's Plan Adopted

CHAPTER 6

Northern Confidence Restored

THE YEAR 1861 HAD TAKEN THE AMERICAN PEOPLE FROM A PEACEFUL existence through the secession movement, creation of the Confederacy, preparation for war, and, finally, into armed conflict. As the old year faded, Stonewall Jackson was not the only one thinking of invading enemy territory. North of the Potomac River, Federal authorities were preparing for a massive offensive into eastern Virginia, a campaign that was part of a plan by Major General George B. McClellan to crush Southern resistance and achieve "a permanent restoration of a peaceful Union."

McClellan presented his plan to President Lincoln on August 2, 1861, two weeks after the Union defeat at Bull Run. The first objective was to drive Confederate troops out of Virginia and occupy Richmond. If possible, he added, he would continue southward and occupy Charleston, South Carolina; Savannah, Georgia; Montgomery and Mobile, Alabama; Pensacola, Florida; and New Orleans, Louisiana, and "crush the rebellion in its very heart." He also urged strong movements along the Mississippi River and in eastern Tennessee to reduce resistance to the Virginia invasion.

"An essential feature of the plan of operations," McClellan added, "will be the employment of a strong naval force, to protect the movement of a fleet of transports intended to convey a considerable body of troops from point to point of the enemy's seacoast. This naval force should also cooperate with the main army in its efforts to seize the important seaboard towns of the rebels."

McClellan recommended that his force, "the main army of operations," should have at least 273,000 men to carry out the proposed action.[1] That was more than five times the number of troops in the Washington area when McClellan took command there July 17.[2]

Lincoln accepted McClellan's plan and, on August 19, Secretary of War Simon Cameron called on Northern governors to forward immediately to Washington "all volunteer regiments, or parts of regiments," within their states.[3] By September 8, McClellan's force had been increased to nearly 85,000, but only 60,000 to 70,000 were ready for duty. At that time, McClellan was concerned that a strong enemy force would strike Washington. He urged reinforcement at once.[4]

By the end of October McClellan had 134,285 troops ready for duty, but he was not satisfied. He said he needed 208,000 effective troops—150,000 to advance into Virginia and 58,000 to defend Washington, Baltimore, and key points along the Potomac River. "This advance," McClellan added, "should not be postponed beyond the 25th of November."[5]

Despite this encouraging response to the call for troops, the public was getting restless over the army's inactivity. By late September, Attorney General Edward Bates observed: "Our people are weary of being kept always and everywhere upon the defensive. We absolutely need some dashing expeditions—some victories, great or small, to stimulate the zeal of the Country."[6]

Nearly a month passed before there was any official hint to government leaders outside Washington that defense was not the only reason for repeated requests for troops. In a letter to Pennsylvania Governor Andrew G. Curtin on October 28, Assistant Secretary of War Thomas A. Scott requested that all available troops be sent to Washington as speedily as possible "to aid in the efforts to crush out this gigantic rebellion."[7]

During this period Army-Navy expeditions were planned to attack key coastal points indicated by McClellan in the plan proposed to Lincoln. In a little more than three weeks two were being organized, one of which was already in motion.

On August 2, the day McClellan presented his plan, Brigadier General Thomas W. Sherman was sent to New York to organize, "in connection with Captain [S. F.] DuPont of the U.S. Navy," a force of 12,000 men. It was to rendezvous on Long Island Sound and be prepared to sail "at the earliest possible moment."[8] The objective was Confederate coastal positions in South Carolina, Georgia, and eastern Florida.

On August 25 Major General Benjamin F. Butler was put in command of a small detachment of troops and ordered to join with a Navy force, commanded by Commodore S. H. Stringham. The objective was to attack Confederate positions at Hatteras Inlet in North Carolina.[9]

The expedition left Fort Monroe, Virginia, the next day and by August 29 had taken two Confederate forts that guarded the inlet. Butler left a garrison and returned to Fort Monroe on August 31 to submit his report. He noted:

In my judgment, it [Hatteras Inlet] is a station second in importance only to Fortress Monroe on this coast. As a depot for coaling and supplies for the blockading squadron it is invaluable.[10]

Following his return Butler was authorized on September 10 to raise a volunteer force in the New England states of up to six regiments.[11] Before the year ended, it became part of an Army-Navy expedition to capture New Orleans.

Sherman, meanwhile, had encountered an unexpected problem. McClellan's request for reinforcements prompted the War Department, on September 14, to order him to "come with all your men to Washington."[12] He began moving his force to the capital, which displeased Lincoln. On September 18 Lincoln told Cameron that the Army-Navy expedition "is in nowise to be abandoned, but must be ready to move by the 1st of or early in October."[13] The expedition finally sailed from Annapolis, Maryland, on October 21.[14]

Two days later Brigadier General Ambrose E. Burnside was ordered to assemble troops in Annapolis for offensive operations on the coast of North Carolina. This expedition did not get under way until early 1862.[15]

Progress of the Sherman-DuPont expedition was slowed by gales and rough seas in late October and early November, so the initial attack was delayed until November 7, when the two forts guarding Port Royal Harbor were captured.[16] By December 10 Sherman's troops had fanned out and held Otter Island, at the entrance to Saint Helena Sound north of Port Royal, and Tybee Island, south of Port Royal at the mouth of the Savannah River.[17]

McClellan's desire to advance by November 25 was frustrated. On November 1 he was named general in chief of all armies to succeed Winfield Scott, who had retired.[18] This new responsibility would limit the time McClellan could devote to the Army of the Potomac. As preparations for its advance slowed, Federal officials began to murmur. In late November McClellan complained: "The necessity for delay has not been my fault. I am doing all I can to get ready to move before winter sets in, but it now begins to look as if we were condemned to a winter of inactivity."[19]

In early December Lincoln asked McClellan how long it would take to advance should that decision be made. McClellan replied that 100,000 troops could be in motion "probably by December 25."[20]

Late in December new anxiety struck Washington. McClellan contracted typhoid fever and was in bed for three weeks. Some authorities were alarmed because, they claimed, details of the proposed campaign were known only to McClellan. Others feared that great confusion would result if McClellan died.[21]

The new year was only twelve days old when McClellan appeared unexpectedly at a meeting that had been called to discuss the situation. Nothing was accomplished and another meeting was scheduled for the next day. Lincoln invited him along with Generals Irvin McDowell and William B. Franklin and Quartermaster General Montgomery C. Meigs. Also present were Secretary of State William H. Seward, Treasury Secretary Salmon P. Chase, and Postmaster General Montgomery Blair.

There was a great deal of whispering and some heated discussions, but this meeting also was fruitless. Afterward, McClellan privately urged Lincoln to "trust me, and said that if he would leave military affairs to me I would be responsible that I could bring matters to a successful issue and free him from all his troubles."[22]

Two weeks passed with no movement and Lincoln lost patience. On January 27 he ordered "a general movement of the land and naval forces of the United States against the insurgent forces," to begin February 22. This was followed by a special war order on January 31 in which Lincoln directed that "all the disposable force of the Army of the Potomac, after providing safely for the defense of Washington, be formed into an expedition for the immediate object of seizing and occupying a point upon the railroad southwestward of what is known as Manassas Junction, all details to be in the discretion of the commander-in-chief." Lincoln again ordered the expedition to move on or before February 22.[23]

McClellan protested and, in a lengthy letter February 3 to the new secretary of war, Edwin M. Stanton, proposed sending a large force down the Potomac River to the Chesapeake Bay and then to Urbanna, Virginia, on the south bank of the Rappahannock River. If the Rebels withdrew from Manassas and moved south to protect Richmond, McClellan said, the rest of the Army of the Potomac would join the Urbanna force and attack Richmond. A rapid movement from Urbanna, he contended, would cut off Confederate troops on the lower Peninsula, between the James and York rivers.

As an alternative, he suggested moving all the way down the Chesapeake Bay to Fort Monroe and then advancing up the Peninsula to attack Richmond. McClellan added that he considered a movement between the York and James rivers safer but less brilliant than the one from Urbanna, but he preferred it to an attack upon Manassas.[24] Lincoln asked McClellan to evaluate the differences between the plans he had proposed and the movement that Lincoln had ordered.[25]

In mid-February, following several conferences, Lincoln "reluctantly consented to abandon his plan of operation for that suggested by me," according to McClellan.[26] On February 27 the War Department began procuring vessels to transport the Army of the Potomac to Fort Monroe, from which it would move up the Peninsula.[27]

Preparations were interrupted, however, by surprising news that reached McClellan on Sunday, March 9. The Confederates were evacuating their lines in Centreville and Manassas. McClellan ordered a general advance the next morning to determine the "exact condition of affairs" and, if possible, to hinder the Confederates if they were retreating toward Richmond.

A small cavalry force reached Confederate lines in Centreville at noon, March 10, but found only empty camps and "heaps of burning military stores and property."[28] The Southerners had withdrawn south of the Rappahannock River.

The new year also brought into sharp focus the Navy's critical need for coal, especially anthracite, for operations along the South Atlantic coast and in the Gulf of Mexico. As the problem worsened, it gave added importance to a major objective in Jackson's invasion plan—to close the coal mines.

On January 4 Flag Officer Samuel F. DuPont, commanding the South Atlantic Blockading Squadron, told Assistant Navy Secretary Gustavus V. Fox that the fleet's coal supply was dwindling at a time when "most important operations are pending."[29] The seriousness of the situation was clearly shown in three additional messages from DuPont to Fox:

February 10: "We are stinted for coal and ammunition."

February 18: "Coal—coal—I am going with the ships unloaded."

March 14: "Now my friend for the last time let me implore you to send coal. I have begged in vain. Two more weeks and this whole fleet will be laid up."[30]

The situation in the Gulf of Mexico was similar. David D. Porter, commanding a mortar fleet there, told Fox on March 11 of his movement from the Atlantic to the Gulf of Mexico with the armed steamer *Harriet Lane,* then added:

When I got to Key West [Florida] there was 95 tons [of coal] on hand, which we took for the *Harriet Lane.* When I left there, there was none. Here there is not a pound belonging to the Navy. Is it right that so material an article as coal, should be scarce at a time when the most important move of the war is about to begin?

On March 28 he wrote:

I don't know whose fault it is, but we are without coal. The *Mississippi* put out her fires today having burnt her last pound, the *Clifton* has five tons, the *Westfield* ten, the *Harriet Lane* 20, the *Pensacola* 20, and all the gun boats are short. He [Flag Officer David G. Farragut] sent a coal vessel here [Southwest Passage on the Mississippi River] from Ship Island loaded with coal. She had 280 tons; we should have had 1500 tons. We can't move without coal.[31]

Butler, commander of Army forces that were to attack New Orleans, also was aware of the need. On December 14, 1861, as he was moving troops from New England to the Gulf of Mexico, he questioned Fox: "Have you forwarded ship load of coal to Ship Island [off the coast of Mississippi]?" Fox replied that he had not. Ship Island was to be the Army's base for the combined attack in late April.[32]

Fox's response apparently prompted Butler to take a unique step in February as the last of his troops were embarking for Ship Island. Instead of loading transports with stone for ballast, he used 3,000 tons of anthracite and had the fuel on board when he reached Ship Island on March 31.

When he met with Farragut to coordinate the move against New Orleans, Butler said the Navy commander "was almost in despair" over the lack of coal. The Navy vessels that would ascend the Mississippi to New Orleans were equipped with furnaces that required anthracite. Butler reported that he had 2,500 to 3,000 tons of anthracite in ballast and offered it to Farragut, which Farragut eagerly accepted.[33]

In a letter to Navy Secretary Gideon Welles on April 8, Farragut reported that Butler had provided the coal. He added, "Now that our own vessels are beginning to arrive, my alarms on that account [coal] are dispelled, and so soon as the vessels can coal and get their stores and munitions of war on board we will be ready to proceed up the river."[34]

As the coal problem became evident, Navy officials spent two months probing for the cause and seeking a solution. On April 3, Fox informed DuPont that "some different arrangements" were being made to correct the problem.[35] In a letter to DuPont the same day, Welles explained that 3,000 tons of coal were to be shipped as soon as possible and that it would be followed with 1,100 tons per week.[36] It was only a temporary solution and the need for coal created more problems in 1862 and 1863.

The "different arrangements" apparently were slow in developing. On November 24, J. G. Miner, an agent of the Navy Department, told Welles, "I have gotten a little method at last into the coal transportation. For the first month's operations, a gross amount of 688 tons."[37]

—————>◦●◦<—————

The government's demand for coal in 1862 was described as enormous by W. Parker Foulke of West Chester, Pennsylvania. "The president of the [Philadelphia and] Reading Railroad informs me that he is transporting 60,000 tons per week over that line, and that he has hard work to supply the requisite facilities," Foulke wrote in a letter on July 24, 1862.[38]

In the Civil War period, the Philadelphia and Reading extended from Philadelphia, Pennsylvania's major port on the Delaware River, to Reading in Berks County, and on to Schuylkill Haven and Pottsville in the anthracite region. A branch extended westward from Reading to Harrisburg.[39]

Coal apparently was no problem in early 1862 for the North Atlantic Blockading Squadron, commanded by Flag Officer Louis M. Goldsborough. The proximity of northern ports made it relatively easy to supply vessels, particularly those assigned to cooperate with Burnside in an attack on the North Carolina coast and with McClellan's move to the Peninsula.

The only hint of trouble came from McClellan. On March 12 he noted that several transports for more than 15,000 troops were at Alexandria, "but they were not coaled up or ready to receive the troops."[40] That problem was quickly resolved and five days later the first troops, Brigadier General Charles S. Hamilton's division, left Alexandria for Fort Monroe.[41]

Meanwhile, successes in early 1862 had given Union authorities and the public new hope. Jackson withdrew from Romney and Union troops moved in. Then, in rapid succession, victories were gained in other areas in a pattern similar to the extended plan McClellan had proposed to Lincoln the previous September.

In February Forts Henry and Donelson in Tennessee fell to Union land and naval forces. Other Union troops gained control of southern Kentucky and middle Tennessee. In North Carolina, combined Union forces captured Confederate fortifications on Roanoke Island.[42]

In March those forces moved south and captured New Bern, North Carolina.[43] Impressive results also were achieved along the coasts of South Carolina, Georgia, and eastern Florida. By the end of the month, Union forces controlled much of the coast from Edisto Island, South Carolina, to St. Augustine, Florida.[44] In Jacksonville, Florida, "loyal citizens" went so far as to adopt a resolution voiding Florida's secession ordinance and calling for a convention to organize a new state government.[45]

Early in March, in southeastern Virginia, the ironclads *Monitor* and *Virginia* (formerly the *Merrimack*) clashed. The *Virginia*, which had inflicted severe damage on wooden Union warships in Hampton Roads, was effectively eliminated as a threat. This allowed McClellan to continue his move to the Peninsula and then on to Richmond.[46] He left Alexandria on April 1 and arrived at Fort Monroe the next day to take personal command of the campaign.[47]

———————

Everything seemed to be going well. Union officials, confident that the end of the war was near, took an unusually bold step April 3. The War Department closed recruiting offices and notified governors that "volunteer recruiting service will cease."[48]

This confidence was strengthened a few days later by news from western Tennessee that Confederate troops had been repulsed with heavy losses in the Battle of Shiloh on April 6–7. The next day, Island No. 10 in the Mississippi River was seized following the surrender of Confederate forces.[49]

On April 10 Lincoln proclaimed: "It has pleased Almighty God to vouchsafe signal victories to the land and naval forces engaged in suppressing an internal rebellion, and at the same time to avert from our country the dangers of foreign intervention and invasion."

He then urged people at their next worship service "to render thanks to our Heavenly Father for these inestimable blessings" and to "reverently invoke Divine guidance for our national counsels, to the end that they may speedily result in the restoration of peace, harmony, and unity throughout our borders, and hasten the establishment of fraternal relations among all the countries of the earth."[50]

Northern confidence peaked a month later. In a proclamation issued on May 12 Lincoln lifted the blockade on Beaufort, North Carolina; Port Royal, South Carolina; and New Orleans, Louisiana.[51] This was premature and the next on-to-Richmond drive was shattered, as it had been at Bull Run in the summer of 1861. As Northern confidence weakened, the attitude of the Confederate public and government grew stronger. McClellan's Peninsula Campaign helped influence Confederate leaders in June 1862 to adopt Jackson's invasion plan. It also led to Lee's command of the Army of Northern Virginia, the union of Lee and Jackson on the battlefield, and, a few months later, the first steps on the Confederate invasion route.

CHAPTER 7

Gloom Deepens in the South

WHILE NORTHERN HOPE AND CONFIDENCE GREW IN EARLY 1862, GLOOM spread over the Confederacy. Southern authorities were deeply concerned over how they could meet the threatened invasion of northeastern Virginia by vastly superior Union forces.

Preparations for the Union advance were no secret. Confederate officials had been alerted almost a month earlier by people General Joseph E. Johnston described as "our friends in Washington."[1] Those spies had been operating since the early days of the war. Their contact in the Southern army was Colonel Thomas Jordan, assistant adjutant general to General P. G. T. Beauregard.[2]

Between November 25 and December 30, 1861, Jordan received eight messages from agents describing preparations for McClellan's proposed on-to-Richmond campaign. The first indicated that the Army of the Potomac would cross the Potomac River and advance against Confederate positions between Centreville and Manassas. Union leaders, it was stated, were confident their troops could be in Richmond within two weeks.[3]

Most of the notes indicated that the Union movement was expected to start within a week to ten days. One writer reported that "those in high authority" expected the move to start "between this [December 23] and the 5th of next month." Another writer quoted McClellan's aide-de-camp as saying, "If the general were well enough the move would be made next week [the first week of January]." Several of the notes contained references to the Butler and Burnside forces that were preparing to move. There was uncertainty, however, about their destinations.[4]

Johnston was worried about the reported Union preparations. He was even more alarmed by an agent's report that McClellan probably would move into Virginia with 180,000 to 185,000 men.[5] He had only 44,563 troops ready for duty in the Potomac District of the Department of Northern Virginia.[6]

Johnston began to consider moving to a defensive line nearer Richmond. He first hinted at this in letters to Secretary of War Judah P. Benjamin in mid-January. On the 14th he described his situation as unsafe and stated that it would remain so "until the destination of the Burnside expedition is known." Four days later, Johnston reported that McClellan's troops had not gone into winter quarters and that the number of his own men "are as few as can safely meet the enemy."[7]

The weather worked in Johnston's favor. The storm that had plagued Jackson in the Shenandoah Valley struck northeastern Virginia with equal fury. "The quantity of rain that fell, and of snow, always melting quickly, made a depth of mud rarely equaled," and the situation would have made military operations south of the Potomac and east of the Blue Ridge almost impossible, he explained.[8] Benjamin told Johnston on January 25: "It seems scarcely possible that in the present condition of roads an attack [by Union forces] can be made."[9]

Johnston met with Jefferson Davis in January to discuss the situation. In a letter to Johnston on February 6, the president stated, "I was fully impressed with the difficulties which you presented when discussing the subject of a change of position to preserve the efficiency of your army."

Davis agreed that road and stream conditions would delay any possible enemy attack, then told Johnston:

> I hope that you will be able to mobilize your army by the removal of heavy ordnance and such stores as are not required for active operations, so that whenever you are required to move it may be without public loss and without impediment to celerity.
>
> In the meantime, as I have heretofore advised you, I am making diligent effort to reinforce your columns. It may still be that you will have the power to meet and repel the enemy, a course of action more acceptable certainly to both of us, but it is not to be disguised that your defective position and proximity to the enemy's base of operations do not permit us to be sanguine of that result. It is therefore necessary to make all due preparations for the opposite course of events.[10]

Ten days later Johnston told Davis: "This army is far weaker now than it has ever been since July 20, 1861. We cannot retreat from this point without heavy loss. If we are beaten this army will be broken up, and Virginia, at least, lost."[11]

Help was on the way, however. On January 23 Congress passed an act authorizing Davis to call on the states for additional troops.[12] On February 2, less than two weeks later, Benjamin issued a call for 254,615 men from the eleven Confederate states, plus 117,000 from Kentucky and Missouri, to serve for three years or the duration of the war. The new recruits were to make up 175 additional regiments and were "to be ready to take the field by March 15th."[13]

On February 14 Benjamin notified the governors that recruiting parties had been sent to their states to obtain the reinforcements. "To expedite completion of those quotas is now of the highest importance to the public defense," Benjamin stated. "You are therefore requested and earnestly solicited to use your executive powers in aid of such recruiting parties."[14]

It was some time before the effect of these steps was realized. In the meantime, the Confederacy faced the situation with growing pessimism. On January 29 Robert Garlick Hill Kean, who became chief of the Confederate Bureau of War a few months later, noted in his diary: "There seems to be a more general feeling of despondency prevailing at this time than ever before since the war began. The weather perhaps alone keeps McClellan from advancing on us here [Richmond]." On February 12 he wrote: "One disaster after another has befallen our army. Our condition is feebler than it has been since last July."[15]

A week later Davis revealed the depth of the Confederate pessimism when he informed Johnston: "I am very anxious to see you. Events have cast on our arms and our hopes the gloomiest shadows, and at such a time we must show redoubled energy and resolution."[16] Davis evidently was concerned over the capture of Forts Henry and Donelson and the threat that led to the capture of Nashville, Tennessee, later in February.

———>●<———

Johnston met with Davis and the Cabinet late in the month to discuss withdrawing his troops to a less-exposed position. No specific orders resulted, but Johnston later recalled that he understood "that the army was to fall back as soon as practicable."

Davis's postmaster general, John H. Reagan, noted that "after a conference between the President and General Johnston, it was agreed that our army should fall back and take a position in the vicinity of Fredericksburg." Davis did not mention a conference but later twice referred to conversations with Johnston. Sometime later, he went to Johnston's headquarters for further discussion and a reconnaissance of the Fredericksburg area.[17]

———>●<———

By the end of February Davis's mood was even gloomier. On the 28th he advised Johnston, "Your opinion that your position may be turned whenever the enemy shall choose to advance, and that he will be ready to take the field before yourself, so clearly indicate prompt effort to disencumber yourself of everything which would interfere with your rapid movement when necessary." He urged Johnston to familiarize himself with the country to his rear "to enable you to select a line of greater natural advantages than that now occupied by your forces."

> As heretofore stated in conversation with you, it is needful that the armies on the north, the east, and the proximate south of this capital should be so disposed as to support each other. With their present strength and position the armies under your command are entirely separated from the others.[18]

Once again Davis felt an urgent need for Lee's presence and decided to recall him from the southeastern coast.[19] Lee arrived in Richmond on March 5.[20] That day Johnston revealed his intention to abandon positions in the Centreville-Manassas area "in two or three days."[21] Difficulty in loading baggage and supplies delayed the start until March 9, but by the 12th a new line had been established in Culpeper County along the right bank of the Rappahannock River.[22]

Davis was shocked. In two dispatches to Johnston on March 15 Davis stated that "your letter of the 13th instant received this day" was the first information he had received of the withdrawal. Until then, Davis asserted, "I was as much in the dark as to your purposes, condition, and necessities as at the time of our conversation on the subject about a month since."[23]

The withdrawal was particularly annoying to Davis because, a few days earlier, he had tried to share with Johnston a new glimmer of hope. The call for recruits was being met enthusiastically in most states and there were indications quotas would soon be met. Georgia, for example, was ready to furnish thirteen regiments and two battalions instead of the twelve regiments requested.[24]

On March 8 Benjamin called on Governor John Letcher of Virginia to immediately summon 40,000 militia. Fifteen thousand were to join Johnston, 12,000 were to be sent to Stonewall Jackson in the Shenandoah Valley, 10,000 were to go to the Peninsula, and 3,000 to the Aquia District.[25] On March 10, Davis wrote Johnston:

> Further assurance given to me this day that you shall be promptly and adequately reenforced, so as to enable you to maintain your position and resume first policy when the roads will permit.[26]

"First policy," Davis explained after the war, "was to carry the war beyond our own border."[27] But there was little hope in early 1862 of such an invasion. In a few months, however, Jackson and Lee provided the stimulus to realize Davis's policy.

——————

In the meantime rumors had spread that Lee would be named secretary of war in a cabinet reorganization, but the post went to George W. Randolph.[28] On March 13 Lee was assigned "under the direction of the President . . . with the conduct of military operations of the Confederacy."[29]

Lee was not happy. He confided to his wife:

> It will give me great pleasure to do everything I can to relieve him [the president] & serve the country, but I do not see either advantage or pleasure in my duties. But I will not complain, but do my best. In the present condition of affairs no one can foresee what may happen, nor in my judgment is it advisable for any one to make any arrangements with a view of permanency or pleasure. The enemy is pushing us back in all directions, & how far he will be

successful depends much upon our efforts & the mercy of Providence. I shall, in all human probability, soon have to take the field.[30]

———>●<———

Not all news from military fronts was so grim. Before the end of March hope began to shine in the Shenandoah Valley, where Jackson would initiate offensive operations. Before that, however, Jackson had to contend with the same situation that prompted Johnston's withdrawal. Union forces in Charles Town and Harpers Ferry, totaling more than 23,000, were preparing to move against Winchester. Jackson had only 5,394 troops present for duty.[31]

On March 8 he informed Johnston, "I greatly desire to hold this place [Winchester] so far as may be consistent with your views and plans." A few days earlier he had been advised to fall back, if necessary, but to "delay the enemy as long as you can." Jackson chose the latter course and boldly asked for more troops.[32]

None were available and, as enemy troops pushed forward, Jackson realized his position was untenable. On March 11 he reluctantly began to evacuate Winchester and move southward. Jackson had little choice; Johnston's withdrawal and the progress of Union troops created a new threat that had to be met quickly.

By March 19 his troops were in Woodstock and Mount Jackson, thirty and forty-two miles south of Winchester, respectively.[33] A Union division, almost 10,000 men, was sent in pursuit but on March 19 halted in Strasburg, twelve miles north of the nearest Confederate position.[34] Two days later Jackson received surprising information. Federal troops were withdrawing from the Valley.[35]

———>●<———

This movement was part of a plan hurriedly devised by Major General George B. McClellan to comply with President Lincoln's directive to leave Washington "entirely secure" before starting for the Peninsula. On March 16 McClellan ordered Major General Nathaniel P. Banks to move his 5th Corps to Manassas. Only a small force was to be left in the Valley—four regiments of infantry and two artillery batteries near Strasburg, and two regiments of cavalry in Winchester.[36]

On March 21 Union troops began to leave Winchester and march eastward.[37] Something went awry, however, and no entrenched force remained in Strasburg. Brigadier General James Shields left on March 20 for Winchester, giving the movement "all the appearance of a retreat." His purpose, he said, was to draw Jackson away from any supporting force that might be near.[38]

Jackson learned of the withdrawal from his cavalry commander, Colonel Turner Ashby, on March 21 and ordered his troops to march north at dawn the next morning. By 2 P.M. March 23 Jackson and his small force approached Kernstown, four miles south of Winchester. Informed by a "usually reliable source" that the enemy force in his front probably did not exceed four regiments, Jackson attacked.[39] Instead of four regiments, the enemy force was Shields's division of almost 10,000 men. After a stubborn fight Jackson withdrew just before nightfall.[40]

Though he was repulsed, Jackson's bold move halted Union troop movements to eastern Virginia. During the fighting, a hurry-up call went out for the return of Williams's division to Winchester. Two of his three brigades returned immediately to the Valley.[41]

―――――――

Jackson's advance and rumors that he had been strongly reinforced aroused Washington. On March 31 Lincoln ordered Brigadier General Louis Blenker's division detached from McClellan and sent to Major General John C. Frémont's Mountain Department.[42] McClellan was disturbed and, on April 1, told Banks, "The change in affairs in the valley of the Shenandoah has rendered necessary a corresponding departure, temporarily at least, from the plan we some days since agreed upon." McClellan assumed that Banks would have a large enough force to drive Jackson southward, but added that Banks probably would find it impossible to send any troops to Manassas for some time.[43]

―――――――

An important event occurred in Jackson's camp three days after the Battle of Kernstown. Jedediah Hotchkiss joined Jackson's staff as topographical engineer.

Hotchkiss had joined the army in June 1861 and served in western Virginia until stricken with typhoid fever two months later. He recuperated in his home at Loch Willow, northwest of Staunton, until March 1862, when he responded to Letcher's call for militia in the Shenandoah Valley. On March 21 he was accepted for engineering duty and five days later was summoned to Jackson's headquarters. Jackson told him, "I want you to make me a map of the Valley, from Harper's Ferry to Lexington, showing all the points of offense and defense in those places." It was the beginning of Hotchkiss's career as topographical engineer, first with Jackson in the Valley, then with the 2nd Corps of the Army of Northern Virginia until the end of the war.[44]

Hotchkiss also had unique knowledge in another field that would help Jackson and his invasion planning. Following graduation in 1846 from Windsor Academy in New York State, Hotchkiss joined several young men in a walking tour of the Lykens Valley, an anthracite region north of Harrisburg, Pennsylvania. Later Hotchkiss obtained a teaching position and resided among the Lykens Valley miners for a year. He studied the geology of coal deposits and mining in that region. At the end of the year Hotchkiss and a fellow teacher went on a walking tour of Pennsylvania's Cumberland Valley and its extension into Virginia.[45] These are the experiences that aided Jackson's planning of the 1863 invasion movement.[46]

Jackson was keenly aware of what Kernstown had achieved. In a letter to his wife on April 11 he stated: "Although I was repulsed in the attempt to recover Winchester . . . the great object which required me to follow up the enemy, as he fell back from Strasburg, seems to have been accomplished very thoroughly. Time has shown that while the field is in possession of the enemy, the most essential fruits of the battle are ours."[47]

Jackson's success was not unnoticed in Richmond. Congress adopted this resolution: "Resolved by the Congress of the Confederate States of America, that the thanks of Congress are due, and they are hereby tendered to Major General T. J. Jackson and the officers and men under his command for their gallant and meritorious service in the successful engagement with a greatly superior force of the enemy near Kernstown, Frederick County, Virginia, on the 23rd day of March, 1862."[48]

It was only the beginning of Jackson's remarkable achievements in the spring of 1862. In May he set out on another northward drive in the Valley and achieved much more. It was in the Valley that Jackson's daring influenced important decisions in Washington and in Richmond, ones that changed the character of the war.

CHAPTER 8

War in Earnest Comes to Virginia

THE HOPE GENERATED BY JACKSON'S ACTION AT KERNSTOWN QUICKLY dimmed. Jackson withdrew his small army to Mount Jackson, forty-two miles south of Winchester. Enemy forces pursued him, but because of the troops' exhaustion, the Union column halted in Woodstock, eight miles north of the Confederates.[1]

At the end of March Jackson was in a precarious position. To the north was Banks's army with 23,000 men and to the west Frémont's Mountain Department force of almost 22,000. Jackson had no more than 6,000 men.[2]

Johnston's withdrawal to Culpeper, the start of McClellan's advance on the Peninsula, and Jackson's endangered position created a dire strategic problem for the South complicated by insufficient manpower. Lee summed up the situation on March 29:

> The enemy is pressing us on all sides and a call for reinforcements comes from every department. It is impossible to place at every point which is threatened a force which shall prove equal to every emergency.[3]

Even more alarming were reports from March 25 to 29 of steam transports loaded with Federal troops moving down the Potomac River, carrying perhaps more than 100,000 men.[4]

On March 25 Lee wrote to Johnston about the probability that the troops were from McClellan's army and were landing at Old Point Comfort in southeastern Virginia for an attack on Richmond or Norfolk. He advised Johnston that 20,000 to 30,000 men might be needed to help repulse the enemy. Johnston was to organize enough troops to hold his line north of Richmond and be ready to move the remainder to defend the capital.[5]

Davis—uncertain whether Union troops would land in Virginia or North Carolina—summoned Johnston to a meeting in Gordonsville. They decided to send two of Johnston's brigades to Richmond as a precaution. One was moved to North Carolina a few days later and the other was sent to Yorktown to join the Army of the Peninsula, commanded by Major General John B. Magruder.[6]

In early April Magruder estimated his force at 11,000 to 12,000.[7] Nearby were 12,000 men in the Department of Norfolk, commanded by Major General Benjamin Huger. On April 10, Huger informed Lee that the terms of service of many of his regiments would expire in the next three weeks and, as a result, some regiments were "much disorganized."[8]

By April 5 it was determined that McClellan's troops had landed at Fort Monroe and were advancing up the Peninsula toward Yorktown. Three of Johnston's divisions—those of Jubal A. Early, D. H. Hill and D. R. Jones—were ordered to the Peninsula.

That left G. W. Smith's division in Fredericksburg, James Longstreet's in Orange Court House, and Richard S. Ewell's on the Rappahannock River, all east of the Blue Ridge. To the west was Jackson's small army (really just another division) in the Shenandoah Valley.[9]

These developments led to two important confrontations. McClellan's advance on the Peninsula created a serious threat to Richmond; the other was Jackson's Valley Campaign, which resulted in brief alarm in Washington.

When McClellan arrived at Fort Monroe on April 2 to take personal command of the Army of the Potomac, he intended "by rapid movements to drive before me or capture the enemy on the Peninsula, open the James River, and press on to Richmond before he [the enemy] should be materially reinforced from other portions of his territory."[10]

He lost no time. The next day he ordered five divisions with two cavalry regiments to begin moving northward at 6 A.M. on April 4. Two more divisions were to move at 6 A.M. on April 5. The columns were to advance toward Yorktown, twenty-four miles northwest of Fort Monroe. No serious opposition was expected.[11]

Trouble developed immediately. A lack of accurate maps was a serious handicap, and heavy rain lashed the area on April 5.[12] Storms continued for four days and McClellan noted that "roads and camps were in awful condition."[13]

The weather was not the only trouble. McClellan was alarmed that the War Department had discontinued recruiting "on the very eve of the advance of the Army of the Potomac into the enemy's country." The closing of recruiting stations, he later claimed, "unnecessarily prolonged the war at least two years."[14]

McClellan faced another problem as well. He was being deprived of troops he had counted on for his drive against Richmond. On April 3 he was forbidden to detach any troops from the forces of Major General John E. Wool, commander at Fort Monroe.[15]

The next day he was informed that "the President, deeming the force to be left in front of Washington insufficient to insure its safety, has directed that McDowell's corps should be detached from the forces operating under your immediate direction." Later that day McClellan was told that two more departments had been created, one the Department of the Shenandoah under Nathaniel P. Banks, the other the Department of the Rappahannock under McDowell.[16]

McClellan had lost two of his five corps. On April 6 he protested to Lincoln, pointing out: "The order forming new departments, if rigidly enforced, deprives me of the power of ordering up wagons and troops absolutely necessary to enable me to advance to Richmond. I have by no means the transportation I must have to move my army even a few miles."[17]

Lincoln replied: "The forwarding of transportation, ammunition, and Woodbury's brigade, is not, and will not, be interfered with. You now have over 100,000 troops with you, independent of General Wool's command. I think you better break the enemy's line from Yorktown to Warwick River at once. This will probably use time as advantageously as you can."[18]

McClellan disagreed. In two dispatches to Washington on April 7 he stated that he had only 85,000 men ready for duty. But, he added, reports indicated that Johnston had arrived at Yorktown with reinforcements and "it seems clear that I shall have the whole force of the enemy on my hands—probably not less than 100,000."[19]

With his force reduced and fearful that he was up against frightful odds, McClellan changed course. Instead of assaulting enemy lines, he decided to lay siege to Yorktown.[20]

Confederate authorities reacted quickly to the Union movement on the Peninsula. On April 4 Lee notified Johnston, "The movement of troops directed from your line must immediately be made to this place [Richmond]."[21] On April 9 the first of Johnston's troops, Early's division, joined Magruder. The addition increased Magruder's force to about 20,000.[22]

At the time the Confederate line was nearly fifteen miles long from Yorktown west to the Warwick River. Magruder's men, supported by laborers, had dug trenches and fortified key positions. Magruder also had used a ruse. By maneuvering troops rapidly along the line and allowing them to be seen frequently by Union observers, he created the impression of a much larger force than he actually had.[23]

Still, Confederate authorities knew Magruder's skill would only delay McClellan's move against Richmond. On April 12 Davis ordered the Peninsula and Norfolk departments combined with the Army of Northern Virginia under Johnston, who would direct both land and naval operations.[24]

At the president's request Johnston went to Yorktown to examine the situation. On his return to Richmond he proposed that instead of trying to delay McClellan's advance, all available troops, including forces from the Carolinas and Georgia, should assemble quickly in front of Richmond and prepare to go on the offensive.

Davis called for a conference with Randolph and Lee, and Johnston was permitted to invite Longstreet and Smith to join him. After a lengthy discussion Davis decided to continue resistance on the Peninsula and Johnston was directed to move most of his troops there.[25]

Johnston assumed the combined command April 17. He had 53,000 troops to face an enemy force of 133,000. He decided to hold his position as long as possible but, when threatened by attack, to withdraw rather than risk a battle against superior forces. On April 18 Johnston gave Longstreet command of the center position of his line, with Magruder on the right and D. H. Hill on the left.[26]

Despite the rain, preliminary preparations for McClellan's siege lines were completed by April 17. Weather continued to be a problem, though, and the work was delayed by storms in late April that prevented the landing of guns and ammunition.[27]

By May 3 Union batteries were ready. "It was intended to open [fire] with all 114 guns and mortars at once, in order to create the greatest possible moral and physical effect," McClellan said. But by that time, the Confederates were gone. They had abandoned their lines on the night of May 3 and were withdrawing westward toward Richmond.[28]

Jubilantly, McClellan reported the news to Stanton early on May 4, including the fact that the Confederates had left behind many cannon and mortars, plus ammunition and other supplies. Stanton congratulated McClellan and added, "I hope soon to hail your arrival at Richmond."[29]

McClellan promptly sent troops in pursuit but Longstreet counterattacked at Williamsburg on May 5. Overnight the Confederates withdrew, and the next day McClellan occupied Williamsburg without opposition.[30] Johnston then began a gradual withdrawal up the Peninsula to better protect Richmond.[31] At the same time Huger was evacuating Norfolk and moving toward Petersburg. Union troops occupied Norfolk on May 10.[32]

The situation alarmed Richmond. On May 10 Randolph directed that all War Department documents, "except those required for constant reference," were to be packed in boxes for possible removal from the capital. "This is intended as a prudent step," he said, "and is not caused by any bad news from the army."[33]

Following the occupation of Williamsburg, McClellan began to move cautiously toward Richmond. By May 16 he had reached White House, a plantation on the Pamunkey River about twenty-five miles short of his goal.[34] Two days later he received some welcome news. McDowell, with 35,000 to 40,000 troops, had been ordered to leave Fredericksburg, march on Richmond, and cooperate with McClellan in attacking the Rebel capital.[35]

McDowell had already sent one division to the Army of the Potomac by water. To replace that detachment, his force was to be increased by Shields's division from the Shenandoah Valley, where the situation appeared to be relatively quiet.[36] Shields was expected to reach Fredericksburg by May 22, and McDowell planned to move two days later.[37]

Shields's troops did arrive on the 22nd but were so exhausted that it was decided to delay the start of McDowell's movement until the 26th.[38] This proved disastrous for Federal hopes.

In the Valley Stonewall Jackson had stirred up unexpected trouble. His rapid advance to Front Royal and Winchester created fear for the safety of Washington, and Federal authorities changed their plans to meet this new threat.

———⟫●⟪———

After Kernstown Jackson's forces halted near Mount Jackson and remained there for more than two weeks.[39] Operations were restricted by periodic snow, rain, and sleet that began early in April and continued until the second week of the month.[40] The situation provided Jackson with time to think about conducting more aggressive action.

The idea also was proposed by Longstreet in a dispatch to Jackson at 10 A.M. April 3. Longstreet, in temporary command while Johnston was in Richmond conferring with Davis on the Peninsula situation, suggested that he join Jackson with "sufficient reinforcements to strike the Federal forces a sudden, severe blow, and thus compel a change in the movements of McClellan's army."

Longstreet explained to Jackson, "The responsibility of the move could not be taken unless I was with the detachment to give it vigor and action to meet my views, or give time to get behind the Rappahannock in case the authorities discovered the move and ordered its recall."[41]

At 10 o'clock that night Jackson reported there had been no sign that day of any enemy movement and added: "It would not be prudent to attack him [Banks] in his present position, but if you can send me 5,000 infantry, 400 rounds of Parrott [artillery] ammunition, and a battery of six pieces of artillery with its chest filled, I will make a stand, and if circumstances justify it I will advance."

In two letters to Longstreet on April 5 Jackson confirmed delivery of the Parrott ammunition, then wrote: "If you send me a force for the purpose of attacking, it should not, if practicable, be less than 17,000 men and twelve pieces of artillery. If this number asked for is not available, any that you may send will, under Providence, have my best efforts expended upon it, and no stone shall be left unturned to give us success. If Banks is defeated it may greatly retard McClellan's movements."[42]

———⟫●⟪———

In the meantime Jackson had been instructed to leave the Valley if the enemy continued to press him. In that event, according to Johnston, Jackson was to move toward Orange Court House, east of the Blue Ridge.[43]

Jackson, however, was having a communication problem and, in a letter to Ewell from near Mount Jackson on April 10, stated, "I am so much cut off from the world that I hope you will not forget to give me such news as you may have." Jackson noted that "all is quiet in [my] front," though Banks was only about six miles away.

Two days later he informed Ewell, "Should I fall back in consequence of the enemy's advancing I will let you know immediately, when, according to the present arrangement, General Johnston expects you to fall back behind the Rapidan, and from that point reinforce me, if necessary."[44]

On April 13 Ewell offered another suggestion—Jackson could cross the Blue Ridge and join him in an attack on Louis Blenker's division, which was north of Ewell and moving toward the Valley to join Banks. The enemy troops were "very much scattered," Ewell wrote, and a successful action might force Banks to withdraw from the Valley. "Such a move would embarrass the attack of McClellan [on the Peninsula]."[45]

In his response that day Jackson noted, "All is quiet in front." In a second dispatch the same day he expressed the opinion that it would not be safe for him to join Ewell because it might give Banks an opportunity to move in the rear of Lee's column. The correspondence between Ewell and Jackson continued for four days; most of it dealt with local geography.

But, in three dispatches on the 17th, Jackson had bad news for Ewell. Union troops had advanced on him near Mount Jackson and he was falling back toward Swift Run Gap. Ewell was told to join Jackson early the next morning at the Gap.[46]

Union troops occupied Mount Jackson and Banks prepared to advance toward New Market the evening of the 17th. As the pressure increased, Jackson continued falling back toward Harrisonburg and Swift Run Gap. By April 21 he had withdrawn to Conrad's Store, about fifteen miles east of Harrisonburg on the road to Swift Run Gap.[47]

———◦◦◦———

Jackson's withdrawal prompted Lee on April 18 to alert Brigadier General Edward Johnson, commander of the Shenandoah Mountain troops. If Jackson was forced to continue the withdrawal, he would do so by way of Swift Run Gap in order to join Ewell and hold the Blue Ridge.

Johnson was directed to keep in touch with Jackson. "If he is compelled to retire to Swift Run Gap it will be necessary for you to move to Staunton. Should you find the enemy marching in too strong a force for you to resist, you must retire toward Waynesboro and endeavor to hold the passage through the Blue Ridge Mountains."[48]

McDowell, meanwhile, had moved to the Fredericksburg area. This not only created the threat of a direct attack on Richmond from the north, but also might jeopardize Confederate forces on the Peninsula.

The only Confederate troops facing McDowell at the time consisted of a brigade under Brigadier General Charles W. Field. As McDowell advanced, Field withdrew to a point about fourteen miles south of Fredericksburg. On April 25 Lee ordered Brigadier General Joseph R. Anderson to move troops from Richmond to the Fredericksburg area and, as senior officer, assume command of operations there.[49]

Under the circumstances, Lee pointed out to Jackson in an April 30 dispatch, a union of forces under Ewell, Johnson, and Jackson was the only way of strengthening Confederate forces in the Valley.[50]

The next day Lee gave guarded approval to a course of action proposed by Jackson. He wanted to join with Johnson to attack Union troops near McDowell, west of Staunton. If successful, Jackson and Johnson then could swing east and join Ewell for an attack on Banks.[51]

These were the first steps in what became Jackson's Valley Campaign. Ewell had crossed the Blue Ridge on April 30 and moved to hold Banks in check near Harrisonburg. Jackson then marched toward McDowell, about twenty-five miles beyond Staunton.

Johnson joined Jackson on May 7 and the next day they attacked troops under brigadier generals Robert H. Milroy and Robert C. Schenck at McDowell. The battle lasted four or five hours and, after dark, Union troops withdrew. Jackson followed them into the mountains for five days, then decided to turn back toward the Valley. He recrossed the Shenandoah Mountain on May 15 and two days later resumed his march toward Harrisonburg.[52]

In the meantime, Shields's division of more than 10,000 men had left Banks in the Valley on May 11 to join McDowell in Fredericksburg. Banks withdrew his remaining troops to the area of Strasburg just south of Winchester.[53]

In a letter to Jackson on May 16 Lee noted the uncertainty of Banks's intentions and that perhaps he was preparing to join McDowell or McClellan. "It is very desirable to prevent him from going either to Fredericksburg or the Peninsula," Lee advised Jackson, then added:

> Whatever movement you make against Banks do it speedily, and if successful drive him back toward the Potomac, and create the impression, as far as practicable, that you design threatening that line.[54]

The same day, in a letter to Ewell, Jackson stated that high streams might delay him, but he intended to move "down the Valley, and it may be that a kind Providence will enable us to unite and strike a successful blow."[55]

On May 17, however, Johnston advised Ewell that "if Banks is fortifying [his position] near Strasburg the attack would be too hazardous. In such an event we must leave him in his works. General Jackson can observe him and you can come eastward. We want troops here [on the Peninsula]. My general idea is to gather here all the troops who do not keep greatly superior forces away from McClellan." Johnston then directed Ewell to "after reading this send it to General Jackson, for whom it is intended as well as for yourself."[56]

Jackson's reaction was clear in a message to Johnston on May 17: "I have been moving down the Valley for the purpose of attacking, but the withdrawal of General Ewell's command will prevent my purpose being executed. If I do not hear from you soon I will continue my march until I get within striking distance of him [Banks]."[57] Jackson also instructed Ewell to "suspend the execution of the order for returning to the east until I receive an answer to my telegram."[58]

On May 18 Ewell and Jackson met.[59] Details of the advance on Banks apparently were worked out and Ewell got written instructions to advance between New Market and Mount Jackson by May 21. On the 19th Ewell was instructed to push the advance "beyond Mount Jackson."[60]

———◦◦◦———

At the time Jackson had 16,000 to 19,000 troops, including those of Ewell and Johnson.[61] During the next two days they edged closer to the enemy positions. On May 22 the entire command began advancing from Luray toward Front Royal. Ewell, camped that night about ten miles south of Front Royal, attacked a Union force there the next afternoon. After a few hours the enemy retreated across both forks of the Shenandoah River and headed for Winchester.[62] Ewell noted in his report that although his division alone carried out the attack, the results "were the fruits of Major General Jackson's personal superintendence and planning."[63]

On learning of the repulse, Banks abandoned his Strasburg position. At 8 P.M. on May 24 he informed Lincoln that he had withdrawn to Winchester as "the safest course." Lincoln responded that the decision was "wise and prudent."[64]

Early the next morning Jackson attacked Banks and drove Union forces from Winchester. The troops retreated in "considerable confusion," according to Banks, but quickly reformed, marched to Martinsburg, and crossed the Potomac River to Williamsport, Maryland.[65]

Jackson was pleased and, in a note to his wife on May 26, remarked: "I do not remember having ever seen such rejoicing as was manifested by the people of Winchester as our army yesterday passed through the town in pursuit of the enemy. Our entrance into Winchester was one of the most stirring scenes of my life."[66]

The Valley Campaign not only had achieved great success but also had established Jackson's method of waging war. John Esten Cooke noted:

His rule was, never to allow an enemy to rest; to attack whenever it was possible, and to press on until all opposition was broken down. A sluggish or unwary adversary was doomed already. When he least expected it, Jackson was before him, attacking with all the advantages of a surprise. It was said that he marched his men nearly to death, and it was true. But these excessive drains upon their physical strength were compensated by victories, by spoils, and by an immense accession to the moral strength of his command.

Nor did he fail to preserve, thus, thousands of lives, which would have been lost by more deliberate and conventional warfare. He always preferred to arrive, by forced marches, in face of an unprepared enemy, and drive them before him, with comparatively small loss, to a more leisurely advance which would find them ready to meet him. He aimed to succeed rather by sweat than blood.[67]

Federal authorities were greatly alarmed by events in the Valley. At Front Royal, Jackson's troops were on a direct road to Washington, and the reported size of his army—exaggerated by fear—added to the alarm in the capital. Something had to be done.

McDowell's orders were changed on May 24, two days before he planned to start his drive toward Richmond. Lincoln ordered him to send 20,000 men, including Shields's division, to the Valley. Other of his troops were to be sent north to defend Washington. "Your object will be to capture the forces of Jackson and Ewell," Lincoln told McDowell. At the same time, John C. Frémont, commander of the Mountain Department, was ordered to move eastward to relieve Banks "and capture or destroy Jackson's and Ewell's forces."[68]

McDowell acted promptly but told Secretary of War Edwin Stanton, "This is a crushing blow to us." He also expressed his feelings to Lincoln: "I am entirely beyond helping distance of General Banks. It will take a week or ten days for the force to get to the Valley by the route which will give it food and forage, and by that time the enemy will have retired. I shall gain nothing for you there, and shall lose much for you here."[69]

The deep concern for the safety of Washington was evident in two telegrams Lincoln sent to McClellan on May 25. In the first, he informed McClellan of Banks's defeat at Winchester. In the second, he briefly described the situation in the Valley, then told McClellan: "I think the time is near when you must either attack Richmond or give up the job and come to the defense of Washington. Let me hear from you instantly."

McClellan replied: "The time is very near when I shall attack Richmond. I have two corps across the Chickahominy, within six miles of Richmond; the others on this side within the same distance." The next evening McClellan advised Lincoln, "We are quietly closing in upon the enemy preparatory to the last struggle."[70] McClellan was almost within sight of his goal. His camp that night was at New Bridge, four to five miles from the Confederate capital.[71]

———————

Confederate authorities felt a measure of concern for the safety of Richmond. With enemy forces so close, Secretary of War Randolph on May 28 ordered that all War Department records not needed for daily use be loaded on railroad cars, so that they could quickly be removed from the city if necessary.[72]

A storm lashed the area on May 30 and high water on the Chickahominy River separated McClellan's army. Shortly after noon on May 31 Johnston attacked the two corps south of the Chickahominy, around Seven Pines and Fair Oaks just east of Richmond. Johnston was wounded by a shell fragment and carried from the field.[73] The battle was renewed the next morning, but by 11 o'clock the fighting ended with no decisive result.[74]

The next afternoon Lee arrived from Richmond to relieve General Smith, who had assumed temporary command. Earlier that day, Davis had notified Lee that Johnston's wound "renders it necessary to interfere temporarily with the duties to which you were assigned in connection with the general services, but only so far as to make you available for command in the field of a particular army."[75] On June 2 Lee was placed in command of the Confederate armies in eastern Virginia and North Carolina.[76]

Despite Davis's words there was nothing temporary about Lee's change of assignment. On June 1 at Fair Oaks he took command of the army he would lead through the rest of the war.

Before he was wounded, Johnston rendered an important service to Jackson. In a letter on May 27 he told Jackson:

> I congratulate you upon new victories and new titles to the thanks of the country and this army.
>
> If you can threaten Baltimore and Washington, do so. It may produce an important diversion. McClellan is near and McDowell reported advancing from Fredericksburg.
>
> Your movements depend, of course, upon the enemy's strength remaining in your neighborhood. Upon that depends the practicability of your advancing to the Potomac and even crossing it. I know of no hostile force to prevent either.[77]

Those words focused attention sharply on Jackson's invasion plan, which had become the "dream of his life."[78] All that he had accomplished in the Valley so far was important to him primarily for its bearing on his favorite policy—to carry the war into the North. On May 30, with his troops along the Potomac west of Harpers Ferry, Jackson looked across the river to Maryland and began to dream in earnest . . . "if I had enough troops."

CHAPTER 9

Jackson's Plan Accepted— Invasion Postponed

DREAMING OF INVASION WAS NOT ENOUGH FOR JACKSON; HE HAD TO do something about it. He had tried after Bull Run in July 1861. He had tried a few months later, before going to the Shenandoah Valley. And he had tried shortly after arriving in the Valley. Now he was about to take an extraordinary step to bring his plan to the attention of authorities in Richmond.

On May 19 he sent a note to his special friend in Congress, Alexander R. Boteler. "According to my promise," he wrote, "I notify you that I am going down the Valley. But I cannot say that I would advise you to come on, as my movements may not be such as would enable you to visit your home. Should you feel at liberty to join me, I hope that you will do so at your earliest convenience."[1]

Boteler was at liberty. Congress had adjourned on April 21 and Boteler was free of most of the political responsibilities that made him, in Jackson's view, "so invaluable in Richmond." He decided to accept the invitation.

On May 30 Jackson appointed Boteler a volunteer aide-de-camp on his staff with the rank of colonel.[2] As a respected and influential congressman, Boteler was close to top Confederate political leaders. Now, in a colonel's uniform, he also was able to meet army officers on an equal status.

His duties began in an unusual and light-hearted manner in the midst of cannonading. "Early in the afternoon of Friday, May 30th," Boteler explained, "the general and his staff were on a hill near Halltown [about three miles south of Harpers Ferry] where one of our batteries was engaged in an artillery duel with some heavy guns of the enemy. After noting for some time the effects of the firing, he dismounted from the old sorrel and seating himself on the ground at the foot of a large tree, immediately in the rear of the battery, he presently assumed a more recumbent attitude and went to sleep. I could not resist the temptation to make a sketch of him.

"I was busily engaged with my pencil when, on looking up, I met his eyes fixed full upon me. Extending his hand for the drawing, he said with a smile: 'Let me see what you have been doing there,' and on my handing him the sketch he remarked: 'My hardest tasks at West Point were the drawing lessons, and I never could do anything in that line to satisfy myself, or, indeed,' he added, laughingly, 'anybody else.'

"'But, colonel,' he continued after a pause, "I have some harder work than this for you to do, and if you'll sit down here, now, I'll tell you what it is.' On placing myself by his side, he said: 'I want you to go to Richmond for me. I must have reinforcements. You can explain to them down there what the situation is here. Get as many men as can be spared, and I'd like you, if you please, to go as soon as you can.'

"After expressing to him my readiness to go at once and to do what I could to have his force increased, I said: 'But you must first tell me, General, what is the situation here.' Whereupon he informed me of McDowell's movement, how he was transferring a large portion of his army from Fredericksburg to the Valley, by way of Manassas Gap, to cut him off; how Fremont, with 15,000 men, was marching from the direction of Romney to effect a junction with McDowell; how Banks had some 4,000 to 5,000 at Williamsport ready to recross the [Potomac] river, and how [Brigadier General Rufus] Saxton had 7,000 more at Harpers Ferry who were being reinforced by [way of] the Baltimore and Ohio Railroad and were prepared to cooperate with the rest of the Federal forces that were closing in around him.

"'McDowell and Fremont,' he said, 'are probably aiming to effect a junction at Strasburg, so as to head us off from the upper valley, and are both nearer to it now than we are; consequently, no time is to be lost. You can say to them in Richmond that I'll send on the prisoners, secure most, if not all the captured property, and with God's blessing will be able to baffle the enemy's plans here with my present force, but that it will have to be increased as soon thereafter as possible.'" Then, according to Boteler, Jackson added:

You may tell them, too, that if my command can be gotten up to 40,000 men a movement may be made beyond the Potomac, which will soon raise the siege of Richmond and transfer this campaign from the banks of the James [River] to those of the Susquehanna.[3]

Jackson was thinking far beyond a mere demonstration as suggested by Johnston and Lee. He was asking for help to take troops into Pennsylvania as a means to end the war and bring independence to the South. It was Jackson's first direct solicitation of official support for his proposed invasion.

Boteler left immediately but was rejoined by Jackson in Charles Town. They rode a train to Winchester, where Boteler was asked to delay his departure while Jackson prepared papers to be taken to Richmond. Then, "bidding him good-bye, I left his room and was soon on the road to Staunton, realizing the discomfort of a midnight ride in the rain.

"When I arrived at Staunton, learning that a portion of the Central Railroad between Gordonsville and Richmond had, a day or two before, been torn up by the enemy, I would, therefore, be obliged to turn off at Charlottesville for Lynchburg, so as to take the Southside Railroad, which would keep me a day or two longer on the route, I telegraphed the Confederate Secretary of War as follows:

'Jackson in a critical position. Send him all the help you can spare. Am on my way to explain situation but the Central Railroad being cut, cannot reach you until day after tomorrow.'"[4]

Jackson's emissary was indeed a man who could put such a request so bluntly and forthrightly to the secretary. "On getting to Richmond by the roundabout way I had to go," Boteler continued, "it was a great gratification to find that the authorities there immediately upon the receipt of my dispatch, had telegraphed to [South] Carolina for additional troops."[5]

Boteler's account provides the key to better understanding the decision to invade the North in 1862. It describes when the decision was made and who was involved in making it. Supporting evidence contains unmistakable proof of Confederate intentions to strike into the North as Jackson proposed. The daily correspondence reveals the action taken by the government to implement Jackson's plan. Such sources also make clear the problems in coordinating the movements and actions of two armies—those of Jackson and Lee—before the invasion could be undertaken.

The major concern, of course, was the defense of Richmond. Following Fair Oaks, or Seven Pines, Union troops occupied a line ten miles or more long east of Richmond. It was divided, however, in the center by the Chickahominy River, a stream that rises northwest of Richmond and flows in a southeasterly arc. It empties into the James River near Williamsburg.

McClellan's left wing was south of the Chickahominy where Confederates had pressed hard on May 31 and June 1. There were no natural barriers between it and Richmond. The right wing was north of the Chickahominy. Troops would have to cross the river if they were to reinforce the left wing or if they were to independently renew the attack on Richmond.

On June 2, the day after taking command of the Army of Northern Virginia, Lee met with his generals to discuss the situation. In a postwar conversation with Colonel Allan, Lee said that "he found it would be necessary to strike a blow, [but] most of the generals were opposed to this; [Brigadier General Chase] Whiting, for instance, was for holding the lines and retiring gradually before the enemy. He [Lee] thought that would never do."

In his determination to strike a blow, Lee gained Davis's crucial support. He arrived during the June 2 meeting and, as he explained later, found "the tone of the conversation quite despondent." When he expressed disappointment at such opinions, "General Lee remarked that he had, before I came in, said very much the same thing."[6]

Davis then rode to the front, where Lee shortly joined him. When Lee asked his opinion of what should be done, Davis replied that he "knew nothing better than the plan he [Lee] had previously explained to me, which was to have been executed by General Johnston, but was not carried out."

Davis also suggested that Jackson be withdrawn from the Valley as soon as possible and united with Lee's army. But, Davis observed, "so far as we were then informed, General Jackson was hotly engaged with a force superior to his own, and, before he could be withdrawn, it was necessary that the enemy should be driven out of the Valley."[7]

At any rate, Lee quickly set in motion the plan he had discussed with Davis. On June 3, the day after their conversation, Lee directed the army's chief engineer, Major W. H. Stevens, to prepare a line of earthworks, rifle pits, and artillery emplacements opposite Union forces on the south side of the Chickahominy. He ordered each division commander to assign 300 men to the project and work began immediately.[8]

This action was unpopular and provoked criticism from some officers and politicians in Richmond. Like the criticism aimed at Lee in the fall of 1861 during his unsuccessful campaign in western Virginia, complaints this time referred to the work as "Lee's diggings" and dubbed him "the king of spades" or "Ole Spade Lee."[9] Critics did not realize that the earthworks were intended to hold McClellan's left wing in check while Lee hit the Union right north of the Chickahominy.

Severe weather, however, interfered with both armies. Under normal conditions, the Chickahominy was a sluggish stream, with swamps and tangled brush and trees along its banks. But heavy rain had flooded the river and land along it was covered with three to four feet of water. Bridges were washed away, roads were masses of mud, and the entire area was impassable, which made "any general movement of troops out of the question."[10]

The storms delayed work on Lee's defenses and it was not until June 21 that satisfactory progress was reported.[11] The weather also had frustrated McClellan's hope of renewing the attack. On the 14th he reported that the ground might be dry enough for troop movements in perhaps two more days.[12] By that time, however, he had something else to worry about. Confederate plans to seize the initiative were developing rapidly.

<hr />

Davis also lost no time in contributing his efforts to the development of those plans.[13] The same day he conferred with Lee, June 2, Davis telegraphed Major General John C. Pemberton, the commander in Charleston, South Carolina, and politely asked whether he could supply some reinforcements.[14] The action seemed to have little, if any, connection with Boteler's telegram, sent to the secretary of war from Staunton on June 1 or 2 requesting troops for Jackson. There was no order or formal request, only a mild inquiry about whether Pemberton could provide any help.

Pemberton expressed reluctance to give up any troops and reported that Union vessels were massing offshore. The next day, June 3, Pemberton went a step further. He wired the secretary of war asking if he could get troops from North Carolina for the defense of Charleston.[15]

Pemberton's fears were well founded. In mid-June Union forces attacked James Island on the south side of Charleston Harbor.[16]

The need for additional troops in Virginia took on added significance after Boteler arrived in Richmond on June 4 and delivered Jackson's message to Davis. In a letter to Jackson dated June 4 Davis first congratulated him for "the brilliant campaign you have conducted against the enemy in the valley of Virginia," then stated:

> Were it practicable to send you reinforcements it should be done, and your past success shows how surely you would, with an adequate force, destroy the wicked designs of the invader of our homes and the assailer of our political rights.
>
> From the Hon. Mr. Boteler I have learned something of your probable movements. At this distance it is not possible to obtain such exact information as would justify a conclusion, but I hope you will not find at Front Royal a force which you cannot overcome.
>
> The only aid which seemed to be in reach was such as could be collected at Staunton. The commanding officer of that place has been directed to gather all [the troops] he could and move down the valley to communicate with you. Such a movement may have an effect on the enemy beyond its real value.
>
> But it is on your skill and daring that reliance is to be placed. The army under your command encourages us to hope for all which men can achieve.[17]

Davis was not given to hasty decisions. He turned to Lee and sought his advice regarding Jackson's proposal. The same day Davis wrote to Jackson, June 4, Lee telegraphed Major A. W. Harman in Staunton to "collect all the troops in that vicinity . . . and march down the valley and communicate with Jackson."[18] The words were almost identical to Davis's in his letter to Jackson.

Also on June 4 Davis telegraphed Pemberton. This time, he was more pointed and emphatic. "The call made on you for troops was the result of pressing necessity," Davis stated. "It was hoped the season would secure you against operations inland, and that you could spare troops without weakening your strength for the defense of Charleston. You can estimate the consequences to the common cause which depends upon success here. Send three regiments, or, if you think it safe to do so, send the larger number named by you."[19]

Pemberton promptly obeyed. At 7 P.M. on June 4 he replied: "Shall order three regiments from Savannah. Am drawing reinforcements from there for Charleston also. The enemy is reinforcing also, both in gunboats and troops. I may have to abandon one city or the other. Shall meet all your requirements promptly." This was followed by another telegram on June 4: "I send four strong regiments under Brigadier General [Alexander] Lawton," Pemberton informed Davis.[20]

Just as Lee had delayed submitting his resignation from the U.S. Army "to reflect fully" on the matter, he withheld overnight his judgment of Jackson's plan. On June 5, the day after he had ordered Harman to Jackson's support, Lee sent a confidential message to Davis. He stated:

> After much reflection I think if it was possible to reinforce Jackson strongly, it would change the character of the War. This can only be done by the troops in Georgia, S.C. & N.C. Jackson could in that event cross Maryland into Penn. It would call all the enemy from our Southern Coast & liberate those states. If those states will give up their troops I think it can be done.[21]

Later that day, Lee expressed his views to the secretary of war, George Randolph:

> I wrote to his Excellency the President this morning about reinforcements for Jackson. The troops from Georgia you propose sending him I believe form a part of General Lawton's brigade. I wish they were mine; but with the North Carolina Battalion, if they can join him, will fill up his ranks. He ought to have more, or these will not materially aid him.[22]

At last, Jackson's plan had been heard and accepted, and moves were made to provide some of the troops he had requested. Lee gave still more evidence of this when he wired Jackson on June 6: "To what point and by what route had troops best be sent to you?"[23] The South had taken the first decisive step to set Jackson's plan in motion.

The decision to reinforce Jackson and provide troops for an invasion of Pennsylvania in the late spring of 1862 marked a significant change in Confederate strategy. For Davis—greatly disappointed when Johnston pulled back, forestalling his "first policy to carry the war beyond our own border"—it sparked new hope and confidence. In Jackson, Davis had a man who not only talked of invasion but was eager to undertake it.

But for Lee, who in early 1861 had vowed to "draw my sword" only in defense of Virginia, it was a distinct change in attitude. Now, as the commander defending Richmond, he realized that defense of the Confederacy no longer could be trusted to mere resistance, in the hope that the Federals would tire of the fighting. It would have to be more aggressive, more determined, if it was to succeed.

Only a few days passed, however, before Lee began to have second thoughts about where and when to best strike the enemy. Some of his doubts may have been prompted by a letter written by Jackson to Johnston on June 6. Jackson knew that Johnston had been wounded but apparently was unaware that Lee had become commander of the army.

After his successful campaign in the northern Shenandoah Valley, Jackson withdrew southward and was in Port Republic when he wrote the letter. Pursuing him were two enemy forces, commanded by Frémont and Shields. In his letter Jackson reported the positions and probable movements of his own and enemy troops, then stated: "At present I do not see that I can do much more than rest my command and devote its time to drilling. If Shields crossed the Blue Ridge shall my entire command, or any part of it, move correspondingly?"[24] The letter did not reach Lee until June 8.

On June 7 Lee advised Randolph to "send [to Jackson] the Georgia regiments you mention. They will be of some help."[25] The next day he forwarded Jackson's letter to Randolph with this endorsement:

"If General Jackson is safe in his position, and cannot undertake offensive operations, which seems to be the case, reinforcements will be lost upon him. I have written him to report what he can do, and to be prepared to unite with the army near Richmond, if called on, but not to omit to strike the enemy if it can be done successfully."[26]

The letter to Jackson to which Lee referred was written on June 8.

I congratulate you upon defeating & then avoiding your enemy. Your march to Winchester has been of great advantage & has been conducted with your accustomed skill & boldness. I hope you will be able to rest and refresh your troops for a few days before compelled to enter upon active service. I desire you to report the probable intentions of the enemy & what steps you can take to thwart them.

Should there be nothing requiring your attention in the Valley so as to prevent your leaving it a few days, & you can make arrangement to deceive the enemy & impress him with the idea of your presence, please let me know, that you may unite at the decisive moment with the army near Richmond. Make your arrangements accordingly, but should an opportunity occur for striking the enemy a successful blow do not let it escape you.[27]

Even as Lee was writing to Randolph, Frémont struck a portion of Jackson's force near Cross Keys, between Harrisonburg and Port Republic. The attack was repulsed.[28]

The next day, on learning of Jackson's success, Lee changed his mind about reinforcements. In a telegram to Randolph on June 9 Lee stated: "I received this morning a telegram from Staunton announcing a glorious victory achieved by the gallant Jackson and his troops. If confirmed it will enable him to take the offensive again. Reinforcements will therefore be important to him. Those you ordered should go in that event."[29]

As Lee was reporting the victory at Cross Keys, Jackson was scoring another success—the defeat of Shields in the battle of Port Republic on June 9. It was the conclusion of Jackson's brilliant Valley Campaign, and once again his thoughts turned to invasion.

In the meantime, Lee had reached an important decision. While he favored Jackson's invasion plan, he realized the grave threat posed by McClellan's large army. If Lee was to attack, he needed a man of Jackson's caliber to help force the issue, rather than generals who talked of gradual withdrawal in the face of the enemy. On June 10, he proposed to Davis that Jackson's invasion move be postponed. Lee wanted Jackson to join forces with him for an assault on McClellan.

"I propose for your consideration," Lee explained, "sending two good brigades from this army to reinforce General Jackson. With his whole force Jackson can then be directed to move rapidly to Ashland [north of Richmond], where I will reinforce him with fresh troops, with directions to sweep down north of the Chickahominy, cut up McClellan's communications and rear, while I attack in front.

"I can hold McClellan in his present position for a week or ten days during this movement, and be getting our troops from the South. I think this is our surest move."

Lee, who knew McClellan well, assured Davis that the Union commander would not leave the safety of his trenches unless forced to do so. He urged Davis to "please consider this immediately and decide. It [the troop movements] must be commenced tonight."

Lee closed the letter with an unusual statement. "I am reconnoitering on our right," Lee informed the president, "and have sent cavalry in McClellan's rear to cut up foraging parties and wagon trains."[30] This decision undoubtedly was made earlier that day when Lee met with his cavalry commander, Brigadier General J. E. B. Stuart.

———⸎———

On June 4 Stuart had written to Lee expressing his opinion that McClellan would not advance until his works south of the Chickahominy were formidable enough to provide a reasonable assurance of victory. It would be a mistake, Stuart implied, to wait for McClellan to make such a move.

At that time, Stuart pointed out, flooding along the Chickahominy "made it impracticable" for an army to cross. Instead, he suggested that artillery with "moderate but determined support" should remain opposite Union forces north of the Chickahominy while Confederate troops "move down with a crushing force upon his front and right flank."[31]

Though the points targeted by Stuart were the reverse of those proposed in Lee's basic plan, the commander was impressed by Stuart's aggressiveness. He met with Stuart, probably on June 7, to discuss the contemplated plan of action and specifically asked Stuart to probe the Union right flank.

Over breakfast the next morning Stuart instructed one of his scouts, John S. Mosby, to seek the information Lee wanted. Mosby said Stuart asked him to take a small force and find out if McClellan was fortifying positions on Totopotomoy Creek. The creek, Mosby explained, was on McClellan's extreme right and emptied into the Pamunkey, a river in the rear of McClellan's line that was being used to supply his army. Mosby and three troopers left immediately.[32]

That evening Stuart and an aide, Major Heros von Borcke, went to meet a Confederate spy who lived inside the Federal lines. Von Borcke wrote that about five miles beyond the last Confederate outpost, they arrived at a small house where Stuart knocked on the door "in a peculiar manner." The two were admitted, but the man Stuart wanted to see was not there. Several hours later, Stuart and von Borcke rode about two miles farther to the spy's home, where they found the man ill in bed. Stuart talked to him about Union troop activities, then returned to camp with von Borcke. Von Borcke said Stuart was "extremely well satisfied with the information he had obtained."[33]

Mosby returned on June 10 with surprising news. He had not only explored the Union right wing but had gotten in the enemy's rear. He found no fortifications, no evidence of any being constructed, and only cavalry pickets on guard. Mosby concluded the position was dangerously exposed and vulnerable to attack. Stuart immediately took Mosby's report to Lee.[34] The two discussed a possible cavalry expedition behind Union lines to seek more detailed information. Stuart suggested riding around the Union army, which Lee did not encourage.[35]

It was unusual for Lee to express himself so forcefully and bluntly as he did in his letter to Davis on June 10. Neither was it surprising for Davis to be reluctant to change the plan for invading Pennsylvania that he had accepted following Lee's endorsement on June 5. "Mr. Davis hesitated and held back," Lee explained to Colonel Allan after the war, "then came out to see him [Lee] and talked the whole matter over, and after considering [the proposal] another day, finally granted his permission."[36]

In a letter to his wife on June 11 Davis provided an inkling of what had transpired in his talks with General Lee. "I will endeavor by movements which are not without great hazard to countervail the enemy's policy," he wrote. "If we succeed in rendering his works useless to him and compel him to meet us on the field, I have much confidence in our ability to give him the pains of invasion and to feed our Army on his territory. We are reinforcing General Jackson and hope to crown his successes with a complete victory over all the enemy in the Valley."

Two days later he told Mrs. Davis that Jackson's victories at Cross Keys and Port Republic "confirm the report of the flight of the enemy [in the Valley] and the danger to our troops has been mainly passed."[37]

On June 11 Lee set in motion the revised plan for attacking McClellan. He directed Stuart to make "a secret movement to the rear of the enemy." Its primary purpose was to learn McClellan's activities and to destroy his wagon trains.

"The utmost vigilance on your part will be necessary to prevent surprise to yourself," Lee cautioned Stuart. "Information received last evening, the points of which I sent you, lead me to infer that there is a stronger force on the enemy's right than was previously reported. Should you find upon investigation that the enemy is moving to his right, or is so strongly posted as to render your expedition inopportune you will, after gaining all the information you can, resume your former position."[38]

Early the next morning Stuart, with 1,200 cavalrymen and two sections of artillery, set out. First he moved northward to create the impression that he was headed for the Valley to join Jackson, then turned eastward to sweep around McClellan's right. He pushed on toward Old Church in Hanover County. It was there that Stuart realized it would be too dangerous to turn back. "These circumstances led me to look with more favor to my favorite scheme, disclosed to you before starting, of passing around [the enemy army]," Stuart noted in his report.

In two days, June 13–14, Stuart carefully scouted enemy positions, gathered valuable information for Lee's proposed attack, fought frequent skirmishes, and lost only one man in the entire operation. He recrossed the Chickahominy on June 15, returned to camp, then reported to Lee. On June 23 Lee described Stuart's action as "a brilliant exploit" and later noted: "A cavalry expedition, under General Stuart, was made around the rear of the Federal Army to ascertain positions and movements. This was executed with great address and daring by that accomplished officer."[39]

In time, Stuart's ride around McClellan's army was acclaimed as one of the incredible achievements of the war.

There were a few who did not agree. They contended that Stuart's ride, although successful in gaining the information Lee wanted, also had alerted McClellan to the danger of attack. Stuart himself realized that skirmishes behind enemy lines may have nullified the secrecy Lee had hoped to maintain. But he pointed out that, besides the destruction of enemy supplies and the disruption of railroad communications, "the success attending this expedition will no doubt cause 10,000 to 15,000 men to be detached from the enemy's main body to guard his communications."[40]

———◆———

Stuart's expedition was the forerunner of other events related to the invasion of Pennsylvania in June 1863. These included successful expeditions around Union forces in August and October 1862, when important information was acquired. Then, in early 1863, Stuart attended meetings of Lee and Jackson as plans were being made to renew the invasion campaign. There was yet another expedition in the rear of the Union army in late June.

⟶≫●≪⟶

Meanwhile Lee had moved to reinforce Jackson. In a telegram to Randolph on June 11 he stated: "It is very desirable and important that the acquisition of troops to the command of Maj. Gen. T. J. Jackson should be kept secret. With this view I have the honor to request that you will use your influence with the Richmond newspapers to prevent any mention of the same in the public prints."[41]

Lee later explained that the troops were to be sent roundabout, "knowing that the news would reach the enemy and induce the belief that Jackson was to be pushed north."[42]

In the second telegram that day, Lee told Jackson: "Gen. Lawton's Brigade, four regiments, is enroute to you, in addition to the regiments that preceded it. Gen. Whiting with eight regiments will start today. Have you sufficient artillery and wagons?"[43]

The telegram was supplemented by a letter also sent June 11. "Your recent successes have been the cause of the liveliest joy in this army as well as in the country," Lee wrote. "The admiration excited by your skill and boldness has been constantly mingled with solicitude for your situation. The practicability of reinforcing you has been the subject of earnest consideration. It has been determined to do so at the expense of weakening this army. Brigadier General Lawton, with six regiments from Georgia, is on the way to you, and Brigadier General Whiting, with eight veteran regiments leaves here today."

The reinforcements, however, were not intended for any northward thrust. Jackson was instructed to post guards in the mountain passes and, "with your main body, move rapidly to Ashland by rail or otherwise, as you may find advantageous, and sweep down between the Chickahominy and Pamunkey, cutting up the enemy's communications, etc., while this army attacks General McClellan in front. He will thus, I think, be forced to come out of his intrenchments where he is strongly posted on the Chickahominy, and apparently preparing to move by gradual approaches on Richmond. Keep me advised of your movements," Lee added, "and if practicable, precede your troops, that we may confer and arrange for simultaneous attack."[44]

Out in the Valley, Jackson was not thinking seriously of an attack on McClellan. He still wanted to invade the North and was not about to put that idea aside without another attempt to convince Confederate authorities of its timeliness. Victories at Cross Keys and Port Republic spurred his desire to strike at the North and, once again, Colonel Boteler was called on to carry Jackson's request to Richmond.

Boteler returned from Richmond after the Battle of Port Republic and obviously before Lee's letter of June 11 reached Jackson. "I found him [Jackson] in fine spirits when, on my return from Richmond, I rejoined his bivouac in Brown's Gap on the Blue Ridge," Boteler wrote. "On the 12th of June, we descended before dawn to the plains of Mount Meridian on the Middle Fork of the Shenandoah, having our headquarters at Wier's [Weyers] Cave."

Jackson was pleased that reinforcements were moving to him. Boteler continued:

> On Friday, June 13th, the day after we came down from Brown's Gap, [Jackson] in expressing to me his pleasure at the success of my mission for more troops, took the occasion to remark that he would be glad if I would return to Richmond and make a formal application to the government to increase his command to 40,000 men, in order that he might carry into effect the movements he had mentioned to me at Halltown. "By that means," Jackson said, "Richmond can be relieved and the campaign transferred to Pennsylvania."
>
> He told me that in making the proposed counter-movement northward he would advance toward the Potomac along the eastern side of the Blue Ridge, making his march secret as much as possible. By rapidly crossing the mountain at the most available gap, he could, by getting in the rear of Banks (who had returned to Winchester), readily dispose of him, and thereby open up the road to Western Maryland and Pennsylvania by way of Williamsport, etc. Ordinarily, Jackson was exceedingly reticent in regard to his plans and purposes, but on this occasion he spoke without reserve and was more communicative than I ever knew him to be.[45]

This conversation also was reported by John Esten Cooke in his biography of Jackson. At the time, Cooke recounted, Jackson was dreaming of an advance into Pennsylvania. So strong was his feeling on the subject, that he, the most reticent and cautious of commanders, could not withhold some intimation of his views. To a confidential friend, on whose prudence he knew he could rely, he said:

"If they will only give me 60,000 men now, I will go right on to Pennsylvania. I will not go down the Valley; I do not wish the people there to be harassed. I will go with 40,000 if the President will give them to me, and my route will be along east of the Blue Ridge. I ought not to have told even you that; but in two weeks I could be at Harrisburg."[46]

Boteler left Jackson's camp on the 13th, rode to Staunton, and, the next morning, took the train to Richmond. In addition to Jackson's verbal message, Boteler also carried a letter from Jackson to Lee that dealt with the suggestions Lee had offered to Jackson five days earlier.

Jackson explained that Lee's letter of June 8 was not received "until this morning," June 13. He then noted that enemy forces he had defeated at Cross Keys and Port Republic had withdrawn toward Winchester and that his cavalry had followed them almost forty miles. "So," Jackson added, "circumstances greatly favor my moving to Richmond in accordance with your plan. I will remain if practicable in this neighborhood [Mount Meridian] until I hear from you, and rest the troops who are greatly fatigued.

> You can halt the reinforcements coming here if you so desire, without interfering with my plans provided the movement to Richmond takes place. So far as I am concerned my opinion is that we should not attempt another march down the Valley to Winchester until we are in a condition under the blessing of Providence to hold the country.[47]

Boteler arrived in Richmond on June 14. It was after office hours, he explained, and "I lost no time in seeing the Secretary of War at his residence. He referred me to President Davis, who, in turn, told me to submit the matter to General Lee. I procured a horse and rode out to the commanding general's headquarters on the lines below Richmond."

Lee was still up and, "after listening to what I had to say, replied by asking me a question I was not prepared to answer. 'Colonel,' said he, 'don't you think General Jackson had better come down here first and help me to drive these troublesome people away from before Richmond?'"

"I think it would be very presumptuous in me, general," Boteler replied, "to answer that question, as it would be hazarding an opinion upon an important military movement which I don't feel competent to give." Lee pressed for an answer and Boteler replied that "if I answer your question at all, it must be in the negative."

"Why so?" Lee asked.

"Because," Boteler replied, "if you bring our Valley boys down here at this season among the pestilential swamps of the Chickahominy the change from their pure mountain air to this miasmatic atmosphere will kill them off faster than the Federals have been doing."

"That will depend upon the time they'd have to stay here," Lee responded, then asked Boteler if he had any other reason to offer.

"Yes," Boteler replied, "and it's that Jackson has been doing so well with an independent command that it seems a pity not to let him have his own way. And then, too, bringing him here will be—to use a homely phrase—like putting all your eggs in one basket." Lee replied: "I see that you appreciate General Jackson as much as I myself do, and it is because of my appreciation of him that I wish to have him here."

Lee then asked Boteler about the condition of Jackson's army and about the recent battles in the Valley. "So," Boteler noted, "seeing there was no chance of getting his assent to Jackson's proposition and that there were other plans in contemplation, I forbore to press the matter further."

As Boteler prepared to depart, Lee asked how long he expected to be in Richmond. On being told two or three days, Lee said, "Come and see me again before you go back; I may have a communication to send by you to General Jackson."[48]

⟶⟫•⟪⟵

Lee promptly forwarded Jackson's letter to Davis with this endorsement: "I think the sooner Jackson can move this way, the better. The first object now is to defeat McClellan. The enemy in the Valley seem at a pause. We may strike them here before they are ready to move up the Valley. They will naturally be cautious and we must be secret and quick. Will you ask the Secretary to make arrangements for moving Jackson down if you agree with me, as soon as his troops are refreshed a little. They must rest in the journey. Please return to me this letter that I may reply."

Davis's reaction was brief and explicit. "Views concurred in, JD" was written on the bottom of the letter. It was returned to Lee who, on June 16, drafted a message for Boteler to take to Jackson.[49]

Boteler returned to Lee's headquarters on June 18 for a brief meeting. Referring to their conversation June 14, Lee said:

The movement proposed by General Jackson will have to be postponed for reasons which I have already communicated to him, and of which you will soon be apprised.

Lee gave Boteler a letter for Jackson, then "suggested that as I was going to leave in the morning to rejoin Jackson I had better stop at Charlottesville and wait there for orders. Of course, I asked no questions," Boteler commented, "though naturally curious to know what would probably be the character of my orders and why I was to wait for them in Charlottesville. But when I got there at noon the next day, I found the town in a fever of excitement, with a cordon of pickets posted around, preventing all egress from the place."

Boteler was told that "at least a dozen trains of empty cars had passed through [Charlottesville] some hours before to the Valley. I had, therefore, no difficulty in divining what was in the wind and that 'great events were on the gale.'"[50]

Indeed. Jackson was ready to move east to help attack McClellan! After the Battle of Port Republic, the Army of the Valley remained at Weyers Cave until June 17 when, "in obedience to instructions from the commanding general of the department, it moved toward Richmond," Jackson stated in his report.[51] That was the day before Boteler's meeting with Lee (when he was given the letter for Jackson) and two days before Boteler arrived at Charlottesville.

————>●<————

Lee's letter of June 16 focused on a communication problem similar to the one in the spring of 1861, when Jackson was in Harpers Ferry.

Referring to Jackson's letter of the 13th, Lee pointed out that "you have only acknowledged my letter of the 8th. I am therefore ignorant whether that of the 11th has reached you." Lee enclosed a copy of that letter. He also added:

I hope you will be able to recruit and refresh your troops sufficiently for the movement proposed in my letter of the 11th. From your account of the position of the enemy, I think it would be difficult for you to engage him in time to unite with this army in the battle for Richmond. Fremont and Shields are apparently retrograding. If this is so, the sooner you unite with this army the better. McClellan is being strengthened. There is much sickness in his ranks but his reinforcements by far exceed his losses.

The present therefore seems to be favorable for a junction of your army and this. If you agree with me the sooner you can make arrangements to do so the better. In moving your troops you could let it be understood that it was to pursue the enemy in your front. Dispose those to hold the Valley so as to deceive the enemy, keeping your cavalry well in their front and at the proper time suddenly descending upon the Pamunkey.

To be efficacious the movement must be secret. Let me know the force you can bring and be careful to guard from friends and foes your purpose and your intention of personally leaving the Valley. The country is full of spies and our plans are immediately carried to the enemy.

Unless McClellan can be driven out of his intrenchments he will move by positions under cover of his heavy guns within shelling distance of Richmond. I know of no surer way of thwarting him than that proposed. I should like to have the advantage of your views and be able to confer with you. Will meet you at some point on your approach to the Chickahominy.[52]

Lee made it quite clear that Jackson's invasion plan had been postponed. It was only temporary, and less than a month later steps were taken to set it in motion. In the meantime Jackson would help Lee drive McClellan from Richmond.

CHAPTER 10

First Policy Resumed

JACKSON'S ARMY REACHED FREDERICK'S HALL, A STATION ON THE Virginia Central Railroad about fifty miles northwest of Richmond, on Saturday, June 21. The men rested through Sunday, in keeping with Jackson's religious philosophy and his determination to avoid fighting or maneuvering on Sunday unless forced to do so.[1]

About 1 A.M. on Monday, Jackson set out on horseback for Richmond to meet with Lee. The conference at Lee's headquarters included three division commanders of the Army of Northern Virginia, Major Generals A. P. Hill, D. H. Hill, and James Longstreet. The five discussed the general plan, especially Jackson's move to Ashland, suggested in Lee's letter of the 11th.

Since Jackson's troops would have the greatest distance to travel for the attack on McClellan's right, timing was a serious factor. Lee later commented, "Jackson appointed a certain day to be up [in position to open the attack], then Lee was to meet him with the mass of the [Confederate] army before Richmond." Lee told Jackson that "he had not given himself time enough, and insisted that he should be allowed 24 hours more." With this understanding, Lee added, "he [Lee] prepared everything and moved a part of his troops over [the Chickahominy] at Mechanicsville to attack in conjunction with Jackson."

Lee made no mention of the date Jackson specified for his movement. According to Colonel Charles Marshall of Lee's staff, the first date mentioned by Jackson was June 23. Longstreet stated that Jackson first specified the morning of the 25th. When Longstreet suggested that a little more time should be allowed, Jackson agreed and designated the morning of the 26th. D. H. Hill had a slightly different version. He stated that Jackson designated "daylight of the 26th," but implied that no change had been made when Longstreet asked Jackson if he "ought not to give yourself more time?"[2]

On June 24, the day after the meeting, Lee issued General Orders No. 75, directing that "Jackson's command will proceed tomorrow from Ashland and encamp at some convenient point west of the [Virginia] Central Railroad. At 3 o'clock Thursday morning, 26th instant, General Jackson will advance on the road leading to Pole Green Church," about five miles northeast of Mechanicsville and on McClellan's extreme right. Then Lee's own troops would move forward to join the attack. A. P. Hill would cross the Chickahominy at Meadow Bridge, leading to Mechanicsville; D. H. Hill would support Jackson; and Longstreet would support A. P. Hill. To the south, opposite McClellan's left, the divisions of Benjamin Huger and John B. Magruder were to hold their positions while making demonstrations to discover if there was any unexpected activity on the Federal side.[3]

During the June 23 conference, Jackson's army was on the march. Boteler explained that Jackson's troops, after resting on Sunday, had left Frederick's Hall for Ashland and arrived "there on the evening of the 25th."[4] There was only one thing wrong: Jackson's troops were a day behind schedule. Lee's detailed order had stipulated that Jackson's troops were to leave Ashland on the 25th and move to positions from which they would advance at 3 A.M. June 26 for the attack on McClellan's right flank.

The bad news reached Lee on the morning of the 26th, the day set for the assault on McClellan's right flank. Lee told Davis that day, "General Jackson this morning states that in consequence of high water & mud, his command only reached Ashland last night."[5]

———⟫•⟪———

A strange sidelight to Lee's planning for the attack surfaced on June 24, when a young man claiming to be a deserter from Jackson's army was brought to McClellan's headquarters. According to McClellan, the man said he had left Jackson's camp near Gordonsville on June 21 and that "Jackson's troops were then moving to Frederick's Hall, along the Virginia Central Railroad, for the purpose of attacking my rear on the 28th."[6]

It was peculiar in more ways than one, since the deserter claimed to have left Jackson's army two days before Lee met with Jackson and the other officers and fixed the date for the attack for June 26. Was the man merely repeating rumors that had circulated in Jackson's camp or was he trying to mislead the enemy?[7]

McClellan was suspicious. In a dispatch to Secretary of War Edwin Stanton at midnight on June 24, he described the incident as "a very peculiar case of desertion." He also asked Stanton for "the most exact information you have as to the position and movements of Jackson."

Stanton's reply on the 25th was not reassuring. Reports and rumors placed Jackson's force in Gordonsville, Port Republic, Harrisonburg, and Luray. "Within the last two days, the evidence is strong that for some purpose the enemy is circulating rumors of Jackson's advance in various directions, with a view to conceal the real point of attack. I think, therefore, that while the warning of the deserter to you may also be a blind, it could not safely be disregarded."[8]

At 10:40 that night, June 25, McClellan informed Stanton that the latest information tended to confirm that Jackson would soon attack the Union right and rear. "Every possible precaution is being taken. If I had another good division I could laugh at Jackson." Ironically, the message was received in Washington at 3 A.M. on the 26th, the precise time at which Jackson was to have begun his advance on McClellan's right.[9]

On June 25 the day before Lee's planned attack, McClellan had felt out Confederate defenses on his left flank immediately in front of Richmond. Numerous heavy earthworks had been completed, he noted, and in 36 of those about 200 guns were mounted. His secret service also had estimated Confederate strength at 180,000 men.

McClellan was preparing to resume the general movement against Richmond. "On the 26th," he added, "the day upon which I had decided as the time for our final advance, the enemy attacked our right in strong force, and turned my attention to the protection of our communications and depots of supply."[10]

———⊰●⊱———

With no word from Jackson, Lee attacked at 3 P.M. It was the start of almost constant fighting—referred to as the Seven Days Battles—that continued through July 1.[11] On the evening of June 27 McClellan began withdrawing to the James River. On the night of July 1, after the fighting on Malvern Hill, his forces completed their retreat to Harrison's Landing, where they encamped under the protection of Federal gunboats.[12]

The Army of Northern Virginia, under its new leader, had pushed the enemy back to about twenty-five miles southeast of Richmond. Lee's troops followed as far as Westover Plantation, within sight of Union camps. He was pleased with the general results but disappointed that another objective of the campaign had not been achieved. "Under ordinary circumstances," he commented, "the Federal Army should have been destroyed."

In directing his first major campaign of the war, Lee encountered a number of difficulties, especially uncoordinated timing and movements of various units, including Jackson's.[13]

Captain E. P. Alexander, Lee's chief of ordnance, felt there were too many independent commands to be efficiently handled. He pointed out that there were seven divisions in the Army of Northern Virginia as well as those of Huger, Theophilus Holmes, and Lafayette McLaws, plus three more divisions in Jackson's force.[14]

Jackson undoubtedly had a tough time adjusting to conditions around Richmond. In the Shenandoah Valley, he was independent and could plan the action, make decisions, and move and fight as he pleased. In Richmond, he had to coordinate his actions with others' and adapt to the role of a subordinate. Then, too, the almost continuous fighting during the Seven Days was quite different from the hit-and-run nature of the Valley Campaign.

As a result of these factors and Jackson's late arrival, Lee reportedly had a low estimate of Jackson's ability after their first action together.[15] This feeling evaporated as Lee and Jackson began their northward movement.

In the quiet days at Westover, after the Seven Days, Jackson became impatient just as he had after First Bull Run nearly a year earlier. He summoned Colonel Boteler to his tent one evening and said, with considerable excitement, "Do you know we are losing valuable time here?"

"How so?" Boteler asked.

Jackson replied, "Why, by repeating the blunder we made after the battle of Manassas, in allowing the enemy leisure to recover from his defeat and ourselves to suffer by inaction. Yes, we are wasting precious time and energies in this malarious region that can be much better employed elsewhere." Then, according to Boteler:

> Jackson went on to tell me it was evident McClellan's army was thoroughly beaten; that it would have to be reinforced and reorganized before it could become effective in the field; that, therefore, so far as it was concerned, the safety of Richmond was assured; that the movement northward [to Pennsylvania] which he had previously advised should be made without further delay; that he wanted me again to bring the matter to President Davis' attention, and that

in doing so to tell the President it was not from any self-seeking he was so persistent in urging the movement, as he was entirely willing to follow any leader in making it whom he [Davis] might think proper to designate.

Boteler asked, "What is the use of my going to Mr. Davis, as he'll probably refer me again to General Lee? So why don't you yourself speak to General Lee upon the subject?"

Jackson said he had already done so but that Lee had said nothing. "Don't think I complain of his silence," Jackson added. "He doubtless has good reasons for it."

Then Boteler asked if Jackson thought Lee might be slow in making up his mind. "Slow!" Jackson exclaimed with sudden energy, and continued:

By no means, colonel; on the contrary, his perception is as quick and unerring as his judgment is infallible. But with the vast responsibilities now resting on him, he is perfectly right in withholding a hasty expression of his opinion and purposes. So great is my confidence in General Lee that I am willing to follow him blindfolded. But I fear he is unable to give me a definite answer now because of influences at Richmond, where, perhaps, the matter has been mentioned by him and may be under consideration. I, therefore, want you to see the President and urge the importance of prompt action.[16]

The account of the meeting was recorded by three other people, two of whom were on Jackson's staff. John Esten Cooke noted that Jackson, while conversing with a confidential friend, exclaimed, "Why don't we advance! Now is the time for an advance into Pennsylvania; McClellan is paralyzed."

Henry Kyd Douglas, Jackson's assistant inspector general, stated that Jackson suggested to Lee and the government that 40,000 troops should be sent to the Shenandoah Valley to clear it of the enemy, then move toward Maryland and threaten Washington. Cooke and Douglas quoted Jackson as saying that if he was not acceptable as the commander, he would serve under Lee or any other officer. Both believed nothing was done about Jackson's proposal because McClellan's army was still a threat to Richmond.[17]

Major R. L. Dabney, assistant adjutant general on Jackson's staff, quoted Jackson as saying the army should leave the Richmond area, move northward, and "carry the horrors of invasion across the border. This is the only way to bring the North to its senses and end the war." Jackson, Dabney noted, presented these views to Boteler and begged him "to impress them on the Government." Jackson's advice was presented to Davis. "What weight was attached to it is unknown," Dabney commented, "but the campaign soon after took the direction which he [Jackson] had indicated."[18]

In his closing remarks, Boteler was more positive. The day after his conversation with Jackson, he went to Richmond and, as he later wrote:

> I saw Mr. Davis, said all that was necessary upon the object of my interview, and soon thereafter had the satisfaction of accompanying Jackson to a more congenial climate and in more active fields of duty.[19]

⸺⸳�⸳⸺

Boteler left little doubt about the outcome of his trip to Richmond. Authorities obviously had decided to activate Jackson's invasion plan. His conviction was fully justified. In a period of two weeks (July 5–19), Davis, two cabinet members, and the army's adjutant and inspector general all expressed the determination to invade the North. Davis was the first. In his congratulatory message to the Army of Northern Virginia on July 5 he stated:

> Well may it be said of you that you have 'done enough for glory,' but duty to a suffering country and to the cause of constitutional liberty claims from you yet further effort. Let it be your pride to relax in nothing which can promote your future efficiency, your one great object being to drive the invader from your soil and carry your standards beyond the outer boundaries of the Confederacy, to wring from an unscrupulous foe the recognition of your birthright, community independence.[20]

The next day, in a letter to his wife, Davis stated that reports had been received that all available enemy forces were to be sent to the James River to enable McClellan to "make one great effort to defeat us here. Our army is greatly reduced but I hope recruits will be promptly sent forward from most of the States."

Then, he added, "There are many causes which will interfere with the execution of the enemy's plans, and some things which they have not dreamed which we may do. If our ranks were full we could end the war in a few weeks."[21]

The next important step by a high-level official was taken on July 14 by General Samuel Cooper, the Confederate adjutant and inspector general. In a circular to all officers assigned to draft men under the Conscription Act of April 16, Cooper said: "You are required to arrest all deserters, and, under certain circumstances, all persons absent from the Army without leave. The public welfare requires you to discharge this duty and the more important duty of enrolling conscripts with the utmost activity, and without fear, favor, or affection." He then stated:

> Our capacity to improve the recent victories now favoring our arms depends mainly upon your exertions to fill the ranks of our armies. If you are zealous and active we shall make our enemy taste the bitterness of war; if you are negligent we shall continue to witness its ravages on our own soil.[22]

The next day, at Davis's request, Cooper sent an urgent message to John C. Pemberton in Charleston informing him:

> It is deemed necessary for ultimate operations in this quarter, which are daily becoming more important, that the army for the defense of Richmond should be speedily reinforced. The President therefore desires that you hasten forward such regiments and brigades of your command as you may be enabled to spare.
>
> In consideration of the present season, when sickness most prevails on the Southern coast, and when the enemy would be least likely to carry on active operations in that quarter, the President, after due reflection, has arrived at the conclusion that you might safely dispense with more than one-half of your effective force.

Cooper wanted Pemberton to realize this was no ordinary request, and added, "I desire to impress upon you the importance of this movement."[23]

Two days later, on July 17, Secretary of War George Randolph sent a confidential circular to governors that spelled out Confederate intentions. "Our armies are so much weakened by desertions, and by the absence of officers and men without leave, that we are unable to reap the fruits of our victories and to invade the territory of the enemy. Unless public opinion comes to our aid we shall fail to fill our ranks in time to avail ourselves of the weakness and disorganization of the enemy." He added:

> I must therefore beg Your Excellency's aid in bringing back to our colors all deserters and absentees. If you will authorize their arrest by State officers, and bring to our assistance the powerful influence of public opinion in your state, we may yet cross the Potomac before a fresh army is raised to oppose us.[24]

Even more significant was the message sent on July 19 by Secretary of State Judah P. Benjamin to Confederate agents John Slidell in Paris and James M. Mason in London. After recounting in glowing terms the victories in the Shenandoah Valley and before Richmond, Benjamin added:

> This Government and people are straining every nerve to continue the campaign with renewed energy before the North can recover from the shock of their bitter disappointment; and if human exertions can compass it, our banners will be unfurled beyond the Potomac in a very short time.[25]

The repeated references by high-level Confederates at this time, to carrying the war across the Potomac is convincing evidence that the decision had been made to execute Jackson's plan.

—————>●●<—————

The expression "across the Potomac" does not mean just moving from Virginia into Maryland. The Potomac flows from the west, past Hancock, Maryland—a mile or two from the Pennsylvania line—then to Harpers Ferry, where it becomes the boundary between Virginia and Maryland. Crossing the Potomac was only a step in Jackson's plan to take the war to the "banks of the Susquehanna."

Of equal significance was the strengthening of Lee's army for the northward thrust. From July 10 to 20, the strength of the Army of Northern Virginia was increased by more than a fifth to about 79,000. In addition, the return for July 20 noted, there were nearly 16,000 troops from the Department of North Carolina in Virginia.[26]

It was about this time that those reinforcements were reaching Lee. He soon would resume President Davis's first policy and carry the war north of the Potomac River.

CHAPTER 11

The Troubled North

MCCLELLAN'S FAILURE TO TAKE RICHMOND, FOLLOWED BY HIS WITH-drawal to Harrison's Landing, virtually wiped out optimism and confidence in the North. Once again, the hope of a quick end to the war was shattered, just as it had been at Bull Run nearly a year earlier.

Lee quickly assessed McClellan's position at Harrison's Landing. In letters to Jefferson Davis on July 3 and 4, he asserted that a movement by McClellan to cross the James River and renew the attack on Richmond "is hardly possible," but that there "is no way to attack him to advantage."[1]

Davis agreed not to expose Southern troops to fire from Union gunboats. He also felt it would be more appropriate to withdraw Lee's troops to better positions and take precautions against an enemy advance on the south side of the James River.[2]

Encouraged by this, Lee on July 8 began breaking contact with McClellan's army. Jackson moved to a position on the Mechanicsville turnpike north of Richmond. The divisions of Longstreet, McLaws, and D. H. Hill were moved east and south of Richmond. Lee told J. E. B. Stuart to cover the withdrawals and to "watch the movements" of McClellan.[3] The next day Lee informed Davis and added that he would "proceed at once to reorganize our forces for active operations."[4]

The decision was timely. The North was troubled—not only by bad news from the field, especially in eastern Virginia—but also by developments on the home front that hurt morale even more than had Bull Run.

125

It was time for the Confederacy to begin the invasion in the hope of achieving a major objective of Stonewall Jackson's plan—to "force the people of the North to understand what it will cost them to hold the South in the Union at the bayonet's point."

Lee expressed a similar idea in early June 1863 as he was preparing the movement that led to the Battle of Gettysburg. At that time, he referred to "demonstrations of a desire for peace" and "recent political movements" in the North. "We should neglect no honorable means of dividing and weakening our enemies that they may feel some of the difficulties experienced by ourselves," Lee wrote.[5] Jackson's wording was different, but the objective clearly was the same.

So the new Confederate strategy in 1862 did not develop in a vaccum.

Early evidence of the situation in the North came from Indiana on June 6, 1862. Governor O. P. Morton informed Secretary of War Edwin Stanton that he "considers the condition of the State of Kentucky at this time as being nearly, if not quite, as unsettled and dangerous as it has been at any former period, and that there is serious danger of the carrying out of threats openly made in various parts of that State to burn some of the river towns in Indiana." He asked Stanton to send "5,000 good guns" at once to arm militiamen along the Ohio River.[6]

Soon the news was even more ominous. In a confidential letter to Stanton on June 25 Morton stated:

> I desire to call your especial attention to certain matters existing in this State which, in my judgment, deeply concern the welfare and interest of both the State and General Governments.
>
> The fact is well established that there is a secret political organization in Indiana, estimated and claimed to be 10,000 strong, the leading objects of which are to embarrass all efforts to recruit men for the military service of the United States, to embitter public sentiment and manufacture public opinion against the levying and collection of taxes to defray the expenses of the present war, and generally to create distrust in and bad feelings toward the Government and its recognized and legally constituted authorities. Another object is to circulate and foster newspapers of extremely doubtful loyalty—papers that sympathize with the rebellion and oppose and disparage continually and persistently the efforts of the Government to put down traitors and crush out treason.
>
> The organization alluded to is confined to no particular locality, but evidently is in operation in every county in the State. Its

members are bound by oaths and their meetings are guarded by armed men.

These facts have been coming to me for some weeks past from all parts of the State, substantiated by evidence which leaves no doubt in my mind of their truth. I am forced to believe that the present is the most critical period in our history since the commencement of the present war.

I deem it of vital importance to the Government that immediate, vigorous, and effective steps be taken to break up these unlawful and dangerous combinations, and to correct the evils complained of. Our efforts to aid and assist in carrying out the wishes of the Government are greatly impeded; our plans are interfered with and thwarted, and the feelings of our patriotic and loyal citizens are estranged and insulted. Such a state of things cannot long exist, and if a change for the better is not effected no one can foresee the result.

Morton recommended that at least 10,000 small arms be sent to the Indiana militia. He also noted that efforts to supply five regiments requested by the War Department were "progressing very slowly," chiefly because of the problems described in his letter.[7]

Morton's warning was among the first official reports of trouble brewing from a secret society, the Knights of the Golden Circle, and its organized opposition to the North and its war efforts. Even worse, the Knights of the Golden Circle and other militant groups that sprang up in the North advocated secession by half a dozen or more northwestern states. Some proposed that those states should form a confederacy of their own, others that they should join the Southern Confederacy.[8]

An exposé of the Knights of the Golden Circle, written in 1861 by an anonymous member of the order, purported to outline the history of secession from 1834 to 1861. The writer pointed out that in 1834, there arose politicians in Charleston, New Orleans, and other Southern cities who favored re-establishing importation of slaves. They contended that the Constitution was tyrannical, since it had prohibited the trade after 1808, and organized groups known as Southern Rights Clubs.

In 1855 a native of Indiana went south, drafted a constitution, bylaws, and rituals for the organization and renamed it the Knights of the

Golden Circle. A year later, some members recommended establishment of a Southern confederacy. Others proposed annexation of Cuba, Mexico, and Nicaragua.

On the basis of reports he had seen in 1860, the writer estimated the total number of "sympathetic Northerners" at 95,000. New York led with 51,000 members, followed by Pennsylvania with 15,000, Indiana with at least 10,000—the figure reported by Morton to Stanton—and Ohio, Illinois, Iowa, and Michigan with about 5,000 each.[9] Activity allegedly related to the Knights of the Golden Circle became evident in late June 1863, when Confederate troops marched through Pennsylvania toward the Susquehanna River.

———————

Morton's mention of recruiting troubles also opened a new source of concern for the North. Other governors, though they made no mention of problems similar to Morton's, were disheartening in their responses to call for troops. Generally, they indicated there would be serious delays in recruiting new men.[10]

This situation and Lee's success against McClellan in late June alarmed President Lincoln. In a letter to Secretary of State William H. Seward on June 28, Lincoln expressed concern over "the present condition of the war."

Lincoln noted that the evacuation of Corinth, Mississippi, by General P. G. T. Beauregard and the flood on the Chickahominy that delayed McClellan had enabled the enemy to concentrate too great a force in Richmond. If McClellan were to be reinforced from Washington, the unprotected Federal capital could fall.

"What should be done," Lincoln wrote, "is to hold what we have in the West, open the Mississippi, and take Chattanooga and East Tennessee without more [troops]. A reasonable force should in every event be kept in Washington for its protection. Then let the country give us 100,000 new troops in the shortest possible time, which, added to McClellan, directly or indirectly, will take Richmond without endangering any other place which we now hold and will substantially end the war." Then he added:

> I expect to maintain this contest until successful, or till I die, or am conquered, or my term expires, or Congress or the country forsakes me; and I would publicly appeal to the country for this new force were it not that I fear a general panic and stampede would follow, so hard is it to have a thing understood as it really is.

He closed: "I think the new force should be all, or nearly all, infantry, principally because such force can be raised more cheaply and quickly."[11]

———————

Lincoln's message touched off some maneuvering by Seward and Stanton. First, Seward met in New York City with Governors Edwin D. Morgan of New York and Andrew G. Curtin of Pennsylvania, and contacted others by telegraph. He wanted them to support an appeal to Lincoln to call for new recruits.[12]

The appeal, dated June 28, was signed by seventeen governors (including two recognized by the Union in loyal sections of Virginia and Tennessee) and the president of the Military Board of Kentucky. The supporters believed "that the decisive moment is near at hand, and to that end the people of the United States are desirous to aid promptly in furnishing all reinforcements that you may deem needful to sustain our Government."[13]

Seward had drafted the message as well as a proclamation for Lincoln to issue calling for 150,000 men, not 100,000, to respond "without delay." Copies of both documents were sent to Stanton on June 30.[14]

While agreeing with the need for more men, Lincoln balked at issuing a proclamation, again fearing public reaction. Instead, he explained in a letter to governors on June 30: "Rather than hazard the misapprehension of our military condition and of groundless alarm by a call for troops by proclamation, I have deemed it best to address you in this form. To accomplish the object stated we require without delay 150,000 men, including those recently called for by the Secretary of War. Thus re-enforced, our gallant Army will be enabled to realize the hopes and expectations of the Government and the people."[15]

The next day, Stanton informed Seward that "discreet persons here suggest that the call should be for 300,000 men—double the number you propose—as the waste will be large." Later that day, Stanton advised Seward that the president had approved the plan but suggested a call for 200,000 men.[16]

Apparently Lincoln was persuaded by Stanton or Seward (or by both) that the number should be 300,000, for he wrote another letter to the governors on July 1, stating that "fully concurring in the wisdom of the views expressed to me in so patriotic a manner by you in the communication of the 28th day of June, I have decided to call into service 300,000 men. I trust that they may be enrolled without delay, so as to bring this unnecessary and injurious civil war to a speedy and satisfactory conclusion."[17]

After thinking it over, Lincoln changed his mind. On the morning of July 3, he expressed an entirely different view in a confidential message to the governors:

> I should not want the half of 300,000 new troops if I could have them now. If I had 50,000 additional troops here now I believe I could substantially close the war in two weeks. But time is everything, and if I get 50,000 new men in a month I shall have lost 20,000 old ones during the same month, having gained only 30,000 with the difference between old and new troops still against me. The quicker you send [the troops] the fewer you will have to send. Time is everything.[18]

The call for speed was lost on the governors. Their replies, while generally enthusiastic, also were discouraging. In some cases, no recruiting officers had been sent to the states. Some governors complained of a lack of weapons for men who did volunteer. The greatest difficulty was long delays governors expected in getting men to Washington. Some mentioned that it would be as late as August or September before they could forward troops. Others preferred to recruit cavalry or artillery units instead of infantry.[19]

———⋙●⋘———

The reaction to Lincoln's call of July 1 was followed by an act of Congress on July 17 authorizing him to enroll state militias into Federal service, covering all able-bodied men between eighteen and forty-five.[20]

Less than three weeks later, on August 4, the War Department issued a call for 300,000 militia immediately to serve for nine months. Each state was assigned a quota under Lincoln's call for 300,000 volunteers; if any state failed to meet its quota by August 15, the deficiency would be "made up by a special draft from the militia."[21] The next day, the order was changed to specify "a draft of 300,000 men" instead of 300,000 militia.[22]

The public reacted swiftly. On August 7 Illinois Governor Richard Yates informed Stanton:

> Since the orders for drafting, large numbers of citizens are leaving this city [Chicago] to escape the draft, and it is strongly urged upon me to ask you for authority to declare martial law. Do not delay, for I fear the people will take into their own hands the power which should only be used under the authority of your Department.[23]

Even more disturbing was an August 8 message to the War Department from Captain James Mooney of the 19th U.S. Infantry, the acting military commandant in Rochester, New York:

Many men are leaving for Canada. Have I authority to arrest under your order published by telegraph today, or shall I wait until I receive official orders?[24]

On August 9 Stanton advised Mooney that "you are authorized to arrest in the cases specified in the order of this Department without waiting for any further orders."[25] An order had been drafted by the War Department on August 8, at Lincoln's direction, allowing the arrest of men leaving the United States or their home county or state to avoid military duty.

In an unusual step, Stanton prepared a news release in his own writing. He pointed out, "The object is to compel every citizen of the United States subject to military duty to bear his share in supporting the Government."[26]

Another problem surfaced in Wisconsin. Governor Edward Salomon on August 14 informed Stanton: "The people of this State are in the greatest excitement about recruiting. Why will the Government insist on drafting, or leave us in suspense about recruiting, when we can furnish the soldiers by continuing recruiting until the 1st of September?"[27] The draft was scheduled to begin on September 3 and continue until the 300,000 quota had been filled.[28]

In the meantime, trouble was brewing in Maryland and Pennsylvania, the two states targeted for the Confederate invasion. On September 2 Governor A. W. Bradford of Maryland informed Stanton that recruiting officers were being threatened in several counties and asked for troops to protect them. On the same day Governor Curtin reported that the draft in Philadelphia "cannot be made there in season" unless there were enough commissioners or provost marshals in the city.[29]

———————

The trouble intensified and led to antiwar demonstrations, outspoken resentment against the government, and more young men fleeing the country. The seriousness of the problem prompted Confederate authorities to turn their attention to the political arena, the fall elections, and the prospects in the North of the so-called peace party. In the summer of

1862, a unique proposal was made by George N. Sanders, a Kentucky politician and secessionist. After the war Sanders explained:

> Soon after General McClellan's retreat before Richmond, and the non-success of Federal arms generally, I wrote to President Davis suggesting that the Congressional and State campaigns [in the] North would be a favorable time to inaugurate a peace movement, [and] offering to go to Canada on that mission. A sufficient idea of the character of my proposal is given briefly in saying that it was based upon the principles of fraternity and guaranteed reciprocal relations.
>
> President Davis promptly responded in writing that the proposition was of the highest importance, and myself the better judge of the ways and means to be employed. Orders were given to General J. E. B. Stuart, commanding the outposts, to pass me through our lines; and disguising myself I at once left Richmond, leaving behind all papers and other witnesses of [my] identity, and passed directly through the Federal lines to Niagara Falls. Here I met Governer Morehead [former Governor Charles S. Morehead] of Kentucky and other leading men, who thought that as the issues of the approaching elections were already made up, with a fair prospect of success for the peace party, any changes would be impolitic.[30]

The North's problems in the summer of 1862 became factors in Lee's invasion plans. In early July, however, his primary concern was still the protection of Richmond. On July 7 he complained to Randolph about an article in the *Richmond Daily Dispatch* identifying the Confederate divisions opposite Union forces at Harrison's Landing. He asked him to curb reports of Confederate troop strength and positions. Randolph promptly asked newspapers to be more circumspect "or they will do much mischief."[31]

McClellan remained a threat to Richmond that could not be ignored. Compounding this was another Union force, Major General John Pope's Army of Virginia north of Richmond.

It was a new army, formed by Lincoln on June 26 to protect Washington and western Virginia, neutralize the forces of Jackson and Ewell, and then help McClellan to capture Richmond. It was composed of three corps—McDowell's in Fredericksburg, Banks's in the Shenandoah Valley, and Frémont's in the Mountain Department, plus troops around Washington under Brigadier General Samuel D. Sturgis.[32]

After taking command, Pope learned that Jackson and Ewell had left the Valley and joined Lee. He also felt it would have been impossible for him to send troops to McClellan without inviting an attack on Washington.

He decided to draw the bulk of his new army east of the Blue Ridge and move toward Gordonsville and Charlottesville. The purpose was to "draw off as much as possible of the Confederate force threatening McClellan, and distract the attention of the enemy in his front so as to reduce as far as practicable the resistance opposed to his advance on Richmond."[33]

CHAPTER 12

Lee and Jackson Begin
the Northward Movement

LEE REACHED AN IMPORTANT POINT IN HIS CIVIL WAR CAREER IN early July. A month earlier, by endorsing Jackson's invasion plan, he had begun changing his strategic policy from defensive to offensive. Now, he was about to set Jackson's plan in motion. It was not an easy transition. Lee had to deal with military developments in the North as well as the threat to Richmond from McClellan's army, still at Harrison's Landing. Pope's presence just added to the problems.

Pope's force was divided in early July. The 1st and 2nd corps were in the Shenandoah Valley, mostly around Middletown about fifteen miles south of Winchester. One division of the 3rd Corps was in Manassas Junction and the other in Falmouth, on the north side of the Rappahannock River opposite Fredericksburg. Pope's strength was listed on June 30 as 67,614.[1]

By July 4 troops in the Valley had been ordered to Sperryville, east of the Blue Ridge.[2] The next day Pope advised Brigadier General Rufus King, commander of one of McDowell's divisions around Fredericksburg, that because of "the critical condition of affairs at Richmond and the danger of an advance by the enemy in this direction," he was to keep a close watch for twenty-five miles in the directions of Richmond and Gordonsville.[3]

On July 10 King advised McDowell's headquarters of reports in Fredericksburg that Jackson was advancing toward Fredericksburg by way of Gordonsville and Orange Court House.[4] Strangely enough, that was three days before Lee ordered Jackson to "proceed to Louisa Court House, and if practicable to Gordonsville, there to oppose a reported advance of the enemy from the direction of Orange Court House."[5]

Three days earlier, on July 7, Pope had moved to push toward Gordonsville. He told Banks to send his cavalry force with a battery of artillery under Brigadier General John P. Hatch to Culpeper Court House and post pickets at Orange Court House. Three days later, he ordered Banks to "push your patrols as far as possible toward Gordonsville."[6]

The correspondence that week disrupted the move that Pope wanted.[7] July 18 brought the most shocking news to Pope: Hatch had set out with infantry, artillery, and a wagon train, in addition to cavalry.[8]

In a letter to Banks on July 19 Pope stated: "The cavalry should have pushed through to Charlottesville within thirty-six hours after my orders were received. It has been a great mistake, and may possibly lead to serious consequences. Had General Hatch pushed forward when and as I directed he would have found no enemy at Gordonsville, and from all accounts none at Charlottesville."[9]

Pope had reason for apprehension. By the time he wrote that letter, Jackson had arrived in Gordonsville with his own and Ewell's division. On July 21 some Confederates pushed four miles northeast of town.[10]

Jackson, evidently aware that his small force was outnumbered, appealed to Lee for reinforcements. Lee, still concerned over McClellan's army, was reluctant to weaken his defense of Richmond without a prospect of striking a blow elsewhere.[11] On July 26 Lee told Jackson, "I am sorry you feel yourself so weak. Can you not take a strong position and resist the advance of Pope?"[12]

Also on July 26 Lee informed Davis that Jackson "seems to be of the opinion that he is too weak to encounter Pope & I fear Pope is too strong to be allowed to remain so near our communications. He ought to be suppressed if possible. I feel that it will be necessary to reinforce him [Jackson] before he can do anything & yet I fear to jeopardize the division of this army, upon which so much depends."[13]

Lee changed his mind a short time later. On July 27 A. P. Hill's division and a Louisiana brigade, more than 18,000 men, were sent to Jackson in Gordonsville. Lee said: "I want Pope to be suppressed. The course indicated in his orders, if the newspapers report them correctly, cannot be permitted and will lead to retaliation on our part.

"Cache your troops as much as possible till you can strike your blow and be prepared to return to me when done if necessary. I will endeavor to keep General McClellan quiet till it is over, if rapidly executed."[14]

Four orders had been issued by Pope between July 18 and 23; they noted that his troops were to subsist on the country in which they were operating. They specified that food and other supplies were to be obtained from residents of the occupied areas. In return, residents were to be given vouchers that could be cashed after the war.

Other orders specified that unit commanders were to arrest all disloyal citizens within their lines. All who were willing to take the oath of allegiance to the United States could remain in their homes, but those who refused were to be moved south and not permitted to return. If any of those who took the oath of allegiance violated it, they were to be shot and their property seized. If a shot was fired from a house at any Union soldier or legitimate follower of Pope's army, the person who fired the shot was to be arrested and the house razed. Strict penalties also were to be imposed on residents in areas where railroad and telegraph lines, or Union wagon trains, were damaged by guerrillas.[15]

Lee's assertions about this tended to focus attention on the necessity to suppress Pope's army, while obscuring the primary purpose of his own army—to invade the North.

Hill's troops began arriving in Gordonsville on July 29 and Jackson prepared to move northward.[16] Four days later Jackson sent Brigadier General William E. Jones with the 7th Virginia Cavalry Regiment to post pickets on the Rapidan River. As Jones approached Orange Court House, he learned that Federal troops held the town. Jones drove them out but, because he was outnumbered, soon withdrew from the area.

The affair alerted Jackson to the fact that only part of Pope's army was at Culpeper, less than twenty miles north of Orange Court House. He seized the initiative before Union reinforcements could arrive. On August 7 he advanced toward Culpeper from around Gordonsville.[17] When advised of the movement, Lee told Jackson: "If your information is correct, your movement against the enemy in Culpeper is judicious. Relying upon your judgment, courage, and discretion, and trusting to the continued blessing of an ever-kind Providence, I hope for victory."[18]

On August 9 Jackson's troops collided with a force under Banks, an old foe from the Valley. The battle was fought at Cedar Run and nearby Cedar Mountain, eight miles south of Culpeper. The Union column repulsed the first attack and seemed to be gaining the upper hand before the Confederates struck back with typical Jackson fury and routed Banks. Jackson's pursuit of the enemy was halted by darkness. The next day Jackson heard that Banks was being heavily reinforced, so "it was imprudent for me to attempt to advance farther."[19]

On August 12 Lee wrote to Jackson:

I congratulate you most heartily on the victory at Cedar Run. I hope your victory is but the precursor of others over our foe in that quarter, which will entirely break up and scatter his army.[20]

While riding with Jackson that day, cartographer Jed Hotchkiss was instructed to "at once make as many maps as I could of the region where we are [near Gordonsville] on to the Potomac."[21] Such confidence was clearly justified by decisions made in Washington that had a drastic effect on McClellan.

⎯⎯⎯⎯

Major General Henry W. Halleck, commander of the Department of the Mississippi, had been appointed Union general in chief on July 11, the position once held by McClellan. Halleck's major concern was McClellan's situation at Harrison's Landing. The next day Halleck went there "to ascertain if there was a possibility of an advance on Richmond."

After meeting with McClellan Halleck returned to Washington, conferred with his staff, and decided that the only practical move was to unite McClellan's troops with Pope's. That way Washington could be protected during operations against enemy troops.

On July 30 Halleck telegraphed McClellan to evacuate his sick as quickly as possible "to enable you to move in any direction."[22] The uncertainty of when McClellan would move and where he would go prompted Halleck to again reinforce Pope. The closest force was in Newport News, where Ambrose Burnside was stationed with troops from the Departments of North Carolina and of the South. On August 1 Halleck ordered Burnside to embark immediately for Aquia Creek and take position near Fredericksburg.[23]

That day McClellan suggested to Halleck that "Burnside's troops, at least a respectable portion of them, should be placed at my disposal."[24] Two days later Halleck telegraphed McClellan: "It is determined to withdraw your army from the Peninsula to Aquia Creek [near Fredericksburg]. You will take immediate measures to effect this, covering the movement the best you can. Its real object and withdrawal should be concealed even from your own officers."[25] Halleck's messages in early August clearly indicated that the attack on Richmond was to be abandoned and that McClellan and Burnside would join Pope to counter the Confederate advance.

Burnside acted promptly. Advance elements of his command landed at Aquia on August 3 and proceeded to Falmouth, north of Fredericksburg. By August 9 he reported that 12,000 troops were in position there.[26] Another week passed, however, before McClellan began a major movement.

McClellan, naturally, was upset by the order to withdraw from the Peninsula. Since mid-July he had referred several times to the possible resumption of his attack on Richmond and requested reinforcements. On August 2, before receiving Halleck's withdrawal order, McClellan ordered a reconnaissance of Malvern Hill, and a brigade set out the next day. After a number of skirmishes, Union troops withdrew during the night of August 6.[27] McClellan's last plea for men, made August 5, brought a terse reply from Halleck: "I have no reinforcements to send you."[28]

Halleck's reply undoubtedly was prompted by reports he had received a few days earlier. "I received information," Halleck noted, "that the enemy was preparing a large force to drive back General Pope and attack either Washington or Baltimore. That gave me serious uneasiness for the safety of the capital and Maryland, and I repeatedly urged upon General McClellan the necessity of promptly moving his army so as to form a junction with General Pope." Halleck also noted that McClellan's movement "was not commenced till the 14th, eleven days after it was ordered."[29]

McClellan later explained that small units actually had started to withdraw on August 7, but a shortage of transport vessels prevented movement of the main army before the 14th. "All troops and material were en route, both by land and water, on the morning of the 16th."[30]

———⟫●⟪———

The early departure of some of McClellan's troops from Harrison's Landing strengthened Lee's determination to reinforce Jackson. On August 13 he sent Longstreet and his entire force to Gordonsville. At the same time, Brigadier General John B. Hood was ordered to Hanover Junction; the next day he was instructed to join Longstreet.[31]

Later Lee explained that Burnside's corps from the Carolinas had united with Pope, and part of McClellan's army was believed to have left Harrison's Landing for the same purpose. "It therefore seemed," Lee stated, "that active operations on the James [River] were no longer contemplated, and that the most effectual way to relieve Richmond from any danger of attack from that quarter would be to reinforce General Jackson and advance upon General Pope."[32]

The mention of an advance against Pope, after references in two earlier letters to Jackson about suppressing him, suggests that Lee's primary objective was Pope's army.[33] Jed Hotchkiss, however, viewed mid-August activities in an entirely different light. In his August 13 diary entry he said that Jackson had told him not to be "afraid of making too many" maps of the area to the Potomac, then added, "General James Longstreet came to Gordonsville today."[34] The August 14 entry was even more enlightening:

> Troops in large numbers are constantly arriving at Gordonsville. Gen. Robert E. Lee came up today and encamped some $2^1/2$ miles from Gordonsville. Jackson went up to see him. Gen. Lee now assumes command of the army here.
>
> Gen. Jackson has been to Richmond and aided in driving McClellan off. Now the whole army comes to help Gen. Jackson in his long cherished move towards Maryland.

The next day Hotchkiss noted, "We all think the move is soon to take place. Troops are constantly arriving at Gordonsville and coming this way." On the 16th Hotchkiss wrote, "Jackson's whole corps went to Mountain Run, along the Southern slope of Clark's Mountain six miles from Orange Court House." Jackson's headquarters then was four miles from Orange Court House.[35]

Shortly after his arrival in Gordonsville, Lee conferred with Jackson and Longstreet. Pope's army was north of the Rapidan River, between that stream and the Rappahannock River. Reports of Union reinforcements prompted Lee to target Pope's left flank. On the 16th Jackson began moving his troops south of Clark's Mountain. Longstreet followed with his force and camped nearby.[36] Stuart, with "secret instructions" from Lee, began moving his cavalry toward Raccoon Ford on the Rapidan.[37]

Lee's plan called for the cavalry to destroy the railroad bridge over the Rappahannock, in the rear of Pope's army, while Longstreet and Jackson crossed the Rapidan and attacked his left flank. Lee had ordered the movement for the 18th but several problems forced a two-day postponement.[38] One was an unexpected movement of Union troops observed from the top of Clark's Mountain, a few miles north of Orange Court House. On August 16 Lee and Jackson saw enemy troops resting on the north side of the Rapidan. Two days later Lee and Longstreet were surprised to see long lines of enemy troops and wagons moving north toward the Rappahannock.[39] Pope was withdrawing from between the two rivers.

Following the fight at Cedar Mountain Pope reported to Halleck on August 12 that enemy forces had withdrawn and that the Confederate rear "is now crossing the Rapidan toward Orange Court House. I shall follow as far as the Rapidan." Halleck immediately cautioned Pope to "beware of a snare. Feigned retreats are secesh [secessionist] tactics."[40]

The next day Halleck ordered Pope not to cross the Rapidan and advised him that Burnside's reinforcements were on the way.[41] On August 16 Pope notified Halleck that his whole force had advanced to positions near the Rapidan. "The weak point of my position," he added, "is the left. There is danger that forces coming from Richmond may unite with Jackson, and interpose [themselves] between me and Fredericksburg."[42]

Halleck immediately advised Pope: "I think it would be very unsafe for your army to cross the Rapidan. It would be far better if you were in rear of the Rappahannock. Do not let your left flank be turned. If threatened too strongly, fall behind the Rappahannock."[43]

Shortly after noon on August 18 Pope reported that heavily reinforced Confederate units were advancing on his left. "I am not able to resist it without being cut off from the direction of Fredericksburg and Manassas. I have, accordingly, in compliance with your instructions, started back all my trains to pass the Rappahannock tonight." Halleck replied, "I fully approve your move." He then advised Pope to "stand firm until I can help you. Fight hard, and aid will soon come."[44]

Pope had good reason to fear the attack on his left. Early on August 18 a Union cavalry patrol had captured Stuart's adjutant general, Major Norman R. Fitzhugh, who carried a letter from Lee reportedly describing the position of Confederate forces and the threat of an attack on Pope's army. The letter was taken to Pope who, after notifying Halleck of the danger, began withdrawing north of the Rappahannock River.[45]

Jackson and Longstreet were ready to attack on the morning of the 18th, but Stuart was not. One of his two brigades—under Lee's nephew, Brigadier General Fitzhugh Lee—was a day late in reaching the rendezvous point near Raccoon Ford on the Rapidan.

Fitzhugh Lee's brigade, then at Hanover Junction, had been ordered to proceed on August 17 to the Raccoon Ford crossing and Stuart expected to meet him there that evening. Stuart rode to Verdiersville, south of the ford, but there was no sign of Fitzhugh Lee. After several hours Stuart became concerned and sent Major Fitzhugh to look for the brigade.[46]

Fitzhugh Lee explained that when he received the orders, he did not understand "that it was necessary to be at this point on that particular afternoon [the 17th]." As a result, he rode "a little out of his direct road in order to reach his wagons and get from them a full supply of rations and ammunition."[47]

Because of this detour, Stuart stated, Fitzhugh Lee's brigade did not reach the rendezvous until the night of the 18th, "a day behind time."[48] On August 19 Robert E. Lee directed Stuart to "rest your men today, refresh your horses, prepare rations, and everything [you need] for the march tomorrow."[49] This time the advance started on schedule. Longstreet, Jackson, and Stuart crossed the Rapidan River on the 20th and pushed forward.[50]

Lee told Davis on August 21: "Crossed Rapidan last night and this morning at Sommerville, Raccoon, and Morton's Fords [positions from the Confederate left to right]. Enemy commenced retreating yesterday. Got beyond Rappahannock, except a portion of his cavalry, which was driven." Lee then asked if Richmond "can be held" if he started troops northward to follow Pope.[51]

Davis was surprised by the Union withdrawal and, in an immediate reply, stated: "The retreat presents a case not originally contemplated." Although his words indicated that the advance had been discussed earlier, he was not prepared to make a quick decision. Instead, he consulted with Major General Gustavus W. Smith, who was in charge of the defense of Richmond. Davis then decided to take precautions against a sudden attack on the Confederate capital.[52]

<hr />

In the meantime Lee had encountered a problem that prompted him to change his plan of attack. By the time Confederate forces had crossed the Rapidan, Lee knew that Pope had learned of his intended attack on the Union left flank. After reviewing the situation, Lee decided:

> It was deemed best to turn their right flank, and General Jackson, in command of our left wing, was put in motion Thursday [the 21st] for the purpose, while General Longstreet threatened their left wing with our right.[53]

The change had dual significance for the Confederate plan. It helped confuse the enemy by creating the impression of an advance into the Shenandoah Valley; more important, Jackson's troops were taking the first steps on the invasion route he had proposed.

CHAPTER 13

North to the Potomac

THE CHANGE IN LEE'S PLAN WAS ACHIEVED WITHOUT DELAYS SUCH as those that hindered the start of the Peninsula Campaign against McClellan or the more recent crossing of the Rapidan River. This time Confederates began moving promptly on the morning of August 21 to shift the attack to Pope's right. Their course was upstream on the south side of the Rappahannock River, opposite Union forces on the north bank.

Jackson was camped that morning in Stevensburg, four or five miles east of Culpeper. Longstreet was near Kelly's Ford, opposite Pope's left flank and about six miles east of Jackson. Except for three regiments that had been left at Kelly's Ford to observe enemy activity, Stuart's cavalry was near Brandy Station.[1]

Two cavalry regiments under Colonel Thomas L. Rosser moved at daylight on the 21st toward Beverly Ford as an advance guard. If possible, he was to establish a position on the north bank.[2]

Jackson's troops marched toward Beverly Ford at the same time. As they approached, they heard firing on the north bank and learned that Rosser was engaged in a skirmish. Shortly, Union forces were reported advancing in strength and, late in the afternoon, Confederate cavalry was withdrawn from the north bank. At that time, Lee explained, it was decided to seek a more favorable crossing upstream.[3]

Meanwhile Longstreet was preparing to push across Kelly's Ford and threaten Pope's left wing when he was ordered to change direction and advance on the south side of the river to Rappahannock Station. As his troops were withdrawing, his rear brigade was attacked by troops that had crossed the river. The enemy was quickly repulsed and Longstreet continued upriver.[4]

The next day, August 22, the movement up the Rappahannock continued. After leaving Beverly Ford, Jackson crossed the Hazel River at Welford's Ford (also known as Welford's Mill), where he detached a brigade under Isaac R. Trimble to guard the flank of his wagon train. Jackson pushed on to Freeman's Ford and, when he found it strongly guarded, continued upriver to a ford at White Sulphur Springs (also called Warrenton Ford). During the afternoon, an infantry regiment and eight guns were sent across the Rappahannock to seize the springs and adjacent heights. Later, Brigadier General Jubal A. Early's brigade was sent across the river to reinforce the group at the springs.[5]

On his arrival at Rappahannock Station Longstreet ordered Hood to move forward with two brigades to support Jackson's troops (Trimble's brigade) at Freeman's Ford. Hood arrived at 4 P.M. in time to help Trimble repulse a force that had crossed the river to attack the wagon train.[6]

Meanwhile Stuart had set out on another raid. On the morning of the 22nd he embarked with Lee's approval on his second successful expedition around an enemy position. With about 1,500 men and two pieces of artillery, Stuart dashed around Pope's right flank and reached Warrenton in the afternoon. He then advanced to Catlett's Station, where he intended to destroy the railroad bridge over Cedar Run and cut lines of communication.[7]

The infantry had rougher going. Heavy rain that began in the afternoon was followed by a violent electrical storm. The Rappahannock rose rapidly. Jackson's troops at White Sulphur Springs were cut off from the main force and exposed. Another downpour the next afternoon delayed their return until a temporary bridge enabled them to recross the river on the night of the 23rd.[8]

The storm created a different problem for Stuart. Despite the storm, he reported, the cavalry pushed on and reached Catlett's Station after dark. Telegraph lines were cut in several places, but the downpour made it impossible to burn the railroad bridge and other attempts to damage it failed.

The raid provided an unexpected benefit. Before reaching Catlett's Station, Stuart sent a staff member, Captain William W. Blackford, to reconnoiter the area. He located Pope's headquarters, occupied by his staff and other officers. The only troops appeared to be those in a guard post at a crossroads a few hundred yards away.

It was dark when Blackford returned with his report—"the darkest night I ever knew," Stuart noted. Stuart and his men advanced, quietly captured the guards, then found themselves "in the midst of the enemy's encampments." A former slave who wandered into the area recognized Stuart, informed him that Pope's tent was nearby, and offered to guide Stuart. The cavalry charged into the area, captured about 300 Federals, and seized a "fabulous amount" of supplies and equipment. Pope was not there, but his dispatch book and a lot of correspondence were seized.[9]

Stuart said the dispatch book "was of peculiar value" and that it "contained information of great importance to us, throwing light upon the strength, movements, and designs of the enemy, and disclosing General Pope's own views against his ability to defend the line of the Rappahannock."

Before daylight on August 23 Stuart and his men retraced their steps to Warrenton. They had been on the road only a short time when Stuart got another surprise. Among the prisoners was Pope's field quartermaster, Major Charles N. Goulding.[10]

Stuart reported to Lee, about five miles from Warrenton, that Goulding had told him troops were being withdrawn from the Kanawha Valley in western Virginia to reinforce Pope. That day, Lee began to use this important intelligence.

In a letter to Davis he wrote that Pope's quartermaster "is reported to state that General [Jacob D.] Cox's forces are being withdrawn from the Kanawha Valley by way of Wheeling. If the campaign could be pushed in this direction it would have the effect of relieving other parts of the country. To do this all available reinforcements should be sent here."

In a letter to the secretary of war, George Randolph, Lee said that "from an intercepted letter" from Pope to McClellan, Cox's force was estimated at 12,000. He added that Stuart reported that Goulding "positively asserts that Cox's troops are being withdrawn by way of Wheeling. Under the foregoing information I have suggested to General [William W.] Loring that he might be usefully employed to the north, and by destruction of several links of the Baltimore and Ohio Railroad serve most advantageously the operations in this direction."

In a third letter on August 23—this one to General Loring, commanding Confederate forces in the Kanawha Valley—Lee repeated the statements about Cox and added: "This may be stated to deceive but I give you the information that you may look to its truth and take advantage of it. Should that be the case, your command could be usefully employed to the north, and if you destroy several links in the Baltimore and Ohio Railroad it would be of great advantage to us."[11]

The letters indicate that Stuart also took some of the captured correspondence to Lee. Later many letters and probably the dispatch book were taken to Lee's headquarters by Major Heros von Borcke, Stuart's aide.[12]

On August 24 Lee informed Davis that a letter written by Pope to Halleck on the 20th reported his command at 45,000, not counting Burnside's reinforcements. Pope also explained that his intention was to hold Confederate forces in check until McClellan could join him.

Lee added, "This letter of Pope's I think makes it certain that McClellan's destination is to join Pope. The whole army [Confederate] I think should be united here as soon as possible." Lee then explained that he would direct Gustavus Smith in Richmond to "send on [Lafayette] McLaws, D. H. Hill & other available troops. Should you not agree with me in the propriety of this step please countermand the order & let me know."[13]

On the 25th Davis replied, "General Smith will comply with your instructions."[14] That day Lee telegraphed Davis: "I believe a portion of McClellan's army has joined Pope. Expedite the advance of our troops."[15]

———•——

Lee was right. McClellan's 3rd Corps, under Major General Samuel P. Heintzelman, arrived in Alexandria on August 22. Heintzelman was met by a member of Halleck's staff with orders for the corps to hurry to Pope's support. Part of a division left by train that afternoon and was soon followed by the rest of the corps. By the 26th the entire corps was around Warrenton Junction.[16] The 5th Corps, commanded by Major General Fitz John Porter, disembarked at Aquia Creek on the 22nd and proceeded by rail to Falmouth. It remained there until the 26th, when it marched to Bealeton Station and to Warrenton Junction the next day.[17]

Another corps—the 6th, commanded by Major General William B. Franklin—disembarked in Alexandria on August 24 and two days later was ordered to advance to Warrenton and report to Pope.[18] These corps provided Pope with as many as 58,000 more men to meet Lee's advance.[19]

———•——

Davis's prompt reply to Lee's request for troops left no doubt about his feelings or determination to support the invasion plan. In his letter of August 26 Davis noted that troops requested by Lee had been ordered to join him, then added:

Confidence in you overcomes the view which would otherwise be taken of the exposed condition of Richmond, and the troops retained for the defense of the capital are surrendered to you on a renewed request.[20]

In the meantime Lee had moved to strengthen Richmond's defenses. In a letter August 25 to Colonel Jeremy F. Gilmer, chief engineer of the Army of Northern Virginia, Lee directed:

Use every exertion to perfect and complete the defenses around and to the approaches to Richmond by land and water. I wish to place them in such a condition that troops can be withdrawn from them with safety to the city, leaving a proper guard, and again restored when necessary.

Your services, as well as those of the engineers with you, are necessary to this army, and I am only willing to dispense with them to insure the safety of Richmond.[21]

<hr />

A significant event occurred on the night of August 24. Earlier that day Lee had moved his headquarters to Jeffersonton, where Jackson was camped. That evening Lee and Jackson were observed by Dr. Hunter McGuire, Jackson's medical director, conferring over some of Pope's captured correspondence. McGuire reported that Jackson was uncharacteristically excited, drawing a map in the sand with the toe of his boot. After Jackson finished, Lee nodded. Dr. McGuire figured that Jackson had suggested a movement and Lee approved it.[22]

After the war Longstreet explained that when Lee realized he could not advantageously attack Pope's lines behind the Rappahannock, he "decided to change his whole plan, and was gratified, on looking at a map to find a very comfortable way of turning Pope out of his position. It was by moving Jackson off to our left, and far to the rear of the Federal army, while I remained in front with thirty thousand men to engage him in case he should offer to fight."[23]

In his report Lee stated: "In pursuance of the plan of operations determined upon, Jackson was directed on the 25th to cross [the Rappahannock River] above Waterloo and move around the enemy's right, so as to strike the Orange and Alexandria Railroad in his rear.

Longstreet in the meantime was to divert his [Pope's] attention by threatening him in front and to follow Jackson as soon as the latter should be sufficiently advanced."[24]

An important step was taken at this time in the Confederate Congress. On August 25 Representative Henry S. Foote of Tennessee introduced a resolution supporting the plan to invade the North. First, it called for Southern forces "everywhere [to] be as active and aggressive" as possible to drive out enemy troops. Then it stated:

> As soon as the forces of the enemy shall have been driven back to their own country, if the deluded Government at Washington should still refuse us peace, it will be our policy at once to invade the territory of the foe, with a view to obtaining, sword in hand, indemnity for the past and security for the future.

The next proposal was for Davis to issue a "formal and explicit proclamation" guaranteeing to the people of the northwestern states free navigation of the Mississippi and Ohio rivers, "provided that they will at once desist from all further participation in this cruel and unnatural war."

Two days later Foote offered an amendment calling for Davis's proclamation to provide for a reciprocal treaty opening Southern markets to those states. The resolution and amendment were referred to the House Committee on Foreign Affairs. The impact of these actions was evident two weeks later as Lee's troops began their invasion of Maryland.[25]

Jackson started the movement on August 25. He explained, "Pursuing the instructions of the commanding general, I left Jeffersonton on the morning of the 25th to throw my command between Washington City and the army of General Pope and to break up his railroad communication with the Federal capital."[26]

Longstreet's report made no mention of any instructions or orders, but he wrote: "On the 25th we relieved a portion of General Jackson's command at Waterloo Bridge. There was more or less skirmishing at this point until the afternoon of the 26th, when the march was resumed, crossing the Rappahannock at Hinson's Mill Ford, six miles above Waterloo."[27]

On the night of the 25th, Stuart met with Lee and received his "final instructions" to accompany Jackson's movement. He moved at 2 o'clock the next morning and advanced rapidly to overtake Jackson's column.[28]

The entire Confederate army was on the move, aiming to drive off Pope and open the way for an advance across the Potomac River. In the lead, Jackson moved with typical speed along a route apparently intended to create the impression that he was headed back to the Shenandoah Valley. From Jeffersonton, he moved west to Amissville, then turned north in the Loudoun Valley with the Blue Ridge to the west and the Bull Run Mountains to the east, screening his troops and their movements from the bulk of Pope's army. After "a severe day's march," Jackson reported, his troops reached the Salem area on the Manassas Gap Railroad and camped there for the night.[29]

Pope was, indeed, misled. Shortly after noon on August 25 he informed Halleck that "a considerable column of infantry and cavalry and artillery" was on the road to Amissville and Luray or Front Royal on the western side of the Blue Ridge. "They can be plainly seen by our lookouts who estimate them at 20,000," McClellan added. "I have General McDowell's corps ready to march, and as soon as I ascertain certainly that they are going into the Shenandoah [Valley] I will push McDowell in their rear."

At 9 o'clock that night, Pope reported to Halleck: "The column of the enemy alluded to in my dispatch of 12:30 P.M. today passed Gaines' Crossroads, and when last seen, near sunset was passing to the northeast in the direction of Salem and Rectortown. I am induced to believe that this column is only covering the flank of the main body, which is moving toward Front Royal and Thornton's Gap [in the Blue Ridge]."[30]

Of course, Jackson was not headed for the Valley. At dawn on the 26th his troops turned eastward, pushed through Thoroughfare Gap in the Bull Run Mountains, and advanced to Gainesville, where they were joined by Stuart. With the cavalry on its right flank, the Confederate force reached Bristoe Station on the Orange and Alexandria Railroad about 9 P.M. on the 26th. Jackson was right where he was supposed to be, "in rear of General Pope's army, separating it from the Federal capital and its base of supply."[31]

In those two days Jackson's "foot cavalry" had marched about fifty miles and was justifiably tired and hungry.[32] But there was more to be done. Seven miles away at Manassas Junction was a large Union supply station that Jackson coveted. About 500 infantrymen with Stuart and part of his cavalry set out on the mission before midnight.

After a skirmish the Confederates seized the station. More than 300 men were captured, along with eight pieces of artillery, horses, ammunition, equipment, tents, and immense supplies of food, clothing, and other material. The Confederates carried off as much of the food as they could and, on the night of the 27th, burned the rest of the supplies before withdrawing. The next morning they rejoined Jackson's main column near where the First Battle of Bull Run had been fought the previous summer.

Late that day Jackson encountered a Union column that had advanced to Groveton, between Gainesville and Centreville. He attacked and the Battle of Groveton continued until about 9 P.M., when Union troops gradually withdrew.[33]

Longstreet's corps, delayed by skirmishes at Waterloo Bridge on August 26 and at Salem on the 27th, reached Thoroughfare Gap on the afternoon of August 28th. It encountered another Union force that resisted until withdrawing just before dark. Early on August 29 Longstreet resumed the advance. Near Gainesville the noise of battle was heard and Longstreet hurried to support Jackson.[34] It was the beginning of the Second Battle of Bull Run on August 29–30, in which Confederates again forced the Union to abandon the field.

On August 31 Lee ordered Jackson to pursue Union forces that were retreating toward Centreville. Late on September 1 Jackson's men caught up with enemy rear guard near Ox Hill, east of Centreville, and the fighting continued until dark. "By the following morning the Federal Army had entirely disappeared and had moved in the direction of Washington," Jackson noted.[35]

⟫●⟪

The Federal resistance at Ox Hill blocked Southern efforts to turn Pope's right and gave him time to retreat to the main fortifications. Because of this inability to bring the Union army to battle outside Washington, Lee decided to resume the broader sweep into Maryland. Any thought that he might have acted hastily in putting the invasion plan into motion immediately after Second Bull Run is quickly dispelled by three significant developments on August 30 and September 2.

The first was a message sent to Davis on the 30th, while the armies were still fighting. Lee stated: "My dispatches will have informed you of the march of this portion [Longstreet's Corps] of the army. Its progress has been necessarily slow, having a large and superior force on its flank, narrow & rough roads to travel, and the difficulties of obtaining forage & provisions to contend with." He then added:

It has so far advanced in safety and has succeeded in deceiving the enemy as to its object. In order that we may obtain the advantages I hope for, we must be in larger force, and I hope every exertion will be made to create troops & to increase our strength & supplies. We have no time to lose & must make every exertion if we expect to reap advantage."[36]

On September 2, following the Union withdrawal from Ox Hill, Lee went to Jackson's headquarters in Chantilly.[37] Lee had endorsed Jackson's invasion plan in early June and a few weeks later postponed it until McClellan could be driven from Richmond. He was now ready to begin the invasion.

After the war Lee explained that "after Chantilly [Ox Hill], he found he could do nothing more against the Yankees, unless he attacked them in their fortifications around Washington, which he did not want to do. He therefore determined to cross the river into Maryland, and thus effect two things—1st, to relieve Virginia from both armies, as he thought such a movement would force the Union army over the [Potomac] river—and 2nd, to live for a time on the abundant supplies in Maryland.

"In reference to this, he talked to Gen. Jackson, who advised him to go into the [Shenandoah] Valley and cross the Potomac at or above Harpers Ferry, cleaning out the [enemy] forces at Winchester, &c." Lee did not agree with this because it would take him too far from the enemy army and might not induce it to cross the Potomac. "He [Lee], therefore, ordered Jackson to take command in advance and cross [the river] in Loudoun County and move toward Frederick, Maryland, destroying the [Chesapeake and Ohio] Canal &c."[38]

The next day Jackson left Ox Hill "and on the 4th bivouacked near Big Spring between Leesburg and the Potomac."[39] As he looked into Maryland, there was no longer any doubt in his mind about his next step.

In early July Davis, the secretaries of war and state, and the army's adjutant and inspector generals had clearly indicated that preparations were being made for Confederate troops to invade the North. Lee also made this perfectly clear in a September 3 letter to Davis:

The present seems to be the most propitious time since the commencement of the war for the Confederate Army to enter Maryland. The two grand armies of the United States that have been operating in Virginia, though now united, are much weakened and demoralized. Their new levies, of which I understand six thousand men have already been posted in Washington, are not organized, and will take some time to prepare for the field. If it is ever desired to give material aid to Maryland and afford her an opportunity of throwing off the oppression to which she is now subject, this would seem the most favorable.

After the enemy had disappeared from the vicinity of Fairfax Court House and taken the road to Alexandria and Washington, I did not think it would be advantageous to follow him farther. I had no intention of attacking him in his fortifications, and am not prepared to invest them. If I had possessed the necessary munitions, I should be unable to supply provisions for the troops. I therefore determined while threatening the approaches to Washington, to draw troops into Loudoun [County] where forage and some provisions can be obtained, menace their [the enemy's] possession of the Shenandoah Valley, and if found practicable, to cross into Maryland. The purpose, if discovered, will have the effect of carrying the enemy north of the Potomac, and if prevented, will not result in much evil.

The army is not properly equipped for an invasion of an enemy's territory. It lacks much of the material of war, is feeble in transportation, the animals being much reduced, and the men are poorly provided with clothes, and in thousands of instances are destitute of shoes. Still we cannot afford to be idle, and though weaker than our opponents in men and military equipments, must endeavor to harass, if we cannot destroy them. I am aware the movement is attended with much risk, yet I do not consider success impossible, and shall endeavor to guard it from loss.

As long as the army of the enemy are employed on this frontier I have no fears for the safety of Richmond, yet I earnestly recommend that advantage be taken of this period of comparative safety to place its defense, both by land and water, in the most perfect condition. A respectable force can be collected to defend its approaches by land, and the Steamer Richmond I hope is now ready to clear the river of hostile vessels. Should General [Braxton] Bragg find it impracticable to operate to advantage on his present frontier [in Tennessee], his army, after leaving sufficient garrisons, could be advantageously employed in opposing the overwhelming numbers which it seems to be the intention of the enemy now to concentrate in Virginia. I have already been told by prisoners that some of [Major General Don Carlos] Buell's cavalry have been joined to General Pope's army, and have reason to believe that the whole of McClellan's, the larger portions of Burnside's and Cox's and a portion of [Major General David] Hunter's are united to it.

What causes me most concern is the fear of getting out of ammunition. I beg you will instruct the Ordnance Department to spare no pains in manufacturing a sufficient amount of the best kind, and to be particular in preparing that for the artillery, to provide three times as much of the long range ammunition as that for smooth bore or short range guns. The points to which I desire the ammunition to be forwarded will be made known to the Department in time. If the Quartermaster Department can furnish any shoes, it would be of the greatest relief.[40]

Colonel A. L. Long, a secretary on Lee's staff, provided an interesting sidelight on this letter. Though it was dated September 3, Long pointed out that Lee had dictated it to him the day before.[41]

Another aide, Major Walter H. Taylor, was more positive and revealing in his account. Following the defeat of Pope's army, Taylor noted:

General Lee now determined to cross the Potomac River and invade the State of Maryland. The advantages and disadvantages of an aggressive campaign had been well weighed, and with the sanction of the authorities at Richmond and the approval of his own judgment, General Lee gave the order for his army to advance.[42]

With his army concentrated along the Potomac on September 4, Lee again wrote Davis, displaying an even greater confidence than that expressed in the September 3 letter:

Since my last communication to you with reference to the movement I propose to make with this army, I am more fully persuaded of the benefits that will result from an expedition into

Maryland, and I shall make the movement at once, unless you should signify your disapprobation. Should the results of the expedition justify it, *I propose to enter Pennsylvania, unless you should deem it unadvisable upon political or other grounds.*

Lee explained that he was trying to supply his troops around Leesburg, but would probably need help in Maryland. "To be able to collect supplies to advantage in Maryland, I think it is important to have the services of someone known to the people and acquainted with the resources of the country. I wish therefore that if ex-Governor [Enoch L.] Lowe can make it convenient, he should come to me at once. As I contemplate entering a part of the State with which Governor Lowe is acquainted, I think he would be of much service to me in many ways."[43]

Lee issued the following order on September 4: "This army is about to engage in most important operations, where any excesses committed will exasperate the people, lead to disastrous results, and enlist the populace on the side of Federal forces in hostility to our own. Quartermasters and commissaries will make all arrangements for purchase of supplies needed by our army, to be issued to the respective commands upon proper requisitions, thereby removing all excuse for depredations."[44]

In a proclamation the same day, Davis called on Southerners to join "on Thursday, the 18th day of September in a day of prayer and thanksgiving to Almighty God" for recent battlefield triumphs. He referred specifically to McClellan's repulse and to victories at Bull Run and Richmond, Kentucky, both on August 30.

In conclusion he asked that prayers be offered "to implore Him to conduct our country safely through the perils which surround us, to the final attainment of the blessings of peace and security."[45]

———❦———

Lee's movement should not have been a surprise to Federal authorities. The press had been speculating for some time that the Confederates would invade Maryland. The government paid little attention; it was convinced that Lee had one object in mind, an attack on Washington.[46]

Again, McClellan was called on, as he had been after First Bull Run. On August 31 Halleck asked McClellan "to assist me in this crisis with your ability and experience. I am utterly tired out." The next day McClellan went to Washington and was told to take charge of it and its defenses.[47]

The following morning Lincoln and Halleck called on him. The president asked McClellan if he would "as a favor to him, resume command and do the best that could be done." At the time, Lincoln and Halleck expressed concern for the safety of Washington.[48] Later that day steps were taken to ship military supplies at the Washington arsenal to New York and a warship was said to be in the Potomac, ready to take Lincoln and the Cabinet to safety if that should become necessary.[49]

McClellan acted promptly and, before daylight on September 3, reported that troops were ready to repulse an attack and "Washington was safe."[50] But Lee had turned away from the capital. Jackson's troops were on the road from Chantilly to Leesburg to begin the invasion of Maryland.

CHAPTER 14

The Invasion Begins

CONFEDERATE CAMPS BUSTLED ON THE MORNING OF SEPTEMBER 5. After a march of several hours the column reached Leesburg, near fords that would provide relatively easy crossing of the Potomac. Jackson, Longstreet, and Stuart met with Lee at his headquarters for final instructions and, shortly after noon, the march resumed.[1]

Lee immediately informed Davis: "This army is about entering Maryland, with a view of affording the people of that state an opportunity of liberating themselves. I am now more desirous that my suggestion as to General Loring's movements shall be carried into effect as soon as possible, so that with the least delay he may move to the lower end of the Valley, about Martinsburg, and guard the approach in that direction."

He was concerned, however, because with his army north of the Potomac, his supply line from Richmond through Leesburg would be exposed. To counter that threat, supply trains were to turn off at Culpeper Court House and move by way of Luray and Front Royal to Winchester. He recommended that ammunition be forwarded by an alternate route, from Richmond to Staunton, then northward to Winchester. "It is not yet certain that the enemy have evacuated the Valley," he added, "but there are reports to that effect, and I have no doubt that they will leave that section as soon as they learn of [my] movement across the Potomac."

Lee's attention to detail extended to a recommendation that railroad bridges be restored over the Rapidan and Rappahannock rivers between his army and Richmond. Lee told Davis, "My reason for desiring this is,

that in the event of falling back, it is my intention to take a position
about Warrenton, where, should the enemy attempt an advance on Richmond, I should be on his flank, or, should he attack me, I should have a
favorable country to operate in, and the bridges being repaired, should be
in full communication with Richmond."[2]

⸺⸻⸺

Spirits were high that afternoon as Southern troops splashed across the
river. Uniforms were tattered and a lot of feet were bare, but the men
were proud and confident. In just a little more than three months under
Lee, they had forced McClellan to abandon his campaign, then defeated
Pope. As they stepped out of the water onto Maryland shores, their bands
played and men sang "Maryland, My Maryland."[3]

In a telegram on September 6 Lee informed Davis that "two divisions
of the army have crossed the Potomac. I hope all will cross today. Navigation of the [Chesapeake and Ohio] Canal has been interrupted and
efforts will be made to break up the Baltimore and Ohio Railroad."[4]

The crossing was completed as Lee had hoped. At last, Southern flags
were unfurled north of the Potomac, as top Confederate officials had pre-
dicted they would be when Jackson's plan was accepted two months earlier. In a message that day announcing the Confederate victory in
Kentucky on August 30, Lee told his men:

> This great victory is simultaneous with your own at Manassas.
> Soldiers, press forward! Let each man feel the responsibility now
> resting on him to pursue vigorously the success vouchsafed to us by
> Heaven. Let the armies of the East and the West vie with each other
> in discipline, bravery, and activity, and our brethren of our sister
> States will soon be released from tyranny, and our independence be
> established upon a sure and abiding basis.[5]

Lee intended to push the invasion as rapidly as possible. On the 7th
Confederate troops advanced northward to Frederick and Lee immediately reported to Davis that his entire army, except for Brigadier General
John G. Walker's division, was in Maryland. He expressed concern, however, about some Marylanders who would not take Confederate money or
IOUs for supplies. Again, he asked to have former Governor Lowe or
"some prominent citizen of Maryland" join him to help resolve this problem. He also pointed out that, despite "individual expressions of kindness

and general sympathy" for the Confederacy, he did not anticipate any general uprising "of the people in our behalf."

In closing Lee added that the only encounter with Union troops in Maryland had been a cavalry skirmish at Poolesville. As far as he could determine, the enemy army remained in the defenses of Washington.[6]

Lee also reported to Randolph on the 7th that Union troops had evacuated Winchester and that a Confederate force had occupied the town. According to rumors, Lee added, the enemy had withdrawn toward Harpers Ferry and Martinsburg and continued the retreat into Pennsylvania.[7]

The belief that the Union would abandon Harpers Ferry and Martinsburg was quickly dispelled, however, and Lee was alerted to the danger of allowing enemy forces to threaten his communication line through the Shenandoah Valley.[8] His first step was to tell Longstreet on the 7th to "organize forces to surround and capture the works and garrison" in Harpers Ferry. Longstreet objected on the grounds that the troops were worn out by hard marching, that rations were short, and that "it would be a bad idea to divide our forces while we were in the enemy's country." Lee did not press the point and Longstreet believed "the Harpers Ferry scheme" had been dropped.

He was surprised the next day at Lee's headquarters, where Lee and Jackson were discussing the plan. Jackson had been directed to move against Harpers Ferry and Longstreet realized that it was useless to offer "any further opposition."[9]

Lee's confidence in the Maryland invasion was clear in a message to Davis on the 8th:

> The present position of affairs, in my opinion, places it in the power of the Government of the Confederate States to propose with propriety to that of the United States the recognition of our independence.
>
> Such a proposition, coming from us at this time, could in no way be regarded as suing for peace; but, being made when it is in our power to inflict injury upon our adversary, would show conclusively to the world that our sole object is the establishment of our independence and the attainment of an honorable peace.
>
> The rejection of this offer would prove to the country that the responsibility of the continuance of the war does not rest upon us, but that the party in power in the United States elect to prosecute it for purposes of their own. The proposal of peace would enable the

people of the United States to determine at their coming elections whether they will support those who favor a prolongation of the war, or those who wish to bring it to a termination, which can but be productive of good to both parties without affecting the honor of either.[10]

In another significant action on September 8, Lee issued a proclamation to Marylanders:

It is right that you should know the purpose that brought the army under my command within the limits of your State, so far as that purpose concerns yourselves. The people of the Confederate States have long watched with the deepest sympathy the wrongs and outrages that have been inflicted upon the citizens of a commonwealth allied to the States of the South by the strongest social, political, and commercial ties. They have seen with profound indignation their sister State deprived of every right and reduced to the condition of a conquered province.

Under the pretense of supporting the Constitution, but in violation of its most valuable provisions, your citizens have been arrested and imprisoned upon no charge and contrary to all forms of law. The faithful and manly protest against this outrage made by the venerable and illustrious Marylander, to whom in better days no citizen appealed for right in vain, was treated with scorn and contempt; the government of your chief city has been usurped by armed strangers; your legislature has been dissolved by the unlawful arrest of its members; freedom of the press and of speech has been suppressed; words have been declared offenses by an arbitrary decree of the Federal Executive, and citizens ordered to be tried by a military commission for what they may dare to speak.

Believing that the people of Maryland possessed a spirit too lofty to submit to such a government, the people of the South have long wished to aid you in throwing off this foreign yoke, to enable you again to enjoy the inalienable rights of freemen, and restore the independence and sovereignty of your State. In obedience to this wish, our army has come among you, and is prepared to assist you with the power of its arms in regaining the rights of which you have been despoiled.

This, citizens of Maryland, is our mission, so far as you are concerned. No constraint upon your free will is intended; no intimidation will be allowed within the limits of this army, at least. Marylanders shall once more enjoy their ancient freedom of thought and speech. We know no enemies among you, and will protect all, of every opinion. It is for you to decide your destiny freely and without constraint. This army will protect your choice, whatever it may be; and while the Southern people will rejoice to welcome you to your natural position among them, they will only welcome you when you come of your own free will.

Lee sent a copy of the proclamation to Davis with a letter on September 12. In the letter Lee explained that, in the absence of ex-Governor Lowe, and because the citizens of Maryland "were embarrassed as to the intentions of the [Confederate] army, I determined to delay no longer in making known our purpose."[11]

Lee's words echoed the intent of a resolution adopted by the Confederate Congress almost nine months earlier, on December 19. Congress called for "speedy and efficient exertions on our part" to relieve suffering that had been inflicted on Marylanders and to facilitate the state in joining the Confederacy "with the free consent of her people."[12]

———————————

A surprising development in Richmond added to the evidence that Jackson's invasion plan had been set in motion. Jefferson Davis went to be with the Army of Northern Virginia in its movement into enemy territory.

The president had traveled about seventy-five miles when he stopped at Rapidan, just south of Culpeper Court House, to write a note, dated September 7, informing Lee of his decision. Lee received it two days later and was startled by Davis's action as well as fearful for his safety.

He sent an aide, Major Walter H. Taylor, to meet Davis and dissuade him from continuing the journey. Taylor also carried a letter from Lee warning the president of the dangers, such as marauding Union cavalry.

I have just received your letter of the 7th instant, from Rapidan, informing me of your intention to come on to Leesburg. While I should feel the greatest satisfaction in having an interview with you, and consulting upon all subjects of interest, I cannot but feel great uneasiness for your safety should you undertake to reach me. You will not only encounter the hardships and fatigues of a very disagreeable journey, but also run the risk of capture by the enemy. I send my aide-de-camp, Major Taylor, back to explain to you the difficulties and dangers of the journey, which I cannot recommend you to undertake.

I am endeavoring to break up the line through Leesburg, which is no longer safe, and turn everything off from Culpeper Court House towards Winchester. I shall move in the direction I originally intended, towards Hagerstown and Chambersburg, for the purpose of opening our line of communication through the Valley, in order to procure sufficient supplies of flour.

I shall not move until tomorrow, or, perhaps next day, but when I do move, the line of communication in this direction will be entirely broken up. I must, therefore, advise that you do not make an attempt that I cannot but regard as hazardous.[13]

Taylor left Frederick on September 9 and arrived in Warrenton the next day. There, he learned that because of a health problem, Davis had returned to Richmond. Taylor immediately telegraphed the president: "I have just arrived here. Left Frederick City at noon yesterday. General Lee expected that I would meet you and Governor Lowe, and gave me dispatches in addition to verbal instructions. The latter would be useless, since you have returned to Richmond. I shall return to the army and forward the dispatches by mail, unless ordered otherwise."[14]

Lee's letter also added evidence of earlier planning when he pointed out that the army's movements would be made "in the direction I originally intended, towards Hagerstown and Chambersburg."

<hr/>

Meanwhile, Foote's resolution in the House of Representatives had stirred debate. With the Confederates north of the Potomac on September 7, it was no longer necessary to call for invasion of enemy territory. A shortened version was adopted on September 12 by a vote of sixty-three to fifteen.[15]

The approved resolution asked Davis to direct military commanders, as soon as they approached or entered states along the Mississippi River or its tributaries, to publish proclamations "assuring the people of those States, as well as others interested, free navigation of the Mississippi River."[16]

Davis apparently knew of the introduction of the resolution. According to James Lyons, a Virginia representative, there were signs that he favored it.[17] Some time before its adoption, Davis began preparing a draft of the proclamation. After being advised that Lee had crossed the Potomac, Davis decided that the text also could be directed at Marylanders.

Copies of Lee's proclamation and the one prepared by Davis passed each other while en route to recipients. Lee's proclamation was directed specifically to Marylanders, but Davis's draft was much broader in context. The president's proclamation could be adapted for use to any state and for Confederate activity in the Mississippi River area.

In a letter to Lee, probably on September 9,[18] the president advised:

You should, in accordance with established usage, announce by proclamation to the people of Maryland, the motives and purposes of your presence among them at the head of an invading army, and you are instructed in such proclamation to make known:

1st. That the Confederate Government is waging this war solely for self-defense; that it has no design of conquest or any other purpose than to secure peace and the abandonment by the United States of their pretensions to govern a people who have never been their subjects, and who prefer self-government to a union with them.

2d. That this Government, at the very moment of its inauguration, sent commissioners to Washington to treat for a peaceful adjustment of all differences, but that these commissioners were not received, nor even allowed to communicate the object of their mission, and that on a subsequent occasion a communication from the President of the Confederacy to President Lincoln remained without answer, although a reply was promised by General Scott, into whose hands the communication was delivered.

3d. That among the pretexts urged for continuance of the war is the assertion that the Confederate Government desires to deprive the United States of the free navigation of the Western rivers, although the truth is that the Confederate Congress by public act, prior to the commencement of the war, enacted that "the peaceful navigation of the Mississippi River is hereby declared free to the citizens of any of the States upon its boundaries or upon the borders of its navigable tributaries," a declaration to which this Government has always been, and is still, ready to adhere.

4th. That now, at a juncture when our arms have been successful, we restrict ourselves to the same just and moderate demand that we made at the darkest period of our reverses, the simple demand that the people of the United States should cease to war upon us and permit us to pursue our own path to happiness, while they in peace pursue theirs.

5th. That we are debarred from the renewal of formal proposals for peace by having no reason to expect that they would be received with the respect mutually due by nations in their intercourse, whether in peace or in war.

6th. That under these circumstances we are driven to protect our own country by transferring the seat of war to that of an enemy who pursues us with a relentless and apparently aimless hostility; that our fields have been laid waste, our people killed, many homes made desolate, and that rapine and murder have ravaged our frontiers; that the sacred right of self-defense demands that if such a war is to continue its consequences shall fall on those who persist in their refusal to make peace.

7th. That the Confederate army, therefore, comes to occupy the territory of their enemies, and to make it the theatre of hostilities; that with the people themselves rests the power to put an end to this invasion of their homes, for, if unable to prevail on the Government of the United States to conclude a genuine peace, their own State Government, in the exercise of its sovereignty, can secure immunity from the desolating effect of warfare on the soil of the State by a separate treaty of peace, which this Government will ever be ready to conclude on the most just and liberal basis.

8th. That the responsibility thus rests on the people of ——— of continuing an unjust and oppressive warfare upon the Confederate States—a warfare which can never end in any other manner than that now proposed. With them is the option of preserving the blessings of peace by the simple abandonment of the design of subjugating a people over whom no right of dominion has ever been conferred by God or man.[19]

Davis's document was timely in relation to the debates on the House resolution and to the Confederate victories in Virginia and Kentucky. Section three dealt specifically with navigation of the Mississippi and its tributaries, as outlined in the resolution. In the fourth section, Davis refers to "now, at a juncture when our arms have been successful," apparently the simultaneous victories in Virginia and Kentucky. The blank space in the eighth section clearly indicates that the proclamation was not intended for Maryland alone, but for use in any other state that would be entered by Confederate invaders.

Davis's draft of the proclamation evidently did not reach Lee until the 12th or the 13th. In a letter to Davis on the 13th, Lee wrote, "You will perceive by the printed address [proclamation] to the people of Maryland, which has been sent you, that I have not gone contrary to the views expressed by you. Should there be anything in it to correct, please let me know."[20]

The invasion seemed to be going well. In four days Lee had crossed the Potomac, pushed on to Frederick, and was ready to move toward Pennsylvania. The only diversion was the need to send a force to clear the Shenandoah Valley route of the Union garrison that had remained unexpectedly at Harpers Ferry.

CHAPTER 15

Frustration and Disappointment

PLANS TO CARRY THE INVASION INTO PENNSYLVANIA WERE DISCLOSED to Major General John G. Walker on September 8, when he reported to Lee near Frederick. Lee explained that Walker's division probably would be detached and, therefore, "an intelligent performance of my [Walker's] duty might require a knowledge of the ulterior purposes and objects of the campaign." First, Walker was to return to the mouth of the Monocacy River, destroy the aqueduct of the Chesapeake and Ohio Canal, then join in the capture of Harpers Ferry. He then was to rejoin the army in Hagerstown. A few days' rest would help the troops, Lee added, and permit stragglers and reinforcements from Richmond to reach the army. Then, according to Walker, Lee said:

> In ten days from now, if the military situation is then what I confidently expect it to be after the capture of Harpers Ferry, I shall concentrate the army at Hagerstown, effectually destroy the Baltimore and Ohio [Rail]road, then march to this point.

Lee was studying a large map at the time, Walker stated, and pointing to Harrisburg, Pennsylvania. His intention, he added, was to destroy the Pennsylvania Railroad bridge over the Susquehanna River. Lee then pointed out that with that line broken and the B&O and canal out of service, "there will remain to the enemy but one route of communication with the West, and that very circuitous by way of the [Great] Lakes. After that I can turn my attention to Philadelphia, Baltimore, or Washington, as may seem best for our interests." When Walker expressed astonishment at the boldness of the plan, Lee said he did not consider the Army of the Potomac to be a serious danger. He then pointed out:

> He [McClellan] is an able general but a very cautious one. His army is in a very demoralized and chaotic condition, and will not be prepared for offensive operations—or he will not think it so— for three or four weeks. Before that time I hope to be on the Susquehanna.[1]

When learning that Confederate troops had turned away from Washington on September 3, McClellan suspected that Lee would cross the Potomac. He was not sure of the objectives. Would he attack Baltimore and Washington? Would Lee continue into Pennsylvania or was he trying to draw defenders away from Washington so that a large army could attack the capital from the south?

McClellan's first step was to seek to have the garrison in Harpers Ferry, "about ten thousand men," transferred to his own army. The general in chief, Henry W. Halleck, received the idea "with ill-concealed contempt" and "said that everything was all right as it was," according to McClellan.[2]

Troubled by uncertainty, McClellan began advancing slowly from Washington on September 5 and continued a cautious march northwestward—as Lee surmised he would.[3] "The purpose of advancing from Washington," McClellan pointed out, "was simply to meet the necessities of the moment by frustrating Lee's invasion of the Northern States."[4]

Lee was not about to be frustrated. On September 9, the day after his meeting with Walker, Lee issued detailed instructions (Special Orders No. 191) for the army to begin advancing the next day. This document, which shortly had a drastic impact on the invasion, stated:

> The army will resume its march tomorrow, taking the Hagerstown Road. General Jackson's command will form the advance, and, after passing Middletown, with such portion as he may select, take the route toward Sharpsburg, cross the Potomac at the most convenient point, and by Friday morning [September 12th] take possession of the Baltimore and Ohio Railroad, capture such of them [enemy troops] as may be at Martinsburg [Virginia], and

intercept such as may attempt to escape from Harpers Ferry.

General Longstreet's command will pursue the main road as far as Boonsborough [Boonsboro], where it will halt, with reserve, supply, and baggage trains of the army.

General McLaws, with his own division and that of General R. H. Anderson, will follow General Longstreet. On reaching Middletown [he] will take the route to Harpers Ferry, and by Friday morning possess himself of the Maryland Heights and endeavor to capture the enemy at Harpers Ferry and vicinity.

General Walker, with his division, after accomplishing the object in which he is now engaged, will cross the Potomac at Cheek's Ford, ascend its right bank to Lovettsville, take possession of Loudoun Heights, if practicable, by Friday morning. He will, as far as practicable, cooperate with Generals McLaws and Jackson, and intercept retreat of the enemy.

General D. H. Hill's division will form the rear guard of the army, pursuing the road taken by the main army. The reserve artillery, ordnance, and supply trains, &c., will precede General Hill.

General Stuart will detach a squadron of cavalry to accompany the commands of Generals Longstreet, Jackson, and McLaws, and, with the main body of the cavalry will cover the route of the army, bringing up all stragglers that may have been left behind.

The commands of Generals Jackson, McLaws, and Walker, after accomplishing the objects for which they have been detached, will join the main body of the army at Boonsboro or Hagerstown.[5]

Lee also had devised a plan, not included in the written orders, for slowing McClellan. He instructed Stuart to divide his main force and move on both of McClellan's flanks as though threatening Baltimore and Washington. Stuart also was instructed to give out news on both flanks "that he [Lee] was behind with his whole force."[6]

———————

Walker, who had left Frederick on the 9th to destroy the canal aqueduct, was shocked when a copy of Lee's order was delivered to him late in the afternoon of the 10th. It "contained the most precise and detailed information respecting the position of every portion of the Confederate army" and the movements that had been ordered. He was alarmed that a copy might fall into enemy hands.

"I was so impressed with the disastrous consequences which might result from its loss," Walker added, "that I pinned it securely in an inside pocket." He was told later that Longstreet also was concerned and stated that he had destroyed the order after memorizing it."[7] Their concern was justified.

Lee's entire force began the advance from Frederick on September 10. Jackson moved west to Williamsport and the next day recrossed the Potomac and camped in the Martinsburg area. Federal forces in Martinsburg had been warned of Jackson's approach and withdrew to Harpers Ferry. The next morning, Jackson's men entered Martinsburg and the following day, September 13, moved within sight of Harpers Ferry.[8]

Walker was unable to disable the canal because of insufficient tools and the approach of Federal troops. Instead, he moved to Point of Rocks, crossed the Potomac, and on the morning of September 13 was approaching Loudoun Heights, the hill east of Harpers Ferry.[9]

McLaws had moved north of the Potomac and by September 13 took Maryland Heights.[10] Meanwhile, Anderson's division, bolstered by half of Longstreet's own division, had been detached to join McLaws for the attack on Harpers Ferry. As soon as the Shenandoah Valley was cleared of Federals and Harpers Ferry captured, the attacking forces were to rejoin the rest of the army at Boonsboro or Hagerstown.[11]

Hagerstown was important to Lee's plan. It was on a main road that led north into Pennsylvania, through Chambersburg and Carlisle and to the Susquehanna opposite Harrisburg. Longstreet, like the others, had taken up the march on September 10 and arrived in Hagerstown the 11th.[12]

Lee, who accompanied Longstreet's force, later explained that one reason for the move to Hagerstown was to seize supplies that were being moved to Pennsylvania. Longstreet again objected to the marching and, according to Lee, said, "General I wish we could stand still and let the d——d Yankees come to us!"[13]

Lee summarized the situation on September 12 in a letter to Davis from Hagerstown.

> Before crossing the Potomac I considered the advantage of entering Maryland east or west of the Blue Ridge. In either case it was my intention to march upon this town. By crossing east of the Blue Ridge, both Washington and Baltimore would be threatened,

which I believed would insure the withdrawal of the mass of the enemy's troops north of the Potomac. I think this has been accomplished.

I had also supposed that as soon as it was known that the army had reached Frederick, the enemy's forces in the Valley of Virginia, which had retired to Harpers Ferry and Martinsburg, would retreat altogether from the State. In this I was disappointed, and you will perceive from the accompanying order of the 9th instant that Generals Jackson and McLaws have been detached with a view of capturing their forces at each place should they not have retired.

The army has been received in this region with sympathy and kindness. We have found in this city about 1,500 barrels of flour. The supply of beef has been very small, and we have been able to procure no bacon. A thousand pairs of shoes and other clothing were obtained in Frederick, 250 pairs in Williamsport, and about 400 pairs in this city. They will not be sufficient to cover the bare feet of the army.

Our advance pickets are at Middleburg, on the Pennsylvania line. I await here the result of the movements upon Harpers Ferry and Martinsburg.[14]

The Confederate presence on the Maryland-Pennsylvania line was reported to Halleck by Pennsylvania Governor Andrew G. Curtin on September 13. "The enemy, in force of 3,000 infantry and some cavalry, occupied Middleburg, on Pennsylvania line, 7 o'clock this evening," he telegraphed. The next day, Curtin informed Lincoln: "The enemy hold possession with infantry and cavalry 4 miles from Greencastle. Heavy cannonading on south. It is supposed to be along Potomac near Harpers Ferry. We are massing forces rapidly, our people responding to the call in a most wonderful manner. Our organization, we hope, will deter movements upon the interior of Pennsylvania.[15]

Curtin had been alerted to the danger on September 6 as Confederate troops were crossing the Potomac and moving toward Frederick. He informed Secretary of War Stanton that a messenger he had sent out reported from Hagerstown that 6,000 Rebels had arrived in Frederick; that Brigadier General Julius White's troops, who had withdrawn from Winchester, were in grave danger in Martinsburg; and that "troops in large numbers" were needed in Pennsylvania's Cumberland Valley.[16]

Another report, received by Curtin from Chambersburg, estimated the number of Confederates troops in Frederick at 3,500 and stated that they needed food and supplies. It also quoted Stonewall Jackson as saying he planned to move through Adams, York, and Lancaster counties. Curtin also expressed the opinion that Jackson would seek supplies in the Cumberland Valley.[17]

Late in the afternoon of the 7th, Curtin informed Stanton, "Jackson occupies Frederick in force and is preparing to move north," and that the militia was being organized to meet him.[18] Reports of the Confederate threat, compounded by rumors, led to repeated requests from Curtin for Federal troops to defend the state.[19] On September 10 he called on Lincoln for at least 80,000, plus available forces from New York and other eastern states. The Pennsylvania militia and 50,000 men he hoped would be mustered in a few days would join them, Curtin added.[20]

Everything still seemed to be going well as Lee wrote Davis on September 12. "The advance of the Federal army was so slow at the time we left Frederick," he remarked later, "as to justify the belief that the reduction of Harpers Ferry would be accomplished and our troops concentrated before they would be called upon to meet it."[21]

McClellan was behaving true to form. On September 10 scouts reported Lee's army to be in the Frederick area, but McClellan was still uncertain whether the Confederates intended to move toward Baltimore or Pennsylvania.[22] Complicating his dilemma was Halleck's advice not to move too many troops from the Washington defenses, especially from forts on the Virginia side.[23]

On the 11th, from his camp in Rockville, Maryland, McClellan informed Halleck that evidence he had accumulated "goes to prove most conclusively that almost the entire rebel army, amounting to not less than 120,000 men, is in the vicinity of Frederick." If so, he added, forts south of Washington were not in danger.[24] A telegram from Lincoln on the 12th added to McClellan's uncertainty. He had been advised by Governor Curtin "that Jackson is crossing the Potomac at Williamsport, and probably the whole rebel army will be drawn from Maryland." The absence of any reports from Harpers Ferry or Martinsburg, Lincoln added, "corroborates the idea that the enemy is recrossing the Potomac. Please do not let him get off without being hurt."[25]

Union advance forces reached Frederick on the afternoon of the 12th and, after a skirmish with Confederate cavalry, took the city. The next day, the Union 12th Corps marched into the Frederick area.[26]

———————

Confederate optimism peaked on September 12. Events of the next two days dimmed Lee's confidence and ended, for the time being, his hopes of a successful invasion. The first gloomy note was in his letter to Davis on September 13. "I wish your views on its [the army's] operations could be realized, but so much depends upon circumstances beyond its control and the aid we may receive, that it is difficult to conjecture the result. To look to the safety of our own frontier and to operate untrammeled in an enemy's territory, you need not be told is very difficult. Every effort, however, will be made to acquire every advantage which our position and means may warrant."

Lee's major concern at the time was the straggling that arose after Second Bull Run. He informed Davis, "Our ranks are very much diminished—I fear from a third to one-half of the original numbers."[27] Later, he estimated his force at fewer than 40,000."[28]

Operations against Harpers Ferry were progressing more slowly than Lee had anticipated. He later explained, "The advance of the Federal army was so slow at the time we left Frederick as to justify the belief that the reduction of Harpers Ferry would be accomplished and our troops concentrated" before he would have to deal with McClellan's main force.[29]

Startling news reached Lee in Hagerstown on the night of September 13. Stuart reported "that McClellan had taken the advance, and was pushing with his whole force, and that [Stuart] was falling back." Later, Lee noted, "An alarming dispatch was also received from [D. H.] Hill to the same effect." He wakened Longstreet and, after discussing the situation, decided to turn back from Hagerstown and move to the support of Stuart and Hill.[30]

Even more alarming was Stuart's next dispatch. A copy of Special Orders No. 191 had been found by a Union soldier in Frederick and turned over to McClellan. A Marylander who had been at McClellan's headquarters at the time told Stuart that after reading the contents, McClellan raised his hands and exclaimed, "Now I know what to do!"[31]

The first thing he did was notify Lincoln:

I have the whole rebel force in front of me, but am confident, and no time shall be lost. I have a difficult task to perform, but with God's blessing will accomplish it. I think Lee has made a gross mistake, and that he will be severely punished for it. The army is in motion as rapidly as possible. I hope for a great success if the plans of the rebels remain unchanged.

I have all the plans of the rebels, and will catch them in their own trap if my men are equal to the emergency. I now feel that I can count on them as of old. All forces of Pennsylvania should be placed to cooperate at Chambersburg.[32]

In a dispatch to Major General William B. Franklin, commander of the 6th Corps, at 6:20 P.M. on September 13, McClellan stated, "I have now full information as to movements and intentions of the enemy." He ordered Franklin to move at daybreak on the 14th on the road through Crampton's Gap.

McClellan's intention, as explained to Franklin, was to move two columns across South Mountain to "cut the enemy in two and beat him in detail." Franklin, with the support of Major General Darius Couch's division, was to relieve endangered Union forces in Harpers Ferry. The right wing of his army, commanded by Ambrose Burnside, was to cross South Mountain on the road to Boonsboro, north of Crampton's Gap.[33]

At 11 P.M. McClellan informed Halleck: "An order from General R. E. Lee, addressed to General D. H. Hill, which has accidentally come into my hands this evening—the authenticity of which is unquestionable—discloses some of the plans of the enemy, and shows most conclusively that the main rebel army is now before us. Unless General Lee has changed his plans, I expect a severe general engagement tomorrow."[34]

McClellan was correct. The next day, after fighting at Crampton's Gap and South Mountain, Union forces held the mountain passes and were in position to press the Confederates the next morning.[35]

⸺⸺⸺•◖◗•⸺⸺⸺

Earlier on September 14 Lee had alerted McLaws (on Maryland Heights, opposite Harpers Ferry) of the threat of attack from Frederick. He urged him to push his operations "as rapidly as possible," but, if Harpers Ferry was not taken, to move toward Boonsboro to meet Longstreet, who was marching south from Hagerstown.[36]

A pessimistic note was dispatched to McLaws at 8 P.M. on the 14th by Colonel R. H. Chilton, assistant adjutant general on Lee's staff. "The day has gone against us and this army will go by Sharpsburg and cross the River. It is necessary for you to abandon your position tonight. Your troops you must have well in hand to unite with this command, which will retire by Sharpsburg."[37]

At 11:15 P.M. Chilton advised McLaws that, in addition, "I will mention that you might cross the Potomac, below Weverton, into Virginia. I believe there is a ford at the Point of Rocks, and at Berlin, below, but do not know whether either is accessible to you."[38]

The thought of an immediate withdrawal across the Potomac was dispelled shortly when Lee learned that Jackson expected Harpers Ferry to capitulate the next morning, September 15. He then decided to concentrate all his forces in Sharpsburg.[39]

———>•<———

Confederate forces on the three hills overlooking Harpers Ferry began firing on the afternoon of the 14th. The next morning the garrison surrendered. In addition to 11,000 men and arms, the Confederates captured seventy-three pieces of artillery and a large amount of supplies.[40]

Jackson left A. P. Hill to complete the surrender details and moved with the rest of his command to rejoin the main army in Sharpsburg. He arrived on the morning of September 16.[41] Walker's division also reached the Sharpsburg area on the 16th. McLaws arrived in the morning of September 17, followed by Hill in the afternoon.[42]

Lee positioned his troops in a line on hills and fields between Sharpsburg and Antietam Creek to meet McClellan's advance. It was there, on September 16–17, that the armies clashed in the Battle of Sharpsburg (or Antietam, as it was known in the North). With a force he estimated at fewer than 40,000, Lee held off repeated attacks by an army of more than 87,000 men. McClellan claimed victory over a force he estimated at 10,000 more than his own army.[43]

Both armies held their positions on the 18th, with no attempt to renew the conflict. After pondering the situation, McClellan ordered an attack at daylight on the 19th, but Lee was gone.[44]

The Confederates were withdrawing from Maryland. During the night of September 18, they crossed the Potomac at Shepherdstown and returned to Virginia.[45] The first attempt to invade the North had ended in disappointment.

Curtin's comment that Pennsylvanians were responding to the call for volunteers "in a most wonderful manner" created concern over a situation in Reading, the seat of Berks County. On September 18 Charles E. Smith, president of the Reading Railroad, notified Assistant Secretary of War John Tucker:

> Our shop hands at Reading have volunteered in a body. Governor Curtin has accepted them and ordered them to Harrisburg. If you cannot stop them our road will stop, and your coal [supply] will stop also. It requires instant attention, as they mean to leave today.[46]

Halting anthracite shipments would have created a serious problem for Northern industry and would have shut down Navy steamships. It also would have achieved a major objective of Jackson's invasion plan.

The problem was quickly solved. The Battle of Sharpsburg and Lee's subsequent withdrawal relieved the urgent need for volunteers in Pennsylvania. By September 23, "the danger of invasion having passed away," soldiers and volunteers were reported returning to their families.[47]

Later Lee explained, "Had the Lost Dispatch [Special Orders No. 191] not been lost, and had McClellan continued his cautious policy for two or three days longer, I would have had all my troops reconcentrated on the Md. side, stragglers up, men rested and I intended then to attack McClellan. It is probable that the loss of the dispatch changed the character of the campaign."[48]

Less than a week later Lee was thinking of renewing the campaign, an idea revealed in a letter to General William Loring on September 25. Loring had overcome enemy forces in the Kanawha Valley and pushed on to recapture Charles Town in western Virginia.[49] In his letter Lee congratulated Loring and told him that "great benefit would be derived if you could permanently destroy the Baltimore and Ohio Railroad," then move on to Clarksburg and Fairmont, Virginia, and destroy bridges there.

"You could then continue your course (if you thought proper) through Morgantown into Washington County, Pennsylvania, and supply your army with everything it wants." Lee closed the letter in this way:

This army is encamped on the Opequon [Creek], below Martinsburg, having returned from its expedition into Maryland. It will depend upon circumstances whether we will be able to recross into Maryland, but, should you operate down the Potomac, endeavor to keep yourself advised of the movements of this army and notify me of your position. Probably a combined movement into Pennsylvania may be concerted.[50]

Lee also informed Davis on September 25 of his advice to Loring but refrained from mentioning, specifically, the possibility of a combined advance into Pennsylvania. He did, however, tell the president, "In a military point of view, the best move, in my opinion, the army could make would be to advance upon Hagerstown and endeavor to defeat the enemy at that point.[51]

Obviously disappointment had been replaced by determination to renew the invasion quickly. In the weeks ahead it became clear that Jackson would be important in developing plans for the move north again.

PART 3

Back to Virginia

CHAPTER 16

After Sharpsburg

WITH HIS ARMY SAFELY SOUTH OF THE POTOMAC RIVER, LEE HAD TO focus on two courses of action. First was the possibility that McClellan would pursue and force another battle. The other was the prospect of strengthening his own army and renewing the invasion should McClellan become cautious again.

In late September there was no sign of boldness by McClellan and Lee began to think about heading north again. This was first shown in his letter to Loring on September 25. On September 28 he informed Davis that if sufficient clothes, shoes, and blankets could be found, "we could yet accomplish a great deal this fall."[1]

He was encouraged by the rising strength of his army, including recruits and returning stragglers. By September 30 it had grown to 52,790.[2] By October 10 it was up to 64,273.[3]

In the meantime, on September 18, Congress had passed an act providing for organization of divisions into army corps and authorizing Davis to appoint lieutenant generals to command them.[4] He asked Lee for recommendations.[5]

Lee responded that he thought two corps would do for his army and recommended Longstreet and Jackson for promotion. Lee said:

> My opinion of the merits of General Jackson has been greatly enhanced during this expedition. He is true, honest, and brave; has a single eye to the good of the service, and spares no exertion to accomplish his object.[6]

The relationship between Lee and Jackson had been firmly cemented and would become more evident as plans were made to renew the invasion. Such plans were noted by Jed Hotchkiss on October 7: "Gen. R. E. Lee came up to our Hd. Qrs. this morning and he and Gen. Jackson are having a long conversation aided [by] my maps of Maryland and Pennsylvania. No doubt another expedition is on foot."[7]

It was. The next day Lee ordered Stuart to take 1,200 to 1,500 cavalrymen into Pennsylvania.

> Cross the Potomac above Williamsport, leave Hagerstown and Greencastle on your right, and proceed to the rear of Chambersburg and endeavor to destroy the railroad bridge over the branch of the Conococheague [Creek].
>
> Any other damage that you can inflict upon the enemy or his means of transportation you will also execute. You are desired to gain all information of the position, force, and probable intention of the enemy which you can, and in your progress into Pennsylvania you will take measures to inform yourself of the various routes that you may take on your return to Virginia.

Stuart was further instructed to keep the mission a secret and "should you be led so far east as to make it better, in your opinion, to continue around to the Potomac, you will have to cross the river in the vicinity of Leesburg."[8] On October 9 Stuart set out.

The Confederates took possession of Chambersburg on the 10th, cut the wires, and blocked railroad lines. The next morning they destroyed large supplies of arms and ammunition there as well as the machine shops, depot buildings, and several loaded trains of the Cumberland Valley Railroad. They could not destroy the iron railroad bridge over Conococheague Creek, north of town, on the road to Harrisburg.

Stuart then turned east toward Gettysburg, rode around the Union army, crossed the Potomac near Leesburg, and returned to camp on October 14. In his written report to Lee, Stuart included an expedition map, made by his engineer officer, Captain William W. Blackford.[9]

Lee wrote to George Randolph on October 14:

> His expedition was eminently successful, and accomplished without other loss than the wounding of one man. He obtained many remounts for his cavalry and artillery, and deserves much credit for his prudence and enterprise.

From the information he was able to obtain, I am inclined to believe that General McClellan has detached no part of his army eastward, but, on the contrary, has been receiving reinforcements. His main army is posted west of the Blue Ridge range, and stretches from Hagerstown to Rockville.[10]

Under the circumstances, Lee was prompted to delay, for the time being, any effort to continue the invasion.

On October 15 Lee wrote Loring, "The season is now so far advanced that I doubt whether an expedition into Western Pennsylvania, which I once proposed to you, can now be advantageously undertaken."[11] The next day Lee added, "The condition of things [has been] so changed since my letter of September 25th, that I do not recommend your advance to the Potomac merely with a view to cooperate with any movement of this army. Circumstances may arise to draw this army in another direction before you could reach the Potomac."[12]

———◦———

Immediately following the Battle of Sharpsburg, McClellan was convinced that the Confederates would not resume the northward movement. On September 20, the day after Lee completed his withdrawal from Maryland, McClellan observed, "The disorganized rebel army has rapidly returned to Virginia, its dreams of invading Pennsylvania dissipated for ever."[13]

In a telegram to Halleck on the 20th McClellan pointed out that Lee would have to depend on Richmond for ammunition and provisions. He suggested that Major General Nathaniel Banks, commander of the defenses of Washington, "be directed to send out a cavalry force to cut their supply communications opposite Washington. This would seriously embarrass their operations, and will aid this army materially."[14]

The suggestion was acted upon two days later in the first of four expeditions by Banks in September and early October.[15] In the same period McClellan sent scouts into Virginia seven times.[16]

McClellan also reacted on his own front. He reoccupied Maryland Heights on September 20, then Harpers Ferry two days later.[17] His confidence faded quickly, however, and on September 23 he told Halleck that his army had been weakened by casualties and that all possible reinforcements should be sent to him from Washington and other points. "A defeat at this juncture would be ruinous to our cause," he added.[18]

He was more pessimistic in a dispatch to Halleck four days later: "This army is not now in condition to undertake another campaign nor to bring on another battle, unless great advantages are offered by some mistake of the enemy, or pressing military exigencies render it necessary." Instead, he would prepare to attack the Confederates if they attempted another crossing of the Potomac.[19]

At the time McClellan had a force of 93,149, about 40,000 more than Lee had. There also were 71,210 troops in the defenses of Washington.[20]

McClellan's timidity again prompted Lincoln to take action. On October 6 Halleck told McClellan: "The President directs that you cross the Potomac and give battle to the enemy or drive him south. Your army must move now while the roads are good." Lincoln also recommended that the move should be made between Washington and the enemy army, rather than in the Shenandoah Valley. If so, he added, McClellan could receive 30,000 reinforcements.[21]

McClellan countered that the move would have to be delayed because of a serious lack of shoes, clothing, blankets, and cavalry forces. He also was alarmed by Stuart's raid into Pennsylvania and felt it was necessary to shift troops to other points in an attempt to disrupt that movement.[22]

McClellan's concern over Stuart's raid was reflected by an interruption of almost a week in the reconnaissance missions in Virginia by Union troops that had been started on September 20. The missions were resumed on October 13 and four expeditions—two from Washington and two from McClellan's army—were carried out in less than two weeks.[23]

The resumption of enemy reconnaissance alerted Lee to the possibility of a Union advance into Virginia. The brief occupation of Thoroughfare Gap in the Bull Run Mountains and the westward movement of other Union troops prompted action on October 22. Lee sent Brigadier General John G. Walker's division east of the Blue Ridge to observe enemy activity and, if possible, repulse any further westward movement.[24]

At the same time Stonewall Jackson moved east of Winchester on the road between Berryville and Charles Town. Jackson was to be prepared to oppose a Union advance from Harpers Ferry or a movement into the Shenandoah Valley from the Washington area.[25]

Lee also noted in a letter to Davis on October 22 that "the time is fast approaching" when it would become necessary to prepare for the winter. Although he was uncertain of the enemy's intention, Lee felt one Confederate force should be south of the Rappahannock River and in front of Richmond, while another remained in the Valley.[26] His uncertainty was dispelled a few days later. On October 26 McClellan's army began crossing the Potomac River on pontoon bridges, almost three weeks after Lincoln had ordered the advance into Virginia. The crossing was completed on November 2.[27]

By the end of October Union troops were observed moving eastward from the mountains. Longstreet's corps was moved across the Blue Ridge to Culpeper Court House and one of Jackson's divisions advanced east of the ridge.[28] Once again Lee put aside thoughts of invading enemy territory and turned his attention to the defense of Richmond.

This was evident in a letter to Davis on November 6. Lee informed the president that enemy forces "are advancing steadily from the Potomac, their right moving along the base of the Blue Ridge, and their left resting on the Orange and Alexandria Railroad [about twenty-five miles east]. I have not yet been able to ascertain the strength of the enemy, but presume it is the whole of McClellan's army, as I learn that his whole force from Harpers Ferry to Hagerstown has been withdrawn from Maryland. He is also moving more rapidly than usual and it looks like a real advance." Lee noted that, if the advance continued, Longstreet and Jackson would move south and unite around Swift Run Gap. He also recommended reinforcing troops south of the James River.[29]

McClellan's intention, he later explained, was to separate Confederate forces and beat them one at a time, to force them to withdraw and open the way for another on-to-Richmond campaign from Fredericksburg, or for his army to move again to the Peninsula.[30]

Time had run out for McClellan, however. On the night of November 7 a messenger arrived with an order from Lincoln removing him from command of the Army of the Potomac. Major General Ambrose E. Burnside assumed command November 9.[31]

Northern morale, boosted by the repulse of the Confederate invasion in September, dimmed again in October and early November. This was not only because of McClellan's renewed caution and replacement but also because of another wave of internal strife on the home front.

Trouble surfaced in October in the anthracite region of northeastern Pennsylvania shortly after Stuart's seizure of Chambersburg and his ride around McClellan's army. News of the situation reached Stanton at 2:30 P.M. October 22.

"The draft is being resisted in several counties of the state," Governor Curtin wrote. "In Schuylkill County, I am just informed that 1,000 armed men are assembled and will not suffer the train to move with the drafted men to this place [Harrisburg]." Curtin requested permission to use troops in the state, especially cavalry at Carlisle Barracks, "to crush this effort instantly." Stanton immediately authorized Curtin to call on the cavalry "and any other military force in your State."[32]

In a message to Stanton at 11 A.M. on October 24 Curtin asked for more troops and said:

> We all think the resistance to draft is the first appearance of a conspiracy, and, unless crushed at once, cannot say how far it may extend. We know there are 5,000 men in the league in three counties, and all work is interrupted by them.[33]

Curtin's reference to "5,000 men in the league" drew attention to a large group of militant Irish coal miners known as the Molly Maguires. The secret organization, an offshoot of the Ancient Order of Hibernians, was reported to have been operating in the coal fields during the 1840s and 1850s. It intensified its activities with the outbreak of the Civil War. Initially, the Molly Maguires joined Peace Democrats in opposing the war. Then, in 1862, their opposition to the draft resulted in a wave of terrorism that extended into the following year.[34]

An 1863 report stated that "committees of these men have waited upon operators and have told them that they must stop work; that they intend to end the war by cutting off the supply of coal and thus embarrass the Government and create coal riots in the large cities. This is a part of the rebel programme."[35]

Charges that labor violence was a Confederate plot, though understandable in wartime, have not been corroborated. Yet a major objective of the invasion plan that Jackson first proposed in late 1861 was to close the mines, disrupt the economy, and "force the people of the North to understand what it will cost them to hold the South in the Union at the bayonet's point." The early troubles created by the Molly Maguires in the anthracite fields in 1861 and 1862 had, indeed, contributed toward Jackson's objective. Production of anthracite in 1862 dropped more than 7 percent below that of 1860.[36]

CHANGES IN ANTHRACITE COAL PRODUCTION AND SHIPMENTS
FROM 1860 TO 1863. FROM EAVENSON, COAL, P. 498.

YEAR	PRODUCTION (net tons)	CHANGE	SHIPMENTS (net tons)	CHANGE
1860	10,983,972		9,534,697	
1861	10,245,156	− 738,816	8,908,775	− 625,922
1862	10,186,435	− 58,721	8,813,736	− 95,039
1863	12,267,446	+ 2,081,011	10,713,926	+ 1,900,190

Curtin's message of October 24 was submitted to Lincoln and Halleck. In response, Stanton told Curtin that the federal government was behind him and reiterated that 1,000 cavalry troops at Carlisle Barracks were retained for Curtin's use. In addition, "one or two regiments that have served through the war" were in Washington and available for service in Pennsylvania if needed.[37] On October 27 Curtin informed Stanton: "I am happy to say that for the present the necessity for use of force in Schuylkill County is over. The presence of Bishop Wood [Bishop James F. Wood of the Philadelphia Roman Catholic Diocese], who kindly went up when requested, has relieved us all."[38]

October and November produced further bad news for the Lincoln administration. In Pennsylvania, Ohio, and Indiana, the 1862 elections were held on October 14, earlier than the customary November date observed in the other states.[39] In all, six states that had gone for Lincoln in 1860 swung into the Democratic column in the off-year elections— New York, Pennsylvania, Indiana, Ohio, Illinois, and Wisconsin.

Democrats gained thirty-one seats in the House of Representatives, increasing their number to seventy-five but failing to gain a majority. The biggest losses were in Illinois, where Republicans lost fourteen seats, and in Indiana, where eight were lost.

In New York Horatio Seymour, a Democrat, was elected governor by a majority of 10,000 votes. In Pennsylvania the tide swung from a 60,000-vote majority for the Republicans in 1860 to a 4,000-vote majority for the Democrats in 1862.[40]

A Democratic newspaper in Pennsylvania, the *Lancaster Intelligencer,* said in a November 11 editorial: "The November elections eclipse, if possible, the October results in the brilliancy of the Democratic victory achieved. The ball set in motion by the Democracy of Pennsylvania, Ohio and Indiana, has been rolling on, increasing in magnitude and velocity."[41] It was typical of growing Democratic confidence in the party's efforts to achieve a peaceful conclusion to the war and save the Union.

The elections were only a little more than a month past when more bad news came from Indiana. On December 22 Stanton was informed by Colonel H. B. Carrington, head of the mustering service headquarters in Indianapolis, that "a secret order exists in this vicinity to incite desertion of soldiers with their arms, to resist arrest of deserters, to stop enlistments, to disorganize the army, to prevent further drafting—in short, a distinct avowal to stop this war."[42]

Burnside was preparing for another move against Richmond. He wanted to remain north of the Rappahannock River, move to Falmouth, then cross the river near Fredericksburg. At that point, Burnside explained, "we will be on the shortest road to Richmond; the taking of which should be the great object of the campaign. The fall of that place would tend more to cripple the rebel cause than almost any other military event."[43]

When Lee learned on November 18 that Union troops were moving toward Fredericksburg, on the south side of the Rappahannock, most of Longstreet's corps headed for that point. Jackson, who had crossed the Blue Ridge and was near Orange Court House, was ordered on November 26 to advance toward Fredericksburg.[44]

During this period invasion apparently was still on Lee's mind. In addition to scouts assigned to report on enemy troop movements, he had sent others into the North to gather information. On November 19, in reporting to Davis the beginning of Burnside's movement toward Fredericksburg, he noted, "My scouts report no transports at Washington and Alexandria."[45]

On December 8 Lee informed Davis, "A scout who has been absent for several weeks returned last night. He has visited the cities from Washington to New York inclusive." The scout had observed troops being assembled on Staten Island, New York, apparently for a seaborne expedition. At the Brooklyn Navy Yard, he was shown ironclads being prepared, and in Washington was told "by a person in the Coast Survey Office" that the expedition intended to attack Mobile, Alabama. The scout also reported that five regiments, infantry and cavalry, had left the Washington area to join Burnside's army. The scout, Lee wrote, felt that the movements were intended for an attack on Richmond by Burnside.[46] Scouting in enemy territory was evident as late as June 1863, when Confederates were marching toward Gettysburg.

—————

Lee and Burnside met at the Battle of Fredericksburg on December 11–13. Union troops who repeatedly attacked Confederate positions on heights west of the city were repulsed, as were attacks south of there. For two days, the armies faced each other before Burnside's forces withdrew across the Rappahannock on December 15.[47]

The battle brought 1862 to a dismal end for the Union. Northern morale was seriously shaken by defeats in eastern Virginia, the major theater of the war. Edward Bates, Lincoln's attorney general, summed up the situation:

We cannot deny that the People have extended to this administration a reasonable degree of supporting confidence and, that Congress with unhesitating liberality, has granted all our demands for men, money, means and appliances—and all this for the avowed purpose of enabling us to suppress the rebellion.

But we have not suppressed the rebellion. We have, during the whole of this year, made no important advance toward its suppression. On the contrary, our present position is, relatively, worse than it was last spring.[48]

As 1862 faded, a nation torn by internal discord and the realities of the war faced the new year of 1863. In Virginia, where the fighting was closest to the line that divided North and South, the opposing armies watched and waited, each in winter quarters set up after the Battle of Fredericksburg.[49]

CHAPTER 17

Planning Resumed

THE WINTER OF 1862–63 WAS THE MOST SIGNIFICANT—AND REVEALING—
period in Confederate preparations to resume the invasion of the North.
In early January, there was little military activity to break the monotony
of winter camps.[1] Important action was taking place, however, in Lee's
headquarters to renew the invasion interrupted at Sharpsburg in September. Jed Hotchkiss, Jackson's mapmaker, observed:

> While tented in his winter quarters back of Fredericksburg, Lee
> was considering a plan of campaign for the coming spring, having
> frequent consultations with Jackson and Stuart.[2]

The meetings with Jackson were not unusual. With his newfound
confidence in Jackson, as expressed to Davis a few months earlier, Lee obviously was seeking the opinions and plans of his 2nd Corps commander.

Stuart's presence was important, especially since he now knew Pennsylvania roads and had the map prepared by Captain Blackford.
Even more important was that from the conferences, Stuart knew
what Lee and Jackson were hoping to do and how they hoped to do it.
This became a factor in June, when Confederate troops were moving
toward Pennsylvania.

Longstreet was not mentioned among the conferees. During the
early winter of 1863, he was laying out lines for fieldworks and rifle pits
covering possible enemy approaches on upper fords of the Rappahannock

River. After the war Longstreet said he did not learn of the invasion plan until his return from North Carolina in May 1863. Lee noted that Longstreet and two of his divisions were detached in February to serve south of the James River and did not rejoin the army until after the Battle of Chancellorsville in the first week of May.[3]

———◦———

During the winter Jackson also focused on the invasion and "spent many hours in consultation with his topographical engineer."[4] Before the war, when Hotchkiss had walked the Cumberland and Virginia valleys, he became familiar with routes that led to Harrisburg, Pennsylvania. More important was his knowledge of anthracite country, gained in the year he had spent in the Lykens Valley as a teacher. Regarding the meetings, Hotchkiss noted:

> Jackson also was thinking about his favorite design for a campaign into Pennsylvania, to break up the mining operations in the anthracite coal fields, and so seriously cripple the enemy by cutting off fuel supplies for his manufacturing establishments, his railways, and his numerous steamships.[5]

———◦———

As the invasion plan developed, Lee had to deal with two serious problems. One was obtaining enough flour and meat for his men. In a letter to Secretary of War George Randolph on November 17, 1862, Lee attributed much of the straggling to insufficient rations. At the time, he pointed out, their "whole ration consisted of bread and meat."[6]

By late December adequate forage for artillery horses also was a problem. Many of the batteries had to be moved to other areas and commanders were ordered to "resuscitate and restore them [the horses] to proper condition for the spring campaign."[7]

In early January Lee again focused on the need for food. In a letter to the commissary general, Colonel L. B. Northrop, Lee pointed out that mills around his camp could not supply enough flour for his troops and that it was necessary to "draw much more subsistence" from Richmond.[8] On January 12 he informed the new secretary of war, James A. Seddon, that, because of poor grazing, available cattle "will hardly carry us through the present month." He asked that salt meat be sent from Richmond for his troops.[9] This need was emphasized soon at a Cabinet meeting in Richmond.

————————

Lee's other problem was the strength of the Army of Northern Virginia. At the end of 1862 he had 70,972 men ready for duty.[10] That was an increase of only 6,699 over the number on October 10. It also was about half the number reported in the part of the Army of the Potomac that his troops faced on December 31.[11]

In a letter to Seddon on January 10 Lee urgently asked for reinforcements and that the public be urged to support this step. He stated that:

> The success with which our efforts have been crowned, under the blessing of God, should not betray our people into the dangerous delusion that the armies now in the field are sufficient to bring this war to a successful and speedy termination.
>
> While the spirit of our soldiers is unabated, their ranks have been greatly thinned by the casualties of battle and the diseases of the camp. More than once have most promising opportunities been lost for want of men to take advantage of them, and victory itself has been made to put on the appearance of defeat, because our diminished and exhausted troops have been unable to renew a successful struggle against fresh numbers of the enemy.
>
> The lives of our soldiers are too precious to be sacrificed in the attainment of successes that inflict no loss upon the enemy beyond the actual loss in battle. Every victory should bring us nearer to the great end which it is the object of this war to reach.

Lee urged that the War Department call on governors to help the recruiting effort and "to arouse the people to a sense of the vital importance of the subject." He added:

> If we would save the honor of our families from pollution, our social system from destruction, let every effort be made, every means employed, to fill and maintain the ranks of our armies, until God, in his mercy, shall bless us with the establishment of our independence.[12]

Two days later Davis told Congress: "If we mark the history of the present year by resolute perseverance in the path we have hitherto pursued, by vigorous effort in the development of our resources for defense, and by the continued exhibition of the same unfaltering courage in our soldiers and able conduct in their leaders as have distinguished the past, we have every reason to expect that this will be the closing year of the war."[13]

That day, January 12, Davis also told Lee that North Carolina Governor Zebulon B. Vance had asked if the general could "come down for a few days and survey the situation" in that state. Davis added that "your presence there would be important; indeed seems necessary," but he advised Lee that the decision was his own.[14]

Vance was worried by an expedition of 10,000 Union troops, backed by cavalry and artillery, from New Bern to Goldsboro from December 11 to 20.[15] This was followed by reports early in January of an enemy force being assembled in New Bern for "a feint on Goldsboro, but really intended" for an attack on Wilmington, an important seaport on the Cape Fear River.[16]

In the aftermath of the Goldsboro expedition and amid signs of an attack on Wilmington, Lee detached from his army a division commanded by Brigadier General Robert Ransom, Jr., and sent it to Richmond. Lee directed that the division could be sent as far south as Petersburg.[17] Then, in a letter to Davis on January 6, Lee expressed his own uneasiness over affairs in North Carolina and suggested that reinforcements be sent there from General P. G. T. Beauregard's command in South Carolina.[18]

On the 13th, after receiving Vance's request, Lee informed Davis that there were signs that Burnside was moving. Lee could not determine what the Union commander intended to do. If Burnside should retire, Lee added, he was prepared to send some troops to North Carolina. But he feared that the enemy wanted to draw troops away from his army so that Burnside could move against Richmond.[19]

A few days later he left for Richmond and was there on January 16, according to a War Department clerk, "doubtless to see about the pressure upon him for reinforcement in North Carolina."[20] Lee and Davis evidently decided that some troops should be ready to move south. That day Lee told his headquarters that the brigades of William D. Pender and James H. Lane should move to Richmond.[21] The order was issued the next day by Colonel Taylor, assistant adjutant general on Lee's staff.[22] Ransom's division also left Petersburg for North Carolina.[23]

Lee apparently also met with the Cabinet on January 16 on another problem that was troubling Confederate leaders—resuming the invasion.

"One of the considerations favoring such a policy," Postmaster General John H. Reagan stated, "was that supplies for our army were much reduced—and these were abundant in the territory of the enemy. Another consideration was that a successful campaign in the territory adjacent to Washington, Baltimore, and Philadelphia might cause the withdrawal of the [Union] troops menacing Vicksburg [Mississippi] and Port Hudson [Louisiana]."

Reagan said that Vicksburg had been threatened since the previous fall and that Lee's proposal for an 1863 invasion—and its link to Vicksburg—was, in his opinion, the most serious matter ever determined by the Cabinet.[24]

Reagan did not mention a date, but events in the Western Theater indicate that Lee's appearance at the meeting was on January 16. On November 2 Major General Ulysses S. Grant had launched his first movement against Vicksburg overland through northern Mississippi. In late December and January, he shifted the axis to the Mississippi River.[25]

This, apparently, was what Reagan meant as "menacing Vicksburg and Port Hudson." According to Grant, "the real work of the campaign and siege of Vicksburg" began after he had taken personal command of the operation on January 30.[26] Grant's movement became a factor later in the Confederate Cabinet's continued consideration of the plan to carry the war north of the Potomac River.

When Lee returned from Richmond, another problem was developing on his front. On January 19 he advised Davis that from information received from scouts, "I believe that their army [Burnside's], instead of being diminished by detachments to North Carolina, has been reinforced since the battle of 13th December [Fredericksburg].

"I therefore have suspended the march of [Pender's and Lane's] brigades ordered to North Carolina until I can ascertain something more definitely. If in your opinion the necessity there is more urgent than here, I will dispatch them immediately."[27]

Two days later Lee informed the president, "A scout just returned from Washington City reports that the impression is prevalent there that General Burnside's army is preparing to advance." Supply transports were in the Potomac River and two regiments of cavalry had just left Washington to join Burnside's army.

Another scout, he said, "just returned from the vicinity of Potomac Creek" east of Fredericksburg, reported wharves were being built in that area and that there were rumors of a railroad being constructed toward Port Royal, on the Rappahannock River about fifteen miles southeast of Fredericksburg, to transport siege guns.

Another scout on the enemy's right flank indicated that the Union army was "under marching orders. I think it is certain that some movement is contemplated by General Burnside, but whether it is toward Richmond or into winter quarters is not clear."[28]

Davis responded, "My opinion is that you would not be justified at this time in making further detachments from your command. We have nothing from North Carolina to develop the purpose of the enemy there, and it may well be that the late storms have interfered with his programme."[29]

Information from Lee's scouts was accurate. On January 20 Burnside began moving troops up the Rappahannock above Fredericksburg. It was part of the plan he had proposed to undertake a general movement toward Richmond. A storm lashed the area that night, flooding streams and making roads impassable. The "Mud March," as it became known, was halted for two days before the troops were ordered on January 23 to return to their camps.[30] Two days later, at his own request, Burnside was relieved and was replaced by Major General Joseph Hooker.[31]

———⟶⊛⟵———

The difficulty in feeding Confederate troops worsened in late January. On the 23rd Lee informed Davis that "unless regular supplies can be obtained, I fear the efficiency of the army will be reduced by many thousand men, when already the army is inferior in numbers to that of the enemy." He also pointed out that only a quarter of a pound of salt meat was available for each man's daily ration.[32]

On the 26th he told Seddon, "As far as I can learn, we have about one week's supply, four days' fresh meat, four days' salt meat. After that is exhausted, I know not whence further supplies can be drawn. The question of provisioning the army is becoming one of greater difficulty every day."[33] In mid-February Seddon advised Lee that meat shipments were being expedited from Atlanta.[34]

In the meantime Lee had decided to seek supplies from the Shenandoah Valley. On January 27 he suggested to Brigadier General William E. Jones, commander in the Valley District, to "collect cattle or salt meat for our use."[35]

In early February invasion planning was interrupted by developments in North Carolina and the Shenandoah Valley. On February 3 Seddon advised Lee that troops in Wilmington, North Carolina, had been returned to Beauregard in Charleston, who anticipated an attack. Seddon asked Lee if he could send any men to North Carolina.[36]

Lee replied on February 4, "I will do so if you think the exigency requires it." But, he pointed out, Hooker might move against Richmond and Lee was trying to prepare to meet that threat. "I would suggest that the troops now in North Carolina should be concentrated as near as possible to Wilmington, leaving their places to be supplied, if necessary, from here."[37]

Seddon responded, "My dispatch was intended to keep you advised of the apprehended movements of the enemy, and to submit to your judgment the propriety of either moving or making preparations for moving some portion of your forces either here [Richmond] or toward North Carolina. I have just ordered, under direction of the President, General D. H. Hill to duty in North Carolina."[38]

A week later Lee expressed his deep concern over manpower. In a letter to Seddon on February 11, he urged:

> I think it very important to increase the strength of all our armies to the maximum by the opening of the next campaign. Now is the time to gather all our strength and to prepare for the struggle which must take place in the next three months.[39]

With Ransom's brigades gone, the January return showed the Army of Northern Virginia at 72,226 officers and men, only 1,254 more than at the end of December.[40] Lee told Seddon that he had sent out details from every brigade to roundup deserters and absentees.[41]

Lee also was concerned about northwestern Virginia. Brigadier General Robert E. Milroy, Union commander west of the Allegheny Mountains, had angered the populace with several harsh orders aimed at Southern sympathizers, including ones requiring oaths of allegiance and demands for money to reimburse loyalists whose property had been damaged or destroyed. Some carried the threat of execution.

On January 7 Alexander R. Boteler, Confederate legislator and aide to Stonewall Jackson, sent copies of Milroy's orders to U.S. Secretary of

War Edwin Stanton. He wanted to alert the Union government to Milroy's "high-handed outrages."[42]

Davis also directed Lee to call upon U.S. authorities "to prevent the savage atrocities" threatened by Milroy. Lee sent a copy of the message to Halleck and asked "whether your Government will tolerate the execution of an order so barbarous and so revolting to every principle of justice and humanity."[43] On January 14 Halleck replied that if the order was authentic, Milroy's action would be disapproved."[44]

Milroy, however, had been ordered in late December to move east and join Brigadier General B. F. Kelley, commander of the defenses of the upper Potomac. By January 4 Milroy and his troops were in Winchester,[45] creating a new concern for Lee.

———————— ·>•<· ————————

On February 13 Lee informed General William Jones in the Valley District, "I have determined to take advantage of the present time to endeavor to restrict General Milroy's possession of the Valley, if he cannot be otherwise disturbed." Jones was told to be ready to join Stuart, who was to be in charge of the operation.[46]

Lee told Seddon that he had heard that Hooker's 9th Corps was moving south on the Potomac. Uncertainty over its destination prompted Lee to move Major General George E. Pickett's division from Longstreet's 1st Corps to Richmond. Major General John B. Hood's division was moved to Hanover Junction, north of Richmond.[47] On February 15 Lee informed Stuart that Union troops had landed in Newport News and advised him to delay sending troops to the Valley. Stuart was to notify Jones of the decision.[48]

Three days later Lee sent Longstreet south to place Pickett and Hood in position to defend Richmond and Petersburg.[49] On February 25 Adjutant General Samuel Cooper notified Longstreet that he had been assigned to command the Department of Virginia and North Carolina. The next day Longstreet established his headquarters in Petersburg.[50]

Longstreet quickly decided to take the offensive, especially against Union forces in New Bern, North Carolina. "If there is a chance of doing anything, we should not be idle," he told D. H. Hill. "We are much more likely to succeed by operating ourselves than by lying still to await the enemy's time for thorough preparation before he moves upon us."[51]

Lee was not enthusiastic. "There are no signs of further embarkation of troops [from Hooker's army] or collection of transports," he told

Longstreet on March 7. "Where the large force said to be landing at New Bern comes from I cannot conceive. I hope you will be able to get accurate information and put yourself in communication with General Beauregard [in Charleston], so as to be prepared for all emergencies. You had better keep yourself advised of the movements of the force at Newport News."[52]

Lee's cautious attitude undoubtedly was prompted by recent events near Fredericksburg and in Richmond. The first occurred in camp on February 23, when Jed Hotchkiss noted:

> I got secret orders from the General [Jackson] to prepare a map of the Valley of Virginia extended to Harrisburg, Pa., and then on to Philadelphia. The preparation [was to be] kept a profound secret.

He went to work immediately on a map of Cumberland County, Pennsylvania. He labored almost daily before completing it on March 10. He also obtained Cumberland County maps from Captain Blackford of Stuart's staff.[53] As well, he used county maps obtained "by agents sent into the southern counties of Pennsylvania for this purpose."[54]

———➤●◄———

On February 26 Lee wrote to Davis, "I have for some time been doubtful of the intentions of the enemy. The weather for the last eight or ten days has been so unfavorable for observation that it has prevented the scouts from obtaining information." It was apparent, he pointed out, that Hooker occupied a line from Falmouth to Aquia. Then he added:

> I believe for the present the purpose [Hooker's] of crossing the Rappahannock is abandoned, and that the late storms or other causes have suspended the movements recently in progress. The dispositions I have described may be intended to continue the remainder of the winter. The weather and condition of the country forbid any military operations. The last fall of snow was fully a foot deep. The rain of last night and today will add to the discomfort of the troops and the hardships of our horses. I had hoped that the latter would have been in good condition for the spring campaign.
>
> As soon as I can ascertain what is the probable intention of the enemy, and feel that I can leave with propriety, I will visit Richmond and consult with you on the condition of things in North Carolina, &c.[55]

Two days later, a momentous decision was made at a Cabinet meeting in Richmond. Postmaster General Reagan noted Grant's intention "to get below Vicksburg. . . . Our means of communications with western Louisiana, Arkansas and Texas largely depended on our command of the Mississippi." The loss of Vicksburg and Port Hudson would mean "bisecting of the Confederacy by the line of the Mississippi, in which event we should be deprived, in a large measure, of the men and supplies west of that river."

As the Union movement down the Mississippi progressed, civil and military authorities appealed for reinforcements to defend Vicksburg. Davis asked Cabinet members to meet with him to consider the situation. "We assembled early—it was Saturday—and remained in session in the anxious discussion until after nightfall," Reagan wrote. He added:

> I shall never forget that scene. The President and members of the Cabinet fully realized the grave character of the question to be considered. General Lee did not meet with us on this occasion, though he often did so in his capacity as Military Adviser to the President, and latterly as general in the field. He was not a man of many words and when he spoke it was in the fulness of conviction. He had expressed his views on the subject of a campaign north of the Potomac.
>
> Every possible contingency was pointed out in our discussion [that Saturday], and it early became apparent to me that I stood almost alone. I urged that we should let it be given out that we intended to send the Army of [Northern] Virginia north of the Potomac, and that we should meantime strengthen the defenses of Richmond, collect supplies for a six months' siege, and at the proper time dispatch 25,000 or 30,000 of General Lee's troops to Vicksburg.
>
> It was observed that this would involve the necessity of abandoning the Shenandoah Valley. I admitted that we might have to do so temporarily, but added that there would remain with General Lee some 50,000 veteran and victorious troops for the protection of Richmond. I further contended that by sending a part of General Lee's army, and a part of the Army of Tennessee confronting

General [Don Carlos] Buell, and by directing General [Joseph] Johnston to collect and forward all the men and supplies he could from the Gulf States, General Grant might be crushed. My plan involved waiting until he got well on the east side of the Mississippi and then to fall on him with such a force as to prevent his recrossing the stream, then to destroy his army.

It was urged in opposition to my view that the best way to protect Vicksburg was to put Washington and Baltimore in danger and thus cause the withdrawal of troops from Grant's army for their defense. To this I demurred. General Grant, I said, had reached a position which would prevent dealing with him in that way, and that what he was doing showed that he intended Vicksburg should fall if his army was not destroyed.

In the end it was determined that General Lee should cross the Potomac and put himself in position to threaten Washington, Baltimore, and Philadelphia, and that General Johnston should get together such men and supplies as he could in the Gulf States and go to the relief of [Lieutenant General John C.] Pemberton."[56]

Reagan went home "an unhappy man, for I believed we had made a great mistake. I remained restless till probably midnight before going to bed, and did not go to sleep that night."

Reagan got up before daylight and wrote a note to Davis describing his feelings, and asking the president to convene the Cabinet the next day. Davis expressed his intention to do so. It was not necessary, Reagan noted, because before Davis sent out his call, the Cabinet members had met in his office. Then it "appeared useless to attempt a further consideration of that subject."[57]

In his memoirs Reagan did not mention the date of the meeting, other than that it was on a Saturday. There is strong evidence that the date was February 28. In his diary entry of Sunday, March 1, J. B. Jones, a clerk in the War Department, wrote: "Met Judge Reagan yesterday, just from Council Board [Cabinet meeting]. I thought he seemed dejected. He said if the enemy succeeded in getting command of the Mississippi River, the Confederacy would be 'cut in two,' and he intimated his preference of giving up Richmond if it would save Texas, etc. for the Confederacy." This clearly describes Reagan's feelings in his own account. On March 10 Jones noted in his diary, "We may cross the Potomac again."[58] Before April Lee and Seddon made that clear.

———➤●◄———

The decision had been made. Lee was to invade the North with two major objectives: to obtain supplies and, by threatening Washington, Baltimore, and possibly Philadelphia, to relieve the pressure on Vicksburg. Details of the plans discussed by Lee, Jackson, and Stuart developed later. March was a time of preparing for the invasion, with the hope of launching it by April 1.

CHAPTER 18

Preparing to Move

WEATHER WAS AN IMPORTANT INFLUENCE ON MILITARY OPERATIONS IN 1863, just as it had been in early 1862. There was heavy rain and snow in January, and February was just as bad. By the end of the month, there had been ten days of rain or snow, while temperatures had ranged from freezing to balmy—typical Virginia winter weather. March opened with more rain.[1]

Weather, however, did not affect the invasion planning. Following the cabinet meeting on February 28, a chain of events showed that preparations were under way. On March 2 an unexpected proposal came from Brigadier General John D. Imboden, commander of the Northwestern Virginia Brigade. He offered Lee a plan for operations west of the Shenandoah Mountains. The first object was to destroy all Baltimore and Ohio Railroad bridges from Oakland to Grafton in western Virginia; to neutralize Union forces in Beverly, Philippi, and Buckhannon; to enlist men for his brigade; to hold the area long enough "to overthrow the local government"; and to aid Confederate sympathizers in that section.

Imboden also suggested that Jones's troops in the Valley District threaten Milroy in Winchester and then move toward Romney, the target of Jackson's first offensive in the winter of 1861–62. In support of this plan Imboden added:

I assure you, general, that at no period since the war commenced has the opportunity ever been so good to gain a foothold in the northwest [section of Virginia]. The expedition [however] cannot be safely undertaken before about the 1st of April, on account of the swollen streams, resulting from the unusually large fall of snow in the mountains this winter.[2]

At the time Imboden had fewer than 1,000 men ready for duty.[3] He asked Lee for reinforcements. "I know how much you need every man," Imboden added, "but I hope the service proposed for these men here would result in weakening the enemy in your front, by cutting one of his main lines of supply, more than you would be weakened by the temporary withdrawal of 600 or 800 men."[4]

The possibility of a movement in western Virginia, similar to the "second column" operation discussed with General William Loring the previous summer, appealed to Lee. On March 11, he informed Imboden that he had approved the plan. "I think, if carried out with your energy and promptness, it will succeed.

"I will endeavor to give you the two regiments you ask, if I can replace them temporarily in this army. If I cannot spare the regiments named, I will endeavor to get you two from General Samuel Jones," commander of the Department of Western Virginia. Lee advised Imboden to urge Jones to develop a movement in the Kanawha Valley that would prevent Union forces from moving reinforcements to the threatened areas. He also informed Imboden that "by the 1st of April, or before that time, I expect this army to be engaged in active operations." He did not mention invasion of the North, but that he did expect Hooker to move against him "as soon as the roads permit."[5]

On March 10 Davis summoned Lee to Richmond. On his second day there, March 14, Lee canceled all furloughs in the Army of Northern Virginia except for extraordinary cases.[6] This action was taken to maintain the army's strength for the new invasion campaign.

Alarming news on March 17 caused Lee to cut short his time in Richmond. Heavy firing had been reported along the Rappahannock River above Fredericksburg and there were indications that enemy forces were attempting to cross at the U.S. Ford. Stuart also reported that a large body of Union cavalry had forced a passage at Kelly's Ford.[7] Fearing a general movement by Hooker, Lee ordered Pickett and Hood to return to Fredericksburg and sent two battalions of artillery from Richmond to Hanover Junction to guard supplies there.[8]

The alarm was premature. At 7 P.M. March 17 Stuart wired Lee in Richmond, "Enemy is retiring. He is badly hurt. We are after him. His dead men and horses strew the roads."[9] The telegram reached Richmond the next day, but Lee had left by special train for his headquarters.[10]

On March 19 Lee explained to Davis, "On my arrival yesterday, learning that the enemy's cavalry had retired across the Rappahannock, and that no effort was being made by their infantry to cross the river, I countermanded the orders for Pickett's and Hood's division to march in this direction." He also noted that he had returned to Richmond the two artillery battalions at Hanover Junction.[11]

Another matter demanded Lee's attention. During his absence, a letter had arrived at camp from Senator Edward Sparrow, chairman of the Military Affairs Committee. It was dated March 11 and asked Lee's opinion of Senate Bill No. 73, which proposed organization of staffs for armies, corps, divisions, brigades, and regiments.

In a reply on March 20 Lee suggested a number of changes and advised that "the more simple the organization of our Army the more suitable will it be to our service, and that every possible reduction in its expense should be made."[12]

The next day he wrote to Davis and repeated his suggested changes in the bill.

> I think it is important, and indeed necessary, to simplify the mechanism of our Army as much as possible, yet still to give it sufficient power to move and regulate the whole body. Our armies are necessarily very large in comparison with those we have heretofore had to manage. Some of our divisions exceed the army General Scott entered the City of Mexico with, and our brigades are larger than his divisions.
>
> The greatest difficulty I find is in causing orders and regulations to be obeyed. This arises not from a spirit of disobedience, but from ignorance. We therefore have need of a corps of officers to teach others their duty, see to the observance of orders, and to the regularity and precision of all movements.
>
> This is accomplished in the French service by their staff corps, educated, instructed and practiced for the purpose. The same

circumstances that produced that corps exist in our own Army. Can you not shape the staff of our Army to produce equally good results?

Lee then offered a proposal for the officers he considered necessary for the staffs of armies and units down to the brigade level. "If you can fill these positions with proper officers, not the relatives and social friends of the commanders, who, however agreeable their company, are not always the most useful, you might have the finest army in the world."[13]

Davis agreed and steps were taken to develop staffs along French lines. On March 24 Colonel William M. Browne, an aide to Davis, wrote to Brigadier General Camille Polignac, a French prince and veteran of the Crimean War who had joined the Confederate army shortly after the outbreak of the Civil War. Browne wanted information on staff organizations in the French and Prussian armies.[14]

Polignac prepared a memorandum and, on March 28, "called on Mr. [Judah P.] Benjamin, who told me my report was read aloud today by the President to the Secretary of War and the adjutant general and gave much satisfaction."[15]

—————>●<—————

Lee took a major step on March 21, three days after his return from Richmond, with General Orders No. 43: "With a view to a resumption of active operations by the 1st of April, the army will at once prepare for the approaching campaign." All surplus baggage was to be sent to Richmond. Leaves of absence beyond March 31 were restricted, and officers were to keep accurate records of all equipment, supplies, and munitions in their commands.

Animals and forage were scarce and the army would be operating out of contact with Southern railroads, so "it will be necessary to reduce transportation of the army to the lowest limit." He then closed:

> The commanding general regrets the necessity for curtailing the comforts of an army which has evinced so much self-denial in the endurance of privations, but feels satisfied that ready acquiescence will be shown in all measures tending to secure success and the more speedy conclusion of the war, and appeals to officers and men to aid him in the accomplishment of this greatly desired object by the strict observance of orders and careful preservation of the property in their hands, daily becoming more valuable by the difficulty of replacing it.[16]

Any hope for an early start was wiped out by more severe weather. Snow fell from March 19 to 21; warm weather moved in on the 22nd, melting the snow, flooding streams, and leaving deep mud. Robert Garlick Hill Kean, head of the Confederate Bureau of War, figured conditions would hold Lee up for at least three weeks.[17]

Lee wrote Seddon on March 25, citing the importance of maintaining rail service between Richmond and his army before it moved north. He suggested that slaves called up to work on fortifications be used to help restore the Virginia Central Railroad. "The necessities of the road are immediate, and I see no other way of supplying them."[18]

The next day Lee advised Imboden, "I am anxious to know how you progress in your preparations for your expedition west of the Allegheny [Mountains], the strength and composition of your forces, &c. The season is now at hand when it should be executed, and as soon as the roads and mountain streams permit, it should move. Inform me when your preparations will be complete and when you expect to move."[19]

Supplying the Army of Northern Virginia still troubled Lee. On March 27 he told Seddon, "The troops of this portion of the army have for some time been confined to reduced rations, consisting of 18 ounces of flour, 4 ounces of bacon of indifferent quality, with occasionally supplies of rice, sugar or molasses.

"The men are cheerful, and I receive but few complaints; still, I do not think it is enough to continue them in health and vigor, and I fear they will be unable to endure the hardships of the approaching campaign."[20]

In his reply on March 31 Seddon pointed out, "The great difficulty just now is not so much in the want of supplies as of the impediments to their ready transportation and distribution. Our roads have almost defied wagon transportation, and our railroads are daily growing less efficient and serviceable. I am invoking the aid of Congress to enable me to enforce the adoption of more regular schedules, and the employment of more trains in freight transportation. *Meantime, I look with hope to the result of successful expeditions into the enemy's country for supplies.*"[21]

Seddon's last reference adds another link in the chain of evidence that the decision to invade the North had been made well before the Battle of Chancellorsville—at the February 28 Cabinet meeting.

March ended with another day of foul weather and a five-inch snowfall for northern Virginia.[22] Six more inches fell on April 4–5.[23]

In the meantime, another complication arose. Lee was sick.[24] In a letter to his wife, Mary, on March 27 he noted "I have felt so unwell since my return [from Richmond] as not to be able to go anywhere. I have been suffering from a heavy cold which I hope is passing away. The weather has been wretched. More unpleasant than any other part of the winter."[25]

On April 3 he wrote Mary, "I am getting better I trust though apparently very slowly & have suffered a great deal since I last wrote. I have had to call upon the doctors who are very kind & attentive & do every thing for me that is possible. I have taken a violent cold, either from going in or coming out of a warm house, perhaps both, which is very difficult to get rid of & very distressing to have."[26]

Two days later, he told his wife:

> I am suffering with a bad cold as I told you, & was threatened, the doctors thought, with some malady which must be dreadful if it resembles its name, but which I have forgotten. They bundled me up on Monday last [March 30] & brought me to Mr. Yerby's [house] where I have a comfortable room.
>
> I have not been so very sick, though have suffered a good deal of pain in my chest, back and arms. It comes on in paroxysms, was quite sharp & seemed to me to be a mixture of your's & Agnes' [his daughter] diseases, from which I infer they are catching & that I fell a victim while in R[ichmond]. But they have passed off, I hope, some fever remains, & I am enjoying a complete saturation of my system with quinine.[27]

In an April 8 memorandum to his military secretary, Major Charles Marshall, Lee noted, "My head is ringing with quinine & I am otherwise so poorly that I do not seem able to think."[28] Lee was confined to his room until April 16, when he returned to camp. In a letter to his wife on the 19th he wrote, "I am feeble and worthless and can do but little."[29]

The condition evidently recurred during the Battle of Gettysburg. On the night of July 2 and the morning of the 3rd Lee displayed a number of symptoms related to the use of quinine. On August 8 he told Davis, "I feel the growing failure of my bodily strength. I have not yet recovered from the attack I experienced last spring."[30]

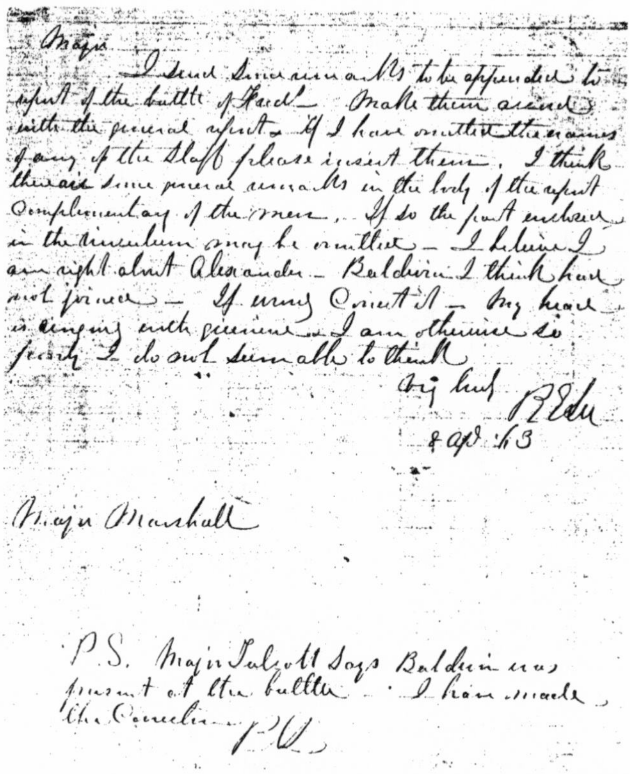

[handwritten letter reproduced as image]

Major
I send some remarks to be appended to the report of the
battle of Fred[ericksburg]. Make them accord with the
general report. If I have omitted the names of any of the
staff please insert them. I think there are some remarks in
the general body of the report complimentary of the men. If
so the part enclosed in the vinculum may be omitted. I
believe I am right about Alexander. Baldwin I think had
not joined. If wrong correct it. My head is ringing with
quinine & I am otherwise so poorly I do not seem able to
think.

                                        Very Truly
                                        R. E. Lee
                                        8 Apl '86
                                        Major Marshall
P.S. Major Talcott says Baldwin was present at the battle.
I have made the correction.

In a letter to his wife on September 4, he wrote, "I have been suffering ever since my last visit to Richmond from a heavy cold which resulted in an attack of rheumatism in my back, which has given me great pain & anxiety, for if I cannot get relief I do not see what is to become of me. I had at one time to go about a great deal & the motion of my horse was extremely painful, so much so that I took to a spring wagon."[31]

On October 28 he wrote to Mary "I do not know what I shall do when winter really comes. I have felt very differently since my attack of last spring, from which I have never recovered. My rheumatism is better though I still suffer. I hope in time it will pass away."[32] On December 4, he told her, "I am much better, though still stiff & painful. I fear I will never be better & must be content."[33]

The condition affected Lee periodically throughout the rest of the war and took his life on October 12, 1870. His death generally was attributed to a heart condition that developed in the attack of March 1863 and worsened during the ensuing years.[34]

———◆———

During his confinement in the spring of 1863 Lee tried to maintain control over the military situation and plans for resuming the invasion. On April 2 he advised Davis that it appeared that the report of Hooker's troop movements were intended "to deceive us." He then added: "When the roads permit of our moving, unless, in the meantime, General Hooker takes the aggressive, I propose to make a blow at Milroy [in western Virginia], which will draw General Hooker out, or at least prevent further reinforcements being sent to the west."[35]

Another problem surfaced a few days later. In a letter on April 6 Seddon asked Lee if he could reinforce the Army of the West—"two or three brigades, say from Pickett's division," and another from Major Samuel Jones's command in the Southwestern Virginia Department.[36]

Lee's reply on April 9 clearly indicated his intention to resume the invasion as soon as possible:

> I do not know that I can add anything to what I have already said on the subject of reinforcing the Army of the West. Should General Hooker's army assume the defensive, the readiest method of relieving the pressure upon General Johnston and General Beauregard [who appeared to be threatened in South Carolina in early April] would be for this army to cross into Maryland. This cannot

be done, however, in the present condition of the roads, nor unless I can obtain a certain amount of provisions and suitable transportation. But this is what I would recommend if practicable.[37]

On April 14 Samuel Cooper wrote Lee about reinforcements for the Army of Tennessee. Cooper figured 12,000 to 15,000 additional men would be needed and asked Lee whether he could split off Hood's or Pickett's division.[38]

Lee demurred. He pointed out that Longstreet had been sent south primarily to gather supplies for the Army of Northern Virginia. "If Pickett's division is withdrawn from him," Lee wrote, "I fear he will be unable to obtain the supplies we hoped to draw from the eastern portion of the department." Lee then briefly outlined a strategic plan to divide his army when it resumed the invasion movement.

> I had expected to recall General Longstreet as soon as he had secured all the subsistence which could be obtained in that region, to hold General Hooker in check, while Milroy could be driven out of the [Shenandoah] Valley. If it is decided that it will be more advantageous to reinforce General Johnston, these operations will have to be suspended. The President, from his position, being able to survey all the scenes of action, can better decide than any one else, and I recommend that he follow the dictates of his good judgment.[39]

In referring to Longstreet, Lee was calling attention to the siege of Suffolk, Virginia, by his corps commander. On April 14th, Longstreet had explained to Lee that he intended to gather supplies for the Army of Northern Virginia in southeastern Virginia, but Union troops had moved to the area and dug in. As a result, the siege continued until May 3, when it was abandoned.[40] On the 16th Lee wrote Davis:

> I do not think that General Hooker will venture to uncover Washington by transferring his army to [the] James River unless the force in front of Alexandria is greater than I suppose, or unless he believes this army incapable of advancing to the Potomac.
>
> My only anxiety arises from the present immobility of the army, owing to the condition of our horses and the scarcity of forage and provisions. I think it all important that we should assume the aggressive by the 1st of May, when we may expect General Hooker's army to be weakened by the expiration of the

term of service of many of his regiments, and before new recruits can be received.

If we could be placed in a condition to make a vigorous advance at that time, I think the Valley could be swept of Milroy and the army opposite me thrown north of the Potomac. I believe greater relief would in this way be afforded to the armies of middle Tennessee and on the Carolina coast than by any other method.[41]

On April 11 Lee showed his desire to begin an aggressive movement as soon as possible. In a letter to Colonel Jeremy F. Gilmer, chief of the Engineer Bureau, he stated, "I have learned that a pontoon train was seen passing through Richmond, on its way to me. I want one of 350 feet span, with rigging and everything complete. I understand there are sixteen boats, with some rigging, now at Gordonsville. An engineer officer had better be sent to examine their condition."

Lee also asked for an officer "who is acquainted with the business, and who could lay the bridge with rapidity." He requested a speedy response and advised Gilmer to "keep the matter as quiet as practicable."[42]

In his reply on April 19 Gilmer informed Lee that a 600-foot pontoon bridge was at Gordonsville and that Captain Hugh T. Douglas, "an expert in the use of pontoon bridges," was there putting the boats and equipment "in complete order." The equipment was to be shipped by rail to Orange Court House.[43]

It remained there until after the Battle of Chancellorsville in the first week of May. Lee wrote Stuart on May 9 that the pontoon boats were at Orange Court House, or Gordonsville, apparently on railroad cars, and that "I have no objection to your taking them if you require them." Lee added that if Stuart needed them, he was to contact Captain Douglas.[44]

Lee was not alone in mid-April in focusing on an early northward movement. On April 13 Jackson issued a comprehensive marching order for his corps:

> Each division will move precisely at the time indicated in the order of march, and if a division or brigade is not ready to move at that time, the next will proceed and take its place, even if a division should be separated thereby.

On the march, the troops are to have a rest of ten minutes each hour. The rate of march is not to exceed one mile in twenty-five minutes, unless otherwise specially ordered. When the troops are halted for the purpose of resting, arms will be stacked and ranks broken, and in no case during the march will the troops be allowed to break ranks without previously stacking arms.

When any part of a battery or train is disabled on a march, the officer in charge must have it removed immediately from the road, so that no part of the command be impeded upon its march. Batteries or trains must not stop in the line of march to water; when any part of a battery or train, for any cause, loses its place in the column, it must not pass any part of the column in regaining its place.

The order included special instructions for making camp, the movement of ambulances, and the care of wounded.[45] Obviously, the order was intended for a long, steady march over many miles without unduly tiring his troops. It was similar to the movement he had described the previous summer as he prepared for the first invasion attempt, when "in two weeks I could be in Harrisburg."

Northern morale suffered again after the enactment on March 3 of another draft law, making all men between twenty and forty-five liable for service.[46] The reaction was quick from the Knights of the Golden Circle. Membership in the secret organization in 1860 was estimated at 95,000. By 1863 one estimate placed it as high as 800,000 to 1,000,000.

In 1864 Joseph Holt, judge advocate general at the War Department, noted that the estimated membership of 500,000 was undoubtedly "considerably exaggerated."[47]

A resident of Reading, Pennsylvania, John S. Richards, reported on March 17, 1863, to Judge Advocate L. C. Turner that he had "authentic information from a variety of sources in regard to organizations that have been formed in various parts of this county [Berks] within the past two weeks to resist the draft." He added that these organizations, "if permitted to exist and increase, may become exceedingly dangerous."[48]

On April 24 Provost Marshal General James B. Fry informed Pennsylvania Governor Andrew G. Curtin that a provost marshal had been assigned to Harrisburg and to the capitals of other Northern states to assure "uniform and harmonious execution of the enrollment act."[49]

About a week later Richards informed Turner that "parties are actively engaged in organizing treasonable lodges" in eastern Berks County. He then asked for the assignment of a provost marshal to that area to help "break up these treasonable societies."[50] Pennsylvania had to deal with a new threat, too—Imboden's raid into western Virginia. Was it the start of another Confederate attempt to invade Pennsylvania?

Imboden had started the movement on April 20 with about 1,800 men and was joined the next day by slightly more than 1,500 from Samuel Jones's force.[51] William E. Jones, commander of the Valley District, left on the 21st with his own force to strike at the B&O Railroad in cooperation with Imboden.[52]

News of the raid quickly reached Washington. At 3:30 P.M. April 21, Henry W. Halleck, the chief of staff, was informed, "Circumstances now tend to indicate that the rebels are preparing to make some movement in force in Western Virginia."[53] Three days later Brigadier General B. S. Roberts, in command of a Union force in Buckhannon, Virginia, told Halleck that reinforcements should be rushed to the area "or the enemy will reach the Baltimore and Ohio Railroad and do great damage." A few hours later Halleck informed Roberts that he had no men to send.[54]

As the Confederates advanced, the alarm spread into Ohio and western Pennsylvania. On April 28 Ohio Governor David Tod sent 850 militiamen with a two-gun artillery battery east to protect Wheeling.[55] At the same time Curtin telegraphed Stanton that the day before, 4,000 Rebel cavalrymen were reported in Morgantown, Virginia, and "coming into Pennsylvania. The Baltimore and Ohio Railroad between Grafton and Cumberland is torn up." Curtin called for as many troops as could be sent to the state."[56]

Lincoln tried to allay the fears of Pennsylvanians. The Confederate action, he advised Curtin on April 28, was "nothing more than a small force of the enemy in the northern part of Virginia to divert us in another quarter."[57] Rumors continued to spread, however, and by May 1 it was reported to Curtin that "the rebel force, estimated at 20,000, is under the command of Stonewall Jackson."[58]

The Confederate raid in western Virginia succeeded in many respects. Curtin's report of the B&O being "torn up" was accurate; all but two B&O bridges in the area were destroyed, and about 2,000 cattle and 1,200 horses had been captured.[59]

Lee later congratulated Imboden, especially over the captured goods. In his endorsement of Imboden's report, Lee added, "The men and officers deserve much credit for the fortitude and endurance exhibited under the hardships and difficulties of the march."[60]

The success of the raid and the fears it had aroused quickly faded. Developments in eastern Virginia had a much greater impact on the war effort and created an even greater alarm as the Confederates again invaded the North.

In late April Lee sought to begin the northward movement by May 1. Manpower was a problem similar to the situation before the Battle of Sharpsburg. He had 60,000 men ready to face an enemy of more than 135,000.[61]

In a letter to Stuart on April 19, Lee explained that he had not determined Hooker's intentions, "but it behooves us to be on the alert." He added that he wished he could send more cavalry to Stuart.[62] The next day, Lee told Stuart that he had appealed to Davis for cavalry reinforcements and added, "I see no evidence of a forward movement" by enemy troops and "everything is quiet in [our] front."[63] On the 21st, Cooper advised Lee, "The President thinks three regiments of cavalry might be safely withdrawn from North Carolina."[64]

The situation changed quickly. On April 27 Lee reported to Davis that there were signs of a Federal movement. He added that he had written to Longstreet "to expedite as much as possible his operations in North Carolina [and southwestern Virginia], as I may be obliged to call him back at any moment."[65]

Shortly after taking command of the Army of the Potomac in late January, Hooker began developing an on-to-Richmond movement. It was discussed with Lincoln at Hooker's camp in the first week of April. When the plan was mentioned, Hooker told Lincoln, "I am going straight to Richmond." A short time later, in a chat with a member of his party, Lincoln commented that it was one of the worst things he had heard during the visit. He had tried to impress on Hooker that the objective was Lee's army, not Richmond, and that the city would fall when Lee's army was neutralized.[66]

Since early April Hooker had been hearing of Longstreet's activities from Major General John J. Peck, commander of Union forces in Suffolk. On April 26 Peck informed Hooker that Suffolk was still under siege and that the Confederates were receiving heavy artillery from Petersburg. He asked Hooker to "advise me in cipher of as much as you deem proper of your operations." Hooker replied: "I have communicated to no one what my intentions are. So much is found out by the enemy in my front with regards to my movements, that I have concealed my designs from my own staff, and I dare not intrust them to the wires, knowing as I do that they are so often tapped."[67]

Three days later Lee reported to Davis that "the enemy crossed the Rappahannock today in large numbers" and that Union cavalry had crossed the Rapidan River in the afternoon. "Their intention, I presume, is to turn our left, and probably to get into our rear. I hope if any reinforcements can be sent, they may be forwarded immediately."[68] Longstreet also was ordered to "move without delay with your command to this place [Richmond] to effect a junction with General Lee."[69]

Hooker's movement precipitated the Battle of Chancellorsville on May 1–4. Lee regrouped on the 5th to attack, but early on the 6th learned that the Union Army was withdrawing to the north side of the Rappahannock. The battle was a remarkable victory for Lee, but it was a victory gained at a terrible price. Stonewall Jackson was wounded on the night of May 2, one bullet striking his right hand, and two others ripping through his left arm. The next day, a Sunday, his left arm was amputated near the shoulder. He seemed to recover quickly and, by Wednesday morning, was regarded sufficiently out of danger to be moved to the home of Thomas Chandler at Guiney's Station, south of Fredericksburg. On Thursday, symptoms of pneumonia developed, and Jackson died on Sunday, May 10.[70]

"A great national calamity has befallen us, and I sympathize with the sorrow you feel," Davis wrote Lee on May 11. "The announcement of the death of General Jackson followed frequent assurances that he was doing very well, and though the loss was one which would have been deeply felt under any circumstances, the shock was increased by its suddenness."[71]

Shortly before Jackson's condition became critical, Lee sent a messenger to him with these words: "Give him my affectionate regards, and tell him to make haste and get well, and come back to me as soon as he can. He has lost his left arm, but I have lost my right arm."[72]

———————————

Confederate authorities had been alarmed by Hooker's advance and by Union cavalry raids on roads and rail lines within ten to twelve miles of Richmond from May 3 to 5. Only one infantry brigade was available to meet the threat, so a force of civilians was organized to help defend the city. By May 6 enemy cavalry had withdrawn and the fear subsided.[73]

Better news arrived that day from Lee. In a dispatch dated May 3, he stated: "This morning the battle was renewed. He [Hooker] was dislodged from all his positions around Chancellorsville, and driven back toward the Rappahannock, over which he is now retreating. We have again to thank Almighty God for a great victory."[74]

The next day Davis replied: "I reverently unite with you in giving praise to God for the success with which He has crowned our arms. The universal rejoicing produced by this happy result will be mingled with a general regret for the good and brave who are numbered among the killed and wounded."[75]

CHAPTER 19

After Chancellorsville

AFTER THE REPULSE OF HOOKER'S ARMY LEE QUICKLY TURNED TO HIS desire to start a new invasion as soon as possible—his third attempt. His goal to start the movement by April 1 had been thwarted by severe weather and his health problem. After Lee's recovery he hoped to start north by May 1, but Hooker's advance checked that. This time he succeeded in taking his army into Pennsylvania. In order to properly follow Lee's progress, it is necessary to summarize what he intended to do and how he hoped to do it. No recorded account of this has been found, but details of the plan, gathered from Lee's correspondence and reports, indicate these intentions:

1. It was to be an offensive campaign of maneuver, not combat. Lee wanted to avoid a general battle if possible, especially in enemy territory.

2. Only one corps would advance to the Susquehanna, cross the river, and if possible, seize Harrisburg and sever the Pennsylvania Railroad. Lee's army was reorganized into three corps, instead of two, in late May.

3. The invading force was to stay north all summer, gathering supplies, moving about, and encouraging Northerners (especially those already involved in peace activities) to seek a halt to the fighting and an end to the war.

4. Meanwhile Lee and his main body would pin down the Army of the Potomac in the immediate defense of Washington.

All of this was part of the plan Jackson had proposed in October 1861. To succeed, Lee wanted reinforcements. This could be accomplished, he pointed out, by these steps:

1. Recalling Longstreet from Richmond and southeastern Virginia.
2. Doubling Stuart's cavalry force.
3. Moving General Beauregard and troops from his command (the Department of South Carolina, Georgia, and Florida) north to help create a major threat to Washington. This was to keep the Union Army from hindering the one Confederate corps from moving into Pennsylvania.

It also is important to know what was going on in other fronts in relation to the Army of Northern Virginia. The situation was as follows:

1. The Union commander in the Department of the Tennessee, Major General Ulysses S. Grant, was progressing against Vicksburg, Mississippi. On May 1, he had won the first of a series of victories that would bring the stronghold itself under direct attack by May 19.
2. The Confederate commander in Vicksburg, Lieutenant General John C. Pemberton, repeatedly called for reinforcements. Some were sought from Lee and Beauregard.
3. Beauregard objected to sending troops to Virginia. He did, however, send 5,000 or more reinforcements to support Pemberton. After the war Beauregard claimed that he was not aware of Lee's detailed invasion plan, but like all after-the-fact statements, especially by Beauregard, this may not have been entirely true. He also expressed his regret that the plan was not carried out as Lee intended.

Lee also faced difficulties in his own army. These resulted in the entire Confederate Army's moving into Pennsylvania.

The Confederate and Union positions in Virginia on May 6 were much the same as they had been before Chancellorsville. Most of Hooker's army was back on the north side of the Rappahannock River and Lee's was on the south bank.[1] On May 7, the day after Hooker withdrew, Lee wrote an important letter to Davis. He urged an increase in the cavalry force and indicated the need for more infantry. Lee pointed out that Hooker had crossed the Rappahannock with 120,000 men, but "our effective strength with which we marched out to meet him, according to the last returns, did not reach 40,000." He then urged Davis to strengthen the Army of Northern Virginia:

This can be done, in my opinion, by bringing troops from the department of South Carolina, Georgia, and Florida. No more can be needed there this summer than enough to maintain the water batteries. Nor do I think that more will be required at Wilmington [North Carolina] than are sufficient for this purpose. If they are kept in their present positions in these departments, they will perish of disease.

I know there will be difficulties raised to their withdrawal. But it will be better to order General Beauregard in with all the forces which can be spared, and to put him in command here [in northern Virginia], than to keep them there inactive and this army inefficient from paucity of numbers. . . .

There are many things about which I would like to consult Your Excellency, and I should be delighted, if your health and convenience suited, if you could visit the army. Should this, however, be inconvenient, I will endeavor to go to Richmond, though I feel my presence here now is essential.[2]

Ill health kept Davis confined to his room,[3] so Lee decided to go to Richmond as soon as possible.

Lee's need for troops reflected an overall problem in the Confederacy in the spring of 1863. As of April 30, Southern land forces totaled 304,236, compared with 567,851 for the Union. In Virginia, Lee had 64,799 men compared with Hooker's 138,378.[4] The Confederacy had a significant superiority only in Beauregard's department.[5]

Longstreet had broken off his siege of Suffolk and started north on May 3 to rejoin Lee. He arrived in Fredericksburg in time to dine with Lee on May 9.[6] Longstreet wrote, "I found him in sadness over the severe wounding of his great lieutenant, General Thomas Jonathan Jackson. With a brave heart, however, General Lee was getting his ranks together, and putting them in condition for other useful work."[7]

Lee and Longstreet discussed the relief of Vicksburg. According to Longstreet, Lee objected to reinforcing Pemberton from Virginia because it would force him to divide the Army of Northern Virginia. Longstreet added that Lee clearly "believed the idea of an offensive campaign was not only important but necessary." Lee asked whether Longstreet did not think that an invasion of Maryland and Pennsylvania by his army would take pressure off Pemberton. Longstreet replied that the movement would be too dangerous. When he realized that Lee was determined to move north, he remarked that the Pennsylvania campaign might succeed if it was offensive in strategy but defensive in tactics. He suggested that, after entering Pennsylvania and menacing Washington, the Confederates "should choose a strong position and force the enemy to attack us. To this he [Lee] readily assented as an important adjunct to his general plan."[8]

Lee disagreed with this statement. In a conversation with Colonel Allan in April 1868, Lee stated that he had heard "a reported conversation of Longstreet's in which the latter stated that Gen. Lee was under a promise to the Lieutenant General not to fight a general battle in Pennsylvania. The General [Lee] said he did not believe it was ever said by Longstreet. That the idea was absurd. He had never made any such promise, and had never thought of doing any such thing."[9]

All of Longstreet's accounts were published after the death of Lee on October 12, 1870. It is evident that Longstreet was unaware that invasion plans had been discussed during the winter days in camp or that top Confederate authorities had accepted Lee's proposal, as described by Postmaster General John H. Reagan in his account of the February 28 Cabinet meeting.[10]

Actually, Longstreet's suggestions in early May were not entirely new. On March 24 he had asked Lee for another division for operations in southeastern Virginia and North Carolina. Lee refused. "If this army is further weakened we must retire to the line of the Annas [rivers] and trust to a battle nearer Richmond for the defense of the capital," Lee replied.[11]

Longstreet said that he did not think such a move was practical, then added: "I have thought since about January 23 last (when I made the suggestion to you) that one army corps could hold the line of the Rappahannock while the other one was operating elsewhere." Longstreet also contended, "The enemy is inclined to make his great effort in the West, but we may break him up in the East and then reinforce in the West in time to crush him there."[12]

Longstreet's correspondence makes it clear he favored an overland campaign from Virginia to relieve Vicksburg. The idea, apparently, had been in his mind for some time, and the victory at Chancellorsville may have fit in with his thoughts about breaking up the enemy in the East, then reinforcing Confederate forces in the West.

In a letter to his uncle, A. B. Longstreet, on July 24, 1863—three weeks after Gettysburg—Longstreet expressed his earliest feelings about the matter.

> The battle was not made as I would have made it. My idea was to throw ourselves between the enemy and Washington, select a strong position, and force the enemy to attack us. So far as it is given to man the ability to judge, we may say with confidence that we should have destroyed the Federal army, marched into Washington, and dictated our terms, or, at least, held Washington and marched over as much of Pennsylvania as we cared to, had we drawn the enemy into attack upon our carefully chosen position in his rear.
>
> General Lee chose the plans adopted; and he is the person appointed to choose and to order. I consider it a part of my duty to express my views to the Commanding-General. If he approves and adopts them, it is well; if he does not, it is my duty to adopt his views, and to execute his orders as faithfully as if they were my own. I cannot help but think that great results would have been obtained had my views been thought better of; yet I am much inclined to accept the present condition as for the best. I hope and trust it is so.[13]

Longstreet's thoughts in this letter have a familiar ring. Before the Battle of Sharpsburg, he was reported to have said to Lee, "I wish we could stand still and let the d——d Yankees come to us."[14]

Longstreet apparently was not aware of the plan that Jackson had proposed earlier and its main target—the anthracite fields of northeastern Pennsylvania. Nor did he appear to realize that its objective was to exert economic pressure on the North and force the Northern people to demand an end to the war.

———◦———

The threat to Vicksburg worsened in the first week of May and the need for reinforcements there continued to mount. On May 5 Beauregard notified Pemberton, "I have sent you two brigades of troops [about 5,000 men] and two batteries. I only regret that I could not send you double the number."[15] On the 7th President Davis noted to Pemberton that Beauregard was insisting that he could not spare more than the 5,000 men sent but "to hold both Vicksburg and Port Hudson is necessary to a connection with Trans-Mississippi. You may expect whatever is in my power to do."[16] The call for troops from Beauregard's army alarmed officials in South Carolina. To them Secretary Seddon replied:

> You do not know, and I could be scarcely justified in stating, the causes that preclude succor from General Lee's army and other points to General Pemberton, but you may rely upon it that only the fullest consideration and under the gravest necessity is the draft made on Charleston and persisted in, despite the earnest remonstrance of gentlemen so highly esteemed as yourselves.[17]

The comment made by Seddon regarding "succor from General Lee's army" provides a second link in the chain of evidence that the Secretary of War was aware that the decision already had been made for Lee to resume the invasion. This supports Seddon's statement made to Lee on March 31 about "successful expeditions into the enemy's territory."

In a coded telegram to Lee on May 9 Seddon proposed sending George Pickett's division to Mississippi. Lee replied, "The adoption of your proposition is hazardous, and it becomes a question between Virginia and the Mississippi. The distance and the uncertainty of the employment of the troops are unfavorable. But, if necessary, order Pickett at once." Davis concurred with Lee's assessment.

In a more detailed letter to Seddon on the 10th, Lee pointed out that Pickett probably could not reach Pemberton before the end of May. "The uncertainty of its [Pickett's division's] arrival and the uncertainty of its application cause me to doubt the policy of sending it. Its removal from this army will be sensibly felt. Unless we can obtain some reinforcements, we may be obliged to withdraw into the defenses around Richmond. You can, therefore, see the odds against us, and decide whether the line of Virginia is more in danger than the line of the Mississippi."[18]

On May 11 Lee decided it was time to strengthen his own army. He wrote Davis: "If I could get in position to advance beyond the Rappahannock, I should certainly draw their troops [Union forces] from the southern coasts. I think you will agree with me that every effort should be made to reinforce this army to oppose the larger force the enemy seems to be concentrating against it."[19] He was more explicit in a letter to Stuart on the same date:

> I shall be glad to get your views as to the increase of the cavalry, and I need not assure you that nothing will be wanted on my part to augment it. If you think a visit to Richmond, on your part, will expedite the organization or equipment of your command, I have no objection, but, on the contrary, recommend it.[20]

A few days later, probably on May 14, Lee and Stuart left for Richmond, and they arrived at the War Department the following day.[21] Also on May 15 an order was issued by the Adjutant and Inspector General's Office "by the command of the Secretary of War," for General Pickett to move to Hanover Junction."[22] On the 16th Lee informed Longstreet that "General Pickett passed through town [Richmond] this morning for Hanover Junction."[23]

On May 16 J. B. Jones, a clerk in the War Department, noted in his diary: "It appears, after the consultation of the generals and the President yesterday, it was resolved not to send Pickett's division to Mississippi, and this morning early the long column marched through the city northward. Gen. Pickett accompanied his division. Two fine regiments of cavalry, the 2nd and 59th North Carolina Regiments, passed through the city this morning likewise." He added:

> There is some purpose on the part of General Lee to have a raid in the enemy's country, surpassing all other raids. If he can organize two columns of cavalry, 5000 each, to move in parallel lines, they may penetrate to the Hudson River; and then the North will discover that it has more to lose by such expeditions than the South. Philadelphia, even, may be taken.[24]

Jones's comments reflected to some degree the move Lee finally undertook the next month, but it turned out to be two columns of the Army of Northern Virginia, not two columns of cavalry. In the comment about the North's discovery, Jones appears to be echoing Jackson's thought in closing his invasion plan in October 1861—to "force the people of the north to understand what it will cost them to hold the South in the Union at the bayonet's point."

Lee remained in Richmond until May 18, when he took the early train to Fredericksburg. When it stopped in Ashland in Hanover County to allow passengers to breakfast at a hotel, Lee visited a family friend. Mrs. John P. McGuire noted in her diary that day that "we had the gratification of a short visit from General Lee. He called and breakfasted with us, while the other passengers breakfasted at the hotel. We were very glad to see that the great and good man was so cheerful."[25]

He had reason to be. The movement by Pickett and the two cavalry regiments was a sign that Davis had endorsed a renewal of the invasion. Lee later stated that the president had promised to bring Beauregard north with all available troops in South Carolina and Georgia to create the impression of an attack on Washington.[26]

Rumors and reports of Lee's proposed movements had begun circulating in the North. At 3:30 P.M. May 14 Major General Daniel Butterfield, Hooker's chief of staff, telegraphed a scout's report to Hooker in Washington. The scout had reported, "The rumor at Culpeper is that General Beauregard is to reinforce Lee as soon as the roads are repaired."[27]

On May 17 Major General John A. Dix, commander at Fort Monroe, informed Halleck, "My man came in from Richmond today. He is satisfied that troops have recently been brought to Richmond from Georgia and South Carolina and sent to Fredericksburg. It was said in Richmond that Lee was to attack Hooker and drive him back to the Potomac."[28] Three days later the *Philadelphia Inquirer* carried a report from a source in Baltimore stating that Lee was planning another invasion of the North.[29]

Jones added in his May 22 diary entry an unusual note about Lee's possible plans. He had just met a friend he had known in Pennsylvania, Robert Tyler, "who offers to wager that General Stuart will be in Philadelphia in a fortnight."[30]

Lee's decision to renew the invasion had become a matter of gossip and speculation. Even Beauregard drafted a plan for the relief of Vicksburg; it was similar to that suggested by Longstreet when he conferred with Lee. Beauregard did not submit the plan himself, but instead he asked General Joseph E. Johnston to present it to the War Department.[31]

The next day, May 16, Beauregard sent a copy of his letter to Johnston to Senator Louis T. Wigfall of Texas, then stated:

I do not think, for several reasons, that the offensive ought to be taken in Virginia at this moment. Amongst those reasons are the difficulty of operating offensively with a large army in an exhausted country like Northern Virginia, and the probability that the threatened danger to Washington would arouse the whole Yankee nation to renewed efforts for the protection of their capital. Should you agree with my views, can you not make a desperate effort to have them adopted at once by the War Department, without saying that they came from me.[32]

News from Vicksburg during this time was not encouraging for the Confederates. On May 19 Pemberton's troops were defeated in the open field and forced to occupy trenches around the city. He added, "Unless a large force is sent at once to relieve it, Vicksburg must before long fall."[33]

The situation remained a significant factor in late May as Lee prepared to take the first steps toward invading Pennsylvania.

CHAPTER 20

The Struggle for Troops

LEE'S RETURN TO CAMP ON MAY 18 FOLLOWING CONFERENCES WITH Davis and Seddon in Richmond was marred by news from the Shenandoah Valley. Robert Milroy's command in Winchester reportedly had crossed the Blue Ridge and was moving eastward. Lee was uncertain whether Milroy was trying to reinforce Hooker or create a diversion for him, but he asked Seddon that day to "please expedite troops from North Carolina. Order the cavalry direct to Culpeper, to Stuart." Seddon replied, "We will expedite troops as far as possible, causing some to march, and sending the others by rail. Two regiments of cavalry, on the way, have been diverted to Culpeper. The residue arriving, will march there also."[1]

The report of enemy activity had been exaggerated. Actually, it was nothing more than scouting expeditions by several hundred Union cavalrymen, and they had not crossed the Blue Ridge.[2] Lee's reaction, however, draws attention to a step he had taken in Richmond to draw troops from North Carolina as well as those previously requested from South Carolina and Georgia.

In a letter to Major General D. H. Hill on May 16, Lee stated:

The extent of the reinforcements you can send to the Army of Northern Virginia must necessarily depend upon the strength of the enemy in your front. As far as I am able to judge, the plan of the enemy is to concentrate as large a force as possible to operate in Virginia. Whether he will unite under General Hooker on the

Rappahannock or operate with different columns I cannot say, but from the information I receive he is withdrawing troops from South Carolina and the country south of James River.

It is of course our best policy to do the same and to endeavor to repel his advance into Virginia. If he weakens his force in North Carolina I think you will be able, by using all your local troops, such portion of your regular cavalry and regular brigades as may be necessary, to repulse and restrain his marauding expeditions and protect the railroads and the farming interests of the country you now hold. Every man not required for this purpose I desire you to send to me and rely upon your good judgment to proportion the means to the object in view.

Lee, however, had noted that Hill could start moving the brigade of Brigadier General Junius Daniel north as part of an exchange for other troops. Brigades under Brigadier Generals John R. Cooke and Robert Ransom belonged to the Army of Northern Virginia, according to Lee, and he expected them to be returned.[3] Lee's reliance on Hill's "good judgment" to determine which other troops would be sent north created a problem that continued for the rest of the month.

In his telegram to Seddon on May 18 Lee referred to "Stuart at Culpeper," indicating that the cavalry had started moving west toward the Blue Ridge. This was the first step along the invasion route. Seddon also revealed that the cavalry reinforcements Lee had requested were on the way.

Stuart's headquarters was moved to Culpeper Court House on May 20th and reinforcements began to arrive immediately.[4] In March he had a force of 6,967 ready for duty; on May 20 the aggregate present was shown as 8,193, with 7,039 ready for duty. By the end of May the aggregate was 11,922, with 10,302 ready for duty.[5] The increases were particularly significant considering the conclusion noted by J. B. Jones in his May 16 diary entry—that Lee was contemplating "a raid into the enemy's country" with two columns of cavalry of 5,000 each.

With his large force in Culpeper, Stuart was ready to keep Lee informed of Union activities or quickly counter any new attempt by Hooker to get around Lee's left for another move on Richmond.

On May 23 General John Imboden, who had successfully raided

northwestern Virginia and aroused fears in Pennsylvania, was sent into the Shenandoah Valley to keep an eye on Milroy. Lee told him to "have your force ready for active operations as soon as possible."[6]

In the meantime Lee had taken two other important steps in his preparations to resume the invasion. On May 19 Brigadier General William N. Pendleton, chief of artillery in the Army of Northern Virginia, wrote to three subordinates that "General Lee wishes the artillery gotten in the best possible condition for service without an hour's delay, and ready to move at very short notice."[7] The next day Lee proposed to Davis that the Army of Northern Virginia be divided into three corps instead of two.

"I have for the past year felt that the corps of this army were too large for one commander," Lee wrote. "Nothing prevented me from proposing to you to reduce their size and increase their number, but my inability to recommend commanders. Each corps contains, when in fighting condition, about 30,000 men. These are more than one man can properly handle and keep under his eye in battle in the country that we have to operate in. . . . The loss of Jackson from the command of one-half the army seems to me a good opportunity to remedy this evil."

He suggested that Longstreet retain command of the 1st Corps; that the 2nd Corps be commanded by Richard S. Ewell, "if you think Ewell is able to do field duty" (he had been wounded during the Second Bull Run campaign); and that the new 3rd Corps be commanded by A. P. Hill. After discussing a number of other officers for prospective promotions, Lee concluded:

> I must now ask you to do in all this matter as seems best to you from your point of view. I have frankly given you my opinion. I hope you will be able to give me your conclusions at your earliest convenience, as it is time I was in motion.[8]

Davis immediately approved Lee's proposal and recommended promotion of Ewell and Hill to lieutenant general. Their commissions were signed May 24.[9]

Ewell and Hill had commanded divisions in Jackson's corps. Hill had been placed in temporary command following the wounding of Jackson at Chancellorsville. Ewell was still at his home in Richmond recuperating in May 1863. Following his graduation from West Point in 1840, Ewell had been stationed briefly at Carlisle Barracks, Pennsylvania.[10] During that time he probably learned something of the country through which his troops would move in June.

On May 23 Lee ordered William E. Jones to leave the Shenandoah Valley with his cavalry and join Stuart in Culpeper.[11] In another letter that day Lee advised Stuart, "I wish you to collect and recruit your cavalry as much as possible, and think it wise to be quiet and watchful for a little time. I do not wish you to let an opportunity escape of dealing the enemy a blow should one offer, but think you had better not undertake an expedition at present." In closing Lee wrote:

> I am obliged to you for your views as to the successor of the great and good Jackson. Unless God in His mercy will raise us up one, I do not know what we shall do. I agree with you on the subject, and I have so expressed myself. It is now in the hands of others.[12]

A few days later a letter from General Johnston reached Richmond and eased, for a time, the deep concern over Vicksburg. He reported that on May 20, Pemberton had repulsed an attack on his trenches with heavy Yankee losses.[13] The assaults resumed without success on May 25; two days later, a truce was called to allow the Union to retrieve its wounded and bury the dead.[14]

The brief optimism felt in Richmond was soon offset by disturbing reports from Lee. First was a letter to Davis on May 30 in which Lee outlined a problem with D. H. Hill. "When in Richmond [May 15–17], I gave General D. H. Hill discretionary instructions to apportion his force to the strength of the enemy, and send me every man he could spare," Lee wrote. Hill, he added, requested positive instructions, but declined to act on them.

"You will see that I am unable to operate under these circumstances," he added, "and request to be relieved from any control of the department from the James to the Cape Fear River. I have, for nearly a month been endeavoring to get this army in a condition to move—to anticipate an expected blow from the enemy. I fear I shall have to receive it here at a disadvantage, or to retreat." After pointing out the problems created by the absence of troops still in southeastern Virginia and North Carolina, Lee told Davis:

> I have given Your excellency all the facts in my possession to enable you to form an opinion as to what is best to be done. I fear the time has passed when I could have taken the offensive with

advantage. From the indications that reached me, the enemy is contemplating another movement. I have not discovered what it is. There may be nothing left for me to do but fall back.[15]

In a confidential message to Seddon on the same day, Lee recommended "that you expedite as much as possible the organization of the citizens of Richmond as a local force for the defense of the city." He also recommended that all troops that could be spared from the departments of South Carolina, Georgia, and Florida, and from the James to the Cape Fear rivers, be moved to Virginia. Lee explained that the recommendations were prompted by information he had received indicating that Hooker probably intended to make a move around the Army of Northern Virginia's left wing, then advance on Richmond.[16]

The last week of May was trying for Lee. He was concerned about Hooker's potential movements, fearful for the safety of Richmond, and busy reorganizing his army. On May 24 he informed A. P. Hill of his promotion and of the plan to reorganize the army into three corps.[17] The next day Ewell was ordered to report to Lee in Fredericksburg.[18] Ewell and his bride of a few days arrived on May 29 and were enthusiastically greeted by troops from his old division and some of Jackson's old division.[19]

Reorganization was completed on May 30. Each corps was composed of three divisions. The 1st Corps divisions were commanded by Major Generals Lafayette McLaws, George E. Pickett, and John B. Hood; the 2nd by Major Generals Robert E. Rodes, Jubal A. Early, and Edward Johnson; and the 3rd by Major Generals R. H. Anderson, Henry Heth, and William D. Pender.[20]

Longstreet ordered Hood's division to move "as early as you can to Verdierville," about ten miles southeast of Culpeper Court House. There, he would be notified by Stuart of any threatening enemy movement.[21]

In the meantime Stuart had proposed to Lee on May 27 a plan for reorganizing his cavalry (six brigades of five regiments each) into brigades of three regiments each, and promotion of officers to command the brigades. Lee replied, "I am very desirous to do everything in my power to give the cavalry an effective organization, but I do not see what good will be accomplished by increasing the number of brigades and commanders without adding something to the effective strength of your command." Lee advised that it would be better to wait until all the promised regiments reached him before reorganizing his brigades.[22]

———>•◦•<———

In a letter on May 31 Davis apparently tried to raise Lee's morale. "I had never fairly comprehended your views and purposes until receipt of your letter of yesterday, and now have to regret that I did not earlier know all that you had communicated to others. I could hardly have misunderstood you, and need not say would have been glad to second your wishes, confiding, as I always do, as well to your judgment as in your information." After a lengthy discussion of the situation south of Virginia and the troops there, Davis wrote:

> I note your request to be relieved of the command of the troops between the James River and Cape Fear. This is one of the few instances in which I have found my thoughts running in the opposite direction from your own. It has several times occurred to me that it would be better for you to control all the operations of the Atlantic slope, and I must ask you to reconsider the matter.
>
> I wish I knew how to relieve you from anxiety concerning movements on the York or James River against Richmond while you are moving toward the north and west.
>
> But even if you could spare troops for the purpose, on whom could you devolve the command with that feeling of security which would be necessary for the full execution of your designs? I readily perceive the disadvantage of standing still, and sorely regret that I cannot give you the means which would make it quite safe to attempt all that we desire.
>
> It is useless to look back, and it would be unkind to annoy you in the midst of your many cares with the reflections which I have not been able to avoid. All the accounts we have of Pemberton's conduct fully sustain the good opinion heretofore entertained of him and I hope has secured for him that confidence of his troops which is so essential to success.[23]

As May ended, the situation in northern Virginia began to change. Lee's outlook brightened in early June, anxiety over the safety of Richmond faded, and he could concentrate on resuming the invasion Jackson had proposed.

CHAPTER 21

Preparing for the Invasion

JUNE WAS A CRITICAL TIME FOR THE ARMY OF NORTHERN VIRGINIA. Confederate troops moved through Maryland to the banks of the Susquehanna River in Pennsylvania and then, on July 1, to Gettysburg, where the great battle was fought.

Lee maintained before and after the campaign that he had not intended to fight a general battle if one could be avoided.[1] So what were his objectives in moving into Pennsylvania in June 1863?

In a conversation with Colonel Allan after the war, Lee stated that by going north, he would draw the enemy away from the Rappahannock River and then, by "exciting their fears for Washington, and, by watching his opportunities, baffle and break up their plans. He did not want to fight unless he could get a good opportunity to hit them in detail." Allan explained:

> He expected to move about, to maneuver and alarm the enemy, threaten their cities, hit any blows he might be able to do without risking a general battle, and then towards fall return nearer his base.

Lee also told Allan that he had no intention of permanent occupation of Pennsylvania, but by referring to his return "towards fall," the general implied that he anticipated remaining north throughout most of the summer.[2] He was not the only one to imply this.

Major Alexander S. Pendleton, known as Sandie, had served as Jackson's assistant adjutant general and remained on Ewell's staff. Several times, he indicated that the invasion plan was being set in motion. On June 4 Pendleton wrote to Kate Corbin, his betrothed, that the Confederate army was on the Rappahannock but that a new movement was contemplated and that he was excited about "our trip to Maryland" and "the hazards and glories of the coming campaign."[3]

In a letter to Kate on June 16 he wrote, "I see a better chance of its [the war's] ending now than for many a day before. The Yankee papers are all despondent, the people scared & our army in fine condition. We will go north for the summer. We are off tomorrow." Two days later he wrote his mother from Martinsburg. "We are not stopping here. We are going to Harrisburg."[4]

Pendleton seemed to echo the words spoken by Jackson in June 1862 to Colonel Boteler. Jackson was hoping for 60,000 men so that he could advance into Pennsylvania. But, he told Boteler, if he could even get 40,000, he would advance on the east side of the Blue Ridge and "in two weeks I could be at Harrisburg."[5]

———⟫●⟪———

An impediment to following this train of thought is the manner in which Civil War history generally is recounted battle by battle. One of the few to recognize this was Colonel Charles Marshall, Lee's aide. In a speech in Baltimore some time after Lee's death in 1870, Marshall referred to Gettysburg and stated that "the history of that battle is still to be written, and the responsibility for the result is yet to be fixed."[6]

Marshall was among the first to identify the invasion movements of 1862 and 1863 as part of a single campaign. He pointed out that one of Lee's prime objectives after taking command was the defense of Richmond.[7] His policy was to keep the enemy occupied at the greatest possible distance, to frustrate Union plans, break up its campaigns, and arouse fear for the safety of Washington, the center of Union politics.

Another of Lee's objectives, Marshall added, was to impress upon Northerners that they had to prepare for a protracted struggle and great sacrifices, with the possibility that all this effort might be of no avail.[8]

There is an unusual significance here that must not be overlooked. Marshall also echoed Jackson's thoughts on a major objective in his 1861 invasion plan. Marshall stated:

> The arguments for peace in the North would have been much more convincing if [a Confederate] victory had placed

Washington, Baltimore and Philadelphia within our reach than if gained in Virginia.

It therefore became important to consider how to accomplish quickly the greatest possible results with the smallest loss, and how to make a limited number of men most effective in attaining both the chief end of bringing a satisfactory peace, and the immediate object of thwarting and frustrating the designs of the enemy.[9]

After Chancellorsville, Marshall noted, it would not have done for Lee to risk another movement toward Richmond by Hooker or for him to attack the larger Union Army opposite Fredericksburg. Therefore, Marshall explained:

> It was desirable for many reasons to force General Hooker to leave the vicinity of Fredericksburg. We were so far from Washington as to make the authorities there feel so secure that they would not hesitate to detach troops to operate against either Richmond or Vicksburg while our army remained confronting that of General Hooker, and the resources of the North in men were such that they could have sent off a sufficient force for either purpose without materially weakening the army at Fredericksburg.
>
> It is an error to compare the possible results of any other plan of operation with the result which actually followed the movement into Pennsylvania. The true standard is to compare the Pennsylvania campaign as it might have been, and as General Lee had reason to believe it would be, with any other plan that he could have adopted in 1863.
>
> If it shall be found that such a campaign was wisely adopted to attain the end proposed, and that it was reasonable to expect that it could be so conducted as to accomplish the end proposed in the way intended, there only remains the enquiry, why was it not conducted in the way in which it was intended? Why did it result in a great battle with the advantage of position on the side of the enemy, when it had not been intended to fight a great battle, or if at all, only on the grounds as General Lee might select?[10]

But what was Lee's plan? He intended to move north in two columns—one would move east of the Blue Ridge Mountains to create a threat to Washington, and the other, a single corps, would cross into the Shenandoah Valley, drive out Union troops, and advance into Pennsylvania.

After the war Gettysburg analysts did not mention the single-campaign theory but focused only on the battle and on the movements that led to it. Typical were the comments of Colonel Long, Lee's military secretary from April 21, 1862, until August 31, 1863. He stated:

By the first of June [1863] General Lee had completed his arrangements for the ensuing campaign. The object of the campaign being the defense of Richmond, General Lee could either continue on the defensive and oppose the Federal advance as he had recently done [at Chancellorsville], or he might assume the offensive and by bold maneuvering oblige the Federal army to recede from its present line of operations to protect its capital or oppose the invasion of Maryland and Pennsylvania. The dispirited condition of the Federal army since its late defeat, and the high tone of that of the Confederates, induced the adoption of the latter plan.

Before the movement began his plans of operation were fully matured and with such precision that the exact locality at which a conflict with the enemy was expected to take place was indicated on his map. The locality was the town of Gettysburg, the scene of the subsequent battle.[11]

Long had been advised of the plan at a meeting with Lee about two weeks before the first Confederate troops moved toward Culpeper on June 3. He said he was told that the first objective would be to draw Hooker from the Rappahannock. Long suggested it might be better to engage Hooker near Manassas. Lee replied that "no results of decisive value to the Confederate States could come from a victory in that locality."

Long said Lee then outlined a plan to invade Pennsylvania toward Chambersburg, York, or Gettysburg. The most likely site of a battle, Lee added, was Gettysburg, nearest his base on the Potomac.

"There was in his mind no thought of reaching Philadelphia, as was frequently feared in the North," Long stated. "Yet, he was satisfied that the Federal army, if defeated in a pitched battle, would be seriously disorganized and forced to retreat across the Susquehanna—an event which would give him control of Maryland and Western Pennsylvania, and probably West Virginia, while it would very likely cause the fall of Washington and the flight of the Federal Government. Lee then added that these results, with probable aid to Vicksburg, fully warranted the hazard of invading the North.

"The proposed scheme of operations," Long added, "was submitted to President Davis in a personal interview, and fully approved by him."[12] This undoubtedly happened while Lee and Stuart were in Richmond from May 15 to 17.

Another member of Lee's staff, Colonel Walter H. Taylor, stated that "his [Lee's] design was to free the State of Virginia, for a time at least, from the presence of the enemy." Taylor also felt that a battle on Northern soil would be inevitable but victory there would gain Lee "far more decisive results than could be hoped for from a like advantage gained in Virginia." Taylor added that any movement into the North would "so far disturb the Federal plans for the summer campaign as to prevent its execution during the season for active operations."[13]

Longstreet, the highest-ranking Confederate to write extensively about Gettysburg, focused on the battle and movements that led to it.[14] He always implied that the decision to invade the North was an alternate offered by Lee to the one he had proposed on his return from Suffolk—to send part of his corps west to relieve Vicksburg.

According to Longstreet, "a few days before we were ready to move [on June 3] General Lee sent for General Ewell to receive his orders. I was present at the time and remarked that if we were ever going to make an offensive battle it should be done south of the Potomac—adding that we might have an opportunity to cross the Rappahannock near Culpeper Court House and make the battle there. I made this suggestion in order to bring about a discussion which I thought would give Ewell a better idea of the plan of operations. My remark had the desired effect and we talked over the possibilities of a battle south of the Potomac.[15]

"As soon as affairs took such shape as to assure me that the advance northward was inevitable," Longstreet wrote, he sent a scout to Washington to find out what he could. Longstreet, like so many others, also felt Lee was going north to seek a battle. "The plan of defensive tactics gave some hope of success," he wrote, "and, in fact, I assured General Lee that the First Corps would receive and defend the battle if he would guard its flanks, leaving his other corps to gather the fruits of success."[16]

These divergent opinions expressed by men so close to Lee complicate the study of Confederate movements that led to Gettysburg. Not everyone was aware of what had been discussed by Lee, Jackson, and Stuart in January and February.

Yet another version was presented by Colonel John S. Mosby, commander of the ranger force that operated in northern Virginia. He was one of the few who recognized the true intent of the Confederate invasion. In an 1891 article he said:

A true history of the Gettysburg campaign has never been written. It has been the accepted idea that General Lee started from Fredericksburg in June, 1863, with a preconceived plan of campaign for the invasion of the North, which should culminate in a great and decisive battle at Gettysburg.

Yet it now appears that even after General Lee had reached the Shenandoah Valley, and cleared it of the enemy, he was doubtful about crossing the Potomac. After having cleared the Shenandoah Valley of the enemy, General Lee waited for some days on events. He sent Ewell into Maryland, but did not decide to follow with the rest of the army until he was convinced that Hooker was about crossing in pursuit. In fact, he seemed to prefer remaining in the Valley as long as he could keep Hooker on the south bank of the Potomac, and allowing Ewell to go into Pennsylvania.

He then said that Lee had told Ewell that north of the Potomac, Ewell's corps "would accomplish as much, unmolested, as the whole army could perform with General Hooker in its front."[17]

In his analysis, Mosby observed that "Lee's dispatches show that by a campaign of maneuvers he expected to win the fruits of a successful battle. His movement was intended as more of a demonstration than a real invasion."[18] It was virtually the same idea that Lee expressed in a conversation with Colonel Allan after the war.[19]

———

Actually Lee had taken the first important step northward on June 1 after reorganizing the Army of Northern Virginia. Jed Hotchkiss—Jackson's topographer, who also had remained on Ewell's staff—noted in his diary on June 1 that there had been a conference at Lee's headquarters that day and "by request I showed him [Ewell] and General A. P. Hill my map. They were much pleased with it and General Ewell gave me a map that General Lee had given him, to copy. General Lee came over to our headquarters [Ewell's] in the P.M."[20]

Hotchkiss did not identify the generals, but they apparently were

Longstreet, Ewell, Hill, and possibly Stuart.[21] Later, in referring to the plan of campaign "as detailed to Colonel Long," Hotchkiss added:

This was, doubtless, the identical campaign that Jackson had in view, and which he probably had discussed with Lee during the preceding winter, when he ordered the preparation of a detailed map extending from the Rappahannock to the Susquehanna.[22]

⸺⸰⸺

In a conversation with Allan after the war Lee implied that Davis had expressed reservations about the plan. Allan quoted Lee as saying:

Mr. Davis did not like the movement northward [and] said he was afraid Lee could not get away, that the enemy would attack. Lee said he had no fears about getting off, the only trouble was about Richmond, but he thought by concealing his movements and managing well, he could get so far north as to threaten Washington before they could check him, & this once done he knew there was no need of further fears about their moving on Richmond.[23]

In early June, however, Lee was still concerned about getting reinforcements from North Carolina and southeastern Virginia, as well as for the safety of Richmond. In a letter to Davis on June 2 he said, "I think Cooke's [brigade] had better be halted on the Chickahominy for the present and Davis' brigade sent to this place to complete Heth's division. I regret losing Ransom's and Jenkins' [brigades] with their veteran troops." He then added:

I hope the forces we can place near Richmond will be able to secure it against attack from the York or James River. The local troops of the city should be organized promptly, and be kept in readiness for service at any moment. If I am able to move, I propose to do so cautiously, watching the result, and not to get beyond recall until I find it safe.[24]

According to Lee's instructions the movement was to begin on Wednesday morning, June 3. Longstreet was to move first, followed by Ewell. Their destination was to be Culpeper, near where Stuart was camped.[25] Hill's corps was to remain near Fredericksburg to watch Hooker and warn Lee of any moves.[26]

The movement started on schedule. On June 3 McLaws began the march. The same day, Hood's division, which had advanced to Verdierville on May 30, resumed the march and joined McLaws in Culpeper.[27]

Rodes's division of Ewell's corps broke camp early on June 4 and headed for Culpeper. His troops marched sixteen miles that day, twenty-one miles on Friday, and four miles on the 6th before he was told to halt and await further orders. Early's and Johnson's divisions left camp on Friday and arrived at Culpeper on June 7.[28]

Lee's plan included support from troops already in the Shenandoah Valley and western Virginia. On June 3 he instructed Samuel Jones to return three regiments and two battalions to Brigadier General Albert G. Jenkins, commander of Confederate cavalry around Staunton. The absent troops constituted almost half of Jenkins's brigade.[29]

On June 7 he directed Jenkins to concentrate at Strasburg or Front Royal by the 10th to cooperate "with a force of infantry." Lee also asked Jenkins for "all the information you have about the position and strength of the enemy at Winchester, Martinsburg, Charlestown, Berryville, and any other point where they may be."[30]

The same day Lee ordered John Imboden, commanding the North-western Brigade, to advance toward Romney. He wanted to attract enemy attention and, if possible, to disrupt the Baltimore and Ohio Railroad. Lee added that Imboden was to "cooperate with any troops you may find operating in the Valley."[31] This was clarified three days later.

A third letter on June 7 went to Major General Isaac R. Trimble, new commander of the Valley District. He urged Trimble to support Jenkins and Imboden and added that if Trimble's health permitted, he should "accompany the troops and take part in their operations."[32]

In the meantime, Stuart, with his enlarged cavalry force, had moved toward Brandy Station, six miles northeast of Culpeper Court House, from where he could cover the army's right flank.[33]

Rumors and reports concerning Confederate movements alarmed Hooker and authorities in Washington. The first hint of trouble came from an observer in Washington, dated June 1. Apparently referring to Stuart's advance to Culpeper, G. S. Smith said he did not figure it was intended to menace Washington, but that the Confederates were again headed toward Maryland or were seeking to distract Hooker while Stuart moved north. Smith concluded, "I have every reason for believing that Stuart is on his way toward Maryland."[34] The next day, Hooker heard from Major General Erasmus D. Keyes, the Union commander in Yorktown, that "the idea prevails [here] that an invasion of Maryland and Pennsylvania is soon to be made."[35]

Hooker, meanwhile, had gained substantial evidence that a Confederate movement was indeed under way. In messages to Secretary of War Edwin Stanton on June 4 and to President Lincoln the next day, he reported that a number of Confederate camps had been moved or had disappeared. He was uncertain whether the movements were intended to protect Richmond or were the beginning of an invasion attempt similar to the one in 1862.

Hooker also wanted to know if he was still expected to cover Washington and Harpers Ferry, as he had been instructed on January 31, or if he was free to pursue the Confederates.[36]

The responses were little help. Halleck informed him on June 5 that Stuart was preparing a column of 15,000 to 20,000 cavalrymen and artillery for a raid, probably within two or three days. Lincoln the same day advised Hooker against crossing the Rappahannock to attack Lee's rear, should the Confederates move north of the river. In his famous words of caution, Lincoln advised Hooker not to risk "being entangled upon the river, like an ox jumped half over a fence and liable to be torn by dogs front and rear, without a fair chance to gore one way or kick the other."

Acting on Lincoln's instructions, Halleck told Hooker he was "entirely free to act as circumstances might require," providing that he remembered "the safety of Washington and Harpers Ferry."[37]

Hooker placed several bridges across the Rappahannock so that he could make a demonstration and "learn, if possible, what the enemy are about." Some prisoners were taken, Hooker told Lincoln, and from them he learned that the movement of enemy camps resulted from the reorganization of their army.[38]

Hooker's action had alerted Lee to the possibility of a Union advance. "It was so devoid of concealment," Lee wrote Davis on June 7, "that I supposed the intention was to ascertain what [Confederate] forces occupied the position at Fredericksburg, or to fix our attention upon that place while they should accomplish some other object." Lee explained that, on the night of June 5, he had ordered Ewell to halt his march

(Rodes's advance toward Culpeper halted the next morning) and, at the same time, had shifted Hill's corps to meet any possible attack.

The next morning, Lee continued, he found no evidence of any further Union advance and told Ewell to resume the march. "My conclusion," he told Davis, "was that the enemy had discovered the withdrawal of our troops from Fredericksburg, and wished to detain us until he could make corresponding changes." That evening, Lee left Fredericksburg to join the advance. Only Hill's corps was left to counter any movement by Hooker.

Lee had other matters on his mind. He wanted Pickett's division back and was demanding reinforcements from North Carolina and other points south.

> I think if I can create an apprehension for the safety of their right flank and the Potomac, more troops will be brought from their lines of operation in the south. But to gain any material advantage, I should, if possible, have a large force, as their army, by all accounts, is represented as very large. If it is true, as stated in the Northern papers, that General Hunter's forces have been reduced by reinforcements sent to the Gulf, it would be well for General Beauregard, with the force made available by this withdrawal, to be sent to reinforce Johnston in the west, or be ordered to reinforce this army.[39]

Later that day Lee telegraphed the president that Hooker reportedly was being reinforced from Suffolk and that "I require all troops that can be spared." He also told Davis that Pickett had been ordered to rejoin Longstreet and suggested that troops around Richmond be moved to cover his withdrawal from Hanover Junction.[40]

By the time Lee's messages reached Richmond, an important step had been taken to reinforce Confederate armies on the major fronts. On June 6 Seddon informed the eight governors east of the Mississippi River:

> Under the instructions of the President, I have the honor to address you on a subject deemed by him of great moment. The numerically superior armies of the enemy confronting us in the field at all the most important points render essential for success in our struggle for liberty and independence greater concentration of our forces, and their withdrawal in a measure from the purpose of local defense to our cities and least exposed States.

Seddon called for 49,500 men—reserve troops over forty-five years of age—to serve for six months for home defense in their own states. Raising these forces, without resorting to a draft, would release many men who could reinforce Confederate armies on the fighting fronts, Seddon said. The call was made under provisions of an act adopted August 13, 1862, by the Confederate Congress.[41]

There was one weakness in this action. The date called on for the men to begin home service, August 1, was almost two months after Lee had requested "all the troops that can be spared" for the invasion movement.

Lee's desire for quick reinforcements was stressed in a confidential letter to Seddon on June 8. After reviewing the situation in North Carolina, Lee stated, "As far as I can judge, there is nothing to be gained by this army remaining quietly on the defensive, which it must do unless it can be reinforced." Lee then repeated his opinion that the southern coast could be held by small forces, thus releasing troops for service on the northern and western fronts. "Unless this can be done, I see little hope of accomplishing anything of importance. All our military preparations and organizations should now be pressed forward with the greatest vigor and every exertion made to obtain some material advantage in this campaign."[42] In his reply two days later Seddon concurred but pointed out, "I have not hesitated in cooperating with your plans, to leave this city [Richmond] almost defenseless." He also noted some hesitance—as Lee had—by Davis to call troops from North Carolina, but added, "I trust he will concur in the policy of encountering some risk to promote the grand results that may be attained by your successful operations."[43]

Back in Culpeper, reports of the proposed movement were filtering down from headquarters. Rodes must have learned what was contemplated and acted accordingly.

In his report he noted that after he had been halted near Culpeper on June 6, he resumed his march the next day, passed through town, and camped about four miles beyond. On June 8 he wrote:

Finding that a long march was ahead of us, and that the supplies had to be closely looked to, I ordered all the baggage, tents, &c., that could be spared to be sent to the rear. By this means, each brigade was enabled to transport three days rations in its train, in addition to an equal amount in the division commissary train, the men also carrying three days' rations each in his haversack; hence, when the division resumed its march, it was supplied with fully nine days' rations.[44]

This time around, there were no written instructions on specific unit movements, so there was no risk of another lost order, as there had been in 1862. Many orders in 1863 were given orally. Some were written, and in a few cases, Lee ordered his officers to destroy letters after they had been memorized.

In the meantime Hooker had decided to move against the Confederate cavalry buildup around Culpeper. On June 6 he ordered all of his cavalry, with some infantry support, to break it up. Hooker ordered Major General Alfred Pleasonton, his cavalry commander, on June 7: "If you should succeed in routing the enemy, you will follow him vigorously as far as it may be to your advantage to do so."[45]

Newspapers in Richmond and other Southern cities reported that Stuart had been surprised—"drastically surprised," as some reported it— by the enemy's advance and the fighting that followed it. The reports touched off a wave of unjust criticism of Stuart that continued long after the war.

Pleasonton's movement was no surprise to Stuart. Lee reviewed the troops at the cavalry camp on June 8 and told Stuart to move across the Rappahannock the following day. The purpose, according to H. B. McClellan of Stuart's staff, was to protect Longstreet's and Ewell's flank as they moved northward. That night several of Stuart's brigades moved closer to the river.[46]

At daylight the area was blanketed by fog but musket fire alerted the Confederates that the enemy had started across the river.[47] It was the beginning of the Battle of Brandy Station. The fighting continued through most of the day before Union forces withdrew across the Rappahannock. During the fighting, Lee sent Ewell to support Stuart, but on reaching Brandy Station with Rodes's division, he found the enemy already retiring.[48]

In a letter to his wife on June 12 Stuart wrote, "God has spared me through another bloody battle, and blessed with victory our arms. . . . The papers are in great error, as usual, about the whole transaction. It was

no surprise. The enemy's movement was known and he was defeated."
The Confederate loss, Stuart added, "does not exceed 500 killed,
wounded and missing."[49]

———⟫●⟪———

The statement that Stuart was not surprised was confirmed by a message
Pleasonton sent to Hooker at 7:40 A.M. June 9: "The enemy is in strong
cavalry force here. We have had a severe fight. They were aware of our
movement, and were prepared."[50] At 8 P.M. he notified Hooker that "having crippled the enemy by desperate fighting, so that he could not follow
me, I returned with my command to the north side of the Rappahannock. Tomorrow morning Stuart was to have started on a raid into Maryland. You may rest satisfied he will not attempt it."[51]

At 8:30 P.M. he informed Hooker that the Union cavalry and infantry
were withdrawing, then added, "Lee reviewed the whole of Stuart's cavalry yesterday."[52] Pleasonton repeated this information in a dispatch on
June 10 to the War Department. He identified the source as a "contra-
band [slave], a servant of an officer in Stuart's artillery." Pleasonton also
referred to "Stuart's raid" and added that it "was intended for Pennsylvania and Pittsburgh."[53]

At 5:30 A.M. June 10 Pleasonton reported, "We had splendid fighting
yesterday, and I think it will prevent Stuart from making his raid, which
he was to have commenced this morning."[54] Pleasonton was correct in
one respect. Stuart did not start his movement on June 10; his orders had
been countermanded.[55] Instead, Ewell's corps started marching on June
10 toward the Shenandoah Valley.

PART 4

On the Road to Gettysburg

CHAPTER 22

Starting North Again

WEDNESDAY, JUNE 10, 1863, MARKED THE BEGINNING OF AN EXTRA-
ordinary period in the history of the Confederacy. It was a time when
"resolute perseverance and vigorous effort" held promise of achieving
the goal Jefferson Davis had envisioned when he told Congress in January, "We have every reason to expect that this will be the closing year of
the war."

Hopes were high that day as Ewell started marching north from the
Brandy Station area. His destination and route were disclosed by Lee in
letters to Generals Imboden and Jenkins on that Wednesday.

To Imboden, Lee expressed pleasure with his prompt movement
toward the Potomac River. "General Ewell will be in command in the
Lower Valley," Lee wrote, and instructed Imboden to "communicate to
him any intelligence which may aid him in his operations, and to carry
out any instructions he may give."

At that time Jenkins's cavalry was near Strasburg, about fifteen miles
south of Winchester, and also on the road from Front Royal. In his letter
Lee noted that Jenkins was at a strategic point. "When you receive notice
from General Ewell of his arrival in the Valley," Lee added, "report to
him for duty. In the meantime, you will keep your scouts out, and collect
all information of the strength and position of the enemy forces at Winchester, Berryville, Martinsburg, and Harpers Ferry, so that you may give
General Ewell the benefit of the latest information."[1]

Ewell had received verbal instructions from Lee for the start of his
movement northward. In a third letter on June 10 Lee informed him of

the orders sent to Imboden and Jenkins, and added: "I request you will keep me advised of your progress, and, as far as you can, notify me of the different stages of your march as you proceed. General Jenkins is establishing a line of couriers between the Valley and my headquarters."[2]

———⊶⊷———

Military matters were not the only things on Lee's mind. He also turned his attention to the major objective of Jackson's plan, to "force the people of the North to understand what it will cost them to hold the South in the Union at the bayonet's point."

Lee felt it was time to pursue peace efforts. In a letter to Davis on June 10 he wrote:

> I beg leave to bring to your attention a subject with reference to which I have thought that the course pursued by writers and speakers among us has had a tendency to interfere with our success. I refer to the manner in which the demonstrations of a desire for peace at the North has been received in our country.
>
> I think there can be no doubt that journalists and others at the South, to whom the Northern people naturally look for a reflection of our opinions, have met these indications in such wise as to weaken the hands of the advocates of a pacific policy on the part of the Federal Government, and give much encouragement to those who urge a continuation of the war.
>
> Recent political movements in the United States, and the comments of influential newspapers upon them, have attracted my attention particularly to this subject, which I deem not unworthy of the consideration of Your Excellency, nor inappropriate to be adverted to by me, in view of its connection with the situation of military affairs.
>
> Conceding to our enemies the superiority claimed by them in numbers, resources, and all the means and appliances for carrying on the war, we have no right to look for exemptions from the military consequences of a vigorous use of these advantages, excepting by such deliverance as the mercy of Heaven may accord to the courage of our soldiers, the justice of our cause, and the constancy and prayers of our people. While making the most of the means of resistance we possess, and gratefully accepting the measure of suc-

cess with which God had blessed our efforts as an earnest of His approval and favor, it is nevertheless the part of wisdom to carefully measure and husband our strength, and not to expect from it more than the ordinary course of affairs is capable of accomplishing. We should not, therefore, conceal from ourselves that our resources in men are constantly diminishing, and the disproportion in this respect between us and our enemies, if they continue united in their efforts to subjugate us, is steadily augmenting.

The decrease of the aggregate of this army, as disclosed by the returns, affords an illustration of this fact. Its effective strength varies from time to time, but the falling off in its aggregate shows that its ranks are growing weaker and that its losses are not supplied by recruits.

Under these circumstances, we should neglect no honorable means of dividing and weakening our enemies, that they may feel some of the difficulties experienced by ourselves. *It seems to me that the most effectual mode of accomplishing this object, now within our reach, is to give all the encouragement we can, consistently with the truth, to the rising peace party of the North.* [Author's italics.]

Nor do I think we should, in this connection, make nice distinction between those who declare for peace unconditionally and those who advocate it as a means of restoring the Union, however much we may prefer the former.

Lee added that "when peace is proposed to us, it will be time enough to discuss its terms." The Confederacy, under those circumstances, would not consider any proposal intended to "bring us back to the Union."[3]

Davis supported these ideas in a letter to Lee on June 19. Lee replied that he was gratified and added, "I do not know that we can do anything to promote the pacific feeling, but our course ought to be shaped as not to discourage it."[4]

Another who recognized the importance of such action was Lee's aide, Charles Marshall. Regarding the 1863 invasion plan, he wrote, "A victory over the Federal Army in Virginia would have tended to strengthen the peace party in the North, only in so far as it would have tended to assure the Northern people that they could not succeed. The 'copperheads' were never weaker than when the Federal armies were successful, and the arguments for peace in the North would have been much more convincing if victory had placed Washington, Baltimore or Philadelphia within our reach."[5]

Evidence of such a peace party came from Governor Richard Yates of Illinois. He wrote Secretary of War Edwin Stanton on June 15, "Day after tomorrow the Democratic Convention for the Northwest is to be held here [Springfield, Illinois], and it is supposed by some that it will inaugurate direct opposition to the Government, if not revolution in our midst." Five days later he informed Stanton, "The convention has adjourned without a conflict, although it adopted peace resolutions."[6]

Others also were considering the possibility of peace. Vice President Alexander H. Stephens, who pointed out that peace resolutions had been adopted at a meeting in New York and that a peace convention had been called in Philadelphia, wrote to Davis from his home at Liberty Hall, Georgia, on June 12. He offered to go to Washington to discuss minor problems such as prisoners of war and noted that his presence might open the way for talks on "securing the blessings of a permanent peace, prosperity and Constitutional Liberty. Should the present position of affairs in your opinion be suitable, of which I am not so well informed as you are, and this suggestion so far meet your approval as to cause you to wish to advise further with me on the subject, you have but to let me know." This was a distinct change in attitude. Stephens added:

> You will remember while we were at Montgomery, when the first commissioners were sent to Washington with a view to settle and adjust all the matters of difference between us and the United States, without a resort to arms, you desired me to be one of those clothed with this high and responsible trust. I then declined, because I saw no prospect of success—did not think, upon a survey of the whole field, that I could effect anything good or useful in any effort I could then make on that line.
>
> You will allow me now to say that at this time I think possibly I might be able to do some good not only on the immediate subject at hand, but were I in conference with the authorities at Washington on any point in relation to the conduct of the war, I am not without hopes that indirectly I could now turn attention to a general adjustment upon such basis as might ultimately be acceptable to both parties and stop the further effusion of blood in a contest so irrational, unchristian, and so inconsistent with all recognized American principles.[7]

Davis swiftly summoned Stephens to Richmond; their meeting would lead to an undertaking in late June along the lines proposed by the vice president.[8]

In the meantime antiwar activists had started trouble in Pennsylvania. On March 3 Congress had approved an act calling for enrollment of men between twenty and forty-five who would be subject to future draft calls.[9] In the first three weeks of June, enrolling officers encountered resistance in three Pennsylvania counties—Greene and Bedford in the southwestern portion of the state, and Schuylkill in the anthracite area northeast of Harrisburg.[10]

Alarmed by the Confederate movement to Culpeper in early June, the Federals began to set up defensive lines in Pennsylvania. The first step was taken on June 7, when General Halleck sent an engineer, Captain C. B. Comstock, to Pittsburgh to prepare the city "against possible rebel raids."[11]

Three days later two new defensive departments were set up. Major General Darius N. Couch was assigned to command of the Department of the Susquehanna, including all Pennsylvania east of Johnstown; Major General William T. H. Brooks commanded the Department of the Monongahela, which covered Pennsylvania west of Johnstown plus three neighboring counties each in western Virginia and Ohio. Both were veterans of the Army of the Potomac.[12]

Bear in mind the development of the Confederate invasion plan. It had been proposed by Stonewall Jackson in 1861, after the First Battle of Bull Run, but no action was taken. In May 1862, after his Valley Campaign, Jackson sent Colonel Boteler to Richmond to present the invasion idea to Davis. Jackson asked for 40,000 men to transfer the action to the banks of the Susquehanna River. Davis sought Lee's opinion. He said that if Jackson could be strongly reinforced, it would change the character of the war. The threat to Richmond was too great, however, so Jackson was called east to join Lee against Union forces threatening the city.

Immediately after the repulse of McClellan, Jackson sent Boteler again to Richmond to urge authorities to take action. They did, as was shown by the correspondence of the president, the secretaries of war and state, and the inspector general in the first two weeks of July, when each mentioned invasion of the North. The initial movement led to the Battle of Sharpsburg, which disrupted the first invasion. This was followed by the conferences of Lee, Jackson, and Stuart in winter camps, meetings in Richmond, and Lee's decision to resume the northward movement as soon as possible.

Events prompted Colonel Marshall of Lee's staff to conclude that the operations were all part of a single campaign "to secure final success." This time the move would indeed take Confederate troops to the banks of the Susquehanna, as Jackson had proposed.

With Pleasonton's cavalry again north of the Rappahannock River and no immediate threat from other Union forces, Ewell resumed the march northward on June 10. Rodes's division led, followed by Johnson and Early.[13] Rodes apparently was told to stay in the lead, so he crossed the Blue Ridge at Chester Gap, passed through Front Royal, forded the Shenandoah River, and halted a few hours near Cedarville.

"Here," Rodes stated in his report, "the lieutenant-general [Ewell] fully unfolded his immediate plans of action to me."

The main features of the plan were the simultaneous attack of Winchester and Berryville, the subsequent attack of Martinsburg, and the immediate entrance into Maryland, via Williamsport or any other point near there which events indicated as best.

My division was ordered to take the Berryville road, via Mill-wood, to attack and seize Berryville; then to advance without delay on Martinsburg, and thence proceed to Maryland, there to await further orders.

Rodes moved north immediately and, after a march of seventeen miles, camped near Millwood on June 12.[14] Meanwhile Jenkins's cavalry brigade had joined Ewell's column at Cedarville and was ordered to move with Rodes. One regiment was detached to help Early and Johnson attack Winchester.[15]

In his diary entry of June 12 Jed Hotchkiss noted, "The passing of a pontoon train [at Front Royal] the day before had made the people anticipate our coming and they came out everywhere to welcome us." The pontoons and equipment were along the Shenandoah River that day, but Ewell decided it would take too long to set up, so his troops forded the river.[16]

News of Ewell's advance and the pontoon bridge created a stir in the War Department in Richmond. Robert G. H. Kean, head of the War Bureau, noted on June 14: "General Ewell's corps are in the Valley about Front Royal. I have as yet no idea why the army is thrown across there. They have a pontoon train along and may be on their way to Pennsylvania or Baltimore."[17]

The mention of pontoon trains by Hotchkiss and Kean, and Lee's references to them in April, provide more evidence that plans for resuming the invasion had been under way before the Battle of Chancellorsville.

The move in the Shenandoah Valley started on schedule June 13. Early advanced toward Winchester on the Valley Pike and Johnson drove off Union pickets on the Front Royal–Winchester road, then moved toward enemy positions east of Winchester. Rodes, with Jenkins's cavalry, headed for Berryville and, after routing enemy troops, prepared to move toward Martinsburg.[18]

Back at Culpeper three brigades of Pickett's division had rejoined Longstreet's corps on June 10. The next day, Longstreet moved his headquarters to Amissville, about fifteen miles north of Culpeper and east of Ewell's route.[19] Stuart noted in his report:

> I was instructed by the commanding general [Lee] to leave a sufficient force on the Rappahannock to watch the enemy in front, and move the main body parallel to the Blue Ridge and on Longstreet's right flank, who was to move near the base of the mountains through Fauquier and Loudoun Counties.[20]

There is no mention of this in Longstreet's report, but in one of his accounts after the war, he stated that his corps "was ordered north along the east base of the Blue Ridge to guard our line of march and cover, in a measure, the Confederate plans, Stuart's cavalry to ride between the First Corps and the Union army."[21] In another account, he stated, "Ewell was started off to the Valley of Virginia to cross the mountains and move in the direction of Winchester, which was occupied by considerable forces under Milroy. I was moving east of the Blue Ridge with Stuart's cavalry on my right so as to occupy the gaps from Ashby's to Harpers Ferry."[22]

Ewell's movements and the statements of Stuart and Longstreet clearly establish the plan for the Army of Northern Virginia to move northward in two columns, one in the Valley and the other east of the Blue Ridge. In the meantime, Lee's 3rd Corps under A. P. Hill remained near Fredericksburg until June 16 to keep an eye on Hooker.[23]

⟶➤●◄⟵

As Lee's troops began marching toward Pennsylvania, it became evident that he had confused the enemy, turned attention away from Richmond, and aroused fear for the safety of Washington. Equally important was the concern rising in states threatened by invasion and increasing antiwar sentiment in the North.

On June 10 as Lee was writing his letter to Davis about "the rising peace party of the North," Hooker repeated the proposal he had made before the Battle of Chancellorsville to move against Richmond. He telegraphed Lincoln: "If it should be the intention [of the enemy] to send a heavy column of infantry to accompany the cavalry on the proposed raid, he can leave nothing behind to interpose any serious obstacle to my rapid advance on Richmond."

He then asked for Lincoln's opinion, but added: "If left to operate from my own judgment, with my present information, I do not hesitate to say that I should adopt this course as being the most speedy and certain mode of giving the rebellion a mortal blow. From information I deem reliable, the only troops remaining in Richmond is the provost-guard, 1,500."[24]

In his reply an hour and a half later Lincoln repeated the advice he had given Hooker in May. "If left to me," he stated, "I would not go south of [the] Rappahannock upon Lee's moving north of it. If you had Richmond invested today, you would not be able to take it in twenty days, meanwhile your communications, and with them your army, would be ruined. I think Lee's army, and not Richmond, is your sure objective point." Halleck informed Hooker that he agreed.[25]

As rumors and reports of enemy movements reached him, Hooker became more concerned. On June 12 he informed Halleck, "It is reported to me from the [observation] balloon that several new rebel camps have made their appearance this morning. There can be no doubt but that the enemy has been greatly reinforced."[26]

Even more alarming was the report Hooker dispatched to Lincoln on the evening of June 14. Longstreet's corps and part of Ewell's had marched from Culpeper on June 7, he stated, and a column followed four days later. Hooker added that "if it is a movement for invasion," he believed that most of the Confederate cavalry was with that enemy force. He estimated the strength of the column as between 70,000 and 80,000. In addition, he stated, Hill's corps "of about 30,000" was still south of the Rappahannock.[27]

Hooker had grossly overestimated Lee's strength. The reorganized army had 76,224 troops, including Stuart's cavalry.[28] Hooker had 104,619 ready for duty.[29]

The situation in the Shenandoah Valley was more favorable for the Confederate advance than it was east of the Blue Ridge. In his sensational Valley Campaign in 1862, Jackson had outwitted three Union armies. In 1863 Jackson's old corps was advancing again in the Valley. This time, there were 22,000 seasoned troops in the unit plus Jenkins's 1,600 cavalrymen.[30]

Facing them was the Union 8th Corps, with 18,629 effectives scattered over almost a dozen points like an open umbrella covering potential invasion routes. The 1st Division, with 12,395 ready for duty, was commanded by Brigadier General Benjamin F. Kelley at Harpers Ferry. One brigade was there and another was at nearby Maryland Heights and Point of Rocks. A third brigade was divided among five points from Charles Town to Martinsburg.

The 2nd Division, under Robert Milroy, with 6,247 men, was concentrated around Winchester. Two brigades, with a few troops from Kelley's command, were at Winchester; the third was at Berryville, between Winchester and the Blue Ridge on a main road leading to Washington.[31]

Milroy was in a precarious situation. On June 13 as Early and Johnson moved toward Winchester, Rodes routed Union forces at Berryville and pushed on toward Martinsburg. "After a fatiguing march of 19 miles" on the 14th, he seized the town.[32]

The Confederate advance aroused serious concern in Pennsylvania. After taking command of the Department of the Susquehanna on June 11 Couch promptly called on Pennsylvanians to furnish all the men necessary for an army corps of infantry, artillery, and cavalry "to prevent serious raids by the enemy." The next day Governor Curtin urged support for Couch's call, stating, "The importance of immediately raising a sufficient force for the defense of the State cannot be overrated."[33]

To help Couch, Curtin took a step on the 12th that irritated Union authorities. He informed Stanton that he had decided to postpone recruiting men to serve for three years, or the duration of the war, in the Federal army. Stanton replied that the War Department could not sanction any postponement of recruiting.[34]

Three days later Couch reported that "comparatively few troops offered [their services] for State defense," and pointed out that "there were not 250 organized men" ready for duty in the department, plus 120 cavalrymen north of Chambersburg to scout enemy activities. As a result, supplies were removed from Carlisle Barracks and farmers in the threatened areas were directed to remove their stock.[35]

There was another problem: There was no money to pay volunteers until Congress appropriated funds. Colonel Thomas A. Scott, superintendent of the Pennsylvania Railroad and a former assistant secretary of war who had been assigned to a staff role in Pennsylvania, wrote Stanton on the 14th, "We find difficulty in getting our people aroused. The difficulty about pay for troops until Congress meets is a serious one." He added that efforts were being made to borrow money for that purpose until Congress could take action.[36]

Money problems could be put aside, but June 14 brought more alarming news. At 4:30 P.M. Curtin wired Stanton that Confederate troops were reported in Martinsburg, about twenty-five miles south of the Pennsylvania-Maryland line. Two hours later Stanton wired back, confirming the report and adding, "They also are at Winchester. It is certain now that there is a general movement toward Pennsylvania, although the rear of Lee's army [Hill's corps] is still south of the Rappahannock."[37]

At the same time Stanton told Couch, "The enemy has appeared at Winchester, and also at Martinsburg. There is no doubt that a general movement is being made toward Pennsylvania, and no effort should be spared to resist him. Hooker is also moving up."[38]

The situation in Pennsylvania was growing more desperate by the hour, and desperate measures were needed to counter the Rebel threat. Curtin turned up the heat. In a telegram received in Washington at 9:30 P.M. June 14 Curtin informed Lincoln:

> I have dispatched Col. T. A. Scott to see you and the Secretary of War. He will arrive in Washington at midnight, and will call on you. The plan for raising troops, although well conceived, we find

ineffectual to produce forces with dispatch equal to the necessities. Colonel Scott will present you my request to authorize a call for 50,000 troops, which we feel very confident will prove successful. I will remain up till I hear from you and the Secretary of War, through Colonel Scott.

I am fully conscious of your anxiety to use all the means in your power to protect this State from invasion, and I will be pardoned for saying that the plan which will be presented by Colonel Scott, in the judgment of all my officers, is the only one practicable for that purpose at present.[39]

At 2:30 A.M. on the 15th Scott wired Curtin that Lincoln would call for men to resist the invasion. Half an hour later Scott telegraphed people in Pittsburgh and Philadelphia—Thomas W. Howe and J. Edgar Thompson—that the "danger is imminent, and the people must be aroused and come forth promptly to prevent the invasion. The rebels are moving north in large force. The advance columns of Lee's army are now at Martinsburg."[40]

A few hours later Lincoln called not for the 50,000 troops proposed by Curtin but for 100,000. He asked for 50,000 militiamen from Pennsylvania, 30,000 from Ohio, and 10,000 each from Maryland and western Virginia. The men were to serve for six months "unless sooner discharged."[41]

Stanton dispatched an appeal for troops at 2:30 in the afternoon to governors of the six New England states and New York, New Jersey, Illinois, Indiana, Iowa, Michigan, Minnesota, and Wisconsin. He asked to be notified immediately of the number that could be forwarded from each.[42]

Lincoln's call sparked an immediate reaction from Simon Cameron, the secretary of war who had preceded Stanton. He telegraphed Lincoln, "I do not believe that you can get troops in time under your call for six months, but if you authorize General Couch to accept them for the emergency, a very large force will be on hand immediately."

Stanton replied, at Lincoln's request:

No one can tell how long the present emergency for troops in Pennsylvania may continue. The present movement is but the execution of Jeff Davis' original plan to make Pennsylvania and the loyal States the theater of war. The rebels are encouraged by the hope of assistance and encouragement held out to them by opposition to the war and resistance to enrollment in Pennsylvania. The law has fixed the period for which troops shall be called. If the emergency is over before that time, they can be discharged; but as human foresight cannot say how long it may take to drive out the rebels, especially if they should get aid and comfort in Pennsylvania, the President thinks he must obey the law."[43]

It is interesting that Stanton's closing words to Cameron seemed to echo Lee's thoughts to Davis five days earlier. Obviously Federal authorities were aware of the danger developing on the home front and the necessity of dealing with it before the invaders could gain advantage.

The next day, June 16, Curtin made an emotional appeal for support from Pennsylvanians.

Our capital is threatened, and we may be disgraced by its fall, while the men who should be driving these outlaws from our soil are quarreling about the possible term of service for six months.

It never was intended to keep them beyond the continuance of the emergency. You all know this by what happened when the militia was called out last autumn. You then trusted your Government and were not deceived. Trust it again now. I will accept men without reference to the six months. If you do not wish to bear the ignominy of shrinking from the defense of your State, come forward at once, close your places of business, and apply your heads to the work.[44]

At the same time H. W. Bradford, the governor of Maryland, appealed for a speedy response for the assigned quota of 10,000 men. "The entire want of an efficient organization of the militia of the State makes it necessary to provide the required force either by volunteers or by draft," he stated. "The term of service will be six months."[45]

Meanwhile an alarming report had been submitted by Mortimer Moulden, provost marshal for Montgomery County, Maryland. He had just returned from the scene of a raid on June 10 by John S. Mosby's men at Seneca, about twenty-five miles upriver from Washington. In his report to Provost Marshal General James B. Fry on June 15 Moulden wrote: "The Chesapeake and Ohio Canal is almost wholly officered and worked by men having little or no sympathy for our Government. The rebel sympathizers in this community [Rockville] are worse than ever in their hatred to the Government."[46]

The problems developing in Pennsylvania and Maryland were typical of those that quickly spread throughout most of the nation. The situation strengthened Lee's strategic plan to render all encouragement possible to "the rising peace party of the North."

CHAPTER 23

The Seeds of Disaster

EVERYTHING SEEMED TO BE GOING WELL FOR THE ARMY OF NORTHERN Virginia on June 14 as it prepared to move toward the Pennsylvania line, just as Jackson had proposed a little more than a year earlier. In the Shenandoah Valley Rodes was advancing toward Martinsburg, Early and Johnson were closing in on Winchester, and Imboden's cavalry was operating around Romney, West Virginia, and Cumberland, Maryland.

At Culpeper Stuart and Longstreet were ready to move north along the eastern base of the Blue Ridge. Their route followed part of the Confederate march in 1862 that led to John Pope's defeat.

Nevertheless a critical element of Lee's plan was missing. Despite his request and the promise he said he had been given by Davis, no troops came from the Carolinas and Georgia. Neither was there any indication that Beauregard was about to come north.

In the meantime nothing official about the situation in Vicksburg had been received in Richmond since the May 24 report of General Joseph E. Johnston, which was mentioned in Davis's letter to Lee two days later. Rumors and unofficial reports of Grant's being repulsed continued to reach Richmond as late as June 23, encouraging hopes for success.[1]

If things worked out as Lee hoped and Washington could be seriously threatened, it was reasonable to assume that a hurried call to Grant for troops could relieve Vicksburg. That was not to be. A little-known incident on the night of June 14 began a fateful week for the Confederacy, one that launched a disaster for the Army of Northern Virginia.

The trouble began as Early and Johnson began their moves to drive Milroy from Winchester. During the day, Lee stated, he had received several encouraging messages from Ewell "about entrapping Milroy and detailing movements" of his troops, including Rodes, who was advancing toward Martinsburg. "Suddenly," Lee added, Ewell "sent a dispatch stating that upon closer inspection he found the works [in Winchester] too strong to be attacked, and asking his [Lee's] instructions!"

Lee was not surprised. He explained that he had known Ewell for a long time and knew of his faults as a military leader. Ewell was indecisive, Lee said, and subject to periods of "quick alternations from elation to despondency." According to Lee, when Ewell assumed command of the 2nd Corps, Lee had talked "long and earnestly" to him about the problem, and hoped Ewell had gotten over his trouble.[2]

Lee explained that he had given Ewell full instructions "and told him that he had sent him ahead, confiding in his judgment, and that he must be guided by his own judgment in any unforeseen emergency."[3] Lee reacted immediately to Ewell's discouraging report. At 10 o'clock that night, he telegraphed Ewell to "use your judgment. If you think it best, push on with two divisions. I will relieve your third division as soon as possible."[4]

Lee talked to Longstreet immediately about the situation and suggested that Ewell needed support. An hour and a half after Lee had wired Ewell to "push on," Longstreet prepared to move his entire corps to Winchester.

A message was sent at 11:30 P.M. to General Hood to move his division "as early as you can tomorrow" for Winchester. Hood was told to let Lee know the earliest hour at which he could move.[5]

At midnight Pickett was directed to follow Hood's division, and McLaws was to report to Lee when he would be ready to move. Colonel J. B. Walton, Longstreet's chief of artillery, was to be prepared to move in the afternoon.[6]

Lee arose early the next morning, June 15, with Winchester still on his mind. At 7 A.M. he wired Davis explaining Ewell's indecision but added, "I presume that he has advanced towards the Potomac, leaving a division in front of Winchester." In addition, "A. P. Hill reported yesterday that the Federal force in front of him withdrew from the south bank of the Rappahannock on the night of the 13th, & by morning had nearly all disappeared. Our scouts report a general movement of the enemy up the Rappahannock, but I have no certain information on that point." Lee's uneasiness was more evident as he informed Davis:

> The uncertainty of the reports as to threatened expeditions of the enemy along the coast of North Carolina, & between the Rappahannock & James Rivers in Virginia, has caused delay in the movements of this army, & it may be too late to accomplish all that was desired.
>
> I still am ignorant as to the extent of the expedition said to be moving up the Peninsula, & hesitate to draw the whole of A. P. Hill's corps to me. Two of Pickett's brigades are at Hanover Junction, so that I am quite weak.[7]

Lee's concern over Winchester was quickly dispelled. In a message at 8:30 P.M. June 15 he informed Longstreet that "a dispatch from Ewell, dated 5 A.M. today, states that Early's division stormed the enemy's works at Winchester, capturing their cannon, &c., with little loss on our side. He was pushing on. I have as yet received no particulars."[8] He also telegraphed the news to Davis.[9] To Ewell, he wired congratulations: "I unite with you in thanks to Almighty God for the victory He has granted to the valor of our troops. Longstreet started today. Hill is in motion. Push on."[10]

⇒⚫⇐

As Lee's concern about the situation in the Valley eased, other matters demanded his attention. He had explained to Longstreet in his letter of June 15:

> I have been waiting for the arrival of Stuart, or of information from him, but as yet have received none. If anything of importance is received, I will write again.
>
> Should nothing render it inadvisable within your knowledge, I wish you would advance Hood on the road by Barbee's Crossroads, &c., to Markham, as arranged today. Your reserve artillery, trains,

&c., may be sent, if you think proper, by Chester Gap. Let McLaws & Pickett follow you as rapidly as they can & should the roads or other circumstances make it advantageous that they should proceed by Front Royal, give them the proper directions accordingly.

Anderson [of A. P. Hill's corps] encamped this evening two miles this side of Germanna, and will pass beyond this place [Culpeper] tomorrow evening. Heth left Fredericksburg today. Hill wrote that Pender was ready and would move as soon as he heard from his scouts that he had sent north of the Rappahannock. As far as heard from, the enemy had all gone.[11]

In a letter to Hill on June 16, Lee stated:

I have received your two dispatches of yesterday and conclude the enemy has entirely disappeared from your front. Gen. Anderson's division arrived here this morning. It will be supplied with provisions and forage, and will resume its march tomorrow. Heth I hope will reach here tomorrow, and as I have not yet heard of Pender being in motion, I presume he will not reach here until the next day.

I wish your corps to follow Longstreet as closely as you can, and, keeping your divisions within supporting distance, your reserve artillery, heavy batteries, and reserve trains might advantageously take the Sperryville road as far as Woodville, and there turn off for Chester Gap to Front Royal, and so down the Valley.

Longstreet's troops have taken the Winchester road as far as Gaines' Crossroads, or some point in that vicinity, where he will turn off to Rocks Ford, across Hedgeman's River, and thence by Edgeworth and Barbee's Crossroads to Markham. He will then either pursue the route by Paris [just east of Ashby's Gap] or fall down into the Valley by the Manassas Gap road according to circumstances. This road is said to furnish good grazing and some dry forage, and will tend to deceive the enemy as to our ultimate destination, at least for a time. Should the route not prove a favorable one, Longstreet will send back word to the marching columns, and they will be turned back on the Chester Gap road. Govern yourself accordingly.

Your divisions as they come up will be furnished with all the provisions and forage which they can take from this place. This being the last point where we will be in railroad communication with Richmond, I recommend that everything which may be found surplus in the baggage of your troops should be sent back from this place. If not here [at Culpeper], I will be found in the advance with General Longstreet.[12]

In referring to movements "as arranged today" in his letter to Longstreet on the 15th, Lee indicated that they had discussed possible actions earlier in the day. In the letters to Longstreet and Hill, it appears that Lee was referring to the most likely routes across the Blue Ridge into the Valley. The advice to Hill to follow Longstreet closely and move down (north) through the Valley seems to indicate that only Stuart's cavalry was to be left east of the mountains. This, however, was not Lee's intention. In a dispatch to Longstreet at 3:30 P.M. June 17 he stated:

> I have heard nothing of the movements of General Hooker from General Stuart or yourself, and, therefore, can form no opinion of the best move against him. If a part of our force could have operated east of the mountains, it would have served more to confuse him, but as you have turned off to the Valley, and I understand all the trains have taken that route, I hope it is for the best.
>
> At any rate, it is too late to change from any information I have. You had better, therefore, push on, relieve Ewell's division as soon as you can, and let him advance into Maryland, at least as far as Hagerstown. Give out it is against Harpers Ferry.[13]

In a letter also dated 3:30 P.M. June 17 Lee told General Ewell, "I think the reports which you have of the forces in Harpers Ferry must be exaggerated. I wish you to move Rodes' division on as far as Hagerstown, and operate in the enemy's country according to the plan proposed. Give out that your movement is for the purpose of enveloping Harpers Ferry." A footnote to this letter states that the copy in Lee's letterbook was made "from memory; draught mislaid."[14]

The two letters of the 17th were addressed from Markham, where Lee apparently had established headquarters on his route north. A dispatch to General Cooper on June 18, however, was marked from Culpeper. Evidently this was an error, or perhaps only part of Lee's headquarters had advanced to Markham. In the letter Lee reported that Rodes had taken Martinsburg and captured several pieces of artillery, more than 200 prisoners, and ammunition and grain.[15]

In a letter to Davis that day Lee stated:

> The enemy has been thrown back from the line of the Rappahannock, and is concentrating, as far as I can learn, in the vicinity of Centreville. The last reports from the scouts indicate that he is moving over toward the Upper Potomac, whether with a view of proceeding to Harpers Ferry, crossing the Potomac River into Maryland, or advancing through the mountains into the Valley, I cannot yet decide.
>
> Longstreet's corps has moved east of the Blue Ridge, with the view of creating embarrassment as to our plans, while Ewell, having driven the enemy from Winchester and Martinsburg, has seized upon the Potomac, so as to enable General Hill's corps to move up from Fredericksburg.

Stuart's cavalry, Lee added, had engaged in some skirmishes but was still holding approaches to gaps in the Blue Ridge. He also reported that Ewell had captured more than 4,000 prisoners, thirty pieces of artillery, and supplies. Milroy, however, "with a small body of organized troops and some stragglers [perhaps fewer than 1,000], escaped into Harpers Ferry."

Milroy had been routed on the 15th by Johnson's division at Stephenson's Depot, about five miles north of Winchester. Johnson reported that his men had captured "2,300 to 2,500 prisoners and about 175 horses, with arms and equipment"—more than half the total noted by Lee.[16]

The context of Lee's letters makes it difficult to follow developments on those critical days from the 15th to the 18th. For example, to Longstreet on the 17th, he noted that "if a part of our force could have operated east of the mountains," it would have confused the enemy. He also advised Longstreet that it was too late to change and he was to push on and relieve Early's division, still at Winchester.

But the next day Lee informed Davis that Longstreet's corps had moved east of the Blue Ridge in order to confuse the enemy. To Hill on the 16th, as noted, Lee stated that Longstreet's troops would move to Markham, then advance to Paris, or into the Valley by the Manassas Gap road.

In his report Longstreet provided no details on the movements of his troops during the period. He merely stated that on June 15, the corps "moved from Culpeper Court House along the eastern slope of the Blue Ridge, and, on the 19th, McLaws' division was posted in Ashby's Gap, Hood's at Snicker's Gap, and Pickett's supporting Hood's and guarding points between the two Gaps."[17]

According to Major Latrobe of Longstreet's staff, the movement started about 9 A.M. June 15, and on the morning of June 19 he was sent with E. P. Alexander, the artillery colonel, to determine the line of battle McLaws was to take in Ashby's Gap. In his diary, he added that on June 20, "Hood, McLaws and Pickett crossed the Shenandoah River at 5 p.m. [I] crossed with McLaws and made headquarters at Millwood."[18] Millwood is in the Shenandoah Valley, about midway between Ashby's Gap and Winchester. These movements were confirmed by Brigadier Generals James L. Kemper of Pickett's division and Joseph B. Kershaw of McLaws's division.[19]

Kershaw also noted that the 16th and 17th were excessively hot and that there were many cases of sunstroke.[20] In Hood's division it was reported that "some 500 men had collapsed from sunstroke, a few dying. The road during the last ten miles was literally lined with fallen soldiers, victims of the heat, humidity and hard marching. The lack of hats and shoes was having a telling effect."[21] In the diary of a soldier in McLaws's division, it was noted that "the heat has been very oppressive" and, as a result, many men had broken down.[22]

A soldier in Hood's 4th Texas Regiment wrote that the trip from Culpeper toward Winchester was "one of the hottest days and one of the hottest marches I have yet experienced. I felt quite sick and giddy with a severe pain in my head as I was climbing the hill after wading the Rappahannock, but it passed off, and I kept with the company, though I saw two dead men during the time and several others fall."[23]

In the meantime Anderson's division of Hill's corps, which had arrived in Culpeper on June 16, started moving westward. On June 19 it passed through Chester Gap to Front Royal, and a few days later the rest of Hill's troops followed into the Valley.[24]

Lee's desire to move toward Pennsylvania as quickly as possible was shown in the advice he had given Ewell and Longstreet to "push on." Unfortunately Ewell lagged and for three days the 2nd Corps was practically at a standstill. Rodes, who had moved his division across the Potomac River at Williamsport, Maryland, late on June 15, explained that his men were fatigued and many were barefoot. "In obedience to orders," he wrote, "the command remained at Williamsport during the 16th, 17th, and 18th, during which time, with the aid of General Jenkins' cavalry, the commissaries and quartermasters obtained large supplies in their respective departments," including powder, leather, cattle, and horses. Practically all the supplies were purchased, Rodes added.[25] On June 19, Rodes moved to Hagerstown and camped along the road to Boonsboro.[26]

On June 16, Johnson advanced from Stephenson's Depot to Shepherdstown and crossed the Potomac two days later. Early had remained in Winchester, guarding prisoners and captured supplies. He left there on June 18 but did not cross the Potomac River (at Shepherdstown, West Virginia) until June 22.[27]

These movements took troops from both Longstreet and Hill into the Valley in support of Ewell. That left only Stuart east of the Blue Ridge as a threat to Hooker and Washington. It was a significant change in Lee's plan to baffle the enemy while creating fear in the Federal capital.

GENERAL ROBERT E. LEE made a most important decision on June 5, 1862, four days after he had been placed in command of the Army of Northern Virginia. Until that time, his strategic policy was aimed only at the defense of Virginia, his native state. On June 5, replying to a request from Jefferson Davis, he endorsed an invasion plan proposed by Stonewall Jackson, and expressed his opinion that if Jackson could be strongly reinforced, "it would change the character of the War." *Massachusetts Commandery Military Order of the Loyal Legion, and the U.S. Army Military History Institute*

LIEUTENANT GENERAL THOMAS J. "STONEWALL" JACKSON
had urged offensive action after the First Battle of Bull Run on July 21,
1861. In mid-October, he suggested a plan to invade the North, put economic pressure on Northern people, and force them to seek an end to the
war, but it went no further than his commanding officer, General G. W.
Smith. In late May 1862, Jackson sent an aide to Richmond to present
the plan to President Davis and other Confederate officials. This time it
was accepted. *Massachusetts Commandery Military Order of the Loyal
Legion, and the U.S. Army Military History Institute*

HON. ALEXANDER R. BOTELER, a Virginia representative in the Confederate Congress and personal friend of General Jackson. On May 30, 1862, Boteler was appointed a volunteer aide-de-camp with the rank of colonel, on Jackson's staff. Boteler left immediately for Richmond to seek reinforcements for Jackson so that he could begin the invasion movement. The plan was approved, but action was delayed by McClellan's advance on the Peninsula. After the repulse of McClellan, Boteler again went to Richmond at Jackson's request, to have the invasion plan set in motion. *Jefferson County, W. Va., Historical Society, courtesy Robert J. Trout*

JEDEDIAH HOTCHKISS, topographical engineer on General Jackson's staff. In addition to his mapmaking ability, Hotchkiss had important knowledge relating to a major objective of Jackson's invasion plan—the closure of the coal mines. In 1846, Hotchkiss took a walking tour of the anthracite region north of Harrisburg, Pennsylvania, then spent a year in the area as a schoolteacher. After that, he walked through the Cumberland Valley, where Confederate troops would advance in 1863. *Massachusetts Commandery Military Order of the Loyal Legion, and the U.S. Army Military History Institute*

MAJOR GENERAL JAMES EWELL BROWN "JEB" STUART, cavalry commander in the Army of Northern Virginia. In the winter camp of January and February 1863, Lee held frequent meetings with Jackson and Stuart to develop plans for renewing the invasion campaign that would end in the Battle of Gettysburg. Following Jackson's death after the Battle of Chancellorsville, Stuart was the only officer, other than Lee, who knew what had been discussed at those meetings. *Massachusetts Commandery Military Order of the Loyal Legion, and the U.S. Army Military History Institute*

MAJOR JOHN S. MOSBY, commander of Mosby's Rangers. He and his men carried out numerous scouting expeditions for Stuart's cavalry. The information they gathered was important for Stuart's ride around McClellan's army on the Peninsula in 1862. In another expedition in 1863, Mosby gained information regarding the route Stuart could follow on the way to the Potomac River. *Massachusetts Commandery Military Order of the Loyal Legion, and the U.S. Army Military History Institute*

LIEUTENANT GENERAL RICHARD S. EWELL was placed in command of the 2nd Corps of the Army of Northern Virginia in its 1863 reorganization following the death of Stonewall Jackson. Ewell was to move north in two columns: Two divisions were to advance through Chambersburg and Carlisle toward the Susquehanna River and, if possible, capture Harrisburg. The other division was to seize the Wrightsville Bridge, downstream from Harrisburg. *Massachusetts Commandery Military Order of the Loyal Legion, and the U.S. Army Military History Institute*

MAJOR GENERAL JUBAL A. EARLY, division commander in the 2nd Corps of the Army of Northern Virginia, whose troops formed the eastern column of Ewell's advance into Pennsylvania. Early's division marched through Adams and York counties toward the Susquehanna River. *Massachusetts Commandery Military Order of the Loyal Legion, and the U.S. Army Military History Institute*

BRIGADIER GENERAL JOHN B. GORDON, commander of a brigade in Early's division, entered Gettysburg with his troops on June 26, 1863. After gathering a small amount of supplies and some food, Gordon moved toward York on June 27 and arrived there on the morning of the 28th. That evening his troops reached Wrightsville and forced Union defenders to retreat across the Susquehanna River bridge. *Massachusetts Commandery Military Order of the Loyal Legion, and the U.S. Army Military History Institute*

LIEUTENANT GENERAL JAMES LONG-
STREET, commander of the 1st Corps,
was to remain east of the mountains with
the rest of the Army of Northern Virginia in order to create fear for the
safety of Washington and hold Union
forces in check. A dispatch from Ewell
on the night of June 14 aroused Lee's
concern, and the next morning
Longstreet began crossing the mountains into the Shenandoah Valley. The
move would lead to a change in plans
and result in the entire army, instead of
one corps, invading Pennsylvania.
*Massachusetts Commandery Military
Order of the Loyal Legion, and the U.S.
Army Military History Institute*

LIEUTENANT GENERAL A. P. HILL, commander of the 3rd Corps, Army of Northern
Virginia. Hill's troops were the first to reach
the Gettysburg area on the morning of July
1, 1863. A division commanded by Major
General Henry Heth had been ordered to
move in that direction, and arrived within
a mile of the town at 9 A.M. A short time
later, they encountered Union troops in
the beginning of the battle General Lee
had hoped to avoid. *Massachusetts Commandery Military Order of the Loyal Legion,
and the U.S. Army Military History Institute*

GENERAL P. G. T. BEAUREGARD, commander of the CSA Department of South Carolina, Georgia, and Florida. In 1863, he objected to sending troops to Lee, and commented "of what earthly use is that 'raid' of Lee's army into Maryland, in violation of all the principles of war?" He did not learn details of Lee's plan until long after the war, when he remarked that "it is to be regretted that General Lee's plan was not carried out as he intended." *Massachusetts Commandery Military Order of the Loyal Legion, and the U.S. Army Military History Institute*

CHAPTER 24

Alarm in Pennsylvania, Confusion in Washington

ALTHOUGH LEE WAS CONCERNED ABOUT THE MOVEMENT OF HIS TROOPS, or the lack of it, alarm was spreading over Pennsylvania. At 10:50 on the night of June 15 Couch alerted Washington: "The enemy are following my pickets 9 miles south of Chambersburg and apparently moving north in three columns; one to Chambersburg, one to Gettysburg, and the other in the direction of the coal mines. I shall have but little to resist them, I fear."[1]

Couch, a native of eastern New York, probably knew of the industrial importance of Pennsylvania coal and recognized the mines as a potential target.[2] His concern for the anthracite fields showed up as he sought to keep Confederates from crossing the Susquehanna River.

As the Confederate advance continued through late June, evidence mounted that the target undoubtedly was the coal mines. On June 30 two strangers described as "supposed spies" were arrested in Pottsville as they moved about the community, "examining the surrounding neighborhood." They were arrested because of contradictory statements about their purpose and papers found on them.[3]

Three days later it was reported that "six Rebel spies were taken at Pottsville this morning and forwarded in irons to Philadelphia." One of them "had sketches of Schuylkill County and all the collieries."[4]

The troops that Couch reported following his pickets south of Chambersburg were the advance of Jenkins's cavalry that had started north after the capture of Winchester, crossed the Potomac above Williamsport, and moved into Pennsylvania.[5] Jenkins was pursuing a wagon train that had left Milroy and was heading for Harrisburg. The Confederate advance had alarmed residents of the area, and early on June 15, the road through Chambersburg toward Harrisburg was crowded. Included were farmers with their livestock and residents of southern Franklin County, Pennsylvania, and Washington County, Maryland.

At 10 o'clock that morning forty or fifty of the wagons dashed north through Chambersburg. About 11 that night Jenkins entered the town and early the next morning took a hill on the Harrisburg road, about four miles north of Chambersburg. While gathering supplies, the Confederates heard reports of Union troops advancing from the north. The rumors caused Jenkins to move back to Greencastle near the Maryland line on June 17.[6]

Rodes said Jenkins had been sent into Pennsylvania to gather supplies and had advanced to Chambersburg, "where he was ordered to remain until my division came up, which he failed to do, because of the reported approach of the enemy in strong force." As a result, "most of the property in that place which would have been of service to the [his] troops, such as boots, hats, leather &c., was removed or concealed" before it could be collected.[7]

Confederate activities from June 14 to 19 were highly confusing to Federal authorities, particularly Hooker. On June 14 Lincoln directed Major General Robert C. Schenck, commander of the Middle Department in Baltimore, to "get Milroy from Winchester to Harpers Ferry if possible. He will be gobbled up if he remains, if he is not already past salvation."[8]

At 8:30 that evening Hooker wired Lincoln that the Army of the Potomac was moving toward Washington, with most of his corps along the Orange and Alexandria Railroad from Catlett's Station northward. At 11:15 P.M. he asked the president if anything further had been heard from Winchester or if, in Lincoln's opinion, Winchester was surrounded. He also expressed reluctance to make any movement "until I am satisfied as to his [the enemy's] whereabouts."[9]

Hooker obviously was confused by a flood of conflicting reports. Among them was one that the whole Army of Northern Virginia was moving toward Harpers Ferry or the Shenandoah Valley. Another reported no enemy troops, except a cavalry brigade at Amissville, were "this side of the mountains." The report did not specify whether it was the Bull Run or Blue Ridge Mountains. Another reported a large force in the rear of Fredericksburg with indications that it was returning there.[10]

Just before midnight on the 14th Lincoln telegraphed Hooker: "You have nearly all the elements for forming an opinion whether Winchester is surrounded that I have. I really fear, almost believe, it is. If I could know that Longstreet and Ewell moved in that direction so long ago as you stated, then I should feel sure that Winchester is strongly invested."[11]

Hooker's confusion also was apparent in a telegram to Halleck at 9:15 the next morning. After briefly describing the location of his own troops, he stated: "Tonight my headquarters will be at Fairfax Station. If your information from the Upper Potomac should be of a character to justify a movement in that direction, I suggest that I may be informed of it at the earliest possible moment."[12]

One of Lee's purposes—to create fear for the safety of Washington—was evident in Halleck's reply less than four hours later. He wrote:

> Garrison of Martinsburg has arrived at Harpers Ferry. Milroy did not obey orders given on the 11th to abandon Winchester, and probably has or will be captured. Harpers Ferry ought to hold out some time. Your army is entirely free to operate as you desire against Lee's army, so long as you keep his main army from Washington.
>
> It is believed that Longstreet and Stuart are crossing the Potomac above and below Harpers Ferry. They certainly should be pursued. The force used for that purpose must depend upon your information of the movements or position of the remainder of Lee's army. Leesburg seems about the best point to move on first.[13]

Lincoln confirmed the loss of Martinsburg and Winchester in a telegram to Hooker at 8:30 P.M. on the 15th. He also told Hooker, "I think the reports authentic that he is crossing the Potomac at Williamsport. We have not heard of his [the enemy's] appearing at Harpers Ferry or on the river anywhere below. I would like to hear from you."[14]

Hooker's response was alarming. The situation, he told Lincoln, "seems to disclose the intentions of the enemy to make an invasion, and, if so, it is not in my power to prevent it. I can, however, make an effort to check him until he has concentrated his forces. I may possibly be able to prevent the junction, and commence the movement tomorrow."

A more detailed explanation was dispatched to Lincoln at 10 P.M.

> I now feel that invasion is his [Lee's] settled purpose. If so, he has more to accomplish, but with more hazard, by striking an easterly direction after crossing than a northerly one. It seems to me that he will be more likely to go north, and to incline to the west. He can have no design to look after his rear. It is an act of desperation on his part, no matter in what force he moves. It will kill copperheadism in the North. If it should be determined for me to make a movement in pursuit, which I am not prepared to recommend at this time, I may possibly be able to move some corps tomorrow.
>
> If they are moving toward Maryland, I can better fight them there than make a running fight. If they come up in front of Washington, I can threaten and cut their communications and Dix [Major General John A. Dix at Fort Monroe] can be reinforced from the south to act in their rear.[15]

At midnight Hooker informed Lincoln that the Army of the Potomac, except for two corps, was near Fairfax Station. He added that A. P. Hill had moved toward Culpeper, "for the purpose, I conclude, of reinforcing Longstreet and Ewell, wherever they may be."[16]

June 16 brought more alarming news from Hooker and increased concern in Washington. At 7 A.M. Hooker told Lincoln that if enemy forces were indeed crossing the Potomac, "a heavy column of ours should be thrown as speedily as possible across the river at Harpers Ferry, while another should be thrown over the most direct line covering Baltimore and Philadelphia."[17]

Four hours later, Hooker wired:

> You have long been aware, Mr. President, that I have not enjoyed the confidence of the major general [Halleck] commanding the army, and I can assure you so long as this continues we may look in vain for success, especially as future operations will require our relations to be more dependent upon each other than heretofore.
>
> It may be possible now to move to prevent the junction of A. P. Hill's corps with those of Ewell and Longstreet. If so, please let instructions to that effect be given me. As will appear to you, the chances for my doing this are much smaller than when I was on the

Rappahannock, for, if he [the enemy] should hold the [mountain] passes stoutly, he can cause me delay. You may depend upon it, we can never discover the whereabouts of the enemy, or divine his intentions so long as he fills the country with a cloud of cavalry. We must break through that to find him.

Lincoln's reply at 10 o'clock that night left no doubt about his stance.

To remove all misunderstanding, I now place you in the strict military relation to General Halleck of a commander of one of the armies to the general-in-chief of all the armies. I have not intended differently, but as it seems to be differently understood, I shall direct him to give you orders and you to obey them.[18]

⎯⎯⎯⎯➤●◄⎯⎯⎯⎯

The problems between Halleck and Hooker showed in their exchanges on June 16. At 11:30 A.M. Halleck wired, "I do not think there is reliable information that the enemy has crossed the Potomac in any force. Where his main corps are, is still uncertain, and I know of no way to ascertain, excepting through your cavalry, which should be kept near enough to the enemy to at least be able to tell where he is. My suggestion of yesterday, to follow the enemy's advance, by moving a considerable force first to Leesburg, and thence as circumstances may require, is the best one I can make."[19]

At 3:50 P.M. Halleck told Hooker, "There is now no doubt that the enemy is surrounding Harpers Ferry, but in what force I have no information. General Schenck says our force there is much less than before reported, and cannot hold out very long. He wished to know whether he may expect relief. He can hope for none, excepting from your army."[20]

At 4 P.M. Hooker asked Halleck whether "our forces at Harpers Ferry are in the town, or on the heights, and from what direction is the enemy making his attack?"[21]

At 7:30 P.M. Hooker told Halleck, "In accordance with your directions, I shall march to the relief of Harpers Ferry." He added that his column would begin at 3 A.M. on the 17th and that he expected to reach his objective in two days.[22]

Halleck's quick reaction certainly added to Hooker's confusion: "I have given no directions for your army to move to Harpers Ferry. I have advised the movement of a force, sufficiently strong enough to meet Longstreet, on Leesburg, to ascertain where the enemy is, and then move to the relief of Harpers Ferry or elsewhere, as circumstances might require. With the remainder of your force in proper position to support this, I want you to push out your cavalry to ascertain something definite about the enemy. You are in command of the Army of the Potomac and will make the particular dispositions as you deem proper. I shall only indicate the objects to be aimed at." Halleck added, "We have no positive information of any large force against Harpers Ferry, and it cannot be known whether it will be necessary to go there until you can feel the enemy and ascertain his whereabouts."[23]

———————

The deep concern at Union headquarters over Confederate movements was reflected in a dispatch on June 17 from Major General Daniel Butterfield, Hooker's chief of staff, to Brigadier General Rufus Ingalls, chief quartermaster of the Army of the Potomac. Ingalls was in Washington at the time, and Butterfield instructed him:

> Try and hunt up somebody from Pennsylvania who knows something, and has a cool enough head to judge what is the actual state of affairs there with regard to the enemy.
>
> Couch reports his pickets driven in. Enemy reported to have appeared at Poolesville, and everywhere else in Maryland, Pennsylvania and Western Virginia. Since we were not allowed to cross [the Rappahannock River] and whip A. P. Hill, while Longstreet and Ewell were moving off through Culpeper and Sperryville, we have lost the opportunity of doing a thing which we knew to a certainty we could accomplish.
>
> My impression now is that there is not a rebel, excepting scouts, this side of the Shenandoah Valley; that Lee is in as much uncertainty as to our whereabouts and what we are doing as we are as to his; that his movements on the Upper Potomac are a cover for a cavalry raid on the north side of the river, and a movement of his troops farther west, where he can turn up at some weak spot.
>
> We cannot go boggling around until we know what we are going after. Get any news you can that you know is definite and reliable, and bring it out with you.[24]

Late on the 16th Pleasonton was told to push forward with his whole cavalry force to find out what Halleck wanted to know. The next morning Pleasonton was instructed instead to move the main body of his cavalry to Aldie, just east of the Bull Run Mountains, and send out reconnaissance forces toward Winchester, Berryville, and Harpers Ferry. He was told that Hooker "relies upon you to give him information of where the enemy is, his force, and his movements."[25]

About the same time Hooker advised Halleck of the cavalry move and said, "As soon as the intentions of the enemy are [made] known to me, I shall be able to advance with rapidity."[26]

By coincidence, Brigadier General Fitzhugh Lee had been sent toward Aldie by Stuart to screen Longstreet's movement. The opposing forces clashed at Aldie on the 17th. Stuart pulled back to Middleburg, west of the Bull Run Mountains on the road to Ashby's Gap.[27]

Pleasonton reported to Hooker on the 18th that he was convinced that "there was no force of consequence" of enemy infantry east of the Blue Ridge. Later in the day he said he would push his reconnaissance toward Upperville and Ashby's Gap.[28] There was more cavalry fighting as Stuart withdrew toward the Gap to screen Longstreet.[29]

This action did little to resolve Federal confusion. Halleck summarized the situation to Hooker on June 19: "It now looks very much as if Lee had been trying to draw your right across the Potomac so as to attack your left. But of that it is impossible to judge until we know where Lee's army is. No large body had appeared either in Maryland or Western Virginia."[30]

Unlike the uncertainty in Washington, confidence seemed to be building in Richmond. J. B. Jones, the War Department clerk, on June 18 noted that the news from Winchester had "exalted our spirits most wonderfully. The whole valley is doubtless in our possession—the Baltimore and Ohio Railroad—and the way is open into Maryland and Pennsylvania. It is believed Hooker's army is utterly demoralized, and that Lee is going on."[31]

Indeed, but Lee still faced many problems. He had to adjust his plans to cope with movements, or the lack of them, in the Valley and along the Blue Ridge.

CHAPTER 25

Change in Plans

LEE DESCRIBED HIS CONCERN OVER THE CHANGES AND DELAYS IN THE invasion plan in a letter to Ewell on June 19. Ewell's forces were divided at the time. Lee wrote:

> I very much regret that you have not the benefit of your whole corps, for, with that north of the Potomac, should we be able to detain General Hooker's army from following you, you would be able to accomplish as much, unmolested, as the whole army could perform with General Hooker in its front.

Lee explained that Hood's division of Longstreet's corps had started for the Valley on the 18th to replace Early "in order that you might have with you your whole corps to operate with in Maryland and Pennsylvania." This movement was changed, however, when Stuart indicated that the enemy appeared to be preparing for an attempt to force a passage through the mountain passes to get in the rear of the 2nd Corps.

Longstreet, Lee added, was to "embarrass the enemy as to our movements" and detain them "east of the mountains until A. P. Hill could get up to your support." Longstreet also was to prevent the enemy from forcing a passage through the mountains and getting into the rear of Ewell's corps, thus separating it from the rest of Lee's army. In conclusion, Lee told Ewell:

> Not knowing what force there is at Harpers Ferry, or what can be collected to oppose your progress, I cannot give definite

instructions, especially as the movements of General Hooker's army are not yet ascertained You must, therefore, be guided in your movements by controlling circumstances around you, endeavor to keep yourself supplied with provisions, send back your surplus, and carry out the plan you proposed, so far as in your judgment may seem fit. If your advance causes Hooker to cross the Potomac, or separate his army in any way, Longstreet can follow you. The last of Hill's divisions had, on the evening of the 18th, advanced a few miles this side of Culpeper Court House, en route to the Valley. I hope all are now well on their way. As soon as I can get definite information as to the movements of General Hooker and the approach of General Hill, I will write again.[1]

Lee's advice to Ewell to "carry out the plan you proposed" raises several questions. What was the plan? How did it relate to Lee's instructions to Ewell on June 17 to "move Rodes' division as far as Hagerstown, and operate in the enemy's country according to the plan proposed"? Or, was it the plan discussed at the meeting of Lee and Ewell on June 11, as noted by Jed Hotchkiss?

Another possibility is that Lee, in his polite way, did not openly reject any suggestion Ewell might have made, in much the same way he had dealt with Longstreet's idea earlier to send troops to Vicksburg rather than invade Pennsylvania At that time, Longstreet felt that Lee had carefully considered the suggestion before deciding on the invasion plan.

———◦◦◦———

Later on the 19th Lee reported to Davis:

General Ewell, with two divisions, has advanced from the Potomac toward Pennsylvania His third division is retained near Shepherdstown for the present, to guard his flank and rear. General Longstreet, on the Ashby's and Snicker's Gaps roads threatens the enemy, who is massed between him and Washington. General Stuart is operating in his front. I hope that the first division of A. P. Hill's corps will reach here today, so Early may be relieved and follow Ewell.

All attempts of the enemy to penetrate the mountains have been repulsed by Stuart's cavalry, who, yesterday again drove him from Middleburg, and, by reports received last evening, the enemy's infantry have evacuated Aldie. Indications seem to be that his main body is proceeding toward the Potomac, whether upon Harpers Ferry or to cross the river east of it, is not yet known. The difficulty of procuring supplies retards and renders more uncertain our future movements.[2]

Lee's intentions were clear in those two letters, but he was unaware that Ewell had halted. On June 18 Rodes was at Williamsport, Johnson was across the Potomac at Sharpsburg, and Early was starting north from Winchester. One of Early's regiments had been left in Winchester, and two others in Staunton, to guard prisoners. His main body reached Shepherdstown on the 19th.[3]

Weather delayed Early. Hotchkiss noted that it had rained on the 18th and that the next night "it rained quite hard and raised the river." On the 20th, he said, "Early is kept back by the high water," and on the 21st he noted, "Early is still on the Virginia shore." More rain fell late in the day and raised the river still higher. Hotchkiss pointed out that "Johnson [was] at Sharpsburg, Rodes at Hagerstown, and Jenkins near Chambersburg."

Hotchkiss recounted two other significant events during that period. On June 18 he was at Rodes's headquarters working on a map of Maryland and Pennsylvania. He noted that Ewell and Major G. Moxley Sorrel of Longstreet's staff had joined Rodes in planning the route of Rodes's division and the 2nd Corps. Hotchkiss, who did not leave Rodes's headquarters until late in the evening, apparently overheard the discussion.

The next day Hotchkiss noted, "Gen. Ewell went to Leetown to see Gen. Longstreet. I went on to Gen. Johnson's headquarters, across the Potomac, as Gen. Ewell said Gen. Johnson might wish to consult me about routes, &c."[4] There is no further evidence of Ewell's meetings with Sorrel and Longstreet or details of what might have been discussed. But it raises interesting questions. Why did a member of Longstreet's staff travel to Ewell's headquarters to discuss movements of the 2nd Corps? Why did Ewell travel to Leetown the next day to see Longstreet? Could Longstreet's action have been prompted by his conference with Lee on the 14th about the situation in Winchester?

In the meantime Ewell had started his troops northward again. Rodes noted that Ewell had come to his headquarters on the 17th or 18th "and gave me additional instructions, to the effect that the division should, on the 19th, resume its march and move slowly toward Chambersburg until the division of General Johnson had crossed the Potomac."

On the 19th Rodes moved to Hagerstown, where he turned toward Boonsboro, as if threatening Harpers Ferry. He halted there and stayed in the Hagerstown-Boonsboro area for two days.[5] Early and Johnson also remained in camp on those days.[6]

Although Ewell had not "pushed on" as Lee desired, he had cleverly leaked out information that his movement was aimed at Harpers Ferry. On June 19 Brigadier General Daniel Tyler, commander at Harpers Ferry, notified Hooker that "three intelligent men deserted from the Eleventh Tennessee Regiment last night at Sharpsburg. They report the force there at about 8,000 of Ewell's corps, which crossed the Rappahannock 25,000 strong. The men last night were ordered to prepare three days' rations, to move this morning, as they were told, on Harpers Ferry or Frederick City [in Maryland]."[7]

There was one serious flaw in this information. The three men he described as deserters evidently were part of a ruse by Ewell to spread false information regarding Harpers Ferry. The 11th Tennessee was not with Ewell's corps. It was in Shelbyville, Tennessee, where it had moved early in January following the Battle of Murfreesboro. The regiment—in Lieutenant General Leonidas Polk's corps of the Army of Tennessee—remained in that area until the Chickamauga Campaign in September.[8]

In a letter on June 19 Davis informed Lee that efforts were being made to return all or parts of two brigades that had been left behind when Pickett was called north with Longstreet to rejoin the Army of Northern Virginia. Both Major General Arnold Elzey, commander at Richmond, and the secretary of war, James Seddon, had been asked to do so, Davis stated, but he was not certain what had been accomplished.

"We have been endeavoring here to organize a force for local defense," Davis explained, "but the delays have been vexatious, and, I think, in no small degree the result of misunderstandings, which better management might have prevented. I hope we shall have better progress hereafter, and think, with good outguards—infantry and cavalry to protect the railroads and give timely notice of an advance of the enemy—it will be possible to defend the city without drawing from the forces in the field more heavily than may be necessary for the duty of outposts and reconnaissance."

In closing Davis wrote, "I rejoice in the success which has attended your advance into the Valley of Virginia, and that Ewell has made so good an introduction to the corps of the gallant Jackson, as the successor of that lamented chief."[9]

Saturday, June 20, was marked by some unusual developments. The first was the movement of Longstreet's corps. In his official report of July 27 Longstreet stated:

> On June 20th, I received a dispatch from headquarters, directing that I should hold myself in readiness to move in the direction of the Potomac, with a view to crossing, &c. As I was ready, and had been expecting an order to execute such purpose, I supposed the intimation meant other preparation, and, knowing of nothing else that I could do to render my preparations complete, I supposed that it was desirable that I should cross the Shenandoah. I therefore passed the river, occupied the banks at the ferries opposite the Gaps [Ashby's and Snicker's] and a road at an intermediate ford, which was practicable for cavalry and infantry.[10]

When viewed alone, this third paragraph of Longstreet's report— written only three weeks after Gettysburg—leads to an unusual question. Why, if Longstreet had been directed merely to be ready to move toward the Potomac, did he twice act on his own suppositions and move westward across the Blue Ridge and the Shenandoah River?

A different view of the situation was provided by Lee in a letter to Davis on June 23. "General Ewell's corps is in motion toward the Susquehanna. General A. P. Hill's corps is moving toward the Potomac; his leading division will reach Shepherdstown today." He then added: "I have withdrawn Longstreet west of the Shenandoah, and, if nothing prevents, he will follow [the other two corps] tomorrow."[11]

In one of his postwar accounts, Longstreet stated that his corps had left Culpeper to cover the march of Hill and Ewell through the Valley and that he had moved along the east side of the Blue Ridge and occupied Snicker's and Ashby's gaps. Stuart "was in my front and on my flank, reconnoitering the movements of the Federals.

"When it was found that Hooker did not intend to attack, I withdrew to the west side and marched to the Potomac. As I was leaving the Blue Ridge I instructed General Stuart to follow me, and to cross the Potomac at Shepherdstown, while I crossed at Williamsport ten miles above." According to Longstreet, Stuart declined on the grounds that he had "discretionary powers" over the movement of his cavalry.[12]

Longstreet's crossing of the Shenandoah River and his attempt to draw Stuart into the Valley to continue the movement toward Pennsylvania would have left no force east of the Blue Ridge to threaten Washington, one of the main objectives of the campaign. Longstreet did mention in one postwar account, "General Beauregard was to be called from his post in the South, with such brigades as could be pulled away temporarily from their Southern service, and thrown forward, with the two brigades of Pickett's division [Jenkins's and Corse's] and such others as could be got together, along the Orange and Alexandria Railroad in threatening attitude towards Washington City."[13] In these accounts, Longstreet gave no indication that he knew of Lee's desire to hold Hooker's troops in check and send Ewell's corps into Pennsylvania.

<hr />

In several letters on June 20 Lee sought to develop another column for the advance, this one west of the Shenandoah Valley. It was much the same as William Loring's proposed movement during the first invasion in 1862. This time, however, Lee wanted a two-pronged attack with one column aimed at western Pennsylvania.

In a letter to John Imboden, the cavalry brigadier, Lee praised the destruction of important railroad bridges around Cumberland, Maryland, and the capture of many cattle and horses for the army. "At this time it is impossible to send a mounted brigade to your assistance," Lee added, "as the whole of the cavalry are required to watch the enemy and guard our movements east of the Blue Ridge and in Maryland.

"Should you find an opportunity, you can yourself advance north of the Potomac, and keep on the left of this army in its advance into Pennsylvania." Imboden was told to "repress all marauding" and to give proper receipts to everyone from whom supplies were obtained.

Lee was determined to avoid another lost order. In conclusion, he told Imboden to "destroy all my letters to you after perusal (having impressed on your memory their main points), to prevent the possibility of their falling into the hands of the enemy."[14]

In a letter to Major General Samuel Jones, commanding the Department of Western Virginia, Lee first reported Imboden's success in destroying B&O bridges, Hooker's movement toward the Potomac, and Ewell's movement into Maryland, with his advance cavalry in Chambersburg. He then said:

> I think the present offers to you a favorable time to threaten Western Virginia, and, if circumstances favor, you might convert the threat into a real attack. A more favorable opportunity will probably not occur during the war, and, if you can accomplish nothing else, you may at least prevent the [Union] troops in that region from being sent to reinforce other points. I would recommend, therefore, that you unite all your available forces, and strike at some vulnerable point.[15]

The letter did not reach Jones until June 26, and the next day he informed Lee, "If the War Department will relieve me from the duty of guarding the salt-works and the line of the Virginia and Tennessee Railroad, I can then go into Northwestern Virginia, perhaps into Pennsylvania, and at least make a diversion in your favor, and damage the enemy seriously."[16]

In another letter on the 20th, this one to Davis, Lee reported Imboden's successes and Ewell's positions north of the Potomac River. He then stated, "I have thought this a favorable time for General Sam Jones to advance into Western Virginia, and have so informed him. Should he not be able to accomplish anything more, he will fix the attention of the enemy in that region, and prevent reinforcements being sent to other points. If any of the brigades that I have left behind for the protection of Richmond can, in your opinion, be spared, I should like them to be sent to me."[17]

The next day, in preparing to move into Pennsylvania, Lee issued strict orders on obtaining supplies in enemy country. He stressed, "No private property shall be injured or destroyed by any person belonging to or connected with the army, or taken, excepting by the officers designated."

He then authorized chiefs of the commissary, quartermaster, ordnance, and medical departments to requisition supplies from "local authorities or inhabitants." All people who complied were to be paid market price and given receipts for the goods. If the locals refused, the department chiefs were authorized to seize supplies.

Officers detached from the main body had the same orders but were to furnish duplicate receipts to the department chiefs. If any Northerner tried to remove or conceal supplies, officers were to seize "such property, and all other property that may be needed by the army." In such cases, the property seized and the owner's identity were to be reported.[18]

Lee wanted to get the supplies so badly needed by his army without upsetting people who might be sympathetic to the South and, perhaps, associated with "the rising peace party of the North." There were two other important considerations: Lee's sense of propriety toward civilians and his realization that plundering degraded discipline in the army.

———————

Back in Richmond, concern over the situation in Mississippi was tempered by Lee's reports. On June 21 Robert Garlick Hill Kean, head of the Bureau of War, noted in his diary, "Yankeedom is in great fright at the advance of Lee's army to the Potomac, and considers this part of Pennsylvania south of the Susquehanna as good as gone."[19]

The similarity is interesting between Kean's statement and one written nearly a week earlier by Darius Couch, commander of the Department of the Susquehanna. In a letter to Stanton on June 15 he wrote, "All is being done that is in our power to resist the invasion, but, as matters look now, all south of the Susquehanna will be swept. Orders are being sent north to run out all horses, &c."[20]

Kean also expressed concern about Confederate plans. In his June 21 diary entry he noted, "General Lee's plans are still wrapped in profound mystery, at least to us in Richmond except doubtless the President and Secretary [of War]. There are two plans which General Lee may have in view, 1st, to occupy the passes in the Blue Ridge in Maryland with the body of his army and send the cavalry and one corps into Pennsylvania. 2nd, to march from Frederick on Baltimore . . . and perhaps Washington. General Lee has doubtless matured his plan of campaign. He saw last year [at Sharpsburg] what was lacking and will provide against it."[21]

Longstreet noted a similar explanation when he wrote that Lee's "early experience with the Richmond authorities taught him to deal cautiously with them in disclosing his views, and to leave for them the privilege and credit of approving, step by step, his apparently hesitant policy, so that his plans were disclosed a little at a time."[22]

Davis bolstered this view in his May 31 letter to Lee regarding D. H. Hill's objections to sending troops to Lee: "I had never fairly comprehended your views and purposes until the receipt of your letter of yesterday and now have to regret that I did not earlier know all that you had communicated to others."[23]

As Lee prepared to advance into Pennsylvania, Hooker cautiously moved to block any threat to Washington. By June 20 three corps paralleled the Potomac west of Washington—the 12th was in Leesburg, the 11th at a ford on Goose Creek, and the 1st at Guilford Station on the Loudoun and Hampshire Railroad. Two others were on the Little River Turnpike, leading from Aldie to Alexandria. The 5th was at Aldie and the 3rd at Gum Springs. Farther south, the 2nd Corps was just east of Thoroughfare Gap in the Bull Run Mountains and the 6th was at Bristoe Station on the Orange and Alexandria Railroad.[24] Some cavalry had advanced to Middleburg.[25]

Hooker was still uneasy. Late in the afternoon of June 20, Pleasonton was instructed "to move tomorrow morning with your entire corps against the enemy's cavalry" and was told that he would have the support of two infantry brigades from Major General George Gordon Meade's 5th Corps. "The commanding general is very anxious that you should ascertain at the earliest possible moment where the main body of the enemy's infantry are to be found at the present time, especially A. P. Hill's corps."[26]

Pleasonton drove Stuart's cavalry through Upperville into Ashby's Gap. He reported that as far as he could determine, the Confederates had no infantry east of the Blue Ridge. From information he had gathered, "Ewell's corps went toward Winchester Wednesday [the 17th]; Longstreet on Friday [the 19th], and another corps (A. P. Hill's, I think) is to move with Longstreet into Maryland."[27]

In his account Stuart explained that the Union cavalry, with infantry support, had been too strong for him to attack and that he gradually withdrew to Ashby's Gap west of Upperville.[28] When he learned of the situation, Longstreet stated, "I succeeded in passing part of McLaws' division across the [Shenandoah] River in time to occupy the Gap before night, and upon advancing a line of sharpshooters the next morning at daylight, the enemy retired." As a result, Longstreet added, McLaws's division returned to the west bank of the Shenandoah River on the 22nd.[29]

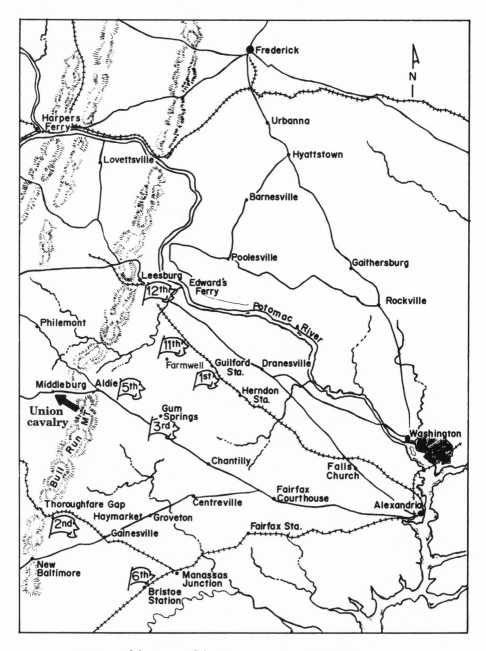

Positions of the Army of the Potomac on June 20, 1863. JOHN HEISER

In his report Stuart explained, "When the mist had sufficiently cleared away next morning [Monday, the 22nd], it was evident the enemy was retiring, and the cavalry was ordered up immediately to the front" and pursued the enemy. When he learned that the Union 5th Corps was in that area, Stuart decided against attacking "and I began to look for some other point at which to direct an effective blow."

Stuart said he then suggested that Lee leave "a brigade or so in my present front, and passing through Hopewell [Gap] or some other gap in the Bull Run Mountains, attain the enemy's rear, passing between his main body and Washington, and cross into Maryland, joining our army north of the Potomac. The commanding general wrote me, authorizing the move if I deemed it practicable, and also what instructions should be given the officer in command of the two brigades left in front of the enemy."[30] Lee confirmed that he had authorized the movement.[31]

Moving into the enemy's rear was not a new idea for Stuart. He had twice circled McClellan's army and made several successful raids behind enemy lines in 1862. Now Lee apparently had sound reason to accept Stuart's suggestion as another means of creating fear in Washington.

—————◆—————

Keeping these events in proper perspective is complicated by the different versions recounted by two members of Lee's staff—Long and Marshall— and by Longstreet. It also is surprising that not one of them seemed aware of Lee's basic intention to send only one corps into Pennsylvania.

According to Longstreet the leading corps, Ewell's, was to cross the Potomac at Williamsport and Shepherdstown. The 3rd Corps, passing behind the Blue Ridge, was to cross at Shepherdstown. The 1st Corps was to draw back from the Blue Ridge and cross the Potomac at Williamsport, to be followed by the cavalry, which was to cross at Shepherdstown.[32] He also noted, "General Lee so far modified the plan of march north as to authorize his cavalry chief to cross the Potomac with part of his command east of the Blue Ridge."[33]

In his account Long stated, "General Lee arrived with Longstreet's corps at Berryville on the 18th where he remained two or three days perfecting his preparations for the invasion of Pennsylvania. About the 21st he continued his advance in two columns, the one composed of the corps of Ewell and Hill, was directed to Shepherdstown, and the other, consisting of Longstreet's corps and the supply train, proceeded to Williamsport."[34]

According to Marshall, "Hill entered the Valley on June 19th, and as soon as his approach was known, Longstreet crossed the Shenandoah and also entered the Valley, thus reuniting the two corps. General Lee then resolved to cross the Potomac, with the object of compelling General Hooker to do the same so as to cover Washington."[35]

It was a trying time for Lee. Ewell's hesitancy in front of Winchester and Longstreet's subsequent crossing of the Blue Ridge had seriously altered the plan outlined in his letter to Ewell. Lee had to meet this reality, not merely modify or perfect his plans as Longstreet and Long stated.

CHAPTER 26

Lee's Deep Concern

LEE DID NOT WASTE TIME. EWELL NOTED ON JUNE 21, "I RECEIVED orders from the general commanding to take Harrisburg, and next morning Rodes and Johnson marched toward Greencastle, Pa."[1] Rodes noted that, according to new verbal instructions from Ewell, he started northward on the 22nd and that Brigadier General Alfred Iverson's brigade "was the first to touch Pennsylvania soil." After a march of thirteen miles Rodes added, "we bivouacked at Greencastle,"[2] about five miles north of the Maryland line.

Lee's order to Ewell apparently was given verbally at a meeting on the 21st, then confirmed in a letter the next day. Colonel Marshall wrote Ewell:

> Your letter of 6 p.m. yesterday has been received. If you are ready to move, you can do so. I think your best course will be toward the Susquehanna, taking the routes by Emmitsburg, Chambersburg, and McConnellsburg. Your trains had better be, as far as possible, kept on the center route.
>
> It will depend upon the quantity of supplies obtained in that country whether the rest of the army can follow. There may be enough for your command, but none for the others. Every exertion should, therefore, be made to locate and secure them. Beef we can drive with us, but bread we cannot carry, and must secure it in the country. . . .

I am much gratified at the success which has attended your movements, and feel assured, if they are conducted with the same energy and circumspection, it will continue. Your progress and direction will, of course, depend upon the development of circumstances. If Harrisburg comes within your means, capture it.

General A. P. Hill arrived yesterday [the 21st] in the vicinity of Berryville. I shall move him on today, if possible. Saturday [the 21st] Longstreet withdrew from the Blue Ridge. Yesterday the enemy pressed our cavalry so hard with infantry and cavalry on the Upperville road that McLaws' division had to be sent back to hold Ashby's Gap. I have not heard from there this morning. General Stuart could not ascertain whether it was intended as a real advance toward the Valley or to ascertain our position.[3]

There is an additional paragraph in the letter, as it appears in the Official Records: "The pontoons will reach Martinsburg today, and will be laid at the point you suggest, 4 or 5 miles below Williamsport, if found suitable. I will write you again if I receive information regarding your movements."[4]

At 3:30 P.M. Ewell got a second letter, this one written by Lee, according to Marshall. It stated:

I have just received your letter of this morning from opposite Shepherdstown. Mine of today, authorizing you to move toward the Susquehanna, I hope has reached you ere this. After dispatching my letter, learning that the enemy had not renewed his attempts of yesterday to break through the Blue Ridge, I directed General R. H. Anderson's division [of Hill's Corps] to commence its march toward Shepherdstown. It will reach there tomorrow.

I also directed General Stuart, should the enemy have so far retired from his front as to permit of the departure of a portion of the cavalry, to march with three brigades across the Potomac, and place himself on your right and in communication with you, keep you advised of the movements of the enemy, and assist in collecting supplies for the army. I have not heard from him since. I also directed Imboden, if opportunity offered, to cross the Potomac, and perform the same offices on your left.[5]

As this letter appears in the Official Records, there also is a closing statement that is not in the letter quoted by Marshall: "I shall endeavor to get General Early's regiments to him as soon as possible. I do not know what has become of the infantry of the Maryland Line. I had intended that to guard Winchester."[6]

The absence of these closing statements from the letters as quoted by Marshall raises some questions. Could Lee have added them after showing copies of the letters to Marshall? Might they have been overlooked or omitted by Marshall for some reason? It also is possible that both statements were included in copies kept in the letterbook at Lee's headquarters.[7]

About the same time, Marshall reported, Lee explained to him that during a conversation with Stuart in Paris, he mentioned that he thought Stuart might leave some cavalry in Snicker's and Ashby's gaps to watch Hooker, and with the rest of the cavalry accompany the army into Pennsylvania. It was then, Marshall said, he was told that Stuart had suggested his plan for moving near Hooker's army.[8]

"General Lee then told me," Marshall wrote, "that he was anxious that there should be no misunderstanding on General Stuart's part, and that there should be no delay in his joining us as soon as General Hooker had crossed" the Potomac. Marshall then added:

He said that in reflecting on the subject, it had occurred to him that it might be possible for General Stuart to cross east of the Blue Ridge and above General Hooker, thus avoiding the delay in returning through Snicker's or Ashby's Gap and crossing above Harpers Ferry. But, Lee added, circumstances might prevent Stuart from crossing east of the Blue Ridge. He said that he desired to impress upon General Stuart the importance of his rejoining the army with the least possible delay as soon as General Hooker had crossed, and he then directed me to write to General Stuart expressing these views.[9]

After the letter was written, Marshall added, it was shown to Lee, who dispatched it to Stuart by way of Longstreet's headquarters. It stated:

I have just received your note of 7:45 this morning to General Longstreet. I judge the efforts of the enemy yesterday were to arrest our progress and ascertain our whereabouts. Perhaps he is satisfied.

Do you know where he is and what he is doing? I fear he will steal a march on us, and get across the Potomac before we are aware. If you find that he is moving northward, and that two brigades can guard the Blue Ridge and take care of your rear, you can move with the other three into Maryland, and take position on General Ewell's right, place yourself in communication with him, guard his flank, keep him informed of the enemy's movements, and collect all the supplies you can for the use of the army. One column of General Ewell's army will probably move toward the Susquehanna by the Emmitsburg route; another by Chambersburg.

Accounts from him last night state that there was no enemy west of Frederick. A cavalry force (about 100) guarded the Monocacy Bridge, which was barricaded. You will, of course, take charge of [Albert] Jenkins' brigade and give him necessary instructions. All supplies taken in Maryland must be by authorized staff officers for their respective departments—by no one else. They will be paid for, or receipts given to the owners. I will send you a general order on this subject, which I wish you to see is strictly complied with.[10]

Longstreet sent Lee's letter at 7 P.M. June 22 with a personal note to Stuart:

General Lee has inclosed to me this letter for you, to be forwarded to you provided you can be spared from my front, and provided I think you can cross the Potomac without disclosing our plans.

He speaks of your leaving, via Hopewell Gap [in the Bull Run Mountains], and passing by the rear of the enemy. If you can get through by this route, I think that you will be less likely to indicate what our plans are than if you should cross by passing to our rear.

I forward the letter of instructions with these suggestions. Please advise me of the condition of affairs before you leave, and order General [Wade] Hampton—whom I suppose you will leave here in command—to report to me at Millwood, either by letter or in person, as may be most agreeable to him.

Longstreet added this postscript:

N.B.—I think that your passage of the Potomac by our rear at the present moment will, in a measure, disclose our plans. You had better not leave us therefore, unless you can take the proposed route in rear of the enemy.

A half hour later, Longstreet informed Lee, "Yours of 4 o'clock this afternoon is received. I have forwarded your letter to General Stuart with the suggestion that he pass by the enemy's rear if he thinks that he may get through. We have nothing of the enemy today."[11]

It is important that in the letter written by Marshall and shown to Lee, there is no reference to crossing the mountains. Stuart is told only, "If you find that he [the enemy] is moving northward, and that two brigades can guard the Blue Ridge and take care of your rear, you can move with the other three into Maryland, and take position on General Ewell's right." But Longstreet wrote Stuart, "He [Lee] speaks of your leaving via Hopewell Gap, and passing by the rear of the enemy."

The only other reference to Hopewell Gap appears in Stuart's report, saying that he had submitted to Lee the plan of passing through Hopewell or some other gap in the Bull Run Mountains, attaining the enemy's rear, and passing between his army and Washington.[12] Apparently Lee noticed that this was not mentioned in the letter Marshall had written, so he may have included it in his forwarding letter to Longstreet.

In reviewing this situation, keep in mind Stuart's presence at the winter planning sessions and in Richmond in mid-May, and realize that other than Lee, only Stuart knew what had been discussed. Stuart also would have been aware if the original invasion plan had broken down, and that his cavalry was the only Confederate force left east of the Blue Ridge that could create an immediate threat to Washington or hold Hooker in check, as Lee had described in his letter to Ewell on June 19.

After the June 22 letter had been forwarded to Stuart, Marshall said Lee fretted about his desire to "guard against the possibility of error," and asked to have the letter repeated. Marshall said:

I remember saying to the General that it could hardly be necessary to repeat the order, as General Stuart had the matter fully explained to himself verbally and my letter had been full and explicit.

Lee's insisted. Marshall drafted another letter at 5 P.M. June 23:

If General Hooker's army remains inactive you can leave two brigades to watch him and withdraw the three others, but should he

not appear to be moving northward I think you had better withdraw this side of the mountains tomorrow night, cross [the
Potomac] at Shepherdstown next day, and move over to Frederick.
You will, however, be able to judge whether you can pass around
their army without hindrance, doing them all the damage you can,
and cross the river east of the mountains.

In either case, after crossing the river you must move on and feel
the right of Ewell's troops, collecting information, provisions, etc. I
think the sooner you cross into Maryland after tomorrow the better.

Stuart also was to tell commanders of the two brigades left behind to
watch the flank and rear of the army and, if the enemy left their front, to
retire west into the Shenandoah Valley. Lee added, "The movements of
Ewell's troops are as stated in my former letter. Hill's First Division will
reach the Potomac today and Longstreet will follow tomorrow."[13]

In his postwar commentary Marshall referred to Stuart's statement in
his report that "the commanding general wrote me, authorizing the move
[Stuart had suggested], if I deemed it practicable, and also what instructions should be given the officers in command of the two brigades left in
front of the army. He also notified me that one column would move via
Gettysburg, the other by Carlisle towards the Susquehanna, and directed
me, after crossing to proceed with all dispatch to join the right (Early) in
Pennsylvania." Marshall then added that "there is no such letter as mentioned by General Stuart" and that Stuart's report was inconsistent with
the letters he had cited.[14]

Another view came from Major H. B. McClellan of Stuart's staff. He
said a courier arrived late on June 23 during a downpour witn a long confidential dispatch from Lee, containing Stuart's orders. McClellan added:

It is much to be regretted that a copy of this letter cannot now
be produced. A diligent search has failed to find it, and as General
Stuart did not forward a copy of it with his report, I presume it was
destroyed during our subsequent march.

But I have many times had occasion to recall its contents, and I
find that my recollection of it is confirmed by several passages in
General Stuart's report.

The letter informed General Stuart that General Early would
move upon York, Pa., and that he was desired to place his cavalry as
speedily as possible with that, the advance division of Lee's right
wing. The letter suggested that, as the roads leading northward

from Shepherdstown and Williamsport were already encumbered by the infantry, the artillery, and the transportation of the army, the delay which would necessarily occur in passing by these would, perhaps, be greater than would ensue if General Stuart passed around the enemy's rear.

The letter further informed him that, if he chose the latter route, General Early would receive instructions to look out for him and endeavor to communicate with him; and York, Pa., was designated as the point in the vicinity of which he was to expect to hear from Early. The whole tenor of the letter gave evidence that the commanding general approved the proposed movement, and thought it might be productive of the best results.

But, McClellan pointed out, responsibility for the decision was placed on Stuart.[15]

While McClellan's account is based on memory, Stuart's report indeed confirms the movement he was authorized to make if he saw fit. Stuart stated that "the main army, I was advised by the commanding general, would move in two columns for the Susquehanna. Early commanded the advance of one of these columns to the eastward, and I was directed to communicate with him as early as practicable after crossing the Potomac, and place my command on his right flank. It was expected that I would find him in York."[16]

In his initial and official reports, Lee stated that Ewell had been instructed to move two divisions through Chambersburg and one to York.[17] There is no mention of York in either letter to Stuart on the 22nd and 23rd. The only reference to Ewell's movements on the 22nd was that "one column of General Ewell's army will probably move toward the Susquehanna by the Emmitsburg route; another by Chambersburg." On the 23rd, it was said, "The movements of Ewell's troops are as stated in my former letter."

Was McClellan's memory accurate or was it swayed by the knowledge that Early actually had gone to York late in June? Was there still another letter sent to Stuart late on the 23rd that mentioned York?

Oddly enough, Colonel Mosby supports McClellan's version. In a postwar letter to Marshall he explained that he had been searching for Lee's letter to Longstreet forwarding the June 22 instructions to Stuart, and asked if Marshall had a copy.

According to Mosby, Marshall replied that "he did not have it. He went on to say that the letter of June 23rd, 5 p.m. from General Lee to

Stuart was revoked by a subsequent one written that night by him in which General Lee ordered Stuart to ride on the right of his column."[18]

Marshall confirmed part of this statement in his own account of the invasion of Pennsylvania: "I have not a copy of the letter from General Lee to General Longstreet enclosing the letter to General Stuart." He said nothing of a third letter.[19]

⟫●⟪

Lee's correspondence from June 19 to 23 clearly shows that the original invasion plan had been changed. His concern showed in two letters to Jefferson Davis on June 23. In one, he stated that "reports of movements of the enemy east of the Blue Ridge cause me to believe he is preparing to cross the Potomac. A pontoon bridge is stated to be laid at Edward's Ferry [about five miles east of Leesburg], and his army corps that he has advanced to Leesburg and the foot of the mountains, appear to be withdrawing. General Stuart last night was within a few miles of Aldie."

Then Lee explained that Ewell's corps was moving toward the Susquehanna, Hill toward the Potomac, and Longstreet was in the Shenandoah Valley, ready to follow. Lee added that sufficient supplies had been gathered to support Ewell's column until June 30 and that "I shall continue to purchase [with Confederate money] all the supplies that are furnished me while north of the Potomac, impressing only when necessary."[20]

In the other letter Lee briefly reviewed the situation south of Virginia, then wrote:

> At this distance, I can see no benefit to be derived from maintaining a large force on the southern coast during the unhealthy months of the summer and autumn, and I think that a part, at least, of the troops in North Carolina, and those under General Beauregard, can be employed at this time to great advantage in Virginia.
>
> If an army could be organized under the command of General Beauregard, and pushed to Culpeper Court House, threatening Washington from that direction, it would not only effect a diversion most favorable for this army, but would, I think, relieve us of any apprehension of an attack upon Richmond during our absence.
>
> The well known anxiety of the Northern Government for the safety of its capital would induce it to retain a large force for its defense, and thus sensibly relieve the opposition to our advance. If success should attend the operations of this army, and what I now

suggest would increase the probability of that result, we might even hope to compel the recall of some of the enemy's troops from the west.

I think it most important that, whatever troops be used for the purpose I have named, General Beauregard be placed in command, and that his department be extended over North Carolina and Virginia. His presence would give magnitude to even a small demonstration, and tend greatly to perplex and confound the enemy. Of course, the larger the force that we can employ the better, but should you think it imprudent to withdraw part of General Beauregard's army for the purpose indicated, I think good results would follow from sending forward, under General Beauregard, such of the troops about Richmond and in North Carolina as could be spared for a short time.

Lee added that, "should you agree with me," the plan should be set in motion immediately.[21]

The same day Lee wrote to Samuel Cooper, the adjutant general, seeking the return of troops from the Army of Northern Virginia that were not needed in Richmond. Referring to the proposal made to Davis, he wrote, "I wish to have every man that can be spared. I think there will be no necessity for keeping a large number of troops at that place, especially if the plan of assembling an army at Culpeper Court House under General Beauregard be adopted."[22]

Two days later, on June 25, Lee again urged Davis to gather an army in Culpeper under General Beauregard. He wrote:

You will see that apprehension for the safety of Washington and their own territory has aroused the Federal Government and people to great exertions, and it is incumbent upon us to call forth all our energies. It is plain that if all the Federal army is concentrated upon this [Lee's army], it will result in our accomplishing nothing, and being compelled to return to Virginia.

If the plan that I suggested the other day of organizing an army, even in effigy, under General Beauregard at Culpeper Court House, can be carried into effect, much relief will be afforded.

I have not sufficient troops to maintain my communications, and, therefore, have to abandon them. I think I can throw General Hooker's army across the Potomac and draw [Union] troops from the south, embarrassing their plan of campaign in a measure, if I can do nothing more and have to return [to Virginia]. I still hope that all things will end well for us at Vicksburg. At any rate, every effort should be made to bring about that result.[23]

Lee's deep concern showed in a second letter to Davis on the 25th. "So strong is my conviction of the necessity of activity on our part in military affairs that you will excuse my adverting to the subject again, notwithstanding what I have said in my previous letter of today. It seems to me that we cannot afford to keep our troops awaiting possible movements of the enemy, but that our true policy is, as far as we can, so to employ our own forces as to give occupation to his at points of our selection."

After reviewing the situation across the Confederacy as well as reports of Union troops being shifted from other areas, Lee concluded, "I think that if the enemy's forces have, in fact, been so far weakened as to render present active operations on his part against them [Confederate forces] improbable, they should go where they can be of immediate services, leaving only a sufficient guard to watch the lines they now hold."

Lee explained that there were several choices for such movements and that reinforcements could help Joseph Johnston or Braxton Bragg in the Western Theater or part of the proposed army under General Beauregard at Culpeper, "or they might accomplish good results by going into Northwestern Virginia. It should never be forgotten that our concentration at any point compels that of the enemy, and, his numbers being limited, tends to relieve all other threatened localities."[24]

Lee's letters of June 23 to Davis and Cooper did not reach Richmond until June 28. Their responses evidently never reached him. Instead, they arrived in Washington on July 4, accompanied by a note to Halleck: "The following dispatches have been intercepted by our scouts." They had been sent by Alexander Butterfield, Hooker's chief of staff.

One of the captured dispatches was a lengthy letter, dated June 28, from Davis to Lee. Davis noted that Grant had been reinforced and had completed entrenchments for the siege of Vicksburg; that Johnston, commander of the Department of the West, was still calling for reinforcements; and that Bragg, commander of the Army of Tennessee, had fallen back to entrenchments in Tullahoma, Tennessee.

Davis also portrayed a dismal picture on other fronts. Beauregard had objected to sending reinforcements west, claiming his whole force was needed to protect his front. Davis also said a large enemy force was reported at White House, east of Richmond, threatening an advance on the capital. He then explained that only Corse's brigade, "in accordance with your orders," had left Hanover Junction but that others were retained and "we are organizing companies for home defense."

"Do not understand me as balancing accounts in the matter of brigades; I only repeat that I have not many to send you, and [not] enough to form an army to threaten, if not to capture, Washington as soon as it is uncovered by Hooker's army."

Lee certainly would have been surprised to know Halleck had Davis's response, but he would have been even more shocked by Cooper's, dated June 29. Cooper wrote, "After reading [Lee's letter], the President was embarrassed to understand that part of it which refers to the plan of assembling an army at Culpeper Court House under General Beauregard.

"This is the first intimation that he has had that such a plan was ever in contemplation, and, taking all things into consideration, he cannot see how it can by any possibility be carried into effect."

Cooper then informed Lee that 20,000 to 30,000 Union troops were reported east of Richmond. He was uncertain whether they were intended as a demonstration or to break up communications and devastate the country.

> Every effort is being made here to be prepared for the enemy at all points, but we must look chiefly to the protection of the capital. In doing this, we may be obliged to hazard something at other points. You can easily estimate your [our?] strength here, and I would suggest for your consideration whether, in this state of things, you might not be able to spare a portion of your force to protect your line of communication against attempted raids by the enemy.[25]

Lee had proposed to Davis on May 7 to bring Beauregard north with sufficient troops to threaten Washington and had discussed the idea with him in Richmond on May 15. It would have been a terrible shock for Lee to be told that this all was news to Davis. After the war Lee confirmed that he had offered such a plan and added: "Mr. Davis promised to do so, but it was never done, probably the difficulties were too great."[26]

In late June the worsening situation in Vicksburg may have influenced Davis's words to Cooper. There was a strange coincidence on June 25 as Lee was making his final appeal to Davis to bring Beauregard's troops north. That day, the president telegraphed Beauregard: "The control of the Mississippi connection between the States east and west of it will be lost unless Johnston is strongly reinforced within the next sixty days. Can you give him further aid, and without the probable loss of Charleston and Savannah? I need not state to you that the issue is vital to the Confederacy."

Beauregard immediately replied that no more troops could be sent from his department without losing the railroad and country between Charleston and Savannah, and possibly the Georgetown district.[27] Early in May, Beauregard had ordered 5,000 infantry and two artillery batteries to go to Pemberton's support in Vicksburg. He subsequently sent Brigadier General Nathan G. Evans's brigade to Mississippi as well.[28]

On July 1, as the battle of Gettysburg was opening, Beauregard wrote to Johnston:

> An effort was lately made to deplete me still more of my forces, but it could only be done at the imminent risk of losing Charleston and Savannah. Of what earthly use is that "raid" of Lee's army into Maryland, in violation of all the principles of war? Is it going to end the struggle, take Washington, or save the Mississippi Valley? Why not have kept [Lee] on the defensive in Virginia, sent Longstreet's 20,000 men (who were not in the battle of Chancellorsville) to reinforce Bragg, who, with the 10,000 I sent you, could have crushed Rosecrans, and then sent about 50,000 men to Memphis and Fort Pillow and then to your assistance?[29]

Beauregard's opinion was unchanged for almost thirty years after the war. In a letter to John S. Mosby on January 6, 1892, however, he wrote:

> I read with much pleasure your two articles in Belford's Magazine on the Gettysburg Campaign, which I had always condemned as dangerous and ill advised, but as explained by you, I withdraw my condemnation of it. It is on the contrary, to be regretted that General Lee's plan was not carried out as he intended.[30]

In 1863, as Lee prepared to push into Pennsylvania, the failure to create an army around Beauregard in Culpeper was another critical break in his invasion plan. With Ewell's corps on the Pennsylvania line and Longstreet and Hill in the Shenandoah Valley moving toward the Potomac, he was left with only three brigades of Stuart's cavalry to achieve what he had explained to Ewell—to hold Hooker in check so that one corps could advance "unmolested" toward the Susquehanna.

CHAPTER 27

The Endangered North

THE SITUATION IN PENNSYLVANIA HAD BECOME CRITICAL BY MID-JUNE. Four days after he had assumed command of the Department of the Susquehanna, General Darius Couch had reported that the enemy apparently was starting to move north in three columns.[1] He was deeply concerned with meeting this threat.

He first sent an aide, Lieutenant Colonel Henry Coppee, to Altoona "to arrange with officers of the Pennsylvania Railroad Company for the defense of that point, the bridges crossing the Juniata [River], as well as the mountain passes, southerly toward Bedford, McConnellsburg, and [Fort] Loudon," west of Chambersburg.[2]

The Pennsylvania Railroad was one of the major lines linking New York and Philadelphia with western states by way of Harrisburg and Pittsburgh. Harrisburg also was a key junction for the Philadelphia and Reading Railroad, the Cumberland Valley Railroad, and the Harrisburg, Portsmouth, Mount Joy, and Lancaster Railroad. Also, the Northern Central Railroad, extending from Baltimore to Sunbury, then connecting upriver with lines into New York State, passed through Bridgeport (now Lemoyne) on the west shore of the Susquehanna, opposite Harrisburg.[3]

It was vital to defend Harrisburg and those rail lines. On June 15 Couch requested Stanton's permission to draw from Philadelphia supplies and tents for 10,000 men, 10,000 rifles with full equipment, and 2,000,000 rounds of small ammunition.[4] About the same time Governor Curtin informed Stanton that "we had 12 naval howitzers, and 60 gunners loaded up today at [the] Philadelphia navy yard, when the

307

Secretary of the Navy ordered them to remain there. We must have those guns and men, with all others we can get, to defend the crossing of the Susquehanna. Urge the Navy Department to order guns to be sent tonight."[5]

In another dispatch Curtin asked permission to call on the public to meet the emergency without regard to time of service, and for Federal authorities to furnish the supplies. "We must have all your facilities to meet the case. The dangers are increased hourly."[6]

On June 16 Couch informed Stanton, "The country is so wild with rumors that I was compelled to use great caution in communicating with you." One, Couch stated, placed Stuart with 20,000 men moving toward Philadelphia. "I have made every exertion to protect bridges across the Susquehanna, but they are to be fired, if it becomes necessary," Couch said. Less than three hours later, he informed Stanton that scouts from the Northern Central Railroad reported that 20,000 to 25,000 Confederate troops were concentrating "to make for Harrisburg."[7] The report undoubtedly referred to Ewell and Jenkins moving toward Chambersburg.

On June 16 and 17 he placed Colonel Emlen Franklin in charge of ferries and fords on the Susquehanna below Columbia and from the Columbia Bridge north to the Dauphin County line. Franklin was directed to bring "all canal boats which can be used by the enemy to the north side [east bank] of the river."[8] On June 20 Brigadier General William F. Smith was directed to "make such dispositions as are necessary for the defense of the river."[9]

The Susquehanna River was the invaders' major obstacle in 1863. Couch considered the area south of the river, on the west bank to the Maryland line, as lost. He intended to prevent the Confederates from crossing the river and reaching the rest of Pennsylvania and other Northern states.

———⟫⟨———

Two branches of the Susquehanna River—the North and West branches—meet at Sunbury and form the main stream that flows south through Pennsylvania and Maryland into the Chesapeake Bay. At Sunbury the river is about half a mile wide. About thirty-five miles south of Sunbury the Juniata River flows from the west into the Susquehanna.

On June 21 General Halleck warned Couch that "movements of the enemy indicate a raid against the Northern Central Railroad." Halleck advised Couch that "forces should be sent down to assist General Schenck [commanding the Middle Department, 8th Corps, with headquarters at Baltimore] in its protection. Blockhouses and stockades should be erected at all the bridges. See the officers of the [rail]road, and get their assistance in building blockhouses and defending bridges."[10] The next day Couch replied: "In case the rebels advance in large force, I believe from my present knowledge of the Susquehanna that we can prevent them crossing from its junction with the Juniata to the Maryland line."[11]

The section of the Susquehanna to which Couch referred passed through a narrow gap between Peters and Cove mountains just below the mouth of the Juniata, then widened rapidly. It was nearly a mile wide in the vicinity of Enola and Marysville, more than three quarters of a mile wide at Harrisburg, one mile wide between Columbia and Wrightsville, and about a mile and a quarter wide a short distance below Columbia.[12]

Five bridges spanned the river in that section. One, more than a mile long, was a combination railroad and public bridge between Columbia and Wrightsville. There were two bridges at Harrisburg; one was a wooden span for public use, the other a railroad crossing. North of Harrisburg were two more railroad bridges. One from Rockville took the Pennsylvania Railroad line west across the Susquehanna to Marysville, toward Pittsburgh. The other bridge, from Dauphin to Marysville, linked the Schuylkill and Susquehanna Railroad—with ties to numerous branch lines in the anthracite coal fields—with the Pennsylvania and Northern Central railroads.[13]

A survey of the river, made in 1861, indicated that the most feasible place to cross would be at Harrisburg. A nearby ford was described as having a "smooth sandy and stone bottom," about two feet deep from the east shore to Forster's Island in midriver and "almost dry shod" to the west shore.[14] The condition, however, was true only during periods of low water. It undoubtedly would have been difficult to cross during and after rainy weather.

The river bottom was mostly a mass of rocks, ledges, and holes, and there were only a few other points where fording was possible in periods of low water. Under those circumstances, it would have been impractical for a military force to have attempted to ford the stream, as the Confederates had on the Shenandoah and Potomac rivers on their way into Maryland.

Further transportation possibilities were provided by the Eastern Division Canal, which flanked the Susquehanna's east shore from the mouth of the Juniata River to Columbia. There, canal boats were able to cross to the west shore above a dam that had been constructed for that purpose. From Wrightsville to Havre de Grace, Maryland, canal boats

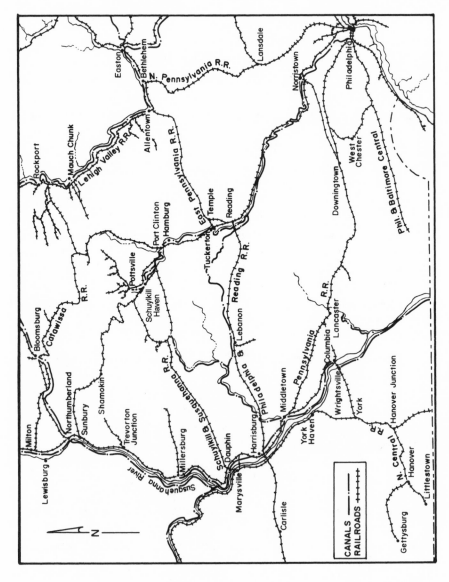

Railroads and Canals of Central Pennsylvania. John Heiser

traveled on the Susquehanna and Tidewater Canal to the Chesapeake Bay.[15] This major water line was linked to numerous lesser canals serving specific areas, particularly the Pennsylvania anthracite coal fields.

———————

Fortifying the Susquehanna was only part of Couch's problem. Even more alarming was a serious shortage of men.

On June 20, with Ewell's 22,000 men moving across Maryland, Couch had only 1,321 men ready for duty in the entire Department of the Susquehanna. Nine staff members were at Harrisburg with 490 troops, 419 were at York, and 403 were at Philadelphia. In the Department of the Monongahela, General Brooks farther west had only 1,027. Only 73 were at Pittsburgh, where trenches were being dug, and 199 in West Virginia.[16] The largest force, 795 men in the 27th New Jersey Regiment, was on the way home from Ohio to be mustered out of service.[17]

Response to appeals by Lincoln, Curtin, and Couch for men had been disappointing. By June 20 only 1,761 emergency militiamen had been mustered into service. By the 30th 7,461 emergency militia, 1,320 ninety-day militia, and 1,769 six-month volunteers had been mustered in.[18] About 2,500 men were added to Couch's force on June 17th from Milroy's command, which had retreated from Winchester by way of Hancock, Maryland, to Bedford, Pennsylvania, but they were badly demoralized.[19]

Milroy, in the meantime, left Baltimore on the morning of the 18th to go to Pennsylvania in search of his men. General Schenck informed Couch of the move and advised him to confer with Milroy regarding the "best course to find and supply these men. They may then be made serviceable for the present for operations in Pennsylvania, offensive or defensive."[20] Milroy located his troops, about 2,500 men, in the vicinity of Bedford. He informed Couch that "all [were] badly supplied with ammunition and rations," and that he was concentrating the force at Bloody Run, about nine miles east of Bedford, as the best point at which to meet enemy forces that might advance into Pennsylvania from McConnellsburg.[21]

Militia regiments from New York began to arrive in Harrisburg.[22] It was the only state to provide any substantial troops to face Lee. By June 30, a total of 12,291 militiamen had been sent to Pennsylvania, plus 400 to Washington.[23]

The governors of Connecticut, Vermont, New Hampshire, Michigan, and Wisconsin reported that they had no organized militia to send to Pennsylvania.[24] Governors elsewhere said generally that it would be impossible to get six-month volunteers in time to be of assistance.[25]

Couch summarized the situation in two letters to Stanton. In the first, on June 22, he had referred to preventing the invaders from crossing the Susquehanna. He added: "You will understand what kind of a force I have, when a few regiments, with a sprinkling of nine-months men in them, are the veterans. The New York troops look very well, but are without much confidence in themselves. My little artillery is all raw; my cavalry the same. I speak of the quality and condition of my troops in order that you may not wonder why I do not boldly face them against the rebels in the Cumberland Valley."[26]

In the second letter, on June 29, Couch stated, "My whole force organized is, perhaps 16,000 men. Five thousand regulars will whip them all to pieces in an open field."[27]

As the situation grew more critical, Couch turned to the development of defensive positions on the west bank of the Susquehanna. "The heights on the right bank of the Susquehanna, opposite Harrisburg, were being fortified, in order to cover that city and the important bridges. Some of the patriotic citizens of that city volunteered to work in the trenches, others were paid."[28]

The main fortification, Fort Washington, was constructed at the end of a ridge overlooking the west shore of the river, just north of Bridgeport. Two other positions were fortified on the same ridge a short distance west. To the south, the engine house of the Cumberland Valley Railroad was fortified, and trenches were dug there as well as along the tracks of North Central Railroad.[29]

Blockhouses had been built on the west bank to guard the two railroad bridges north of Harrisburg. Only fifty or sixty men of the Invalid Corps were on duty there when Brigadier General Charles Yates arrived June 22 with two regiments of the New York State National Guard, about 1,000 men.[30] Preparations for guarding the Columbia-Wrightsville bridge were begun on June 15, when Captain C. C. Haldeman was authorized to raise troops for the defense of Columbia.[31] The bridge leading to Wrightsville was a unique toll bridge, since it was a covered bridge for both highway and railroad travel. On the downstream side was a two-level covered path for towing canal boats across the river above the dam.[32]

Couch then turned his attention to the potential invasion routes he had previously mentioned—through Chambersburg, Gettysburg, and toward the coal mines.[33] The fear that he would have "but little to resist them" was evident in the forces he had to place on those routes. On

June 19 two New York militia regiments plus some cavalry and artillery were sent to the Chambersburg area.[34] On the 21st Major Granville O. Haller of Couch's staff was sent to Gettysburg to take command of a small force there.[35] Milroy, at Bloody Run, was in position to cover any possible attempt by Imboden's force to push toward the Susquehanna River from McConnellsburg.[36]

On June 21 Milroy informed Couch that a scout had reported 40,000 Confederate troops at Hagerstown with eighteen pieces of artillery, and 300 enemy cavalrymen at Mercersburg. Couch relayed the information to Stanton and added, "There is no doubt a force of infantry is on our border."[37]

To the east of the endangered area, a Confederate cavalry raid had aroused similar concern from General Schenck, the commander in Baltimore. On June 17 the Confederates crossed the Potomac River just above the Point of Rocks, cut telegraph lines to Washington, tore up some B&O track, skirmished with Union troops, and recrossed the Potomac late that night.[38]

Though the raid had a more significant purpose, as will be seen, it prompted Schenck to report to Halleck that enemy scouts had advanced close to Westminster, twenty miles northwest of Baltimore. "I suggest that Couch's forces at Harrisburg may be more needed here than there," he added.[39]

The Confederate troopers obviously had achieved one of Lee's objectives—to alarm the enemy—even before the main body had crossed into Pennsylvania.

⸺⸺➤●◄⸺⸺

The details of Lee's plan and those described by Stonewall Jackson in plans he had proposed more than a year earlier were remarkably similar. Lee explained that his intention was to maneuver, threaten Union cities, and hit any blows he could without risking a general battle. In his letter to Davis on June 10, 1863, Lee stated, "We should neglect no honorable means of dividing and weakening our enemies that they may feel some of the difficulties experienced by ourselves . . . and give all the encouragement we can to the rising peace party of the North."

A similar idea was expressed by Jackson in 1861 when he stated that by making unrelenting war amid their homes, he would "force the people of the North to understand what it will cost them to hold the South in the Union at the bayonet's point."

Lee and Jackson had mentioned creating fear for the safety of Washington and the possibility of forcing the Federal government to flee. Both also had fixed Harrisburg as a major target, Lee in his letter of June 19 to Ewell, and Jackson when he sent Colonel Boteler to Richmond in 1862 with his request for 40,000 to 60,000 troops to carry out the invasion.

Jackson also had emphasized breaking up railroads as "lines of interior commercial intercourse"; Confederate troops eagerly did this in 1863. A major feature of Jackson's plan, halting anthracite production, was not mentioned by Lee. Couch knew of its importance, and Richmond also became aware of the possibility that Lee, after seizing Harrisburg, probably would turn to the coal fields.

These similarities strongly suggest that the campaign had been planned by Lee and Jackson during the winter camp meetings early in 1863. Stuart's presence there clued him in to the plan and what was intended, something that had to be kept in mind as the Army of Northern Virginia moved into Pennsylvania.

CHAPTER 28

Marching into Pennsylvania

THE ARMY OF NORTHERN VIRGINIA WAS READY TO TAKE THE FINAL STEP in the plan that it was hoped would at last bring peace and independence to the Confederacy. With the first of Ewell's troops across the Pennsylvania line on June 22, Longstreet took an unusual step. He issued orders that seemed to echo Lee's recent correspondence:

> The movements of the army at this time are of the highest moment to our country. Success in the ends in view will go far to restore to us the blessings of peace, while defeat would inevitably prolong and aggravate all the wretchedness entailed by war upon the South. Success will not only avenge our wrongs upon our foes, but what is dearer still, it will, we hope, send us on the wings of peace to revisit our homes. Defeat, on the other hand, will bring back upon these lovely valleys and mountains the cruel ravages of a heartless invader. Thus it becomes the anxious wish, as it is the duty of every soldier, that no pains or labor should be spared which may be essential to success.

Longstreet especially wanted to prevent straggling and called on everyone to enforce "good order and punctuality." He also directed that a field officer and surgeon follow each regiment to guard against straggling.[1]

In a dispatch the next morning, June 23, Lee told Longstreet, "I wish you to get your corps ready to move in the morning. Let your ordnance officers make arrangements to turn in damaged ammunition and have it replaced by a fresh supply, as it would be useless to take the former along." He also informed Longstreet that Anderson's division of Hill's corps was in motion and that the other two had been ordered to move.[2]

Longstreet immediately ordered his divisions and reserve artillery to move "tomorrow morning at 3 o'clock for Hagerstown, Md., via Berryville, Smithfield and Williamsport." Pickett's division led the movement, followed by the artillery, Hood's division, then McLaws's, in that order. The daily march was to be about fifteen miles, with a two-hour halt at midday.[3]

In the meantime Ewell, whose corps was leading the advance, was acting on Lee's letter of June 22. He was to move toward the Susquehanna River in three columns via Emmitsburg, Maryland, and Chambersburg and McConnellsburg, Pennsylvania. If possible, he was to capture Harrisburg.[4]

On June 22 Jenkins's cavalry and Rodes's and Johnson's infantry were in the Greencastle area of Pennsylvania; Early's division was about three miles from Boonsboro, Maryland. Ewell detached the 17th Virginia Cavalry Regiment from Jenkins's brigade to accompany Early.[5]

That night Rodes, Early, and Ewell gathered between Boonsboro and Hagerstown to discuss the advance. Ewell then rode to Rodes's camp in Greencastle. "From June 23rd," Rodes commented, "the movements of my command were executed under the immediate supervision of the commander of the corps."[6]

On June 23 Jenkins and his cavalry rode into Chambersburg at 10 A.M. Most of his force continued through town and camped a few miles north along the road to Shippensburg, Carlisle, and Harrisburg. Shortly after his arrival, Jenkins demanded provisions from Chambersburg residents. In keeping with Lee's order for obtaining supplies in enemy territory, the names of all who responded reportedly were recorded by Jenkins's aides. Apparently overlooked by the Confederates, however, was the action of a group of residents who raided a warehouse along the railroad line and carried off a large amount of crackers, beans, and bacon.

In Greencastle requisitions were made about the same time by Rodes's officers. They managed to secure some saddles, bridles, and leather.[7] On the same day Brigadier General George H. Steuart's brigade was detached from Johnson's division and ordered to McConnellsburg to collect horses, cattle, and other supplies.[8] Lee also advised Imboden that day, "General Ewell, in advancing toward the Susquehanna, will probably have one column on the McConnellsburg road. Should you be able to cross the Potomac, you must keep on his [Ewell's] left, giving him information of your presence, and aid in collecting supplies."[9]

Not all the news was good on the 23rd. Lee wrote President Davis that day, "Reports of movements of the enemy east of the Blue Ridge cause me to believe that he is preparing to cross the Potomac. A pontoon bridge is said to be laid at Edwards Ferry, and his army corps that he has advanced to Leesburg and the foot of the mountains, appear to be withdrawing."[10] Edwards Ferry was about five miles east of Leesburg, Virginia. The force to which Lee referred evidently was the 11th Corps, which moved to the south bank of the Potomac at Edwards Ferry on June 24.[11]

About 9 A.M. that day Confederate infantry followed a band playing "The Bonnie Blue Flag" into Chambersburg.[12] Rodes's division had marched fourteen miles from Greencastle in leading the advance into Pennsylvania. Except for one regiment left in town as a guard, the men continued northward for almost three miles on the Harrisburg Road to Conococheague Creek and camped near Jenkins's cavalry, which had stopped the day before.[13]

Ewell was in the rear of the column in his carriage. He set up his headquarters in the Franklin Hotel and called on Chambersburg authorities to supply large quantities of food, cooking supplies, clothing, and other goods.[14] Ewell reported that "a [wagon] train was loaded with ordnance and medical stores and sent back," as were 3,000 cattle, evidently to Army headquarters.[15] Jed Hotchkiss briefly noted that he had procured maps and engineering supplies in Chambersburg.[16]

Johnson's division followed Rodes through Chambersburg on the march northward.[17] Steuart's brigade, on its way to McConnellsburg, had marched ten miles to Mercersburg and halted there about midday before continuing across North Mountain.[18]

The Confederates did not take one of the routes mentioned by Lee, through Emmitsburg. Instead, Early, who had advanced to Waynesboro on the 23rd, continued on a route paralleling Rodes and Johnson. On the 24th he marched through Quincy and Altodale to Greenwood, about eight miles east of Chambersburg on the Gettysburg pike, where he camped.[19] There is no explanation for the change, but it may have been made to keep in closer touch with Ewell's other divisions.

Ewell provided a sidelight on the situation in a letter to his niece Elizabeth in Williamsburg, Virginia, whose mother was a native of York,

Pennsylvania. Writing from Chambersburg on June 24 Ewell stated, "I don't know yet if we will go to York—anyhow we will be tolerably close to it. I will let your relations off tolerably easy on your account—probably not taking more than a few forks and spoons and trifles of that sort—no houseburning or anything like it."[20]

———➤●◄———

On June 25 Ewell ordered Early "to cross the South Mountain to Gettysburg, and then proceed to York, and cut the Northern Central Railroad, and also destroy the bridge across the Susquehanna at Wrightsville and Columbia."[21] Destroy the bridge? This is another order that clouds the history of this campaign. For example, Lee stated that when Ewell was told to advance toward Harrisburg, "the expedition of General Early to York was designed in part to prepare for this undertaking by breaking the railroad between Baltimore and Harrisburg, and seizing the bridge over the Susquehanna at Wrightsville."[22] There is no specific mention of destroying or seizing the bridge in Ewell's report.[23] Early, however, stated in his report that later, in giving instructions to a brigade commander, John B. Gordon, he twice directed the latter to "secure it [the bridge] at both ends, if possible."[24]

Later Gordon explained that Ewell's "written orders were full, accurate, and lucid; but his verbal orders or directions, especially under intense excitement, no man could comprehend. At such times his eyes would flash with a peculiar brilliancy, and his brain far outran his tongue. His thoughts would leap across great gaps which his words never touched, but which he expected his listener to fill up by intuition, but woe to the subordinate who failed to understand him."[25] Gordon's comments seemed to echo Lee's postwar thoughts about Ewell.[26]

———➤●◄———

Meanwhile Longstreet's corps and some of Hill's troops had marched to the south bank of the Potomac above Harpers Ferry—Longstreet's troops opposite Williamsport and Hill's at Shepherdstown. Before leaving Frederick, Longstreet had sent a scout named Harrison to Washington to gather "information that he knew would be of value to me" and to report it as soon as possible.[27] Major Ralph J. Moses, Longstreet's chief commissary, said Harrison was one of two scouts in Longstreet's employ who traveled "regularly between Washington and our headquarters."[28]

On June 24 Stuart also was preparing to move toward the Potomac, to his continuing controversy and criticism. His cavalry was concentrated at Rector's Cross Roads west of the Bull Run Mountains. In accordance with Lee's instructions, as he understood them, Robertson's and Jones's brigades were covering Ashby's and Snicker's gaps in the Blue Ridge, and the others—Wade Hampton's, Fitzhugh Lee's, and William Henry Fitzhugh Lee's—would move north in the plan Stuart had proposed. Rations for three days were prepared, and that night Stuart's three brigades rendezvoused secretly at Salem Depot, on the Manassas Gap Railroad.[29]

Preparations were similar to those for Stuart's first ride around McClellan's army in 1862. On a raid around McClellan after the Battle of Sharpsburg, Stuart had brought back information and a map of the roads in Pennsylvania.

At 9 A.M. June 17 Lieutenant Colonel E. V. White, with 125 men of his 35th Virginia Cavalry Battalion, crossed the Potomac three miles above Point of Rocks. They broke telegraph lines between Washington and Hooker's army, tore up some railroad track, and engaged in several skirmishes. White told Stuart the next day that they had covered fifty-seven miles in twenty-five hours and noted that "appearances indicate that they [the enemy] expect soon to evacuate the country."[30] This was the raid that had alarmed General Schenck, the Union commander at Baltimore.[31]

In order to get more accurate information about Hooker's positions and possible movements, Stuart took the same step he had taken before his ride around McClellan during the Seven Days. He sent Mosby on a series of scouting expeditions.[32]

On his return Mosby told Stuart that Hooker's headquarters was at Fairfax Court House and that his army was not moving. Seven of the eight Union corps were scattered over three counties along the Potomac—Fairfax, Prince William, and Loudoun. Mosby then added:

> I had located each corps and reported it to Stuart. They were so widely scattered that it was easy for a column of cavalry to pass between them. No corps was nearer than ten miles of another corps. I pointed out to Stuart the opportunity to strike a damaging blow and suggested to him to cross the Bull Run Mountains and pass through the middle of Hooker's army into Maryland. There was no force to oppose him at Seneca Ford about twenty miles above Washington where I had recently crossed.

Mosby explained that after he had given this report to Stuart, he was told that Lee was eager to know if Hooker was moving to cross the Potomac. "He did not ask me to go, but I volunteered to return and find out for him. With two men I recrossed the mountain, and on the morning of June 23rd was again riding between the camps of the different corps in Fairfax and Loudoun [counties]. All was quiet, there was no sign of a movement. Hooker was waiting for Lee."[33]

⸺⸙⸺

During this period Hooker was virtually motionless south of the Potomac River, between the mountains and Washington. On June 22 and 23 only two of his divisions were moving. Major General Julius Stahel's cavalry division of Pleasonton's corps was shifting its position from east of the mountains to Fairfax Court House, and the 1st Division of the 5th Corps was returning from Upperville to Aldie.

On June 24, as Stuart was preparing to ride around the Union army, the 11th Corps advanced from Trappe Rock on Goose Creek to the south bank of the Potomac at Edwards Ferry. One division of the 6th Corps moved from Germantown to Centreville and Stahel's cavalry division shifted from Fairfax Court House to Dranesville.[34]

In his postwar account Mosby commented, "If Stuart had started a day earlier, or if our army [Longstreet's and Hill's corps] had delayed a day longer, Stuart would have had no difficulty in reaching the north bank of the Potomac on the 25th, ahead of Hooker. There would have been nothing in front to oppose him."[35]

Time, however, was not on Stuart's side. As he began his move toward the Potomac, the Union 1st, 3rd, and 11th corps, with the Artillery Reserve, were crossing at Edwards Ferry. Others were heading in that direction, and Major General Winfield Scott Hancock's 2nd Corps was on the road from Thoroughfare Gap to Gum Springs.[36] Hancock seriously disrupted Stuart's intentions and forced him to change plans.

In fairness to Stuart, he and his five brigades had been left virtually alone in northern Virginia when Lee's infantry was crossing into Maryland. He had four choices: He could stay in position in order to check Hooker if a move was made against Richmond, he could move to threaten Washington and Baltimore, he could ride around the Union army to gain information about its movement and possibly delay its pursuit of Lee, or he could withdraw west of the Blue Ridge and follow Lee's infantry northward along the valley.

He chose the third course. As directed, he left two brigades to guard Snicker's and Ashby's gaps and moved north with the other three. At this point, it is necessary to recall the variations noted earlier in letters sent to Stuart on June 22 and 23 and the confusion they must have caused.

In one letter, Stuart was told that if Hooker moved across the Potomac unexpectedly, he [Stuart] was to cross into Maryland and take position on Ewell's right. In a note from Longstreet, Stuart was told that in order not to disclose Confederate plans, it would be better for him to move by the rear of enemy forces rather than follow the Confederate army. In another dispatch, Stuart was informed that Early's objective was York, where he could possibly meet the Confederate right column.[37] The language of the letters, especially "if you can" and "you will be able to judge," must have led Stuart to believe that he was to determine the best course to follow.

At 1 A.M. on June 25 Stuart's troops moved out on a noiseless ride across the Bull Run Mountains. Hancock still held Thoroughfare Gap, so Stuart's men moved south to Glasscock's Gap. In the meantime, Mosby had been sent out by Stuart on another mission. He was to go to the Dranesville area northwest of Washington to locate a good crossing of the Potomac and report to Stuart at Gum Springs later in the day.[38]

Stuart apparently hoped to pass through the gap, turn north toward Haymarket, then move to Gum Springs and on to the Potomac and into Maryland. It would have taken him to Hooker's rear, on a course that would have led almost directly to Early's route in Adams and York counties, Pennsylvania.

It was not to be. As Stuart's men approached Haymarket, Hancock's troops already were in the town and marching toward Gum Springs. After a skirmish, Stuart halted, grazed his horses, and rested his men. The road he had intended to use was filled with Hancock's troops and Stuart had to change his plans.

Instead of pushing on from Haymarket, Stuart moved south to Buckland Mills to deceive the enemy, then set out on a circuitous route that took him farther eastward than he had intended to go. Late in the afternoon of the 27th his troops reached Dranesville, about 15 miles west of Washington. He then crossed the river at Rowser's Ford and reached the north bank of the Potomac just before midnight. Stuart explained, "I realized the importance of joining our army in Pennsylvania, and resumed the march northward early on the 28th."[39]

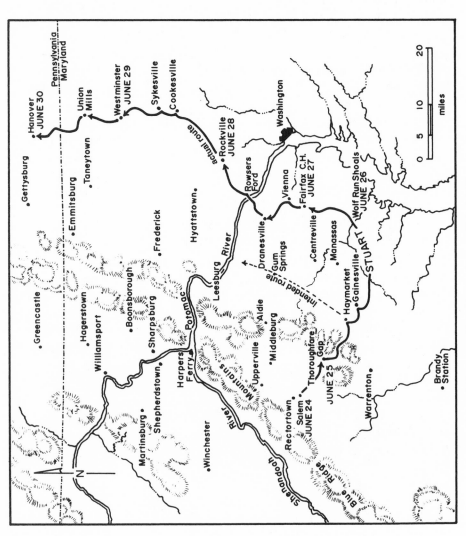

Stuart's Route to Gettysburg, June to July 1863. JOHN HEISER

Stuart's cavalry was the last Confederate units to cross the Potomac. Instead of being in the advance to cover Lee's right flank and keeping Lee informed, Stuart had been forced far to the east and in Hooker's rear.

It was this movement that provoked the postwar wave of criticism against Stuart. Some said he disobeyed orders or took advantage of the discretion given him. Others claimed that Stuart's flair for the spectacular had led him on a wild goose chase. A few even hinted that Stuart needed something to bolster his reputation, which they believed had been tarnished by the Federal attack on his camp at Brandy Station.

Stuart was mortally wounded in 1864 and thus was never able to properly explain the situation. Stuart, with his knowledge of Confederate plans gained in meetings with Lee and Jackson after Sharpsburg and during the winter of 1862–63, evidently was the only officer who truly knew Lee's intentions.

Stuart also must have been aware that problems around Winchester and Longstreet's move into the Shenandoah Valley had resulted in a change in plans. Without Beauregard's troops to threaten Washington, Stuart must have realized that his cavalry was the only force left in position to cause fear for the capital's safety.

It is evident that Stuart had not gone off on a daring dash, as some critics claimed, but actually was trying to help Lee carry out the changed invasion campaign. As criticism of Stuart arose after the war, detractors may have misinterpreted statements in Lee's report of the campaign, in which he simply stated that no report of Federal movements had been received, and the absence of the cavalry rendered it impossible to obtain accurate information.[40] After the war Lee supposedly commented that "Stuart's failure to carry out his instructions forced the battle of Gettysburg,"[41] but it is not entirely certain that this was said as a criticism of Stuart's conduct.

Lee knew that a Union pontoon bridge had been placed across the Potomac. One thing he did not know was that Stuart actually had sent two reports in late June that Union forces were indeed moving northward. According to Major McClellan, Stuart's assistant adjutant general, as Stuart approached Haymarket on June 25, he discovered that Hancock was marching northward on the road on which he had expected to move.

After brief artillery fire Stuart, "not wishing to disclose his force, withdrew from Hancock's vicinity after capturing some prisoners and satisfying himself concerning the movement of that corps.

"This information was at once started to General Lee by a courier bearing a dispatch written by General Stuart himself. It is plain from General Lee's report that this messenger did not reach him; and unfortunate that the dispatch was not duplicated."[42] Two days later Stuart sent another report to Lee about Union movements:

> I took possession of Fairfax C. H. [Court House] this morning at nine o'clock, together with a large quantity of stores. The main body of Hooker's army has gone toward Leesburg, except the garrison of Alexandria and Washington, which has retreated within the fortifications.

From his comments it is evident Lee did not receive either of Stuart's dispatches. There is no explanation why. There was, however, an unusual development regarding the June 27 dispatch: The message or a copy was received in Richmond on July 1.[43]

Stuart did make his best effort to keep Lee informed and he obviously was trying to do his best to support the invasion and his part in it.

CHAPTER 29

To the Banks of the Susquehanna

LATE JUNE WAS A CRUCIAL PERIOD FOR THE CONFEDERATES, A TIME when hope peaked before developments led to disappointment and defeat.

On June 24 everything seemed to be going well for the Army of Northern Virginia. All three corps had started on schedule for their designated objectives, Harrisburg and York. Two of Ewell's divisions were in Chambersburg and the third was camped eight miles east on the road to Gettysburg and York. Longstreet and Hill were ready to cross into Maryland and Pennsylvania to support Ewell.[1] At the same time Stuart was preparing to start around Hooker and join Ewell's right as quickly as possible.

On Thursday, June 25, Longstreet and Hill began crossing the Potomac at Williamsport and Shepherdstown. The two corps reunited the next day at Hagerstown for their advance into Pennsylvania.[2]

Ewell was ready to start his main column toward Harrisburg, as Lee had ordered. Jenkins's cavalry brigade led the march; some of his troopers had reached Shippensburg by Tuesday, June 23. They spent two days gathering "badly needed drugs and food." These probably were among the supplies Ewell had mentioned as having been shipped back, probably by a wagon train.[3]

The presence of Union troops near Shippensburg prompted Rodes to order Brigadier General Junius Daniel to go there because General Jenkins "was threatened by the enemy." Daniel arrived there at 5 A.M. on the 25th.[4]

According to Jed Hotchkiss, he was summoned to corps headquarters on the 25th and Ewell asked him for maps that would be needed in planning "the movements of the next four days." Hotchkiss also noted that Early and Rodes came to headquarters that day and "Early was to go to Gettysburg, York and the Wrightsville-Columbia Bridge."[5] This evidently was the meeting mentioned by Early at which he said he was instructed to proceed to Gettysburg, York, and Wrightsville and destroy the bridge across the Susquehanna.[6]

Heavy rain began on the night of June 25 and continued intermittently until the morning of the 27th. Despite muddy roads, Johnson and the rest of Rodes's division started early on the 26th toward Carlisle. They camped that night in the Shippensburg area. At 6 A.M. on the 27th Rodes and Johnson began marching toward Carlisle on parallel roads. Leading the advance was Jenkins, who entered Carlisle about 10 A.M.

The Carlisle burgess, William M. Penrose; his assistant, Robert Allison; and a group of citizens went to meet Jenkins. They requested the enemy to "make no dash upon the town" that would frighten residents, especially women and children. Jenkins assured them that the residents would not be molested, then asked for food for 1,500 men and forage for their horses. The request was quickly filled.[7]

Rodes and Johnson reached Carlisle about three hours after Jenkins. Johnson's men encamped about three miles west of town. One of Rodes's brigades camped at Dickinson College; another moved to Trindle Road just east of town; his main body went to Carlisle Barracks, the Union Army post on the Harrisburg road.[8]

Steuart's brigade of Johnson's division arrived from McConnellsburg a short time later. It had been detached at Greencastle to go to Fulton County for supplies. Steuart brought in some cattle and horses.[9]

Jenkins had advanced about six miles east of Carlisle. Later, Ewell sent his engineer officer, Captain H. B. Richardson, to join Jenkins and reconnoiter the approaches to and the defenses of Harrisburg.[10] Jenkins camped on the 27th at Hickorytown on the Trindle Road about midway between Carlisle and Mechanicsburg. Richardson was accompanied by another member of Ewell's staff, a Major Clark. They were to obtain information about crossings of the Susquehanna River, particularly the depth and current; the availability of material for rebuilding or repairing bridges; and the conditions of fords.[11]

In the meantime, after meeting with Ewell, Early prepared to start his troops toward Adams and York counties. Most of his unnecessary baggage and supplies were sent back to Chambersburg. On the 26th he marched across South Mountain on the way to Gettysburg.[12] Before leaving, however, Early burned the iron works of U.S. Representative Thaddeus Stevens near Greenwood. "This I did on my own responsibility," Early stated, "as neither General Lee nor General Ewell knew I would encounter these works." The company store was emptied but houses and property of employees were not molested, he added.[13]

After crossing South Mountain and approaching Cashtown, Early heard that there was possibly a Union force in Gettysburg. He sent Gordon's brigade with a cavalry battalion to check it out while the rest of the division moved left and north of Gettysburg to cut off any enemy withdrawal.[14]

Small Union forces in the path of the invaders hastily withdrew. General Knipe already had withdrawn from the Shippensburg area to New Kingstown, about five miles east of Carlisle. On the 27th, Couch ordered him to fall back again to avoid being outflanked.[15]

Captain D. H. Hastings, with a small cavalry force, noted that "being satisfied that the rebels were in considerable force a few miles west of the Carlisle Barracks, and having no means of defense, I retired from that position last night [the 25th], bringing with me all the munitions of war and movable public property."[16]

At Gettysburg, Major Haller reported to Couch that one of his regiments, three miles from Gettysburg, had been forced to fall back. Haller explained he feared he had too few to resist the Confederate advance and began to withdraw. At 8 P.M. June 26 he informed Couch that "the rebels were in Gettysburg" and that he had ordered all troops to withdraw to York.[17]

As Gordon approached Gettysburg, the cavalry had a brush with Union militiamen who were withdrawing from the area. Gordon's force then entered the town without resistance on the afternoon of the 26th. In the meantime Early had moved with the rest of his troops to Mummasburg, about five miles northwest of Gettysburg. A short while later Early rode to Gettysburg and called on town authorities for a large amount of supplies and some money. They refused.[18] A search produced only a few supplies, but 2,000 rations were found on a train and given to Gordon. The cars and a railroad bridge near Gettysburg were burned. The advance toward York was to continue the next morning, June 27.

White, with his cavalry, was to move to Hanover Junction and then toward York, burning railroad buildings at the Junction and all possible railroad bridges in the area. Gordon was ordered to move at the same time along the macadamized road to York.[19]

Early's timing corresponded perfectly with that of Ewell's other divisions, which had reached Carlisle on June 27. On the morning of the 27th Gordon's brigade, with additional artillery and cavalry, moved east toward York. He halted several miles west of the city and camped there. Early, with the rest of his division, left Mummasburg at daylight and marched beyond East Berlin, about ten miles west of York on a road parallel to the one used by Gordon. Early then rode to Gordon's camp and learned that indications were that no Union troops were in York. Gordon was directed to advance into York, and if there was no opposition, to continue to "the Wrightsville and Columbia bridge and get possession of it at both ends and hold it until I came up."[20]

In the meantime Longstreet's and Hill's corps had reached the Chambersburg area and were in position to support either or both of Ewell's columns or to move against Hooker if he should follow them into Pennsylvania.

Heth's division of Hill's corps was the first to enter Chambersburg. It turned at the town square and moved eastward on the road toward Gettysburg. Hill and his staff then rode into town, followed shortly by Lee and his aides. The two rode away from the group and "held a short, whispered consultation."

Among the people watching was Benjamin S. Huber, who had just returned after carrying a message to Harrisburg. He was concerned about the direction Lee would take. If he continued north, toward Carlisle, then Harrisburg and Philadelphia would be threatened. If he turned east in the square, he would be moving toward Gettysburg on the road to Baltimore. As soon as Lee's route was determined, Huber would have to return to Harrisburg with a report for Washington.

A few moments later the generals concluded their conversation. Lee rode to the center of the square and turned right toward Gettysburg. The supposition was that Baltimore was the target. Huber rode immediately to the base of North Mountain and to Newport, where he took a train to Harrisburg. He arrived before daylight on the 27th and reported to Curtin and Couch. The news was immediately telegraphed to Washington.

The significance of Lee's move had been misinterpreted. In turning right at the square, Lee was merely going east to establish his headquarters in a grove just outside town on the road to Gettysburg.[21]

Heth's troops also had turned off at the square and marched east on the Gettysburg road. They were followed in the afternoon of June 26 and the next morning by the divisions of Major Generals William D. Pender and Richard H. Anderson. By June 27 the entire corps had reached Fayetteville, about seven miles east of Chambersburg, and camped there for two days.[22]

During the afternoon and late into the evening of the 27th most of Longstreet's troops marched through Chambersburg and camped just north of town along Conococheague Creek.[23] A few, however, remained about five miles south of Chambersburg, and did not march through the town until June 28, when they joined the others camped along the creek.[24]

It is important at this point to recognize that Lee's army was in position to carry out Stonewall Jackson's plan expressed a little more than a year earlier—that if he had 40,000 to 60,000 more men, he could be in Harrisburg in two weeks. On June 27, 1863, Lee was in Pennsylvania with more than 60,000 troops. Less than two weeks—the time designated by Jackson—had passed since the capture of Winchester. Two of Ewell's divisions were in Carlisle within a day's march of the state capital. His third division was near York, also only a day from the Susquehanna. If they could seize the two bridges in Harrisburg and the one from Wrightsville to Columbia, Jackson's plan could be carried out. Lee also could give all aid possible to "the rising peace party of the North."

There was confidence in Orders No. 73, issued by Lee on the 27th. "The commanding general has observed with marked satisfaction the conduct of the troops on the march," Lee wrote, "and confidently anticipated results commensurate with the high spirit they have manifested. No troops could have displayed greater fortitude or better performed the arduous marches of the past ten days."

Lee then expressed regret over a few violations of his order for proper behavior in enemy territory, and added: "It must be remembered that we make war only upon armed men, and that we cannot take vengeance for the wrongs our people have suffered without lowering ourselves in the eyes of all whose abhorrence has been excited by the atrocities of our enemies, and offending against Him to whom vengeance belongeth, without whose favor and support our efforts must all prove in vain."[25]

Lee's confidence also showed in his conversation with Isaac Trimble on the afternoon of the 27th, as noted earlier. Lee said, "Ewell's forces are by this time in Harrisburg; if not, go and join him and help him to take the place." He also repeated his intention to attack the enemy in detail, create a panic, and virtually destroy Hooker. But he also was aware that he might have to face the entire Army of the Potomac and, if so, that a battle might be fought near Gettysburg.[26]

Lee was worried over Stuart's whereabouts and his ignorance of Hooker's movements. Colonel Marshall said Lee expressed apprehension several times over the possibility that Hooker might be threatening Richmond and that this was due entirely to "his hearing nothing from General Stuart." After Gettysburg, Stuart told Marshall about the June 27 dispatch that he had sent to Lee. Marshall added, "We never got that dispatch."

Another member of Lee's staff, Colonel Long, also pointed out that "on reaching Chambersburg, General Lee, not having heard from Stuart, was under the impression that the Federal army had not yet crossed the Potomac." According to Trimble, on June 27 Lee also stated that he had not heard of enemy troops crossing the Potomac, "but was waiting for word from General Stuart about movements of the Union army."[27]

Evidence indicates that Stuart had sent an earlier dispatch, then one on the 27th, but that they had never reached Lee. It also is clear that the absence of Stuart resulted from Union movements on the route he had intended to follow, not from any personal desires, as critics later charged.

In fact, after starting his movement on schedule with those of Lee's other elements on June 25, Stuart had to turn off to avoid getting tangled with Union forces advancing toward the Potomac. After moving south to Buckland Mills to deceive the enemy, Stuart and three brigades moved east to Brentsville, then to Wolf Run Shoals on the 26th. The next day, he advanced on a route to Fairfax Station, to Fairfax Court House, to Dranesville, and before midnight to Rowser's Ford between Washington and Seneca.[28]

In evaluating Stuart's movements, recognize that on the night of June 27, his was the only part of the invasion force south of the Potomac. All the others were approaching the Susquehanna.

One of Couch's chief concerns was protection of the main river crossings. Western approaches to the bridges leading into Harrisburg were being fortified, but Couch feared that was inadequate. He directed that if the bridges could not be held, the army should be ready to burn them quickly.[29]

Couch had taken action earlier to protect the bridge between Wrightsville and Columbia. On June 24 Colonel J. G. Frick was ordered to Columbia to take the necessary steps to secure all the Susquehanna River bridges and fords in Lancaster County.[30] While the Confederates were still at York, Frick had arranged to blow up one span of the mile-long bridge in an effort to prevent the invaders from reaching Columbia.[31]

Concern about another bridge over the Susquehanna—at Conowingo, Maryland—prompted General Schenck in Baltimore to tell Couch that "I cannot reach the Conowingo bridge, and have nothing there. You should burn it, if you have not already done so."[32] Union authorities were determined to prevent the Confederates from penetrating east of the river.

—————————⟫●⟪—————————

Uncertainty about Confederate movements created much greater confusion for Hooker and other Union leaders. On June 24 he received a recommendation to move his army "at once to the neighborhood of Harpers Ferry" from Brigadier General Gouverneur K. Warren, Hooker's chief engineer. He pointed out that "the whole of Lee's army is reported to be on the Potomac above that place, part of it across the river, and threatening an advance upon Harrisburg."

Warren noted that at Harpers Ferry, "we can protect Washington as well, and Baltimore better than here [at Fairfax Court House] and preserve our communications and routes of supply." He described the move as "the shortest line to reach Lee's army" and noted that it "will enable us to operate on his communications, if he advances; to throw overwhelming forces on either portion of his army that he allows the river to divide; and is too strong a position for him to attack us in, even if we make heavy detachments." Warren suggested the move "would prevent Lee from detaching a corps to invade Pennsylvania with, as it would expose the rest of his army to our attack in superior force."

Warren said his recommendations were "based upon the idea that we are not to try and go around his army, and drive it out of Maryland, as we did last year, but to paralyze all its movements by threatening its flank and rear if it advances, and gain time to collect reinforcements sufficient to render us the stronger army of the two, if we are not so already."[33]

At 11:35 that night Hooker ordered Major General Oliver O. Howard, commander of the 11th Corps, to march the next morning for Sandy Hook, near Harpers Ferry. Howard was told that other troops would join him to guard the bridge and depots at Edwards Ferry.[34]

In a letter to Halleck on the 24th Hooker speculated that Ewell was over the river and heading northward. He did not know if any other Confederate troops had crossed the river, but if he found out that they had, "I will commence moving, myself." He also stated that troops were on the way to Harpers Ferry and that he might send a corps or two across the river, possibly to cut Ewell off from the rest of Lee's army. "If the enemy should conclude not to throw any additional force over the river, I desire to make Washington secure, and, with all the force I can muster, strike for his line of retreat in the direction of Richmond."

Hooker's extreme uncertainty about enemy movements and his own ideas for countering them was summed up in the final words of this letter. "I request that my orders be sent me today, for outside of the Army of the Potomac I don't know whether I am standing on my head or feet."[35] Later, this situation prompted a surprising action by Hooker.

Hooker was not alone in his deep concern. At 8:55 A.M. on the 24th Lincoln had telegraphed Couch: "Have you any reports of the enemy moving into Pennsylvania? And, if any, how many?" At 9:30 A.M. Couch replied, "Rebel cavalry are this side [north] of Chambersburg." He added that reports indicated A. P. Hill and Longstreet probably had crossed the Potomac with 40,000 men and that Ewell was at Greencastle with 30,000 men and thirty pieces of artillery. Lee's headquarters, he told Lincoln, were at Millwood, twelve miles from Winchester.[36]

On June 24, as noted, Hooker began moving cautiously toward the Potomac River. The next day, he began crossing the river at Edwards Ferry. The 1st Corps advanced about ten miles north to Barnesville, Maryland; the 3rd Corps from Gum Springs to the mouth of the Monocacy River; Howard's 11th Corps to Jefferson, Maryland, northeast of Harpers Ferry; the Artillery Reserve from Fairfax Court House to near Poolesville, Maryland; and Stahel's cavalry toward Frederick.

The 2nd Division of the 6th Corps moved from Bristoe Station to Centreville, Virginia. Some troops—two brigades of Samuel Crawford's division and Stannard's Vermont Brigade—left the Washington defenses to join Hooker's troops.[37]

Another important step on June 25 was the assignment of Major General John F. Reynolds to command of the right wing of the Army of the Potomac. It was composed of Reynolds's 1st Corps, Major General Daniel Sickles's 3rd Corps, and Howard's 11th Corps.[38]

A short time later Reynolds took two gaps in South Mountain on roads leading toward Baltimore and Washington.[39] Reynolds was informed that Howard had reached Point of Rocks and that he would move toward Middletown, Maryland, not Sandy Hook.[40]

Reynolds also learned that the other corps of Hooker's army—the 2nd, 5th, 6th, and 12th—and Hooker's headquarters would begin moving into Maryland early on the 26th.[41]

On June 26 Reynolds's wing advanced farther into Maryland, the 1st Corps to Jefferson, the 3rd to Point of Rocks, and the 11th to Middletown. The 2nd Corps was north of Edwards Ferry; the 5th Corps within four miles of the mouth of the Monocacy; the 6th Corps at Dranesville, on the road to Edwards Ferry; the 12th Corps at the mouth of the Monocacy; and Hooker's headquarters at Poolesville.[42]

The Union movement into Maryland continued on June 27. Headquarters was moved to Frederick. The 1st and 3rd corps advanced to Middletown, the 2nd to Barnesville, the 5th to near Frederick, the 6th to near Poolesville, the 12th to Knoxville. The 11th Corps remained at Middletown.[43]

In the meantime Hooker became anxious about conditions at Harpers Ferry. He asked Halleck on June 26, "Is there any reason why Maryland Heights should not be abandoned after the public stores and property are removed?" He then informed Halleck that he intended to go there the next day "to satisfy myself on that point. It must be borne in mind that I am here with a force inferior in numbers to that of the enemy, and must have every available man to use in the field."[44]

The next morning Hooker left for Harpers Ferry to review the situation.[45] Halleck told Hooker, "Maryland Heights have always been regarded as an important point to be held by us, and much expense and labor incurred in fortifying them. I cannot approve their abandonment, except in case of absolute necessity."[46]

Hooker obviously was disturbed by this. He immediately replied from Sandy Hook:

> I find 10,000 men here [at Harpers Ferry] in condition to take the field. Here they are of no earthly account. They cannot defend a ford of the river, and, as far as Harpers Ferry is concerned, there is nothing of it. As for the fortifications, the work of the troops, they remain when the troops are withdrawn. No enemy will ever take possession of them. This is my opinion. All the public property could have been secured tonight, and the troops marched to where they could have been of some service. Now they are but a bait for the rebels, should they return.

He requested that his comments be passed on to Stanton and Lincoln.[47] In a message at 1 P.M. on the 27th Hooker told Halleck:

> My original instructions require me to cover Harpers Ferry and Washington. I have now imposed upon me, in addition, an enemy in my front of more than my number. I beg to be understood, respectfully, but firmly, that I am unable to comply with this condition with the means at my disposal, and earnestly request that I may at once be relieved from the position I occupy.[48]

Hooker's request was immediately accepted and Major General George Gordon Meade was appointed commander of the Army of the Potomac.[49] In his response to the order on June 28 Meade said:

> As a soldier, I obey it, and to the utmost of my ability, will execute it. Totally unexpected as it has been, and in ignorance of the exact condition of the troops and position of the enemy, I can only now say that it appears to me I must move toward the Susquehanna, keeping Washington and Baltimore well covered, and if the enemy is checked in his attempt to cross the Susquehanna, or if he turns toward Baltimore, to give him battle. I trust every available man that can be spared will be sent to me, as from all accounts the enemy is in strong force.[50]

It was an unusual coincidence that placed Meade in command of the army on the same day that the Confederates reached the high water mark of their invasion, the day that indeed took them to the banks of the Susquehanna.

———◆———

The Confederates were amazed by the attitude of many civilians in the areas through which they marched. On reaching Carlisle, Jed Hotchkiss noted that the people there "were not as sullen as those at Chambersburg."[51]

John B. Gordon wrote to his wife on June 23: "These people are apparently very indifferent as to the result of this war. I am satisfied that the mass of these near the Maryland line, would be delighted to see the war end on almost any basis."

In another letter, dated July 7, he told his wife that when he rode through York on the 28th, "it would have astonished you, darling, to see how much afraid of us these people were." As he rode ahead of his brigade through the streets, "great crowds of ladies and gent[lemen], boys and girls, crowded the streets and sidewalks and houses. So dense was the crowd, and so excited that I could scarcely get along the street."[52]

Captain William J. Seymour, an aide of Brigadier General Harry T. Hays, brigade commander in Early's division, wrote: "Soon after we entered the State of Pennsylvania, General Early was waited upon by a deputation of citizens who informed him that there were thousands of men in that part of the State who were opposed to the war & who belonged to a secret society called the 'Knights of the Golden Circle.' The distinctive signs, grips and countersigns [of the society] were imparted to the General, who, in turn, gave them to his officers.

"Much to our surprise, hundreds of people in the towns through which we passed greeted us with these signs, and we joyfully accepted them as proofs of the anti-war feeling that pervaded the country." They soon learned that the people were not as friendly as the signs would seem to indicate, but that "these professions and demonstrations were hollow and hypocritical." The people actually had been victims of a scam.

"Just in advance of our army," Seymour explained, "two Yankees from one of the New England States travelled through the county, professing to be high officers of a New York lodge of the 'Knights of the Golden Circle,' and that they were empowered to receive any number of persons on payment of five dollars per capita. They represented that the Northern Society was closely connected with a similar society in the South, and that the persons and property of all members would be respected by the Confederate Army. In this way, thousands of people were induced to pay their money for the privilege of being accounted as friends of the South; hence our apparently cordial greeting along our line of march."[53] Early also noted, "As we moved through the country, people made mysterious signs to us."[54]

On June 27, with Ewell's two columns just a day's march from the Susquehanna, there were increasing signs that two of Jackson's objectives were creating concern east of the river. One was to seize and, if necessary, destroy the commerce of Philadelphia and other large cities. The other was to make Northerners understand what it would cost them to hold the South in the Union.[55]

In Philadelphia Major General N. J. T. Dana reported that the city was "almost defenseless," with no more than 400 men on guard and 600 convalescent troops in hospitals. One of the important factories there was that of Alfred Jenks & Son, which produced arms for Union troops. Dana was instructed to use tugs, barges, or other river vessels to remove gun-manufacturing machinery beyond reach of the enemy, if necessary.[56]

In Wilmington, Delaware, where gunpowder was made, Major General Henry DuPont and Governor William Cannon asked for two New York artillery batteries to defend the city and powder works. Two cavalry companies also were sent to guard the Conowingo bridge, south of the Pennsylvania-Maryland line.[57]

Public concern also rose in four other states east of the Susquehanna—Maryland, New Jersey, New York, and Rhode Island. On June 24 Stanton received a report that only 662 men were on duty in eight forts to defend New York Harbor against naval invasion. Three days later Navy Secretary Gideon Welles was informed that so many troops from the fort garrisons "had been forwarded to the seat of war" that the harbor was endangered. Welles was requested to assign the ironclad *Roanoke* to the harbor's defense.[58]

Similar alarm was felt in Rhode Island over Narragansett Bay and the cities of Providence, Fall River, and other towns. In a letter to Lincoln Governor James Y. Smith requested authority to construct, arm, and man suitable earthworks at the expense of the federal government.[59]

New Jersey Governor Joel Parker reported to Lincoln that his people feared invasion of their state. "We think that the enemy should be driven from Pennsylvania," he said, and that the "apathy [here] should be removed."[60] On June 30 martial law was declared in Baltimore and neighboring counties.[61]

Public concern manifested itself in some unusual ways, including calls for McClellan to again command the Army of the Potomac or other points such as Philadelphia.[62]

In Pennsylvania the primary defensive measures were focused on the bridges at Harrisburg and Columbia, toward which Ewell's columns were advancing. Couch's concern for the safety of Harrisburg was clear in his first report to Meade on June 29. He pointed out that 25,000 enemy troops "are between here [Harrisburg] and Baltimore. I have only 15,000 men, such as they are, on my whole line—say 9,000 here [at Harrisburg]."[63]

Defensive positions had been built on the river hills near Columbia and "fairly bristled with men,"[64] but there was a problem. Most were private citizens and some were armed only with shotguns.[65]

The 27th Pennsylvania Militia arrived at Columbia on June 24, and Colonel Frick's first step was to send four companies across the river to Wrightsville. The next morning, four more companies were sent across to a position near the York turnpike, about half a mile from Wrightsville.[66]

In the afternoon of June 27 Confederates were reported near York, so the two remaining militia companies were sent to Wrightsville to defend the bridge. On June 28 troops began digging rifle pits on either side of the turnpike. If these defenses were unable to halt the Confederates, one span of the Columbia-Wrightsville bridge was rigged with explosives, as previously ordered, to keep the invaders from crossing into Lancaster County.[67]

———›‹›‹‹‹———

Sunday, June 28, dawned clear and bright.[68] In Carlisle and on the outskirts of York Ewell's men were ready to move. The other two corps of the Army of Northern Virginia remained in camp—Longstreet just north of Chambersburg and Hill near Fayetteville, on the road to Gettysburg. Lee also remained on the eastern outskirts of Chambersburg. Early that day, Ewell's advance units—Jenkins's cavalry and Gordon's brigade—began separate movements toward the Susquehanna. Otherwise, Ewell's troops remained at Carlisle observing the Sabbath in a Stonewall Jackson manner. The Reverend Beverly Tucker Lacy, who had arrived at Jackson's headquarters back on March 1 "to remain awhile," preached at two services on the Carlisle Barracks grounds. This was followed by "quite an animating scene" at which the Confederate flag was raised, and Rodes, Trimble, and Daniel spoke.[69]

After the flag ceremony four staff officers—Sandie Pendleton, William Allan, Hunter McGuire, and Benjamin C. "Clem" Fishburne—obtained passes to go into Carlisle to attend services. At the Presbyterian church, they were "politely received and shown to their seats." The congregation was made up largely of Southern troops. After church, the officers learned that the minister was from Alabama and knew some of the soldiers in the congregation that day.

The four officers then went to Dickinson College, where a professor gave them a tour. In the library, they were joined by other professors and some of their friends, and all enjoyed "a very amiable conversation." Eventually the conversation turned to the war, "which was discussed in a most pleasant manner."[70] The rest of Ewell's troops in Carlisle were ready to move to Harrisburg the next day.[71]

⟶➤●◄⟵

In the meantime Jenkins began reconnoitering Harrisburg's defenses. As he approached Mechanicsburg, pickets were sent out to check nearby roads to avoid any surprises. As he approached the junction of West Main and York streets, Jenkins divided his force into two columns. The leading one turned north on the Hogestown road and moved north to the Harrisburg pike, then east to Oyster Point, on the western outskirts of what is now Camp Hill. Jenkins then sent two scouts into Mechanicsburg to seek its surrender. The scouts reported that there were no enemy troops in town.

Jenkins, with his troops, then rode into town, met with Mayor George Hummel, and demanded surrender of the town's flag and rations for 1,500 men. The flag was taken at the mayor's home, and residents quickly responded to the request for food.[72] "It was very humiliating, and yet amusing, to see persons walk up with these baskets of ham, bread, butter, and whatever else they choose to bring," C. B. Niesley, a local resident, wrote to his parents on July 1. "On Monday [June 29] a lieutenant of a battery came in and requested rations for 150 men. They have been all over the county, as far as we can hear, taking horses and anything they could use.

"There has been considerable fighting down near Oisters [Oyster] Point. We could hear the firing distinctly. This morning I heard from Churchtown. They have their headquarters at my farm, using things as they see proper. Thus far they have not disturbed private property or families."[73] The fighting Niesley mentioned was during Jenkins's advance in preparation for what was to have been Ewell's crossing of the Susquehanna and capture of Harrisburg.

While a few of Jenkins's troops remained east of Mechanicsburg, tearing up railroad tracks, the other two columns moved toward the Harrisburg defenses. The column that had moved north on the Hogestown road advanced to Salem Church and Sporting Hill along the Harrisburg pike. The other approached the junction of Trindle Road and the Harrisburg pike, near what are now 32nd and Market streets in Camp Hill.

Both columns encountered skirmishes on June 28 and 29 in what is regarded as the northernmost clash involving Confederate troops in Pennsylvania.[74] During this time, Jenkins and three of Ewell's staff officers had moved to a hill south of Bridgeport and were studying the Harrisburg defenses through field glasses. Two men in a rowboat, apparently checking river conditions, reportedly were picked up by Union troops.[75] Jenkins and the men in the boat obviously were carrying out Ewell's instructions to make a thorough study of Harrisburg, its approaches, and its defenses.

Movements in York County on Sunday, June 28, led to the deepest penetration of Northern territory by Lee's troops. At daylight, both of Early's columns—Gordon's brigade just west of York, and the rest of the division near Dover, northwest of the city—began marching. During this period, the York mayor and a number of residents met Gordon and surrendered the town to him. Before entering, Gordon sent a provost guard "to occupy the city, and take down the Federal flag left flying over the principal street."[76]

Early's main column marched through Weiglestown to the York-Harrisburg road. Robert Hoke's brigade, under the temporary command of Colonel Isaac E. Avery, marched into York to occupy it and preserve order. Early said, "I here met with General Gordon, and repeated to him my instructions to proceed to the Susquehanna and secure the Columbia bridge, if possible, and he moved in that direction with his command." Later, Early noted that he also told Gordon that he preferred the bridge be kept intact.[77] Gordon's brigade advanced into the city.

On his arrival, Early requisitioned 2,000 pairs of shoes, 1,000 hats, 1,000 pairs of socks, three days' rations, and $100,000. All the supplies, except 500 to 800 pairs of shoes, were furnished. City officials said that most of the town's money had been sent away and they were unable to provide the total requested.[78] But a receipt furnished by Early's quartermaster, Major C. E. Snodgrass, showed that they had received $28,610 from the town.[79]

Gordon and his troops entered York on Sunday morning as church bells were ringing and well-dressed men, women, and children were on their way to services. The civilians' appearance "strangely contrasted with that of my marching soldiers," Gordon commented. The soldiers were covered with road dust and some were without shoes. "Confederate pride, to say

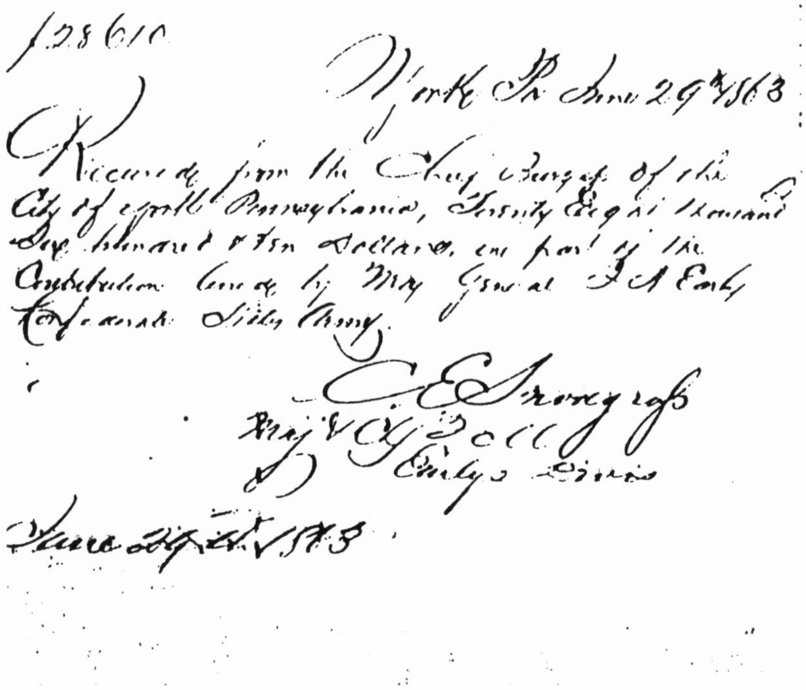

$28610

York Pa. June 29th 1863

Received from the Chief Burgess of the City of York Pennsylvania, Twenty Eight thousand Six hundred & ten Dollars, as part of the Contribution levied by Maj General J. A. Early Confederate States Army.

C. E. Snodgrass
Maj & QM, Early's Divis.

June 29th 1863

Courtesy MHI Archives, Documents of the Loyal Legion of the United States, Massachusetts Commandery nothing of Southern gallantry, was subjected to the sorest trial by the consternation produced among the ladies of York," the general added.

Gordon rode a short distance ahead of his troops and turned his horse so that he could speak to a crowd of young ladies on the sidewalk. As he turned, "a cry of alarm came from their midst; but after a few words of assurance from me, quiet and apparent confidence were restored." Gordon assured them that "under the orders of the Confederate commander-in-chief, both private property and non-combatants were safe." This was followed by an unusual incident in which, Gordon explained:

> A young girl, probably twelve years of age, ran up to my horse and handed me a large bouquet of flowers, in the center of which was a note, in delicate handwriting, purporting to give the numbers and describe the position of the Union forces at Wrightsville, toward which I was advancing.
>
> I carefully read and reread this strange note. It bore no signature, and contained no assurance of sympathy for the Southern cause, but it was so terse and explicit in its terms as to compel my confidence.

The note also suggested that Gordon, as he neared Wrightsville, should stop on a ridge and carefully examine the Union position at the bridge. In the late afternoon, as he approached the town, he halted on the ridge and, with his field glasses, scanned the situation "to verify the truth of the mysterious communication, or detect its misrepresentations." Gordon was amazed by what he saw.

> There, in full view before us, was the town, just as described, nestling on the banks of the Susquehanna. There was the blue line of soldiers guarding the approach, drawn up, as indicated, along an intervening ridge and across the pike. There was the long bridge spanning the Susquehanna and connecting the town with Columbia on the other bank. Most important of all, there was the deep gorge or ravine running off to the right and extending around the left flank of the Federal line and to the river below the bridge.
>
> Not an inaccurate detail in that note could be discovered. I did not hesitate, therefore, to adopt its suggestion of moving down the gorge in order to throw my command on the flank, or possibly in the rear, of the Union troops and force them to a rapid retreat or surrender.[80]

The note described the defensive preparations. Since this work was carried on well into Saturday night, Gordon knew it could not have been written by a casual observer. It evidently was the work of a scout who was under Lee's orders to get information to Gordon as quickly as possible. The scout would have been advised that Confederates would be moving through York, just as Stuart had been told by Lee to join a column from Ewell's corps there.

In an address before the Military Historical Society of Massachusetts after the war, Lieutenant Colonel George B. Davis of the 1st Massachusetts Cavalry noted that before the invasion, maps of Pennsylvania "were procured without difficulty by [Confederate] agents sent into the southern counties of Pennsylvania for this purpose."[81]

As noted, Lee had informed Jefferson Davis in letters on November 19 and December 8, 1862, that scouts had been sent north to gather all information possible. He wrote that his scouts had reported no evidence of troop transports being prepared in Washington or Alexandria. He also wrote that a scout "who had been absent several weeks" had just returned with information from New York, Staten Island, the Brooklyn Navy Yard, Washington, and the Coast Survey Office.[82] Lee's spy system apparently was widespread and it would not have been surprising had a scout been placed at the Wrightsville bridge and others perhaps in Harrisburg.

As Gordon studied the area along the river, he focused on the ravine mentioned in the note. He remembered that he had been directed to cross the Susquehanna River, if possible, and added:

> My immediate object was to move rapidly down that ravine to the river, then along its right bank to the bridge, seize it, and cross to the Columbia side. Once across, I intended to mount my men, if practicable, so as to pass rapidly through Lancaster in the direction of Philadelphia, and thus compel [the Union commander] to send a portion of his army to the defense of that city.[83]

His intention was interrupted, however, by Frick's trench line across the turnpike on the approach to the bridge and the threat of an attack from that direction. He immediately sent out a force to make a demonstration along the enemy line, while three regiments were sent "to the right by a circuitous route in order to turn these works, and, if possible, gain the enemy's rear, cut off his retreat, and seize the bridge." Gordon's opening artillery fire caused the enemy force to retreat rapidly across the river and try to destroy the bridge.[84] As the last of the Union men passed the arch where explosives had been placed, the fuses were lit, but the explosion did no serious damage to the bridge.[85] Barrels of kerosene were then rolled out on the bridge and ignited. This tactic worked better; Gordon's column had gotten almost halfway across the bridge before the flames drove it back. A lack of firefighting equipment frustrated Confederate attempts to save the bridge.

But when the flames reached a lumberyard in Wrightsville and spread to nearby buildings—including several houses—buckets, tubs, pails, and pans were quickly provided by residents and Confederate soldiers prevented destruction of more property.[86]

———————

The bridge destruction also frustrated Early's invasion plans. On the 28th, just before dark, he rode out of York toward Columbia to determine the result of Gordon's expedition. He had gone only a short distance when he saw the smoke from the bridge. He expressed his regret and explained:

> Notwithstanding my orders [given verbally by Ewell] to destroy the bridge, I had found the country so defenseless, and the militia which Curtin had called into service so utterly inefficient, that I determined to cross the Susquehanna, levy a contribution on the rich town of Lancaster, cut the [Pennsylvania] Central Railroad, and then move up in rear of Harrisburg while General Ewell was advancing against that city from the other side.

Early also intended to mount his troops on "the horses which had been accumulated in large numbers on the east side of the river by the farmers who had fled before us." He added that his project had been thwarted by the destruction of the bridge, "as the river was otherwise impassable, being very wide and deep at this point. I therefore ordered General Gordon to move his command back to York next day, and returned myself to that place that night."[87]

Although not the northernmost point reached by Confederate soldiers, Wrightsville was the deepest penetration into the industrial heart of the North. Gordon's troops had gotten onto the Wrightsville-Columbia bridge. If they could have seized it, Early could have increased the pressure for Northerners to end the war.

CHAPTER 30

And Then Back to Gettysburg

CRITICAL DEVELOPMENTS LATE ON JUNE 28 DRASTICALLY CHANGED Confederate plans and ended Lee's hopes of moving into the heart of the North. Then began unexpected movements that led to Gettysburg.

News of the burning of the Wrightsville-Columbia bridge had not reached headquarters when Lee decided to order Ewell to move directly on Harrisburg. Longstreet was to move to Ewell's support the next morning. Hill was "to move eastward to the Susquehanna, cross the river below Harrisburg, and seize the railroad between Harrisburg and Philadelphia." The idea was to divert Union reinforcements that might be coming from the north. Colonel Marshall expected "that there would be such alarm created by these movements that the Federal Government would be obliged to withdraw its army from Virginia and abandon any plan that it might have for an attack on Richmond."[1]

Ewell and Hill acted promptly. Ewell noted in his report that he was "starting on the 29th for that place [Harrisburg]."[2] In his report Hill pointed out that his corps—three infantry divisions and five battalions of artillery—was camped near Fayetteville on the road from Chambersburg to Gettysburg. He added:

> On the morning of June 29th I was directed to move on this road in the direction of York, and to cross the Susquehanna, menacing the communications of Harrisburg and Philadelphia, and to cooperate with General Ewell, acting as circumstances might require. Accordingly, on the 29th I moved General Heth's division to Cashtown, some 8 miles from Gettysburg.[3]

345

After dispatching the orders to Ewell and Hill, Marshall returned to his tent. He was then summoned by Lee, who said that the movements would have to be changed. With Lee at the time was Longstreet's scout, Harrison, who brought alarming news from Washington that he first transmitted to Longstreet, then to Lee. He said that the Army of the Potomac had advanced to Frederick, Maryland, and some troops were moving toward the mountains. Even more important was that Meade had replaced Hooker as commander.[4]

Marshall said that Lee inferred that Meade intended to enter the Cumberland Valley, cut communications with Virginia through Hagerstown, and disrupt Lee's ammunition supply. Lee then revealed his decision to change troop movements. Marshall stated that Lee was insistent "that the enemy's army should be kept east of the mountains, and consequently he [Lee] determined to move his own army to the east side of the Blue Ridge so as to threaten Washington and Baltimore, and detain the federal force on that side of the mountains to protect those cities."

Marshall was directed to immediately countermand the orders that had just been sent to Ewell and Hill, and ordered Hill "to move eastward on the road through Cashtown or Gettysburg as circumstances might direct." Longstreet was ordered to follow the next morning.[5]

⸺⸺⸺●⸺⸺⸺

A confusing aspect of these orders shows in a dispatch Lee sent to Ewell from Chambersburg, dated June 28 at 7:30 A.M.

> I wrote you last night, stating that General Hooker was reported to have crossed the Potomac, and is advancing by way of Middletown, the head of his column being at that point in Frederick County [Maryland]. I directed you in that letter to move your forces to this point [Chambersburg].
>
> If you have not already progressed on the road, and if you have no good reason against it, I desire you to move in the direction of Gettysburg, via Heidlersburg, where you will have turnpike most of the way, and you can thus join your other divisions to Early's, which is east of the mountains. I think it preferable to keep on the east side of the mountains. When you come to Heidlersburg, you can either move directly on Gettysburg, or turn down to Cashtown.

A footnote states that the letter, as it appears in Lee's letterbook, "was copied from memory."[6]

Ewell clearly was being told to move toward Gettysburg or Cashtown after Lee had learned about the Union movement toward Pennsylvania. But Lee did not know about that until the night of June 28. In a note attached to a copy of the letter to Ewell, Longstreet points out that the time should have been 7:30 A.M. on the 29th, not the 28th.

He also stated that Ewell was preparing to begin marching on Harrisburg on the 29th when he received "this counter order sent after the report of the scout was made." Longstreet said the original intent was for Ewell to concentrate at Chambersburg, but that this "was changed in the later dispatch to Gettysburg."[7]

In the meantime Gordon started moving back toward York as ordered by General Early. Before leaving Wrightsville on Monday, Gordon and a number of his soldiers were guests of Mrs. L. L. Rewalt for breakfast. She explained that, although she had no sympathy for the Southern cause, she wanted to express her appreciation for what Gordon's men had done the night before to save her house from burning.[8] By nightfall on the 29th, Early's men were back in York.[9]

This period was marked by difficult and sometimes confusing problems for George Gordon Meade, the new Union commander. He proposed to keep Washington and Baltimore well covered while he moved toward the Susquehanna and, if necessary, battled the enemy.[10] Halleck concurred and put Schenck's and Couch's troops at Meade's disposal. Halleck added a note of caution: "It is most probable that Lee will concentrate his forces this side of the Susquehanna."[11]

Meade was reasonably sure of Lee's position and estimated enemy strength at more than 100,000 men of all arms. "Reliable intelligence," he stated, "placed the advance [Ewell's corps] on the Susquehanna at Harrisburg and Columbia; Longstreet's corps at Chambersburg, and Hill's corps between that place and Cashtown." This was correct, except that Ewell's troops had not crossed the Susquehanna to Harrisburg or Columbia, but were still at Carlisle and on the road to Wrightsville.

On the other hand, Meade was uncertain of the exact Union situation. On the morning of the 28th, he noted, "my own army, of which the most recent returns showed an aggregate of a little over 100,000, was situated in and around Frederick, Md., extending from Harpers Ferry to the mouth of the Monocacy [River], and from Middletown to Frederick." Much of the day, Meade explained, was spent "in ascertaining the position and strength of the different corps." He also brought forward the cavalry that had been covering the Union rear in its passage across the Potomac and that had been strengthened by reinforcements from the defenses of Washington.[12]

Meade took an unusual step at 1 P.M. on Sunday, June 28. To Halleck, he raised a question about the problem that had annoyed Hooker and provoked the latter's request to be relieved of command. Meade asked: "Am I permitted, under existing circumstances, to withdraw a portion of the garrison of Harpers Ferry, providing I leave sufficient force to hold Maryland Heights?" Halleck replied: "The garrison at Harpers Ferry is under your orders. You can diminish or increase it as you think the circumstances justify."[13] Meade immediately ordered Major General William French to move 7,000 men to Frederick and along the Baltimore and Ohio Railroad. The rest of French's men were to remove public property and take it to Washington.[14]

At 8:15 P.M. Meade informed Halleck that the 1st, 2nd, 5th, 11th, and 12th corps, plus the Artillery Reserve, were around Frederick. The 3rd was at Middletown, about six miles west of Frederick, and the 6th Corps near New Market, east of Frederick. "My intention is now to move tomorrow on three lines to Emmitsburg and Westminster, having the army on the road from Emmitsburg through Westminster, or as near there as we can march," he said. Meade also requested Halleck's "views as to the movement proposed."[15] Halleck replied: "So far as I can judge, without a better knowledge of the enemy's positions, your proposed movement seems good."[16]

Meade did not wait for the response; he issued marching orders for 4 o'clock the next morning, June 29. The 1st and 11th corps were to move to Emmitsburg, the 3rd and 12th to Taneytown, and the 2nd to Frizzellburg. The other two corps were to move at 8 A.M., the 5th to Uniontown and the 6th to New Windsor. The artillery was to precede the 12th Corps at 4 A.M. and various other units were to march four hours later. Headquarters was to move at 8 A.M. for Middleburg.[17] The positions would be along what became known as the Pipe Creek Line.

In the meantime Lee and Meade were concerned about where Stuart was and what he was doing. Lee felt completely in the dark, as his repeated questions to subordinates indicated. Meade was confused by conflicting reports regarding Stuart.

To Halleck at 1 P.M. on the 28th, Meade cited "reliable intelligence" that "leads to the belief that Stuart has crossed at Williamsport, and is moving toward Hagerstown, in rear of Lee's army. All accounts agree in giving Lee so large a force that I cannot believe he has left any considerable body of troops on the south side of the Potomac. Please give me your views fully."[18]

Meade's information was not reliable, of course. Stuart, Wade Hampton, Fitzhugh Lee, and John Chambliss had crossed the Potomac at Rowser's Ford, about two miles southeast of Seneca, Maryland, late on June 27 and early on the 28th.[19] The other two brigades, under William E. Jones and Beverly H. Robertson, had been left south of the Potomac and were at Berryville on June 29. Later Robertson, with three of Jones's regiments, moved by way of Williamsport and Chambersburg to Cashtown, where they arrived on July 3.[20]

In a dispatch at 12:30 P.M. on the 28th Halleck provided Meade with convincing evidence that Stuart's cavalry had not crossed the Potomac River at Williamsport. "A brigade of Fitzhugh Lee's cavalry has crossed the Potomac near Seneca Falls, and is making for the railroad to cut off your supplies. There is another brigade of rebel cavalry south of the Potomac, which may follow. We have no cavalry here to operate against them."[21] At 2 P.M. Meade replied: "Dispatch received in relation to crossing of enemy cavalry at Seneca Creek. Have ordered two brigades and battery to proceed at once in search and pursuit."[22]

Communications continued throughout the day between Halleck and Meade. Halleck was concerned over the unexpected movement of the 2nd Massachusetts Cavalry, which he said had moved "contrary to my orders" from Poolesville, Maryland, where it had been assigned to keep an eye on the Potomac below Edwards Ferry. Halleck emphasized that there was no cavalry available in Washington to send out.[23] Meade ordered the regiment back to Poolesville.[24]

The most alarming news reached Meade from Halleck at 3 P.M. "It is just reported that your train of one hundred and fifty wagons has been captured by Fitzhugh Lee near Rockville. Unless cavalry is sent to guard your communications with Washington, they will be cut off. It is reported that there is still a considerable rebel force south of the Potomac."[25]

"Do you consider the information at all to be depended upon concerning a force of the enemy south of the Potomac?" Meade replied. "All our information here tends to show that Lee's entire army passed through

Hagerstown, the rear passing yesterday a.m."[26] Halleck responded, "I doubt if there is any large force south of the Potomac, probably a few thousand cavalry, enough to render it necessary to have a strong rear guard to protect the trains and picket the river."[27]

Early in the evening Meade informed Halleck that Brigadier General Adolph von Steinwehr had reported from South Mountain that 3,000 of Stuart's cavalry had passed through Williamsport the previous afternoon. Major General John Sedgwick, "on the march from Poolesville, reports that 3,000 of the enemy's cavalry, with some artillery, are in his rear. My impression is that Stuart has divided his force, with a view of harassing our right and left flanks."[28] Less than an hour later, Meade added: "There seems to be no doubt that 3,000 of the enemy's cavalry have been on our right, between us and Washington today."[29]

As confusion over the position and movement of Confederate cavalry increased, an important step was taken at Meade's headquarters. Major General Daniel Butterfield, Meade's chief of staff, sent a message to Major Thomas T. Eckert, the telegraph superintendent in Washington: "The major general commanding desires to know if any reliable information can be given as to the direction taken by the [enemy] cavalry force that were at Rockville, the hour they left, the names of any generals or colonels, and the designation of any regiments. Did they return to recross the river, or proceed north, by what road and when?"[30]

━━━━━━━━

Actually, the main Confederate cavalry column was composed of the three brigades with Stuart that were advancing well to the right of Lee's army. As noted, Stuart had been forced to change plans and was advancing farther to the east. His route had taken him to Dranesville, and from there to Rowser's Ford on the night of June 27. On the 28th a lock gate on the Chesapeake and Ohio Canal was broken and a number of boats intercepted. The cavalry then moved forward to Rockville, on the direct line from Washington to the Army of the Potomac. After some skirmishing that forced a Union withdrawal, Stuart took the town. In order to disrupt Union communications, miles of telegraph lines in the area were torn down.

Shortly after seizing Rockville, the troopers spotted a long train of wagons approaching from Washington. It was about eight miles long, with the last wagon only three or four miles from Washington. Stuart's men swooped down on this tempting prize. Some wagons, upset as drivers sought to escape, had to be burned, but more than 125 were seized, many loaded with oats intended for Meade's horses.

As the Confederate force continued to ride northward, Stuart was determined to "reach our column with as little delay as possible, to acquaint the commanding general with the nature of the enemy's movements," which Stuart described as moving northward through Frederick. The wagon train hindered a rapid advance, but Stuart kept in mind Lee's letter of June 22, with orders to "collect all the supplies you can for the use of the army."[31]

Meade's advance toward Pennsylvania was set in motion early on Monday, June 29. "On the evening of that day," Meade reported, "the army was in position, the left at Emmitsburg and the right at New Windsor."[32] Actually, only five of the seven regular corps had reached their designated positions that evening. The 1st and 11th were at Emmitsburg, the 3rd and 12th at Taneytown, and the 6th near New Windsor.[33]

The 5th Corps, assigned to Uniontown, marched northeast fifteen miles from Frederick to Liberty, about midway to its designated position.[34] The 2nd Corps, which was to move to Frizzellburg, halted at 10 P.M. a mile beyond Uniontown after a march of thirty miles. Hancock explained that the order for him to move at 4 A.M. had been delayed by an accident, so he did not get on the road until 8 A.M. The 2nd Corps remained at Uniontown on the 29th and 30th.[35]

Meade also reported that three of his cavalry divisions were in key positions along his line. The 1st Division, commanded by Brigadier General John Buford, was on his left flank; the 2nd, commanded by Brigadier General David Gregg, was near Westminster on the right flank; and the 3rd, under Brigadier General Judson Kilpatrick, was in front of the Union line.[36]

While his troops were moving, Meade notified corps commanders of the order of march for the 30th. The 12th Corps was to advance to Littlestown, Pennsylvania, passing the 3rd Corps at Taneytown. The 5th was to cross Pipe Creek on the road between Littlestown and Westminster. The 6th was to pass through Westminster and advance northeastward to Manchester. The 1st was to advance from Emmitsburg "half way to Gettysburg" to the Marsh Creek crossing. The Reserve Artillery was to follow the 12th Corps, and the engineer and bridge train was to move near the 5th Corps. Meade's headquarters also would be moved from Middleburg to Taneytown.[37]

Meade described to Halleck the positions to which his army was moving: "If Lee is moving for Baltimore, I expect to get between his main army and that place. If he is crossing the Susquehanna, I shall rely upon General Couch, with his force, holding him until I can fall upon his rear and give him battle, which I shall endeavor to do. My endeavor will be in my movements to hold my force well together, with the hope of falling upon some portion of Lee's army in detail."[38]

Meade's uncertainty about Lee's position and movements was more evident in a dispatch to Couch on the 30th. "I am in position between Emmitsburg and Westminster, advancing upon the enemy," he wrote, explaining that he knew A. P. Hill's corps was at Cashtown, between Chambersburg and Gettysburg, but added: "I am without definite and positive information as to the whereabouts of Longstreet and Ewell. The latter I presume to be in front of you." Meade urgently requested reliable information "about the disposition of the enemy and his movements."[39]

Shortly after noon on June 30 Halleck told Couch, "Every possible effort should be made to hold the enemy in check on the Susquehanna till General Meade can give him battle. I have no direct communication with General Meade, but he wishes you to be in readiness to act in concert with him. You will probably be able to learn his movements from the country people."[40]

Also on the 30th Couch told Meade, "Part of the rebel force has left the vicinity of Carlisle, with fifty pieces of artillery, and passed toward Shippensburg. This looks like concentrating a portion of their troops down the Cumberland Valley. Eight thousand of their men left York, and went toward Carlisle."

The message was sent in care of Stanton.[41] Stuart's troopers had disrupted telegraph communications between Meade's headquarters and Federal and state military officials in Washington and Harrisburg.[42]

⎯⎯⎯⎯⎯►◄⎯⎯⎯⎯⎯

Couch's report evidently had not reached Meade when the latter sent a significant message from Taneytown to Halleck at 4:30 P.M. on the 30th.

Reports he had received "seemed to place Ewell in the vicinity of York and Harrisburg," with Longstreet at Chambersburg and A. P. Hill "moving between Chambersburg and York." He added that Stuart's cavalry, "estimated to be 6,000 to 8,000 strong, had passed through Westminster and Hanover. The people [here] are all so frightened that accurate information is not to be obtained."

Meade updated Halleck on the movements of his corps and closed with a report that his cavalry had driven a Confederate regiment out of Gettysburg. He also said another Union cavalry force was "engaged with Stuart at Hanover this a.m." A similar dispatch was sent to Couch an hour later, but the one to Halleck did not reach Washington until 4 A.M. on July 1.[43]

At 11:30 P.M. on the 30th Stanton provided Meade with more accurate information on Confederate movements. Brigadier General Herman Haupt, chief of military railroads, was in Harrisburg at that time and had reported:

> Lee is falling back suddenly from the vicinity of Harrisburg, and concentrating all his forces. York has been evacuated. Carlisle is being evacuated. The concentration appears to be at or near Chambersburg. The object apparently a sudden movement against Meade, of which he should be advised by courier immediately. A courier might reach Frederick by way of Western Maryland Railroad to Westminster. This information comes from T. A. Scott, and I think is reliable.[44]

Haupt's report was accurate and to the point. By June 30 Confederate forces had left the Harrisburg and York areas and were moving toward Meade's army.

<hr>

On the morning of June 29 Lee had begun moving the Army of Northern Virginia toward Gettysburg. Meade's intentions at the time were unknown, so the initial instructions to corps commanders were not specific. The destination generally was indicated as Cashtown or Gettysburg.[45]

Hill moved first. Heth's division advanced from Fayetteville to Cashtown on June 29 and was followed the next day by Pender. Anderson's division remained at Fayetteville until July 1. Longstreet followed Hill on the 30th but Pickett's division stayed in Chambersburg as a rear guard.[46]

On June 29 and 30 Ewell was moving in three columns under Lee's orders to rejoin the rest of the army in the Cashtown area. Johnson left Carlisle on the 29th and marched west of South Mountain to Green Village, then east to Scotland and on to Gettysburg, arriving late on July 1.[47]

Ewell, traveling with Rodes, was starting to move toward Harrisburg on June 29 when he received orders to turn back. Rodes marched south from Carlisle into Adams County and reached Heidlersburg the night of June 30. Early had started moving west toward East Berlin, about five miles east of Heidlersburg.[48]

Early camped on the 30th about three miles from Heidlersburg and went to see Ewell. There, he was told that the army was concentrating at or near Cashtown and to move in that direction. After passing through Heidlersburg the next morning, Ewell told Early that Hill was moving from Cashtown toward Gettysburg, that Rodes had turned off his designated route at Middletown (now Biglerville) and also was moving toward Gettysburg.[49]

The new orders may have caused some difficulty, but the three corps of the Army of Northern Virginia clearly were on the way to Gettysburg, where they would meet Meade in the battle Lee had hoped to avoid. Lee had another serious problem; he had not heard from Stuart. Heth later remarked that he had seen Lee several times between the 27th and 30th and that the first thing he would say was "Have you heard anything about my cavalry? I hope no disaster has overtaken my cavalry."[50]

Stuart had suffered no disaster, but his determination to reach Ewell as quickly as possible had been frustrated, particularly by Union cavalry near Westminster, Maryland, on June 29 and the next day at Hanover, Pennsylvania. About 10 A.M. on the 30th, according to Stuart, "the head of the column reached Hanover, and found a large column of [enemy] cavalry passing through, going toward the gap in the mountains which I intended using." The enemy force was the rear of General Kilpatrick's cavalry division, operating on Meade's right.[51] Periodic fighting between the two forces continued until late afternoon.[52]

Stuart also noted that the captured wagon train had become a serious problem and he decided to detour to the right to Jefferson, on a road leading to York. "I was satisfied," he explained, "from every accessible source of information, as well as from the lapse of time, that the Army of Northern Virginia must be near the Susquehanna."

Fitzhugh Lee was instructed to push on with the train for York. Stuart and the rest of the troops made a night ride toward Dover. Many slept in their saddles. In Dover on the 1st, Stuart stated: "I was unable to find our forces. The most I could learn was that General Early had marched his division in the direction of Shippensburg, which the best information I could get seemed to indicate as the point of concentration." After a brief rest Stuart pushed on, passing through Dillsburg to Carlisle, reaching that point in the afternoon.[53]

Before reaching Carlisle Stuart learned that it was occupied by about 3,000 Union men who had been sent there after Ewell began his march toward Gettysburg. Fitzhugh Lee was sent forward to seek rations and to demand the town's surrender. Some minor skirmishing arose, but the only serious damage was the burning of the cavalry buildings at Carlisle Barracks.[54]

Before leaving Dover Stuart had sent an aide, Major A. R. Venable, to follow Early's route and seek Lee for definite information about the army's whereabouts. Later in the day, a member of Fitzhugh Lee's staff was sent toward Gettysburg for the same purpose.[55]

On the night of July 1 Venable returned with news that the army was at Gettysburg and that a battle was on. Stuart immediately sent Hampton toward Gettysburg and directed the other brigades to prepare to move there. Lee, meantime, had received a report on the afternoon of July 1 of Stuart's arrival at Carlisle and ordered him to ride to Gettysburg and take position on the Confederate left.[56]

The first meeting of Union and Confederate troops at Gettysburg was on June 30, the day before the main battle began. Heth ordered Brigadier General James J. Pettigrew's brigade to go to Gettysburg for supplies, especially shoes.[57] Apparently, Heth was not aware that Gordon had gone through Gettysburg on June 26 and had searched the town for supplies with little success.[58]

On his approach to Gettysburg Pettigrew discovered a Union cavalry force. The sound of drums in the distance alerted him to the possibility of enemy infantry nearby. Under the circumstances Pettigrew did not deem it advisable to enter the town, so he returned to Cashtown and reported to Heth.[59]

That evening Hill arrived at Cashtown and heard Pettigrew's report. Heth said that if Hill had no objection, he would take the whole division to Gettysburg to secure the shoes he believed were there. Hill approved and Heth set out at 5 A.M. July 1.[60]

Pettigrew's action, however, had alerted Meade to a Confederate threat. The cavalry Pettigrew had seen were two of Buford's brigades. Buford said his troops had entered Gettysburg on the afternoon of June 30 "just in time to meet the enemy entering town" and drove him back before Pettigrew could gain a foothold. He immediately reported the situation to Meade, and Reynolds moved toward Gettysburg.[61]

Heth's and Reynolds' movements precipitated the three-day battle that began July 1. Unlike most Civil War battles, Gettysburg was a "meeting" engagement; neither army was concentrated in a defensive position and the battle developed as units reached the scene. Gettysburg was like the hub of a giant wheel, with major roads leading into it from Hagerstown, Chambersburg, Carlisle, Harrisburg, York, Baltimore, Taneytown, and Emmitsburg. Several other roads led into Gettysburg from nearby towns. Troops could move into the area from all directions.

The first day's action was a classic meeting engagement. When Heth's troops began moving from Cashtown, he explained, "I was ignorant of what force was at or near Gettysburg, and supposed it consisted of cavalry, most probably supported by a brigade or two of infantry."[62]

Buford's cavalry was the first Union force Heth encountered. But the "brigade or two of infantry" that Heth thought was supporting Buford was the advance of Reynolds's 1st Corps, a unit of three divisions ordered up to Gettysburg on the night of June 30.[63]

The initial contact was along the Chambersburg road, about three miles northwest of Gettysburg. The battle Lee had hoped to avoid got quickly under way about 8 A.M. along a line west of town, extending from McPherson's Ridge northward.[64] Reynolds was mortally wounded and was succeeded by Major General Abner Doubleday as commander of the 1st Corps. Before he was wounded, Reynolds had called Oliver O. Howard's 11th Corps to his support.[65]

Fighting continued into the early afternoon when Rodes and Early of Ewell's corps moved south and formed a line at right angles to Hill's force.[66] The Federals were outnumbered and outflanked, so Howard pulled the two corps to Cemetery Ridge south of town.[67]

Johnson, who had taken a longer route from Carlisle, did not reach the Gettysburg area until late that night. He then took a position on Ewell's left. Early's division in the center and Rodes's on the right completed Ewell's line facing Cemetery Hill.[68]

In the meantime Lee had arrived on the scene and established his headquarters where the Chambersburg road crossed Seminary Ridge, about a mile west of Gettysburg.[69] Before leaving his headquarters at

Greenwood early on July 1 Lee had ordered Imboden to relieve Pickett in Chambersburg so that the division could move to Gettysburg.[70]

Longstreet, following Hill, set out from Chambersburg on June 30, except for Pickett's division, which remained in Chambersburg, and Law's brigade of Hood's division, which had been sent to New Guilford to guard the Emmitsburg road. As he moved toward Gettysburg on July 1, Longstreet explained, "Our march was greatly delayed by Johnson's division which came into the road from Shippensburg, and the long wagon trains that followed him." His troops did not reach the battlefield until the morning of July 2.[71]

Unlike Lee Meade was not in the Gettysburg area on July 1. Early in the evening, he ordered the rest of his army to Gettysburg. He arrived at 1 A.M. July 2. All but one of Meade's corps, the 6th, had arrived by early July 2. By this time, the Union line had been established on Cemetery Ridge, from Culp's and Cemetery hills on the right to the Round Tops, two hills on Meade's left. The 6th Corps arrived at 2 P.M. and was placed in reserve.[72]

The Confederate line was on Seminary Ridge, to the west of and almost parallel to Cemetery Ridge. Ewell, on the left, faced Culp's and Cemetery hills. Hill was in the center and Longstreet, on his arrival, was sent to the right.[73]

The stage was set for two critical days of fighting. Only Pickett and Stuart were missing from the Confederate lines on the morning of July 2.

Lee readied an attack on the Union left on July 2. He explained that, though he had not wanted a general battle, the successes on the first day and "the valuable results that would ensue from the defeat of the army of General Meade" made him think it "advisable to renew the attack."

Lee had wanted to attack early but preparations were not completed until the afternoon. The plan was for Ewell to attack the high ground on the Union right and for Hill to threaten the center. The major attack was to be made by Longstreet, with the hope of gaining control of the strategic south end of Cemetery Ridge.[74]

Timing ultimately doomed the plan. Ewell was ordered to delay his attack until he heard Longstreet's guns on the right; he did not hear the firing until 5 P.M.[75] because Longstreet had encountered problems. First, he felt he needed to wait until Law's brigade returned from New Guilford about noon. Then, as engineers started to guide his troops into an attack position, it was discovered that the route was in plain view of the enemy. A more concealed route was found. McLaws was in position by 4 P.M., but Hood then had to be shifted to the right before the attack began.[76]

Longstreet's attack was further complicated when Major General Daniel Sickles of the Union 3rd Corps, in violation of Meade's orders, pulled out of the Cemetery Ridge line and advanced a half mile or more west to higher ground.[77]

Longstreet's delay and Sickles's advance resulted in terrific fighting in the Wheat Field, the Peach Orchard, Devil's Den, and the slopes of Little Round Top that climaxed the second day of the Battle of Gettysburg. It certainly was a difficult one for Lee. Captain William Blackford, of Stuart's staff, wrote:

> When Stuart arrived upon the left flank on the morning of the 2nd, there followed several cavalry combats, and during the evening I was sent to General Lee to report what had happened. I found General Lee at his headquarters near the town, but he was in his tent and I was told by one of his staff that I could not see him; so, I gave my report to this officer, either Venable or Taylor, I think it was, who took it in to General Lee, and then I sat half an hour with them telling of our expedition. When coming on errands of this kind before, I had usually given my report to General Lee in person, but on this occasion I supposed he was too busy to see me.
>
> I was a little surprised to see him come out of his tent and go to the rear several times while I was there, and he walked so much as if he was weak and in pain that I asked one of the gentlemen present what was the matter with him, and he told me General Lee was suffering a good deal from an attack of diarrhea. . . .Now who in such a condition would not be affected in vigor of both mind and body, and will not this account for several things which were behind time, or not pushed forward as they should have been on the 3rd of July?[78]

Blackford's observation that Lee appeared to be "weak and in pain" draws attention to Lee's letter of April 8, 1863, to Colonel Marshall. At that time, Lee was confined to bed with what he thought was a severe cold and was suffering sharp pain in his chest, back, and arms. In the letter, Lee noted, "My head is ringing with quinine & I am otherwise so poorly I do not seem able to think." The attack, at first thought to be rheumatism, was the forerunner of a heart condition, the symptoms of which were evident repeatedly after his illness in the spring of 1863 and led to his death in 1870.[79]

Gordon, frequently in contact with Lee after the war, added another bit of evidence about Lee's condition on the night of July 2. He noted that Lee's "nearest approach to fault-finding" regarding Gettysburg "was his statement that his own sight was not perfect, and that he was so dull that, in attempting to use the eyes of others, he found himself often misled."[80]

That opens the way to another possibility—that Lee was self-medicating with quinine. Among the symptoms attributed to its use is ringing in the head or ears, described in part by Lee in his letter of April 8. Other problems include muscular weakness and severe bowel trouble, as noted by Blackford on the night of July 2, and disturbed vision, as mentioned by Gordon.[81]

***

Pickett was relieved by Imboden and arrived with three brigades during the afternoon of July 2, but was not involved in the fighting on that day.[82] Stuart left Carlisle at 1 A.M. July 2 and reached the Gettysburg area in time to thwart an attempt by Kilpatrick to move by way of Hunterstown and strike Ewell's rear.[83]

Meanwhile preparations were made to renew the attack. Lee called for simultaneous attacks on the morning of July 3 by Ewell on the enemy's right and by Longstreet on the center. Pickett's fresh troops would lead Longstreet's advance and were to be supported by Heth and two brigades of Pender's division of Hill's corps.[84] Pender was out of action, so his men were being led by Isaac Trimble.

Stuart moved his cavalry to the left of and in advance of Ewell's troops, east of the Union line on Cemetery Ridge. Stuart's force was increased in the morning of July 3 by Jenkins's brigade on its return from east of Mechanicsburg.[85]

Once again the timing was off. Ewell's attack on July 2 had been intended as a diversion in support of Longstreet. Ewell was to renew his attack at daylight on the 3rd to continue creating a diversion in Longstreet's favor. Enemy forces struck first, however, and Johnson's division had to repulse the attack before starting its own advance. Half an hour after Johnson started the diversion, Ewell learned that Longstreet would not attack until 10 A.M.[86]

Longstreet relates further confusion. In his report he stated that on the morning of July 3, he was preparing to renew his attack, aiming to pass around Round Top on the left of the Union line. "A few moments after my orders for the execution of this plan were given," Longstreet stated, "the commanding general joined me, and ordered a column of attack to be formed of Pickett's, Heth's, and part of Pender's divisions, the assault to be made directly at the enemy's main position."

Longstreet referred to it as Cemetery Hill, on the center right of the Union line on Cemetery Ridge. He added that Pickett was instructed to form his line so that the center of the assaulting column would hit the Union defenses.[87]

In his reports Lee said the general plan was unchanged from that of the previous day. Longstreet, reinforced by three of Pickett's brigades, was to attack the next morning, July 3, and Ewell was to assail the Union right at the same time.[88]

⸻⸻≫●≪⸻⸻

The conflicting time elements and orders noted by Longstreet and Ewell allow for much speculation. Could Lee's physical condition have impaired his judgment? Might it also have prompted the comment attributed to him after the fighting on July 3, that "It was all my fault"?

It must be recognized that both Ewell and Longstreet had stated that orders were given to start the third day's attack "the next morning." According to Longstreet, early in the afternoon of the 3rd, "Pickett, who had been charged with the duty of arranging the lines behind our batteries, reported that his troops were in order, and on the most sheltered ground." The artillery was ordered to open fire, and continued the bombardment until its supply of ammunition was nearly exhausted. Pickett was then ordered to begin advancing toward the enemy line.[89]

With Pickett's men leading the advance, Confederate troops crossed nearly a mile of open ground between the two lines. In a terrific struggle, the Confederates reached the Union line and penetrated it for a brief time before being driven back by a powerful Union counterattack. "Pickett's Charge" was the last major struggle on the fields of Gettysburg. The only other actions that afternoon were three clashes of cavalry on both flanks of the opposing armies.

Gettysburg was over. Reports indicated that the two armies had suffered a total of 55,112 casualties—7,058 killed, 33,264 wounded, and 10,790 missing. Meade's army had 3,155 killed, 14,529 wounded, and

5,365 missing, for a total of 23,049. Lee's army had 3,903 killed, 18,735 wounded, and 5,425 missing, for a total of 28,063.[90] By March 18, 1864, the bodies of 3,354 Union soldiers had been buried in the Gettysburg national cemetery, dedicated by President Lincoln on November 19, 1863.[91]

For Lee and the Army of Northern Virginia, the invasion campaign had reached its climax. "Owing to the strength of the enemy's position, and the reduction of our ammunition, a renewal of the engagement could not be hazarded, and the difficulty of procuring supplies rendered it impossible to continue longer where we were," Lee wrote. The next day, July 4, Lee ordered the army back to Virginia.[92]

CHAPTER 31

After the Battle

THE BATTLE LEE HAD HOPED TO AVOID HAD REPULSED THE TIDE OF INVA-
sion. One of the important objectives of Lee's plan—to force Union
authorities to recall troops from Mississippi to protect the Federal capital—had failed, and Vicksburg surrendered to Ulysses S. Grant on July 4.

The Confederate withdrawal from Gettysburg began the same day,
with the removal of wagons bearing prisoners and wounded soldiers who
could be moved. The trains moved on the Cashtown and Fairfield roads
toward Williamsport, Maryland. It was hoped they could cross the
Potomac on a pontoon bridge left at nearby Falling Waters, West Virginia, a short distance below Williamsport.

Late that night the army began moving on the Fairfield road toward
Hagerstown. Ewell's corps, in the rear, did not leave Gettysburg until
late on the morning of July 5. The troops began arriving at Hagerstown
on the afternoon of the 6th and the movement was completed the
next morning.

Lee faced another delay. He noted, "The Potomac was found to be so
much swollen by the rains that had fallen almost incessantly since our
entrance into Maryland as to be unfordable. Our communications with
the south side were thus interrupted, and it was difficult to procure either
ammunition or subsistence. The trains with the wounded were compelled to await at Williamsport the subsiding of the river and the construction of boats, as the pontoon bridge left at Falling Waters had been
partially destroyed by the enemy."[1]

In his report Meade stated that reconnaissance on the morning of July 4 indicated that the Confederates generally were still in position opposite the Union line. The next day he learned that the enemy "was in full retreat" by the Fairfield and Cashtown roads. He sent the 6th Corps in pursuit on the Fairfield road and a cavalry force on the Cashtown road.

The rest of his army on July 5 and 6 was caring for the wounded and burying the dead. He added that Major General William H. French sent a cavalry force to destroy the pontoon bridge at Falling Waters. French explained that his men had destroyed the bridge, then pointed out that the Confederates also had "floored the railroad bridge at Harpers Ferry," and that his men had destroyed the trestle work on each side of it. They also destroyed a bridge over the nearby canal.[2]

In a letter on July 7 Lee told Davis that in making the move from Gettysburg, "we were obliged to leave a large number of our wounded who were unable to travel, and many arms that had been collected on the field at Gettysburg." He explained that his troops had moved toward Hagerstown "to protect our trains with the sick and wounded."[3]

The next day from his headquarters near Hagerstown Lee wrote:

My letter of yesterday will have informed you of the position of this army. Though reduced in numbers by the hardships of battles through which it has passed since leaving the Rappahannock its condition is good and its confidence unimpaired. When crossing the Potomac into Maryland, I had calculated upon the river remaining fordable during the summer, so as to enable me to recross at my pleasure, but a series of storms commencing the day after our entrance into Maryland had placed the river beyond fording stage and the present storms will keep it so for at least a week.

I shall therefore have to accept battle if the enemy offers it, whether I wish to or not, and as the result is in the hands of the Sovereign Ruler of the universe and known to him only, I deem it prudent to make every arrangement in our power to meet any emergency that may arrive. From information gathered from the [news]papers I believe that the troops from North Carolina and the coast of Virginia, under Generals Foster and Dix, have been ordered to the Potomac and that recently additional reinforcements have been sent from the coast of South Carolina to General Banks.

If I am correct in my opinion this will liberate most of the troops in those regions and should not your Excellency have already done so I earnestly recommend that all that can be spared be concentrated on the Upper Rappahannock under General Beauregard with directions to cross that river and make a demonstration upon Washington. This course will answer the double purpose of affording protection to the capital at Richmond and relieving the pressure upon this army.

Lee concluded: "I hope your Excellency will understand that I am not in the least discouraged or that my faith in the protection of an All Merciful Providence, or in the fortitude of this army is at all shaken. But though conscious that the enemy has been much shattered in the recent battle, I am aware that he can be easily reinforced, while no addition can be made to our numbers. The measure therefore that I have recommended is altogether one of a prudential nature."[4]

In a postscript Lee added that he had learned from a letter in the *New York Times* that a bearer of dispatches from Davis had been captured at Hagerstown on July 2. "The dispatches," he added, "are said to be of the greatest importance & to have a great bearing on coming events." Lee undoubtedly was referring to Davis's and Cooper's responses to his letters of June 23 and 25 repeating his request to bring Beauregard north with troops to threaten Washington.[5]

On the 10th, Lee told the president:

The Potomac continues to be past fording, and owing to the rapidity of the stream and the limited facilities we have for crossing, the prisoners and wounded are not yet over. I hope they will all be across today.

I have not yet received any definite intelligence of the movements or designs of the enemy. A scout reports that a column which followed us across the mountains has reached Waynesboro in Pennsylvania and other bodies are reported as moving by way of Frederick from Emmitsburg, as if approaching in this direction.

If these reports be correct, it would appear to be the intention of the enemy to deliver battle, and we have no alternative but to accept it if offered. The army is in good condition, and we have a good supply of ammunition. With the blessing of Heaven, I trust that the courage and fortitude of the army will be found sufficient to relieve us from the embarrassment caused by the unlooked for natural difficulties of our situation, if not to secure more valuable and substantial results.[6]

———————

At this point, while general communications between Lee and Richmond were impossible, Davis managed to get a telegram to Lee on July 9. It stated: "Intelligence of the presence of the enemy near Williamsport has induced me, with a view to cover your communication, to order General Samuel Jones, with 3,000 infantry and two batteries of artillery, to proceed to Winchester, where he will receive your orders."[7]

There is no evidence of how the telegram was transmitted or how it got across the flooded Potomac, but Lee received it. In a telegram to Davis dated July 10, Lee stated: "Your telegram of July 9th has been received. I thank you for the troops sent. My letter will inform you the state of things. The army is in good health and condition and hold a position between Hagerstown and Williamsport. The enemy is gradually making appearance against us. I have sent all the prisoners and most of the wounded across the river."[8]

A few boats had been found and were being used to ferry men into West Virginia. In the meantime Union cavalry attempted to attack the wagons but was held back by Imboden. During this action Stuart arrived and drove the enemy away. On July 8 another enemy cavalry force advanced toward Hagerstown but was repulsed by Stuart and pursued as far as Boonsboro. Except for this action, there was only skirmishing between small bodies of Union and Confederate troops.

When the main body of the Union Army arrived in the area on July 12, Lee's men took a previously selected position covering the Potomac River from Williamsport to Falling Waters, where it remained for two days. Lee said Meade was busy constructing entrenchments but manifested "no disposition to attack."

By July 13 the Potomac, though still deep, was considered fordable and Lee decided "to await an attack no longer." A pontoon bridge had been completed at Falling Waters, "new boats having been constructed and some of the old recovered. Orders were accordingly given to cross the Potomac that night, Ewell's corps by the ford at Williamsport, and those of Longstreet and Hill on the bridge." The cavalry would bring up the rear.

Once again weather delayed Lee. "The movement was much retarded by a severe rain storm and the darkness of the night," Lee pointed out. "Ewell's corps, having the advantage of a turnpike road, marched with less difficulty and crossed by 8 o'clock the following morning." Longstreet's and Hill's troops were delayed by "the passage of artillery, ammunition wagons and ambulances which could not ford the river," so they did not start crossing the bridge until daylight on the 14th. The movement was completed by 1 P.M., when the bridge was removed.[9]

Longstreet graphically described his men's problems. The rain sometimes fell in "blinding sheets," and the road at some points was "ankle-deep with mud." Complicating his problem was a wagon filled with wounded men that missed the end of the bridge and plunged into the river. Fortunately, Longstreet stated, everyone was rescued.[10]

Ewell also had a difficult time. His report stated that on the night of the 14th, he was ordered to ford at Williamsport. This evidently was an error; he meant the 13th, for his description of the weather conformed to those of Lee and Longstreet.

He had been instructed to send his ammunition chests across the river in boats, but when he reached the river, he could find no boats, "nor any one in charge. It was dark and raining. The entrance to the river would have been impracticable for artillery in daylight, and, as well as I could ascertain, the exit was worse." On the recommendation of Lieutenant Colonel James L. Corley, chief quartermaster of the Army of Northern Virginia, the artillery and a reserve ambulance train were sent to the pontoon bridge to cross the river.

"Just before midnight," he stated, "my advance [Rodes's division] commenced crossing. The men had directions to sling their cartridge boxes over their shoulders, but many rounds of ammunition were necessarily lost, as the water was up to their armpits, sometimes deeper." By 8 A.M., his whole corps, except for those sent to the pontoon bridge, had waded across the river.[11]

In Richmond, the government, the press, and the public were in the dark regarding events in Mississippi and Pennsylvania. Telegraphic communication between Richmond and Vicksburg as well as Lee's army had been cut. It took days for couriers from Mississippi to reach Richmond. The flooded Potomac made it difficult for couriers and reporters to get back to Virginia with news. For almost two weeks Richmond was flooded with rumors and vague reports about what had happened in Pennsylvania.

On June 28 Robert Garlick Hill Kean, head of the Bureau of War, noted in his diary, "We are still without distinct news from either Vicksburg or Lee's army." He also called attention to another problem. About 25,000 Union troops were reported in Williamsburg, apparently intent on moving up the James River toward Richmond. The movement was repulsed in skirmishing before reaching the Richmond area. In his entry of June 29, Kean noted: "General Lee wants Beauregard to collect an army in Virginia to protect his communications. It will hardly be attempted."[12]

Unexpected support was headed for Lee early in July, however, from Ohio. Brigadier General John Hunt Morgan, whose cavalry division raided northward from middle Tennessee, had been ordered to confine his activity to Kentucky, but he made an unauthorized raid into Ohio "to join General Lee if the latter should still be in Pennsylvania." A strong Union column clashed with the raiders on July 19 and captured them a week later.[13]

On July 1 J. B. Jones, the War Department clerk, noted in his diary that a report had been received from "officers from the Federal flag of truce boat that came up to City Point [now Hopewell, Virginia] yesterday" that Harrisburg and York had been captured.[14]

The *Richmond Whig* reported July 1: "A despatch was received at the War Department yesterday, from City Point, with eight hundred exchanged prisoners. The same despatch stated that news was brought by the flag [of truce] boat of the occupation of Harrisburg by our troops, also of York, Pennsylvania. No further particulars were given." The story did say that the report "is partly confirmed by information from other sources."

The *Whig* also commented editorially:

> Gen. Lee has maneuvered Hooker's army out of Virginia and changed the theatre of hostilities from our own soil to that of the enemy, or the equivocal ground of Maryland. This is a great relief—for it has been the chief misfortune of the war, so far as Virginia is concerned, that from the outset she has had to bear the destroying presence of both armies. Hooker is compelled to keep between Lee and Washington, which enables the latter to subsist his army very readily from the country about and beyond him.
>
> What Gen. Lee's plan is we do not know, and would not hint at if we knew. It is enough for us to know who formed it and who is

executing it, to feel the assurance that it is wisely designed and will be skillfully carried out. The policy of invasion was not forced upon him by the exigencies of his situation, by pressure of public opinion, nor by orders from superior authority. It was deliberately chosen by himself. He knew what he had to encounter, and what he had to rely on. Weighing everything he determined to take the step, and the Executive sanctioned his determination.

It was a movement liable to grave contingencies and perils, and that could only have been justified by the reasonable prospects of securing great advantages. We believe, therefore, that grand eventualities are embraced in the plan, and we entertain the most sanguine hope that they will be accomplished, because we repose so implicit a confidence in the great strategist who designed, and the great soldier who directs, the movement.[15]

———

By contrast the *Richmond Daily Dispatch* of the same date reported, "It appears that our troops occupy points in three counties of Pennsylvania—Fulton, Franklin and Adams." The article continued with descriptions of the counties and noted that Connellsville and Uniontown were in southwestern Pennsylvania, near Pittsburgh. General Imboden "is, or has been, operating over there."[16] The differences are typical of the extreme problems the press faced in searching for facts instead of rumors and for whatever reliable news could be obtained from north of the flooded Potomac.

———

On Thursday morning, July 2, the *Whig* expressed some doubt about the capture of Harrisburg.

For several days past we have had a constantly recurring report of the occupation of Harrisburg, Pennsylvania, by the Confederates, but, up to this time, no confirmation of the report has been received. On Tuesday [July 1st], as stated yesterday, a despatch from City Point announced that news was brought by the flag of truce boat of the capture of both Harrisburg and York.

The *Petersburg Press,* of yesterday, alludes to the report, and adds, "We have received a private message from a reliable source stating that there is no doubt whatever of the facts." There is no doubt of the fact, as far as York is concerned, but we apprehend that the reported occupation of Harrisburg is rather in advance of the "fact." At all events, though the probabilities incline us to believe the report, we prefer to await further advices before hurrahing over the capture of the Capital of Pennsylvania.

Despite such prudence the *Whig* carried an unusual commentary that day, headlined "The Coal Fields of Pennsylvania." It stated:

If it be true that the Confederate forces occupy Harrisburg, the attention of the Commanding General will no doubt be directed to the coal fields, which lie within forty or fifty miles of the city. His first aim will be to cut all the railroad connections, and thus put a stop to the transportation of fuel.

The next paragraph emphasized the importance of anthracite coal:

The Anthracite coal is found in large quantities in no other part of the world but Pennsylvania. Enormous quantities are used in the United States navy, in countless workshops and manufactories of the North, in the river boats, and even upon locomotives. The bituminous coal which is found near Pittsburgh, would not answer the purpose, even if it could bear the cost of transportation. Our troops already hold the railroads and canal leading from the Cumberland coal fields.

All that is needed is to seize the anthracite fields, destroy the roads and the machinery of the pits, set fire to the various mines and leave them. Northern industry will thus be paralyzed at a single blow. His next [aim] will be to destroy the most costly and not easily replaced machinery of the pits. Whether he would stop at this is questionable. He might set fire to the pits, withdraw the force sent out on this special duty, and leave the heart of Pennsylvania on fire, never to be quenched until a river is turned into the pits or the vast supply of coal is reduced to ashes.

The commentary concluded:

These views may have induced General Lee to move upon Harrisburg. We doubt whether he would fire the mines, but the destruction of the Mauch Chunk Railroads, and pit implements would be as legitimate as blowing up tunnels and aqueducts or burning bridges. Of one thing we may be sure—that whatever is best to be done will be done by General Lee, and if he thinks fit to destroy the Pennsylvania mines, they will certainly be destroyed. Should he leave them untouched, it will be for the best of reasons. But it is impossible not to indulge the hope that he will avail himself of the tremendous power which the possession of the coal fields, even temporarily, would confer.[17]

Whoever wrote the articles and editorials in the *Whig* of July 1 and 2, or furnished the information for them, was familiar with Pennsylvania. They accurately described the key cities mentioned in Lee's plans. Even more important, they focused accurately on the three major points of the invasion plan proposed by Stonewall Jackson in late 1861—closing the anthracite mines, disrupting commerce, and hindering manufacturing. The result was intended to bring economic pressure on the North as a means to end the war.[18]

In considering the *Whig's* possible sources of information, two other points should be recognized. One is that the *Whig* office was known as "a favorite meeting place of Confederate congressmen."[19] The other is that J. B. Jones had published a Philadelphia weekly newspaper, the *Southern Monitor,* from 1857 until early 1861, when he went south to join the Confederate movement.[20]

Briefly after he had joined the War Department, he occasionally mentioned in his diary that he had prepared material for the press. On June 4, 1861, he stated that he hoped "by this means to relieve the Secretary of the useless and painful labor of dictating negative replies to numberless communications. This had the sanction of both the President and the Secretary."

On June 17, after General Joseph E. Johnston had evacuated Harpers Ferry, Jones explained that he knew why Johnston had done so "and prepared a short editorial for one of the papers." It was shown to the secretary of war, who, Jones stated, "was well pleased with it." On June 26 Jones noted: "The President revised one of my articles for the press today, suggesting some slight modifications which, perhaps, improved it. It was not a political article, but designed exclusively to advance the cause by inciting the people of Virginia and elsewhere to volunteer for the war."

The last mention regarding the press was on July 1, 1861, when Jones wrote that the secretary of war "had been piqued at the effect produced by an article I had written on the subject of the difficulty of getting arms from Georgia with the volunteers from that state. My article had been read and approved by the Secretary; nevertheless he now regretted it had been written." The situation prompted Jones to add, "I resolved to meddle no more."[21]

There is no evidence that Jones, or perhaps congressmen, provided information for the *Whig* article and editorial, but the possibility cannot be overlooked.

—————

Rumors and confusing reports continued to reach Richmond through the first week of July, according to the diaries of Jones and Kean of the War Department. On July 3 Jones noted, "We have nothing further from the North or the West." The next day, he wrote that Colonel Josiah Gorgas, chief of the Ordnance Bureau, was unable "to send much ammunition to General Lee."

On July 5 he noted, "We have just received intelligence of a great battle at Gettysburg, Pennsylvania. I have not heard the day, but the news was brought by flag of truce boat to City Point last night. The Yankee papers, I am told, claim a victory, but acknowledge a loss of five or six generals, among them Meade."

The next day Jones wrote that they had "received Baltimore and New York papers with accounts of the battle at Gettysburg. The Governor of Pennsylvania says it was 'indecisive,' which means, as we read it, that Meade's army was defeated." He added, "There is a rumor in the city, generally credited, that another battle was fought in Pennsylvania on Friday [July 3rd], and that the enemy was annihilated." Jones concluded the day's entry: "There may be later news from Lee; or Vicksburg may be relieved; or New Orleans taken; or an armistice; or nothing."[22]

—————

In his entry of July 7 Kean noted that Vicksburg had capitulated on the 4, then wrote:

> General Lee has delivered a great battle at Gettysburg, Pennsylvania, with Meade's army. It began on Thursday, July 2nd. We have only Yankee accounts, but these inspire hope of a victory. The battle

has evidently lasted several days, the last struggle probably taking place on Sunday, July 5th.

A telegram from the operator in Martinsburg states on the 6th that General Lee has captured 40,000 of the enemy; that [A. P.] Hill in the center fell back as if borne back by the enemy who fell into the trap, while Longstreet and Ewell closed in on the flanks and made this capture, and that the prisoners were under escort of Pickett's division, having refused to be paroled. This I do not yet believe. We have no official news from this great battle.[23]

In his entry of the same date Jones noted, "The fighting near Gettysburg began on Wednesday, July 1st, continued until Sunday, the 5th, and perhaps longer." Jones then repeated, with only a single exception, the paragraph noted by Kean regarding the Confederate trap that resulted in the capture of 40,000 Union prisoners. Instead of echoing the doubt expressed by Kean, Jones remarked that "this might possibly be true."[24]

———

As the rumors and unconfirmed reports swirled in Richmond, the general attitude changed from day to day. The newspapers of July 7 reported that Lee had triumphed at Gettysburg, that the Union Army was retreating toward Baltimore, and "General Lee is pursuing."[25]

The impact of changing reports is shown in Jones's comments of July 8. At one point, he stated, "The hills around Gettysburg are said to be covered with the dead and wounded of the Yankee Army of the Potomac." He then noted:

The fighting of these four days is regarded as the severest of the war, and the slaughter unprecedented; especially is this so for the enemy. The New York and Pennsylvania papers are reported to have declared for Peace.

Jones's concern was evident in the next paragraph: "The absence of dispatches from General Lee himself is beginning to create distrust, and doubts of decisive success at Gettysburg. His couriers may have been captured, or he may be delaying to announce something else he has in contemplation."

Jones also learned that an officer on the truce boat had reported that Lee was retiring. His reaction was that such a move was "simply impossible," in view of the Potomac River flooding.

Jones then noted: "Alas! We have sad tidings from the West. Gen. Johnston telegraphs from Jackson, Mississippi, that Vicksburg capitulated on the 4th inst. This is a terrible blow, and has produced much despondency."

He closed the day's entry with the sentiment that James A. Seddon, the secretary of war, "has caught the prevailing alarm at the silence of Lee" and had sought a solution from Davis, but got none. "If Lee falls back again, it will be the darkest day for the Confederacy we have yet seen."[26]

<hr>

The fighting at Gettysburg, and the confusion it created in Richmond, not only stymied Lee's invasion plans but also disrupted the mission to Washington that Vice President Alexander H. Stephens had proposed to Davis on June 12.[27] The purpose was generally referred to as a peace mission, but according to Stephens, that was not the case. The primary objective was to deal with the treatment of prisoners of war and the exchange of prisoners, he said.

But, as he explained to Davis, "while a mission might be despatched on a minor point, the greater one could possibly, with prudence, discretion, and skill, be opened to view and brought into discussion, in a way that would lead eventually to successful results."

When he arrived in Richmond on June 22 or 23, Stephens was astounded by the change in the military situation. Lee's army was no longer on the Rappahannock and Stephens knew nothing of the plan to invade Pennsylvania or that part of Lee's army already had crossed the Potomac. He also was surprised to learn from Seddon that the danger to Vicksburg had become more serious.

Stephens met with Davis, then with Davis and the Cabinet. Everyone, according to Stephens, agreed "that the prospect of success was increased by the position and projected movements of General Lee's army." The initial arrangement was for Stephens to follow the army's route and communicate with Washington authorities from Lee's headquarters. Heavy rain and poor road conditions changed this plan.[28]

On July 3 Stephens, accompanied by Robert Ould, commissioner for the exchange of prisoners, left Richmond aboard a small steamer, the *Torpedo*, which was flying a flag of truce. It was to sail down the James River to Hampton Roads, then north on the Chesapeake Bay to the Potomac River and upstream to Washington.[29]

Stephens had two copies of a letter, dated July 2, one addressed to President Lincoln from President Davis, the other addressed to Lincoln as commander in chief from Davis as commander in chief. Stephens also had a letter from Davis outlining his mission. Stephens was to present Lincoln with whichever letter copy he deemed appropriate. Davis advised Stephens that the letter to Lincoln was worded so "as to avoid any political difficulties in its reception."

Intended exclusively as one of those communications between belligerents which public law recognizes as necessary and proper between hostile forces, care has been taken to give no pretext for refusing to receive it on the ground that it would involve a tacit recognition of the independence of the Confederacy. Your mission is simply one of humanity, and has no political aspect.

Stephens was advised to establish "the cartel for the exchange of prisoners on such basis as to avoid the constant difficulties and complaints which arise, and to prevent for the future what we deem the unfair conduct of our enemies in evading the delivery of the prisoners who fall into their hands; in retarding it by sending them on circuitous routes, and by detaining them sometimes for months in camps and prisons; and in persisting in taking captive non-combatants."[30]

Early on the afternoon of July 4 as the steamer neared Newport News, it was approached by a small Union vessel that raised a white flag. The *Torpedo* was not allowed to proceed. Requests for a route to Washington were sent to Rear Admiral S. P. Lee, commanding the North Atlantic Blockading Squadron, and to the commanding officer at Fort Monroe.

The messages were forwarded to Washington and the *Torpedo* remained in the Newport News area until July 6, when Navy Secretary Gideon Welles responded, "The request of Alexander H. Stephens is inadmissible. The customary agents and channels are adequate for all needful military communication and conference between U.S. forces and the insurgents."

On his return to Richmond on July 8 Stephens recounted for Davis the problems with Union authorities and stated: "Deeply impressed as I was with the views and feelings in undertaking the mission and asking [for] the conference, I can but express my profound regret at the result of the effort made to obtain it, and I can but entertain the belief that if the conference sought had been granted mutual good could have been effected by it."[31]

The hope of an agreement on prisoner of war problems, and possibly opening conversations that might lead to peace, had been rejected. A few days later Stephens left Richmond for his home in Georgia.

————————

Meanwhile reports of skirmishing around Hagerstown and Frederick continued to reach Richmond. On July 15, according to J. B. Jones, "there was a rumor of another battle beyond the Potomac, this morning, but it has not been confirmed." The next day he wrote: "This is another blue day in the calendar. Nothing from Lee, or Johnston, or Bragg; and no news is generally bad news."[32]

Then on July 17, two weeks after the fighting at Gettysburg, the bad news finally reached Richmond. Newspapers that day reported an official dispatch from Lee that the Army of Northern Virginia had withdrawn into Virginia.[33]

"At last we have the authentic announcement that General Lee has crossed the Potomac," Jones wrote in his diary that day. "Thus the armies of the Confederate States are recoiling at all points, and a settled gloom is apparent on many weak faces. Whether Lee will come hither or not, no one knows, but some tremble for the fate of Richmond." Jones then noted that if Meade should detach a major force to attack Richmond, Lee might cross the Potomac again.[34]

He was not alone in considering the possibility. In letters to his wife from near Hagerstown on July 10 and 13, J. E. B. Stuart wrote: "We got the better of the fight at Gettysburg but retired because the position we took could not be held. We have now a fresh supply of ammunition and will give battle again.

"We return without defeat, to recuperate and reinforce, when, no doubt the role will be reenacted. We must invade again—it is the only path to peace."[35]

————————

Three years after the war Lee grew concerned about criticism directed at him and stated that "critics talked much of that which they knew little about." At one point, he mentioned that "Stuart's failure to carry out his instructions forced the battle of Gettysburg."[36]

Lee obviously was referring to the lack of information from Stuart regarding enemy movements. All of the cavalry movements are described in Stuart's report, but there is no mention of the two dispatches that had been sent late in June reporting Hooker's movements.

Colonel Marshall described a conversation with Stuart when the latter personally delivered his report. He said that he told Stuart "how General Lee, being confident that he [Stuart] would give him immediate information of Hooker's crossing [of the Potomac], had assumed from not receiving the information that Hooker had not crossed and acted on that belief." Marshall added:

> Stuart said that when he crossed at Rowser's Ferry [Ford], and found that Hooker had crossed the day before above him, he had sent a dispatch to General Lee by way of Ashby's Gap. We never got that dispatch.[37]

As postwar interest in the Civil War mounted, participants quickly responded to publishers' requests for articles and books. As the volume of accounts grew, criticism of Stuart increased to the point where some claimed that he had gone off on a wild dash of his own. Stuart had not survived the war and could not respond. One of his staff members, Major Henry B. McClellan, rose to Stuart's defense after the war.

In preparing his memoirs McClellan stated, "General Early is, so far as I know, the only prominent General who has expressed the opinion that General Stuart's movement was not a misfortune to the Confederate cause." In a series of letters to Early, beginning in November 1877, McClellan had sought Early's opinion about certain matters.

In a letter to Early on February 21, 1878, McClellan stated: "I agree with you that Lee did not intend to imply the censure of Stuart which others have drawn from his language. Under this general head of want of information several other charges are made, either directly or inferentially, which I think ought to be met."

In referring to Stuart's crossing of the Potomac, McClellan quoted from an article by Early stating: "When Hooker was crossing the Potomac at Edwards Ferry, it was simply impossible for Stuart to cross the stream between that point and Harpers Ferry. Stuart's only alternatives, therefore, were to cross west of the Blue Ridge at Shepherdstown or Williamsport, or east of Hooker's crossing. He selected the latter in accordance with the discretion given him."

Early had pointed out that by moving west of South Mountain, Stuart's cavalry could not have obtained or reported any more information than individual scouts. On the other hand, Early concluded, "Stuart's movement on the other flank greatly perplexed and bewildered the Federal commanders, and compelled them to move slower."

McClellan then explained: "We may dismiss at once the inconsiderate charge that Stuart disobeyed or exceeded the orders given him by General Lee, for General Lee states [in his report] that Stuart acted 'in the exercise of the discretion given to him.' Stuart had submitted his plans to his commander in a personal interview. Those plans were approved, and he was authorized to carry them out if in his opinion it seemed best to do so."

McClellan then called attention to the inactivity of the brigades under Beverly Robertson and William Jones, which had been left behind to cover the Blue Ridge gaps. If the brigades had moved from Rector's Crossroads on the 26th, McClellan wrote, "they would have been in position on the 28th to have stopped Buford's [Union cavalry] northward march on that day, and so to have occupied him from reaching Gettysburg on the 30th. It would be difficult to explain why these two brigades remained in the vicinity of Rector's Crossroads from the 25th to the 29th without discovering or reporting to the Commanding General anything concerning the movements of the enemy, or why these brigades were found at Berryville on July 1st."[38]

<hr/>

Among Stuart critics was Longstreet, the highest-ranking Confederate who wrote about the Gettysburg campaign. In one account, he said he had instructed Stuart "to follow me," and to cross the Potomac at Shepherdstown while Longstreet crossed at Williamsport. When Stuart objected on the grounds that he had discretionary power, Longstreet said the cavalry "hurried around beyond Hooker's army and we saw nothing more of him until the evening of the 2nd of July when he came down from York and joined us, having made a complete circuit of the Federal army."[39] In another account Longstreet stated that Stuart "rode on a raid, so that when the cavalry was most needed it was far away from the army." He added that "our plans, adopted after deep study, were suddenly given over to gratify the youthful cavalryman's wish for a nomadic ride."[40]

McClellan obviously had sent a copy of his extract to Longstreet on July 20, 1878, and requested his opinion. In his response eight days later, Longstreet wrote: "Your favor of the 20th instant with catalogue of your interesting Institute was duly received. Your request that I make a candid criticism of your paper upon the Gettysburg campaign I shall cheerfully undertake, so far at least to express a candid opinion." He added:

> Your paper, as it was intended, is a complete vindication of Gen. Stuart. It shows Gen. Lee's authority for the movements of his cavalry and that these movements were all conducted rapidly and vigorously executed.
>
> That Stuart left more cavalry with us than we actually used, a fact not known to me heretofore, and that therefore it was particularly unjust, not to say cruel, in all who have assailed Stuart as the cause of the failure of the Gettysburg campaign.[41]

After the war John B. Gordon and Marshall drew attention to several missing pieces of the Gettysburg puzzle. Gordon wrote:

> It is a great loss to history and to posterity that General Lee did not write his recollections as General Grant did. From correspondence and personal interviews with him, I know that he was profoundly impressed with the belief that it was his duty to write, and he expended much time and labor in getting the material for such a work.
>
> From his reports, which are models of official papers, were necessarily excluded the free and full comments upon plans, movements, men, failures, and the reasons for such failures, as they appeared to him, and of which he was the most competent witness.[42]

Marshall explained that it was his duty to compile Lee's official reports. Regarding Gettysburg, Marshall pointed out that the official reports of the corps, division, and brigade commanders, and those of the artillery and cavalry commanders and medical staff were a major source of information. He added that when Lee read the prepared copy of that and other reports, he "would peruse it carefully, [and] make such alterations as his personal knowledge suggested." But, Marshall added:

> It is well known that he [Lee] assumed the entire responsibility of the issue in the Battle of Gettysburg, and thus covered the errors and omissions of all his officers. He declined to embody in his report anything that might seem to cast the blame of the result

upon others, and in answer to my appeal to allow some statements which I deemed material to remain in the report.

He said he disliked in such a communication to say aught to the prejudice of others, unless the truth of such statements had been established by an investigation in which those affected by them had been afforded an opportunity to defend or justify their actions.[43]

These comments draw attention to a remark by Lee after the war when he was trying to assemble material for his proposed book. It was then that he stated to Colonel Allan that "the imperfect, halting way in which his corps commanders (especially Ewell) fought the battle [of Gettysburg], gave victory (which he says trembled for 3 days in the balance) finally to the foe."[44] This raises several important questions: What if Stonewall Jackson had not been fatally wounded at Chancellorsville? What if he had been with Lee on the march into Pennsylvania and had fought with his usual tenacity? The answers never will be known, but, in closing, keep in mind that Jackson had first proposed an invasion plan in late 1861 and that it had been repeated in 1862, endorsed by Lee, and approved in July 1862. The first attempt had been started almost immediately, but was repulsed at Antietam following the lost order incident.

Then in winter camp in January and February 1863 plans for renewing the invasion were made at frequent meetings of Lee, Jackson, and Stuart. Lee's hopes for an early start were disrupted, first by his illness, then by the Battle of Chancellorsville. One can only wonder what the outcome might have been if Jackson had been there to march north with Lee on the route of the invasion plan he had proposed.

NOTES

Prologue: Looking Back before the Battle

1. United States War Department, *The War of the Rebellion: Official Records of the Union and Confederate Armies,* U.S. Government Printing Office, Washington, D.C., 1880–1901; Series 1, Vol. 27, Pt. 2; reports of Robert E. Lee, p. 316, Richard S. Ewell, p. 439, Jubal A. Early, pp. 464–66 (hereafter cited as *O.R.;* Series 1, unless otherwise noted).

2. E. P. Alexander, *Military Memoirs of a Confederate,* Charles Scribner's Sons, New York, 1907, reprinted by Press of Morningside, Dayton, Ohio, pp. 368–69, quoted from "Returns of May 31" (hereafter cited as Alexander, *Memoirs*). The report lists the strength of J. E. B. Stuart's cavalry division as 10,292 men in seven brigades, those of Wade Hampton, Beverly H. Robertson, William E. Jones, Fitzhugh Lee, William Henry Fitzhugh Lee, Alfred Jenkins, and John Imboden. Three of those—Hampton's and the two Lees'—were with Stuart for the move behind the Union Army. Various sources estimate the strength of that force at 2,000 to 5,000 men.

3. *O.R.,* Vol. 27, Pt. 3, p. 243.

4. *O.R.,* Vol. 27, Pt. 3, p. 407; June 29, 1863, letter of Major General Darius N. Couch to the secretary of war.

5. *O.R.,* Vol. 27, Pt. 2, pp. 693–94.

6. J. B. Jones, *A Rebel War Clerk's Diary,* Old Hickory Bookshop, New York, 1935, Vol. 1, p. 366 (hereafter cited as Jones, *Diary*).

7. *Southern Historical Society Papers,* Vol. 26, pp. 116–28, published in 1898 by the Southern Historical Society, Richmond, Virginia (hereafter cited as *SHSP*).

8. *O.R.,* Vol. 27, Pt. 2, Lee's report, p. 316.

9. Mark M. Boatner, *The Civil War Dictionary,* David McKay Company, 1959, p. 339 (hereafter cited as Boatner, *Dictionary*).

10. *O.R.,* Vol. 27, Pt. 2, Lee's report, p. 322.

11. Gettysburg National Park Service archives.

12. The magnitude of Gettysburg campaign and battle accounts is shown in the bibliography prepared by Richard A. Sauers, *The Gettysburg Campaign, June 3–August*

1, 1863, published in 1982 by Greenwood Press, Westport, Connecticut. The compiler refers to "the overwhelming quantity of published material" and appropriately describes Gettysburg as "the most written-about battle in American history." There are almost 2,800 books, newspaper and magazine articles, and other sources cited, beginning in 1863 and continuing through 1982. That is an average of twenty-four a year. Equally interesting is the fact that material was published in every one of those 119 years.

13. *O.R.,* Vol. 27, Pt. 2, Lee's Report, pp. 308, 318. Lee's intentions, as described in detail in chapters 17 and 18, indicate that plans for the 1863 campaign had been developed at meetings of Lee, Jackson, and Stuart at the Army of Northern Virginia's winter camp in January and February, and approved in Richmond at the end of February. In late March, Lee expressed his intention to start the movement by April 1. On March 31, Secretary of War James A. Seddon wrote to Lee of his hope for success in the army's "expeditions into the enemy's country."

Start of the campaign was delayed, however, by bad weather in March, then by illness that kept Lee in bed for more than a week in late March and early April. After his recovery, Lee decided "we should resume the aggressive by the 1st of May." Three days earlier, Jackson had issued specific marching orders for every unit of his corps—ones for a long, hard march. This time, the start of the movement was interrupted by the Union advance that led to the Battle of Chancellorsville from May 1 to 4.

14. William Allan, *Conversations with Gen. R. E. Lee,* handwritten notebook, Cyrus Hall McCormick Library, Washington and Lee University, Lexington, Virginia, conversation of April 15, 1868, pp. 5–6 (hereafter cited as Allan, *Conversations with Lee*). A typescript is in the Southern Historical Collection at the University of North Carolina, Chapel Hill.

Although Allan's notebook remained in his family until 1946, the text of two conversations was quoted or printed in full in important publications before that time. They were as follows:

An Aide-de-Camp of Lee, being the papers of Colonel Charles Marshall, sometime aide-de-camp, military secretary, and assistant adjutant-general on the staff of Robert E. Lee, 1861–1865, edited by Major General Sir Frederick Maurice and published by Little, Brown and Company, Boston, in 1927 (hereafter cited as Marshall, *Aide-de-Camp*).

R. E. Lee, a Biography, by Douglas Southall Freeman, four volumes, published in 1934–35 by Charles Scribner's Sons, New York and London (hereafter cited as Freeman, *Lee Biography*).

Lee's Lieutenants, a Study in Command, by Douglas Southall Freeman, three volumes, published in 1942–44 by Charles Scribner's Sons (hereafter cited as Freeman, *Lee's Lieutenants*).

In Marshall, *Aide-de-Camp,* pp. 248–52, Maurice notes that among Marshall's papers there was a memorandum dated April 15, 1868, of a conversation Allan had with Lee on that date regarding the capture of Harpers Ferry and the battles of Fredericksburg and Gettysburg.

In Freeman, *Lee Biography,* Vol. 3, pp. 20–21, a statement is attributed to Longstreet concerning the Gettysburg campaign. On pp. 160–61, reference is made to problems Lee encountered during the Battle of Gettysburg. Footnotes on pp. 21 and 161 cite the source as "Allan's memorandum in Marshall [page] 250."

In *Lee's Lieutenants,* Vol. 2, Appendix I, p. 716, Freeman points out that, following the publication of the *Lee Biography,* Allan's son, Dr. William Allan of

Charlotte, North Carolina, made available to him "two highly interesting memoranda" of conversations with Lee in Lexington on February 15, 1868. One was with Allan, the other with E. C. Gordon, Lee's clerk at Washington College. Both dealt with McClellan's acquisition of Lee's lost order before the Battle of Antietam on September 17, 1862. Freeman added, "the two documents are of sufficient importance to justify publication in full."

Both documents are printed in Appendix I, pp. 716–23. They are somewhat different in context, but both deal with Lee's reaction to a magazine article written by former Lieutenant General D. H. Hill about the lost order. Gordon enclosed a copy of his conversation with Lee on February 15, 1868, so that Allan could make a copy of it, "or such parts of it as you may want."

Allan's report of the February 15, 1868, conversation is the first of seven in his notebook. Gordon's memorandum is transcribed—in a different handwriting—in the notebook following Allan's seventh and last entry of his conversation with Lee on February 19, 1870. This is followed by a copy of Gordon's transmittal letter of November 18, 1886.

15. *O.R.,* Vol. 27, Pt. 3, Lee to Ewell, p. 905. Lee's statement about sending only one corps into Pennsylvania leads to an interesting question. If so, why was Ewell in command of it instead of Longstreet, the more experienced corps commander? The key to the answer is found in Note 13 above. Plans laid early in 1863 clearly indicated that Jackson's corps would lead the invasion. When the movement began, Jackson's troops were in the lead, but with a new commander. Ewell had been promoted from division to corps commander following Jackson's death after the Battle of Chancellorsville.

Why was Longstreet not substituted? Longstreet, with part of his corps, had been sent in mid-February to southeastern Virginia to guard against a Union attack on Richmond from the south and to gather supplies for the rest of the army. Longstreet was recalled in early May and personally rejoined Lee on May 9. But on June 7, Lee informed President Davis that only two of Longstreet's three divisions were with him. The other, Pickett's, was still at Hanover Junction, about twenty miles north of Richmond, *O.R.,* Vol. 27, Pt. 2, p. 293. Three days later, Seddon wrote to Lee that another brigade was being sent to the Junction so that Pickett could move north to join Longstreet, *O.R.,* Vol. 27, Pt. 3, p. 882.

16. Walter H. Taylor, *General Lee, His Campaigns in Virginia, 1861–1865,* a memoir that was not originally intended for publication, but was printed in 1906 by Nusbaum Book and News Company, Norfolk, Virginia; reprinted by Press of Morningside Bookshop, Dayton, Ohio, 1975. The letter from Lee appears in the Appendix, p. 309 (hereafter cited as Taylor, *Lee*).

17. A handwritten copy of this letter is in the Virginia Historical Society's collection of *Lee Papers,* Mss1L51c737, p. 37 (hereafter cited as VHS, *Lee's Papers*). The letter is quoted in the publishers' note, p. 3, of A. L. Long's *Memoirs of Robert E. Lee, His Military and Personal History,* edited by Marcus J. Wright and published in 1887 by J. M. Stoddart & Company, New York, Philadelphia and Washington (hereafter cited as Long, *Memoirs*).

18. James Longstreet, *From Manassas to Appomattox,* p. 654, J. B. Lippincott, Philadelphia, 1896, reprinted by Indiana University Press, Bloomington, Indiana, 1960 Centennial Edition (hereafter cited as Longstreet, *M to A*).

19. VHS, *Lee's Papers.*

20. Allan, *Conversations with Lee,* December 17, 1868, p. 1.

21. Allan, *Conversations with Lee,* April 15, 1868, p. 7.

22.   VHS, *Osmun Latrobe Papers.*

23.   Longstreet, *M to A,* Preface, pp. xxvii and xxix.

PART 1: INVASION PROPOSED

Chapter 1: The Road to War

1.   Marshall, *Aide-de-Camp,* pp. 67–68.

2.   *Lee's Dispatches, Unpublished Letters of General Robert E. Lee, C.S.A., to Jefferson Davis and the War Department of the Confederate States of America, 1862–65, from the Private Collection of Wemberley Jones de Renne, of Warmsloe, Georgia.* Edited by Douglas Southall Freeman, with additional dispatches by Grady McWhiney, and published in 1957 by G. P. Putnam's Sons, New York pp. 5–6 (hereafter cited as *Lee's Dispatches*). *The Wartime Papers of R. E. Lee,* Clifford Dowdey and Louis R. Manarin, editors, published by the Virginia Civil War Commission, 1961, pp. 183–84 (hereafter cited as *Lee's Wartime Papers*).

3.   Lenoir Chambers, *Stonewall Jackson,* published by William Morrow & Company, New York, 1959, Vol. 1, p. 31 (hereafter cited as Chambers, *Jackson*).

4.   John Esten Cooke, *Stonewall Jackson, A Military Biography,* published by D. Appleton and Company, New York, 1866, p. 11 (hereafter cited as Cooke, *Jackson*). A lengthy letter written by Jackson to Bennett on July 28, 1861, shortly after the First Battle of Bull Run, appears in Appendix I, pp. 465–66. It deals with Jackson's brigade in the battle and is signed, "Your much attached friend, T. J. Jackson."

        A member of Jackson's staff, Alexander S. Pendleton, identifies Bennett's wife as Jackson's cousin. W. G. Bean, *Stonewall's Man: Sandie Pendleton,* published by the University of North Carolina Press, Chapel Hill, 1959, footnote, p. 43 (hereafter cited as Bean, *Sandie Pendleton*).

        In Appendix III, Cooke, *Jackson,* p. 470, Cooke offered an interesting insight into Jackson's movements in mid-April 1862. It stated: "Note to Page 128 [in his book]. The period of the incident here related is incorrectly given. Ashby's horse was shot on Jackson's last retreat, just before the battles of Cross Keys and Port Republic. The date of the event was accurately stated in the original MS of this work; but a very gallant officer who took a prominent part in these scenes assured the writer that it occurred on the first retreat—his memory misleading him. As Jackson's report was not then at hand, the alteration was made. Circumstances connected with the publication of the work prevent a remoulding of the statement; this note will sufficiently guard the reader from an erroneous impression. The misstatement is not a serious one; but truth is always important."

5.   Chambers, *Jackson,* Vol. 1, pp. 50–51; R. L. Dabney, *Life and Campaigns of Lieut. Gen. Thomas J. Jackson,* published by Blalock & Company, New York, 1866, p. 31 (hereafter cited as Dabney, *Life and Campaigns*).

6.   Chambers, *Jackson,* Vol. 1, p. 53.

7.   Manuscript, *Cadet Record of Thomas Jonathan Jackson,* compiled by Lowell Reidenbaugh, St. Louis, Missouri, from U.S. Military Academy records at West Point, New York.

8.   *Biographical Register of the Officers and Graduates of the U.S. Military Academy at West Point, N.Y., 1802 to 1867,* by Major General George W. Cullum, published by the Association of Graduates of the United States Military Academy, Supplement, Vol. 9, p. 20.

9. Lieutenant Colonel G. F. R. Henderson, *Stonewall Jackson and the American Civil War*, two volumes, published in 1900 by Longmans, Green, and Company, New York, London, and Bombay, India, Vol. 1, pp. 29, 46–47 (hereafter cited as Henderson, *Jackson*).

10. *Memoirs of Stonewall Jackson by his widow, Mary Anna Jackson*, originally printed by Courier-Journal Job Printing Company, Louisville, Kentucky, 1895, reprinted in 1976 by Morningside Bookshop, Dayton, Ohio, pp. 49–51 (hereafter cited as Mrs. Jackson, *Memoirs*); Henderson, *Jackson*, Vol. 1, pp. 53–55.

11. Chambers, *Jackson*, Vol. 1, pp. 206–13; Cooke, *Jackson*, pp. 19–20.

12. Cooke, *Jackson*, p. 21; Henderson, *Jackson*, Vol. 1, pp. 59–61; Chambers, *Jackson*, Vol. 1, pp. 240–44; Mrs. Jackson, *Memoirs*, pp. 57–58.

13. Cooke, *Jackson*, pp. 22–23.

14. Cooke, *Jackson*, pp. 35–36; Henderson, *Jackson*, Vol. 1, pp. 103–4; Mrs. Jackson, *Memoirs*, p. 144.

15. *O.R.*, Vol. 2, pp. 784–87.

16. Details in Note 27.

17. Fitzhugh Lee, *Great Commanders: General Lee*, published by D. Appleton and Company, New York, 1898, pp. 23, 51–55 (hereafter cited as Fitzhugh Lee, *General Lee*).

18. Fitzhugh Lee, *General Lee*, pp. 74–76.

19. Bruce Catton, *The Coming Fury*, Vol. 1 of the *Centennial History of the Civil War*, published by Doubleday & Company, Inc., New York, 1961, p. 203 (hereafter cited as Catton, *Coming Fury*). Catton noted that the letters to his wife, dated January 23, 1861, and to his daughter Agnes, on January 29, 1861, are in the *Robert E. Lee Papers*, Library of Congress.

Lee's letter to his wife is quoted in Freeman, *Lee Biography*, Vol. 1, p. 420. In the footnote, Freeman states that he received a copy of the letter from a Lee descendant, Mrs. Mary Custis Lee de Butts. The letter also is quoted in Fitzhugh Lee, *General Lee*, p. 84. The letter, in slightly different wording, however, also is found on pp. 120–21 of *Life and Letters of Robert Edward Lee, Soldier and Man*, by J. William Jones, D.D., and published in 1906 by the Neale Publishing Company, New York and Washington (hereafter cited as J. W. Jones, *Lee's Letters*).

20. Long, *Memoirs*, pp. 88–89; Freeman, *Lee Biography*, Vol. 1, pp. 420–21.

21. *O.R.*, Vol. 1, p. 586.

22. Allan, *Conversations with Lee*, February 25 and March 10, 1868.

23. *Lee's Wartime Papers*, pp. 8–9.

24. *Lee's Wartime Papers*, pp. 9–10; J. W. Jones, *Lee's Letters*, pp. 133–34.

25. Allan, *Conversations with Lee*, February 25, 1868, p. 5; J. W. Jones, *Lee's Letters*, p. 132; *Philadelphia Weekly Times*, November 17, 1877, p. 1.

26. Allan, *Conversations with Lee*, February 25, 1868, p. 4. Judge Robertson's name is spelled Robinson in Allan's account. Freeman, *Lee Biography*, Vol. 1, p. 637, Appendix I–3. More than a month earlier, on March 15, Leroy P. Walker, secretary of war in the new Confederate government, notified Lee that he had been appointed a brigadier general in the Confederate Army. Lee was requested to signify his "acceptance or non-acceptance," *O.R.*, Ser. 4, Vol. 1, pp. 165–66. There is no evidence Lee received the note or replied to it.

27. Scott told Robertson that he would not accept the appointment offered him by Virginia and added: "I have served my country, under the flag of the Union, for more than fifty years, and so long as God permits me to live, I will defend that flag with my sword, even if my own native State assails it," General Marcus J. Wright,

Great Commanders: General Scott, published by D. Appleton and Company, New York, 1893, p. 714; Charles Winslow Elliott, *Winfield Scott, the Soldier and the Man,* published by the MacMillan Company, New York, 1937, p. 104; John G. Nicolay and John Hay, *Abraham Lincoln, A History,* published by the Century Company, New York, 1904, Vol. 4, pp. 302–3.

On April 20, Walker sent an agent, D. G. Duncan, to Washington "to keep the [War] Department fully advised of all that transpires," *O.R.,* Vol. 51, Pt. 2, p. 20. On April 24, in a telegram sent to Montgomery from Richmond, Duncan informed Walker that "General Scott is determined to stand by Union and his Oath," *O.R.,* Vol. 51, Pt. 2, p. 29.

On April 23, Alexander H. Stephens had telegraphed Davis from Richmond that "General Scott not resigned, and I believe will not from the best information I get," *O.R.,* Vol. 51, Pt. 2, p. 26.

28. Allan, *Conversations with Lee,* February 25, 1868, pp. 4–5.
29. *O.R.,* Vol. 51, Pt. 2, p. 27.
30. Long, *Memoirs,* pp. 96–98; Fitzhugh Lee, *General Lee,* pp. 89–92; Freeman, *Lee Biography,* Vol. 1, pp. 465–68.
31. Long, *Memoirs,* text of the letter as quoted on p. 102. The friend is not identified.
32. *Lee's Wartime Papers,* pp. 12–13, 15.
33. Jed Hotchkiss, *Confederate Military History,* Vol. 3, Virginia, published by Confederate Publishing Company, Atlanta, Georgia, 1899, reprinted in 1975 by Press of Morningside Bookshop, Dayton, Ohio, p. 22 (hereafter cited as Hotchkiss, *CMH, Virginia*).
34. *O.R.,* Ser. 4, Vol. 1, pp. 1, 42–44, 70, 80.
35. Hotchkiss, *CMH, Virginia,* p. 36.
36. *O.R.,* Ser. 4, Vol. 1, pp. 90, 77.
37. Emory M. Thomas, *The Confederate Nation,* published by Harper & Row, Publishers, Inc., New York, 1979, p. 85 (hereafter cited as Thomas, *Confederate Nation*).
38. *O.R.,* Ser. 4, Vol. 1, p. 90; Hotchkiss, *CMH, Virginia,* p. 36; Jefferson Davis, *The Rise and Fall of the Confederate Government,* two volumes, published by D. Appleton and Company, New York, 1881, reprinted by Thomas Yoseloff, New York, 1958, Vol. 1, pp. 248–50 (hereafter cited as Jefferson Davis, *Rise and Fall*).
39. *O.R.,* Vol. 1, p. 254.
40. *O.R.,* Ser. 4, Vol. 1, pp. 92–101.
41. *O.R.,* Ser. 4, Vol. 1, pp. 120, 136–47.
42. Hotchkiss, *CMH, Virginia,* pp 36–37.
43. *O.R.,* Ser. 3, Vol. 1, pp. 67–69.
44. *O.R.,* Ser. 3, Vol. 1, p. 76.
45. *O.R.,* Ser. 4, Vol. 1, p. 223; *Proceedings of the Virginia State Convention,* edited by George H. Reese, published by the Virginia State Library, 1965, Vol. 4, pp. 144–46 (hereafter cited as *Virginia Convention Proceedings*).
46. Jubal A. Early, *War Memoirs,* published by Charles W. Button, Lynchburg, Virginia, 1912, reprinted by Indiana University Press, Bloomington, Indiana, Civil War Centennial Series, 1960, and by Kraus Reprint, Millwood, New York, 1981, Preface, p. xxxiii (hereafter cited as Early, *Memoirs*).

Chapter 2: In Defense of Virginia

1. *O.R.,* Vol. 2, pp. 3–5, 21–22; Hotchkiss, *CMH, Virginia,* p. 40.
2. *O.R.,* Vol. 51, Pt. 2, p. 22; Hotchkiss, *CMH, Virginia,* p. 41.

3.   *O.R.,* Ser. 4, Vol. 1, pp. 244, 294; *Virginia Convention Proceedings,* Vol. 4, p. 493.

4.   *O.R.,* Ser. 4, Vol. 1, pp. 255, 342–43; Jefferson Davis, *Rise and Fall,* Vol. 2, p. 3.

5.   *Calendar of Virginia State Papers and Other Manuscripts, January 1, 1836 to April 15, 1869,* arranged, edited, and printed under the authority and direction of H. W. Flournoy, secretary of the commonwealth and state librarian (hereafter cited as Flournoy, *Virginia State Papers*). Under the ordinance, Governor John Letcher issued a proclamation on June 14, 1861, declaring voters had ratified secession. He noted that the votes reported did not include returns from a number of counties, especially in northwestern Virginia. He estimated the vote in counties not heard from as 3,234 in favor of secession and 11,961 opposed. Vol. 11, pp. 155–56 of the above publication, reprinted in 1968 by Kraus Reprint Corporation of New York. Letcher's reported and estimated votes show a total of 129,184 for and 32,334 against ratification of the secession ordinance.

6.   *O.R.,* Vol. 2, Lee to Cooke and Ruggles, pp. 777–78.

7.   *O.R.,* Vol. 2, Letcher to Lee, p. 784.

8.   *O.R.,* Vol. 2, Lee to Jackson, pp. 784–85.

9.   Cooke, *Jackson,* p. 36; Henderson, *Jackson,* Vol. 1, p. 115.

10. *O.R.,* Vol. 2, Jackson to Lee, pp. 809–10; Lee to Jackson, pp. 809–10.

11. John D. Imboden, *Battles and Leaders of the Civil War,* edited by Clarence C. Buell and Robert U. Johnson, published by the Century Company, New York, 1884–89, reprinted by Thomas Yoseloff, Inc., New York, 1956, Vol. 1, p. 120 (hereafter cited as *B&L*).

12. *O.R.,* Vol. 2, pp. 813, 827.

13. *O.R.,* Vol. 2, Lee and Jackson letters, May 7–12, pp. 813–14, 822–25, 832, 836.

14. *O.R.,* Vol. 2, Lee and Jackson letters, May 11–12, pp. 832, 836. Bean, *Sandie Pendleton,* footnote, p. 43. Bennett's role as Virginia state auditor and his concern over men of northwestern Virginia who had been arrested for voting for secession is found in *O.R.,* Ser. 2, Vol. 2, pp. 1390–96.

15. *O.R.,* Vol. 2, pp. 840, 863.

16. *O.R.,* Vol. 2, pp. 844–45, 871. Johnston had resigned from the U.S. Army on April 22, 1861, and was appointed a brigadier general in the Confederate Army on May 14, 1861. The next day, he was assigned to the command at Harpers Ferry but was delayed by illness en route there. In his official report, *O.R.,* Vol. 2, p. 470, Johnston states that he assumed command at Harpers Ferry on May 23.

17. Mrs. Jackson, *Memoirs,* p. 158; Dabney, *Life and Campaigns,* p. 196.

18. *O.R.,* Vol. 2, p. 652.

19. *O.R.,* Vol. 2, p. 648, Scott to McClellan; *O.R.,* Vol. 2, pp. 49–50, McClellan's report.

20. *O.R.,* Vol. 2, pp. 40–43.

21. *O.R.,* Vol. 2, p. 881.

22. *O.R.,* Vol. 2, pp. 471–72, Johnston's report; *O.R.,* Vol. 2, pp. 923–25, General Samuel Cooper, Confederate Army adjutant and inspector general, to Johnston; Cooke, *Jackson,* p. 48; Henry Kyd Douglas, *I Rode with Stonewall,* published by the University of North Carolina Press, Chapel Hill, 1940, p. 18 (hereafter cited as Douglas, *Stonewall*).

23. *O.R.,* Vol. 2, p. 185, Johnston's report; *O.R.,* Vol. 2, pp. 185–86, Jackson's report; *O.R.,* Vol. 2, p. 157, Patterson's report; Cooke, *Jackson,* pp. 50–51; Henderson, *Jackson,* Vol. 1, pp. 128–30. Henderson states that Stuart had only fifty men in the actual attack.

24. *O.R.,* Vol. 2, pp. 185–86, Jackson's report.

25. *O.R.*, Vol. 2, p. 185, Johnston to Cooper, July 4, 1861.

26. A few days after the skirmish at Falling Waters, Jackson received a letter from Lee enclosing a promotion to the rank of brigadier general. The letter was dated July 3 and the promotion from the secretary of war was dated June 17, Mrs. Jackson, *Memoirs*, pp. 166–67. Boatner, *Dictionary*, p. 432. Cooke, *Jackson*, p. 55. An order assigning "Brig. Gen. T. J. Jackson" to duty with Johnston's Army of the Shenandoah was dated July 4, *O.R.*, Vol. 2, p. 963. Stuart's promotion, Hotchkiss, *CMH, Virginia*, p. 667, biographical section.

27. *O.R.*, Vol. 2, Union returns, p. 309; Beauregard's strength, p. 568; Johnston's strength, p. 187; Johnston ordered to unite with Beauregard, pp. 477–78.

28. Henderson, *Jackson*, Vol. 1, p. 145. The wording varies in different accounts, but the reports are carefully analyzed in Freeman, *Lee's Lieutenants*, Vol. 1, p. 82, and Appendix V, pp. 733–34.

29. McDowell, in letters to army headquarters on July 21–22, referred to his troops as "a confused mob, entirely disorganized," and as "pouring through this place [Fairfax Court House] in a state of utter disorganization," *O.R.*, Vol. 2, p. 316. Dabney, *Life and Campaigns*, p. 209. Robert Selph Henry, *The Story of the Confederacy*, revised edition published in 1943 by the New Home Library, New York, p. 60 (hereafter cited as Henry, *Confederacy*).

30. Cooke, *Jackson*, p. 76. In a footnote, Cooke wrote that he had received "valuable information about this battle" from Stuart, Hampton, and Pendleton. Henderson, *Jackson*, Vol. 1, p. 154.

31. Mrs. Jackson, *Memoirs*, p. 185.

Chapter 3: After Bull Run

1.   J. T. Headley, *The Great Rebellion: A History of the Civil War in the United States*, Vol. 1, p. 120. Vol. 1 published by Hurlbut, Scranton & Company, Hartford, Connecticut, 1864; Vol. 2 by American Publishing Company, Hartford, Connecticut, 1866 (hereafter cited as Headley); Cooke, *Jackson*, p. 79.

2.   *O.R.*, Vol. 2, p. 204; George B. McClellan, McClellan's Own Story, p. 63, published by Charles L. Webster & Company, New York, 1887 (hereafter cited as McClellan, *Own Story*).

3.   *O.R.*, Vol. 2, p. 746.

4.   *O.R.*, Vol. 2, pp. 752–53.

5.   *O.R.*, Vol. 2, p. 753.

6.   McClellan, *Own Story*, pp. 55, 66.

7.   *O.R.*, Vol. 2, p. 763.

8.   *O.R.*, Vol. 5, p. 766.

9.   McClellan, *Own Story*, p. 66–67.

10. *O.R.*, Vol. 5, pp. 766–67. The exact date of Lee's departure is not clear. July 28 is indicated in Freeman, *Lee Biography*, Vol. 1, p. 541. Colonel Walter H. Taylor, who accompanied Lee, stated Lee left Richmond "in the latter days of July," Taylor, *Lee*, p. 27. Lee reached Huntersville in western Virginia on August 3, *Lee's Wartime Papers*, p. 61.

11. *O.R.*, Vol. 5, p. 829, Davis to Johnston.

12. *O.R.*, Vol. 5, pp. 828–29; *O.R.*, Vol. 51, Pt. 2, p. 269.

13. These letters are found in *O.R.*, Vol. 5, and Vol. 51, Pt. 2.

14. *O.R.*, Vol. 5, p. 864, letter dated September 19 to Davis from Mason Mathews, a

representative in the Virginia General Assembly. Mathews had visited camps of Generals Floyd and Wise and described conditions in both as disastrous. *O.R.*, Vol. 5, pp. 865–66, letter on same date to Davis from W. N. Syme, a resident of Lewisburg in Greenbrier County. Syme described the fighting at Camp Gauley and the retreats of both Confederate forces, then stated that he feared "our county and town are in great danger of falling into the hands of the enemy."

15. Walter H. Taylor, *Four Years with General Lee*, pp. 26–31, D. Appleton & Company, New York, 1877, reprinted by Indiana University Press, Bloomington, Indiana, and Bonanza Books, New York, 1962 (hereafter cited as Taylor, *Four Years*); Robert E. Lee, Jr., *Recollections and Letters of Robert E. Lee*, pp. 44–47, Doubleday, Page & Company, New York, 1904, revised edition published by Broadfoot Publishing Company, Wilmington, North Carolina, 1988 (hereafter cited as R. E. Lee, Jr., *Recollections and Letters*); Freeman, *Lee Biography*, pp. 564–74.

16. *O.R.*, Vol. 5, p. 868, Lee to Wise.

17. *O.R.*, Vol. 5, pp. 163, 184. The order was dated September 21, but did not reach Wise until the 25th. On January 22, 1862, Wise was assigned to command Confederate troops on Roanoke Island, North Carolina, *O.R.*, Vol. 9, p. 139.

18. Henry, *Confederacy*, p. 65; Freeman, *Lee Biography*, Vol. 1, p. 602 (in footnote, he cites Long, *Memoirs*, p. 130; Fitzhugh Lee, *General Lee*, p. 125; and the *Richmond Dispatch*, July 9, 1862, p. 2, col. l); J. Cutler Andrews, *The South Reports the Civil War*, p. 118, Princeton University Press, Princeton, New Jersey, 1970 (hereafter cited as Andrews, *South Reports*).

19. *Lee's Wartime Papers*, letter from Lee to his wife, pp. 79–80. Andrews, *South Reports*, p. 115. Two of the editors are identified as John M. Daniel of the Richmond *Examiner* and Robert Henry Glass of the Lynchburg *Republican*. Daniel is identified as Major J. M. Daniel, assistant adjutant general, p. 62, *Confederate Staff Officers*, by Joseph Crute, Jr., Derwent Books, Powhatan, Virginia, 1982 (hereafter cited as *Confederate Staff Officers*). Glass's role is described in Andrews, *South Reports*, pp. 115–18. He also had the rank of major, but left the army at the end of October 1861.

Wise also had an editor on his staff, Nathaniel Tyler of the Richmond *Enquirer*, who served as an aide-de-camp, *Confederate Staff Officers*, p. 214; Andrews, *South Reports*, p. 27.

20. *O.R.*, Vol. 5, pp. 908–9.

21. *O.R.*, Vol. 51, Pt. 2, pp. 361–62.

22. Freeman, *Lee Biography*, Vol. 1, p. 602, states that Lee and Taylor arrived in Richmond on October 31; in footnote, Freeman cites the *Richmond Dispatch* of November 1, 1861, p. 2, col. 2.

23. Jefferson Davis, *Rise and Fall*, Vol. 1, p. 436.

24. *O.R.*, Vol. 6, p. 309.

25. Jefferson Davis, *Rise and Fall*, Vol. 1, p. 437.

26. Dabney, *Life and Campaigns*, pp. 245–46.

27. Mrs. Jackson, *Memoirs*, letter dated October 1, 1861, pp. 194–95. *O.R.*, Vol. 5, 884–87, report of conference at Centreville, Virginia, prepared by Smith, and endorsed by Beauregard and Johnston. Smith is not mentioned in Jackson's letter to his wife.

The Department of Northern Virginia, composed of the Potomac, Aquia, and Valley districts, was established on October 22, 1861, *O.R.*, Vol. 5, 913, General Orders No. 15, Adjutant and Inspector General's Office. Several months later, in 1862, the organization would be identified as the Army of Northern Virginia.

28. *O.R.,* Vol. 5, pp. 889–90. Benjamin had replaced Secretary Leroy P. Walker, who, on September 10, had tendered his resignation to be effective the 16th, *O.R.,* Ser. 4, Vol. 1, pp. 602–3.

29. *O.R.,* Vol. 5, pp. 919–20. As a member of Congress and a volunteer aide on Jackson's staff in the spring of 1862, Boteler had an important role in conveying Jackson's strategic plans to authorities and gaining their approval.

30. *O.R.,* Vol. 5, p. 909, Benjamin to Jackson, October 21.

31. *O.R.,* Vol. 5, p. 913, General Orders No. 15.

32. *O.R.,* Vol. 51, Pt. 2, pp. 129–30. Trimble was promoted to brigadier general on August 9, 1861, and to major general on April 23, 1863.

33. *O.R.,* Vol. 2, p. 896, Lee's Special Order No. 196. *Lee's Dispatches,* pp. 33–34, letter to Brigadier General Milledge L. Bonham. *O.R.,* Vol. 2, pp. 901–2, Beauregard's letter to Davis. Alfred Roman, *The Military Operations of General Beauregard in the War Between the States 1861 to 1865,* two volumes, published in 1884 by Harper & Brothers, New York, reprinted in 1994 by Da Capo Press, Inc., New York, Vol. 1, pp. 65–68 (hereafter cited as Roman, *General Beauregard*). T. Harry Williams, *P. G. T. Beauregard, Napoleon in Gray,* published in 1955 by Louisiana State University Press, Baton Rouge, Louisiana, pp. 66–68 (hereafter cited as Williams, *P. G. T. Beauregard*).

34. *O.R.,* Vol. 2, p. 324, McDowell's report.

35. *O.R.,* Vol. 2, pp. 162–63, Patterson's letter to Army headquarters; p. 166, Scott's letter to Patterson.

36. *O.R.,* Vol. 2, pp. 195, 200, 202–3, 205; McClellan, *Own Story,* p. 62.

37. *O.R.,* Vol. 2, p. 485, Beauregard's report.

38. *O.R.,* Vol. 2, pp. 506–7, Chesnut to Beauregard.

39. *O.R.,* Vol. 2, p. 505, Davis's notation.

40. *O.R.,* Vol. 51, Pt. 2, pp. 275–76, Beauregard to Johnston.

41. *O.R.,* Vol. 5, pp. 833–34, Davis to Johnston.

42. *O.R.,* Vol. 5, pp. 881–82, Johnston to Benjamin, September 26; p. 883, Benjamin to Johnston, September 29.

43. *O.R.,* Vol. 5, pp. 884–87, Gustavus W. Smith's report.

44. Jefferson Davis, *Rise and Fall,* Vol. 1, pp. 450–52.

45. Henderson, *Jackson,* Vol. 1, pp. 174–76, Smith's letter to Henderson.

46. Cooke, *Jackson,* pp. 86–88.

47. In chapter 9.

48. In chapter 13, cited, *O.R.,* Vol. 12, Pt. 3, p. 940. In chapter 15, cited, *O.R.,* Vol. 19, Pt. 2, pp. 625–26. In chapter 16, cited, *O.R.,* Vol. 19, Pt. 2, p. 666, Lee's reference to "the expedition I once proposed to you."

49. In chapter 15, cited, *B&L,* Vol. 2, pp. 604–6, Major General John G. Walker's article, *Jackson's Capture of Harpers Ferry.* In Prologue, pp. 2–3, Trimble's mention of the 1863 objective, cited, *SHSP,* Vol. 26, pp. 116–28.

50. In chapter 21, cited, Allan, *Conversations with Lee,* April 15, 1868.

51. In chapter 22, cited, *O.R.,* Vol. 27, Pt. 3, pp. 880–81, *Lee's Wartime Papers,* 507–9.

Chapter 4: King Coal versus King Cotton

1. Jefferson Davis, *Rise and Fall,* Vol. 1, p. 564.

2. *O.R.,* Ser. 3, Vol. 1, pp. 89–90, 122.

3. Raimondo Luraghi, *The Rise and Fall of the Plantation South,* pp. 60–61, 98–99,

published by New Viewpoints, a division of Franklin Watts, New York, 1978 (hereafter cited as Luraghi, *Plantation South*).

4. The U.S. Department of Agriculture was established in 1862. Before that, agricultural policy came under the U.S. Patent Office.

5. S. T. Shugart, acting commissioner, *U.S. Patent Office, Annual Report for 1860*, dated January 29, 1861, p. 18, Government Printing Office, Washington, D.C. (hereafter cited as Shugart, *Report*).

6. D. P. Holloway, commissioner, *U.S. Patent Office, Annual Report for 1861*, dated January 30, 1862, pp. 84–85, Government Printing Office, Washington, D.C. (hereafter cited as Holloway, *Report*).

7. Holloway, *Report*, p. 382. Holloway's suggestion aroused some interest in developing silk production, but it did not gain momentum until after the Civil War. By 1867, attempts to establish the ailanthus silkworm of China here and in France proved unsuccessful. A short time later, Leopold Trouvelot, a French naturalist, came to the United States and began experiments he hoped would produce a cross-bred silkworm. Working in Medford, Massachusetts, he was attempting to cross native moths with moths he had brought from France known as gypsy moths. In 1869, some gypsy moth larvae escaped or eggs were whisked out of his laboratory window by a gust of wind. It was the beginning of the gypsy moth problem that plagues the northeastern United States today. At first, damage done by the moths' leaf-eating caterpillars was barely noticeable. But in the summer of 1924, serious defoliation was reported in 825 acres of woodland in Massachusetts, Maine, and New Hampshire. Twenty years later, more than 250,000 acres of woodland were defoliated in eight northeastern states. Since then, the battle against this pest has spread over millions of acres—a constant reminder of a problem that had its roots in the Civil War. *Sunday Patriot-News*, Harrisburg, Pennsylvania, September 6, 1970, pp. A3 and A13. (The article was prepared by the author, who was then public information officer for the Pennsylvania Department of Agriculture.)

8. Holloway, *Report*, p. 85.

9. Holloway, *Report*, pp. 7–8.

10. Howard N. Eavenson, *The First Century and a Quarter of American Coal Industry*, p. 434, privately printed in 1942, Koppers Building, Pittsburgh, Pennsylvania (hereafter cited as Eavenson, *Coal*).

11. Eavenson, *Coal*, p. 431.

12. Eavenson, *Coal*, pp. 428, 431.

13. Eavenson, *Coal*, p. 498.

14. Pennsylvania Geological and Survey Bureau, Harrisburg, Pennsylvania.

15. Christopher T. Baer, *Canals and Railroads of the Mid-Atlantic States 1800–1860*, anthracite coal field maps, pp. 31–39, editors Glenn Porter and William H. Mulligan, Jr., published 1981 by the Regional Economic History Research Center, Eleutherian Mills–Hagley Foundation, Inc., Wilmington, Delaware (hereafter cited as Baer, *Canals and Railroads*).

16. Jay Oliver Rhodes, division engineer for the Philadelphia & Reading Coal & Iron Company, unpublished manuscript of a history of anthracite coal, pp. 99–100. The manuscript was written in the 1930s and is now at the Historical Society of Schuylkill County, Pottsville, Pennsylvania.

17. Eavenson, *Coal*, pp. 141–43.

18. Frank M. Bennett, *The Steam Navy of the United States*, pp. 8–11, 137–41, and Appendix B, published by W. T. Nicholson Press, 1896, reprinted by Greenwood Press, Westport, Connecticut, 1971 (hereafter cited as Bennett, *Steam Navy*).

19. Fletcher Pratt, *The Navy: A History,* p. 424, published by Garden City Publishing Company, Inc., Garden City, New York, 1941, copyright, Doubleday, Doran & Company, Garden City, New York (hereafter cited as Pratt, *Navy History*).
20. Bennett, *Steam Navy,* Appendix B; Pratt, *Navy History,* pp. 424–30.
21. U.S. Navy Department, *Official Records of the Union and Confederate Navies in the War of the Rebellion,* thirty volumes, published by the Government Printing Office, Washington, D.C., 1894–1927, Vol. 13, p. 479 (hereafter cited as *Navy O.R.*).
22. *Navy O.R.,* Vols. 12 and 13. Details will be presented later in proper time periods.
23. Baer, *Canals and Railroads,* pp. 74–77.
24. Baer, *Canals and Railroads,* pp. 66, 74.
25. Baer, *Canals and Railroads,* pp. 53–54, 56–57, and supplemental map for 1860. The Pennsylvania Main Line Canal between Pittsburgh and Philadelphia was divided by the Appalachian Mountains in western Pennsylvania. Linking the eastern and western divisions of the canal was a portage railroad from Hollidaysburg, east of the mountains, to Johnstown on the west side. Smaller boats and rafts could be hauled over the railroad on flat cars or sets of wheels (trucks). Larger boats had to be unloaded. Several freight lines used divided boats so that each of two sections could be loaded onto trucks for the trip over the portage railroad. This canal system also served as many as 100 passengers a day during busy periods. Passenger boats had the right-of-way on the canal and were scheduled to complete the run between Philadelphia and Pittsburgh in four days. Robert McCullough and Walter Leuba, *The Pennsylvania Main Line Canal,* pp. 86–100, published by Morristown Cove Herald, Martinsburg, Pennsylvania, 1962 (hereafter cited as McCullough and Leuba, *Main Line Canal*).
26. Baer, *Canals and Railroads,* pp. 70–71, 76–77, and supplemental map for 1860.
27. *Thirty-Fifth Annual Report of the President and Directors to the Stockholders of the Baltimore and Ohio Railroad Company, for the year ending September 30, 1861,* printed by William M. Innes, Adams Express Building, Baltimore, Maryland (hereafter cited as *B&O Report*), p. 36, report of W. P. Smith, master of transportation.
28. *B&O Report,* pp. 6–7, report of John W. Garrett, B&O president.
29. *B&O Report,* p. 13, Garrett's report; p. 42, report of John L. Wilson, master of road.
30. *B&O Report,* pp. 30–31, Smith's report.
31. Imboden, *B&L,* Vol. 1, pp. 122–23.
32. *B&O Report,* p. 46, report of the master of road.
33. Imboden, *B&L,* Vol. 1, p. 123.
34. *O.R.,* Vol. 2, p. 472, Johnston's report; *O.R.,* Vol. 2, p. 949, letter, Johnston to Cooper; Dabney, *Life and Campaigns,* pp. 200–201.
35. Mrs. Jackson, *Memoirs,* p. 167.
36. William E. Bain, editor, *B&O in the Civil War,* from the papers of William Prescott Smith, master of transportation for the B&O, 1860–66, pp. 155–56, published by Sage Books, Denver, Colorado, 1966; source of this material is the collection of Smith's papers at the University of Louisville, Kentucky, p. 6 (hereafter cited as Bain, *B&O*). *O.R.,* Vol. 5, pp. 858–59, Lieutenant Colonel Turner Ashby in September 1861 informed Cooper that his troops were responsible for "protecting Mr. Sharpe, Government Agent, now removing engines, &c., from [the] Baltimore and Ohio Road to Strasburg."

Chapter 5: Jackson's Romney Campaign
1. *O.R.,* Vol. 5, p. 936, Special Orders No, 486.
2. *O.R.,* Vol. 5, pp. 921–22, Jackson to Benjamin.

3. *O.R.,* Vol. 5, pp. 378–80, Kelley's report.

4. *O.R.,* Vol. 5, pp. 93–7, Jackson to Benjamin; Mrs. Jackson, *Memoirs,* pp. 200–202; Cooke, *Jackson,* pp. 84–86; Douglas, *I Rode with Stonewall,* pp. 15–17; Bean, *Sandie Pendleton,* p. 49.

5. *O.R.,* Vol. 5, p. 937, Jackson to Benjamin.

6. *O.R.,* Vol. 5, p. 939, Benjamin to Jackson.

7. *O.R.,* Vol. 5, p. 940, Johnston to Cooper, Cooper to Johnston, November 7; *O.R.,* Vol. 5, pp. 945–47, Davis to Johnston; Jefferson Davis, *Rise and Fall,* Vol. 1, pp. 457–59.

8. *O.R.,* Vol. 5, pp. 965–66, Jackson to Benjamin, outlines plan for attack on Romney.

9. *O.R.,* Vol. 5, p. 966, Johnston's endorsement of plan; Jefferson Davis, *Rise and Fall,* Vol. 1, p. 454.

10. *O.R.,* Vol. 5, p. 969, reference to seizure of Cumberland, Maryland, appears in Benjamin's letter to Loring, November 24. The seizure of Cumberland was proposed earlier to Davis in a letter from Navy Commander C. H. McBlair. He felt that holding Cumberland was important because of its position on the Baltimore and Ohio Railroad; letter, McBlair to Jefferson Davis, October 31, *O.R.,* Vol. 5, pp. 931–32.

11. *O.R.,* Vol. 5, pp. 968–69, Benjamin's letter to Loring.

12. *O.R.,* Vol. 5, pp. 983–84, Loring to Benjamin.

13. *O.R.,* Vol. 5, p. 982, Cooper to Loring.

14. *O.R.,* Vol. 5, p. 982, Benjamin to Jackson.

15. Cooke, *Jackson,* p. 88; also noted previously in chapter 4.

16. Cooke, *Jackson,* p. 88; Henderson, *Jackson,* Vol. 1, p. 186. Both, obviously, were unaware of Davis's brief reference to approval of Jackson's plan.

17. *O.R.* Ser. 4, Vol. 1, pp. 805–6; *Journal of the Congress, Confederate States of America,* 1861–1865, Government Printing Office, Washington, D.C., 1904, Vol. 1, pp. 534, 575, 587, 589 (hereafter cited as *Journal, Confederate Congress*).

18. *Journal, Confederate Congress,* Vol. 1, p. 589.

19. Douglas, *I Rode with Stonewall,* p. 24.

20. *Alexander Robinson Boteler Biography,* Magazine of the Jefferson County (West Virginia) Historical Society, Vol. 20, pp. 19–27 (hereafter cited as *Boteler Biography*).

21. *The Annals of the War, Written by Leading Participants, North and South,* originally published in *The Philadelphia Times,* book published in 1879 by the Times Publishing Company, Philadelphia, Pennsylvania, republished in 1974 by Civil War Times Illustrated, Gettysburg, Pennsylvania, article by Alexander R. Boteler, pp. 220–27 (hereafter cited as *Annals of the War*); Sandburg, *War Years,* Vol. 1, pp. 116–19.

22. *Boteler Biography,* p. 24. It is stated that in May 1861, Boteler was elected as a delegate to the Virginia General Assembly from Jefferson County, but before he took office, the people of his 10th Congressional District selected him as their representative. Immediately, the state convention appointed him to a vacancy in the provisional Congress then sitting in Richmond. A list of members of the provisional Congress from February 4, 1861, to February 17, 1862, notes that Alexander R. Boteler was admitted November 27, 1861. *O.R.,* Ser. 4, Vol. 3, p. 1187.

23. Douglas, *I Rode with Stonewall,* pp. 27–28.

24. *O.R.,* Vol. 5, pp. 976–77, Jackson's letter to Major Rhett, assistant adjutant general of the Department of Northern Virginia. Jackson noted that "with but comparatively little exception both tracks [of the B&O] have been by our Government taken up from the Furnace Hill, near Harper's Ferry, to Martinsburg, and about

7 1/2 miles of one of the tracks has also been removed west of Martinsburg. Captain Sharpe, assistant quartermaster, has repaired a locomotive for the purpose of removing the track more rapidly, and today [December 2] I expect it to commence running, and Captain Sharpe expects to be able with it to remove one mile per day of the single track. I have made a detail of 50 men from the militia for the purpose of expediting the work as rapidly as possible." As late as December 27, B&O rails reportedly were piled up at Charles Town and Halltown south of the Potomac, Assistant Adjutant General R. Morris Copeland, of Major General Nathaniel P. Banks's staff, to U.S. War Department, *O.R.,* Vol. 5, p. 693.

25. *O.R.,* Vol. 5, p. 390, Jackson's report of operations in the Valley; Hotchkiss, *CMH, Virginia,* p. 199. Hotchkiss fixes the dates of the operation as December 6 and 7.

26. *O.R.,* Vol. 5, pp. 988–89, Jackson's letter to Secretary of War Judah P. Benjamin.

27. *O.R.,* Vol. 5, pp. 395–96, Jackson's letter to General Johnston.

28. *O.R.,* Vol. 5, p. 390, Jackson's report; Hotchkiss, *CMH, Virginia,* p. 199.

29. *O.R.,* Vol. 5, pp. 398–99, Banks's report.

30. *O.R.,* Vol. 5, p. 687, Thomas to Kelley; *O.R.,* Vol. 5, p. 688, Banks to Leonard.

31. On December 4, Cooper told Loring to "direct the four regiments under Colonel Taliaferro to proceed to Winchester," *O.R.,* Vol. 5, p. 980. Taliaferro's brigade arrived in Winchester on December 8, *O.R.,* Vol. 5, pp. 988–89, Jackson's letter to Benjamin. Loring's arrival, *O.R.,* Vol. 5, pp. 1004–5, Jackson's letter to Rhett.

32. *O.R.,* Vol. 5, pp. 1004–5, Jackson letter to Rhett dated December 24. This letter indicates that it was started before Loring's arrival. The last two paragraphs contain the report of Loring's arrival (noted in 31 above) and Jackson's determination to "march on the enemy." According to Jed Hotchkiss, Loring and his troops arrived in Winchester on Christmas Day. Hotchkiss, *CMH, Virginia,* p. 200.

33. *O.R.,* Vol. 5, p. 1005–6, Jackson's letter to Rhett, December 24.

34. *O.R.* Vol. 5, p. 974, return of the Department of Northern Virginia for November 1861; *O.R.,* Vol. 5, p. 1015, return for December 1861.

35. *O.R.,* Vol. 5, p. 390, Jackson's report. This includes several units from outlying posts that joined the column on January 2. According to Jed Hotchkiss, the number was about 9,000. Hotchkiss, *CMH, Virginia,* p. 201.

36. *O.R.,* Vol. 5, p. 392; Hotchkiss, *CMH, Virginia,* p. 201; Bean, *Sandie Pendleton,* p. 52; Cooke, *Jackson,* pp. 90–92.

37. *O.R.,* Vol. 5, pp. 390–93, Jackson's report.

38. *O.R.,* Vol. 5, p. 393, Jackson's report.

39. *O.R.,* Vol. 5, pp. 1046–48. Jackson subsequently filed charges against Loring on February 7, *O.R.,* Vol. 5, pp. 1065–66. Loring filed an answer five days later, *O.R.,* Vol. 5, pp. 1070–71.

Jackson's secrecy regarding his military operations may have created the rift between him and Loring. Loring knew that Romney was the objective, as pointed out in the copy of Jackson's letter sent to him by Benjamin. But Loring does not seem to have been apprised of any details by Jackson. In an informal conversation with Hotchkiss on Saturday, April 4, 1863, Charles J. Faulkner, assistant adjutant general on Jackson's staff, referred to the Bath expedition of January 1862. "He talked of Gen. Jackson's reticence in regard to it," Faulkner stated, "not even informing Gen. Loring, the second in command, of the object of the expedition, when he was going, or anything of the kind." Faulkner also stated that Jackson's brother-in-law and adjutant general had no knowledge of the details; p. 126, *Make Me a Map of the Valley, the War Journal of Stonewall Jackson's Topographer,* edited by Archie P. McDonald and published in 1973 by Southern Methodist University, Dallas, Texas (hereafter cited as Hotchkiss, *Diary*).

Except for his report of the Battle of Kernstown, Jackson had not prepared reports of his campaigns of 1862. Lee demanded reports; in January 1863, Faulkner was assigned to Jackson's staff, with the rank of lieutenant colonel, to assist in the completion of this work; Bean, *Sandie Pendleton*, p. 101. Faulkner, a native of Virginia who was U.S. minister to France before the war, was arrested May 17, 1861, on his return to the United States, and was imprisoned in New York; *O.R.*, Ser. 2, Vol. 2, pp. 3, 102, and *O.R.*, Ser. 4, Vol. 1, pp. 736–37. He was released and returned to Virginia early in 1862; *O.R.*, Ser. 2, Vol. 3, p. 813.

40. *O.R.*, Vol. 5, p. 1053.
41. *O.R.*, Vol. 5, pp. 1059–60.
42. Mrs. Jackson, *Memoirs*, p. 232.
43. *O.R.*, Vol. 5, p. 1060.
44. Douglas, *I Rode with Stonewall*, p. 25.
45. Douglas, *I Rode with Stonewall*, pp. 25–26.
46. Douglas, *I Rode with Stonewall*, p. 26; Freeman, *Lee's Lieutenants*, Vol. 1, p. 128.
47. *O.R.*, Vol. 5, pp. 1062–63.
48. Douglas, *I Rode with Stonewall*, pp. 26–27.
49. *O.R.*, Vol. 5, p. 1059. In the letter to Johnston, Benjamin states that he enclosed "a memorandum from the President for your consideration and reflection." A footnote states that the memorandum was not found.
50. *O.R.*, Vol. 51, Pt. 2, pp. 465–66.
51. *O.R.*, Vol. 5, p. 1068, Special Orders No. 33 of the War Department.
52. *O.R.* Vol. 5, p. 1086, return of the Department of Northern Virginia for February 1862.
53. *O.R.*, Vol. 51, Pt. 2, p. 479, Special Orders No. 45 of the War Department.
54. *O.R.*, Vol. 10, Pt. 2, p. 504.
55. Douglas, *I Rode with Stonewall*, pp. 27–28.

PART 2: JACKSON'S PLAN ADOPTED

Chapter 6: Northern Confidence Restored

1. *O.R.* Vol. 5, pp. 6–9, McClellan's report; McClellan, *Own Story*, pp. 101–5. In his report, *O.R.* Vol. 5, p. 6, the date is shown as August 4. In McClellan, *Own Story*, p. 101, McClellan states that the date of the report was erroneously given as August 4. He explains that the memorandum was dated August 2 and was "submitted to the President at his own request."
2. *O.R.*, Vol. 5, p. 11. McClellan in his report listed the number of troops in and around Washington as about 50,000 infantry, fewer than 1,000 cavalry, and 650 artillerymen.
3. *O.R.*, Ser. 3, Vol. 1, p. 426. This request was directed to the governors of New York, New Jersey, Pennsylvania, Michigan, and the six New England states. A week earlier, on August 12, Secretary of War Simon Cameron asked the governors of Wisconsin, Michigan, Indiana, Illinois, and Ohio to report how many regiments were organized and how many could be "ready for marching orders this week." Correspondence relative to requests for troops continued from August 12, 1861, to January 3, 1862, and appear in *O.R.*, Ser. 3, Vol. 1, pp. 426–777.

4. *O.R.,* Vol. 5, pp. 587–89, McClellan, *Own Story,* pp. 106–7, McClellan to Cameron; *O.R.,* vol 5, p. 12, McClellan's report. In the report, McClellan also noted that 9,290 men were absent because of illness and that 1,156 were in confinement.

5. *O.R.,* Vol. 5, pp. 9–11, McClellan's report, the letter to Cameron is not dated, but in the report McClellan states it was written "in the latter part of October."

6. *The Diary of Edward Bates 1859–1866,* edited by Howard K. Beale, published by DaCapo Press, New York, 1971, September 30 entry, p. 194 (hereafter cited as Edward Bates, *Diary*).

7. *O.R.,* Ser. 3, Vol. 1, p. 605.

8. *O.R.,* Vol. 6, p. 168, letters of Assistant Secretary of War Thomas A. Scott to William T. Sherman, August 2, 10, and 11.

9. *O.R.,* Vol. 4, p. 579, Assistant Adjutant General E. D. Townsend to Major General John E. Wool, commanding at Fort Monroe, August 13; p. 580, Special Orders No. 13, issued August 25 by Wool directing Major General Benjamin F. Butler to take a force of about 860 and join with Commodore S. H. Stringham of the Navy for the expedition. Fort Monroe, Virginia, remained in U.S. possession from the outbreak of the war. *O.R.,* Vol. 1, p. 485, Vol. 2, pp. 54, 643, 765.

10. *O.R.,* Vol. 4, pp. 580–81, Wool's report; pp. 581–86, Butler's report.

11. *O.R.,* Ser. 3, Vol. 1, p. 815.

12. *O.R.,* Vol. 6, p. 171, Townsend to Sherman.

13. *O.R.,* Vol. 6, p. 171, Lincoln to Cameron.

14. *O.R.,* Vol. 6, p. 3, Sherman's report.

15. *O.R.,* Vol. 5, p. 626, Special Orders No. 115, Army of the Potomac, October 23; Vol. 9, pp. 951–53, instructions for movement.

16. *O.R.,* Vol. 6, pp. 3–6, Sherman's reports.

17. *O.R.,* Vol. 6, pp. 198–99, Sherman to Adjutant General Lorenzo Thomas.

18. *O.R.,* Vol. 5, p. 639.

19. McClellan, *Own Story,* pp. 176–77, private letter.

20. *O.R.,* Vol. 11, Pt. 3, pp. 6–7, memorandum, Lincoln to McClellan, about December 1, with McClellan's reply.

21. McClellan, *Own Story,* p. 155. Lincoln referred to McClellan's illness in letters to Major General Henry W. Halleck on December 31, 1861, and January 1, 1862, and to Brigadier General Don Carlos Buell on December 31, 1861, *O.R.* Vol. 7, pp. 524 and 526. In a letter to Brigadier General John Pope on December 28, 1861, Halleck stated, "General McClellan is now sick. This is confidential, and must not be repeated," *O.R.,* Vol. 8, p. 470.

22. McClellan, *Own Story,* pp. 156–59. McClellan first learned of the meeting from Edwin M. Stanton, who was appointed secretary of war a few days later.

23. *O.R.,* Vol. 5, p. 41.

24. *O.R.,* Vol. 5, pp. 42–45; McClellan, *Own Story,* pp. 229–36.

25. *O.R.,* Vol. 5, p. 41; McClellan, *Own Story,* p. 229; February 3 letter, Lincoln to McClellan.

26. *O.R.,* Vol. 5, pp. 45–46; McClellan, *Own Story,* pp. 162–63.

27. *O.R.,* Vol. 5, p. 46. McClellan's report includes portions of John Tucker's report.

28. *O.R.,* Vol. 5, p. 51, McClellan's report.

29. *Confidential Correspondence of Gustavus Vasa Fox, Assistant Secretary of the Navy 1861–65,* edited by Robert Means Thompson and Richard Wainwright, printed by the DeVinne Press, New York, for the Naval History Society, Vol. 1, printed in 1918, pp. 87–89 (hereafter cited as Fox, *Confidential Correspondence*).

30. Fox, *Confidential Correspondence*, Vol. 1, pp. 103, 107, 113–14.

31. Fox, *Confidential Correspondence*, Vol. 2 (printed in 1919), pp. 86–87, letter of March 11; pp. 92–93, letter of March 28.

32. *Private and Official Correspondence of Gen. Benjamin F. Butler during the Civil War*, copyright Jessie Ames Marshall (Butler's granddaughter), 1917, published by the Plimpton Press, Norwood, Massachusetts, p. 297 (hereafter cited as Butler, *Correspondence*).

33. *Butler's Book, a Review by Benjamin F. Butler of His Legal, Political and Military Careers*, published by A. M. Thayer & Company, Boston, Massachusetts, 1892, pp. 354–55 (hereafter cited as *Butler's Book*).

34. *Navy O.R.*, Vol. 18, p. 109.

35. Fox, *Confidential Correspondence*, Vol. 1, p. 114.

36. *Navy O.R.*, Vol. 12, p. 707.

37. *Navy O.R.*, Vol. 13, p. 816.

38. *Harrisburg Civil War Round Table Collection*, William Mangold Collection, U.S. Army Military History Institute, Carlisle, Pennsylvania (hereafter cited as *MHI, Harrisburg CWRT Collection*).

    The Foulke letter was addressed to George W. Stroud and was primarily concerned with obtaining signatures on right-of-way documents for the Mahonoy and Broad Mountain Railroad, which was under construction in 1862. Foulke noted that this railroad was expected to be operating in two or three weeks.

39. Baer, *Canals and Railroads*, 1860 supplement map.

40. McClellan, *Own Story*, p. 239.

41. *O.R.*, Vol. 11, Pt. 1, p. 6; McClellan, *Own Story*, p. 239.

42. Henry, *Confederacy*, pp. 475–76, table of events.

43. *O.R.*, Vol. 9, pp 197–201, Burnside's report.

44. *O.R.*, Vol. 6, pp. 254–55, General Thomas West Sherman to Stanton.

45. *O.R.*, Vol. 6, pp. 250–52, Sherman to Thomas.

46. *O.R.*, Vol. 5, pp. 50–51, 64.

47. *O.R.*, Vol. 11, Pt. 1, p. 6; McClellan, *Own Story*, p. 254.

48. *O.R.*, Ser. 3, Vol. 2, pp. 2–3.

49. *O.R.*, Vol. 10, Pt. 1, p. 108, Grant's report; *O.R.*, Vol. 8, pp. 78–84, Pope's report.

50. *O.R.*, Ser. 3, Vol. 2, p. 14.

51. *O.R.*, Ser. 3, Vol. 2, p. 31; New Orleans had been captured April 25 by Navy forces and occupied May 1 by Butler's troops, *O.R.*, Vol. 6, p. 437.

Chapter 7: Gloom Deepens in the South

1. *O.R.*, Vol. 5, pp. 1006–7.

2. Reports of the operation of this spy ring are covered in detail in *O.R.*, Ser. 2, Vol. 2, Treatment of Suspected and Disloyal Persons, North and South. Among the cases reported are those of Mrs. Rose O'Neal Greenhow, pp. 561–77; William T. Smithson, a prominent Washington banker who operated under the code name Charles R. Cables, pp. 1354–57; Michael Thompson, a Washington attorney; Lewis L. McArthur, a clerk in Thompson's office, pp. 1307–13; and Mrs. Augusta Heath Morris, pp. 1346–51.

    In a letter to Dr. J. F. Mason (sent in care of Major R. G. Rhett, assistant adjutant general on Johnston's staff), Mrs. Morris stated that she was sent to Washington by Generals Johnston and Beauregard "with the consent of the President." She also stated that she had obtained the plans of McClellan, p. 1348.

Jordan's role is explained in his letter of October 29, 1861, to Confederate Secretary of War Judah P. Benjamin, *O.R.,* Vol. 5, pp. 928–29, and *O.R.,* Ser. 2, Vol. 2, pp. 564–65. He stated that he had met with Mrs. Greenhow before leaving Washington and arranged for her to correspond with "Thomas John Rayford," his code name. Jordan noted that Mrs. Greenhow supplied information on Union troop movements four days before the First Battle of Bull Run. Jordan also noted that an agent identified as Dr. Aaron Van Camp had just come to the Confederate camp from Washington with information about U.S. Navy movements.

Beauregard, in a letter on March 24, 1863, to Miss Augusta J. Evans of Mobile, Alabama, stated that the first message from Mrs. Greenhow was brought by a young lady "about the 10th of July, 1861." Beauregard added that a second dispatch (in cipher) from Mrs. Greenhow was delivered July 16 by a special messenger. Beauregard said it warned that a Union force of at least 55,000 was preparing to advance that day on the Confederates at Manassas. Beauregard's account was in a letter sent on March 14, 1863, to Miss Augusta J. Evans of Mobile, Alabama, *O.R.,* Vol. 51, Pt. 2, pp. 688–89.

3. *O.R.,* Vol. 5, pp. 978–79. Jordan's letter to Benjamin states, "A secret agent was sent to Washington, and a trusty citizen of Maryland has returned with some notes from friends." Enclosed were two notes, dated November 25 and 30. Both mention efforts would be made to hide the Union plan to move quickly.

4. *O.R.,* Vol. 5, pp. 1006–7, Johnston to Benjamin forwarding notes of December 22 and 23; *O.R.,* Vol. 5, p. 1019, Johnston's memorandum to Benjamin outlining information in notes of December 28 and 30 and two undated; *O.R.,* Ser. 2, Vol. 2, pp. 565–66 and *O.R.,* Vol. 5, p. 1038, Jordan to Benjamin, contain the full text of the December 28 note mentioned by Johnston and a note from Mrs. Greenhow dated December 26.

5. *O.R.,* Ser. 2, Vol. 2, pp. 565–66.

6. *O.R.,* Vol. 5, p. 1015, return of the Army of Northern Virginia for December 1861.

7. *O.R.,* Vol. 5, pp. 1028, 1036–37, Johnston to Benjamin.

8. Joseph E. Johnston, *Narrative of Military Operations,* D. Appleton and Company, New York, 1874, pp. 84–85 (hereafter cited as Johnston, *Narrative*).

9. *O.R.,* Vol. 5, p. 1045.

10. *O.R.,* Vol. 5, pp. 1063–64.

11. *O.R.,* Vol. 5, p. 1074. Johnston refers to the loss of Beauregard, commander of the Potomac District in the Department of Northern Virginia, who, on January 26, 1862, had been assigned to duty at Columbus, Kentucky, *O.R.,* Vol. 5, p. 1048, Benjamin to Johnston; p. 1051, Johnston's reply, January 29, and *O.R.,* Vol. 5, p. 1053, General Orders No. 17, January 30.

12. *O.R.,* Ser. 4, Vol. 1, p. 869.

13. *O.R.,* Ser. 4, Vol. 1, pp. 902–6.

14. *O.R.,* Ser. 4, Vol. 1, pp. 930–31.

15. *Inside the Confederate Government: The Diary of Robert Garlick Hill Kean, head of the Bureau of War,* edited by Edward Younger, published 1957 by Oxford University Press, Inc., New York, reprinted 1973 by Greenwood Press, Westport, Connecticut, pp. 22–24 (hereafter cited as Kean, *Inside the Confederate Government*).

16. *O.R.,* Vol. 5, p. 1077, Davis to Johnston.

17. Johnston, *Narrative,* p. 96. John H. Reagan, *Memoirs with Special Reference to Secession and the Civil War,* the Neale Publishing Company, New York and Washington, D.C., 1906, reprinted in 1973 by AMS Press, Inc., New York, pp. 117–18 (hereafter cited as Reagan, *Memoirs*). Davis, *Rise and Fall,* Vol. 1, pp. 464–65.

18. *O.R.,* Vol. 5, pp. 1083–84.

19. *O.R.,* Vol. 6, p. 400.

20. *O.R.,* Vol. 53, p. 221; *Lee's Wartime Papers,* p. 123; Major General John C. Pemberton assumed command of the Department of South Carolina, etc., *O.R.* Vol. 6, p. 402; Lee's letter to Johnston, March 5, 1862, at Richmond, *O.R.,* Vol. 5, p. 1090.

21. *O.R.,* Vol. 5, pp. 1090–91, Johnston to Brigadier General Chase Whiting, commanding a division on Johnston's right; *O.R.,* Vol. 51, Pt. 2, p. 487, confidential dispatch to Brigadier General Samuel G. French.

22. *O.R.,* Vol. 5, pp. 526–27, Johnston's report.

23. *O.R.,* Vol. 51, Pt. 2, pp. 1073–74, Johnston's report of March 13 to Davis; Davis's replies, *O.R.,* Vol. 5, pp. 527–28.

24. Georgia's responses, *O.R.,* Ser. 4, Vol. 1, pp. 913, 929–30, 948, 1013; other states, *O.R.,* Vol. 52, Pt. 2, pp. 127–29, 921–22, 948, 973–77, 980–82; also *O.R.,* Vol. 6, p. 830, and *O.R.,* Vol. 10, Pt. 2, pp. 333–34.

25. *O.R.,* Vol. 51, Pt. 2, p. 495, call to Virginia for 40,000 militia.

26. *O.R.,* Vol. 5, p. 1096.

27. Davis, *Rise and Fall,* Vol. 1, p. 464.

28. *O.R.,* Vol. 5, p. 1083, note added to letter of Johnston to Whiting; Freeman, *Lee Biography,* Vol. 2, p. 4.

29. *O.R.,* Vol. 5, p. 1099; *Lee's Wartime Papers,* p. 127.

30. *Lee's Wartime Papers,* pp. 127–28.

31. *O.R.,* Vol. 5, p. 732, return of the Army of the Potomac; *O.R.,* Vol. 5, p. 1086, return of the Army of Northern Virginia.

32. *O.R.,* Vol. 5, pp. 1094–95.

33. *O.R.,* Vol. 5, p. 1098, letter, Johnston to Cooper; Hotchkiss, *CMH, Virginia,* p. 216; William Allan, *History of the Campaign of Gen. T. J. (Stonewall) Jackson in the Shenandoah Valley of Virginia from November 4, 1861, to June 17, 1862,* J. B. Lippincott, Philadelphia, Pennsylvania, 1880, reprinted in 1987 by Morningside House, Inc., Dayton, Ohio, pp. 40–41 (hereafter cited as Allan, *Jackson's Valley Campaign*).

34. *O.R.,* Vol. 12, Pt. 1, p. 338, Shields's report; the strength of Shields's division was reported on March 17 as 9,549 available troops, *O.R.,* Vol. 12, Pt. 3, pp. 4–5.

35. *O.R.,* Vol. 12, Pt. 1, p. 379, Jackson to Johnston.

36. McClellan's instructions to Banks, *O.R.,* Vol. 5, p. 56, *O.R.,* Vol. 12, Pt. 1, p. 164.

37. *O.R.,* Vol. 12, Pt. 1, p. 378, abstract of record of events in Williams's division.

38. *O.R.* Vol. 12, Pt. 1, p. 338–39, Shields to Major R. Morris Copeland, assistant adjutant general, at 5th Corps headquarters.

39. *O.R.,* Vol. 12, Pt. 1, pp. 380–81, Jackson's report; *O.R.,* Vol. 12, Pt. 1, p. 385, Ashby's report.

40. *O.R.,* Vol. 12, Pt. 1, pp. 335–38, Shields's report; pp. 380–84, Jackson's report.

41. *O.R.,* Vol. 12, Pt. 1, p. 378, Williams's division abstract.

42. *O.R.,* Vol. 11, Pt. 3, p. 52, Stanton to McClellan; p. 53, McClellan to Gen. E. V. Sumner; p. 56, Special Orders No. 99.

43. *O.R.,* Vol. 12, Pt. 1, p. 234–35, and *O.R.,* Vol. 5, p. 59, McClellan to Banks.

44. Hotchkiss, *Diary,* Introduction, pp. xviii–xxi; March 26, 1862, entry, p. 10.

45. Hotchkiss, *Diary,* Introduction, pp. xvi–xvii.

46. In chapter 17.

47. Mrs. Jackson, *Memoirs,* pp. 248–49.

48. *O.R.,* Vol. 12, Pt. 1, p. 384; Mrs. Jackson, *Memoirs,* p. 250.

Chapter 8: War in Earnest Comes to Virginia

1. *O.R.,* Vol. 12, Pt. 1, p. 470, Jackson's report; p. 342, Shields's report.
2. *O.R.,* Vol. 12, Pt. 3, p. 50, Banks's report; p. 37, Fremont's return of March 30.
    Shortly before the Battle of Kernstown, Jackson began to receive militia that had been called out by Governor John Letcher. Some were unarmed and on March 31 Jackson asked Colonel S. Bassett French, an aide of Gov. Letcher, for pikes, *O.R.,* Vol. 12, Pt. 3, pp. 841–42. In a note dated April 9, French informed Lee that he hoped 1,000 pikes could be sent to Jackson. He also mentioned that about 4,000 militia had joined Jackson's force, *O.R.,* Vol. 12, Pt. 3, p. 842.
3. *Lee's Wartime Papers,* p. 140, letter to Major General John B. Magruder, commander at Yorktown.
4. Johnston, *Narrative,* p. 108.
5. *O.R.,* Vol. 11, Pt. 3, p. 397; *Lee's Wartime Papers,* pp. 134–35.
6. Johnston, *Narrative,* p. 109.
7. *O.R.,* Vol. 11, Pt. 1, p. 405, Magruder's report. Davis estimated Magruder's force early in April at 7,000 to 8,000 but added that reinforcements had increased it to 12,000, Davis, *Rise and Fall,* Vol. 2, pp. 84–85.
8. *O.R.,* Vol. 9, p. 38, returns of the Department of Norfolk for January showed a total of 12,983 men present; *O.R.,* Vol. 11, Pt. 3, pp. 435–36, Huger's letter to Lee.
9. Johnston, *Narrative,* pp. 109–10.
10. *O.R.,* Vol. 11, Pt. 1, p. 8, McClellan's report.
11. *O.R.,* Vol. 11, Pt. 1, pp. 9–10, McClellan's report; it also notes that there were skirmishes at Big Bethel and Howard's Bridge.
12. *O.R.,* Vol. 11, Pt. 1, p. 9, McClellan's report, reference to maps; p. 10, heavy rain reported.
13. McClellan, *Own Story,* p. 276.
14. McClellan, *Own Story,* pp. 258–59.
15. *O.R.,* Vol. 11, Pt. 3, p. 65, message from the War Department to Generals Wool and McClellan.
16. *O.R.,* Vol. 11, Pt. 3, pp. 66–68, two letters from Thomas to McClellan.
17. *O.R.,* Vol. 11, Pt. 3, pp. 73–74.
18. *O.R.,* Vol. 11, Pt. 1, p. 14, letter, Lincoln to McClellan. Brigadier General Daniel P. Woodbury's engineer brigade, on March 23, had been ordered to provide the means of landing troops and equipment from transports, *O.R.,* Vol. 11, Pt. 3, p. 59, Special Orders No. 5.
19. *O.R.,* Vol. 11, Pt. 1, pp. 11–12, two letters, one to Lincoln, the other to Stanton. In the letter to Lincoln, McClellan pointed out that only 53,000 men had joined him at the time, but others were moving up as rapidly as possible.
20. *O.R.,* Vol. 11, Pt. 1, p. 12, McClellan's report; McClellan, *Own Story,* pp. 264–67. The decision was disclosed to Stanton on April 7. "It will be necessary," McClellan wrote, "to resort to the use of heavy guns and siege operations before we assault."
21. *O.R.,* Vol. 11, Pt. 3, p. 420. This refers to Lee's letter of March 25 to Johnston. A more detailed description of the situation, especially if Johnston's line north of Richmond was threatened, is found in two letters of Lee to Johnston on March 28, *O.R.,* Vol. 11, Pt. 3, pp. 408–9.
22. Davis, *Rise and Fall,* Vol. 2, p. 85; Early, *Memoirs,* p. 58.
23. Early, *Memoirs,* p. 59.
24. *O.R.,* Vol. 11, Pt. 3, p. 438, and *O.R.,* Vol. 12, Pt. 3, p. 846, Special Orders No. 6.
25. Davis, *Rise and Fall,* Vol. 2, pp. 86–88; Johnston, *Narrative,* p. 110–13.

26. *O.R.,* Vol. 11, Pt. 1, p. 275, Johnston's report; Johnston, *Narrative,* pp. 117–18; *O.R.,* Vol. 11, Pt. 3, p. 48, Johnston's order of April 18.

27. *O.R.,* Vol. 11, Pt. 1, pp. 17–18; McClellan, *Own Story,* pp. 274–75.

28. McClellan, *Own Story,* pp. 286–88; *O.R.,* Vol. 11, Pt. 1, p. 18.

29. *O.R.,* Vol. 11, Pt. 3, pp. 133–34.

30. *O.R.,* Vol. 11, Pt. 1, p. 449, McClellan's report; McClellan, *Own Story,* pp. 319–33.

31. Johnston, *Narrative,* pp. 126–28.

32. *O.R.,* Vol. 11, Pt. 3, p. 490, Randolph on May 3 directed Major General Benjamin Huger to prepare for a speedy evacuation from Norfolk to Petersburg; Norfolk was occupied by Union troops May 10, *O.R.* Vol. 11, Pt. 1, p. 634, Wool's report.

33. *O.R.,* Vol. 11, Pt. 3, p. 504, Randolph to Cooper.

34. McClellan, *Own Story,* p. 341.

35. *O.R.,* Vol. 11, Pt. 1, p. 27; McClellan, *Own Story,* p. 345–46, Stanton to McClellan.

36. *O.R.,* Vol. 12, Pt. 3, p. 122. Stanton transferred Shields's division to the Department of the Rappahannock on May 1.

Shields on May 5 reported to McDowell that he had been ordered to remain in the Valley until Banks's troops occupied a position near Strasburg. Shields also reported that his division had 11,000 men ready for duty, *O.R.,* Vol. 12, Pt. 3, p. 34.

37. *O.R.,* Vol. 11, Pt. 3, p. 186, McDowell to McClellan.

38. McClellan, *Own Story,* pp. 350–51, Lincoln's letter to McClellan.

39. *O.R.,* Vol. 12, Pt. 1, p. 470, Jackson's report.

40. Allan, *Jackson's Valley Campaign,* p. 61; Hotchkiss, *Diary,* pp. 15–30, weather described in entries of March 30 to April 21.

41. Longstreet, *M to A,* p. 65. Reference to Longstreet's letter of April 3 is made in Jackson's letter of that date (*O.R.,* Vol. 12, Pt. 3, pp. 842–43) but marked "not found" in footnote. Douglas Southall Freeman refers to Longstreet's suggestion to Jackson, but adds that "unfortunately, the dispatch that contains this proposal has been lost," Freeman, *Lee's Lieutenants,* Vol. 1, p. 167.

42. *O.R.,* Vol. 12, Pt. 3, Jackson's letters of April 3 and 5, pp. 842–44; *O.R.,* Vol. 11, Pt. 3, p. 448, Johnston's General Orders No. 1 of April 18.

43. *O.R.,* Vol. 11, Pt. 3, pp. 419–20, Johnston's letter of April 4 to Lee.

44. *O.R.,* Vol. 12, Pt. 3, pp. 845–46, Jackson's letters of April 10 and 12 to Ewell. In the April 12 letter, Jackson refers to Ewell's letter "of yesterday" but the footnote states that it was not found.

45. *O.R.,* Vol. 12, Pt. 3, pp. 846–47, Ewell to Jackson.

46. *O.R.,* Vol. 12, Pt. 2, pp. 848–53. One of the letters appears twice in the *O.R.,* on pp. 846 and 853. The instructions are the same, but the date line differs. The one on page 846 shows the date as April 12; the other as April 17. Both are timed at 9:15 P.M., and both were sent from "near New Market." Other letters from Jackson to Ewell at the time period were sent from "near Mount Jackson."

The two letters have the same endorsement: "Received between 7:30 and 8:30 on the 18th April, 1862." Another letter on p. 853, dated April 17, 1862, at 2:50 P.M., informs Ewell that "Lieutenant Meade, the bearer of this letter, is directed to guide you to Swift Run Gap." The first letter, dated April 12, contains the statement "I will send Lieutenant Meade to guide you." This sentence is not in the April 17 letter.

47. *O.R.,* Vol. 12, Pt. 1, p. 426, Banks's report; Pt. 3, p. 854, Jackson's letter to Ewell.

48. *O.R.,* Vol. 12, Pt. 3, pp. 853–54, Lee to Johnson.
49. *O.R.,* Vol. 12, Pt. 3, p. 856, Lee's letter to Field, and Field's telegram to Ewell; p. 867, Lee to Anderson.
50. *O.R.,* Vol. 12, Pt. 3, p. 875, Lee to Jackson.
51. *O.R.,* Vol. 12, Pt. 3, p. 872, Jackson to Lee, April 29; Lee's response, p. 878.
52. *O.R.,* Vol. 12, Pt. 1; reports of Jackson, pp. 470–73; Johnson, pp. 482–84; Milroy, pp. 465–67; Schenck, pp. 462–65. Milroy and Schenck stated that they withdrew on the night of May 8 because ammunition had been exhausted.

    Jackson's pursuit and his return to the Valley is outlined in Douglas, p. 49; his return to the Valley, *O.R.,* Vol. 12, Pt. 1, p. 701, Jackson's report.

    The Shenandoah Mountain is shown on two maps—p. 85, No. 1, and p. 94, No. 2—in *The Official Military Atlas of the Civil War,* prepared by Major George B. Davis, U.S. Army, and Leslie J. Perry and Joseph W. Kirkley, civilian experts, and published by the U.S. Government Printing Office, Washington, D.C., 1891–95; republished in 1978 by the National Historical Society, Gettysburg, Pennsylvania, and printed by Arno Press, Inc., and Crown Publishers, Inc. (hereafter cited as *Official Military Atlas of the Civil War*).
53. *O.R.,* Vol. 12, Pt. 3, pp. 153, 160–61, Shields's letters to McDowell; *O.R.,* Vol. 12, Pt. 1, p. 522, Banks's letter of May 14 to Stanton from Strasburg. Banks had withdrawn from Harrisonburg to New Market on May 5 (*O.R.,* Vol. 12, Pt. 3, p. 135), and arrived at Strasburg on May 13, as disclosed in letters to Stanton (*O.R.,* Vol. 12, Pt. 3, p. 183).
54. *O.R.,* Vol. 12, Pt. 3, pp. 892–93, Lee to Jackson.
55. *O.R.,* Vol. 12, Pt. 3, p. 893, Jackson to Ewell.
56. *O.R.,* Vol. 12, Pt. 3, pp. 896–97, Johnston to Ewell.
57. *O.R.,* Vol. 12, Pt. 3, pp. 894–95, Jackson to Johnston.
58. *O.R.,* Vol. 12, Pt. 3, p. 897, Jackson to Ewell.
59. Hotchkiss, *Diary,* p. 46.
60. *O.R.,* Vol. 12, Pt. 3, pp. 897–98, Jackson's dispatches to Ewell, May 18 and 19.
61. Returns of May 3 showed a total of 8,397 available troops in Jackson's command, *O.R.,* Vol. 12, Pt. 3, p. 879. Johnson's strength was estimated by Colonel Abner Smead, Johnson's inspector general, at 3,000 effective men, Allan, *Jackson's Valley Campaign,* p. 66; a report submitted on March 18 by Edward Willis, acting assistant adjutant general on Johnson's staff, showed an aggregate of 2,784 troops present, *O.R.,* Vol. 12, Pt. 3, pp. 828–29. Ewell's strength on April 16 was reported as "somewhat over 8,000 troops" plus about 500 cavalrymen, *O.R.,* Vol. 12, Pt. 3, p. 851, Ewell to Cooper. One of Ewell's four brigades remained at Gordonsville when he moved to the Valley, *O.R.,* Vol. 12, Pt. 3, pp. 888, 890–92, Ewell to Brigadier General L. O'Bryan Branch.
62. *O.R.,* Vol. 12, Pt. 1, pp. 701–3, Jackson's report.
63. *O.R.,* Vol. 12, Pt. 1, pp. 778–80, Ewell's report.
64. *O.R.,* Vol. 12, Pt. 1, p. 527, Banks to Lincoln. Lincoln's reaction was reported in Stanton's dispatch to Banks on May 24, *O.R.,* Vol. 12, Pt. 1, p. 528.
65. *O.R.,* Vol. 12, Pt. 1, pp. 528–30, Banks's dispatches to Stanton, May 25 and 26.
66. Mrs. Jackson, *Memoirs,* p. 265.
67. Cooke, *Jackson,* pp. 451–52.
68. *O.R.,* Vol. 12, Pt. 3, p. 219, Lincoln to McDowell, May 24; p. 231, Stanton to McDowell, May 25.

69. *O.R.,* Vol. 12, pp. 220–21, McDowell's dispatches to Stanton and Lincoln in the evening of May 24.

70. *O.R.,* Vol. 11, Pt. 1, pp. 31–32; McClellan, *Own Story,* p. 367; *O.R.,* Vol. 11, Pt. 1, p. 33, McClellan's telegram to Lincoln at 7:30 P.M. May 26.

71. McClellan, *Own Story,* pp. 396–97, private letter written at New Bridge at 8 P.M. May 26.

72. *O.R.,* Vol. 11, Pt. 3, p. 557, Randolph's memorandum.

73. *O.R.,* Vol. 11, Pt. 1, pp. 933–35, Johnston's report.

74. Long, *Memoirs,* p. 159; Marshall, *Aide-de-Camp,* p. 58.

75. *O.R.,* Vol. 11, Pt. 3, pp. 568–69,

76. *O.R.,* Vol. 11, Pt. 3, p. 571, Special Orders No. 126 of the War Department.

77. Douglas, *Stonewall,* p. 65.

78. Cooke, *Jackson,* p. 88, as noted in chapter 3, p. 44.

Chapter 9: Jackson's Plan Accepted—Invasion Postponed

1. Duke University, Manuscript Department of Perkins Library, Ms. 581, *Alexander R. Boteler Papers* (hereafter cited as Duke University, *Boteler Papers*).

2. *O.R.,* Vol. 12, Pt. 3, pp. 903–4.

3. *SHSP,* Vol. 40, pp. 164–65, Boteler's paper on Jackson's 1862 campaign.

4. *SHSP,* Vol. 40, p. 168.

5. *SHSP,* Vol. 40, p. 169.

6. Allan, *Conversations with Lee,* December 17, 1868. Davis fixes the date of the meeting as June 2, "the day after Lee assumed command," Davis, *Rise and Fall,* Vol. 2, pp. 130–31. That was two days before Boteler presented Jackson's request for enough troops to invade the North. Davis explained that he was riding out to the army when he noticed horses in front of a house and recognized one as Lee's mount.

   Colonel Long of Lee's staff stated that the conference was held at a house on the Nine Mile road, that the army's principal officers were present, and they generally agreed "that the line then occupied should be abandoned for one nearer Richmond which was considered more defensible," Long, *Memoirs,* p. 163.

7. That plan apparently originated in a conference between Davis and Lee sometime before the Battle of Fair Oaks, or Seven Pines. Davis expressed dissatisfaction "with the condition of affairs" and asked for Lee's advice. Instead of making a direct reply, Lee asked Davis what he thought should be done. The latter replied, "McClellan should be attacked on the other side of the Chickahominy [north of the river] before he matured his preparations for a siege of Richmond." He was not surprised by Lee's prompt agreement because, Davis explained, the idea had been suggested by Lee during a previous conversation.

   When Lee offered to discuss the idea with Johnston, Davis agreed. Lee returned with the information that Johnston "proposed, on the next Thursday [May 29th] to move against the right flank and rear of the enemy." This was to be followed by an attack on the enemy's front. Davis, *Rise and Fall,* Vol. 2, p. 120.

8. *O.R.,* Vol. 11, Pt. 3, Lee to Stevens, pp. 571–72; General Orders No. 62, p. 573.

9. Marshall, *Aide-de-Camp,* p. 79; Freeman, *Lee Biography,* Vol. 2, p. 863; *Mary Chesnut's Civil War,* edited by C. Vann Woodward, published by Yale University Press, New Haven, Connecticut, and London, 1981, p. 388 (hereafter cited as *Mary Chesnut*).

10. *O.R.,* Vol. 11, Pt. 1, pp. 38–46, McClellan's report. McClellan, *Own Story,* pp. 378–88. Hotchkiss, *Diary,* pp. 49, 50–56, reports rain on May 30, June 1, 2, 3, 4, 5, 9, and 10; the June 5 entry notes that the river was "higher than it had been in 25 years," and the June 12 entry notes that the river still was "rather high for crossing" at a ford.

11. Marshall, *Aide-de-Camp,* p. 79.

12. McClellan, *Own Story,* p. 389, message to Stanton, June 14.

13. *O.R.,* Vol. 51, Pt. 2, p. 565, Davis's message to "The Army of Richmond."

14. *O.R.,* Vol. 14, p. 534.

15. *O.R.,* Vol. 14, p. 535, Pemberton to Davis, and Pemberton to Randolph. The request for troops from Pemberton's department was not new. As early as April 30, as McClellan moved up the Peninsula, Lee called on Pemberton for "additional troops to oppose the advance of the enemy." This competition for men continued for more than a month before Pemberton, on May 26, grudgingly informed Lee that only two regiments could be sent to Richmond, *O.R.,* Vol. 14, pp. 480–82, 491, 518–20.

16. *O.R.,* Vol. 14, pp. 85–88, Pemberton's report; pp. 42–50, report of Major General David Hunter, U.S. Army, Department of the South.

17. *O.R.,* Vol. 12, Pt. 3, p. 905.

18. *O.R.,* Vol. 12, Pt. 3, pp. 905–6, noted in Lee's letter to Randolph.

19. *O.R.,* Vol. 14, p. 539.

20. *O.R.,* Vol. 14, p. 539, two messages from Pemberton to Davis.

21. *Lee's Dispatches, Unpublished Letters of General Robert E. Lee, C.S.A., to Jefferson Davis and the War Department of The Confederate States of America, 1862–65, from the Private Collection of Wyemberley Jones de Renne, of Warmsloe, Georgia.* Edited by Douglas Southall Freeman, with additional dispatches by Grady McWhiney and published in 1957 by G. P. Putnam's Sons, New York (hereafter cited as *Lee's Dispatches*), pp. 5–6; *Lee's Wartime Papers,* pp. 183–84.

22. *O.R.,* Vol. 12, Pt. 3, pp. 905–6.

23. VHS, *Lee's Telegraph Book.*

24. *O.R.,* Vol. 12, Pt. 3, pp. 906–7.

25. *O.R.,* Vol. 12, Pt. 3, p. 907.

26. *O.R.,* Vol. 12, Pt. 3, p. 907, Lee's endorsement appended to Jackson's letter. *O.R.,* Vol. 12, Pt. 3, p. 908, Lee's letter to Jackson on June 8.

27. *Lee's Wartime Papers,* p. 187.

28. Hotchkiss, *Diary,* p. 54. Hotchkiss observed the action from a hill overlooking the battlefield.

29. *O.R.,* Vol. 11, Pt. 3, p. 584; *Lee's Wartime Papers,* p. 188.

30. *O.R.,* Vol. 51, Pt. 2, p. 1074; *Lee's Wartime Papers,* p. 188.

31. Huntington Library, San Marino, California, Stuart's letter (SA248). On June 3, the day after the meeting among Lee, Davis, and generals of the Army of Northern Virginia on the Nine Mile road, Longstreet went to Lee and suggested a move against McClellan's right flank. Longstreet wrote that Lee "gave a patient hearing to the suggestion, without indicating approval or disapproval, Longstreet, *M to A,* p. 114.

32. *The Memoirs of Colonel John S. Mosby,* edited by Charles Wells Russell and published by Little, Brown and Company, Boston, Massachusetts, 1917, p. 110 (hereafter cited as Mosby, *Memoirs*); *SHSP,* Vol. 26, p. 247; Mosby's letter to his daughter, Pauline, pp. 24–25, *The Letters of John S. Mosby,* edited by Adele H.

Mitchell, published in 1986 by the Stuart–Mosby Historical Society (hereafter cited as *Mosby's Letters*).

33. Heros von Borcke, *Memoirs of the Confederate War for Independence,* first printing, 1866, reprinted by Peter Smith, New York, 1938, Vol. 1, pp. 34–36 (hereafter cited as von Borcke, *Memoirs*).

34. Mosby, *Memoirs,* pp. 110–11.

35. *O.R.,* Vol. 1, Pt. 1, p. 1038, Stuart's report.

36. Allan, *Conversations with Lee,* December 17, 1868. In the eight days after Lee assumed command of the Army of Northern Virginia on June 1, Confederate plans changed several times. On June 2, Lee talked of striking McClellan's line, and Davis suggested that Jackson, when available, should be brought east for the attack (as noted in 7 above). On June 4, Davis received from Boteler Jackson's proposal to invade the North and sought Lee's opinion. On June 5, Lee endorsed it.

　　On June 7, Davis again visited Lee's headquarters. Apparently a question arose over which plan should be adopted. Long observed: "The relations between General Lee and Mr. Davis are very friendly. The general is ever willing to receive the suggestions of the President, while the President exhibits the greatest confidence in General Lee's experience and ability, and does not hamper him with executive interference." Long, *Memoirs,* pp. 167–68. Evidently, Lee suggested postponing Jackson's invasion plan, and Davis agreed to the change the next day. The agreement on the plan to attack McClellan is made clear in Lee's letter of June 10 to Davis, *O.R.,* Vol. 51, Pt. 2, p. 1074 (as noted in 28 above).

37. *Jefferson Davis, Constitutionalist, His Letters, Papers and Speeches,* collected and edited by Dunbar Rowland, Jackson, Mississippi, printed for the Mississippi Department of Archives and History, 1923, Vol. 5, pp. 272, 277–78 (hereafter cited as Rowland, *Jefferson Davis*).

38. *Lee's Wartime Papers,* p. 192.

39. *O.R.,* Vol. 11, Pt. 1, pp. 1036–40, Stuart's report; *O.R.,* Vol. 11, Pt. 2, Lee's report of the Seven Days Battles, p. 490; *O.R.,* Vol. 11, Pt. 1, p. 1042, General Orders No. 74, Army of Northern Virginia; Mosby, *Memoirs,* p. 112; *SHSP,* Vol. 26, p. 248.

40. Alexander, *Memoirs,* p. 114; *O.R.,* Vol. 11, Pt. 1, p. 1039, Stuart's report.

41. *O.R.,* Vol. 11, Pt. 3, p. 590; *Lee's Wartime Papers,* p. 191.

42. Allan, *Conversations with Lee,* December 17, 1868.

43. VHS, *Lee's Telegraph Book.*

44. *O.R.,* Vol. 11, Pt. 3, pp. 589–90; *O.R.,* Vol. 12, Pt. 3, p. 910.

45. *SHSP,* Vol. 40, pp. 172–73.

46. Cooke, *Jackson,* pp. 200–201.

47. *Lee's Wartime Papers,* p. 193. The original of this letter is at Duke University.

48. *SHSP,* Vol. 40, pp. 173–74

49. *Lee's Wartime Papers,* p. 193, endorsements of Lee and Davis are appended to the original letter.

50. *SHSP,* Vol. 40, pp. 174, 176. The account on page 174 ends with, "General Lee, in accordance with his request, during which, referring to our former conversation he said: * * * ." Lee's response does not appear until the middle of page 176. The transposition makes Lee's statement appear as part of another quoted conversation. The printing error may have come from a mistake in assembling type or several pages of text may have been out of place. The error was discovered some time later; the misplaced portion of type was moved to its proper place, and the portion of the

account beginning with Lee's statement "The movement proposed by General Jackson will have to be postponed . . ." was reprinted in *SHSP,* Vol. 42, pp. 174–80. The only explanation appears in small type under the title: See Vol. XL [40].

51. *O.R.,* Vol. 12, Pt. 1, pp. 711–16, Jackson's report. This statement is in the last paragraph on p. 716.
52. *O.R.,* Vol. 11, Pt. 3, p. 602; *O.R.,* Vol. 12, Pt. 3, p. 913; *Lee's Wartime Papers,* p. 194.

Chapter 10: First Policy Resumed

1. *SHSP,* Vol. 40, p. 178.
2. Henderson, Vol. 1, pp. 395–97; Freeman, *Lee Biography,* Vol. 2, pp.108–9; Allan, *Conversations with Lee,* December 17, 1868; Marshall, *Aide-de-Camp,* p. 84; D. H. Hill, *B&L,* Vol. 2, p. 347; Longstreet, *M to A,* pp. 121–22.
3. *O.R.,* Vol. 11, Pt. 2, pp. 498–99.
4. *SHSP,* Vol. 40, p. 178.
5. *Lee's Dispatches,* pp. 15–16.
6. McClellan, *Own Story,* p. 390–91.
7. There are numerous instances of deserters or contrabands coming into Federal lines with information that seemed plausible but was intended to mislead the enemy. They are common in the *O.R.* and obviously were intended to buy time for Confederate forces.

   An example of an attempt to confuse the Yankees is found in Lee's instructions of June 16, when he directed Jackson to begin the movement from the Valley to unite with Lee's army. "In moving your troops," Lee wrote, "let it be understood that it was to pursue the enemy in your front." *O.R.,* Vol. 12, Pt. 3, p. 602.
8. McClellan, *Own Story,* p. 391; *O.R.,* Vol. 11, Pt. 1, p. 49.
9. *O.R.,* Vol. 11, Pt. 3, p. 254.
10. *O.R.,* Vol. 11, Pt. 1, pp. 49–51.
11. *O.R.* 11, Pt. 2, pp. 622–30, D. H. Hill's report; pp. 834–40, A. P. Hill's report. The battles were those of Mechanicsville, June 26; Gaines Mill or Cold Harbor, June 27; White House, June 28; Savage Station on the York River Railroad, June 29; Turkey Creek Bridge, Glendale, and Frayser's Farm, June 30; and Malvern Hill, July 1.
12. *O.R.,* Vol. 11, Pt. 2, pp. 489–98, Lee's report; *O.R.,* Vol. 11, Pt. 2, pp. 19–23, McClellan's report.
13. *O.R.,* Vol. 11, Pt. 2, p. 496–97, Lee's report.
14. *Fighting for the Confederacy, the Personal Recollections of General Edward Porter Alexander,* edited by Gary W. Gallagher, published in 1989 by the University of North Carolina Press, Chapel Hill, and London, p. 104 (hereafter cited as Alexander, *Fighting for the Confederacy*). An eighth division, commanded by Brigadier General David R. Jones. was not mentioned by Alexander.
15. Hotchkiss, *Diary,* p.118, entry of March 6, 1863.
16. *SHSP,* Vol. 40, pp. 180–81.
17. John Esten Cooke, *Hammer and Rapier,* published in 1870 by Carleton, Publisher, Madison Square, New York, and by Low, Son & Company, London, p. 247 (hereafter cited as Cooke, *Hammer and Rapier*); Douglas, *Stonewall,* p. 113.
18. Dabney, *Life and Campaigns,* pp. 486–87.
19. *SHSP,* Vol. 40, p. 182.

20. *O.R.,* Vol. 11, Pt. 3, p. 690.

21. Rowland, *Jefferson Davis Papers,* Vol. 5, pp. 290–91.

22. *O.R.,* Ser. 4, Vol. 2, pp. 5–6, Cooper's instructions to enrolling officers.

23. *O.R.,* Vol. 11, Pt. 3, p. 642. In the context of the other sources cited in this section, the "importance" of reinforcements from Pemberton clearly was not just to secure Richmond, but also to strengthen the strike force for invading the North.

24. *O.R.,* Ser. 4, Vol. 2, p. 7, Cooper's circular to governors.

25. *The Messages and Papers of Jefferson Davis and the Confederacy, Including Diplomatic Correspondence, 1861–1865,* edited and compiled by James D. Richardson, published in 1905 by United States Publishing Company, Nashville, Tennessee, and reprinted in 1966 by Chelsea House–Robert Hector, New York, in association with R. R. Bowker, Vol. 2, p. 267 (hereafter cited as Davis, *Messages and Papers*).

26. *O.R.,* Vol. 11, Pt. 3, p. 645. This is one of the few instances in which the return notes such an increase in a short period of time.

Chapter 11: The Troubled North

1. *Lee's Dispatches,* pp. 24–27.

2. *O.R.,* Vol. 11, Pt. 3, pp. 631–33, two letters dated July 5 from Davis to Lee.

3. *O.R.,* Vol. 11, Pt. 3, pp. 636–37.

4. *Lee's Dispatches,* pp. 28–32.

5. *O.R.,* Vol. 27, Pt. 3, pp. 850–52; *Lee's Wartime Papers,* pp. 507–8.

6. *O.R.,* Ser. 3, Vol. 2, pp. 109–10.

7. *O.R.,* Ser. 3, Vol. 2, pp. 176–77.

8. *O.R.,* Ser. 2, Vol. 7, pp. 930–53. The activities of the Knights of the Golden Circle and other militant organizations are described by Joseph Holt, judge advocate general of the U.S. Army, in a "detailed report of testimony furnished me from different sources in regard to the secret associations and conspiracies against the Government formed principally in the Western States by traitors and disloyal persons." Establishment of a Northwestern Confederacy is described on pp. 950–51 as part of a section headed "Its Specific Purposes and Operations."

    Activities of the Knights of the Golden Circle and similar groups are described at length in *Dark Lanterns, Secret Political Societies, Conspiracies, and Treason Trials in the Civil War,* by Frank L. Klement, Louisiana State University Press, Baton Rouge, Louisiana, and London, 1984 (hereafter cited as Klement, *Dark Lanterns*).

9. *An Authentic Exposition of the K. G. C., Knights of the Golden Circle, a History of Secession from 1834 to 1861,* by an anonymous member of the order; published in 1861 by C. O. Perrine, Indianapolis, Indiana, pp. 5–22 (hereafter cited as *Knights of the Golden Circle*).

10. *O.R.,* Ser. 3, Vol. 2, pp. 179–80. Lincoln was concerned over persistent rumors and reports that Beauregard and his troops were on the way to Richmond or had actually arrived there. *O.R.,* Vol. 11, Pt. 3, pp. 201, 240–41, 252–53, 334, and *O.R.,* Vol. 12, Pt. 3, pp. 396, 421.

11. *O.R.,* Ser. 3, Vol. 2, p. 181.

12. *O.R.,* Ser. 3, Vol. 2, p. 180.

13. *O.R.,* Ser. 3, Vol. 2, pp. 181–82.

14. *O.R.,* Ser. 3, Vol. 2, Stanton to Seward, and Seward to Stanton, p. 181; Seward to Stanton, p. 182; Seward to Stanton, and Stanton to Seward, p. 186; Stanton to Seward, p. 187.

15. *O.R.,* Ser. 3, Vol. 2, p. 183.

16. *O.R.,* Ser. 3, Vol. 2, p. 186.
17. *O.R.,* Ser. 3, Vol. 2, pp. 187–88.
18. *O.R.,* Ser. 3, Vol. 2, pp. 200–201.
19. *O.R.,* Ser. 3, Vol. 2, pp. 201–90, responses of governors.
20. *O.R.,* Ser. 3, Vol. 2, pp. 280–82.
21. *O.R.,* Ser. 3, Vol. 2, pp. 291–92.
22. *O.R.,* Ser. 3, Vol. 2, pp. 295–96.
23. *O.R.,* Ser. 3, Vol. 2, p. 316.
24. *O.R.,* Ser. 3, Vol. 2, p. 329.
25. *O.R.,* Ser. 3, Vol. 2, p. 345.
26. *O.R.,* Ser. 3, Vol. 2, p. 370, General Orders No. 104. *O.R.,* Ser. 3, Vol. 2, p. 322, news release sent to Northern papers.
27. *O.R.,* Ser. 3, Vol. 2, p. 387, Governor Salomon of Wisconsin to Stanton.
28. *O.R.,* Ser. 3, Vol. 2, pp. 380–81, 389.
29. *O.R.,* Ser. 3, Vol. 2, pp. 506–8.
30. Rowland, *Jefferson Davis Letters,* Vol. 7, p. 327.
31. *O.R.,* Vol. 11, Pt. 3, pp. 635–36, Lee to Randolph and Randolph's endorsement.
32. *O.R.,* Vol. 12, Pt. 3, p. 435. This was supplemented by General Orders No. 103, dated August 12, issued by the War Department, *O.R.,* Vol. 12, Pt. 3, p. 568.
33. *B&L,* Vol. 2, pp. 449–54.

Chapter 12: Lee and Jackson Begin the Northward Movement

1. *O.R.,* Vol. 12, Pt. 2, pp. 20–21, Pope's report. Pope estimated his effective strength at 38,000 plus 5,000 cavalrymen. The June 30 return, *O.R.,* Ser. 3, Vol. 2, p. 185, lists the total effective strength as 67,614, plus 9,000 in the Kanawha District.
2. *O.R.,* Vol. 12, Pt. 2, p. 21, Pope's report. The moves also are described in Pope's letter to Wool, *O.R.,* Vol. 12, Pt. 3, pp. 453–54.
3. *O.R.,* Vol. 12, Pt. 3, p. 454.
4. *O.R.,* Vol. 12, Pt. 3, p. 463.
5. *O.R.,* Vol. 12, Pt. 3, p. 915, Special Orders No. 150, dated July 12, 1862.
6. *O.R.,* Vol. 12, Pt. 3, pp. 458, 465.
7. *O.R.,* Vol. 12, Pt. 3, p. 470, Colonel George D. Ruggles, Pope's chief of staff, to Banks. Ruggles attributed the problem to "the hurry and confusion of organizing my office for an early departure for the field."
8. *O.R.,* Vol. 12, Pt. 3, pp. 481–82, Banks's letter to Pope.
9. *O.R.,* Vol. 12, Pt. 3, p. 484.
10. *O.R.,* Vol. 12, Pt. 2, p. 181; Hotchkiss, *Diary,* pp. 62–63, entries of July 18, 19, and 21; Douglas, *Stonewall,* p. 120.
11. *O.R.,* Vol. 12, Pt. 3, pp. 916–17, two letters, Lee to Jackson, on July 23 and 25. Letters from Jackson were not found, according to footnotes on those pages.
12. *O.R.,* Vol. 12, Pt. 3, pp. 917–18, Lee's reply to a letter from Jackson dated July 23. The footnote also indicated that this letter of Jackson's was not found.
13. *Lee's Wartime Papers,* p. 238; *Lee's Dispatches,* pp. 38–40.
14. *O.R.,* Vol. 12, Pt. 3, pp. 918–19; *Lee's Wartime Papers,* pp. 239–40; Special Orders No. 164, dated July 27, 1862, directed Hill to move with his own and the Louisiana troops to Gordonsville, *O.R.,* Vol. 12, Pt. 3, p. 919.
15. *O.R.,* Vol. 12, Pt. 2, pp. 51–52. The first was General Orders No. 7, issued July 10, 1862, and the second, General Orders No. 11, on July 23, 1862.
16. Hotchkiss, *Diary,* p. 63, July 29 entry; *General A. P. Hill: The Story of a Confeder-*

ate Warrior, by James I. Robertson, Jr., published 1987 by Random House, New York, p. 99 (hereafter cited as Robertson, *A. P. Hill*).

17. *O.R.*, Vol. 12, Pt. 2, p. 178, Lee's report; p. 181, Jackson's report.
18. *O.R.*, Vol. 12, Pt. 3, p. 926.
19. *O.R.*, Vol. 12, Pt. 2, pp. 181–85, Jackson's report; Hotchkiss, *Diary*, pp. 66–67, entries of August 9 and 10.
20. *O.R.*, Vol. 12, Pt. 2, p. 185.
21. Hotchkiss, *Diary*, p. 68, August 12 entry.
22. *O.R.*, Vol. 12, Pt. 2, p. 5, Halleck's report; *O.R.*, Vol. 11, Pt. 1, pp. 76–77, McClellan's report; McClellan, *Own Story*, p. 491. Halleck's assignment as general in chief, Lincoln's order, *O.R.*, Ser. 3, Vol. 2, p. 217.
23. *O.R.*, Vol. 12, Pt. 3, p. 524.
24. *O.R.*, Vol. 11, Pt. 2, p. 935, McClellan's letter to Halleck.
25. *O.R.*, Vol. 11, Pt. 2, pp. 80–81, McClellan's report; McClellan, *Own Story*, pp. 495–96.
26. *O.R.*, Vol. 12, Pt. 3, two messages, Burnside to Halleck, pp. 528–29, 554.
27. *O.R.*, Vol. 11. Pt. 1, pp. 76–81, McClellan's report; *O.R.*, Vol. 11, Pt. 2, pp. 951–56, reports of Union officers; pp. 956–57, Lee's report; McClellan, *Own Story*, pp. 492–98.
28. *O.R.*, Vol. 11, Pt. 3, p. 359; McClellan, *Own Story*, p. 493.
29. *O.R.*, Vol. 12, Pt. 3, pp. 5–6, Halleck's report.
30. McClellan, *Own Story*, pp. 498–505.
31. *O.R.*, Vol. 11, Pt. 3, p. 675, Special Orders No. 181, August 13; *O.R.*, Vol. 12, Pt. 3, p. 930, Lee to Hood.
32. *O.R.*, Vol. 12, Pt. 2, pp. 551–52, Lee's report for August 12 to September 2.
33. *O.R.*, Vol. 12, Pt. 3, pp. 917–19, Lee's letters to Jackson on July 23 and 27.
34. Hotchkiss, *Diary*, p. 68, August 13. Longstreet had been ordered to Gordonsville on August 13. He apparently left in advance of his troops and arrived in the late afternoon. Lee addressed a letter to him there at 9 A.M. August 14. The letter opened with a reference to "your note of 6 p.m. yesterday," *O.R.*, Vol. 11, Pt. 3, p. 676.
35. Hotchkiss, *Diary*, pp. 68–69, entries of August 14, 15, and 16.
36. Freeman, *Lee Biography*, Vol. 2, p. 279; *O.R.*, Vol. 12, Pt. 2, p. 552, Lee's report; Henderson, Vol. 2, p. 111.
37. *O.R.*, Vol. 12, Pt. 2, p. 725, Stuart's report.
38. *O.R.*, Vol. 12, Pt. 2, p. 552, Lee's report; p. 729, Special Orders No. 189, August 19, 1862, directed that the move was to begin at dawn August 20. Lee explained in his report that the movement had been planned for August 18, but "the necessary preparations not having been completed, its execution was postponed to the 20th." Longstreet also stated that the move originally was planned for August 18, but was modified because of a Union movement, Longstreet, *M to A*, pp. 160, 163.
39. Marshall, *Aide-de-Camp*, p. 124. Long, *Memoirs*, pp. 186–87. Hotchkiss also noted that he and Stuart had ascended Clark's Mountain and observed enemy activities, Hotchkiss, *Diary*, p. 69, entry of August 17. Longstreet, *M to A*, pp. 161–62.
40. *O.R.*, Vol. 12, Pt. 3, p. 564.
41. *O.R.*, Vol. 12, Pt. 3, p. 569.
42. *O.R.*, Vol. 12, Pt. 3, p. 575. According to Longstreet, part of Lee's plan was "to strike in between General Pope's left and the reinforcements that could join him [Pope] from Fredericksburg," Longstreet, *M to A*, p. 159.

43. *O.R.,* Vol. 12, Pt. 3, p. 576.

44. *O.R.,* Vol. 12, Pt. 3, p. 591. In his report submitted to Halleck on September 3, Pope stated that on August 17, he learned that Lee had assembled "nearly the whole of the rebel army" within eight miles of his front. That night he began withdrawing his own army across the Rappahannock River in an effort to thwart the reported intention of the Confederates to attack Washington. The withdrawal, he added, continued through August 18, *O.R.,* Vol. 12, Pt. 2, pp. 12–13.

45. *O.R.,* Vol. 12, Pt. 2, p. 725–26, Stuart's report. Stuart notes the capture of Major Fitzhugh, but makes no mention of the letter. Pope's report, *O.R.,* Vol. 12, Pt. 2, p. 29, states that the letter, dated August 13 at Gordonsville, was "an autograph letter of General Robert E. Lee to General Stuart."

In a letter on August 13, Lee directed Stuart to check on the authenticity of a report that Burnside's troops had united with Pope's army. If true, Stuart was to leave a detail to observe enemy activity and move with the main cavalry force to Gordonsville. He was to report to Longstreet "in the event of his [Lee's] absence." But the letter was not written by Lee. It was written by his aide, Major Walter H. Taylor, and opens with "I am directed by General Lee to say," *O.R.,* Vol. 12, Pt. 3, p. 928.

46. *O.R.,* Vol. 12, Pt. 2, pp. 725–26, Stuart's report.

47. *Fitzhugh Lee,* p. 183.

48. *O.R.,* Vol. 12, Pt. 2, 725–26, Stuart's report.

49. *O.R.,* Vol. 12, Pt. 2, p. 728, Lee to Stuart.

50. *O.R.,* Vol. 12, Pt. 2, p. 552, Lee's report.

51. *O.R.,* Vol. 51, Pt. 2, p. 609; *Lee's Wartime Papers,* p. 261.

52. *O.R.,* Vol. 12, Pt. 3, pp. 938–39. Davis echoed Lee's advice to Smith a week earlier before leaving Richmond for Gordonsville. In placing Smith in charge of the defense of Richmond, Lee said, "I deem no instructions necessary beyond the necessity of holding Richmond to the last extremity should any attack be made upon it," *O.R.,* Vol. 12, Pt. 3, pp. 930–31, August 14.

53. *Lee's Wartime Papers,* pp. 261–62, letter to Davis.

Chapter 13: North to the Potomac

1. *O.R.,* Vol. 12, Pt. 2, pp. 552–60, Lee's report; pp. 641–48, Jackson's report; pp. 563–68, Longstreet's report; pp. 729–33, Stuart's report.

2. *O.R.,* Vol. 12, Pt. 2, p. 730, Stuart's report.

3. *O.R.,* Vol. 12, Pt. 2, p. 730, Stuart's report; p. 642, Jackson's report; p. 552, Lee's report.

4. *O.R.,* Vol. 12, Pt. 2, p. 563, Longstreet's report; p. 552, Lee's report; Longstreet, *M to A,* p. 163.

5. *O.R.,* Vol. 12, Pt. 2, p. 642, Jackson's report; pp. 703–16, Early's report

6. *O.R.,* Vol. 12, Pt. 2, p. 563, Longstreet's report; pp. 718–19, Trimble's report.

7. *O.R.,* Vol. 12, Pt. 2, pp. 730–31, Stuart's report.

8. *O.R.,* Vol. 12, Pt. 2, p. 642, Jackson's report; pp. 705–7, Early's report.

9. *O.R.* Vol. 12, Pt. 2, pp. 730–31, Stuart's report; *War Years with Jeb Stuart,* by Lieutenant Colonel William W. Blackford, published 1945 by Charles Scribner's Sons, New York, pp. 98–107 (hereafter cited as Blackford, *War Years*).

10. *O.R.,* Vol. 12, Pt. 2, p. 732, Stuart's report.

11. *O.R.,* Vol. 12, Pt. 3, pp. 940–42, Lee's letters to Davis, Randolph, and Loring.

At 11 P.M. August 8, Pope had instructed Cox to leave 2,500 men, with some cavalry for scouting and picketing, in the Kanawha Valley and move the remainder of his force east to join his army. Three days later, Pope ordered Cox to leave 5,000 men in western Virginia. On August 12, Cox notified Pope that steps were being taken to send troops east. On August 21, Cox informed Stanton that his troops were moving toward Washington "as fast as the railroad can furnish the transportation." On August 22, Cox advised Pope that most of the troops had been shipped, *O.R.*, Vol. 12, Pt. 3, pp. 551, 560–61, 567, 619, 629.

12. Von Borcke, *Memoirs*, Vol. 1, p. 133. Von Borcke stated that he took "captured dispatches and papers" to Lee's headquarters on the evening of August 25. Obviously, after hurriedly checking them, Stuart had taken those he considered most important to Lee on August 23. These prompted Lee's letters of that date to Davis, Randolph, and Loring. (These documents apparently were used by Lee in a conference with Jackson on the evening of August 24 that will be described later in the text.)

13. *O.R.*, Vol. 12, Pt. 3, p. 942; *Lee's Dispatches*, p. 263, Lee's letter to Davis; Pope to Halleck, *O.R.*, Vol. 12, Pt. 3, p. 603.

14. *O.R.*, Vol. 12, Pt. 3, p. 944.

15. *Lee's Dispatches*, p. 264.

16. *O.R.*, Vol. 12, Pt. 2, pp. 411–15, Heintzelman's report.

17. *O.R.*, Vol. 12, Pt. 2, p. 465, itinerary of the 5th Corps from August 15 to 31.

18. *O.R.*, Vol. 13, Pt. 3, p. 651, Franklin's letter to Halleck, and p. 676, Halleck's instructions to Franklin.

19. *O.R.*, Vol. 11, Pt. 3, p. 367. August 10 return of the Army of the Potomac shows the number of men ready for duty in the three corps as 42,500 and the aggregate as 58,006.

20. *O.R.*, Vol. 12, Pt. 3, p. 945.

21. *O.R.*, Vol. 12, Pt. 3, p. 944.

22. Henderson, *Jackson*, Vol. 2, pp. 123–24. Henderson states this information was in a letter he received from Dr. McGuire.

23. *B&L*, Vol. 2, pp. 512–26, "Our March around Pope," by Longstreet.

24. *O.R.*, Vol. 12, Pt. 2, pp. 553–54, Lee's report.

25. *Journal, Confederate Congress*, Vol. 5, pp. 314, 320–21.

26. *O.R.*, Vol. 12, Pt. 2, p. 643, Jackson's report.

27. *O.R.*, Vol. 12, Pt. 2, p. 564, Longstreet's report.

28. *O.R.*, Vol. 12, Pt. 2, p. 734, Stuart's report.

29. *O.R.*, Vol. 12, Pt. 2, p. 643, Jackson's report.

30. *O.R.*, Vol. 12, Pt. 3, p. 653, two dispatches from Pope to Halleck. The cavalry mentioned by Pope evidently was the 2nd Virginia, commanded by Colonel Thomas T. Munford, which had been assigned to Jackson's column for the advance, *O.R.*, Vol. 12, Pt. 2, p. 733, Stuart's report; p. 747, Munford's report.

31. *O.R.*, Vol. 12, Pt. 2, p. 643, Jackson's report; Douglas, *Stonewall*, pp. 134–35.

32. Cooke, *Jackson*, p. 277.

33. *O.R.*, Vol. 12, Pt. 2, pp. 643–44, Jackson's report; pp. 720–21, Trimble's report; Douglas, *Stonewall*, pp. 135–36.

34. *O.R.*, Vol. 12, Pt. 2, p. 564, Longstreet's report. Lee and his staff accompanied Longstreet's corps on the move that led to the Second Battle of Bull Run, Long, *Memoirs*, p. 191.

35. *O.R.*, Vol. 12, Pt. 2, p. 647, Jackson's report; p. 558, Lee's report.

36. *Lee's Dispatches*, pp. 266–67.

37. Hotchkiss, *Diary*, p. 98, entry of September 2.

38. Allan, *Conversations with Lee,* February 16, 1868.
39. *O.R.,* Vol. 12, Pt. 2, pp. 647–48, Jackson's report.
40. *O.R.,* Vol. 19, Pt. 2, pp. 590–91.
41. Long, *Memoirs,* p. 204. The entire letter is on pp. 516–18.
42. Taylor, *Lee,* p. 118; *Fitzhugh Lee,* p. 197.
43. *O.R.,* Vol. 19, Pt. 2, pp. 591–92.
44. *O.R.,* Vol. 19, Pt. 2, pp. 592–93, General Orders No. 102, September 4, 1862.
45. *The Messages and Papers of Jefferson Davis and the Confederacy,* two volumes, com-
    piled and edited by James D. Richardson, published in 1905 by United States
    Publishing Company, reprinted in 1966 by Chelsea House–Robert Hector, New
    York, in association with R. R. Bowker (hereafter cited as *Messages and Papers of
    Davis and Confederacy*), Vol. 1, pp. 268–69.

    At Richmond, Kentucky, on August 30, the Confederate Army of Kentucky,
    commanded by Major General Edmund Kirby Smith, routed the Union Army of
    Kentucky, commanded by Major General William Nelson. Smith reported taking
    about 5,000 prisoners. According to Union reports, its forces retreated in confu-
    sion and casualties totaled 4,303 men captured or missing, *O.R.,* Vol. 16, Pt. 1, pp.
    906–52.
46. Andrews, *North Reports,* p. 270. As early as August 21, the Baltimore correspon-
    dent of the *New York Herald* predicted that Jackson would cross the Potomac at
    Leesburg and attack Maryland.

    Another correspondent, Uriah H. Painter of the *Philadelphia Inquirer,* got
    more definite information. While seeking to gather news in the field before the
    Second Battle of Bull Run, he had been taken prisoner by Confederate troops.
    Painter, who was wearing civilian clothes, escaped after obtaining important infor-
    mation concerning Lee's movements. He immediately went to Washington, where
    he reported to the War Department that Confederate troops were about to invade
    Maryland.
47. *O.R.,* Vol. 11, Pt. 1, pp. 102–4; McClellan, *Own Story,* pp. 524–25, 534.
48. *O.R.,* Vol. 11, Pt. 1, p. 105; McClellan, *Own Story,* p. 535.
49. *O.R.,* Vol. 11, Pt. 3, p. 802, McClellan to Halleck, and p. 805, Halleck's reply.
    McClellan told Halleck that an aide, Lieutenant Horace Porter, informed him that
    Brigadier General James W. Ripley, the union chief of ordnance, said he had just
    received an order to "ship everything from this arsenal to New York." Halleck
    replied that "at least 50,000 or 60,000 arms will be left and a large number of
    artillery pieces." McClellan, *Own Story,* p. 536, regarding warship in the Potomac.
50. *O.R.,* Vol. 11, Pt. 1, p. 105, McClellan's report, "I felt sure this day that we could
    repulse any attack made by the enemy on the south side of the Potomac."

Chapter 14: The Invasion Begins

1. Von Borcke, *Memoirs,* Vol. 1, p. 183–84. Von Borcke accompanied Stuart to the
   meeting; he noted that Longstreet and Jackson were there when Stuart arrived.
2. *O.R.,* Vol. 19, Pt. 2, pp. 593–94, letter to Davis, September 5.
3. Hotchkiss, *Diary,* pp. 78–79, entry of September 5.
4. *Lee's Wartime Papers,* p. 296.
5. *O.R.,* Vol. 19, Pt. 2, p. 596, General Orders No. 103.
6. *O.R.,* Vol. 19, Pt. 2, pp. 596–97; *Lee's Wartime Papers,* pp. 297–98; *B&L,* Vol. 2,
   p. 604, Walker's article on the capture of Harpers Ferry. Walker had been assigned
   to the Richmond defenses and remained there until after McClellan's army withdrew. He then moved north with two of his three brigades to join Lee and reached

the Manassas area after the fighting. He continued northward to Leesburg, arriving there on the night of September 6.

7. *O.R.,* Vol. 19, Pt. 1, pp. 139–40, letter to Randolph that was received in Richmond on September 10; *O.R.,* Vol. 19, Pt. 2, p. 594, Lieutenant Colonel Funk's report of the occupation of Winchester, forwarded to the War Department on September 5.

8. *O.R.,* Vol. 19, Pt. 1, p. 145, Lee's report.

9. Longstreet, *M to A,* pp. 201–2; *B&L,* Vol. 2, p. 663, Longstreet's article, "The Invasion of Maryland."

10. *O.R.,* Vol. 19, Pt. 2, p. 600.

11. *O.R.,* Vol. 19, Pt. 2, pp. 601–2; *Lee's Wartime Papers,* pp. 299–300; *O.R.,* Vol. 19, Pt. 2, pp. 604–5, Lee's letter with a copy of the proclamation.

12. *Journal, Confederate Congress,* Vol. 1, pp. 534–89, previously quoted in Chapter 5.

13. *O.R.,* Vol. 19, Pt. 2, pp. 602–3, Lee to Davis.

14. Taylor, *Lee,* pp. 119–21; Taylor, *Four Years,* p. 66; *O.R.,* Vol. 51, Pt. 2, p. 617, Taylor's telegram to Davis.

15. *Journal, Confederate Congress,* Vol. 5, pp. 314, 320–21, 334–35, 372.

16. *O.R.,* Ser. 4, Vol. 2, p. 82.

17. Rowland, *Jefferson Davis* Papers, Vol. 8, p. 253, letter of James Lyons to W. T. Walthall, August 20, 1878.

18. *O.R.,* Vol. 19, Pt. 2, pp. 598–99, Davis to Lee. The dateline in the text is "Richmond, Va. September 7[?], 1862." The question mark evidently implies that the figure 7 was not clear. The correct date may have been September 9, a conclusion supported by the following facts:

    In his letter to Davis on September 9, Lee wrote, "I have just received your letter of the 7th instant from Rapidan." Also, Taylor, in his account, stated that he left Frederick on September 9 and arrived in Warrenton the next day, where he learned that Davis had returned to Richmond.

    The evidence indicates that Davis was at Rapidan, not Richmond, on September 7 and, having returned to Richmond, was in the capital on September 9 to send the text of a suggested proclamation to Lee.

19. *O.R.,* Vol. 19, Pt. 2, pp. 598–99.

20. *O.R.,* Vol. 19, Pt. 2, pp. 605–6.

Chapter 15: Frustration and Disappointment

1. *B&L,* Vol. 2, pp. 604–6, "Jackson's Capture of Harpers Ferry."

2. McClellan, *Own Story,* pp. 549–50. McClellan wrote, "Secretary Seward came to my quarters one evening" before he went to the front and "asked my opinion of the condition of affairs at Harpers Ferry." In his account of the meeting, he twice mentioned "Mr. Seward" and his role in the conversation, and the visit to Halleck.

3. *O.R.,* Vol. 19, Pt. 1, pp. 38–40, McClellan's report.

4. McClellan, *Own Story,* p. 553.

5. *O.R.,* Vol. 19, Pt. 2, pp. 603–4, Special Orders No. 191. Mention of Boonsboro and Frederick in this order, and in letters of the same period, frequently refer to the towns as Boonsborough and Fredericktown.

6. Allan, *Conversations with Lee,* February 15, 1868.

7. *B&L,* Vol. 2, pp. 606–7. Walker stated that Longstreet told him that after memorizing the order, he "chewed it up." After the war, Longstreet wrote that after it was carefully read, the order was "used as some persons use a little cut of tobacco," Longstreet, *M to A,* p. 213.

8. *O.R.,* Vol. 19, Pt. 1, p. 953, Jackson's report.
9. *O.R.,* Vol. 19, Pt. 1, p. 912, Walker's report.
10. *O.R.,* Vol. 19, Pt. 1, pp. 852–53, McLaws's report.
11. *O.R.,* Vol. 19, Pt. 1, p. 145, Lee's report; p. 839, Longstreet's report.
12. *O.R.,* Vol. 19, Pt. 1, p. 839, Longstreet's report.
13. Allan, *Conversations with Lee,* February 15, 1868.
14. *O.R.,* Vol. 19, Pt. 2, pp. 604–5. This was the letter in which Lee enclosed the copy of his proclamation to Marylanders, as noted in the previous chapter.
15. *O.R.,* Vol. 19, Pt. 2, pp. 287, 293.
16. *O.R.,* Vol. 51, Pt. 1, p. 791.
17. *O.R.,* Vol. 19, Pt. 2, p. 203, Curtin to Wool, with copy to Stanton.
18. *O.R.,* Vol. 19, Pt. 2, p. 204.
19. *O.R.,* Vol. 19, Pt. 2, pp. 204–88.
20. *O.R.,* Vol. 19, Pt. 2, p. 268.
21. *O.R.,* Vol. 19, Pt. 1, p. 145, Lee's report.
22. McClellan, *Own Story,* p. 557.
23. *O.R.,* Vol. 19, Pt. 1, p. 40; McClellan, *Own Story,* pp. 554–55.
24. *O.R.,* Vol. 19, Pt. 2, pp. 254–55.
25. *O.R.,* Vol. 19, Pt. 1, p. 41; McClellan, *Own Story,* p. 555.
26. *O.R.,* Vol. 19, Pt. 1, p. 26, McClellan's report; p. 416, Longstreet's report; pp. 208–9, Pleasonton's report.
27. *O.R.,* Vol. 19, Pt. 2, pp. 605–6.
28. *O.R.,* Vol. 19, Pt. 1, p. 151, Lee's report.
29. *O.R.,* Vol. 19, Pt. 1, p. 145, Lee's report.
30. Allan, *Conversations with Lee,* February 15, 1868. On September 13, a Union cavalry division under Brigadier General Alfred Pleasonton had started along the Hagerstown road toward South Mountain. It had proceeded only three or four miles when it encountered some of Stuart's cavalry, and a sharp skirmish ensued. The Confederates withdrew toward Turner's Gap, *O.R.,* Vol. 19, Pt. 1, pp. 208–9, Pleasonton's report; pp. 816–17, Stuart's report.
31. Allan, *Conversations with Lee,* February 15, 1868; memorandum of conversation on same date with E. C. Gordon, Lee's clerk. The order was addressed to Major General D. H. Hill and was signed by Colonel R. H. Chilton, assistant adjutant general on Lee's staff. *B&L,* Vol. 2, p. 603, "The Finding of Lee's Lost Order," by Silas Colgrove, who, at the time of writing, was a Union brevet brigadier general.
    Lee later explained that "he had the orders sent from his own headquarters to Hill, as the latter was now under his immediate command, and it was perfectly proper for General Jackson to do too, to inform Hill that he was not longer under his [Jackson's] orders," Allan, *Conversations with Lee,* February 15, 1868.
32. *O.R.,* Vol. 19, Pt. 2, p. 281, dispatch dated September 13, 1862—12m [midnight].
33. *O.R.,* Vol. 19, Pt. 1, pp. 45–46, McClellan's report.
34. *O.R.,* Vol. 19, Pt. 2, pp. 281–82. The authenticity was established by Williams's adjutant general, Colonel E. S. Pittman, who had served with Chilton before the war and recognized Chilton's signature and handwriting, *B&L.,* Vol. 2, p. 603, Colegrove's article.
    The order was written and signed by Chilton because of a serious injury suffered by Lee on the day after Pope's army had retreated from Manassas. Lee had dismounted, with his horse's bridle looped over his arm, and was talking to Longstreet. When a group of prisoners and their guards suddenly crossed a nearby

railroad embankment, the movement startled the horse, which tossed its head and jumped, throwing Lee to the ground. Both wrists were sprained and bones were broken in his right hand. Six weeks after the accident, Lee wrote to his wife, "My hands are improving slowly. I am now able to sign my name," *Recollections and Letters of General Robert E. Lee,* by his son, Captain Robert E. Lee, published 1904 by Garden City Publishing Company, Inc., Garden City, New York, and reprinted in 1988 by Broadfoot Publishing Company, Wilmington, North Carolina, p. 79 (hereafter cited as *Recollections and Letters of Gen. Lee*). The accident also is recounted in Taylor, *Lee,* p. 115.

35. *O.R.,* Vol. 19, Pt. 1, pp. 374–76, Franklin's report; pp, 416–18, Burnside's report.
36. *O.R.,* Vol. 19, Pt. 2, p. 608.
37. *O.R.,* Vol. 51, Pt. 2, pp. 618–19.
38. *O.R.,* Vol. 19, Pt. 2, p. 608, Chilton to McLaws.
39. *O.R.,* Vol. 19, Pt. 1, pp. 140–41, Lee's report to Davis, September 16; p. 951, dispatch from Jackson at 8:15 P.M. September 14.
40. *O.R.,* Vol. 19, Pt. 1, p. 951, two dispatches from Jackson, September 15 and 16; pp. 852–57, McLaws's report; pp. 912–14, Walker's report.
41. *O.R.,* Vol. 19, Pt. 1, p. 955, Jackson's report.
42. *O.R.,* Vol. 19, Pt. 1, p. 914, Walker's report; p. 857, McLaws's report; p. 982, A. P. Hill's report
43. *O.R.,* Vol. 19, Pt. 1, p. 151, Lee's report; p. 67, McClellan's report; McClellan, *Own Story,* p. 613.
44. *O.R.,* Vol. 19, Pt. 1, p. 67, McClellan's report.
45. *O.R.,* Vol. 19, Pt. 1, p. 151, Lee's report.
46. *O.R.,* Vol. 19, Pt. 2, p. 329.
47. Reading, Pennsylvania, *Daily Times,* September 23, 1862.
48. Allan, *Conversations with Lee,* February 15, 1868.
49. *O.R.,* Vol. 19, Pt. 1, pp. 1070–71, Loring's report to Randolph.
50. *O.R.,* Vol. 19, Pt. 2, pp. 625–26.
51. *O.R.,* Vol. 19, Pt. 2, pp. 626–27.

PART 3: BACK TO VIRGINIA

Chapter 16: After Sharpsburg

1. *O.R.,* Vol. 19, Pt. 2, p. 633. Lee's letter to Loring noted in chapter 15.
2. *O.R.,* Vol. 19, Pt. 2, p. 639, field return of the Army of Northern Virginia for September 30.
3. *O.R.,* Vol. 19, Pt. 2, p. 660, field return of the Army of Northern Virginia for October 10. The September 30 return did not list any cavalry force, but the October 10 return included a cavalry division of 5,761 men.
4. *O.R.,* Ser. 4, Vol. 2, p. 198.
5. *O.R.,* Vol. 19, Pt. 2, pp. 633–34.
6. *O.R.,* Vol. 19, Pt. 2, pp. 643–45, Lee to Davis. Longstreet and Jackson were promoted to lieutenant generals in October. Longstreet refers to it as "about this time," Longstreet, *M to A,* p. 290.

Jackson learned of his promotion on October 11 and, in a letter to his wife on October 20, advised her not to "trouble yourself about representations that are made to your husband. It appears to me that it would be better for you not to have anything written about me," Mrs. Jackson, *Memoirs,* pp. 348–50.

As late as October 22, Lee addressed correspondence to "Major General Jackson" and "Major General Longstreet," *O.R.*, Vol. 19, Pt. 2, pp. 674, 676. The first correspondence in which the two were addressed as lieutenant general was sent from Lee on October 28, *O.R.*, Vol. 19, Pt. 2, pp. 685–86.

Lee formally announced the promotions November 6, when he also listed promotions and assignments made in organizing the two commands into army corps, *O.R.*, Vol. 19, Pt. 2, pp. 698–99.

7. Hotchkiss, *Diary,* p. 87, entry of October 7.
8. *O.R.*, Vol. 19, Pt. 2, p. 55, Lee's letter to Stuart.
9. *O.R.*, Vol. 19, Pt. 2, pp. 52–54, Stuart's report.
10. *O.R.*, Vol. 19, Pt. 2, p. 51.
11. *O.R.*, Vol. 19, Pt. 2, p. 666.
12. *O.R.*, Vol. 19, Pt. 2, pp. 667–68. Loring had been relieved of command October 15 and ordered to Richmond, pp. 666–67.
13. McClellan, *Own Story,* p. 613.
14. *O.R.*, Vol. 19, Pt. 1, p. 69, McClellan's report; McClellan, *Own Story,* p. 622.
15. *O.R.*, Vol. 19, Pt. 2, pp. 3–4, skirmish at Ashby's Gap, September 22; pp. 5–6, expedition from Centreville to Bristoe Station and Warrenton Junction, September 25–28; pp. 7–9, expedition from Centreville to Warrenton and Buckland Mills, September 29; pp. 27–28, reconnaissance from Fairfax Court House to Aldie, October 8–9.
16. *O.R.*, Vol. 19, Pt. 2, p. 4, reconnaissance from Shepherdstown, September 25; p. 9, skirmish near Glenville in western Virginia, September 30; pp. 10–14, reconnaissance from Sharpsburg to Shepherdstown and Martinsburg, October 1; 14–15, reconnaissance from Harpers Ferry to Leesburg, October 1–2; pp. 16–25, operations at Blue Gap (or Hanging Rock), Little Cacapon Bridge, and Paw Paw Tunnel, October 2–4; pp. 25–26, reconnaissance from Loudoun Heights to Neersville and Hillsborough, October 4–6; pp. 26–27, reconnaissance from Conrad's Ferry to Leesburg, October 8.
17. *O.R.*, Vol. 19, Pt. 1, p. 69.
18. *O.R.*, Vol. 19, Pt. 1, p. 70.
19. *O.R.*, Vol. 19, Pt. 1, pp. 70–71.
20. *O.R.*, Vol. 19, Pt. 2, pp. 336–37.
21. *O.R.*, Vol. 19, Pt. 1, p. 72.
22. *O.R.*, Vol. 19, Pt. 1, pp. 72–75.
23. *O.R.*, Vol. 19, Pt. 2, pp. 81–101, reconnaissance from Sharpsburg and Harpers Ferry to Smithfield and Charles Town, October 16–17; expedition to Thoroughfare Gap, October 17–18; reconnaissance from Loudoun Heights to Lovettsville, October 21; and skirmishes at Manassas Junction and near Bristoe Station, October 24.
24. *O.R.*, Vol. 19, Pt. 1, p. 152, Lee's report; *O.R.*, Vol. 19, Pt. 2, p. 676, Lee to Longstreet.
25. *O.R.*, Vol. 19, Pt. 1, p. 152, Lee's report.
26. *O.R.*, Vol. 19, Pt. 2, p. 675.
27. *O.R.*, Vol. 19, Pt. 1, pp. 86–87.
28. *O.R.*, Vol. 19, Pt. 1, p. 152, Lee's report.
29. *O.R.*, Vol. 19, Pt. 2, pp. 697–98.
30. McClellan, *Own Story,* p. 646.
31. McClellan, *Own Story,* pp. 648, 650–52; *O.R.*, Vol. 19, Pt. 2, p. 545, Lincoln to McClellan; p. 557, Burnside's General Order No. 1.

32. *O.R.,* Vol. 19, Pt. 2, pp. 468–69.

33. *O.R.,* Vol. 19, Pt. 2, p. 479.

34. *The Molly Maguires,* by Wayne G. Broehl, Jr., published by Harvard University Press, Cambridge, Massachusetts, 1964, pp. 86–87 (hereafter cited as Broehl, *Molly Maguires*).

35. *O.R.,* Ser. 3, Vol. 3, pp. 1008–9, letter, November 9, 1863, to Lincoln from Charles Albright, a Mauch Chunk, Pennsylvania, attorney who commanded the 34th Pennsylvania Militia, *O.R.,* Vol. 27, Pt. 2, p. 216, and at Reading, Pennsylvania, Department of Susquehanna report of August 31, 1863, *O.R.,* Vol. 29, Pt. 2, p. 137.

    After the war, Albright was attorney for the Lehigh & Wilkes-Barre Coal Company and helped prosecute a number of Molly Maguires, Broehl, *Molly Maguires,* pp. 93, 272, 274, 292, 295, 324, 343.

36. Eavenson, *Coal,* p. 498, production records. The shipments are listed in the *Annual Report of the Geological Survey of Pennsylvania for 1886,* Part 3, Anthracite Coal Regions, published in 1887 by the Board of Commissioners for the Geological Survey, p. 1033 (hereafter cited as *Pennsylvania, Geological Survey*).

    The report lists shipments by railroad and canal in long tons—2,240 pounds, compared with the normal 2,000 pounds per ton. The trend was developed from production records, Eavenson, *Coal,* p. 498, and *Pennsylvania, Geological Survey,* p. 1033.

37. *O.R.,* Vol. 19, Pt. 2, p. 479.

38. *O.R.,* Vol. 19, Pt. 2, p. 500. Bishop Wood met with miners in Pottsville during the time of draft resistance. "He taught them their duty under the laws, and as good citizens," according to Benjamin Bannan, publisher and editor of the Pottsville *Miners' Journal.*

    Bannan, draft commissioner for Schuylkill County, also helped develop a temporary solution, especially in Cass Township. After saying the draft could not be executed in Cass Township "without a bloody conflict," he took advantage of an unusual requirement of the law—that volunteers who had enlisted in county towns or cities had to be credited to townships in which they resided. He obtained affidavits showing that the draft quota for Cass Township had been filled by volunteers, and at once issued an order releasing conscripts of Cass Township from reporting for duty, Broehl, *Molly Maguires,* p. 89.

39. *New York Times,* October 15–18 and 25; November 5.

40. Carl Sandburg, *Abraham Lincoln: The War Years,* four volumes, published by Harcourt, Brace & Company, New York, 1939, Vol. 1, pp. 610–14 (hereafter cited as Sandburg, *Lincoln, The War Years*). *Congressional Quarterly's Guide to U.S. Elections,* published in 1975 by Congressional Quarterly, Inc., Washington, D.C., pp. 607–11.

41. Lancaster [Pennsylvania] *Intelligencer,* November 11, 1862, p. 2, col. 2.

42. *O.R.,* Ser. 2, Vol. 5, p. 108.

43. *O.R.,* Vol. 21, p. 99, Burnside's report.

44. *O.R.,* Vol. 21, pp. 553–55, Lee's report.

45. *O.R.,* Vol. 21, pp. 1020–21.

46. *O.R.,* Vol. 21, pp. 1052–53.

47. *O.R.,* Vol. 21, pp. 546–56, Lee's report.

48. Edward Bates, *Diary,* p. 272.

49. Hotchkiss, *CMH, Virginia,* p. 373.

Chapter 17: Planning Resumed

1. Andrews, *South Reports,* pp. 286–87.
2. Hotchkiss, *CMH, Virginia,* p. 375.
3. Longstreet, *M to A,* p. 331; *B&L,* Vol. 3, p. 246; *Annals of the War,* p. 416; *O.R., Vol. 25,* Pt. 1, p. 795, Lee's report.
4. Henderson, *Jackson,* Vol. 2, p. 386.
5. Hotchkiss, *CMH, Virginia,* p. 375–76.
6. *O.R.,* Vol. 21, p. 1016.
7. *O.R.,* Vol. 21, p. 1077, Special Orders No. 277, December 24, 1862.
8. *O.R.,* Vol. 51, Pt. 2, p. 667.
9. *O.R.,* Vol. 51, Pt. 2, p. 669. *O.R.,* Ser. 4, Vol. 2, pp. 178, 1074. George W. Randolph resigned as secretary of war on November 17 and was replaced four days later by James A. Seddon. Davis submitted Seddon's nomination to the Senate on January 15, 1863, p. 358.
10. *O.R.,* Vol. 21, p. 1082, December 31, 1862, return of the Army of Northern Virginia.
11. *O.R.,* Vol. 21, p. 924, December 31, 1862, return of the Army of the Potomac. Not included were 6,342 troops in the defenses of the Upper Potomac and 63,068 around Washington that had been reported in the return of December 10, p. 1121.
12. *O.R.,* Vol. 21, pp. 1085–86.
13. *O.R.,* Ser. 4, Vol. 2, p. 337.
14. *O.R.,* Vol. 21, p. 1088.
15. *O.R.,* Vol. 18, pp. 52–59, report of Major General John G. Foster, commander of the Union Department of North Carolina.
16. *O.R.,* Vol. 18, pp. 814–15, Seddon's letter of January 3 to Lee.
17. *O.R.,* Vol. 18, pp. 820–21, 825, Lee to Seddon, January 5 and 6.
18. *Lee's Wartime Papers,* pp. 387–88.
19. *O.R.,* Vol. 21, pp. 1091–92.
20. Jones, *Diary,* Vol. 1, p. 239.
21. VHS, *Lee's Telegraph Book.*
22. *O.R.,* Vol. 21, p. 1095, Special Orders No. 17, January 17, 1863.
23. *O.R.,* Vol. 18, p. 850, on January 16, Seddon notified Major General Gustavus W. Smith at Goldsboro that Lee had placed Ransom's division under Smith's control; p. 855, Smith on January 21 reported to Seddon that Ransom's troops were in North Carolina.
24. Reagan, *Memoirs,* pp. 150–51
25. *Personal Memoirs of U. S. Grant,* two volumes, published by Charles L. Webster & Company, New York, 1892, Vol. 1, pp. 422–42, (hereafter cited as Grant, *Personal Memoirs*); *O.R.,* Vol. 24, Pt. 1, pp. 44–47, Grant's report.
26. Grant, *Personal Memoirs,* p. 442.
27. *O.R.,* Vol. 21, pp. 1096–97; *Lee's Wartime Papers,* pp. 391–92.
28. *O.R.,* Vol. 21, pp. 1103–4.
29. *O.R.,* Vol. 21, p. 1108, Davis to Lee, January 22.
30. *O.R.,* Vol. 19, p. 99; *O.R.,* Vol. 21, pp. 752–55, Burnside's reports and extracts from units involved.
31. *O.R.,* Vol. 21, pp. 1004–5, War Department, General Orders No. 20, January 25.
32. *O.R.,* Vol. 21, p. 1110.
33. *O.R.,* Vol. 25, Pt. 2, pp. 597–98.
34. *O.R.,* Vol. 25, Pt. 2, pp. 612–13.

35. *O.R.,* Vol. 25, Pt. 2, p. 598, Lee to Jones; *O.R.,* Vol. 51, Pt. 2, p. 676, Lee to Seddon.

36. *O.R.,* Vol. 14, p. 759.

37. *O.R.,* Vol. 14, pp. 762–63.

38. *O.R.,* Vol. 14, pp. 763–64, Seddon to Lee. Hill, commander of a division in Jackson's 2nd Corps, had been ordered on January 14 to Richmond and to report to Cooper, *O.R.,* Vol. 21, p. 1093. On February 7, he was assigned to command of troops in North Carolina, Special Orders No. 32, adjutant and inspector general's office, *O.R.,* Vol. 18, p. 872.

39. *O.R.,* Vol. 51, Pt. 2, 680.

40. *O.R.,* Vol. 25, Pt. 2, pp. 601–2, Army of Northern Virginia return for January 1863; *O.R.,* Vol. 21, p. 1082, return of December 31, 1862.

41. *O.R.,* Vol. 51, Pt. 2, p. 680, Lee's letter to Seddon.

42. *O.R.,* Ser. 3, Vol. 3, p. 8.

43. *O.R.,* Ser. 3, Vol. 3, pp. 8, 10–11.

44. *O.R.,* Ser. 3, Vol. 3, p. 15.

45. *O.R.,* Vol. 21, pp. 946, 956–57.

46. *O.R.,* Vol. 25, Pt. 2, pp. 621–22, Lee's letters to Stuart and Jones.

47. *O.R.,* Vol. 25, Pt. 2, pp. 622–23, two letters to Seddon; p. 624, letter February 15 to Seddon; p. 627, February 16 letters to Davis and Seddon.

    The troops were the Army of the Potomac's 9th Corps, commanded by Major General William F. Smith. The 1st Division began the transfer to Newport News on February 6, followed by the 2nd on February 9 and the 3rd on February 10, *O.R.,* Vol. 18, p. 149. On March 16, Burnside resumed command of the corps, then went to take command of the Department of Ohio, *O.R.,* Vol. 23, Pt. 2, p. 147.

48. *O.R.,* Vol. 25, Pt. 2, pp. 623–24.

49. *O.R.,* Vol. 25, Pt. 2, p. 632.

50. *O.R.,* Vol. 18, p. 895.

51. *O.R.,* Vol. 18, pp. 898, 902–3.

52. *O.R.,* Vol. 18, pp. 911–12.

53. Hotchkiss, *Diary,* pp. 116–19, entries of February 23–28 and March 2, 4, 10.

54. *The Gettysburg Papers,* Vol. 1, compiled by Ken Bandy and Florence Freeland, published in 1978 by the Press of Morningside Bookshop, Dayton, Ohio, pp. 1–40. *The Strategy of the Gettysburg Campaign,* by Brevet Lieutenant Colonel George B. Davis, 1st Massachusetts Cavalry, April 5, 1898, reprinted from Vol. 3, *Military Historical Society of Massachusetts Papers* (hereafter cited as *Gettysburg Papers*). The reference to Hotchkiss is on p. 5.

55. *O.R.,* Vol. 25, Pt. 2, pp. 642–43.

56. Reagan, *Memoirs,* pp. 151–52.

57. Reagan, *Memoirs,* p. 122.

58. Jones, *Diary,* Vol. 1, pp. 265–66, 271–72.

Chapter 18: Preparing to Move

1. Hotchkiss, *Diary,* pp. 110–19; Jones, *Diary,* Vol. 1, pp. 243–48.

2. *O.R.,* Vol. 25, Pt. 2, pp. 652–53, Imboden to Lee.

3. *O.R.,* Vol. 25, Pt. 2, p. 657, March 3, 1863, return of the Northwestern Brigade.

4. *O.R.,* Vol. 25, Pt. 2, pp. 652–53, Imboden to Lee. On March 6, Seddon informed Samuel Jones that a member of Imboden's cavalry, Captain John H. McNeill, had

discussed the plan with Imboden and then applied for authority to "make a dash on the Baltimore and Ohio Railroad." The plan was viewed favorably by Seddon and Jones, *O.R.*, Vol. 25, Pt. 2, pp. 656–61.

5. *O.R.*, Vol. 25, Pt. 2, p. 661, Lee to Imboden.

6. VHS, *Lee's Telegraph Book.*

7. VHS, *Lee's Telegraph Book.*

8. *O.R.*, Vol. 18, pp. 924–25, Longstreet's letter to Lee; pp. 925–26, Longstreet's letter to D. H. Hill.

9. *O.R.*, Vol. 51, Pt. 2, p. 685.

10. Jones, *Diary*, Vol. 1, pp. 276–77, entry of March 18, 1863.

11. *O.R.*, Vol. 25, Pt. 2, p. 675, Lee to Davis; pp. 675–76, Lee to Major General Arnold Elzey, commanding at Richmond; p. 672, Lee to Cooper, requesting that Pickett's and Hood's divisions be detained until further notice.

12. *O.R.*, Ser. 4, Vol. 2, pp. 446–47.

13. *O.R.*, Ser. 4, Vol. 2, pp. 447–48.

14. *The Diary of Camille Polignac*, U.S. Army History Institute, *Civil War Times Illustrated Collection*, entry of March 25, 1863, hereafter cited as Polignac, *Diary*).

   Polignac was given the rank of lieutenant colonel on July 16, 1861, and served for a time on Beauregard's staff. On January 10, 1863, he was promoted to brigadier general, Boatner, *Dictionary*, p. 637.

   Browne was an aide to the president, *O.R.*, Ser. 4, Vol. 2, pp. 215–16.

15. Polignac, *Diary*, entries of March 25, 26, 27, and 28.

16. *O.R.*, Vol. 25, Pt. 2, pp. 681–82.

17. Hotchkiss, *Diary*, pp. 121–22; Jones, *Diary*, Vol. 1, 277; Kean, *Inside the Confederate Government*, pp. 45–46.

18. *O.R.*, Vol. 25, Pt. 2, pp. 683–84. In his reply on April 1, Seddon explained that the act passed by the Virginia General Assembly to call out slaves to work on fortifications "does not permit a diversion" of slaves from public defense works, *O.R.*, Vol. 51, Pt. 2, p. 690.

19. *O.R.*, Vol. 25, Pt. 2, pp. 685–86. Lee also noted that he had written to Brigadier General William E. Jones that he was to threaten Union forces at Romney, New Creek, and Cumberland to prevent them from moving west, and to Brigadier General Samuel Jones to send two infantry regiments to Imboden and also to threaten Union forces in the Kanawha Valley.

20. *O.R.*, Vol. 25, Pt. 2, pp. 686–87.

21. *O.R.*, Vol. 25, Pt. 2, pp. 693–94. The sentence referring to expeditions into the enemy's country was italicized by the author.

22. Hotchkiss, *Diary*, p. 124.

23. Hotchkiss, *Diary*, p. 126; Jones, *Diary*, Vol. 1, p. 287.

24. Hotchkiss, *Diary*, p. 124, entry of March 29, "General Lee is sick and General J[ackson] went over to see him in the P.M."

25. *Lee's Wartime Papers*, pp. 419–20.

26. *Lee's Wartime Papers*, pp. 426–27.

27. *Lee's Wartime Papers*, pp. 427–29.

28. This letter is in the collection of Michael J. Hammerson of London, who graciously made it available to the author.

29. *Lee's Wartime Papers*, pp. 437–38.

30. *O.R.*, Vol. 51, Pt. 2, pp. 752–53; *Lee's Wartime Papers*, pp. 589–90.

31. *Lee's Wartime Papers*, pp. 595–96.

32. *Lee's Wartime Papers*, pp. 615–16.

33. *Lee's Wartime Papers*, pp. 631–32.
34. Freeman, *Lee Biography*, Vol. 4, pp. 524–25.
35. *O.R.*, Vol. 25, Pt. 2, pp. 700–701.
36. *O.R.*, Vol. 25, Pt. 2, pp. 708–9.
37. *O.R.*, Vol. 25, Pt. 2, pp. 713–14.
38. *O.R.*, Vol. 25, Pt. 2, p. 720.
39. *O.R.*, Vol. 25, Pt. 2, pp. 725–26.
40. *O.R.*, Vol. 18, pp. 269–72, report of Major General John A. Dix, commander of the Union Department of Virginia, with record of events from April 11 to May 4; pp. 329–30, report of Major General Samuel G. French.
41. *O.R.*, Vol. 25, Pt. 2, pp. 724–25.
42. *O.R.*, Vol. 25, Pt. 2, p. 715.
43. *O.R.*, Vol. 25, Pt. 2, p. 735.
44. *O.R.*, Vol. 25, Pt. 2, pp. 788–89.
45. *O.R.*, Vol. 25, Pt. 2, pp. 719–20, General Orders No. 26, headquarters, 2nd Corps, Army of Northern Virginia.
46. *O.R.*, Ser. 3, Vol. 3, pp. 1046–53, report of James B. Fry, provost marshal general, to Stanton.
47. *The Trials for Treason at Indianapolis, Disclosing Plans for Establishing a Northwestern Confederacy*, edited by Benn Pitman, recorder to the Military Commission, and published in 1865 by Moore, Wilstach & Baldwin, Cincinnati, Ohio, with the approval of the judge advocate general and the secretary of war, approval signed by Charles A. Dana, assistant secretary of war; pp. 325–26, from a report of Colonel Joseph Holt, judge advocate general of the U.S. War Department (hereafter cited as *Trials for Treason*). *O.R.*, Ser 2, Vol. 7, p. 935, Holt's report.
48. *O.R.*, Ser. 3, Vol. 3, p. 75.
49. *O.R.*, Ser. 3, Vol. 3, p. 166
50. *O.R.*, Ser. 3, Vol. 3, p. 187.
51. *O.R.*, Vol. 25, Pt. 1, pp. 98–99, Imboden's report.
52. *O.R.*, Vol. 25, Pt. 1, pp. 113–14, William E. Jones's report.
53. *O.R.*, Vol. 25, Pt. 2, pp. 241–42, letter, Major General Robert C. Schenck to Stanton.
54. *O.R.*, Vol. 25, Pt. 2, p. 246, Roberts's letter and Halleck's reply.
55. *O.R.*, Vol. 25, Pt. 2, p. 279.
56. *O.R.*, Vol. 25, Pt. 2, p. 278.
57. *O.R.*, Vol. 25, Pt. 2, p. 279.
58. *O.R.*, Vol. 25, Pt. 2, p. 347.
59. *O.R.*, Vol. 25, Pt. 1, pp. 98–105, Imboden's report; pp. 113–15, William E. Jones's report.
60. *O.R.*, Vol. 25, Pt. 2, p. 819, Lee to Imboden on May 23; *O.R.*, Vol. 25, Pt. 1, p. 105, Lee's endorsement of Imboden's report.
61. *O.R.*, Ser. 4, Vol. 2, p. 530, March 31, 1863, return of Confederate armies; *O.R.*, Vol. 25, Pt. 2, p. 696, March 1863, return of Army of Northern Virginia, includes Valley District, but only two of Longstreet's five divisions; *O.R.*, Vol. 25, Pt. 2, p. 180, March 31, 1863, return of Army of the Potomac.
62. *O.R.*, Vol. 25, Pt. 2, pp. 736–37.
63. *O.R.*, Vol. 25, Pt. 2, p. 738.
64. *O.R.*, Vol. 25, Pt. 2, p. 741.
65. *O.R.*, Vol. 25, Pt. 2, pp. 752–53.
66. *O.R.*, Vol. 51, Pt. 1, p. 1000, Lincoln to Hooker and Hooker's reply. Sandburg,

Lincoln, The War Years, Vol. 2, pp. 84–92; in Lincoln's party was his wife, their son Tad, Attorney General Edward Bates, Dr. Anson G. Henry, and Noah Brooks. The comments about Hooker's objectives were made during a conversation with Brooks.

The latter, a newspaperman and long-time friend of Lincoln's, had come to Washington during the second year of the Civil War as a correspondent for the Sacramento (California) *Union,* Andrews, *North Reports,* p. 54.

67. *O.R.,* Vol. 25, Pt. 2, pp. 256–57, Peck's letter and Hooker's reply; pp. 190–92, earlier reports by Peck.

68. *O.R.,* Vol. 25, Pt. 2, pp. 756–57.

69. *O.R.,* Vol. 25, Pt. 2, p. 760.

70. Cooke, *Jackson,* pp. 439–45; Henderson, *Jackson,* Vol. 2, pp. 453–54, 470–71; Mrs. Jackson, *Memoirs,* pp. 447–57.

71. *O.R.,* Vol. 25, Pt. 2, p. 791.

72. Mrs. Jackson, *Memoirs,* p. 454.

73. Kean, *Inside the Confederate Government,* pp. 55–56; Jones, *Diary,* Vol. 1, pp. 306–10; *O.R.,* Vol. 25, Pt. 2, pp. 775–76, Seddon to Lee.

74. *O.R.,* Vol. 25, Pt. 2, p. 768.

75. *O.R.,* Vol. 25, Pt. 1, p. 805.

Chapter 19: After Chancellorsville

1. *O.R.,* Vol. 25, Pt. 1, pp. 794–95, 804, Lee's report; p. 671, Major General Henry W. Slocum's report.

2. *O.R.,* Vol. 25, Pt. 2, pp. 782–83.

3. Jones, *Diary,* Vol. 1, p. 269, March 7 entry, "the President is sick"; p. 306, May 3, "the President's health is still precarious"; p. 318, May 9, "the President still absents himself from the Executive Office, his health being precarious."

   In a letter on May 20 to Governor Joseph E. Brown of Georgia, Davis confirmed this problem, writing, "Continued illness, which has confined me to my room during several weeks, has prevented a more prompt reply to your letter of the 4th ultimo [April]" *O.R.,* Vol. 52, Pt. 2, pp. 473–74.

4. *O.R.,* Ser. 4, Vol. 2, p. 530, returns of the Confederate Army on April 30 showed an aggregate present of 360,097; Ser. 3, Vol. 3, p. 179, returns of the U.S. Army on April 30 listed the aggregate present as 675,904.

5. *O.R.,* Vol. 14, p. 909, April 23 return of Beauregard's army; p. 434, March return of Major General David Hunter, commander of the Union Department of the South, listed 20,097 men present and ready for duty; p. 451, the April 30 return showed 16,828 enlisted men present for duty.

   O.R., Ser. 4, Vol. 2, p. 530, returns of Confederate Army; *O.R.,* Ser. 3, Vol. 3, p. 179, return of Union Army lists 18,326 present for duty in the Department of the South; *O.R.,* Vol. 14, p. 338, the aggregate present is listed as 16,989; another report, p. 451, lists the number of enlisted men as 16,828.

6. VHS, *Latrobe Diary.*

7. Longstreet, *M to A,* p. 328.

8. Longstreet, *M to A,* pp. 330–31; *SHSP,* Vol. 5, pp. 54–57; *Annals of the War,* pp. 416–17; *The Century Magazine,* Vol. 33, p. 623; *B&L,* Vol. 3, pp. 245–47.

9. Allan, *Conversations with Lee,* April 15, 1868.

10. Longstreet's first article was published in the November 3, 1877, edition of the Philadelphia *Weekly Times.* This was reprinted in the *Southern Historical Society*

Papers, Vol. 5, in 1878, and *Annals of the War,* 1879. Another article was printed in *The Century Magazine* in February 1887. His book, *M to A,* was published in 1896.

11. *O.R.,* Vol. 18, p. 942, Longstreet to Lee; pp. 943–44, Lee to Longstreet.

12. *O.R.,* Vol. 18, pp. 958–60, two letters, Longstreet to Lee, April 3 and 4.

13. *SHSP,* Vol. 5, pp. 54–55; *Annals of the War,* pp. 414–15.

14. Allan, *Conversations with Lee,* February 15, 1868, previously noted in chapter 15.

15. *O.R.,* Vol. 24, Pt. 3, p. 833.

16. *O.R.,* Vol. 24, Pt. 3, p. 842.

17. *O.R.,* Vol. 14, p. 940.

18. *O.R.,* Vol. 25, Pt. 2, p. 790.

19. *O.R.,* Vol. 25, Pt. 2, pp. 791–92.

20. *O.R.,* Vol. 25, Pt. 2, p. 792.

21. Jones, *Diary,* Vol. 1, p. 325. Jones noted that Major General Samuel G. French, too, was at the War Department that day, but that his visit involved a disagreement between French and Longstreet.

22. *O.R.,* Vol. 25, Pt. 2, p. 802, Special Orders No. 116.

23. VHS, *Lee's Telegraph Book.*

24. Jones, *Diary,* Vol. 1, pp. 325–26.

25. *Diary of a Southern Refugee,* by "A Lady of Virginia," and published in 1868 by E. J. Hale & Son, New York, p. 214, entry of Monday, May 18 (hereafter cited as *Diary of a Southern Refugee*).

26. Allan, *Conversations with Lee,* February 19, 1870.

27. *O.R.,* Vol. 25, Pt. 2, p. 479; Hooker was summoned to Washington on May 13 to meet with Lincoln, p. 474.

28. *O.R.,* Vol. 18, p. 720.

29. Andrews, *North Reports,* p. 407.

30. Jones, *Diary,* Vol. 1, p. 329.

31. *O.R.,* Vol. 23, Pt. 2, pp. 836–37.

32. *O.R.,* Vol. 23, Pt. 2, p. 839. Wigfall had served briefly on Beauregard's staff early in the war.

33. *O.R.,* Vol. 24, Pt. 3, pp. 891–92.

Chapter 20: The Struggle for Troops

1. *O.R.,* Vol. 25, Pt. 2, p. 807.

2. *O.R.,* Vol. 25, Pt. 1, pp. 140–44.

3. *O.R.,* Vol. 18, p. 1063.

4. Blackford, *War Years,* p. 210; Von Borcke, *Memoirs,* Vol. 2, pp. 262–63.

5. *O.R.,* Vol. 25, Pt. 2, pp. 696, 814, 846. According to the report of Lafayette Guild, the medical director, Lee's army suffered 10,281 casualties—1,581 killed and 8,700 wounded —in the Battle of Chancellorsville. *O.R.,* Vol. 25, Pt. 1, p. 807.

6. *O.R.,* Vol. 25, Pt. 2, p. 819.

7. *O.R.,* Vol. 25, Pt. 2, pp. 809–10. The officers were Colonel E. P. Alexander and Colonel J. B. Walton of the 1st Corps and Colonel R. Lindsay Walker, identified as an artillery officer in the 3rd Corps. The organization of the Army of Northern Virginia at the time of Chancellorsville (*O.R.,* Vol. 25, Pt. 1, p. 791) identifies Walker as the chief artillery officer of the Light Division, commanded by A. P. Hill following Jackson's wounding. Lee's Special Orders No. 146, of May 30, 1863, reorganizing the army (*O.R.,* Vol. 25, Pt. 2, p. 840) stated that the chief of artillery

was to designate the artillery battalions to serve with the three corps. On June 4, on the recommendation of the chief, Brigadier General William N. Pendleton, Walker was assigned to the 3rd Corps, *O.R.,* Vol. 27, Pt. 3, p. 859.

8. *O.R.,* Vol. 25, Pt. 2, pp. 810–11.
9. Kean, *Inside the Confederate Government,* p. 64; Jones, *Diary,* Vol. 1, p. 352, entry of May 25.
10. *The Making of a Soldier, Letters of General R. S. Ewell,* arranged and edited by Captain Percy Gatling Hamlin of the Medical Corps, Maryland National Guard, published in 1935 by Whittet & Shepperson, Richmond, Virginia (hereafter cited as Ewell, *Making of a Soldier*). Ewell graduated from the U.S. Military Academy in July 1840, was assigned to the First Dragoons, and ordered to Carlisle Barracks. A few months later, on November 20, he was ordered to Fort Wayne, "between Arkansas and the Cherokee Nation," pp. 37–39, Ewell's letter to his brother, Ben, on February 2, 1841.
11. *O.R.,* Vol. 25, Pt. 2, pp. 819–20.
12. *O.R.,* Vol. 25, Pt. 2, pp. 820–21.
13. *O.R.,* Vol. 24, Pt. 3, p. 916.
14. *O.R.,* Vol. 24, Pt. 1, pp. 276–77, Pemberton's report.
15. *O.R.,* Vol. 25, Pt. 2, pp. 832–33.
16. *O.R.,* Vol. 25, Pt. 2, p. 834.
17. *Lee's Dispatches,* p. 91.
18. *O.R.,* Vol. 25, Pt. 2, pp. 824–25.
19. Hotchkiss, *Diary,* pp. 145–46. The day after he heard of his promotion, Ewell and his cousin, Lizinka Campbell Brown, a widow, were married, p. 103, Ewell, *Making of a Soldier.*
20. *O.R.,* Vol. 25, Pt. 2, p. 840, Special Orders No. 146, reorganizing the Army of Northern Virginia; p. 839, letter from Longstreet's headquarters to Hood.
21. *The Letters of Major General J. E. B. Stuart,* edited by Adele H. Mitchell and published in 1990 by the Stuart-Mosby Historical Society, pp. 320–22 (hereafter cited as Stuart-Mosby Historical Society, *Letters of J. E. B. Stuart*).
22. *O.R.,* Vol. 25, Pt. 2, pp. 836–37.
23. *O.R.,* Vol. 25, Pt. 2, pp. 841–43.

Chapter 21: Preparing for the Invasion

1. *O.R.,* Vol. 27, Pt. 2, pp. 308, 318, Lee's reports.
2. Allan, *Conversations with Lee,* April 15, 1868.
3. Bean, *Sandie Pendleton,* pp. 131–32.
4. Bean, *Sandie Pendleton,* p. 134, letter to Kate. The source of this information is cited in Bean's book as the William N. Pendleton Papers (No. 1466) in the Southern Historical Collection at the University of North Carolina, Pendleton's reference to Harrisburg does not appear in the book, but is in his letter of June 18 in the Pendleton Papers.
5. Quoted previously in chapter 9.
6. Marshall, *Aide-de-Camp,* p. 174.
7. Marshall, *Aide-de-Camp,* p. 183.
8. Marshall, *Aide-de-Camp,* p. 74.
9. Marshall, *Aide-de-Camp,* pp. 187–88.
10. Marshall, *Aide-de-Camp,* pp. 190–94.

11. Long, *Memoirs*, pp. 267–68.
12. Long, *Memoirs*, pp. 268–69.
13. Taylor, *Lee*, p. 180; *Four Years*, pp. 90–91.
14. Lee died October 12, 1870, before he could begin writing a history of the Army of Northern Virginia. Of the five top commanders who served with him until the Battle of Gettysburg (Jackson, Longstreet, Stuart, A. P. Hill, and Ewell), only Longstreet and Ewell survived the war. Ewell, who died January 25, 1872, wrote nothing about the war, except for occasional mention of it in personal correspondence.
15. *B&L*, Vol. 3, pp. 247–49, Longstreet's article, *Lee's Invasion of Pennsylvania*. This article also was published in *The Century Magazine*, Vol. 33, No. 4, p. 623, in February 1887.
16. Longstreet, *M to A*, pp. 333–34.
17. John S. Mosby, *Stuart's Cavalry in the Gettysburg Campaign*, a two-part article in the October and November 1891 issues of *Belfords Monthly and Democratic Review*, produced by Belford & Company, Publishers, of New York (hereafter cited as Mosby, *Belfords Monthly*); Part 1, in the October issue, pp. 149–52. This magazine is in the archives of the Museum of the Confederacy in Richmond.

    Mosby provided a more detailed account of the Gettysburg Campaign in his book, *Stuart's Cavalry in the Gettysburg Campaign*, published by Moffat, Yard & Company, New York, in 1908, and reprinted in 1984 by Confederate Printers, Falls Church, Virginia. In the book, Mosby on several occasions referred to the article in *Belfords Monthly*, first, in the Preface, p. v, and then in the text, p. 195. In the second reference, in countering criticism of Stuart, Mosby stated, "He knew that his orders had required him to leave General Lee in Virginia, and join Ewell in Pennsylvania, and that he had full authority to pass through Hooker's army and cross the Potomac at Seneca." In closing, Mosby raised the question "How could Stuart pass around Hooker and at the same time keep between Hooker and Lee?" p. 221.
18. Mosby, *Belfords Monthly*, Pt. 1, p. 152.
19. Allan, *Conversations with Lee*, April 15, 1868, as quoted in this chapter's first page.
20. Hotchkiss, *Diary*, p. 146.
21. A letter from Stuart to Major Walter H. Taylor of Lee's staff, datelined "Headquarters Cavalry Division, Army of Northern Virginia, June 1st, 1863" (Stuart-Mosby Historical Society, *Letters of J. E. B. Stuart*, pp. 322–23), raises some doubt about his presence at the meeting of "the generals." While it establishes that he was at his headquarters for a time that day, it does not clearly eliminate the possibility that he also attended the session at Lee's headquarters.
22. Hotchkiss, *CMH, Virginia*, p. 396.
23. Allan, *Conversations with Lee*, February 19, 1870.
24. *O.R.*, Vol. 25, Pt. 2, pp. 848–49.
25. *O.R.*, Vol. 27, Pt. 2, p. 293.
26. *O.R.*, Vol. 27, Pt. 3, pp. 859–60.
27. *O.R.*, Vol. 27, Pt. 2, p. 293.
28. *O.R.*, Vol. 27, Pt. 2, pp. 545–46, Rodes's report; p. 293, Lee's report.
29. *O.R.*, Vol. 27, Pt. 3, p. 858, two letters, one from Lee, one from Colonel Long of Lee's staff. *O.R.*, Vol. 25, Pt. 2, p. 763, organization of Jenkins's brigade.
30. *O.R.*, Vol. 27, Pt. 3, pp. 865–66.
31. *O.R.*, Vol. 27, Pt. 3, p. 865, Lee to Imboden, and p. 866, Lee to Jones, both on June 7.

32. *O.R.,* Vol. 25, Pt. 2, p. 840, Special Orders No. 146 of May 30, 1863, for reorganization of the Army of Northern Virginia; *O.R.,* Vol. 27, Pt. 3, pp. 866–67.

 Trimble had been seriously wounded in the Second Battle of Bull Run in 1862 and, in the spring of 1863, suffered from an attack of erysipelas. On May 15, he informed Lee that he was nearly recovered. Five days later, Lee offered him the command of the Valley "if your health permits," *O.R.,* Vol. 25, Pt. 2, pp. 801, 812.

33. H. B. McClellan, *I Rode with Jeb Stuart,* p. 263.

34. *O.R.,* Vol. 27, Pt. 3, p. 3, G. S. Smith to Pleasonton, who forwarded the message to Hooker on June 3. Early in April, Assistant Secretary of War P. H. Watson had sent Smith to Pleasonton, then commanding a cavalry division. Smith reported to Pleasonton, who sent him to Hooker's headquarters, *O.R.,* Vol. 25, Pt. 2, pp. 196–97, Pleasonton to Watson. Smith may have been a Union spy who had penetrated to Richmond that spring, or else was a pro-Union refugee who had escaped from the Confederate capital into Federal lines. No identification is mentioned in the *O.R.* references.

35. *O.R.,* Vol. 25, Pt. 2, p. 595.

36. *O.R.,* Vol. 27, Pt. 1, pp. 29–30.

37. *O.R.,* Vol. 27, Pt. 1, pp. 31–32.

38. *O.R.,* Vol. 27, Pt. 1, pp. 32–33, telegram to Lincoln at 9:15 P.M. June 5.

39. *O.R.,* Vol. 27, Pt. 2, pp. 293–94.

40. *Lee's Dispatches,* pp. 101–2.

41. *O.R.,* Ser. 4, Vol. 2, pp. 580–82. Seddon informed the governors that this action could be taken under two laws enacted by Congress—one to provide for local defense and special service, approved August 21, 1861 (*O.R.,* Ser. 4, Vol. 1, p. 579); the other to form volunteer companies for local defense, approved October 13, 1862 (*O.R.,* Ser. 4, Vol. 2, pp. 206–7).

42. *O.R.,* Vol. 27, Pt. 3, pp. 868–69.

43. *O.R.,* Vol. 27, Pt. 3, p. 882.

44. *O.R.,* Vol. 27, Pt. 2, pp. 545–46.

45. *O.R.,* Vol. 27, Pt. 3, pp. 27–28; instructions regarding supporting units on pp. 29–34.

46. H. B. McClellan, *I Rode with Jeb Stuart,* p. 262.

47. Blackford, *War Years,* p. 213; *O.R.,* Vol. 27, Pt. 2, pp. 679–80, Stuart's report. The fog is not mentioned in the report.

48. *O.R.,* Vol. 27, Pt. 2, pp. 439–40, Ewell's report.

49. Stuart-Mosby Historical Society, *Letters of J. E. B. Stuart,* pp. 263–65. The actual number of killed, wounded, and missing was listed as 485 in Stuart's report, *O.R.,* Vol. 27, Pt. 2, p. 719. Ninety more casualties were reported later by Colonel E. V. White, commander of the 35th Virginia Cavalry Battalion, *O.R.,* Vol. 27, Pt. 2, pp. 768–70. Total Union casualties were 866, *O.R.,* Vol. 27, Pt. 1, pp. 168–70.

50. *O.R.,* Vol. 27, Pt. 3, p. 38.

51. *O.R.,* Vol. 27, Pt. 1, p. 903.

52. *O.R.,* Vol. 27, Pt. 3, p. 40.

53. *O.R.,* Vol. 27, Pt. 3, pp. 47–48, letter addressed to Seth Williams, assistant adjutant general on Hooker's staff, was received at the War Department at 9 P.M. June 9.

54. *O.R.,* Vol. 27, Pt. 1, p. 904.

55. Stuart-Mosby Historical Society, *Letters of J. E. B. Stuart,* pp. 323–25, closing paragraph of letter to his wife.

PART 4: ON THE ROAD TO GETTYSBURG

Chapter 22: Starting North Again

1. *O.R.,* Vol. 27, Pt. 3, pp. 878–79.
2. In chapter 21, statements of Longstreet, Mosby, and Hotchkiss. *O.R.,* Vol. 27, Pt. 3, p. 879, Lee's letter to Ewell.
3. *O.R.,* Vol. 27, Pt. 3, pp. 880–82.
4. *O.R.,* Vol. 27, Pt. 3, p. 904, Davis to Lee, June 19; pp. 930–31, Lee to Davis, June 25.
5. Marshall, *Aide-de-Camp,* pp. 186–87.
6. *O.R.,* Vol. 27, Pt. 3, pp. 140, 241.
7. Alexander H. Stephens, *A Constitutional View of the War Between the States,* two volumes, published in 1868 by the National Publishing Company, Philadelphia, Pennsylvania; Cincinnati, Ohio; and Atlanta, Georgia; and by Zeigler, McCurdy & Company, Chicago, Illinois, and St. Louis, Missouri (hereafter cited as Stephens, *Constitutional View of the War Between the States*), Vol. 2, pp. 557–61; *Messages and Papers of Davis and Confederacy,* Vol. 1, pp. 339–41.
8. Rowland, *Jefferson Davis Papers,* Vol. 5, p. 525.
9. *O.R.,* Ser. 3, Vol. 3, pp. 88–93.
10. *O.R.,* Ser. 3, Vol. 3, pp. 321–22, 324–25, 330–32.
11. *O.R.,* Vol. 27, Pt. 3, p. 32.
12. *O.R.,* Vol. 27, Pt. 3, pp. 54–55, 68–69.
13. Hotchkiss, *Diary,* p. 150, entry of June 10.
14. *O.R.,* Vol. 27, Pt. 2, pp. 546–47, Rodes's report.
15. *O.R.,* Vol. 27, Pt. 2, pp. 439–40, Ewell's report.
16. Hotchkiss, *Diary,* p. 151, entry of June 12.
17. Kean, *Inside the Confederate Government,* p. 73.
18. *O.R.,* Vol. 27, Pt. 2, p. 440, Ewell's report; p. 459, Early's report; p. 547–48, Rodes's report.
19. Hotchkiss, *Diary,* p. 150, entry of June 11.
20. *O.R.,* Vol. 27, Pt. 2, p. 687, Stuart's report.
21. Longstreet, *M to A,* p. 340.
22. *The Century Magazine,* Vol. 33, No. 44, February 1887, Longstreet's article, *Lee's Invasion of Pennsylvania,* p. 623.
23. *O.R.,* Vol. 27, Pt. 2, p. 306, Lee's report.
24. *O.R.,* Vol. 27, Pt. 1, pp. 34–35.
25. *O.R.,* Vol. 27, Pt. 1, p. 35, telegrams from Lincoln and Halleck.
26. *O.R.,* Vol. 27, Pt. 1, p. 36.
27. *O.R.,* Vol. 27, Pt. 1, p. 39.
28. Alexander, *Memoirs,* p. 368, based on returns of the Army of Northern Virginia for May 31, *O.R.,* Ser. 4, Vol. 2, p. 615.
29. *O.R.,* Vol. 25, Pt. 2, p. 574.
30. Alexander, *Memoirs,* p. 368; Jenkins's force, *O.R.,* Vol. 27, Pt. 2, p. 547, Rodes's report.
31. *O.R.,* Vol. 25, Pt. 2, pp. 589–92, returns of May 31.
32. *O.R.,* Vol. 27, Pt. 2, pp. 547–49, Rodes's report.
33. *O.R.,* Vol. 27, Pt. 3, pp. 68–69, Couch's order; pp. 79–80, Curtin's proclamation.

34. *O.R.,* Vol. 27, Pt. 3, p. 76, Curtin to Stanton; p. 77, Stanton's reply.
35. *O.R.,* Vol. 27, Pt. 2, pp. 211–12, Couch's report.
36. *O.R.,* Vol. 27, Pt. 3, p. 111. Scott's position as superintendent of the Pennsylvania Railroad is noted in Sandburg, *The War Years,* Vol. 1, p. 77. In *O.R.,* Ser. 3, Vol. 4, p. 1049, a letter written by Scott on January 13, 1865, identifies him as vice president of the railroad.
37. *O.R.,* Vol. 27, Pt. 3, p. 112.
38. *O.R.,* Vol. 27, Pt. 3, p. 113.
39. *O.R.,* Vol. 27, Pt. 3, p. 113.
40. *O.R.,* Vol. 27, Pt. 3, p. 134, Scott to Curtin; p. 135, Scott to Howe and Thompson.
41. *O.R.,* Ser. 3, Vol. 3, pp. 360–61; Vol. 27, Pt. 3, pp. 136–37.
42. *O.R.,* Vol. 27, Pt. 3, p. 137.
43. *O.R.,* Vol. 27, Pt. 3, pp. 141–42.
44. *O.R.,* Vol. 27, Pt. 3, p. 169.
45. *O.R.,* Vol. 27, Pt. 3, pp. 169–70.
46. *O.R.,* Ser. 3, Vol. 3, p. 363; *O.R.,* Vol. 27, Pt. 2, p. 787, Mosby's report.

Chapter 23: The Seeds of Disaster

1. Jones, *Diary,* Vol. 1, pp. 332–44, entries from May 27 to June 10; p. 359, entry of June 23, "Grant again repulsed in a furious attempt to take Vicksburg."
2. Allan, *Conversations with Lee,* March 3, 1868. Lee also noted that in 1864, during the Wilderness Campaign, he found Ewell "prostrate on the ground" on May 17 or 18. While Lee indicates that it was the result of another attack of despondency, all the records refer to the situation in that period as related to Ewell's "sickness." On May 29, Early was put in command of the 2nd Corps because of the "temporary absence of General Ewell" due to sickness, *O.R.,* Vol. 36, Pt. 3, p. 846; on June 13, Ewell was assigned to command of the Department of Richmond, *O.R.,* Vol. 40, Pt. 2, p. 646. During this period, in a conversation with Ewell, Lee remarked that he had been "constantly uneasy about you since last fall," Hamlin, *Making of a Soldier,* p. 128; Early, *Memoirs,* p. 361.
3. Allan, *Conversations with Lee,* March 3, 1868.
4. VHS, *Lee's Telegraph Book.*
5. *O.R.,* Vol. 27, Pt. 3, p. 887.
6. *O.R.,* Vol. 27, Pt. 3, p. 888.
7. *Lee's Wartime Papers,* pp. 514–15.
8. *O.R.,* Vol. 27, Pt. 3, p. 890.
9. VHS, *Lee's Telegraph Book; Lee's Wartime Papers,* p. 515; *Lee's Dispatches,* p. 102.
10. VHS, *Lee's Telegraph Book.*
11. *O.R.,* Vol. 27, Pt. 3, p. 890.
12. *O.R.,* Vol. 27, Pt. 3, p. 896.
13. *O.R.,* Vol. 27, Pt. 3, p. 900.
14. *O.R.,* Vol. 27, Pt. 3, pp. 900–901.
15. *O.R.,* Vol. 27, Pt. 2, p. 296.
16. *O.R.,* Vol. 27, Pt. 2, pp. 295–96, Lee to Davis; pp. 501–2, Johnson's report.
17. *O.R.,* Vol. 27, Pt. 2, p. 357, Longstreet's report, July 27, 1863.
18. VHS, *Latrobe Diary.*
19. *O.R.,* Vol. 27, Pt. 3, p. 1090, itinerary of Kemper's Brigade.
20. *O.R.,* Vol. 27, Pt. 2, p. 366, Kershaw's report.

21. Colonel Harold B. Simpson, *Gaines Mill to Appomattox, Waco and McLennan County [Texas] in Hood's Texas Brigade,* published in 1963 by Texian Press, Waco, Texas, p. 130–31. This is a history of Company E, 4th Texas Regiment.

22. *A Life for the Confederacy, as Recorded in the Pocket Diaries of Pvt. Robert A. Moore, Co. G, 17th Mississippi Regiment, Confederate Guards,* Holly Springs, Mississippi, edited by James W. Silver and published in 1959 by McCowat-Mercer Press, Inc., Jackson, Tennessee, p. 151.

23. John C. West, *A Texan in Search of a Fight, being the diary and letters of a private soldier in Hood's Texas Brigade,* published in 1901 and reprinted in 1969 by Texian Press, Waco, Texas, p. 75.

24. *O.R.,* Vol. 27, Pt. 2, pp. 313–14, Lee's report.

25. *O.R.,* Vol. 27, Pt. 2, p. 550, Rodes's report.

26. *O.R.,* Vol. 27, Pt. 2, p. 462, Ewell's report.

27. *O.R.,* Vol. 27, Pt. 2, p. 503, Johnson's report; p. 464, Early's report.

Chapter 24: Alarm in Pennsylvania, Confusion in Washington

1.   *O.R.,* Vol. 27, Pt. 3, p. 131.

2.   Historical Times, *Civil War Encyclopedia,* p. 187. Couch graduated from West Point in 1846 along with Thomas J. Jackson. He also had served as a naturalist on a Smithsonian Institution expedition to Mexico during a leave of absence in 1853.

3.   Pottsville *Miners' Journal,* July 4, 1863. The article refers to the arrest on "Tuesday last" (June 30).

4.   New York *Herald,* July 1, 1863.

5.   *O.R.,* Vol. 27, Pt. 2, p. 548, Rodes's report.

6.   Hoke, *Great Invasion,* pp. 97–113. Hoke observed much of the activity from the second floor of his residence on the public square, p. 96.

7.   *O.R.,* Vol. 27, Pt. 2, p. 551, Rodes's report.

8.   *O.R.,* Vol. 51, Pt. 1, p. 1055.

9.   *O.R.,* Vol. 27, Pt. 1, pp. 39–40.

10. *O.R.,* Vol. 27, Pt. 3, pp. 101–2.

11. *O.R.,* Vol. 27, Pt. 1, p. 40.

12. *O.R.,* Vol. 27, Pt. 1, pp. 40–41.

13. *O.R.,* Vol. 27, Pt. 1, pp. 41–42. Halleck said that information from Pleasonton was unsatisfactory and contradictory.

14. *O.R.,* Vol. 27, Pt. 1, p. 43.

15. *O.R.,* Vol. 27, Pt. 1, pp. 43–44.

16. *O.R.,* Vol. 27, Pt. 1, p. 44.

17. *O.R.,* Vol. 27, Pt. 1, p. 44.

18. *O.R.,* Vol. 27, Pt. 1, p. 45, Hooker to Lincoln; p. 47, Lincoln's response.

19. *O.R.,* Vol. 27, Pt. 1, p. 45.

20. *O.R.,* Vol. 27, Pt. 1, pp. 45–46.

21. *O.R.,* Vol. 27, Pt. 1, p. 46.

22. *O.R.,* Vol. 27, Pt. 1, p. 46.

23. *O.R.,* Vol. 27, Pt. 1, p. 47.

24. *O.R.,* Vol. 27, Pt. 3, pp. 174–75.

25. *O.R.,* Vol. 27, Pt. 3, pp. 171–72, letter to Pleasonton from Brigadier General Seth Williams, assistant adjutant general on Hooker's staff.

26. *O.R.,* Vol. 27, Pt. 1, p. 48.

27. *O.R.,* Vol. 27, Pt. 2, p. 688, Stuart's report; p. 306, Lee's report; *O.R.,* Vol. 27, Pt. 1, p. 50, Hooker to Halleck.
28. *O.R.,* Vol. 27, Pt. 1, pp. 907–8.
29. *O.R.,* Vol. 27, Pt. 2, pp. 688–89.
30. *O.R.,* Vol. 27, Pt. 1, pp. 52–53.
31. Jones, *Diary,* Vol. 1, p. 352.

Chapter 25: Change in Plans

1. *O.R.,* Vol. 27, Pt. 3, p. 905.
2. *O.R.,* Vol. 27, Pt. 2, p. 296.
3. *O.R.,* Vol. 27, Pt. 2, from the reports of Rodes, p. 550; Johnson, p. 503; Early, p. 464.
4. Hotchkiss, *Diary,* pp. 153–54.
5. *O.R.,* Vol. 27, Pt. 2, pp. 550–51, Rodes's report.
6. *O.R.,* Vol. 27, Pt. 2, p. 442, Ewell's report.
7. *O.R.,* Vol. 27, Pt. 2, p. 24.
8. *Military Annals of Tennessee, Confederate,* edited by John B. Lindsley and published in 1886 by J. M. Lindsley & Company, Nashville, Tennessee, pp. 295–96. The 11th Regiment is listed in the Army of Tennessee in reports of January 21, April 1, July 31, and August 31, 1863, *O.R.,* Vol. 23, Pt. 2, pp. 613, 734, 941, 958.
9. *O.R.,* Vol. 27, Pt. 3, p. 904.
10. *O.R.,* Vol. 27, Pt. 2, p. 357.
11. *O.R.,* Vol. 27, Pt. 2, p. 297, Lee to Davis.
12. *SHSP,* Vol. 5, p. 58
13. Longstreet, *M to A,* p. 336.
14. *O.R.,* Vol. 27, Pt. 3, pp. 905–6.
15. *O.R.,* Vol. 27, Pt. 3, p. 906.
16. *O.R.,* Vol. 27, Pt. 3, pp. 941–42.
17. *O.R.,* Vol. 27, Pt. 2, pp. 296–97.
18. *O.R.,* Vol. 27, Pt. 3, pp. 921–23, General Orders No. 72.
19. Kean, *Inside the Confederate Government,* p. 75.
20. *O.R.,* Vol. 27, Pt. 3, p. 129, Couch to Stanton.
21. Kean, *Inside the Confederate Government,* p. 75.
22. Longstreet, *M to A,* pp. 336–37.
23. *O.R.,* Vol. 25, Pt. 2, pp. 841–42, Davis to Lee; p. 832, Lee to Davis, May 30, regarding the problem of drawing troops from D. H. Hill's command. Both letters are quoted previously in chapter 19.
24. *O.R.,* Vol. 27, Pt. 1, p. 142, itinerary of the Army of the Potomac, June 3 to July 31, 1863.
25. *O.R.,* Vol. 27, Pt. 1, p. 911, Pleasonton's report.
26. *O.R.,* Vol. 27, Pt. 3, pp. 227–28, letter of Daniel Butterfield, Hooker's chief of staff, to "Commanding Officer, Cavalry Corps"; p. 229, order to Meade.
27. *O.R.,* Vol. 27, Pt. 1, pp. 911–12, Pleasonton to General S. Williams.
28. *O.R.,* Vol. 27, Pt. 2, pp. 690–91, Stuart's report.
29. *O.R.,* Vol. 27, Pt. 2, p. 357, Longstreet's report.
30. *O.R.,* Vol. 27, Pt. 2, pp. 691–92, Stuart's report.
31. *O.R.,* Vol. 27, Pt. 2, p. 316, Lee's report.
32. Longstreet, *M to A,* p. 340.

33. Longstreet, *M to A,* p. 341.
34. Long, *Memoirs,* p. 271.
35. Marshall, *Aide-de-Camp,* pp. 198–99. It is not clear from the statements of Long and Marshall exactly when Lee arrived in the Shenandoah Valley. Long said he arrived at Berryville on June 18. Marshall states that Lee left Paris, at the eastern base of Ashby's Gap, on the afternoon of June 21 and camped near Millwood that night. Millwood and Berryville are west of the Shenandoah River on separate roads leading to Winchester. Millwood is about five miles south of Berryville.

    The accurate dates are determined, however, by two letters from Lee to Davis and another to Samuel Jones, commanding the Department of Western Virginia. The first letter to Davis was datelined "Headquarters, near Millwood, Va., June 19, 1863," VHS, *Lee's Letter Book; Lee's Wartime Papers,* p. 320. The second letter was datelined "Berryville, June 20, 1863," *O.R.,* Vol. 27, Pt. 2, pp. 296–97. The letter to Jones also was written from Berryville on June 20, *O.R.,* Vol. 27, Pt. 3, p. 906.

Chapter 26: Lee's Deep Concern

1. *O.R.,* Vol. 27, Pt. 2, p. 443, Ewell's report.
2. *O.R.,* Vol. 27, Pt. 2, pp. 550–51, Rodes's report.
3. Marshall, *Aide-de-Camp,* pp. 199–201.
4. *O.R.,* Vol. 27, Pt. 3, p. 914.
5. Marshall, *Aide-de-Camp,* p. 203.
6. *O.R.,* Vol. 27, Pt. 3, pp. 914–15.
7. *Lee's Wartime Papers,* pp. 524–25. The source of both letters is identified as VHS, *Lee's Letter Book.*
8. Marshall, *Aide-de-Camp,* p. 201; *O.R.,* Vol. 27, Pt. 2, p. 692, Stuart's report.
9. Marshall, *Aide-de-Camp,* pp. 201–2.
10. Marshall, *Aide-de-Camp,* pp. 202–3; *O.R.,* Vol. 27, Pt. 3, p. 913.
11. Marshall, *Aide-de-Camp,* pp. 204–6; *O.R.,* Vol. 27, Pt. 3, p. 915.
12. *O.R.,* Vol. 27, Pt. 2, p. 692, Stuart's report.
13. Marshall, *Aide-de-Camp,* pp. 207–9; *O.R.,* Vol. 27, Pt. 3, p. 923.
14. Marshall, *Aide-de-Camp,* pp. 210–11.
15. McClellan, *I Rode with Jeb Stuart,* pp. 315–17.
16. *O.R.,* Vol. 27, Pt. 2, p. 707, Stuart's report.
17. *O.R.,* Vol. 27, Pt. 2, pp. 307, 316, Lee's report.
18. MHI, Mosby's letter of February 19, 1896, to Lunsford L. Lomax, who was among former Confederate officers helping compile documents for publication in the *Official Records* (*O.R.,* Preface, p. xi). In the letter, Mosby referred to correspondence with Marshall in the spring of 1887.
19. Marshall, *Aide-de-Camp,* p. 204.
20. *O.R.,* Vol. 27, Pt. 2, p. 297; *Lee's Wartime Papers,* pp. 529–30.
21. *O.R.,* Vol. 27, Pt. 3, pp. 924–25.
22. *O.R.,* Vol. 27, Pt. 3, pp. 925–26.
23. *O.R.,* Vol. 27, Pt. 3, pp. 930–31.
24. *O.R.,* Vol. 27, Pt. 3, pp. 931–33.
25. *O.R.,* Vol. 27, Pt. 1, pp. 75–77. It created a situation somewhat similar to the lost order incident of 1862, only this time, the consequences were not as drastic. Halleck, however, did pass the information to a subordinate in the area in which Beauregard was operating.

On July 5, Halleck informed Brigadier General Quincey A. Gillmore, commander of the Union Department of the South, that "according to latest reports, Generals Magruder and Smith were pressing toward New Orleans and endeavoring to separate General Banks from that city. The conditions of affairs here is such that we cannot at present reinforce General Banks from the north. It is therefore proposed that you immediately send to New Orleans such forces as you can temporarily spare from your proposed operations.

"You will perceive from the intercepted dispatches of Jeff. Davis and General Cooper, copies of which were sent to you by mail, that General Beauregard would dispatch troops to reinforce General Johnston, the moment any of ours left the vicinity of Charleston for the Mississippi River. It is therefore important that you conceal as much as possible the departure of any troops you may send to New Orleans." *O.R.*, Vol. 28, Pt. 2, p. 14.

26.	Allan, *Conversations with Lee,* February 19, 1870.
27.	*O.R.,* Vol. 28, Pt. 2, pp. 162–63.
28.	*O.R.,* Vol. 28, Pt. 1, pp. 66–67.
29.	*O.R.,* Vol. 28, Pt. 2, p. 173.
30.	Mosby, *Stuart's Cavalry in the Gettysburg Campaign,* Introduction, pp. vii–viii.

Chapter 27: The Endangered North

1.	In chapter 24; *O.R.,* Vol. 27, Pt. 3, p. 131, Couch's letter to Stanton.
2.	*O.R.,* Vol. 27, Pt. 2, p. 212, Couch's report.
3.	Baer, *Canals and Railroads,* pp. 64–68 and 1860 map.
4.	*O.R.,* Vol. 27, Pt. 3, p. 132.
5.	*O.R.,* Vol. 27, Pt. 3, p. 135–36.
6.	*O.R.,* Vol. 27, Pt. 3, p. 144.
7.	*O.R.,* Vol. 27, Pt. 3, p. 163.
8.	*O.R.,* Vol. 27, Pt. 3, pp. 160, 186, Special Orders Nos. 4 and 6.
9.	*O.R.,* Vol. 27, Pt. 3, p. 240, Special Orders No. 10.
10.	*O.R.,* Vol. 27, Pt. 3, p. 251.
11.	*O.R.,* Vol. 27, Pt. 3, p. 264.
12.	U.S. Geological Survey Department maps at the Pennsylvania Bureau of Topographic and Geological Survey, Department of Environmental Resources, Harrisburg, Pennsylvania.
13.	Maps at the Pennsylvania State Archives; Baer, *Canals and Railroads,* p. 66 and 1860 map.
14.	*Confederate Invasion of the West Shore—1863,* by Robert Grant Crist and published in 1963 by the Lemoyne Trust Company, Lemoyne, Pennsylvania, p. 7 (hereafter cited as Crist, *Confederate Invasion*). This paper was presented at a meeting of the Cumberland County Historical Society and Hamilton Library Association, Carlisle, Pennsylvania, on March 23, 1962. The source of this information is cited as *Military Survey of the Susquehanna River—1861: A Report to Brig. Gen. Pleasonton, Commanding the Philadelphia Home Guard,* in the Manuscript Division of the Historical Society of Pennsylvania, Philadelphia, Pennsylvania.
15.	Baer, *Canals and Railroads,* pp. 53–54 and 1860 map.
16.	*O.R.,* Vol. 27, Pt. 3, p. 263, returns of the Departments of the Susquehanna and Monongahela.
17.	*O.R.,* Vol. 27, Pt. 3, pp. 184–85, Colonel G. W. Mindil, commander of the 27th New Jersey Regiment, on June 15 reported to Stanton from Cincinnati, Ohio, that

his 800 men were on their way home to be mustered out, but that their services were offered for Pennsylvania's defense; Stanton instructed him to proceed to Pittsburgh, but to be prepared to stop in Wheeling if they should be needed there; p. 1080, Mindil notified New Jersey Governor Joel Parker on June 20 that his regiment had been accepted for Pennsylvania's defense and that it was in Wheeling, but added that it "will be home shortly."

18. *O.R.,* Vol. 27, Pt. 2, pp. 215–16, Couch's report.
19. *O.R.,* Vol. 27, Pt. 2, p. 212, Couch's report.
20. *O.R.,* Vol. 27, Pt. 3, p. 201.
21. *O.R.,* Vol. 27, Pt. 3, p. 235.
22. *O.R.,* Vol. 27, Pt. 2, p. 212, Couch's report.
23. *O.R.,* Vol. 27, Pt. 2, p. 219, report of the New York adjutant general.
24. *O.R.,* Vol. 27, Pt. 3, pp. 142–43, 201, 222–23.
25. *O.R.,* Vol. 27, Pt. 3, p. 142.
26. *O.R.,* Vol. 27, Pt. 3, p. 264.
27. *O.R.,* Vol. 27, Pt. 3, p. 407.
28. *O.R.,* Vol. 27, Pt. 2, p. 212, Couch's report.
29. Crist, *Confederate Invasion,* pp. 16–21; Wilbur S. Nye, *Here Come the Rebels!* published in 1965 by the Louisiana State University Press, reprinted in 1984 by Morningside House, Inc., Dayton, Ohio, pp. 222–27 (hereafter cited as Nye, *Here Come the Rebels*).
30. *O.R.,* Vol. 27, Pt. 2, p. 230, report of Yates.
31. *O.R.,* Vol. 27, Pt. 3, p. 132, Special Orders No. 3.
32. Nye, *Here Come the Rebels,* p. 285.
33. In chapter 24; *O.R.,* Vol. 27, Pt. 3, p. 131.
34. *O.R.,* Vol. 27, Pt. 2, p. 212, Couch's report; p. 232, report of Brigadier General William Hall, 3rd Brigade, New York National Guard; p. 245, report of Brigadier General Jesse C. Smith, 11th Brigade, New York National Guard; Nye, *Here Come the Rebels,* pp. 237–39; *Shippensburg in the Civil War,* published in 1964 by the Shippensburg Historical Society, Shippensburg, Pennsylvania, pp. 24–25 (hereafter cited as *Shippensburg*).
35. *O.R.,* Vol. 27, Pt. 2, p. 212, Couch's report.
36. *O.R.,* Vol. 27, Pt. 3, p. 238.
37. *O.R.,* Vol. 27, Pt. 3, p. 251, Milroy to Couch; p. 253, Couch to Stanton.
38. *O.R.,* Vol. 27, Pt. 2, pp. 770–71, White's report.
39. *O.R.,* Vol. 27, Pt. 3, p. 233.

Chapter 28: Marching into Pennsylvania

1. *O.R.,* Vol. 51, Pt. 2, p. 725, General Orders No. 10.
2. *O.R.,* Vol. 51, Pt. 2, p. 726; *O.R.,* Vol. 27, Pt. 3, pp. 914–15, Lee to Ewell, and p. 923, Lee to Stuart.
3. *O.R.,* Vol. 51, Pt. 2, pp.725–26.
4. In chapter 25; *O.R.,* Vol. 27, Pt. 3, p. 914; Marshall, *Aide-de-Camp,* pp. 199–201.
5. *O.R.,* Vol. 27, Pt. 2, p. 443, Ewell's report; p. 464, Early's report.
6. *O.R.,* Vol. 27, Pt. 2, p. 551, Rodes's report.
7. Hoke, *Great Invasion,* pp. 132–35.
8. *O.R.,* Vol. 27, Pt. 2, p. 503, Johnson's report.
9. *O.R.,* Vol. 27, Pt. 3, p. 924.
10. *O.R.,* Vol. 27, Pt. 2, p. 297.

11. *O.R.,* Vol. 27, Pt. 1, p. 143, itinerary of the Army of the Potomac.

12. Hoke, *Great Invasion,* p. 135.

13. *O.R.,* Vol. 27, Pt. 2, p. 551, Rodes's report.

14. Hoke, *Great Invasion,* pp. 135–46.

15. *O.R.,* Vol. 27, Pt. 2, p. 443, Ewell's report.

16. Hotchkiss, *Diary,* p. 134.

17. Hoke, *Great Invasion,* p. 135; *O.R.,* Vol. 27, Pt. 2, p. 551, Rodes's report.

18. Hoke, *Great Invasion,* p. 147.

19. *O.R.,* Vol. 27, Pt. 2, p. 464, Early's report.

20. Hamlin, *Making of a Soldier,* p. 121.

21. *O.R.,* Vol. 27, Pt. 2, pp. 464–65, Early's report; Hoke, *Great Invasion,* p. 157.

22. *O.R.,* Vol. 27, Pt. 2, p. 316, Lee's report.

23. *O.R.,* Vol. 27, Pt. 2, p. 443, Ewell's report.

24. *O.R.,* Vol. 27, Pt. 2, p. 466, Early's report.

25. *Reminiscences of the Civil War,* by John B. Gordon, published in 1903 by Charles Scribners Sons, New York, pp. 38–39 (hereafter cited as Gordon, *Reminiscences*).

26. In chapter 26; Allan, *Conversations with Lee,* March 3, 1868.

27. *O.R.,* Vol. 27, Pt. 2, pp. 306–7, Lee's report; p. 358, Longstreet's report; *O.R.,* Vol. 27, Pt. 3, p. 1090, itinerary of Kemper's Brigade; *B&L,* Vol. 3, p. 249. There is no mention of the crossing in Hill's report, but Captain C. B. Brunson of Hill's Reserve Artillery Battalion noted that his force reached Shepherdstown on June 24 and crossed the Potomac the next day, *O.R.,* Vol. 27, Pt. 2, p. 677.

28. Selected passage from the *Ralph J. Moses Autobiography,* No. 529 in the Southern Historical Collection, Library of the University of North Carolina, Chapel Hill, p. 60 (hereafter cited as Moses, *Autobiography*).

29. *O.R.,* Vol. 27, Pt. 2, p. 692, Stuart's report.

30. *O.R.,* Vol. 27, Pt. 2, pp. 770–71, White's report.

31. In chapter 27.

32. *O.R.,* Vol. 27, Pt. 2, p. 692, Stuart's report.

33. Mosby, *Stuart's Cavalry in the Gettysburg Campaign,* pp. 76–78. Mosby's reference to "the seven corps" must have been an oversight in which Pleasonton's force was not recognized as the "cavalry corps" of the Army of the Potomac. Mosby pointed out that the Union right was on the Potomac near Leesburg, the left at Thoroughfare Gap, "and Pleasonton with his cavalry and Meade's corps" in the center at Aldie.

34. *O.R.,* Vol. 27, Pt. 1, pp. 142–43, Army of the Potomac itinerary.

35. Mosby, *Bedford's Monthly,* November 1891, p. 266.

36. *O.R.,* Vol. 27, Pt. 1, p. 143, Army of the Potomac itinerary.

37. In chapter 25.

38. *O.R.,* Vol. 27, Pt. 2, p. 692, Stuart's report.

39. *O.R.,* Vol. 27, Pt. 2, pp. 693–94, Stuart's report.

40. *O.R.,* Vol. 27, Pt. 2, p. 307, Lee's report; p. 462, Stuart's report.

41. Allan, *Conversations with Lee,* April 15, 1868.

42. H. B. McClellan, *Stuart,* p. 321.

43. Jones, *Diary,* Vol. 1, p. 366.

Chapter 29: To the Banks of the Susquehanna

1. *O.R.,* Vol. 27, Pt. 2, pp. 307, 316, Lee's reports; p. 358, Longstreet's report.

2. *O.R.,* Vol. 27, Pt. 2, p. 358, Longstreet's report; p. 307, Lee's report; Hoke, *Great Invasion,* p. 153.

3. *Shippensburg,* p. 28; previously noted in chapter 26; *O.R.,* Vol. 27, Pt. 2, p. 443, Ewell's report.

4. *O.R.,* Vol. 27, Pt. 2, pp. 55–56, report of Daniel; *Shippensburg,* pp. 27–28.

5. Hotchkiss, *Diary,* pp. 154–55.

6. In chapter 27.

7. Hotchkiss, *Diary,* p. 155; Nye, *Here Come the Rebels,* p. 303; Hoke, *Great Invasion,* p. 173.

8. Hotchkiss, *Diary,* p. 155; Nye, *Here Come the Rebels,* pp. 303–5.

9. *O.R.,* Vol. 27, Pt. 2, p. 443, Ewell's report.

10. Hotchkiss, *Diary,* p. 155; Nye, *Here Come the Rebels,* pp. 307–8; *O.R.,* Vol. 27, Pt. 2, p. 443, Ewell's report.

11. Nye, *Here Come the Rebels,* p. 308; Hotchkiss, *Diary,* pp. 155–56. Another officer, Captain Johnson, is mentioned as being with Richardson and Clark. Neither Clark nor Johnson is identified by initials or first name, or by title. They are presumably members of Ewell's staff.

12. Early, *Memoirs,* p. 255.

13. Early, *Memoirs,* pp. 255–56.

14. *O.R.,* Vol. 27, Pt. 22, p. 465, Early's report; Early, *Memoirs,* p. 256.

15. *O.R.,* Vol. 27, Pt. 3, p. 362.

16. *O.R.,* Vol. 27, Pt. 3, p. 344, Hastings to Adjutant General Lorenzo Thomas.

17. *O.R.,* Vol. 27, Pt. 3, p. 344.

18. *O.R.,* Vol. 27, Pt. 2, p. 465, Early's report; Early, *Memoirs,* pp. 256–58; Hoke, *Great Invasion,* pp. 171–72.

19. *O.R.,* Vol. 27, Pt. 2, pp. 465–66, Early's report.

20. Early, *Memoirs,* pp. 258–59.

21. Hoke, *Great Invasion,* pp. 160–63, 169. Hoke was looking from a second-floor window of his house on the northeast corner of the square when the officers arrived. As soon as Lee was recognized, he and others dashed into the street to observe the meeting with Hill and the movements that followed.

    Hoke explained that a courier system had been set up to keep officials in Harrisburg informed of enemy movements, pp. 158–59. A former county judge, F. M. Kimmell, had been placed in charge of the operation by Curtin. Since telegraph lines to Washington had been cut, it was impossible to notify Federal authorities of enemy activity. Instead, a number of young couriers from Chambersburg and Franklin County took the information directly to Harrisburg. Most of the dispatches were verbal, but ones of significant importance were written on slips of paper. Couriers carrying such slips were ordered to swallow dispatches if capture seemed imminent.

22. Hoke, *Great Invasion,* p. 174; *O.R.,* Vol. 27, Pt. 2, p. 677, report of Captain E. B. Brunson, commanding the Reserve Artillery Battalion.

23. Hoke, *Great Invasion,* p. 174; *O.R.,* Vol. 2, p. 358, Longstreet's report.

24. *O.R.,* Vol. 27, Pt. 22, p. 366, report of Brigadier General Joseph B. Kershaw.

25. *O.R.,* Vol. 27, Pt. 3, pp. 942–43.

26. Prologue.

27. Marshall, *Aide-de-Camp,* pp. 216–18; Long, *Memoirs,* p. 274; Prologue.

28. *O.R.,* Vol. 27, Pt. 2, pp. 692–93, Stuart's report.

29. *O.R.,* Vol. 27, Pt. 3, p. 388.

30. *O.R.,* Vol. 27, Pt. 3, pp. 297–98.

31. *O.R.,* Vol. 27, Pt. 2, p. 278, Frick's report.

32. *O.R.,* Vol. 27, Pt. 3, p. 401.

33. *O.R.,* Vol. 27, Pt. 3, p. 292, Warren to Hooker.

34. *O.R.,* Vol. 27, Pt. 2, pp. 290–91, Hooker to Howard.
35. *O.R.,* Vol. 27, Pt. 1, pp. 55–56, Hooker to Halleck.
36. *O.R.,* Vol. 27, Pt. 3, p. 295.
37. *O.R.,* Vol. 27, Pt. 1, p. 143, Army of the Potomac itinerary.
38. *O.R.,* Vol. 27, Pt. 3, p. 305. The first references to the right wing of the Army of the Potomac appear in two letters by Reynolds on June 25 to Brigadier General Seth Williams, assistant adjutant general on Hooker's staff. Both letters are addressed from "Headquarters Right Wing, Poolesville [Maryland]," *O.R.,* Vol. 27, Pt. 3, p. 320.
39. *O.R.,* Vol. 27, Pt. 3, p. 307.
40. *O.R.,* Vol. 27, Pt. 3, p. 306.
41. *O.R.,* Vol. 27, Pt. 3, p. 314, Hooker's orders.
42. *O.R.,* Vol. 27, Pt. 1, p. 143, Army of the Potomac itinerary.
43. *O.R.,* Vol. 27, Pt. 1, p. 143, Army of the Potomac itinerary.
44. *O.R.,* Vol. 27, Pt. 1, p. 58.
45. *O.R.,* Vol. 27, Pt. 1, p. 59, Daniel Butterfield, chief of staff, to Halleck and War Department.
46. *O.R.,* Vol. 27, Pt. 1, p. 59.
47. *O.R.,* Vol. 27, Pt. 1, p. 60.
48. *O.R.,* Vol. 27, Pt. 1, p. 60.
49. *O.R.,* Vol. 27, Pt. 3, p. 362, War Department General Orders No. 194.
50. *O.R.,* Vol. 27, Pt. 1, pp. 61–62.
51. Hotchkiss, *Diary,* p. 155.
52. *John B. Gordon Papers,* The University of Georgia Libraries, Athens, Georgia.
53. *The Civil War Memoirs of Captain William J. Seymour, Reminiscences of a Louisiana Tiger,* edited by Terry L. Jones, published in 1991 by the Louisiana State University Press, pp. 68–69.
54. Early, *Memoirs,* p. 265.
55. In chapter 3.
56. *O.R.,* Vol. 27, Pt. 3, p. 347, Dana assigned to duty in Philadelphia; pp. 365–66, Dana to John S. Schultze, assistant adjutant general, Department of the Susquehanna; p. 408, Stanton to Dana, June 29.
57. *O.R.,* Vol. 27, Pt. 3, p. 403, Schenck to Halleck, Thomas S. Burrows at Conowingo Bridge, and DuPont.
58. *O.R.,* Vol. 27, Pt. 3, p. 298, E. D. Morgan, former governor of New York, to Stanton; pp. 367–68, Mayor George Opdyke of New York to Welles.
59. *O.R.,* Ser. 3, Vol. 3, p. 421.
60. *O.R.,* Vol. 27, Pt. 3, p. 409.
61. *O.R.,* Vol. 27, pp. 437–38, Schenck's order and proclamation.
62. *O.R.,* Vol. 27, Pt. 3, p. 168, Lieutenant Colonel Ambrose Thompson, in New York, to Lincoln; p. 391, C. A. Walborn, postmaster of Philadelphia, to Stanton; p. 410, S. F. Miller from Louisville, Kentucky, to Lincoln; p. 435, J. Edgar Thomson, Philadelphia, to Lincoln; p. 436, A. K. McClure, Philadelphia, to Lincoln.
63. *O.R.,* Vol. 27, Pt. 3, pp. 407–8.
64. *Lancaster County 1841–1941,* by Frederic Shriver Klein, associate professor of history, Franklin and Marshall College, Lancaster, Pennsylvania, published in 1941 by the Lancaster County National Bank, p. 46 (hereafter cited as Klein, *Lancaster County*).
65. *O.R.,* Vol. 27, Pt. 2, p. 213, Couch's report.
66. *O.R.,* Vol. 27, Pt. 2, p. 277, Frick's report.

67. *O.R.,* Vol. 27, Pt. 2, p. 996, Haller's report; p. 278, Frick's report; Nye, *Here Come the Rebels,* p. 290.
68. Hotchkiss, *Diary,* p. 155.
69. Hotchkiss, *Diary,* pp. 117, 155; Bean, *Sandie Pendleton,* p. 136.
70. Bean, *Sandie Pendleton,* pp. 136–37.
71. *O.R.,* Vol. 27, Pt. 2, p. 443, Ewell's report.
72. Nye, *Here Come the Rebels,* pp. 328–30; *A History of Mechanicsburg and the Surrounding Area,* by Norman D. Keefer, published in 1976 by the Mechanicsburg Area Historical Committee, pp. 48–49 (hereafter cited as Keefer, *Mechanicsburg History*).
73. MHI Archives, *Civil War Round Table Collection,* Rhoda Hoerner papers. The name C. B. Niesley appears in the index of *History of Cumberland and Adams Counties, Pennsylvania,* published in 1886 by Warner, Beers & Company, Chicago, reprinted in 1874 by Unigraphic, Inc., Evansville, Indiana, and sponsored by the Cumberland County Historical Society, Carlisle, Pennsylvania, and Adams County Historical Society, Gettysburg, Pennsylvania (hereafter cited as *Cumberland and Adams Counties History*). On pp. 255–56, Niesley is identified as the secretary of the Allen and East Pennsborough Society for the Recovery of Stolen Horses and Mules and the Detection of Thieves.
74. *O.R.,* Vol. 27, Pt. 2, pp. 220–21, report of Brigadier General William F. Smith; p. 234, report of Brigadier General John Ewen; Nye, *Here Come the Rebels,* pp. 333–41.
75. Nye, *Here Come the Rebels,* p. 342; *The Gettysburg Campaign: A Study in Command,* by Edwin B. Coddington, published in 1968 by Charles Scribner's Sons, reprinted in 1979 by Morningside Press, Dayton, Ohio, p. 188 (hereafter cited as Coddington, *Gettysburg Campaign*). *Martial Deeds of Pennsylvania,* by Samuel P. Bates, published in 1873 by T. H. Davis & Company, Philadelphia, Pennsylvania, p. 182 (hereafter cited as Bates, *Martial Deeds*).
76. *O.R.,* Vol. 27, Pt. 2, p. 491, Gordon's report. The exact time of the surrender is not clear. In another account, Gordon stated that the mayor and other people of York met his command on Sunday morning, June 28, on the pike just before his troops entered the city, Gordon, *Reminiscences,* p. 142. In his report, Early stated that the surrender was made on the night of June 27, *O.R.,* Vol. 27, Pt. 2, p. 466; but later stated that it had occurred early on June 28 as Gordon was approaching York, Early, *Memoirs,* p. 259.
77. *O.R.,* Vol. 27, Pt. 2, p. 466, Early's report; Early, *Memoirs,* p. 259.
78. *O.R.,* Vol. 27, Pt. 2, p. 466, Early's report.
79. MHI Archives, *Documents of the Loyal Legion of the United States, Massachusetts Commandery.*
80. Gordon, *Reminiscences,* pp. 142–44.
81. *Gettysburg Papers,* Vol. 1, p. 5.
82. In chapter 16. The letters quoted there are in *O.R.,* Vol. 21, pp. 1020–21, 1052–53.
83. Gordon, *Reminiscences,* p. 147. Although he could not have known on June 28 that Meade had replaced Hooker as commander of the Army of the Potomac, Gordon in this postwar account referred to Meade as the Union commander.
84. *O.R.,* Vol. 27, Pt. 2, pp. 491–92, Gordon's report.
85. *O.R.,* Vol. 27, Pt. 2, pp. 278–79, Frick's report.
86. Gordon, *Reminiscences,* pp. 147–48; *O.R.,* Vol. 27, Pt. 2, p. 492.
87. *O.R.,* Vol. 27, Pt. 2, p. 467, Early's report; Early, *Memoirs,* pp. 260–61.

Chapter 30: And Then Back to Gettysburg

1. Marshall, *Aide-de-Camp*, p. 218.
2. *O.R.*, Vol. 27, Pt. 2, p. 443, Ewell's report.
3. *O.R.*, Vol. 27, Pt. 2, p. 606, Hill's report.
4. Marshall, *Aide-de-Camp*, pp. 218–19. Marshall referred to the enemy advance as having reached "Frederickstown." He meant Frederick, northwest of Washington, on the route followed by most of the Union forces.
5. Marshall, *Aide-de-Camp*, pp. 219–20.
6. *O.R.*, Vol. 27, Pt. 3, pp. 943–44.
7. Southern Historical Collection, Wilson Library, University of North Carolina, Chapel Hill, *James Longstreet Papers*, No. 3081.
8. Gordon, *Reminiscences*, p. 149.
9. *O.R.*, Vol. 27, Pt. 2, p. 467, Early's report; p. 492, Gordon's report.
10. In chapter 27; *O.R.*, Vol. 27, Pt. 1, pp. 61–62.
11. *O.R.*, Vol. 27, Pt. 1, p. 62, Halleck to Meade at 1 P.M.
12. *O.R.*, Vol. 27, Pt. 1, p. 114, Meade's report.
13. *O.R.*, Vol. 27, Pt. 1, pp. 62–63, Meade to Halleck, sent at 1 P.M. and received in Washington at 2:20 P.M.; p. 63, Halleck's response.
14. *O.R.*, Vol. 27, Pt. 1, p. 114, Meade's report; *O.R.*, Vol. 27, Pt. 3, pp. 378, 382, 401–2, Meade's letters to French.
15. *O.R.*, Vol. 27, Pt. 1, pp. 64–65, Meade's letter to Halleck.
16. *O.R.*, Vol. 27, Pt. 1, p. 66, Halleck's response.
17. *O.R.*, Vol. 27, Pt. 3, pp. 375–76, Meade's orders.
18. *O.R.*, Vol. 27, Pt. 1, p. 62.
19. *O.R.*, Vol. 27, Pt. 2, p. 693, Stuart's report; Blackford, *War Years*, p. 223; H. B. McClellan, *I Rode with Jeb Stuart*, p. 323; Chambliss had taken command of William Henry Fitzhugh Lee's brigade following the latter's wounding at Brandy Station, p. 283.
20. *O.R.*, Vol. 27, Pt. 2, pp. 751–52, Jones's report; Blackford, *War Years*, pp. 228–29, notes that Robertson's and Jones's forces remained at Upperville and did not join Lee's army until after the Battle of Gettysburg.
21. *O.R.*, Vol. 27, Pt. 1, p. 62, Halleck to Meade.
22. *O.R.*, Vol. 27, Pt. 1, p. 62, Meade to Halleck.
23. *O.R.*, Vol. 27, Pt. 1, pp. 63–64, one dispatch was sent at 2 P.M., the other at 7:20 P.M.
24. *O.R.*, Vol. 27, Pt. 1, p. 63, Meade to Halleck at 3 P.M.
25. *O.R.*, Vol. 27, Pt. 1, p. 63.
26. *O.R.*, Vol. 27, Pt. 1, p. 64, Meade's dispatch sent at 3 P.M., received in Washington at 4:55 P.M.
27. *O.R.*, Vol. 27, Pt. 1, p. 66, Halleck's dispatch sent at 7:20 P.M.
28. *O.R.*, Vol. 27, Pt. 1, p. 66, sent at 7:25 P.M.
29. *O.R.*, Vol. 27, Pt. 1, pp. 64–65, sent at 8:15 P.M.
30. *O.R.*, Vol. 27, Pt. 1, p. 64.
31. *O.R.*, Vol. 27, Pt. 2, pp. 685–86, Stuart's report; Blackford, *War Years*, pp. 223–25; H. B. McClellan, *I Rode with Jeb Stuart*, pp. 323–25.
32. *O.R.*, Vol. 27, Pt. 1, p. 114, Meade's report.
33. *O.R.*, Vol. 27, Pt. 1, p. 243, Doubleday's report; p. 702, Howard's report; p. 592, Birney's report; p. 666, report of Brigadier General Horatio G. Wright, command-

ing 1st Division, 6th Corps. (Report of Major General John Sedgwick, commander of the 6th Corps, pp. 663–64, deals only with the fighting).

34. *O.R.,* Vol. 27, Pt. 1, p. 595, Major General George Sykes's report.

35. *O.R.,* Vol. 27, Pt. 1, p. 367, Hancock's report.

36. *O.R.,* Vol. 27, Pt. 1, p. 114, Meade's report.

37. *O.R.,* Vol. 27, Pt. 3, p. 402, Meade's circular.

38. *O.R.,* Vol. 27, Pt. 1, pp. 66–67. A notation with the letter states that it was found on the body of a soldier killed June 30 near Glen Rock, Pennsylvania, south of York, near the Maryland line.

39. *O.R.,* Vol. 27, Pt. 1, pp. 67–68.

40. *O.R.,* Vol. 27, Pt. 3, p. 433, Halleck to Couch.

41. *O.R.,* Vol. 27, Pt. 3, p. 433, Couch to Halleck.

42. *O.R.,* Vol. 27, Pt. 1, p. 67. This explanation appears near the end of Meade's letter of June 29 to Halleck.

43. *O.R.,* Vol. 27, Pt. 1, pp. 68–69, Meade to Halleck. The note about a similar letter to Couch appears at the end of the letter to Halleck.

44. *O.R.,* Vol. 27, Pt. 1, p. 69, Stanton to Meade.

45. *O.R.,* Vol. 27, Pt. 2, p. 317, Lee's report.

46. *O.R.,* Vol. 27, Pt. 2, p. 606, Hill's report.

47. *O.R.,* Vol. 27, pp. 443–44, Ewell's report; p. 503, Johnson's report; p. 558, report of Brigadier General James A. Walker, commanding the Stonewall Brigade.

48. *O.R.,* Vol. 27, Pt. 2, pp. 443–44, Ewell's report.

49. *O.R.,* Vol. 27, Pt. 2, pp. 467–68, Early's report.

50. *SHSP,* Vol. 4, p. 156, Heth's paper, *"Causes of Lee's Defeat at Gettysburg"*; *The Memoirs of Henry Heth,* edited by James L. Morrison, Jr., published in 1974 by Greenwood Press, Westport, Connecticut, and London, p. 174 (hereafter cited as Heth, *Memoirs*).

51. *O.R.,*Vol. 27, Pt. 2, pp. 695–96, Stuart's report; H. B. McClellan, *I Rode with Jeb Stuart,* pp. 327–29; Blackford, *War Years,* pp. 225–28.

52. *Encounter at Hanover,* published in 1963 by the Historical Publication Committee of the Hanover Chamber of Commerce, p. 84.

53. *O.R.,* Vol. 27, Pt. 2, p. 696, Stuart's report.

54. *O.R.,* Vol. 27, Pt. 2, pp. 696–97, Stuart's report.

55. H. B. McClellan, *I Rode with Jeb Stuart,* p. 330; Blackford, *War Years,* p. 228.

56. *O.R.,* Vol. 27, Pt. 2, p. 697, Stuart's report; p. 308, Lee's preliminary report.

57. *O.R.,* Vol. 27, Pt. 2, p. 637, Heth's report.

58. In chapter 28.

59. *O.R.,* Vol. 27, Pt. 2, p. 637, Heth's report.

60. *O.R.,* Vol. 27, Pt. 2, p. 637; Heth, *Memoirs,* p. 173.

61. *O.R.,* Vol. 27, Pt. 1, p. 114, Meade's report; p. 926, Buford's report.

62. *O.R.,* Vol. 27, Pt. 2, p. 637, Heth's report.

63. *O.R.,* Vol. 27, Pt. 1, p. 114, Meade's report.

64. *O.R.,* Vol. 27, Pt. 2, pp. 307, 317, Lee's report; p. 606, Hill's report.

65. *O.R.,* Vol. 27, Pt. 1, pp. 114–15, Meade's report.

66. *O.R.,* Vol. 27, Pt. 2, p. 317, Lee's report.

67. *O.R.,* Vol. 27, Pt. 1, p. 115, Meade's report.

68. *O.R.,* Vol. 27, Pt. 2, p. 504, Johnson's report; p. 470, Early's report.

69. Marshall, *Aide-de-Camp,* pp. 227–28.

70. *O.R.,* Vol. 27, Pt. 3, pp. 947–48, Lee to Imboden.

71. *O.R.,* Vol. 27, Pt. 2, p. 358, Longstreet's report.
72. *O.R.,* Vol. 27, Pt. 1, pp. 115–16, Meade's report.
73. *O.R.,* Vol. 27, Pt. 2, p. 318, Lee's report.
74. *O.R.,* Vol. 27, Pt. 2, p. 308, Lee's preliminary report of July 31, 1863; pp. 318–19, Lee's report of January 1864.
75. *O.R.,* Vol. 27, Pt. 2, p. 446, Ewell's report.
76. *O.R.,* Vol. 27, Pt. 2, p. 358, Longstreet's report.
77. *O.R.,* Vol. 27, Pt. 1, p. 116, Meade's report.
78. Blackford, *War Years,* p. 230.
79. In chapter 18; *Lee's Wartime Papers,* pp. 589–90, Lee to Davis; pp. 595–96, letter to his wife, September 14, 1863; pp. 625–26, letter to his wife, October 20, 1863; *Civil War Times Illustrated,* Vol. 18, No. 8, December 1979, article by Harris D. Riley, Jr., M.D., *Robert E. Lee's Battles with Disease.*
80. Gordon, *Reminiscences,* p. 176.
81. *Textbook of Materia Medica,* by A. S. Blumgarten, M.D., F.A.C.P., fourth edition, published in 1928 by the MacMillan Company, pp. 403, 407; *Drug Evaluations,* sixth edition, published in 1986 by the American Medical Association, Chicago, Illinois, p. 1584; *Goodman and Gilman's The Pharmacological Basis of Therapeutics,* eighth edition, published in 1990 by Pergamon Press; and the 1993 edition of the *Physicians' Desk Reference.*
82. *O.R.,* Vol. 27, Pt. 2, p. 320, Longstreet's report; p. 385, Major Charles S. Peyton of Garnett's brigade states in his report that his troops did not reach the field until 9 A.M. July 3; pp. 387–88, Major James Dearing states that his artillery battalion reached the battlefield area about dusk on the 2nd and bivouacked in the rear of the 1st Corps; Long, *Memoirs,* p. 388, states that Pickett's division "was fresh, having taken no part in the previous days fighting," July 2.
83. *O.R.,* Vol. 27, Pt. 2, p. 697, Stuart's report; H. B. McClellan, *I Rode with Jeb Stuart,* p. 331; Blackford, *War Years,* p. 228.
84. *O.R.,* Vol. 27, Pt. 2, p. 320, Lee's report; p. 359, Longstreet's report; p. 608, Hill's report.
85. *O.R.,* Vol. 27, Pt. 2, p. 697, Stuart's report.
86. *O.R.,* Vol. 27, Pt. 2, p. 447, Ewell's report.
87. *O.R.,* Vol. 27, Pt. 2, p. 359, Longstreet's report; Longstreet, *M to A,* pp. 385–88.
88. *O.R.,* Vol. 27, Pt. 2, pp. 308, 320, Lee's reports.
89. *O.R.,* Vol. 27, Pt. 2, pp. 359–60, Longstreet stated that it was about 2 P.M. when Pickett was in position, and the artillery was ordered to open fire; p. 608, A. P. Hill stated in his report that the cannonade started at 1 P.M.; p. 447, Ewell's report stated that it was "after 2 o'clock." Meade said the Confederate artillery opened fire "at 1 P.M. on the 3rd," *O.R.,* Vol. 27, Pt. 1, p. 117.
90. Boatner, *Dictionary,* p. 339.
91. *Revised Report of the Select Committee Relative to the Soldiers' National Cemetery,* published in 1865 by the Pennsylvania House of Representatives, p. 149, report of Samuel Weaver, superintendent of the exhuming of Union dead in the Gettysburg battlefield.
92. *O.R.,* Vol. 27, Pt. 2, p. 309, Lee's preliminary report; p. 311, Lee's General Orders No. 74, July 4, 1863.

Chapter 31: After the Battle

1. *O.R.,* Vol. 27, Pt. 2, pp. 309–10, 322–23, Lee's reports.
2. *O.R.,* Vol. 27, Pt. 1, pp. 117–18, Meade's report; p. 489, French's report.

3. *Lee's Wartime Papers,* pp. 540–41.
4. *Lee's Wartime Papers,* pp. 543–44; copy of letter at MHI, *Alvan C. Gillem Papers.*
5. *Lee's Wartime Papers,* p. 544. Lee's previous requests are noted in chapter 24 and chapter 25.
6. *Lee's Wartime Papers,* p. 545.
7. *O.R.,* Vol. 27, Pt. 3, p. 986.
8. *Lee's Wartime Papers,* p. 546.
9. *O.R.,* Vol. 27, Pt. 2, pp. 309–10, 323, Lee's reports.
10. Longstreet, *M to A,* pp. 429–30.
11. *O.R.,* Vol. 27, Pt. 2, pp. 448–49, Ewell's report. Hotchkiss, *Diary,* p. 161, notes that on July 13, the wagon trains, including his wagon, had crossed the pontoon bridge, and added, "It rained throughout the day and very hard at night." In his July 14 entry, Hotchkiss stated: "Everything came safely over. General Ewell came up to our camp at 4 A.M. and we moved to a dry place in the woods. The day was quite pleasant and we all dried ourselves." He also described July 15 as "a fine warm day."
12. Kean, *Inside the Confederate Government,* pp. 76–77; Richmond defenses also noted in Jones, *Diary,* Vol. 1, pp. 367–69.
13. Basil W. Duke, *Morgan's Cavalry,* published in 1909 by the Neale Publishing Company, New York and Washington, D.C., pp. 297, 339–40.
14. Jones, *Diary,* Vol. 1, p. 366.
15. *Richmond Whig,* July 1, 1863.
16. *Richmond Daily Dispatch,* July 1, 1863.
17. *Richmond Whig,* July 2, 1863.
18. In chapters 3 and 4.
19. Andrews, *The South Reports,* p. 28.
20. *Historical Times Civil War Encyclopedia,* p. 402.
21. Jones, *Diary,* Vol. 1, pp. 18–19, 24, 36–38, 52, 55.
22. Jones, *Diary,* Vol. 1, pp. 369–71.
23. Kean, *Inside the Confederate Government,* pp. 78–79.
24. Jones, *Diary,* Vol. 1, p. 371.
25. *Richmond Whig* and *Richmond Daily Dispatch,* July 7, 1863.
26. Jones, *Diary,* Vol. 1, pp. 373–74.
27. In chapter 21; Stephens, *Constitutional View of the War Between the States,* Vol. 2, pp. 557–61; *Messages and Papers of Davis and Confederacy,* Vol. 1, pp. 339–41.
28. Stephens, *Constitutional View of the War Between the States,* Vol. 2, pp. 558–66.
29. *O.R.,* Ser. 2, Vol. 6, p. 94.
30. Davis, *Rise and Fall,* Vol. 2, pp. 591–95; *Messages and Papers of Davis and Confederacy,* Vol. 1, pp. 341–44.
31. *O.R.,* Ser. 2, Vol. 6, pp. 94–95, Stephens's report to Davis; pp. 79–84, Federal messages regarding Stephens's request to proceed to Washington.
32. Jones, *Diary,* Vol. 1, pp. 379–80, entries of July 15 and 16.
33. Andrews, *South Reports,* p. 318.
34. Jones, *Diary,* Vol. 1, pp. 381–82, entry of July 17.
35. Stuart-Mosby Historical Society, *Letters of J. E. B. Stuart,* pp. 326–28.
36. Allan, *Conversations with Lee,* April 15, 1868.
37. Marshall, *Aide-de-Camp,* p. 216.
38. MHI, H. B. McClellan's letters to Jubal Early, February 15 and 21, 1878, *Box B, Military Order of the Loyal Legion of the United States—Massachusetts Commandery Collection.* The extract from his manuscript also is in this collection and is addressed to Jubal Early. McClellan, however, may have erred in dating the

notation to Early as February 9, 1877. It should have been 1878. In his notation to Early, McClellan noted, "I have received my MS. from Philadelphia." In his letter of February 15, 1878, he stated, "I have recalled my MS., and the opportunity is presented for revision."

The material in the extract was included in a book—*The Life and Campaigns of Major General J. E. B. Stuart*—published in 1885 by Houghton, Mifflin and Company, Boston and New York, and J. W. Randolph and English, Richmond, Virginia.

The title was changed, however, to *I Rode with Jeb Stuart,* when the book was republished in 1958 as part of the Civil War Centennial Series by the Indiana University Press, Bloomington, Indiana, and again in 1976 by the Kraus Reprint Company of Millwood, New York.

39.   *SHSP,* Vol. 5, p. 64; *Century Magazine,* Vol. 33, No. 4, p. 624.
40.   Longstreet, *M to A,* p. 343.
41.   VHS, Longstreet's letter to H. B. McClellan, July 28, 1878.
42.   Gordon, *Reminiscences,* p. 166.
43.   Marshall, *Aide-de-Camp,* pp. 178–81.
44.   Allan, *Conversations with Lee,* April 15, 1868.

BIBLIOGRAPHY

OFFICIAL PUBLICATIONS

Calendar of Virginia State Papers and Other Manuscripts, Jan. 1, 1836 to April 15, 1869. Arranged, edited, and printed under direction of H. W. Flourney, secretary of the commonwealth and state librarian of Virginia. Reprint, Kraus Reprint Corporation, New York, 1968.

Congressional Quarterly's Guide to U.S. Elections. Congressional Quarterly, Inc., Washington, D.C., 1965.

Journal of the Congress, Confederate States of America, 1861–65. Seven vols. Government Printing Office, Washington, D.C., 1904.

Messages and Papers of Jefferson Davis and the Confederacy, Including Diplomatic Correspondence, 1861–1865. Two vols. Permission to publish granted to James D. Richardson by Congress on April 17, 1900. Reprint, 1966, Chelsea House–Robert Hector Publishers, New York, in association with R. R. Bowker.

The Official Atlas of the Civil War. Major George B. Davis, U.S. Army, and civilian experts Leslie J. Perry and Joseph W. Kirkley. Government Printing Office, Washington, D.C., 1891–5. Reprint, the National Historical Society, Gettysburg, Pennsylvania, 1978.

Pennsylvania House of Representatives. Samuel Weaver. *Revised Report of the Select Committee Relative to the Soldiers' National Cemetery [at Gettysburg],* 1865.

Proceedings of the Virginia State Convention. George H. Reese, ed. Virginia State Library, 1965.

U.S. Navy Department. *Official Records of the Union and Confederate Navies in the War of the Rebellion.* Thirty-one vols. Government Printing Office, Washington, D.C., 1894–1927.

U.S. Patent Office. *Annual Report of S. T. Shugart, Acting Commissioner, for 1860.* Government Printing Office, Washington, D.C., January 29, 1861. Includes agriculture report for 1860.

———. *Annual Report of D. P. Holloway, Commissioner, for 1861.* Government Printing Office, January 30, 1862. Includes agriculture report for 1861. (The Department of Agriculture was established later in 1862.)

U.S. War Department. *The War of the Rebellion: A Compilation of the Official Records of the Union and Confederate Armies.* 128 vols. Government Printing Office, Washington, D.C., 1880–1901.

BOOKS

Alexander, Edward P. *Miliary Memoirs of a Confederate.* Charles Scribner's Sons, New York, 1907. Reprint, Press of Morningside Bookshop, Dayton, Ohio, 1977.

————. *Fighting for the Confederacy: The Personal Recollections of General Edward Porter Alexander.* Gary W. Gallagher, ed. The University of North Carolina Press, Chapel Hill, North Carolina, 1989.

Allan, William. *History of the Campaign of Gen. T. J. (Stonewall) Jackson in the Shenandoah Valley of Virginia from November 4, 1861, to June 17, 1862.* J. B. Lippincott, Philadelphia, Pennsylvania, 1880. Reprint, Press of Morningside Bookshop, Dayton, Ohio, 1987.

Andrews, Cutler. *The North Reports the Civil War.* University of Pittsburgh Press, 1955.

————. *The South Reports the Civil War.* Princeton University Press, Princeton, New Jersey, 1970.

Annals of the War, written by leading participants, North and South. Times Publishing Company, Philadelphia, Pennsylvania, 1879. Reprint, Civil War Times Illustrated, Gettysburg, Pennsylvania, 1974.

An Authentic Exposition of the K.G.C., Knights of the Golden Circle: A History of Secession from 1834 to 1861 by an Anonymous Member of the Order. C. O. Perrine, Indianapolis, Indiana, 1861.

Baer, Christopher T. *Canals and Railroads of the Mid-Atlantic States 1800–1860.* Glenn Porter and William H. Mulligan, Jr., eds. The Regional Economic History Research Center, Eleutherian Mills–Hagley Foundation, Inc., Wilmington, Delaware, 1981.

Bain, William E., ed. *B&O in the Civil War, from the papers of William Prescott Smith, master of transportation for the B&O Railroad, 1860–66.* Sage Books, Denver, Colorado, 1966. Source quoted by author is the collection of Smith's papers at the University of Louisville, Kentucky.

Bates, Samuel P. *Martial Deeds of Pennsylvania.* T. H. Davis & Company, Philadelphia, Pennsylvania, 1873.

Beale, Howard K. *The Diary of Edward Bates [U.S. Attorney General], 1859–1866.* Da Capo Press, New York, 1971.

Bean, W. G. *Stonewall's Man: Sandie Pendleton.* University of North Carolina Press, Chapel Hill, 1959.

Bennett, Frank M. *The Steam Navy of the United States.* W. T. Nicholson Press, 1896. Reprint, Greenwood Press, Westport, Connecticut, 1971.

Blackford, Lieutenant Colonel William W., C.S.A. *War Years with Jeb Stuart.* Charles Scribner's Sons, New York, 1945.

Boatner, Mark M. *The Civil War Dictionary.* David McKay, Inc., New York, 1959.

Broehl, Wayne G., Jr. *The Molly Maguires.* Harvard University Press, Cambridge, Massachusetts, 1964.

Buell, Clarence C., and Johnson, Robert C., eds. *Battles and Leaders of the Civil War.* Four vols. Century Company, New York, 1884–89. Reprint, Thomas Yoseloff, Inc., New York, 1956.

Butler, Benjamin F. *Butler's Book: A Review of His Legal, Political and Military Career.* A. M. Thayer & Company, Boston, 1892.

Catton, Bruce. *The Centennial History of the Civil War.* Three vols. Doubleday & Company, Inc., New York, 1961–63.

Chambers, Lenoir. *Stonewall Jackson.* Two vols. William Morrow & Company, New York, 1957.

Coddington, Edwin B. *The Gettysburg Campaign: A Study in Command.* Charles Scribner's Sons, 1968. Reprint, Press of Morningside Bookshop, Dayton, Ohio, 1979.

Cooke, John Esten. *Stonewall Jackson: A Military Biography.* D. Appleton and Company, New York, 1866.

———. *Hammer and Rapier.* Carleton, Publisher, Madison Square, New York, and Low, Son & Company, London, 1870.

Crist, Robert Grant. *Confederate Invasion of the West Shore—1863.* Lemoyne Trust Company, Lemoyne, Pennsylvania, 1963.

Cullum, Brevet Major General George W. *Biographical Register of the Officers and Graduates from 1802 to 1867 of the U.S. Military Academy.* Nine vols. James Miller, New York, 1879.

Dabney, R. L. *Life and Campaigns of Lieut. Gen. Thomas J. Jackson.* Blalock & Company, New York, 1866.

Davis, Jefferson. *The Rise and Fall of the Confederate Government.* Two vols. D. Appleton and Company, New York, 1881. Reprint, Thomas Yoseloff, New York, 1958.

Diary of a Southern Refugee, by a Lady of Virginia. E. J. Hale & Son, New York, 1868.

Douglas, Henry Kyd. *I Rode with Stonewall.* University of North Carolina Press, Chapel Hill, 1940.

Dowdey, Clifford, and Manerin, Louis R., eds. *The Wartime Papers of R. E. Lee.* Virginia Civil War Commission. Little, Brown and Company, Boston, 1961.

Duke, Basil W. *Morgan's Cavalry.* The Neale Publishing Company, New York, 1909.

Early, Jubal A. *War Memoirs.* Charles W. Button, Lynchburg, Virginia, 1912. Reprint, Indiana University Press, Bloomington, Indiana, Civil War Centennial Series, 1960; Kraus Reprint, Millwood, New York, 1981.

Eavenson, Howard N. *The First Century and a Quarter of American Coal Industry.* Privately printed, 1942, Pittsburgh, Pennsylvania.

Encounter at Hanover: Prelude to Gettysburg. Historical Publication Committee of the Hanover, Pennsylvania, Chamber of Commerce, 1963.

Freeman, Douglas Southall. *R. E. Lee: A Biography.* Four vols. Charles Scribner's Sons, New York, 1934–35.

———. *Lee's Lieutenants: A Study in Command.* Three vols. Charles Scribner's Sons, New York, 1942–44.

———, ed. *Lee's Dispatches.* Unpublished letters of General Robert E. Lee, C.S.A., to Jefferson Davis and the War Department of the Confederate States of America, 1862–65, from the private collection of Wyemberley Jones de Renne of Warmsloe, Georgia. G. P. Putnam's Sons, New York, 1957.

The Gettysburg Papers. Two vols. Compiled by Ken Bandy and Florence Freeland. Press of Morningside Bookshop, Dayton, Ohio, 1978.

Gordon, Lieutenant General John B., C.S.A. *Reminiscences of the Civil War.* Charles Scribner's Sons, New York, 1903.

Headley, J. T. *The Great Rebellion: A History of the Civil War in the United States.* Two vols. Vol. 1 published by Hurlbut, Scranton & Company, Hartford, Connecticut, 1864; Vol. 2 by American Publishing Company, Hartford, 1866.

Henderson, Lieutenant Colonel G. F. R. *Stonewall Jackson and the American Civil War.* Two vols. Longmans, Green, and Company, New York, 1900.

Henry, Robert Selph. *The Story of the Confederacy*. Bobbs-Merrill Company, 1931, 1936. Reprint, New Home Library, New York, 1943.

Heth, Henry. *Memoirs*. James L. Morrison, Jr., ed. Greenwood Press, Westport, Connecticut, 1974.

History of Cumberland and Adams Counties, Pennsylvania. Sponsored by the Cumberland County Historical Society, Carlisle, Pennsylvania, and Adams County Historical Society, Gettysburg, Pennsylvania. Warner, Beers & Company, Chicago, Illinois, 1886. Reprint, Unigraphic, Inc., Evansville, Indiana, 1974.

Hoke, Jacob. *The Great Invasion of 1863; or, General Lee in Pennsylvania*. W. J. Shuey, Dayton, Ohio, 1887. Reprint, Thomas Yoseloff, New York, 1959.

Hotchkiss, Jedediah. *Confederate Military History, Vol. III, Virginia*. Confederate Publishing Co., Atlanta, Georgia, 1899. Reprint, Press of Morningside Bookshop, Dayton, Ohio, 1979.

Inside the Confederate Government: The Diary of Garlick Hill Kean, Head of the Bureau of War. Edward Younger, ed. Oxford University Press, Inc., New York, 1957. Reprint, Greenwood Press, Westport, Connecticut, 1973.

Jackson, Mary Anna. *Memoirs of Stonewall Jackson by His Widow*. Courier-Journal Job Printing Company, Louisville, Kentucky, 1895. Reprint, Press of Morningside Bookshop, Dayton, Ohio, 1976.

Johnston, Joseph E. *Narrative of Military Operations*. D. Appleton and Company, New York, 1874.

Jones J. B. *A Rebel War Clerk's Diary at the Confederate States Capital*. Two vols. Old Hickory Bookshop, New York, 1935.

Jones, J. William, D.D. *Life and Letters of Robert Edward Lee, Soldier and Man*. The Neale Publishing Company, New York, 1906.

Keefer, Norman D. *A History of Mechanicsburg (Pa.) and the Surrounding Area*. Mechanicsburg Area Historical Committee, 1976.

Klement, Frank L. *Dark Lanterns: Secret Political Societies, Conspiracies, and Treason Trials in the Civil War*. Louisiana State University Press, Baton Rouge, Louisiana, 1984.

Lancaster County 1841–1941. Frederick Shriver Klein, associate professor of history, Franklin and Marshall College, Lancaster, Pennsylvania. Lancaster County National Bank, 1941.

Lee, Fitzhugh, *Great Commanders: General Lee*. D. Appleton, New York, 1898.

Lee, Robert E., Jr. *Recollections and Letters of Robert E. Lee*. Doubleday, Page & Company, New York, 1904. Reprint, Broadfoot Company, Wilmington, North Carolina, 1988.

The Letters of John S. Mosby. Adele H. Mitchell, ed. Stuart-Mosby Historical Society, 1986.

The Letters of Major General J. E. B. Stuart. Adele H. Mitchell, ed. Stuart-Mosby Historical Society, 1990.

Long, A. L. *Memoirs of Robert E. Lee: His Military and Personal History*. Marcus J. Wright, ed. J. M. Stoddart & Company, New York, 1887.

Longstreet, James. *From Manassas to Appomattox*. J. B. Lippincott, Philadelphia, 1896. Reprint, Civil War Centennial Series, Indiana University Press, Bloomington, Indiana, 1960; Kraus Reprint Co., 1969.

Luraghi, Raimondo. *The Rise and Fall of the Plantation South*. New Viewpoints, a division of Franklin Watts, New York, 1978.

McClellan, George B. *McClellan's Own Story.* Charles L. Webster & Company, New York, 1897.

McClellan, H. B. *The Life and Campaigns of Major General J. E. B. Stuart.* Houghton, Mifflin, Boston, 1885. Reprinted as *I Rode with Jeb Stuart* by Indiana University Press, Bloomington, Indiana, 1958, as part of the Civil War Centennial Series, and in 1976 by Kraus Reprint Company, Millwood, New York.

McDonald, Archie P., ed. *Make Me a Map of the Valley: The War Journal of Stonewall Jackson's Topographer.* Southern Methodist University Press, 1973.

The Making of a Soldier: Letters of General R. S. Ewell. Captain Percy Gatling Hamlin, M.D., Medical Corps, Maryland National Guard, ed. Whittet & Shepperson, Richmond, Virginia, 1935.

Marshall, Charles. *An Aide-de-Camp of Lee, being the papers of Colonel Charles Marshall, sometime aide-de-camp, military secretary, and assistant adjutant general on the staff of Robert E. Lee, 1860–65.* General Sir Frederick Maurice, ed. Little, Brown and Company, Boston, Massachusetts, 1927.

Marshall, Jessie Ames, ed. *Private and Official Correspondence of Gen. Benjamin F. Butler during the Period of the Civil War.* Plimpton Press, Norwood, Massachusetts, 1917.

Mary Chestnut's Civil War. C. Vann Woodward, ed. Yale University Press, New Haven, Connecticut, 1981.

The Memoirs of Colonel John S. Mosby. Charles Wells Russell, ed. Little Brown and Company, Boston, 1917.

Mosby, John S. *Stuart's Cavalry in the Gettysburg Campaign.* Moffat, Yard & Company, New York, 1908. Reprint, Confederate Printers, Falls Church, Virginia, 1984.

Nicolay, John G., and Hay, John. *Abraham Lincoln: A History.* The Century Company, New York, 1904.

Nye, Wilbur Sturtevant. *Here Come the Rebels!* Louisiana State University Press, 1965. Reprint, Press of Morningside Bookshop, Dayton, Ohio, 1984.

Personal Memoirs of U. S. Grant. Two vols. Charles L. Webster, New York, 1892.

Pitman, Benn, ed. *The Trials for Treason at Indianapolis, Disclosing Plans for Establishing a Northwestern Confederacy.* Moore, Wilstach & Baldwin, Cincinnati, Ohio, 1865.

Pratt, Fletcher. *The Navy: A History.* Garden City Publishing Company, Inc., Garden City, New York, 1941.

Reagan, John W. *Memoirs with Reference to Secession and the Civil War.* The Neale Publishing Company, New York, 1906. Reprint, AMS Press, Inc., New York, 1973.

Robertson, James I., Jr. *General A. P. Hill: The Story of a Confederate Warrior.* Random House, New York, 1987.

Roman, Alfred. *The Military Operations of General Beauregard in the War Between the States, 1861 to 1865.* Two vols. Harper & Brothers, New York, 1884. Reprint, Da Capo Press, Inc., New York, 1994.

Rowland, Dunbar, ed. *Jefferson Davis, Constitutionalist: His Letters, Papers and Speeches.* Ten vols. The Mississippi Department of Archives and History, 1923.

Sandburg, Carl. *Abraham Lincoln: The War Years.* Four vols. Harcourt, Brace & Company, New York, 1939.

Sauers, Richard A. *The Gettysburg Campaign, June 3–August 15, 1863: A Comprehensive, Selectively Annotated Bibliography.* Greenwood Press, Westport, Connecticut, 1982.

Seymour, Captain William J. *Civil War Memoirs: Reminiscences of a Louisiana Tiger.* Terry L. Jones, ed. Louisiana State University Press, Baton Rouge, Louisiana, 1991.

Shippensburg in the Civil War. Shippensburg Historical Society, 1964.

Stephens, Alexander, H. *A Constitutional View of the War Between the States: Its Causes, Character, Conduct and Results.* Two vols. National Publishing Company, Philadelphia, Pennsylvania; and Ziegler, McCurdy & Co., Chicago, Illinois, 1868.

Taylor, Walter H. *General Lee: His Campaigns in Virginia, 1861–1865, with Personal Reminiscences.* Nusbaum Book and News Company, Norfolk, Virginia, 1906. Reprint, Press of Morningside Bookshop, Dayton, Ohio, 1965.

———. *Four Years with General Lee.* D. Appleton and Company, New York, 1878. Reprint, Indiana University Press, Bloomington, Indiana, and Bonanza Books, New York, 1962.

Thomas, Emory M. *The Confederate Nation.* Harper & Row, Publishers, Inc., New York, 1979.

Thompson, Robert Means, and Richard Wainwright, eds. *Confidential Correspondence of Gustavas Vasa Fox, Assistant Secretary of the Navy, 1861–65.* DeVinne Press, New York, 1918.

Von Borcke, Heros. *Memoirs of the Confederate War for Independence.* Two vols. First published in 1866. Reprint, Peter Smith, New York, 1938.

Williams, T. Harry. *P. G. T. Beauregard: Napoleon in Gray.* Louisiana State University Press, Baton Rouge, Louisiana, 1955.

Wright, Marcus J. *Great Commanders: General Scott.* D. Appleton and Company, New York, 1894.

UNIT HISTORIES

A Life for the Confederacy, as Recorded in the Pocket Diaries of Pvt. Robert A. Moore, Co. G, 17th Mississippi Regiment, Confederate Guards. James W. Silver, ed. McCowat-Mercer Press, Inc., Jackson, Tennessee, 1959.

Military Annals of Tennessee, Confederate. John B. Lindsley, ed. J. M. Lindsley & Company, Nashville, Tennessee, 1886.

Simpson, Colonel Harold B. *Gaines Mill to Appomattox, Waco and McClennan County [Texas] in Hood's Texas Brigade. A History of Co. B, 4th Texas Regiment.* Texian Press, Waco, Texas, 1963.

West, John C. *A Texan in Search of a Fight, Being the Diary and Letters of a Private Soldier in Hood's Texas Brigade.* Texian Press, Waco, Texas, 1901. Reprinted in 1969.

MEDICAL INFORMATION

Blumgarten, A. S., M.D., F.A.C.P. *Textbook of Materia Medica.* fourth edition. The MacMillan Company, New York, 1928.

Drug Evaluations. Sixth edition, American Medical Association, Chicago, Illinois, 1986.

Goodman and Gilman's The Pharmacological Basis of Therapeutics. Eight edition, Pergamon Press, a member of the Maxwell McMillan Pergamon Publishing Corporation, New York, 1990.

Physicians' Desk Reference. Forty-seventh edition, 1993.

MANUSCRIPTS

Allan, William. *Conversations with R. E. Lee.* A handwritten notebook, Cyrus Hall McCormick Library, Washington and Lee University, Lexington, Virginia. Transcript in the *Southern Historical Collection,* No. 2764, University of North Carolina, Chapel Hill.

Annual Report of the Geological Survey of Pennsylvania for 1886, Part 3, Anthracite Coal Regions, published in 1887 by the Board of Commissioners for the Geological Survey.

Baltimore and Ohio Railroad Company. *Annual Report for Fiscal Years Ending Sept. 30, 1861, and Sept. 30, 1862.*

Pennsylvania Geological and Survey Bureau, Harrisburg, Pennsylvania. *Annual Report of the Geological Survey of Pennsylvania for 1886. Part 3, Anthracite Coal Regions.* Published by Board of Commissioners for the Geological Survey, 1887.

Reidenbaugh, Lowell. *Cadet Record of Thomas Jonathan Jackson.* St. Louis, Missouri. Compiled from U.S. Military Academy records, West Point, New York.

LETTERS AND OTHER PAPERS

Alexander R. Boteler's Papers. Manuscript Department (Ms. 581), Perkins Library, Duke University, Durham, North Carolina.

The Diary of Camille Polignac. Civil War Times Illustrated Collection, U.S. Army Military History Institute, Carlisle, Pennsylvania.

Documents of the Loyal Legion of the United States, Massachusetts Commandery Collection. U.S. Army Military History Institute, Carlisle, Pennsylvania.

John B. Gordon Papers. The University of Georgia Libraries, Athens, Georgia.

Michael J. Hammerson Collection. London, Lee's letter.

Harrisburg Civil War Round Table Collection. U.S. Army Military History Institute, Carlisle, Pennsylvania.

Osman Latrobe Papers. Virginia Historical Society, Richmond, Virginia.

Lee's Headquarters Papers. Virginia Historical Society, Richmond, Virginia.

Lee's Letter Book. Virginia Historical Society, Richmond, Virginia.

Lee's Letters. Virginia Historical Society, Richmond, Virginia.

Lee's Telegraph Book. Virginia Historical Society, Richmond, Virginia.

James Longstreet's Letters. Virginia Historical Society, Richmond, Virginia.

James Longstreet's Papers. Southern Historical Collection, No. 3081, University of North Carolina, Chapel Hill.

Military Survey of the Susquehanna River—1861. Manuscript Division, Historical Society of Pennsylvania, Philadelphia, Pennsylvania.

John S. Mosby Papers. U.S. Army Military History Institute, Carlisle, Pennsylvania.

Ralph J. Moses Autobiography. Southern Historical Collection, No. 529, University of North Carolina, Chapel Hill.

Papers of the Military Historical Society of Massachusetts.

William N. Pendleton Papers. Southern Historical Collection, No. 1466, University of North Carolina, Chapel Hill.

Stuart's Letters. The Huntington Library, San Marino, Calif.

MAGAZINES

Belford Monthly and Democratic Review. Belford & Company, Publishers, New York, in the archives of the Museum of the Confederacy, Richmond, Virginia. Two-part article in October and November 1891, John S. Mosby, "Stuart's Cavalry in the Gettysburg Campaign."

Century Illustrated Monthly Magazine. Forty-seven vols. The Century Company, New York, and F. Worne & Company, London.

Journal of the Lancaster County Historical Society. Vol. 84, No. 3, 1980. Article, "The Defense of Columbia," June, 1863.

Magazine of Jefferson County (W. Va.) Historical Society. "Alexander R. Boteler's Biography," Vol. 20.

Southern Historical Society Papers, 1839–1914. Fifty-two vols. R. A. Brock, ed., secretary of the Southern Historical Society. Published by the Southern Historical Society, Richmond, Virginia.

NEWSPAPERS

New York *Herald*
New York Times
Harrisburg (Pennsylvania) *Sunday Patriot-News*
Lancaster (Pennsylvania) *Intelligencer*
Lancaster (Pennsylvania) *Intelligencer Journal**
Philadelphia Inquirer
Philadelphia *Weekly Times*
Pottsville (Pennsylvania) *Miners' Journal*
Reading (Pennsylvania) *Daily Times*
Lynchburg (Virginia) *Republican*
Richmond Daily Dispatch
Richmond Examiner
Richmond Enquirer
Richmond Whig

* The *Lancaster News Journal,* a morning paper, and the *Lancaster Intelligencer,* an evening paper, were combined in 1928 as the *Intelligencer Journal,* a morning paper.

INDEX